CANADA

HANDBOOKS TO THE MODERN WORLD
General Editor: James Warren

WESTERN EUROPE
THE SOVIET UNION AND EASTERN EUROPE
THE MIDDLE EAST
AFRICA
ASIA
ASIA AND THE PACIFIC (2 volumes)
THE UNITED STATES (3 volumes)
CANADA

HANDBOOKS TO THE MODERN WORLD

CANADA

Edited by

MEL WATKINS

Facts On File
New York

Canada
Copyright © 1993 by Facts On File, Inc.

Facts On File, Inc.
460 Park Avenue South
New York NY 10016
USA

Library of Congress Cataloging-in-Publication Data
Canada / edited by Mel Watkins.
        p.   cm.—(Handbooks to the modern world)
    Includes index.
    ISBN 0-8160-1831-6
    1. Canada.   I. Watkins, Mel.   II. Series: Handbooks to the modern
world (Facts on File, Inc.)
F1008.C2   1991
971—dc20   91-45584

A British CIP catalogue record for this book is available from the British Library.

Facts On File books are available at special discounts when purchased in bulk quantities for businesses, associations, institutions or sales promotions. Please call our Special Sales Department in New York at 212/683-2244 (dial 800/322-8755 except in NY).

Composition and manufacturing by the Maple-Vail Book Manufacturing Group
Printed in the United States of America

10 9 8 7 6 5 4 3 2 1

This book is printed on acid-free paper.

CONTRIBUTORS

THOMAS S. AXWORTHY is executive director of the CRB Foundation in Montreal, and an adjunct lecturer at the John F. Kennedy School of Government, Harvard University. He was principal secretary to Prime Minister Pierre Trudeau from 1981 to 1984.

CARL E. BEIGIE was chief economist for McLean McCarthy, Inc. in Toronto. He held the position of adjunct professor of business economics and academic director of the Executive MBA program in the Faculty of Management at the University of Toronto. Mr. Beigie serves as chairman of the board of the Canadian Foundation for Economic Education and is a director of the Ontario Housing Corporation. He was the founding executive director and later resident of Canada's C. D. Howe Institute. From 1968 to 1971, following two years on the economics faculty of the University of Western Ontario, he worked for the Irving Trust Co. in New York, becoming assistant vice president and international economist. From 1983 to early 1988, he was director and chief economist at Dominion Securities Inc. in Toronto. He taught as an adjunct professor in the Faculty of Management of McGill University from 1973 to 1990.

JOHN R. CALVERT has been employed since 1978 as a senior research officer for the Canadian Union of Public Employees, Canada's largest trade union. He studied at the University of Western Ontario and, subsequently, at the London School of Economics, where he received his doctorate in 1976. He is the author of *Government Limited* (1984) and coeditor of *The Facts on Free Trade* (1988). He has also written numerous articles on Canadian labor relations. Calvert is currently on the editorial board of *Labour/le Travail,* a journal of Canadian labor history.

WILLIAM CHRISTIAN is professor of political studies at the University of Guelph. He received his B.A. and M.A. from the University of Toronto and his Ph.D. from the London School of Economics. He has also taught at the University of Toronto and Mount Allison University, and was an academic visitor at the London School of Economics. He is coauthor of *Political Parties and Ideologies in Canada* (3rd edition, 1990), and was a consultant for the Royal Commission on Election Reform and Party Financing.

G. BRUCE DOERN is professor, School of Public Administration, Carleton University, Ottawa. A former director of the school, he is the author or editor of more than 20 books on various aspects of Canadian and comparative public policy, including *The Politics of Energy* (1984), *Faith and Fear: The Free Trade Story* (1991) and *Getting It Green* (1990). He has also served as a research coordinator for the Royal Commission on The Economic Union and Canada's Development Prospects (1983–85), and as a scholar in residence at the C.D. Howe Research Institute (1990–91).

PIERRE FOURNIER is director of research for Levosgne, Beaubien and Geoffrion, Inc. He was professor of political science at the Université du Québec à Montréal. He is a specialist in Canadian and Quebec politics, and economic and constitutional matters in particular. He obtained a Ph.D. from the University of Toronto in 1975. His main publications include *Le patronat québécois au pouvoir: 1970–76* (1977), *Le Capitalisme au Québec* (1978), *Capitalisme et politique au Québec* (1979), *L'entreprise québécoise* (1987), *Le Québec militaire* (1989) and *Autopsie du Lac Meech* (1990). He has also been active in research and as a consultant to a number of governmental bodies, including the Office de planification et de développement du Québec, the Macdonald Royal Commission, the Commission consultative sur les relations de travail and the Commission d'enquête sur le système de santé et les services sociaux du Québec.

R. DOUGLAS FRANCIS is professor of Canadian history at the University of Calgary. He is the author of *Images of the West* (1989) and *Frank H. Underhill: Intellectual Provocateur* (1986), and coauthor of a two-volume history of Canada entitled *Origins* (1988) and *Destinies* (1988). He is also the editor of a number of anthologies in Canadian history. Educated at York University in Toronto (B.A.; Ph.D.) and the University of Toronto (M.A.), he has taught at York and the University of British Columbia as well as the University of Calgary. He is currently visiting professor of Canadian studies at the University of Tsukuba, Japan.

GERALD L. GALL has been a professor of law at the University of Alberta since 1971. He has also taught in the faculties of business and arts and science and has taught each summer since 1971 at the University of Prince Edward Island. He is the author of *The Canadian Legal System* and the editor of a collection of essays entitled *Civil Liberties in Canada: Entering the 1980s.* He has recently written a number of articles relating to the topic of multiculturalism and the Canadian Charter of Rights and Freedoms. Professor Gall is a former executive director and honorary member of the board of the directors of the Canadian Institute for the Administration of Justice, and is presently a member of its board. He is a former national vice chairman of the Constitutional Law Section of the Canadian Bar Association, is presently a member of the management board of the Centre for Constitutional Studies at the University of Alberta, and is a member of the board of directors and the national council of the Canadian Human Rights Foundation. He is also a former chairman of the Administration of Justice Section of the Canadian Association of Law Teachers and a former cochairman of that association's Special Committee on the Appointment of Judges. He is currently a member of the Alberta Universities Coordinating Council Professional Examinations Board in Law and its executive committee, and is a former member of the Canadian Human Rights Tribunal and the National Parole Board. He is also a barrister and solicitor in the province of Ontario.

WILBUR GRASHAM graduated from the University of Toronto in engineering physics and spent several years as a field geophysicist in northern Quebec and Greenland. He then joined the staff of the National Research Council Laboratories in Ottawa and worked four years on underwater acoustics. He also served as secretary of the council's Associate Committee on Geodesy and Geophysics. With an interest in the role of science in policy and administration, he returned to the University of Toronto to take an M.A. in political economy, eventually joining the political science staff at the university, where he remained until he retired as professor emeritus. During those years he taught mainly Canadian Government and Canadian Public Administration, as well as introductory statistics for students of economics and political science. The focus of his present research is the history of Canadian public administration, with particular reference to its roots in British concepts and practice.

THOMAS I. GUNTON is deputy minister of finance, Government of British Columbia, and former director of the School of Resource and Environmental Management at Simon Fraser University in Vancouver, British Columbia. Gunton graduated with his Ph.D. in planning from the University of British Columbia and his Master's from the University of Waterloo. He has published extensively in the area of resource policy and economic development. His publications include *Resource Rents and Public Policy,* co-edited with John Richards. Gunton has also had extensive professional experience, including his holding the position of assistant deputy minister in the Department of Energy and Mines for the government of Manitoba. He has appeared as an expert witness before numerous resource agencies, including the National Energy Board, the Ontario Energy Board and private-sector arbitrations.

ROBERT HALASZ has been editor of the *Funk & Wagnalls New Encyclopedia Yearbook* and of *World Progress,* a current-events quarterly. He contributes to a number of reference works, including *Current Biography* and the *Dictionary of the Middle Ages.*

JOHN HUTCHESON is associate professor in the Division of Social Sciences at York University, Toronto, and coordinator of Canadian studies. He is the author of *Dominance and Dependency: Liberalism and National Policies in the North Atlantic Triangle* (1978), and coeditor (with Ian Parker and Patrick Crawley) of *The Strategy of Canadian Culture in the 21st Century* (1988). From 1982 to 1988 he was editor of *The Canadian Forum.*

ROGER HUTCHINSON is Professor of Church and Society at Emmanuel College in the Toronto School of Theology at the University of Toronto. He has written a number of articles on religion in Canada and served as coeditor and contributor to *A Long and Faithful March: "Towards the Christian Revolution" 1930's–1980's* (1989) with Harold Wells; and *Christian Faith and Economic Justice: Toward a Canadian Perspective* (1988) with Cranford

Pratt. He is the author of *Prophets, Pastors and Public Choices: Canadian Churches and the MacKenzie Valley Pipeline Debate* (1992).

HEATHER JARMAN is the president of her own business, which provides services for writers, musicians and other professionals. After receiving a B.A. in archaeology and anthropology at the University of California, Berkeley, she moved to Cambridge, England and was appointed to a post on the British Academy Early History of Agriculture Project at Cambridge University. From 1976 to 1983, she was general manager of The Academy of Ancient Music, and at the same time she began to do regular research and editing for Hugh Brody, mostly on Canadian subjects. In 1987, she was assistant consultant to the Museum of Mankind (British Museum) for their Living Arctic exhibition, a celebration of the Canadian North.

JOHN KIRTON is an associate professor of political science, codirector of research for the Centre for International Studies, and a fellow of Trinity College at the University of Toronto. Educated at the University of Toronto, Carleton University's Norman Paterson School of International Affairs, and Johns Hopkins University's Paul Nitze School of Advanced International Studies (from which he received his Ph.D. in 1977), he is coauthor (with David Dewitt) of *Canada as a Principal Power* (1983), editor of *Canada, the United States and Space* (1985), and coeditor of *The International Joint Commission Seventy Years On* (1982), *Canada and the New Internationalism* (1988), and *Canadian Foreign Policy: Selected Cases* (1992). In addition to consulting for the private and public sector in the field of media analysis of international and public affairs, he is currently a vice president of the Couchiching Institute of Public Affairs, and a member of the Foreign Policy Committee of the Canadian National Roundtable on the Environment and the Economy.

SEYMOUR MARTIN LIPSET is Hazel Professor of Public Policy at George Mason University and Senior Fellow at the Hoover Institution at Stanford University. He is the author of many books, including *Continental Divide: The Values and Institutions of the United States and Canada* (1990), *Agrarian Socialism* (1971), *The Confidence Gap* (2nd edition, 1987), *Political Man* and *The First New Nation* (1979). He is president of the American Sociological Association, a former president of the American Political Science Association and World Association for Public Opinion Research. He has been elected to membership in various honor societies such as the National Academy of Science and the American Academy of Arts and Sciences. He has received the Gold Medal of the International Council for Canadian Studies.

PETER LYON is reader in international relations and academic secretary of the Institute of Commonwealth Studies at the University of London. He lectures on international politics at the London School of Economics and Political Science, as well as at other universities and institutions. A former president of the British Association for Canadian Studies, he is editor of *The Round Table: The Commonwealth Journal of International Affairs,* and has written extensively on Commonwealth, Third World and Canadian themes, especially those relating to foreign and defense policy matters. He is vice president of the Royal Commonwealth Society, governor of the Commonwealth Trust, and a frequent lecturer on Canadian and international affairs. He is author-editor of, inter alia, *Britain and Canada: Survey of a Changing Relationship*.

JAMES R. MACGREGOR has been providing tourism consulting services to the public and private sectors in Canada since 1971. He has prepared numerous regional tourism development and marketing strategies in many countries and has worked with dozens of communities to identify their tourism and economic development opportunities. Most recently he has edited the document "An Action Strategy for Sustainable Tourism Development," which has become Canada's national tourism policy. MacGregor is a leading expert in Japanese travel to North America and has completed an extensive research project on the Japanese consumer at the International Institute for International Training at Mount Fuji. He is a lecturer at the University of Calgary's Environmental Studies Program and the Simon Fraser University Tourism Foundation Management Program and has recently completed an ecotourism strategy for the Philippines.

M. PATRICIA MARCHAK is professor of sociology and dean of Arts at the University of British Columbia, Canada; she is a former head of the Department of Anthropology and Sociology. She is the author of numerous articles on political trends, regional development and industry. Her books include *Ideological Perspectives on Canada* (3rd edition, 1987), *In Whose Interests* (1979), *Green Gold: The Forest Industry in British Columbia* (1983), and *The Integrated Circus: The New Right and the Restructuring of Global Markets* (1991); and (as coeditor) *Uncommon Property: The Fishing and Fish-Processing Industries in British Columbia* (1987).

LORNA R. MARSDEN is president and vice chancellor of Wilfrid Laurier University, Waterloo, Ontario. She was a Liberal senator in the Canadian Parliament from 1984 to 1992. She chaired the Senate Standing Committee on Social Affairs, Science and Technology. She received her Ph.D. from Princeton University and has taught in the Department of Sociology at the University of Toronto since 1972. Her academic work has focused on economic sociology, and particularly the situation of women in Canada. Since 1970, she has been active in the women's movement, serving as president of the National Action Committee on the Status of Women from 1975 to 1977. She is the coauthor of *The Fragile Federation: Social Change in Canada* (1979) and *Lives of Their Own: The Individualization of Women's Lives* (1990).

ANTHONY C. MASI has been a member of the Department of Sociology, McGill University, since 1979, and director of the Faculty of Arts Computer Laboratory since 1987. Masi was a visiting professor in Italy at the University of Bari (1986–87) and the University of Pisa (1990). In addition to scholarly publications he has prepared briefs and reports for the federal government of Canada, the regional government of Apulia in southeastern Italy, and private industry.

ALEXANDER N. MCLEOD was medalist at Queen's University, Littauer Fellow at Harvard, and later a professor at Atkinson College of York University, Toronto, from which he retired in 1977 as professor emeritus. He has been a staff member of the International Monetary Fund, and was monetary adviser to the United Nations Commissioner in Libya in preparation for Libya's independence. He was director of research for the Saudi Arabian Monetary Agency, chief economist of the Toronto-Dominion Bank, and monetary adviser to the government of Botswana. McLeod now writes and works in support of national and international policies that are socially responsible and economically sound.

KENNETH MCNAUGHT is professor emeritus of history at the University of Toronto. Born in Toronto in 1918, he was educated at Upper Canada College and the University of Toronto, where he received a Ph.D. in 1950. He has taught at various universities in Canada, Britain, Germany and the United States. McNaught has written widely on public affairs in Canada and the United States, and is the author of numerous books, including *A Prophet in Politics: The Biography of J.S. Woodsworth* (1959), *The Penguin History of Canada* (1988), and *Manifest Destiny: A Short History of the United States* (1963).

LIONEL ORLIKOW is director of the Winnipeg Education Centre, at the University of Manitoba, an inner-city teacher education program that prepares aboriginals, recent immigrants to Canada and other low-income residents as elementary-degree teachers. Formerly deputy minister of education for the province of Manitoba, he earned a Ph.D. from the University of Chicago and an M.Ed. from Harvard University. Orlikow served as editor of *Learning* magazine, a publication of the Canadian Association for Adult Education, and as an elected school trustee in the Winnipeg School Division.

CRANFORD PRATT is professor emeritus of political science at the University of Toronto and Fellow of the Royal Society of Canada. After several decades of teaching, research and publishing on African political and developmental themes, he has for more than a decade concentrated on Canadian foreign policy, particularly in relationship to the Third World. He contributed to and edited *Human Rights and Canadian Foreign Policy* (1988; with Robert Matthews), and *Internationalism Under Strain: The North-South Policies of Canada, the Netherlands, Norway, and Sweden* (1989), and *Middle Power Internationalism: The North-South Dimension* (1990).

DONALD J. SAVOIE is the author of several books, including *The Politics of Public Spending in Canada* (1990), *Regional Economic Development: Canada's Search for Solutions* (1986), *Federal-Provincial Collaboration: The Canada-New Brunswick General Development Agreement* (1981), and *Regional Policy in a Changing World* (1990). He has also published widely in leading journals of political science, public policy, public administration and Canadian studies. He currently holds the Clement-Cormier Chair in Economic Development at the Université de Moncton, where he also teaches public administration. He was appointed a member of the Economic Council of Canada in 1990, named to the editorial board of the Canadian Public Administration in 1985, and elected to the national executive of the Institute of Public Administration of Canada in 1985 and 1990. Savoie has served as adviser and consultant to a number of federal, provincial and territorial departments and agencies.

LEONARD SHIFRIN, a lawyer by training, writes a syndicated national-affairs column focused on social policy, which appears in major newspapers across Canada. He has been involved in the social-policy field since the 1960s, and is a former executive director of Canada's National Council of Welfare. His commentaries on health, social security and tax issues have also appeared in magazines, journals and books, as well as on radio and television.

DONALD V. SMILEY, recently deceased, was distinguished research professor of political science emeritus at York University, Toronto. He was a member of the Royal Society of Canada and former president of the Canadian Political Science Association. He served as adviser to the Royal Commission on Bilingualism and Biculturalism, the Royal Commission on Canada's Economic Projects and other federal and provincial agencies. He was the author of numerous books, monographs and articles on Canadian government.

GARTH STEVENSON is professor of politics at Brock University in St. Catharines, Ontario, where he teaches courses on federalism, Quebec politics and the economic role of the state. He earned a B.A. and M.A. from McGill University, and a Ph.D. from Princeton University. His publications include *Unfulfilled Union* (3rd edition, 1989), *The Politics of Canada's Airlines* (1987) and *Rail Transport and Australian Federalism* (1987).

BOB STIRLING is professor of sociology and social studies at the University of Regina. His education includes agricultural economics (B.S.A.) and sociology (M.A. and Ph.D.). He also maintains an active interest in a family farm. He has studied and written about a number of agricultural topics such as the energy efficiency of prairie agriculture, community change and viability, and rationalization of the grain-handling industry.

DIXON THOMPSON is professor of environmental science in the Faculty of Environmental Design at the University of Calgary. He has worked for Environment Canada, the Science Council, the Commission on Canadian Studies, and the Environment Council of Alberta, and was a member of the Board of Nova's Research and Development subsidiary. He is a member of the Rawson Academy of Aquatic Science and is on the board of directors of the Rawson Academy and Resource Futures International. He contributes to projects in Peru, Colombia, Costa Rica and Mexico.

HAROLD TROPER is professor of history at the Ontario Institute for Studies in Education at the University of Toronto. He holds an M.A. from the University of Cincinnati and a Ph.D. from the University of Toronto. He has written widely on the history of Canadian immigration and interethnic relations. He is the author or coauthor of nine books, including *Immigrants: A Portrait of the Urban Experience, 1896–1930* (1975); *None Is Too Many: Canada and the Jews of Europe 1933–1945* (1983); and *Old Wounds: Jews, Ukrainians and the Hunt for Nazi War Criminals in Canada* (1989).

RONALD WARDHAUGH is professor of linguistics at the University of Toronto, where he teaches courses on various topics in sociolinguistics and the sociology of language. He has published a number of books, including *Language and Nationhood: the Canadian Experience* (1983) and *Languages in Competition* (1987).

MEL WATKINS is professor of economics and political science at University College, University of Toronto. He teaches in the area of Canadian Studies and has published extensively on the economic history of Canada and Canadian political economy. He was the chief author of the 1968 Canadian government report on foreign ownership (known popularly as the Watkins Report). In 1987–88 he was a special adviser to the Canadian Labour Congress on free trade. He is a consultant to the Ontario Métis Aboriginal Association. He is an editor of *This Magazine,* for which he writes a regular column.

EDWARD R. WEICK is an Ottawa-based socioeconomic consultant whose special interests are the Canadian and circumpolar north, Native people and environmental issues. He has worked with corporations, government departments, government task forces and special inquiries. During the 1970s he was socioeconomic adviser to the Mackenzie Valley Pipeline Inquiry (Berger Commission). Subsequently, he worked as socioeconomic coordinator of a three-company group responsible for preparing an environmental impact statement on oil and gas production in the Beaufort Sea. While with the government of Canada, he played an important role in developing government policy for Canada's northern territories. As a private consultant, Weick has recently worked in the field of Native self-government and advises Yukon Indian people on the implementation of their land claim and the Inuit of northern Quebec on economic planning.

CONTENTS

CONTENTS

PART FOUR: ECONOMICS

PART FIVE: SOCIAL AFFAIRS

MAPS

PREFACE

Like so much of the world, Canada is in an extraordinary state of flux in the 1990s. The powerful forces of economic integration, or globalization, are at play. (It should be recalled that it was a Canadian, the communications guru Marshall McLuhan, who coined the phrase "global village"; he used to insist, incidentally, that villages were not necessarily fun places to be.) A key dimension for Canada is, in fact, continentalization, first through the 1988 Free Trade Agreement with the United States, followed by steps to incorporate Mexico (and perhaps the hemisphere as a whole) in an American-led continental bloc.

The global recession of the early '90s hit Canada early, and it hit hard. Radical restructuring of the Canadian economy is taking place within the free trade framework; though it is certainly too soon to judge the final outcome, the manufacturing sector centered in Ontario has experienced severe loss of jobs.

At the same time, equally powerful forces of political disintegration are tearing at the Canadian fabric. (Are they, if only in part, the other side of that coin of economic integration?) Quebec separatism continues to gather force, while English-speaking Canada shows a limited willingness to compromise and find a new federalism. Quebecers (or Québécois) have twice before elected a provincial government committed to separation; they now seem poised to elect members of similar persuasion to the federal parliament.

With a most unpopular Conservative government (20% or less approval rate in the public opinion polls), Canada is being governed by default. Support from those at the right of the political spectrum who have abandoned the Conservatives is shifting in English-speaking Canada to a further-right Reform Party, which is intransigent in opposing the devolution of powers to Quebec. The crisis of ungovernability may persist.

There are further political happenings of note. For the first time ever, Ontario—the largest province and the industrial heartland of Canada—has elected a social democratic (New Democratic or NDP) government. It has since been joined by NDP governments in British Columbia and Saskatchewan. With the majority of Canadians now governed at the provincial level by left-wing governments—albeit only slightly left-of-center—the issue of what governments can any longer do in these generally neoconservative times is being put to the test. In addition, aboriginal peoples, long oppressed but mostly quiescent, have pushed their way to the front of the political stage and are, finally, getting a serious hearing from other Canadians.

I have no crystal ball, and it is always possible that Canada will continue to muddle through; certainly there are worse fates. Compared to much of the world, Canada is prosperous. It is a good place to live and a most interesting place to be. It is a fascinating country to write about and, I hope, to read about.

Canada has, of course, much in common with other developed industrialized societies, notably with the United States. (It even calls its currency the dollar, but it has a different, and lesser, value than the American dollar; in this volume, unless otherwise specified, money figures are in Canadian dollars.) But the essays in this book are also about the ways in which Canada is unique and specific relative to the world community.

I am indebted to Andrew C. Kimmens, who conceived this volume, and to James Warren and William Meyers, of Facts On File, who saw it through editorially to completion. This book was too long in the making; I am particularly grateful to those contributors who, having met their original deadlines, were rewarded by having to update and did so cheerfully. As always, University College at the University of Toronto was a most pleasant place to work, and my family was most tolerant of the time taken.

Mel Watkins
Toronto, Canada

PART ONE

THE PROVINCES
AND TERRITORIES
OF CANADA

PROVINCIAL AND TERRITORIAL GOVERNMENT

PROVINCIAL GOVERNMENT

Constitution: The 10 provinces of Canada are linked together in a federal system set out by an act of the British Parliament, the British North America Act, 1867, now renamed the Constitution Act of 1867 by the Constitution Act of 1982. The Act outlines the distribution of powers between the two levels of government. The original bias of confederation leaned toward a strong central government, allowing 16 areas of jurisdiction to provincial legislatures and 29 to Parliament. The federal government, located in Ottawa, was given powers to disallow provincial statutes within one year of their passage, to appoint provincial lieutenant governors, to declare provincial works for the general advantage of Canada or several provinces and to appoint judges to superior, district and county courts. However, in practice, provincial governments have staked claims to wider jurisdiction, the central government has rarely exercised some of its powers (e.g., disallowance), and a more equal relationship has evolved.

Provincial governments are primarily responsible for public education, health and social services, highways and local government (through municipalities). Provincial courts rule in matters of both civil and criminal law. Taxation powers are limited to direct taxation, such as personal and corporation income tax, consumer taxes and certain property taxes. However, the Constitution Act, 1982, granted provinces unrestricted powers of taxation in the field of natural resources. In the areas of agriculture and immigration the federal government and provincial governments share jurisdiction, but the federal government can prevail if provincial policy conflicts with federal interests. Jurisdiction over property and civil rights has led to provincial control of labor relations and marketing and business contracts. Of increasing importance in the postwar period has been provincial control of public land and thus ownership of natural resources.

Government institutions: Provincial government is modeled on the British parliamentary system with an elected legislature to which the premier and cabinet are responsible. The lieutenant governor represents the Crown and

3

is appointed by the federal cabinet. Officially the lieutenant governor is defined as part of the legislature and also as formal head of the executive, with powers to appoint and dismiss provincial premiers and ministers; summon, prorogue and dissolve provincial legislatures; and give assent to provincial legislation. In practice, the lieutenant governor has become a figurehead acting on the advice of the premier and cabinet. The power to reserve a bill for consideration by the federal cabinet is politically not exercisable today.

The members of the cabinet, which includes the premier, also form the executive council, the body that has legal status in contrast to the cabinet, which has political status. The premier, as leader of the party that controls the legislature and chief member of the executive council, controls public policy and administration. The cabinet ministers are appointed from among members of the majority party in the legislature. In 1987 the size of provincial cabinets ranged from 11 members in Prince Edward Island (PEI) to 28 in Quebec, with an average of around 20. Most ministers are assigned a department and its related policy area, such as health, education, labor, social services, energy, environment, natural resources, economic development, agriculture, transportation, tourism and recreation, justice, finance, municipal affairs, consumer protection, and intergovernmental affairs. Some ministers have more than one department; some departments have more than one minister. Since 1960, as provincial governments have expanded their areas of activity and control, cabinet committee systems have been adopted to improve policy planning and coordination.

Provincial legislatures, usually called the Legislative Assembly, are today all composed of a single elected chamber, although five were originally bicameral. Electoral districts or ridings each return one member to the legislature (except PEI and British Columbia). In 1987 PEI had the smallest legislature, at 32, and Ontario the largest, at 125. The procedure for making provincial law requires that a bill undergo a first and second reading, detailed review in committee and a final third reading. The legislature also approves provincial budgets. The modern emphasis on executive government curtails independent action by the Legislative Assembly. Bills involving expenditure or taxation can be introduced only by ministers. The passage of other bills introduced by members who are not ministers is possible but is exceptional, and minority government is rare. All provinces except PEI publish a Hansard report of debates and proceedings.

Federal representation: Representation in the Senate, the upper house of Parliament, was constitutionally fixed to give equitable regional representation. The original intent was to prevent Ontario, the most populous province, from having a greater say in decisions about tariffs, taxation and railways than Quebec and the Maritimes (PEI, Nova Scotia, New Brunswick), which were more important to the national economy than their population suggested. Thus, the 104 senators are made up of 24 from the Maritimes, 24 from Quebec, 24 from Ontario, 24 from the western provinces (Manitoba, Saskatchewan, Alberta, British Columbia), six from Newfoundland and one each from the Yukon Territory and the Northwest

Territories. Senators are appointed by the governor general on the advice of the prime minister. The 1987 Meech Lake Accord would have had the prime minister select senators from lists provided by provincial premiers. In western provinces the proposal that the senate should consist of an equal number of elected senators from each province is popular. Senate reform is a hotly contested aspect of constitutional debate.

Representation in the House of Commons, the elected lower house of Parliament, is on the basis of population. The number of seats, currently 295, is subject to redistribution after each decennial census. Members of Parliament are elected from single-member constituencies.

Judicial system: The provincial judicial system consists basically of two types of courts: superior courts and provincial courts. The federal government appoints judges to the superior courts; the province makes appointments to the provincial courts. Superior courts are usually divided into trial and appeal divisions. The trial division can hear all civil suits except those within the jurisdiction of federal courts. In criminal matters they hear trials of serious offenses, for which a jury is either mandatory or may be requested (except in Alberta). The appellate division hears appeals from the trial division of the superior court and from lower courts, and its decisions can be appealed to the Supreme Court of Canada. Nova Scotia, Ontario and British Columbia have retained country or district courts, which at one time operated in all provinces, to hear certain serious criminal trials and civil cases involving specified amounts of money.

Provincial courts as a rule handle lesser criminal cases, though they may try more serious offenses if the accused so chooses. They also make preliminary inquiries of indictable offenses. All provinces deal separately with family matters, juvenile offenses, small claims and probate, but there is considerable variation in whether they come under the jurisdiction of entirely separate courts or under a division of the superior or provincial courts.

Provincial revenue: Under the Constitution Act, 1867, Parliament exercises unlimited taxing powers, the provinces being restricted to direct taxation. In 1988–89 taxation contributed 61% of provincial revenues. For most of the provinces personal and corporate income tax is collected by the federal government on behalf of the provinces. This system is now threatened by the opting-out of Quebec, Ontario and Alberta from the corporate tax collection agreements, and the agreement that all provinces will join Quebec in implementing their own personal income tax collection systems. In 1993 provinces will be able to choose their own schedule of rates, income brackets, and non-refundable tax credits, i.e., credits deductible from taxes otherwise payable, including the basic credit and the married, child, age, and disability credits (which in Canada have recently replaced deductions from income). Each province will be able to make this tax more or less progressive.

Provinces also levy a number of other direct taxes, of which the sales tax is the most important. Only Quebec has agreed to integrate its sales tax collection with the federal Goods and Services Tax instituted in January

1991. Since this has a much broader base than provincial sales taxes, it would increase revenue and convert sales taxes into provincial Goods and Services taxes. Non-tax revenues contributed 18% to provincial coffers in 1985–86. They included motor vehicle user charges, natural resource levies and liquor store profits.

Provincial governments also rely on federal transfer payments. In 1989– 90 cash transfers totaled $24.3 billion, almost 20% of provincial revenues. Transfer payments fall broadly into two categories: general purpose and specific purpose transfers. Insured health care and social welfare grants are specific purpose transfers, while equalization grants are general purpose and thus unconditional. Established in 1957, equalization payments were de- signed to enable the poorer provinces with small revenue bases to maintain public services and taxation levels comparable to the richer provinces. The list of sources of revenue equalized now contains 33 items. Calculations for 1990–91 resulted in all provinces except Ontario, Alberta and British Co- lumbia receiving equalization grants, totaling approximately $8.2 billion. Other general grants brought the total to $9.86 billion in general purpose cash transfers. In addition there were Established Programs Financing (EPF) transfers of $8.22 billion and $6.27 billion specific purpose cash transfers.

Health care: The Constitution Act, 1867 gave the provinces jurisdiction over hospitals, asylums, charities and charitable institutions. All provinces now administer well-developed programs of health care, old-age pensions and unemployment insurance in addition to a whole range of other social welfare benefits. However, the processes of industrialization and urbaniza- tion following World War I produced chronic social problems throughout the nation, so that at an early stage the federal government was drawn into participating with provinces in financing social services. Initially, in order to preserve the terms of the Constitution, the federal government offered conditional grants to share the cost of provincially administered programs. It was under this arrangement that the first old-age pension scheme was introduced in 1927. Since then, three constitutional amendments have se- cured some federal jurisdiction in certain areas of social welfare. In 1940 the federal government gained exclusive jurisdiction for a national unem- ployment scheme. The 1951 amendment permitted national old-age pen- sions with concurrent jurisdiction under provincial paramountcy. This was extended in 1964 to include supplementary benefits, which were to be part of the Canada Pension Plan introduced a year later.

Health programs began operation on a shared-cost basis. In 1957 the federal government offered to contribute to a comprehensive, universal pro- vincial hospital insurance scheme. By 1961 all 10 provinces were partici- pating, and in 1966 the Medical Care Act extended the 1957 benefits to include doctors' services. Until 1977 federal payments matched provincial spending dollar for dollar. At that time, Parliament altered the arrange- ment to transfer a lump sum based on a three-year moving average of the gross national product (GNP) and per capita cash payment. The use of these funds is no longer limited to use on hospital and doctors' services. Although this system gave provinces greater flexibility, the financial outcome was that the federal government no longer contributed a full 50% of rapidly increasing hospital costs. In the early 1980s doctors and hospitals in some provinces tried to supplement the limited resources by charging extra fees direct to patients. The Canada Health Act of 1984 has been largely successful in halting this erosion of the principle of universal accessibility by deducting the amount collected in extra payments from the federal transfer payment.

A mixed bag of other social benefits provided by the federal government includes payments to mothers under the 1944 Family Allowance Act; the program long included all children under the age of 18, but universality was abandoned in the 1992 federal budget in favor of monthly payments to low-income families; the Canada Assistance Plan of 1966, which provides cost-share support for provincial social assistance programs; a means-tested benefit for old-age pensioners paid under the 1967 Guaranteed Income Supplement program; and the Spouse's Allowance brought in in 1975 for old-age pensioners' spouses aged 60 to 64.

Education: Since education falls entirely under provincial jurisdiction, 10 different systems have developed. Nevertheless, many similarities exist. In all provinces a minister of education together with a department of education determine provincial policy for public elementary and secondary schools, which are run by local school boards and funded by some combination of local taxation and provincial grants. In 1986–87 pupils in public schools made up nearly 95% of the total 4.94 million enrollment in all elementary and secondary schools in Canada. The other 5% attended private schools administered by religious organizations or other groups, which usually operate within the guidelines determined by provincial departments of education. The exception to provincial jurisdiction is the education of status Indian children, which is the responsibility of the federal government but increasingly has involved provincial cooperation and more recently greater involvement of Indian communities.

Post-secondary educational bodies include degree-granting universities and liberal-arts colleges and a disparate group of non-degree-granting institutions such as community colleges, hospital nursing schools and adult education courses. Originally entirely private, this whole category of education has increasingly come under provincial control since the mid-1960s.

The federal government played a very minor role in education prior to World War II. Since then considerations of the state of the national economy, regional financial disparities and national unity have drawn the federal government into greater participation. Three areas have attracted federal attention. During the 1960s Parliament passed legislation to provide financial aid for technical and vocational training, second-language instruction and post-secondary education. Under the Fiscal Arrangements Act (1967, revised 1977), unconditional federal grants were paid to provinces to cover 50% of the operating costs of post-secondary education.

In 1977 the Established Programs Financing arrangements provided that federal aid to post-secondary education, hospital insurance, medicare and nursing home care should no longer be a percentage of actual provincial expenditure, but should be based on payments in 1975–76 and increased in proportion to growth of population and GNP. But the federal government also partially vacated the personal income tax field (13.5 tax points) and the corporation income tax field (1 tax point), and the yield of these vacated points to a province was subtracted from the EPF payment. In the mid-'80s the government limited the automatic GNP increase of the basic EPF calculation; in 1990–91 it was reduced to 0%. Since the tax yield deducted is expected to grow as GNP increases, the net yield of the EPF is expected to decline. Quebec will be the most seriously affected. Because of long-standing opting out agreements, its EPF net cash transfer will be 0 by 1996. The start of this pull-back of federal aid during a recession has enabled the federal government to plan for decreases in its deficit but at considerable cost to the provincial attempts to control theirs.

In 1990 the annual increase in the Canada Assistance Plan grant of half of actual provincial social assistance expenditures was limited to 5% for the wealthier provinces. In the 1991 federal budget the limit was extended to 1994–95. British Columbia challenged the federal government's right to change the agreed arrangements unilaterally and was upheld by the British Columbia court. But on appeal by the Canadian government to the Supreme Court of Canada, British Columbia lost 7 to 0.

TERRITORIAL GOVERNMENT

The two territories of Canada are governed by the federal government, which has delegated legislative powers to territorial governments in the Northwest Territories and Yukon Acts. The head of each territorial government is a federally appointed commissioner, who reports directly to the federal Minister of Indian Affairs and Northern Development. Each territory elects a Legislative Assembly, from which an Executive Council is drawn. In the Northwest Territories the commissioner is not required to act on the advice of the Executive Council or the Legislative Assembly, but does so by tradition. In the Yukon, as of 1979, executive power was transferred by the federal government to the Executive Council, and the commissioner is instructed to follow its decisions except in matters of particular concern to Ottawa. The legislative powers of the commissioners-in-council are similar to those assigned to the provinces under the Constitution Act, 1867. The federal government retains control over lands, natural resources, taxation and claims of native rights, but the trend is toward delegation of greater powers to the territorial governments.

ALBERTA

GEOGRAPHY

Features: Alberta is the westernmost of the three Prairies Provinces. It is divided from British Columbia on the west by the Rocky Mountains and from Saskatchewan on the east by an arbitrary straight line. Alberta comprises four distinct biophysical regions. The Foothills Region along the southwestern border of the province consists of a series of ridges rising to a maximum height of 12,293 ft/3,747 m. Much of this mountainous territory lies in national and provincial parks and provincial forest reserves. The latter are zoned for watershed, wildlife, recreation, mining, commercial grazing, forestry and multipurpose uses.

The greater area of Alberta is part of the Interior Plain of North America. Both the Prairie Region in southern Alberta and the Parkland Region in the central part of the province benefit from soils developed on glacial deposits. The fertility of these soils, together with gently undulating topography, create excellent conditions for agricultural activities. However, low rainfall and high evaporation in the Prairie Region are major limiting factors to its productivity. Since the 19th century, irrigation has been used to alleviate the chronic water deficit.

The Boreal Forest Region occupies the northern half of the province. Rivers and lakes dominate the landscape. The area is unsuitable for agriculture except in the Peace River region, where parkland conditions create the world's most northerly grain-growing area. Many of the province's natural resources are concentrated here, including forests, fur-bearing mammals, fish, coal, oil, natural gas, sand, gravel, peat moss, iron ore and oil sands deposits.

Area: 255,284 sq. mi./661,185 sq. km., including 6,485 sq. mi./16,796 sq. km. of inland water.

Mean maximum and minimum temperatures: Calgary 61.2°F/16.5°C (July), 12.0°F/ − 10.9°C (January); Edmonton 61.2°F/16.5°C (July), 5.5°F/ − 14.7°C (January); Fort McMurray 61.3°F/16.3°C (July), − 7.2°F/ − 11.5°C (January).

Relative humidity: 52%−77%.

9

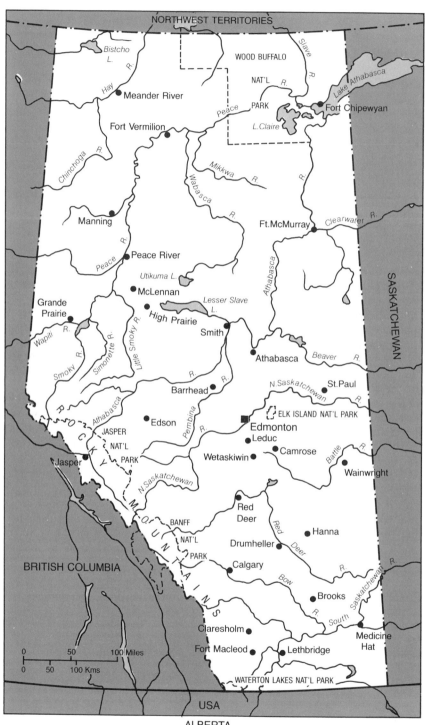

NORTHWEST TERRITORIES

Bistcho L.

WOOD BUFFALO

NAT'L

PARK

Hay R.

Meander River

Peace R.

Slave R.

Lake Athabasca

Fort Chipewyan

Fort Vermilion

L.Claire

Chinchoga R.

Mikkwa R.

Wabasca R.

R.

Manning

Ft.McMurray

Clearwater R.

Peace R.

Peace River

Athabasca R.

Utikuma L.

McLennan

Grande
Prairie

Lesser Slave L.

High Prairie

Smith

Wapiti R.

Smoky R.

Simonette R.

Little Smoky R.

Athabasca

Beaver R.

St.Paul

Barrhead

R.

R.

N.Saskatchewan R.

R O C K Y

Athabasca

Edson

ELK ISLAND NAT'L PARK

JASPER

NAT'L

PARK

Pembina R.

Edmonton

Leduc

Camrose

Wainwright

Jasper

Wetaskiwin

Battle R.

N.Saskatchewan

Red
Deer

BANFF

NAT'L

PARK

Drumheller

Hanna

Red Deer R.

M O U N T A I N S

BRITISH COLUMBIA

Calgary

Brooks

Bow R.

South Saskatchewan R.

Claresholm

Medicine
Hat

Fort Macleod

Lethbridge

WATERTON LAKES NAT'L PARK

SASKATCHEWAN

0   50   100 Miles
0   50   100 Kms

USA

ALBERTA

Mean annual precipitation: Edmonton 18 in./416 mm., including 54 in./ 136 cm. of snow; Calgary 16.7 in./424 mm., including 60 in./152 cm. of snow; Fort McMurray 18.6 in./472 mm., including 65 in./164 cm. of snow. Precipitation in the southeast is lower, averaging 11.8 in./300 mm.

POPULATION

Total population (1986 census): 2,375,300. Estimated population, 1990: 2,471,600.

Chief towns and population (1990): Calgary (692,885), Edmonton, the capital (605,538), Lethbridge (60,610; 1989), Red Deer (55,907), Medicine Hat (42,290), St. Albert (38,318), Fort McMurray (35,000) and Grande Prairie (26,648). Population density 9.27 per sq. mi./3.5 per sq. km.

Distribution: Expansion of urban population has been a major feature of Alberta's development in the period after World War II and especially in the 1970s. In 1951 only 46% of the population lived in urban areas. By 1986 the proportion had increased to nearly 80% of the population, the majority of which is concentrated in the two metropolitan centers of Edmonton and Calgary.

Ethnic composition: There is a great diversity of ethnic groups and religions. As in the rest of Canada, people whose origins were in whole or in part in the British Isles, including Ireland, constitute a large proportion (36.3% in the 1986 census), but the number of French is uncharacteristically small (5.5%), surpassed by that of German only (7.6%) and just larger than that of Ukrainian only (4.5%) descent. Native peoples, including Inuit, North American Indians and Métis, make up 2.1%, and Scandinavian, Dutch, Polish and Italian a further 6.5%. South Asians, Chinese, Filipinos, Vietnamese and other Asians are 4.6%. There are more than 1,200 ethnocultural groups eligible to receive support from the province for cultural and linguistic programs.

Language: Canada is officially bilingual English and French, but many Westerners are opposed to official bilingualism. In the 1986 census 82.3% of the population claimed English as their mother tongue and 92.0% gave it as their home language or one of their home languages. A total of 2.4% gave French as their mother tongue and 1.1% as their home language, and 15.3% gave Inuit, one of the Indian languages, or some other language, mostly European, as mother tongue and 6.9% as home language.

Religions: Approximately 56% of the 1981 population belonged to various Protestant denominations, including United Church of Canada, Anglican and Lutheran, and 26% were Roman Catholic.

11

CONSTITUTION AND GOVERNMENT

In 1905 Alberta and Saskatchewan were created by acts of the Parliament of Canada out of parts of the Northwest Territories. In both the Alberta Act and the Saskatchewan Act the Dominion Government (as the federal government was then called) retained for itself control over the natural resources of the new provinces. These were not transferred to the two provinces until 1930, and the delay is a continuing source of provincial resentment against the national government. Alberta was the last province to have its legislation disallowed or reserved for Dominion Government approval. These powers were used against Social Credit legislation, the last time in 1943. Alberta was the first province to establish the office of ombudsman to mediate between members of the public and the government, and the province has its own bill of rights.

Executive: In March 1991 Premier Donald R. Getty's Conservative cabinet had 27 members. Most ministers presided over one or more departments of government. Two are listed as associates, i.e., second ministers of departments for which others have primary responsibility. Others are listed as also having responsibility for an organization or policy area not having departmental status. There were 24 departments and 25 agencies, presumably with varying degrees of independence. Several of these provide financial or related services to the public, for example Treasury Branches, a profit-making savings and loan operation, or the Hail and Crop Insurance Corporation. Others regulate or provide services, such as the Alberta Government Telephones Commission. But most prominently agencies serve the dominant concerns of the Alberta economy: the Oil and Sands Research Authority, the Petroleum Marketing Commission and the Water Resources Commission.

Political parties: Alberta politics has been characterized by a succession of governing parties with overwhelming majorities remaining in power for long periods, after which they are defeated and virtually eliminated from the legislature by a new party. Since Alberta became a province in 1905, only four parties have come to power: Liberal (1905–1921), United Farmers of Alberta (1921–1935), Social Credit (1935–1971) and Progressive Conservative (1971–present). The 1989 election returned 59 Progressive Conservatives, 16 New Democrats (the official opposition) and 8 Liberals. Social Credit, which dominated the province for 36 years and formed until 1991 the government of neighboring British Columbia, ran six candidates who all were at the bottom of the poll.

Local government: Like the other Prairie provinces, Alberta entered the depression of the 1930s with municipal governments and school authorities for its rural areas that had grown out of the needs of an agricultural society before the coming of the automobile. The enduring achievement of William Aberhart's Social Credit party was to transform the overlapping jumble of small rural municipal units into larger, more efficient units. The new units shared boundaries with new school divisions, which replaced districts based on one-room schools. Financial and administrative coordination between school boards and municipalities became possible. The County Act went further and allowed the joining of a municipal district and a coterminous school division into a multipurpose authority in which a committee of county council augmented by representatives of smaller municipalities took over the functions of the school division. Thirty such counties have been formed and thirty coterminous municipal districts remain. In addition there are improvement districts where population is too sparse for normal municipal institutions and special areas in the most arid portion of the province. Originally the government hoped to incorporate hospitals into the system of multipurpose authorities, but these required areas too large to fit and are organized in separate districts.

The government record in urban matters has not been so innovative. A New Towns Act enabled the provincial government to ease the creation of instant urban communities growing out of the oil boom after 1947. But the metropolitan areas of Edmonton and Calgary were permitted, although not encouraged, to expand with little control, and the consequent loss of prime farm land has scarcely been addressed.

Lloydminster, a community that straddled the new Alberta-Saskatchewan boundary when the provinces were created, is governed as a unit and is now a city in both provinces.

Federal representation: Alberta has six seats in the Senate, a constitutionally determined fixed number. Members are appointed by the governor general on the advice of the prime minister. However, the government of Alberta favors an elected Senate, and without constitutional authority arranged an election to fill a vacant Alberta seat. After some delay the victor, Stan Waters, was appointed to the Senate by Prime Minister Brian Mulroney in June 1990, to become the first "elected" senator. Waters died in 1991.

Judicial system: Superior Courts, with judges appointed by the federal government, consist of the Court of Appeal, which sits in Edmonton and Calgary with a chief justice and 13 other judges, and the Court of Queen's Bench, which sits in Edmonton and Calgary with 60 judges and in addition in Lethbridge and Red Deer with two judges each.

Provincial Courts, with judges appointed by the provincial government, include the Provincial Court, which sits in Calgary and Edmonton and 16 other centers; the Family and Youth Division of the Provincial Court, which sits in Calgary, Edmonton, Medicine Hat and Red Deer; and the Civil Division, sitting in Edmonton and Calgary.

RECENT HISTORY

In common with the other three Western provinces and against a background of physical isolation and frontier experience, Alberta's political history has been characterized by habitual resentment against central Canada and the federal government, an attitude often termed "western alienation."

A major turning point in Alberta's history was the discovery of oil at Leduc, near Edmonton, in 1947. From then until 1985 its fortunes were seen no longer to rely on agriculture, but on the development of its oil and natural gas resources. Under Premier William Aberhart's student and successor as Social Credit premier, Ernest Manning—whose ultraconservatism and belief in the virtues of capitalism created conditions that attracted a large influx of businessmen—Alberta became the fastest-growing province in Canada.

In 1968, after 25 years as premier, Manning resigned. His successor, Harry Strom, did not last long by Albertan standards, and in 1971 the Progressive Conservative party was elected with Peter Lougheed at its head. Apart from a new emphasis on youth and vigor, there was little change of ideology or policy, nor did clashes with the federal government cease. Alberta's position as a supplier of raw materials to the more highly industrialized provinces of Ontario and Quebec gave it a political advantage and economic base, which Lougheed could use to secure greater provincial jurisdiction. Other factors contributing to western alienation were resentment over the bilingual issue in a province with a tiny minority of French speakers, and the weak or nonexistent representation in the federal Liberal cabinet and caucus, especially compared to the strong French and Quebec contingent. One collision with central Canada came in 1973 when Alberta demanded a high price for its oil in line with the OPEC increases. A much more serious rift occurred in 1980 over energy pricing and revenue-sharing as proposed by the National Energy Program. Through this program the federal government attempted to achieve oil self-sufficiency for Canada, a greater share of the economic benefits of western oil for itself and other regions of Canada, and a higher level of Canadian ownership of the industry. However, Lougheed succeeded in negotiating changes to the NEP and to Prime Minister Pierre Elliott Trudeau's constitutional package in time to quiet the growing separatist movement.

Some sources of discontent apparently evaporated with the national election of the Mulroney Conservative government in 1984, and many others might have been resolved by the Meech Lake Accord of 1987 had it not failed to receive approval of all provinces. This conceded a shifting of powers from Ottawa to the provinces and an end to the National Energy Program. On the major issue of free trade, Conservative premier Donald Getty, elected in 1985, for once came out in agreement with the federal government. After the worldwide 50% fall in oil prices in 1985–86, internal Alberta policy has emphasized agriculture and the creation of jobs as priorities over energy resource development.

ECONOMY

The discovery of oil in the Leduc fields in 1947 marked the transition from a predominantly agricultural to a predominantly petroleum-based economy. The ramifications quickly spread throughout all aspects of social, economic and political life. With a history of successive governments dedicated to the free enterprise system, foreign investors and residents were not slow to recognize the new opportunities presented by the vast oil and gas resources. Population, especially urban, increased by 160% between 1947 and 1980; per capita personal income rose to the highest in Canada in the early 1980s; and through a combination of taxes and royalties the government grew wealthy overnight. In response to the demands of the oil industry, the construction, manufacturing and business services sectors of the economy expanded accordingly. In 1986 per capita production, as measured by gross domestic product (GDP), was $22,960, the highest in Canada.

In spite of avowed opposition to big government bureaucracy and socialism, both the Social Credit and Conservative parties have put their tremendous oil revenues to use building a vast infrastructure of roads, schools, universities and hospitals and have particularly prided themselves on the high level of social services offered to residents. The personal income tax rate is the lowest in Canada, and Alberta is the only province without a retail sales tax.

Foreseeing the eventual decline of the nonrenewable resource base, the Alberta Heritage Savings Trust Fund was created in 1976. Initially the fund received 30% of nonrenewable resource revenues and invested in a range of projects, some designed to yield an immediate commercial return and others, such as agricultural and medical research, to provide long-term economic or social benefits. In fact, the Heritage Fund is already being used to cushion the province against financial difficulties caused by major fluctuations in world oil prices. Budgetary deficits following the 1981 worldwide recession and the drastic 50% fall in oil prices in 1985–86 led the government first to reduce and finally, in April 1987, to cap the nonrenewable resource revenue transferred to the fund until Alberta is able to achieve a balanced budget. At the same time, a 1982 amendment to the Heritage Fund Act permitted the transfer of investment earnings from the fund to the province's general revenues. Between 1982 and 1988 an additional $11 billion—more than a full year's budgetary expenditure—has been provided from this source.

Despite financial assistance from the Heritage Fund, the 1980s required adjustments to a leaner economic diet. In 1989, private and public investment totaled $19.9 billion, below its 1981 high of $21.8 billion. The financial sector has undergone a period of consolidation and retrenchment, especially since the shock in 1985 of the collapse of two Schedule A chartered banks based in Alberta which had made unwise loans in the energy and real estate sectors. Both agriculture and oil depend on external markets; prices and revenues are largely determined by outside economic and political forces. More attention is now being paid to efficiency and productivity in order to maintain competitiveness in world markets. Moreover, government encouragement for an industrial core within the province, thus reducing the export of raw materials and jobs, has begun to bear fruit. Between 1975 and 1984 manufacturing grew in value by 27.4% in real terms compared to a national growth rate over the same period of 7.4%.

Agriculture: As a contributor of only 3.5% of the 1989 GDP, agriculture lags behind mining, manufacturing and construction. This figure, however, belies the importance of agriculture in the provincial and Canadian economies. Twenty percent of Canada's total agricultural output comes from Alberta. Due to its relatively small population and food consumption, the farming industry accounts for more than $2 billion in foreign exports annually, with wheat alone in 1990 being the third most important export, after crude petroleum and natural gas. As an employer of 7.6% of the Alberta labor force (1989), agriculture nearly matches manufacturing and surpasses mining. Furthermore, the early widespread cultivation of wheat established many of the settlement and transportation patterns that remain dominant today. Unfortunately even the bumper crop of 1991 cannot compensate for the low price of wheat owing to the trade war between the United States and the European Community.

More than 50 million acres/20.2 million hectares are devoted to crop and livestock production, with approximately 27 million acres/11 million hectares classified as cultivated. It is estimated that another 20 million acres/8.1 million hectares could be added to the farmland inventory in the future. There are around 58,000 farms in Alberta at an average capital investment per farm of $630,000. The trend is to larger, more efficient farms through consolidation of existing operations. Twenty years ago the average farm size was 550 acres/223 hectares, at present it is about 870 acres/350 hectares. Annual farm cash receipts have also increased substantially, from approximately $600 million in the early 1960s to $3.97 billion in 1989, when they were divided almost equally between crops and livestock (46% crops).

Most of the cultivated area in Alberta (1990) is seeded to wheat, barley, tame hay, canola, oats, rye, mixed grains and flaxseed, in that order. Receipts from the sale of wheat, oats, barley, canola and flaxseed account for over 90% of the total farm cash receipts from crops. In keeping with international demand for a growing variety of agricultural products, specialty crops, which include alfalfa, sugar beet, mustard seed, beans, vegetables, potatoes, forage seed and honey, are becoming more important, especially in the irrigated districts of southern Alberta. Total crop production has more than doubled in the past 20 years, rising from 10.38 million tons/ 9.4 million tonnes in 1961 to more than 23.15 million tons/21 million tonnes in an average year during the 1980s. Livestock production has also grown significantly. Alberta maintains the largest livestock population of the western provinces, accounting for 48% of the cattle and calves, 41% of the hogs and nearly 55% of the sheep and lambs.

Mineral production: The fuels production and mining industries completely overshadow other sectors of the GDP, representing 27% in 1985. Although it employs only about 6% of the labor force, a vast number of jobs in other sectors rely on a booming petroleum industry. In 1989 Alberta produced 82% of Canada's crude oil and synthetic equivalent and 86% of its natural gas.

Until the major oil strike at Leduc in 1947, the chief oil-producing region of Alberta was Turner Valley. The Leduc discovery led to intensive exploration programs and the development of major reserves at Redwater,

Swan Hills, West Pembina, Rainbow Lake and the central Foothills Region. In 1990 established reserves of conventional crude stood at 3.7 billion barrels/583 million cu. m. In 1989 net production of crude oil and equivalent liquids was 345 million barrels/54.8 million cu. m., amounting to nearly $6.9 billion. In 1989, 39% was exported to other Canadian provinces and 36% to U.S. refineries, and the remainder was consumed in Alberta.

Further sources of oil are the oil sands deposits that underlie 23,000 sq. mi./60,000 sq. km. of northern and eastern Alberta. An estimated 12 trillion cu. ft./338 billion cu. m. of bitumen are in place in the four deposits. The importance and potential of these relatively untapped reserves have increased dramatically in recent years as conventional crude oil supplies have decreased and sophisticated recovery techniques have been developed. The largest oil sands deposit lies adjacent to the Athabasca River, where beds of oil sands are exposed at the surface and can be exploited by open-pit mining. However, 95% of deposits in the Athabasca area and all reserves in the Cold Lake, Peace River and Wabasca areas are too deep to be recovered by this method. They have required the development of what are known as "in-situ" techniques. Underscoring the importance attached to oil sands development, the Alberta government in 1976 established the Alberta Oil Sands Technology and Research Authority (AOSTRA). AOSTRA has received $351 million from the Alberta Heritage Savings Trust Fund. Its involvement ranges from academic and institutional research to support for large-scale field pilots and demonstration units in cooperation with the private sector. In 1986 there were seven commercial-scale in-situ steam drive recovery projects operating in the Cold Lake area, and one in Peace River. In addition, 59 experimental oil sands and heavy oil schemes were operating in Alberta, most of them involving in-situ recovery techniques. However, the relatively low price of oil since 1986 has caused companies to slow down or postpone further development of major projects.

Total remaining established reserves of marketable natural gas at the end of 1989 were estimated at 60.6 trillion cu. ft./1.70 trillion cu. m. Of the 2.54 trillion cu. ft./71.9 billion cu. m. produced in 1989 and valued at $4.02 billion, 21.9% was consumed within Alberta, 35.7% was shipped to other Canadian provinces and 41.8% was exported to the United States. An oversupply of natural gas in the United States from 1988, which resulted in a decline in price and in drilling and exports, was expected to last into 1989 or 1990, but volume of production and export rose again in 1988 and later. Nearly 500 processing plants for natural gas produce sulfur, in 1990 Alberta's fifth largest export, as well as liquid co-products such as propane, butanes and pentanes-plus.

Coal mining declined from a high output in 1946 to its lowest value in 1962. Then the opening of two new markets, Japanese steel producers and domestic thermal electric power plants, initiated a recovery. In 1986 production totaled 27.58 million tons/25.02 million tonnes at a total value of $438 million, making Alberta Canada's second largest producer. Of this 69% was subbituminous coal from the Plains region, used primarily "as-mined" in thermal power generating stations close to the mine sites. The remaining 31% was bituminous from the Mountains and Foothills regions, used mainly in coking and steel production. Remaining established reserves of coal estimated at 26.34 billion tons/23.9 billion tonnes and ultimate potential reserves at 871 billion tons/790 billion tonnes. Future uses for these reserves have been identified as feedstock for synthetic natural gas plants, manufacturing liquid fuels, enhanced oil recovery and oil sands recovery, and, with new technologies to reduce sulfuric oxide emissions, electricity production.

Alberta is also richly endowed with nonfuel mineral resources. Construction aggregates constitute by far the largest volume of industrial mineral production, which also includes raw materials for cement, ceramics and building products manufacture. However, their value is exceeded by nonmetallics and Alberta is one of the world's largest producers of sulfur, producing 97% of Canada's total. In addition, potential has been identified for development of deposits of nonmetallic minerals (bentonite, peat moss and dolomite) and metallic minerals (uranium, molybdenite, copper, lead, zinc, iron ore, magnesium, titanium, vanadium and nickel).

Manufacturing: Alberta lagged behind other provinces in manufacturing due to its small population and greater distance from markets. The recent transformation in this sector is due to population expansion, low taxes and energy costs plus readily available skilled labor and local financing. Manufacturing ranks second among the goods-producing industries in terms of GDP and provided employment for 86,800 people in 1988 (7.8% of the labor force). The 1990 value of manufacturing shipments totaled $18.95 billion, with food and beverage production at 25%, followed by refined petroleum production making up 19% and chemicals and chemical products at 17%. Since the mid-1970s, provincial government policy has been to encourage growth and diversification in the manufacturing sector. Annual investment in manufacturing plants increased from $441 million in 1975 to $1.12 billion in 1984. Diversification can be seen in the rapid expansion of chemicals manufacturing, petroleum refining and plastics processing and the emergence of advanced manufacturers of electrical, telecommunications and aerospace products. The government supports technological research through the Alberta Research Council, the Alberta Microelectronics Centre, the Alberta Laser Institute and the Food Processing Development Centre.

Forestry: Although forestry contributes only a small fraction to the GDP, Alberta's forests are the largest remaining timber source in North America, covering some 143,000 sq. mi./378,000 sq. km. The annual cut is in the order of 200 million cu. ft./6 million cu. m. coniferous and 18 million cu. ft./500,000 cu. m. deciduous, with potential for increased levels in the future. In 1984 an agreement between the federal and provincial governments was signed to develop Alberta's forest resources and industries over the next five years. Forest-based industries in 1990 accounted for about 5%

of the value of manufacturing shipments in the province, and a number of new forest projects have been started.

Service sector: The service sector stands out as Alberta's largest employer with 33.4% of the labor force in 1986, when it contributed about 15% of the GDP. Tourism plays an increasingly important role. In 1986 the industry supported the equivalent of 74,000 full-time jobs and generated revenues of $2.3 billion, approximately four times the amount earned by the industry a decade earlier. Calgary hosted the Twenty-fifth Olympic Winter Games in 1988.

Foreign trade: In 1990 Alberta exported $15.6 billion worth of goods and services, over one-fifth (21.5%) of the GDP. Exports in 1986 had been the lowest since 1981 due to the low price of oil. In 1990 crude oil represented the largest export earner at 33.9% of the total. Two of the next five highest earners were also related to the energy sector: natural gas (16.8%) and coal (3.3%). Wheat was the third highest at 5.5%, followed by organic chemicals (4.0%) and sulfur (3.9%). $1.0 billion worth of manufactured products excluding food and beverages were exported in 1990. Alberta exports to 120 countries on six continents. Its most important customer by far is the United States, which in 1990 took 74.8% of the total of $15.4 billion, including $7.9 billion via pipeline. The Asia/Pacific Rim countries, particularly Japan and mainland China, have become the second largest market. In Europe, the third largest export region, the Soviet Union had become Alberta's fourth most important customer.

Employment: Alberta's labor force numbered just over 1.3 million in 1991, the fourth largest in Canada. The participation rate of about 72% ranks highest in Canada. Unemployment had run at under 4% prior to the recession in 1981. Between 1982 and 1986 rates hovered around 10% to 11%. When he ran for the office of premier, Donald Getty made job creation one of the major issues of his campaign, and he continued to emphasize it as a government priority. The unemployment rate dropped to 8.0% in 1988 and to 7.0% in 1990, as compared to 8.1% for Canada overall.

Prices: Alberta's annual rate of inflation is below the national average. The consumer price index for all items in 1990 (1986 = 100) was 117.8 in Edmonton and 117.6 in Calgary, compared to 119 for Canada overall.

SOCIAL SERVICES

Welfare: Oil revenues allowed Alberta to provide a high level of social services starting in the late 1940s. Some of the earliest programs included free medical and hospital care for those receiving old age assistance, mothers' allowances, and pensions for the blind. Today the Social Allowance Program provides funding for basic necessities such as food, clothing and shelter from six regional and 52 district offices throughout the province. Child welfare covers adoptions, foster care, protection and services for unmarried mothers and handicapped children. The Family and Community Support Services program is jointly funded by the province and municipalities. It is designed to encourage and finance community projects that will prevent or ease social problems. Income supplements are available through Alberta Widow's Pension, Assured Income for the Severely Handicapped and, for senior citizens, Alberta Assured Income Plan. Assistance for the Métis population is based on the 1939 Métis Betterment Act, which established seven exclusively Métis colonies on marginal arable land and provided for government aid for housing, health, education, electricity and highways to settlements.

Health: Alberta belongs to the federal medicare scheme and operates the Alberta Health Care Insurance Plan, which provides basic health and hospitalization for all citizens at a modest monthly premium. Subsidized rates are available for low-income individuals and families. Senior citizens receive free coverage. In March 1986 there were 123 public general hospitals, two federal general hospitals, 44 auxiliary hospitals, two mental health hospitals and 87 nursing homes. Preventive health services are provided by 27 local health authorities and two city health departments. Their free services include prenatal classes, children's clinics, immunization programs and dental services. Government funding agencies such as the Alberta Heritage Foundation for Medical Research and the Medical Research Council of Canada provide support for a wide range of research projects.

Housing: The province provides rental housing for senior citizens and low-income families. Serviced lots are available to purchase through the Alberta Mortgage and Housing Corporation. Additional mobile home loan insurance may be obtained on loans provided by private sector lenders. Mortgage financing for lower-income families and rental housing centers is also available.

EDUCATION

The provincial government and local public boards (or county education committees) and separate (e.g., Roman Catholic or other religious) boards share responsibility for education. Basic education (grades 1–12) comes under the jurisdiction of Alberta Education, which oversees curriculum and teacher certification. Local boards employ teachers and operate schools at elementary, junior high school and senior high school levels. In 1982–83 a reorganization provided five regional offices to oversee and support all schools both public and private regarding delivery of programs.

There are more than 160 private schools, with more than 13,000 students. Many of the private schools have affiliation with religious denominations. Public and separate (Roman Catholic) boards are funded from provincial grants and local property taxes and their schools are free for all children. In 1986–87, 426,987 students were enrolled in grades 1–12. Preschool programs are available, though not compulsory, through Alberta Early Childhood Services.

The advanced education system in Alberta has 34 postsecondary institutions. About 85% of funding for these institutions comes from provincial grants, the remainder from tuition fees and private grants. Of the four universities, Athabasca is an open university providing undergraduate courses by correspondence. In 1986–87 it had 10,772 part-time students. Alberta (in Edmonton), Calgary and Lethbridge universities had a combined enrollment of 43,207 full-time students. The Banff Centre (1,360 part-time students in 1986–87) gives professional training in the arts and management and environmental studies. Technical and vocational training is provided by three technical institutes (11,302 full-time students in 1985–86), four Alberta Vocation Centres (17,369 full-time students in 1985–86), the Alberta Petroleum Industry Training Centre, the Community Vocational Centres and six hospital-based schools of nursing. Apprenticeship and certification programs cover 51 designated trades. With 10% of Canada's population, Alberta trains about 22% of Canada's apprentices. Eleven public (18,166 full-time students in 1986–87) and four private colleges offer a variety of certificate/diploma programs, university transfer and apprenticeship programs. There are 85 Further Education Councils administering noncredit courses, and five Community Consortia which were established in 1981–82 to provide postsecondary credit programs in areas of the province that are remote from other such institutions.

MASS MEDIA

Newspapers and periodicals: The nine daily newspapers are mainly owned by national or international chains. They are the Edmonton *Journal,* Calgary *Herald* and Medicine Hat *News,* all part of the Southam newspaper group; the Edmonton *Sun* and Calgary *Sun* owned by the Toronto Sun Publishing Co.; the Lethbridge *Herald,* part of the Thomson newspaper empire; and the Grande Prairie *Daily Herald-Tribune* and Fort McMurray *Today,* owned by Bowes Publishers Ltd. The exception is the Red Deer *Advocate,* which is not owned by a Canadian chain. They have a total circulation of about 550,000, reaching almost 85% of all households in the province.

About 130 weekly newspapers are published, with a gross circulation of over one million. Some general magazines are *Alberta Report* (neoconservative, provincial rights) and *NeWest Review* (arts). In addition, several trade journals serve the petroleum industry and other industries.

Broadcasting: Alberta is served by 41 AM and 15 FM radio broadcast originating stations and by 84 stations overall, including rebroadcast, in 1991. They are all privately owned except for CBC network stations in Edmonton and Calgary, the University of Alberta student station (CJSR) and the Alberta government-owned CKUA, which is part of the ACCESS television and radio network for educational broadcasting. The 11 television stations, of mixed national and local ownership, operate in major centers with 113 rebroadcast stations ensuring coverage throughout the province. Urban areas receive cable television.

BIOGRAPHICAL SKETCHES

Donald R. Getty.   Born in Westmount, Quebec, in 1933, Getty was elected premier of Alberta in 1985 and is a Member of Legislative Assembly (MLA) for Stettler. He graduated from the University of Western Ontario in London in 1955 with a degree in Honors Business Administration. After graduation Getty worked in the oil industry in Edmonton until 1967, when he joined an investment firm as a partner. During the same period he distinguished himself as quarterback with the Canadian Football League team the Edmonton Eskimos. In 1967 Getty was one of six Progressive Conservative Party members elected to the Alberta legislature. When the party formed the government four years later, Getty was appointed minister of federal and intergovernmental affairs and subsequently minister of energy and natural resources. He did not stand for reelection in 1979, preferring to return to private life. Between 1979 and 1985 he was president of D. Getty Investments Ltd. and served on boards of directors of a large variety of companies. He was also a member of the board of governors of the Resources of Canada Fund. Getty reentered politics in 1985 by successfully contesting the leadership of the Progressive Conservative Party following the resignation of Premier Peter Lougheed. He was defeated in the general election of March 1989 but remained as premier and was reelected to the legislature in a by-election after a sitting member resigned.

Dick Johnston.   Born in Lethbridge, Alberta, Johnston was appointed provincial treasurer in May 1986. He holds a B.A. from the University of Calgary and an M.B.A. from the University of Alberta and is a fellow of the Institute of Chartered Accountants of Alberta. He was first elected to the Alberta legislature for Lethbridge East in March 1975. Since then he has served in the Cabinet as minister of municipal affairs (1975–79), minister of federal and intergovernmental affairs (1979–82), minister of advanced education (1982–83) and minister responsible for the status of women (1983–86).

Raymond Martin.   Leader of the opposition. Born August 8, 1941 in Drumheller, Alberta, he was educated at the University of Alberta and the University of Calgary and became a high school teacher and guidance counselor. He was first elected to the Alberta legislature in 1982, was reelected in 1986 and 1989, and has served as chairman of the Public Accounts Committee. In 1984 he was elected leader of the New Democratic Party.

NEW BRUNSWICK

GEOGRAPHY

Features: New Brunswick is the largest of the three Maritime Provinces. It is bordered by water on most of three sides, but on the north and west it joins to Quebec and Maine, thus providing a land connection between the Maritimes and continental North America. Its watery eastern boundary is made up of the Gulf of St. Lawrence and, dividing it from Prince Edward Island, Northumberland Strait. At the southeast corner the narrow Isthmus of Chignecto links New Brunswick to Nova Scotia, while the Bay of Fundy and Chignecto Bay complete the southern boundary.

Topographically, New Brunswick is unremarkable. A gently rolling plateau in the central and eastern portions of the province rises to 2,690 ft./ 820 m. in the northern uplands. Rugged hills along the southern coast slope down to tidal marshes and a lowland plain. The significant geographic feature is the extensive river system, particularly the Saint John and the Miramichi rivers, which have always formed the focus for settlement. It is also important as a source of power and originally provided access to the interior, which allowed the early development of the timber trade. Eighty-six percent of the surface of New Brunswick is covered by forest, which is the province's greatest natural resource. Although only 7% of the land surface is cleared, the suitability of soils in the upper Saint John region for growing potatoes gives agriculture an important place in the economy. Volcanic rocks in the Bathurst to Newcastle area contain the zinc-lead-copper deposits that are the basis of New Brunswick's mining industry, and some of the more recent carboniferous sediments in the central and eastern parts of the province contain coal and oil-bearing shales.

Area: 28,354 sq. mi./73,436 sq. km., including 519 sq. mi./1,344 sq. km. of inland water. Makes up 0.7% of total area of Canada.

Mean maximum and minimum temperatures: Saint John: 62.4°F/16.9°C (July), 18.0°F/ − 7.8°C (January).

Relative humidity: Fredericton: 62%–80%.

Mean annual rainfall: 51 in./1,278 mm.

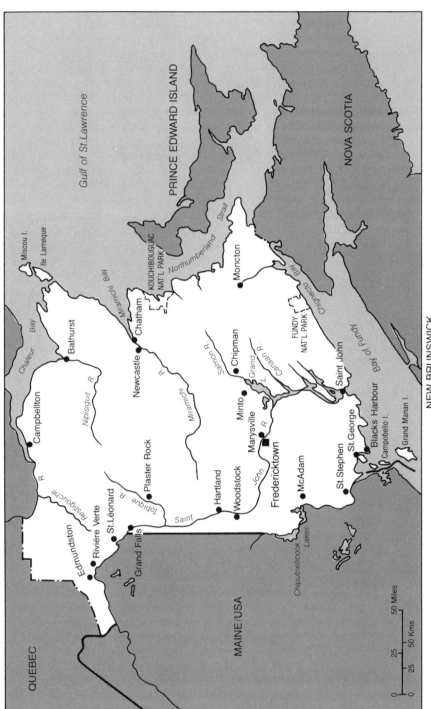

QUEBEC

Edmundston

St.Léonard

Rivière Verte

Grand Falls

Restigouche R.

Campbellton

Chaleur Bay

Nipisiguit R.

Bathurst

Ile Lameque

Miscou I.

Gulf of St.Lawrence

PRINCE EDWARD ISLAND

Miramichi Bay

KOUCHIBOUGUAC
NAT'L PARK

Northumberland Strait

Chatham

Newcastle

Miramichi R.

Plaster Rock

Tobique R.

Salmon R.

Hartland

Woodstock

Saint R.

Chiputneticook Lakes

John R.

Marysville

Fredericktown

Minto

Chipman

Grand L.

Canaan R.

Moncton

FUNDY
NAT'L PARK

Chignecto Bay

Saint John

NOVA SCOTIA

McAdam

St.Stephen

St.George

Blacks Harbour

Campobello I.

Grand Manan I.

Bay of Fundy

MAINE/USA

0   25   50 Miles

0   25   50 Kms

NEW BRUNSWICK

POPULATION

Total population (1986 census): 710,400. Estimated population, 1990: 724,600.

Chief towns and population (1986 census): Saint John (76,381), Moncton (55,468), Fredericton, the capital (44,352), Bathurst (14,683), Edmundston (11,497), Campbellton (9,073). Saint John metropolitan area, estimated, October 1990 (124,200).

Distribution: New Brunswick's period of urbanization occurred between 1941 and 1971. Since then the proportion of officially designated urban population has declined from 62% to 49.4% in 1986, making New Brunswick the second most rural province in Canada after Prince Edward Island.

Ethnic composition (1981 census): New Brunswick was originally part of the Algonquian cultural area, and today 3,983 Micmac and 3,152 Maliseet reside in the province. Acadian French were the earliest European settlers. They are concentrated in the northwestern, northeastern and southern corners of the province and constitute 33.8% (including those who are partly French) of the population. In common with the two other Maritime Provinces, Acadians have their own political organization, the Société des acadiens du Nouveau-Brunswick, which is funded mainly by the federal government. They are also served by a continually improving cultural and French-language infrastructure. The largest ethnic group, at 51.3%, are people of British, or partly British origin, many of whom are descended from Loyalist refugees from the American Revolution, but also including subsequent immigrants from Ireland and Scotland. They live primarily in the south and southwest. In addition 10% of the population are mixed British and French. Other significant groups are German, Dutch and Scandinavian.

Language: In the 1986 census 65.3% gave English as their mother tongue and 33.5% French; 3.5% named English plus one or more other languages; 1.3% gave only other languages. New Brunswick is the only officially bilingual province in Canada; between 1971 and 1981 the bilingual proportion of the population increased from 21.5% to 26.5%.

Religion (1981 census): The British-French ethnic and language division in New Brunswick is reflected in a Protestant-Catholic demarcation. In 1981 Roman Catholics made up 53.9% of the population, of which 68.2% were of French origin, the remainder being of Irish and other extraction. The various Protestant denominations totaled 42.9%, being mainly Baptist (14%), United (13.4%) and Anglican (10.9%).

CONSTITUTION AND GOVERNMENT

Executive: The Cabinet consists of 18 ministers including the premier, reduced from 24 following the 1991 election. In addition to members heading the usual provincial departments, one cabinet member is chairman of a Crown corporation, the New Brunswick Electric Power Commission. In 1970 a cabinet committee system was introduced. The four main committees (1990) are the Executive Committee (reviews legislative proposals, deals with federal-provincial relations), the Board of Management, and the Economic and Social Policy and Programs Committees (policy-making and resource allocation within their fields). There are 13 semi-independent agencies, boards, commissions, and crown (public) corporations. In addition there are over 30 agencies, boards and commissions attached to departments.

Legislature: The Legislative Assembly consists of 58 members elected from single-member constituencies. Any Canadian citizen of full age and six months' residence is entitled to vote. Business is conducted in French and English, New Brunswick having been the first province to install a simultaneous translation system.

Political parties: On the whole New Brunswick typifies the ideal two-party system: the two major parties—Liberal and Conservative—have alternated in power at regular intervals and often, especially since 1960, split the vote almost equally. The longest term of a single premier, that of the Conservative Richard Hatfield, lasted from 1970 to 1987. His 17 years in office ended with a landslide victory for the Liberals at the October 1987 provincial election, in which they won all 58 seats in the Legislative Assembly. Third parties have had little success in New Brunswick, although the Parti Acadien did well in two constituencies in 1978 and the New Democratic Party (NDP) took 10.2% of the vote in 1982 and elected one candidate then and another in a by-election in 1984. But in 1991 the Confederation of Regions, a party hostile to both the New Brunswick accommodation of the French language and the socialist program of the NDP, won eight seats and 21% of the vote, only two years after its New Brunswick founding convention.

Local government: The Equal Opportunity program of 1964–67 restricted usual municipal jurisdiction to primarily services for property, including water, sewer, fire protection and local police services. The provincial government assumed complete administrative and financial responsibility for education, health, welfare and judicial services. It abolished the 15 county councils and limited municipal taxes, so that New Brunswick property owners enjoy the lowest local tax rates in the country.

Federal representation: New Brunswick has 10 seats in the Senate. In the November 1988 federal election its number of seats in the House of Commons was increased from 10 to 15; these are evenly split 5 each among the Conservative, Liberal and NDP parties.

Judicial system: New Brunswick originally had a normal provincial judicial structure, but in 1979 the county or district courts were amalgamated with courts of the Queen's Bench. Under the Official Languages Act, French and English speakers are guaranteed judicial services in their own languages. The position of ombudsman was created in 1967.

RECENT HISTORY

The overriding motivation for much recent political activity in New Brunswick has been regional economic disparity reinforced along ethnic and religious lines. These differences only emerged as major issues after 1960, when francophone Acadians—descendants of French settlers of the region—began to find their political voice.

Until the election of Louis Robichaud in 1960, New Brunswick had had only one Acadian premier. Robichaud's Liberal party victory over the incumbent Conservatives was not based on a particularly revolutionary platform, and it was not until the 1963 election that Robichaud pledged "equal opportunities" to everyone, regardless of where in the province they lived. The Program for Equal Opportunity that the reelected Liberals implemented between 1964 and 1967 was based on the report of the Byrne Royal Commission. Byrne concluded that many of the poorer municipalities were incapable of providing an adequate standard of basic services and recommended that the province take responsibility for education, welfare, health and the administration of justice.

In many ways the Program for Equal Opportunity resembled Quebec's Quiet Revolution. Although aimed at abolishing regional disparities, the coincidence of Acadian Roman Catholics with poor rural areas meant that the thrust of the program was to improve the social and economic conditions of francophone residents at the expense of a largely anglophone elite.

Despite vociferous attacks, Robichaud retained the support of the majority of New Brunswickers, and until 1970 the government continued with legislation to provide more favorable socioeconomic conditions for Acadians. A natural adjunct to the Equal Opportunity Program was the New Brunswick Official Languages Act, introduced in 1968. Under the Act public services would be available in both French and English, giving Acadians equal access to education, the courts, government agencies, the civil service and the legislature.

More tax increases notwithstanding, the province continued to experience economic problems, which, together with frequent labor disputes and a number of other controversies, brought about the defeat of the Liberals in the 1970 election. After an extremely narrow victory for the Conservatives, their leader Richard Hatfield went on to become the longest serving premier in New Brunswick history. Clearly he enjoyed the support of the Acadian population, whose welfare took high priority for the Hatfield administration. The passage of Bill 88 tended to defuse the separatist Acadian cause. This bill and associated legislation provided for distinct cultural and social institutions for the English and French communities and two autonomous unilingual school systems. The Hatfield government also reformed family law as in Ontario, passed the Employment Termination Act and the Right to Information Act, and introduced much needed electoral reforms.

On the other hand, Hatfield was unable to improve the poor economic situation he inherited from Robichaud. Having promised to reduce taxation in his 1974 election campaign, Hatfield was forced to cut funding to schools, hospitals and social services. The implementation of bilingual legislation and government-driven economic development put heavy demands on the provincial budget. Part of these were met from federal sources, and by 1982–83 the federal share of provincial revenues was about 44.4%. Nevertheless, financial difficulties persisted. After a Conservative victory in the 1982 election, Hatfield expanded his cabinet, adding more women and francophones, but by then his progressive social stance was insufficient to obscure the worsening economic situation and numerous political scandals. On top of the rest, in 1984–85 public hearings on bilingualism served to expose the extent of anglophone hostility toward a perceived francophone threat to the anglophone community's job opportunities and longstanding majority power.

In the absence of any leadership review mechanism, Hatfield went on to lead the Conservative party in the 1987 election. The Liberals, under their dynamic young leader Frank McKenna, took every single seat in the legislature. McKenna naturally saw his victory as a "license for change," and he made an aggressive attack on the province's economic problems with encouraging initial results. On the social front, his policies continued in the Hatfield tradition of progressive social programs, including promoting the rights of women and ensuring protection for francophones. McKenna became a strong advocate of Maritime cooperation, but he rejected the possibility of provincial union. In February 1991 he launched a drive for extension of the Trans-Canada Pipeline to carry Alberta natural gas to the Maritimes and reduce their dependence on imported oil.

McKenna maintained his support for Acadian equality of opportunity in the face of a more organized anglophone backlash. With the Conservative Party routed and in tatters, many of its supporters backed a new political party, Confederation of Regions. Its primary objective is to reverse New Brunswick's record of official bilingualism. At the election of September 23, 1991, the Liberal representation in the legislature was reduced to 46 with three ministers defeated. Three Conservatives and one New Democrat were elected. The Confederation of Regions with eight members became the official opposition.

ECONOMY

In a climate of great enthusiasm for centrally directed regional development, Premier Louis Robichaud tapped readily available federal funds to modernize primary industries and promote industrialization. The government invested directly in mining, forestry, fisheries and secondary manufacturing. It also tried to create an environment more conducive to industrialization by increasing its electricity-generating capacity and providing better transport facilities and transport subsidies for New Brunswick products. The decline of secondary industry was halted, a new mining industry was born and other primary industries were updated, but the economy developed little internal momentum. By the mid-1980s its vital statistics still placed it firmly third from the bottom in the provincial hierarchy, a large gap separating it from its more prosperous colleagues to the west.

In contrast to the heavy government involvement in planning and funding development schemes of the '70s and '80s, Premier Frank McKenna looked to private and foreign investment to drive economic expansion in the 1990s. His new economic plan, "Toward 2000," is an exercise in public relations and marketing, its glossy format designed to attract attention in head offices of national and international corporations. In order to encourage business migration, the Department of Commerce and Technology visits Hong Kong regularly and also promotes New Brunswick in Taiwan, Korea, Singapore and Japan. The same objective was the motivation in October 1989 for McKenna's meetings with industrialists and businessmen in France, West Germany and Great Britain. Economic strategy also targets for development small businesses, which contributed most of the growth in manufacturing jobs in 1988. New Brunswick advertises a long list of attractions to the foreign investor and small entrepreneur alike. One of those most emphasized is a trained and skilled work force, which the government intends to enhance through its new New Brunswick Youth Strategy scheme and through greater assistance in retraining the unemployed. Various government financial-incentive schemes include an investment tax-credit program, loans, bond or loan guarantees, venture-capital support and grants for small-business development. In addition to these direct subsidies to new private investments, the government is continuing to construct new highways and hospitals, a province-wide fiber-optic communications system and more electricity generating plants. Research and development infrastructure also claims a share of the provincial budget.

Results so far seem to justify the aggressive sales campaign. By 1989, although the province was third from the bottom with a GDP of $12.6 billion (at market prices) and per capita income of $16,097 (Canadian average was $21,092), the New Brunswick economy was heralded as the strongest in Atlantic Canada. Growth estimated at 3.3% for the year exceeded the Canadian average of 2.8%, and real growth in constant dollars was estimated at 2.2%. In 1990 as compared with earlier years the economy experienced weaker growth, primarily due to the declining demand in forest-related and mining industries. The strong growth that had taken place is attributed to a more diversified economic base and robust mineral prices, but particularly to the huge increase in business investments. After a rise of 12.6% in 1988, the rise for 1989 was 28%, in nominal terms, in non-residential construction spending and a remarkable 30% growth in expenditure on machinery and equipment. Current predictions are for a healthy economy at the end of the 1990s. The weakening of the economy that came in 1990 was in line with recessionary trends in the United States and Canada. Construction activity continued to be a major component of growth, led by energy generation projects.

Forestry: With 86% of New Brunswick's land surface covered by productive forest, it is not surprising that forestry provides the mainstay of the provincial economy. Its contribution to the GDP in 1986 belies its over-whelming importance. Direct employment in forestry is the highest of the primary industries. More importantly, one-sixth of all jobs in the province can be attributed to the forestry industry, as can one-third of employment in manufacturing, almost one-quarter of goods produced and nearly half of exports. Forestry forms an important part of the industrial core of all cities except Fredericton and Moncton, and of 67 single-industry communities, 33 are wood-based. But owing to the depressed housing market in Canada and the northeastern United States, and to the decline in demand for pulp products combined with new capacity, the sales of lumber and pulp and paper products have fallen in 1990–91 and can be expected to remain slow. In 1990 the United States took only 62% of foreign lumber exports, a decrease from the recent high of 83%. Despite the current successful process of diversification of its economic base, forecasts for the next decade show New Brunswick's economy continuing to center on its primary industries and the manufacturing sector they supply. New investments are mainly in pulp and paper mills and the mining sector. During 1989–91 various investment projects came into production, including Repap's $370 million second coated paper machine in Newcastle and a new Acuma press-wood plant, which began production in October 1990.

Productive forest covers 24,000 sq. mi./62,000 sq. km., containing an estimated 515.9 cubic meters of wood, 65% of which is softwood and 35% hardwood. Ownership is divided among the Crown (8.15 million acres/3.3 million hectares), corporate freehold (2.82 million acres/1.14 million hectares) and private freehold (5.2 million acres/2.1 million hectares). Since the early 1970s the government has taken an active part in the long-term preservation of New Brunswick's forest resources, relying heavily on federal financial assistance for programs of reforestation, training in forestry management and silviculture, and research and development. Education and research centers include a forestry faculty at the University of New Brunswick and the new Hugh John Fleming Forestry Centre in Fredericton.

Mining: In contrast to forestry, mining is a relative newcomer as an important component in New Brunswick's economy. It was only in the 1950s, with the discovery of extensive base-metal reserves in the Bathurst-Dalhousie region, that mining began to make a significant contribution. It is now a billion-a-year industry with value of production reaching $910 million in 1988 (its value was $864 million in 1985) and is one of the main areas of new investment. Employment exceeded 3,000 in 1988. Since many of the mineral deposits occur in the poorest regions of the province, mining activities serve both to contribute to and provide economic justification for rural development schemes.

A long list of important minerals includes zinc, silver, lead, copper, antimony, bismuth, potash, peat, tungsten, sulfur and coal. Gold has been discovered near the Bay of Fundy, and one mine began production in 1986. Figures for 1988 show large increases in the value of mined minerals: zinc up 30% from 1987 to $379 million, copper up 76% to $30 million and potash up 49%. Overall production in 1988 was valued at $699 million.

Exploration also rose in 1988, assisted by a hefty tax concession of 150% of costs.

In addition to its direct contributions to New Brunswick's economy, the mining sector supplies part of the energy requirement of the province. Spurred by the energy crisis of the early and mid-1970s, a long dormant coal mining industry was revitalized through strip mining. Despite the much greater role played by hydroelectric and nuclear power plants, coal is maintaining its niche in the provincial energy plan. In 1989 New Brunswick Coal, a subsidiary of the New Brunswick Electric Power Commission, committed $19 million for the modernization of Minto Mine to supply a second coal-fired unit at the Grand Lake power plant and in 1990 a similar amount was committed for a dragline. At the same time, a federally funded research and development project based at NBEPC Chatham Generating Station is testing systems for reducing sulfur emissions from coal-fired electric generating plants. Known reserves of oil, gas and oil shales have not yet been systematically exploited, although New Brunswick has the largest oil refinery in Canada.

Although the record growth figures of the late 1980s are unlikely to be repeated, it is predicted that mining will play a key role in New Brunswick's economic development of the 1990s. In addition to maintaining high investment in primary mining activities, the province is seeking to enhance its value by attracting investment in manufacturing activities that will use New Brunswick's native minerals.

Tourism: Known as Canada's "Picture Province," New Brunswick has turned tourism into a major industry. In 1986 more than 4.4 million tourists visited the province. Tourist revenues in 1990 are estimated at $612 million, and employment equaled 22,500 person years, both up 4.2% over 1989. In addition to its natural attractions including two national and 58 provincial parks (163,000 acres/66,000 hectares), beaches, ocean and freshwater fishing and game hunting, the provincial government has built two very popular historical settlements and maintains 60 museums. In order to attract new investment, financial assistance is offered under the Canada/ New Brunswick Subsidiary Agreement on Tourism Development. Capital investment in 1988 came to $40 million.

Manufacturing: New Brunswick manufacturing shipments in 1990 reached over $6.1 billion. In 1987 the industry reported a dramatic 122% increase in capital spending, much of it in pulp and paper mills. In that year the province had 1,477 manufacturing firms employing 42,300 people; the number employed declined to 37,000 in 1989. Manufacturing is largely based on processing primary products extracted locally. At 43% of manufacturing production, forest products constitute the largest share of output. More than 100 small, scattered mills produce such wood products as lumber, shingles, plywood and furniture. The 11 pulp and paper mills, which require high capital investment and a large work force, have significantly affected the pattern of urban development. Recently the industry completed a $780 million modernization program and the province is home to Miramichi Pulp and Paper, the most modern coated paper mill in the world. The maximum value of shipments of manufactured wood products was, in 1988, $497,279,000; and of paper and allied products $1,900,000,000, in 1989.

In second place is the food and beverage sector, which contributed 22% of manufacturing shipments in 1989. In 1990 the value of food processing shipments alone amounted to $1.2 billion. Part of New Brunswick's potato crop supplies McCain Foods Limited, the world's largest producer of frozen potato products. Other record-breakers rely on the fishing industry: New Brunswick has the world's largest lobster pound and the world's largest sardine cannery. Altogether there were 152 fish processing plants employing over 10,000 workers producing $330 million of fish products in 1988. Two-thirds of the output was exported. In 1991, of $193 million in exports, the United States took $146.5 million and Japan $19 million.

The third important component of New Brunswick's manufacturing success is the award of a federal contract worth $6.2 billion to a Saint John shipbuilding firm for the construction of 9 navy patrol frigates. HMCS *Halifax*, the first of these and the first new Canadian warship in 20 years, began sea trials in August 1990. The project employs about 3,400 workers and should continue as a stable source of growth into the 1990s. However, new government cuts in defense expenditure will slow the pace of construction.

Part of the government's economic plan proposes to diversify the manufacturing base by attracting more high technology industry to the province. To lure and assist such companies, the government has established a number of research and development centers, including the New Brunswick Research and Productivity Council, the Manufacturing Technology Centre and a microelectronics research center (CADMI).

Agriculture and fishing: Like the economy in the other Maritime Provinces, New Brunswick's economy relies heavily on primary industry. Although forestry and mining regularly contribute more to the GDP, in terms of employment both agriculture and fishing exceed mining. In addition, they provide the raw materials of the food processing industry, second only to forest products in the manufacturing sector. The history of agriculture in New Brunswick follows the pattern of most industrialized countries. Between 1941 and 1986 the number of farm holdings declined from 31,899 to 3,554, the area of improved land dropped from 864,500 acres/350,000 hectares to 417,215 acres/168,913 hectares and direct employment fell from 26,834 in 1951 to about 6,000 in 1988. On the other hand, total production has remained constant, and employment in food processing and transport has risen to an estimated 18,000. Farm cash income totaled $275 million in 1990, a growth over five years of 27.2%. Potatoes, which are raised mostly in the upper Saint John River valley, contributed $78.2 million (28%) to farm income. They are the province's chief agricultural export and make up 20% of the national total. Half of this production is processed within the province. Apart from potatoes and a small area of field crops and maple production, farming in New Brunswick is based on animals. Dairy production, centered in the Saint John River valley and the southeastern sections of New Brunswick, contributed 21.4% of farm income; 26.7% came from beef, poultry and hogs; and a further 5.6% from eggs. Investment in 1986 amounted to $658 million. Construction of the $50 million Cavendish processing plant expected in 1992 should dramatically increase potato processing in the province.

New Brunswick's fishing industry was in decline until the 1960s, when it was revitalized by the introduction of modern methods and vessels. It received another boost in 1977 when the fishing limit was extended to 200 nautical mi./370 km. Today nearly 6,000 fishermen harvest more than 50 species of fish and shellfish worth (in 1990) $99.5 million, around 8% of the value of Canadian east coast fisheries production. In terms of processed value, lobster is most important, contributing about one-third of the total; crab comes second at about one-fifth; herring makes up one-tenth; and scallop and cod are also important species. The recent decline in fish stocks is a source of considerable worry for the industry. On the other hand, aquaculture is growing rapidly with new salmon hatcheries and an Aquaculture Industrial Park to service the developing industry. Sales for 1990 are estimated at $75 million. Currently 48 active salmon culture sites employ over 500 people.

Although now forecast to grow more slowly than the goods-producing sector, in 1987 the services sector contributed 64% of the GDP and 70% of total wages and salaries in the province. In 1986 one-third of the 267,000 jobs were in community, business and personal services, including educational and medical services. The second biggest employer is the retail and wholesale trade, of which the annual retail value in 1988 was $4.1 billion.

Foreign trade: In 1989 the value of exports totaled $3.2 billion. Forest products outperform all other commodities, with woodpulp at the top ($655.3 million) and paper plus paperboard only marginally behind ($600.7 million). Petroleum oils other than crude ($582.6 million), fish and fish products ($246 million) and electricity ($198.6 million) complete the top five. The United States is New Brunswick's major market.

Employment: In common with the other Atlantic provinces, New Brunswick suffers from a chronic unemployment problem. Premier Frank McKenna's declared mission has been to stimulate job creation for the province's potential labor force of 546,000 (1987) persons over 15 years. Since a high of 15.2% in 1985, the unemployment rate decreased to 12.1% in 1990, still third highest in Canada.

Prices: The consumer price index average increase for New Brunswick was 4.6% in 1990, the fifth consecutive year in which consumer inflation was below the Canadian average.

SOCIAL SERVICES

Health: Basic health services are free to all residents under the nationally coordinated programs. The province has 36 hospitals and 21 medical clinics and is currently investing in extensive work on several hospitals. The doctor-patient ratio averages 1:900. Psychiatric care is offered in the home, and several regional hospitals provide chronic care units. Senior citizens benefit from provincial assistance for prescription drugs and 64 subsidized nursing homes. Public health services are responsible for nursing, inspection, control of communicable diseases, maternal and child health care, home care, nutrition, tuberculosis screening and the operation of a home dialysis program. Health and social services together claim 34% of the provincial budget.

EDUCATION

The Program for Equal Opportunities of the 1960s not only set the objective of instruction for francophones in their own language, but also reorganized educational responsibilities to make its achievement more realistic. Responsibility for funding of local schools was shifted from municipalities to the province, so that the level of resources available for education no longer depended on the wealth, or lack of it, locally. However, it was not until the late 1970s that Bill 88 provided for two autonomous unilingual school systems. Today each system reports to a different deputy minister in the Department of Education. In 1986 education received 21.5% of the provincial budget.

New Brunswick is divided into 41 school districts administering 434 (in 1986–87) elementary and high schools covering grades 1 to 12. In 1986–87, 46,318 francophone students attended 154 schools under 15 school boards, while 92,705 anglophone students attended 280 schools under 26 boards.

Responsibility for higher education is divided between the Department of Community Colleges and the Maritime Higher Education Commission. The 10 community colleges offer specialized training in a wide variety of subjects and provide full and part-time adult education courses. Their enrollment in 1986–87 numbered 3,946 students in French-language programs and 8,043 in English.

The University of New Brunswick (UNB), founded in 1785 by Loyalists, is the province's largest and oldest degree-conferring institution, with the main campus in Fredericton and a subsidiary in Saint John. Catholic-affiliated Saint Thomas University shares UNB's Fredericton campus. Mount Allison University, affiliated with the United Church, is located at Sackville. All three offer anglophone programs to a total of 10,731 full-time students (1986–87). Francophone programs are provided to 3,405 full-time students at Université de Moncton and affiliated centers in Edmundston and Shippegan.

MASS MEDIA

Newspapers and periodicals: In 1987 New Brunswick had six daily newspapers. The K. C. Irving interests own the English-language Saint John *Telegraph-Journal* and *Times-Globe* Fredericton *Gleaner* and Moncton *Times-*

Transcript. The provincial media situation was dramatically unbalanced by the bankruptcy in 1982 of the Acadian daily newspaper, *L'Evangeline.* It was not until 1984 that a new French-language daily, *L'Acadie Nouvelle,* began publication.

There were 23 weekly newspapers in 1987, seven in French or bilingual. One of the older Canadian magazines, *Atlantic Advocate,* is published in Fredericton.

Broadcasting: Of the 38 radio stations serving New Brunswick, 16 are privately owned, three are owned by the Canadian Broadcasting Corporation and two are university stations. Three stations broadcast in French, three are bilingual and the CBC International Service at Sackville puts out programs in several languages. Television programs come from three major sources: CBC and CTB (English language) and Radio-Québec (French language). Urban centers receive cable television, carrying the main American networks, and several pay-TV channels are also available.

BIOGRAPHICAL SKETCHES

Frank McKenna. McKenna was sworn in as the 27th premier of New Brunswick in October 1987. He is also the minister responsible for the Advisory Council on the Status of Women and the minister responsible for regional development. Born in 1948, McKenna received his Bachelor of Arts from St. Francis Xavier University, took his Bachelor of Laws from the University of New Brunswick and carried out postgraduate studies in political science at Queen's University. His outstanding academic performance was rewarded by scholarships and numerous prizes. Following university he joined a Chatham law firm and specialized in criminal law. He was first elected Member of Legislative Assembly (MLA) for Chatham in 1982 and became leader of the Liberal Party of New Brunswick in 1985. In 1988 McKenna received the Vanier Award for Outstanding Young Canadians and honorary doctorate degrees from the Université de Moncton (D.Sc.Pol.) and the University of New Brunswick (LLD). He is the author of academic research papers on amending the Canadian constitution as well as on New Brunswick and offshore mineral rights.

Allan Maher. Minister of finance and minister responsible for the Board of Management. Allan Maher was appointed minister of finance and minister responsible for the New Brunswick Liquor Corporation in October 1987, and he kept his finance portfolio after the 1991 election. Born in 1938, he attended a senior leaders' course with the Air Cadet League, and he studied at the New England Institute of Anatomy. A funeral director by profession, he was first elected MLA for Dalhousie in 1978 and was reelected in 1982 and 1987. He was a caucus whip and has served on several legislative committees.

Edmund Blanchard. Minister of intergovernmental affairs, minister of justice, and attorney general. Born May 31, 1954, in Atholville, New Brunswick, he was educated at Dalhousie University. A lawyer, he was first elected to the New Brunswick legislature in 1987 and was appointed minister of state for mines in 1989.

Danny Cameron. Acting leader of the opposition and MLA for York South. Born 1925 in Osgoode, Ontario, he reads and speaks some French. In the election of 1991 he defeated a Liberal minister. He had been president of the South York Progressive Conservative (PC) Association for 10 years, but he ran as a Confederation of Regions candidate. He was chosen as acting leader by the caucus of 8 Confederation of Regions MLA's, pending a convention after the leader, Arch Pafford, failed to win a seat.

MANITOBA

Features: Located in central Canada, Manitoba is bordered on the north by the Northwest Territories and Hudson Bay, on the east by Ontario, on the south by the U.S. states of Minnesota and North Dakota, and on the west by Saskatchewan. It consists of four geological regions: Lake Agassiz Lowland, Western Upland, Precambrian Upland, and Hudson Bay Lowland. Three large lakes, Winnipeg, Winnipegosis and Manitoba, cover much of Lake Agassiz Lowland and are the remnants of Lake Agassiz, a prehistoric body of water that occupied south-central Manitoba during the last ice age and accounts for the remarkable flatness of this area, much of which was a huge swamp. An extensive system of drainage ditches, including the Red River Floodway, has made this prairie region suitable for cultivation. It includes Winnipeg and the Red River Valley and contains most of the province's agriculture, industry and population.

Occupying southwestern Manitoba, the Western Upland, with rolling ground moraine broken in places by hilly end moraines, has a relief generally favorable for cultivation. In this region is Manitoba's highest point, Mount Baldy, 2,727 ft./831 m. The natural vegetation, as in the Lake Agassiz Lowland, is open grassland. To the north lies the Precambrian Upland, the rocky granite Canadian Shield. Here the terrain is very rugged and is laced with streams, rivers, thousands of lakes and large tracts of swamp. Forest, consisting mainly of spruce, covers most of this region, which is the principal source of Manitoba's mineral wealth, pulpwood, fish and fur-bearing animals. Flat sedimentary rocks underlie the Hudson Bay Lowland, which consists mainly of Arctic tundra.

All of Manitoba's waters ultimately flow to Hudson Bay. The Red and Assiniboine rivers flow north and east, respectively, through productive farmland; meet at Winnipeg; and continue as the Red into Lake Winnipeg. Flowing west from Ontario and east from Saskatchewan, respectively, the Winnipeg and Saskatchewan rivers also empty into Lake Winnipeg. Three principal northern rivers—the Nelson, Churchill and Hayes—receive waters from Manitoba's lakes and run northeast, emptying into Hudson Bay.

Area: 250,946 sq. mi./649,947 sq. km., including 39,225 sq. mi./101,592 sq. km. of inland water. The province makes up 6.5% of the total area of Canada.

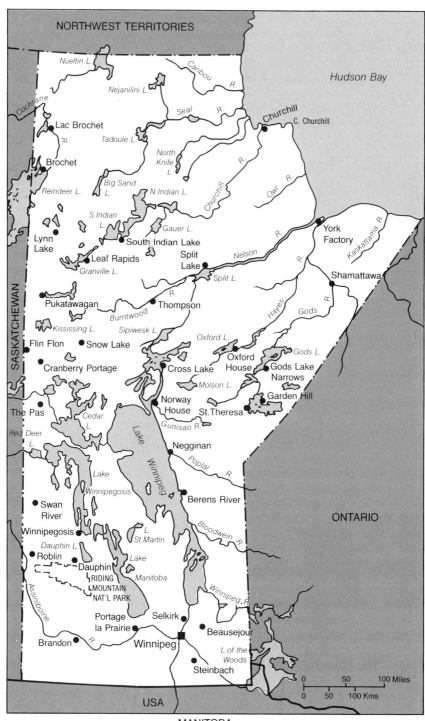

NORTHWEST TERRITORIES

Hudson Bay

Nueltin L.

Caribou

R.

Nejanilini L.

Seal

R.

Cochrane

Churchill

C. Churchill

Lac Brochet

R.

Tadoule L.

North Knife L.

Brochet

Churchill

R.

Owl

R.

Big Sand L.

Reindeer L.

N.Indian L.

S.Indian L.

York Factory

Kaskattama

R.

Gauer L.

Lynn Lake

South Indian Lake

Split Lake

Shamattawa

Nelson

R.

Leaf Rapids

Granville L.

Split L.

R.

SASKATCHEWAN

Pukatawagan

Burntwood

Thompson

Hayes

R.

Gods

R.

Kississing L.

Sipiwesk L.

Flin Flon

Snow Lake

Oxford L.

Gods L.

Cranberry Portage

Cross Lake

Oxford House

Gods Lake Narrows

The Pas

Cedar L.

Molson L.

Garden Hill

Norway House

St.Theresa

Red Deer L.

Gunisao R.

Negginan

Lake Winnipeg

Poplar

R.

Lake Winnipegosis

Berens River

ONTARIO

Swan River

Bloodwein

R.

Winnipegosis

L. St.Martin

Dauphin L.

Lake Manitoba

Roblin

Dauphin

RIDING MOUNTAIN NAT'L PARK

Assiniboine

R.

Winnipeg R.

Portage la Prairie

Selkirk

Beausejour

Brandon

Winnipeg

L.of the Woods

Steinbach

0   50   100 Miles
0   50   100 Kms

USA

MANITOBA

Mean maximum and minimum temperatures: Winnipeg 67°F/19.g°C (July), −3°F/−19.3°C (January); Churchill 53°F/11.8°C (July), −17.5°F/−27.5°C (January).

Mean annual precipitation: Winnipeg 21 in./526.5 mm., of which 49 in./ 125.5 cm. is snow.

POPULATION

Total population (1986 census): 1,071,232. Estimated population, 1990: 1,092,600. Population density averaged 4.3 per sq. mi./1.6 per sq. km.

Chief towns and population (1986 census): Winnipeg, the capital (594,551), Brandon (38,708) Thompson (14,701), Portage la Prairie (13,198) and Flin Flon (7,243). Winnipeg metropolitan area estimated, June 1, 1990 (647,100).

Distribution: The area west of a line drawn from The Pas, in the north-west, diagonally to the southeast corner of the province contains 95% of the population. Winnipeg contains well over half the provincial population and is the largest city in Canada west of Toronto. In 1986, 72% of the Manitoba population was urban.

Ethnic composition: Taking into account both single and multiple origin, in 1986 46% of the population was British (including Irish); 12% German; 10% Ukrainian; 9% French; and 4% each Polish, Scandinavian, Dutch, and North American Indian. Métis (mixed white and Indian) came to 2% of the population. A total of 40,655 Indians were living on reservations in 1986. The non-British element is proportionally larger in rural areas.

Language: In 1986, English was the mother tongue and home language of 73% and 87% of the population, respectively. French was the language of 5% and 3%, respectively. Other languages accounted for the remaining 22% and 10%. In spite of a provision of the Manitoba Act of 1870, making both French and English official languages in the legislature and courts, a provincial act in 1890 made English the only official language. This legislation remained in force for almost 100 years but was overturned by the Supreme Court of Canada in 1979 and since 1984 the provincial government has recognized French and English as equal in status. However, opposition to the granting of what is seen as a preferred status to French by those with other non-English linguistic backgrounds has not fully subsided.

Religion: The largest single denomination in 1981 was the Roman Catholic church, whose adherents constituted 26.5% of the population, followed by the United Church, the largest Protestant denomination (24%). Anglicans comprised 11%, Mennonites 7%, Lutherans 6%, Ukrainian Catholics 5%, Greek Orthodox 3%, and Jews 1%.

CONSTITUTION AND GOVERNMENT

Manitoba came into being July 15, 1870 as a province of Canada, upon proclamation of the Manitoba Act, an act of the Parliament of Canada. It was the first province to be added to the original four in the Canadian confederation. Like the other provinces, its relation to the federal government is now determined by the Constitution Act of 1982. Formally its government is headed by a lieutenant governor who represents the Queen, who is sovereign of Canada as well as sovereign of Great Britain, but in practice the chief executive is the premier, who heads an executive council or cabinet. As in the other Canadian provinces, the executive is responsible for the legislature and needs the support of the majority of the legislature to stay in power.

Executive: In March 1991 the premier presided over a cabinet of 18 members. There were 18 departments and 11 crown (public) corporations and other semi-independent agencies and boards. The most important crown corporation is Manitoba Hydro, which serves over 300,000 farm and residential consumers and almost 50,000 power and general service users.

Legislature: There is a single-chambered Legislative Assembly of 57 members, with each member representing a separate constituency. The party that can command majority support in the legislature forms the government, and the next largest becomes the official opposition. Elections are normally held every four years but may be called earlier upon the recommendation of the premier or if the government loses a vote in the legislature on a major issue.

Political parties: The traditional parties in Manitoba were the Liberal and Conservative (since 1943, Progressive Conservative) parties, but between 1922 and 1932 the governing party was the United Farmers of Manitoba, renamed in 1927 the Progressive Party; and a Liberal-Progressive coalition ruled the province from 1932 until 1958 (sometimes with partners). The New Democratic Party first came to power in 1969 and in successive elections almost entirely displaced the Liberals until 1988, when the Liberals made a comeback. From 1969 to 1988 party support tended to polarize on class/income lines, with the "haves" and "Anglos" inclined to support the Conservatives, and the "have-nots" and "ethnics" the NDP.

Local government: As of 1989, Manitoba had five incorporated cities, 35 incorporated towns, 39 incorporated villages and 105 rural municipalities. The rural municipalities range in size from four to 22 townships (a township is six miles square). Municipalities are directed by locally elected councils, subject to some provincial control. There are 17 local-government districts in settled areas that are not incorporated municipalities; they perform the same general functions as municipalities and are headed by administrators who act on the advice of elected councils but are subject to the final authority of the minister of municipal affairs. In northern Manitoba, the Department of Northern Affairs has jurisdiction in those areas not incorporated or organized as local-government districts. Many of the larger nonorganized communities have elected community councils, but because of a very limited tax base most of their funds come from the provincial government.

Federal representation: Manitoba is represented in Parliament by six federally appointed senators and 14 elected members of the House of Commons. The 1988 federal elections sent seven Conservatives, five Liberals, and two New Democratic Party members to the House of Commons.

Judicial system: The Manitoba Court of Appeals, which sits in Winnipeg, is the highest court in the province. It has a chief justice and six other judges, appointed by the federal government. The Court of Queen's Bench, the province's highest trial court, has a chief justice, an associate chief justice, and (in 1989) 23 other judges, all federally appointed. This court has jurisdiction in civil matters with no set monetary limit and most indictable criminal offenses. The criminal division sits permanently in Winnipeg and five other towns. There is also a family division, consisting of a chief justice and five associate justices, that has jurisdiction over divorce and family-maintenance cases in most of the province. Queen's Bench justices also handle surrogate matters, such as the probating of wills, and small claims. Provincial Court, which in 1989 sat in 19 permanent and 54 circuit locations, has provincially appointed judges. This court has jurisdiction in summary conviction cases and indictable offenses elected to be tried by the provincial judge. It is responsible for child protection in most areas and family cases in some areas. The family division also acts as youth court throughout Manitoba.

RECENT HISTORY

In 1958 the Liberal-Progressive coalition was defeated by the Conservative Party, partly because legislative seats were redistributed so that rural overrepresentation was ended and Winnipeg received its fair share of seats; and partly because of the popularity in western Canada of the federal party's standard-bearer, Prime Minister John Diefenbaker. The new provincial government, headed by Duff Roblin, introduced hospital insurance, old-age pensions and other progressive measures. Improvements in highways and other public works were undertaken. But Roblin's successor in 1967, Walter Weir, was more conservative, and in 1969 the electorate turned the Conservatives out and bypassed the Liberals in favor of the New Democratic party.

Under the new premier, Ed Schreyer, the NDP expanded hospitals, included nursing homes in hospital-insurance coverage, introduced a pharmacy plan for the elderly, and first cut, then eliminated, medicare premiums. New neighborhood health clinics were established, welfare allowances were raised repeatedly, and there was a vast expansion in public housing. Auto insurance was made public and premiums were reduced. In order to redistribute income, personal and corporate income taxes were raised while the property tax fell. In order to preserve jobs, the government took over some failing private enterprises. The NDP was returned to office in 1973. During Schreyer's second term, family-law reforms provided for an equal division of assets in the case of divorce. The pharmacy program was extended to all citizens, the tax system was again revised to favor low-income earners, and more funds were allocated to ambulance service and day care for children. Language rights for French speakers were enlarged in the public schools. In addition, the public insurance agency extended its activities to all fields except life insurance, and rent control was introduced.

In 1977, the Conservatives unseated the NDP. The new premier, Sterling Lyon, had campaigned on a platform of tax cuts and severe retrenchment in government operations, promising to get rid of unprofitable government takeovers. Accordingly, the new regime reduced social and health services, abolished rent control, froze spending on public works and sold some of the companies the government had previously bought. Personal and corporate income taxes were cut.

In the 1981 elections, the NDP won a narrow victory over the Conservatives, while the Liberals were virtually wiped out. Under the new premier, Howard Pawley, the government was driven by revenue losses due to recession to put a hiring and wage freeze on the public service and cut government spending in some areas, despite the party's fight against such actions while in opposition. It instituted a payroll tax and raised the sales tax. The government also reintroduced rent control, created a public petroleum corporation, and expanded health benefits. A contentious issue was how far to extend bilingualism, which had been mandated by the federal courts, to government services; the NDP's support for bilingualism was unpopular.

The Pawley government won another term in March 1986, when the NDP won 30 seats, the Conservatives 26, and the Liberals one. However, by-elections resulting from vacancies reduced its margin, and a new election was forced in May 1988 after an NDP member deserted the government and voted against the budget. The government's support had fallen because of increased taxes and auto rates; mismanagement of public corporations was also an issue. This time the Conservatives won 25 seats, the Liberals 20 and the NDP only 12. Gary Filmon became premier of a Conservative government. The Liberal leader, Sharon Carstairs, became the first woman to head the official opposition in a province.

ECONOMY

Manitoba is more prosperous than the Atlantic provinces but less so than Ontario and the far western provinces, Alberta and British Columbia. It has a diversified economy, with agriculture, mining, manufacturing, services and trade all being important. The estimated gross provincial product was $23.9 billion in 1990. In 1990, services accounted for about 23% of the gross provincial product; finance, insurance and real estate 22.2%; transportation and communications, 9.1%; trade, 10.2%; manufacturing, 10.7%; agriculture (including fishing, hunting and trapping) 4.8%; public administration, 8.4%; construction, 4.1%; mining and forestry 3.9%; and utilities, 3%. Per capita personal income was an estimated $19,258 in 1990. The average family income in 1990 was $46,351, compared to the Canadian average of $50,468.

Agriculture: The 1986 census reported 27,336 farms in Manitoba, with an average area of 700 acres/284 hectares per farm and the total farmed area (in 1987) 19.1 million acres/7.7 million hectares. Total cash receipts from farming came to $1.97 billion in 1990, including direct payments of $169.3 million, when net farm income was $545 million. The chief crop, wheat, is grown throughout southern Manitoba and accounts for about 40% of crop value. In 1988, when cash receipts from farming came to $2.06 billion wheat accounted for $387.8 million, plus an additional $49.3 million from the Canadian Wheat Board, which has the authority to buy the province's wheat (and oats and barley) for export. The 1988 wheat crop came to 2.6 million tons/2.4 million tonnes.

The 1990 crop was 6.1 million tons/5.5 million tonnes but cash receipts were only $565.5 million, and net cash income only $462 million, the lowest since 1981, owing to the fall in wheat prices. Other major crops are barley, rapeseed (canola), flaxseed, oats and rye. Manitoba farmers received $131.2 million in grain stabilization payments in 1988 but zero in 1990.

Livestock and animal products accounted for $773.4 million in cash receipts in 1990. Of this sector, cattle came to $270 million, hogs to $254 million and dairy products to $118 million. The 200-acre Union Stockyards in the Winnipeg area of St. Boniface (formerly a separate city) is the largest in Canada.

Forestry: Slightly more than half (129,127 sq. mi./334,440 sq. km.) of Manitoba's area is officially classified as forest land. Of this land, 95% is owned by the provincial government, and most of it is in central and northern Manitoba. The most common commercial tree species are black spruce, jack pine, trembling aspen (poplar), white spruce, balsam poplar and white birch. A total of 63.6 million cu. ft./1.83 million cu. m. of wood was harvested from public land in 1989–90, with more than 90% converted to pulpwood or sawlogs. The value added by forestry at factor cost—market value, minus costs of factors that went into its production—in 1987 was only $21.4 million. The value of shipments was $62.7 million.

Fishing: Although 39,225 sq. mi./101,592 sq. km. of Manitoba is inland water, and more than half of this area is exploited by commercial fisheries, the catch was worth only about $28.3 million in 1987–88. Whitefish, pike, walleye and sauger predominate among the 14 species or groups of species that enter into the commercial catch. Lakes Winnipeg, Winnipegosis and Manitoba accounted for 71% of the 1987–88 commercial catch of 28.9 million lb./13.1 million kg.

Mining: Nonfuel mineral production was valued at $1.6 billion in 1988, a record for the province and a 77% increase in value over 1987 production, which was also a record. However in 1990 value fell to $1.2 billion. Nickel, mined and smelted at Thompson and Namew Lake, is Manitoba's most valuable mineral. Production in 1988 was an estimated 157.9 million lb./70.2 million kg. valued at $1.05 billion. This fell to 150.3 million lb./68.2 million kg., valued at $707.4 million, in 1990. Next in importance among metals is copper, which is mined in the Flin Flon, Snow Lake and Leaf Rapids areas, and smelted at Flin Flon. Production in 1990 was 122.5 million lb./55.6 million kg. The 1990 value was 178.1 million. Zinc is mined in the same areas as copper and refined at Flin Flon. Production in 1990 was 162.4 million lb./73.7 million kg., worth $142.0 million. Gold mines near Lynn Lake, Flin Flon and Sherridon produced 5,249 lb./2,382 kg. in 1990, worth $34.3 million. Other metals mined or produced were silver, cobalt, tantalum, selenium, cadmium and tellurium. Among nonmetals, cement ($34.8 million) and sand and gravel ($36.2 million) were most valuable in 1990. Stone, lime, gypsum and clay were also produced.

Energy: Manitoba Hydro, a public corporation, is responsible for the generation, transmission, distribution and sale of electricity except for the inner section of Winnipeg, which is served by the city-owned Winnipeg Hydro. The two operate as an integrated system. Plentiful hydroelectric power, mostly from rivers in northern Manitoba, provides at least 95% of the electricity generated in the province in a year of normal precipitation. The installed generating capacity is 3.9 million kilowatts, and net/generation within the province was 18.8 billion kilowatt hours of electricity in 1989. Manitoba exports electricity to Saskatchewan, Ontario, Minnesota and North Dakota and also imports from the United States and other provinces. Work was begun on a massive new generating station in 1985, the fifth on the Nelson River and the largest in Manitoba.

Crude oil is produced in southwestern Manitoba, particularly in the Virden, Pierson, Daly and Waskada areas. In 1989, production was 25.5 million cu. ft./723,000 cu. m., worth $90 million. The province's reserves were estimated at 268 million cu. ft./7.6 million cu. m. Natural gas from Alberta, used for residential, industrial and commercial heating, provided about 35% of Manitoba's energy requirements in 1989, compared with 41% from oil and 23% from electricity. About 60% of Manitoba homes are heated by gas.

Manufacturing: In 1988 there were about 1,300 manufacturing establishments. In 1990 manufacturing employed some 54,000 people (10.7% of provincial employment) and produced goods valued at about $7.2 billion. The most important sector in 1990 was food processing (1.77 billion and 25%), and following in decreasing order were transportation equipment; primary metal industries; printing and publishing; machinery; wood, furniture and fixtures; clothing and textiles; and paper and allied products. Winnipeg accounted for 73% of manufacturing shipments. An estimated 48% of manufacturing output is exported to other parts of Canada and another 10% to markets outside Canada.

Transportation: Winnipeg is a major center for the Canadian National and Canadian Pacific railways, and both companies have extensive yards in the city. Another 510 mi./820 km. railway line stretches from The Pas to the Hudson Bay port of Churchill by way of Thompson, allowing for the export of wheat and nickel. Air Canada operates domestic and international flights daily through Winnipeg. Canadian Airlines International also operates frequent flights through Winnipeg and also serves The Pas, Flin Flon, Thompson, Gillam and Churchill. Six other lines connected Winnipeg to points in Manitoba as of 1989. Northwest had daily flights connecting Winnipeg to Minneapolis-St. Paul, Minnesota, and Aspen Airways connected daily to Grand Forks, North Dakota and Denver, Colorado. In all, there were 104 licensed commercial air carriers in Manitoba in 1989. A total of 2,138,007 passengers passed through the Winnipeg airport in 1987.

In 1989, Manitoba had 4,566 mi./7,349 km. of trunk highways and 7,642 mi./12,229 km. of provincial roads (mostly gravel). The number of registered vehicles was 890,885, including 532,645 passenger cars. The province operates seven ferries serving communities on Lake Winnipeg and northern Manitoba. Churchill, the sole port, handled 633,600 tons of cargo in 1986, most of it grain.

Wholesale and retail trade: Wholesale trade in 1986 amounted to $16.7 billion in 1986. Retail trade totaled $6.22 billion in 1989, and $6.32 billion in 1990.

Foreign trade: Exports leaving Manitoba in 1990 totaled $3.55 billion in value, of which exports to the United States accounted for 61%, with Japan second at 8.7%. Imports entering Manitoba were valued at nearly $2.7 billion, with the United States accounting for 86%. Nickel was the most valuable export, estimated at $637 million and 30% of total production and 18% of Manitoba exports. Grains and cereals came next at 17.6%, oilseeds and oil third at 7.5%.

Banking and finance: In 1988, Manitoba had 340 bank branches, of which the Royal Bank of Canada had 98, the Canadian Imperial Bank of Commerce 79, and the Bank of Montreal 67. Winnipeg has one of the nation's four stock exchanges. Total public and private investment was $5 billion in 1988.

Construction: A total of $836.9 million worth of building permits were issued in Manitoba in 1989, but this fell to $731.5 million in 1990. Winnipeg accounted for 79% (1989) and 66% (1990) in value. Construction (1990) was valued at $3.7 billion.

Tourism: Riding Mount National Park, 168 mi./270 km. northwest of Winnipeg, contains 1,150 sq. mi./2,978 sq. km. of rolling woodland, lakes and streams. There are two National Historic Parks and three National Historic Sites. In 1988, the 139 provincial parks occupied a total of 5,083 sq. mi./13,164 sq. km. The International Peace Garden straddles the Manitoba-North Dakota border and includes 1,451 acres/588 hectares. Non-resident tourists contributed $457 million to the economy in 1989, when out-of-province visitors numbered 2.6 million.

Public finance: The 1991–92 budget called for $5.24 billion in spending, of which 33% was to go for health, 18% for education and training and 10.5% for payments on the public debt. Revenue was projected at $4.77 billion plus $145 million transferred from the fiscal stabilization fund ($125 million) and lottery revenues ($20 million). The chief sources of revenue were expected to be personal and corporation income tax, 26%, other provincial collections, 40%, and federal transfer payments and receipts, 34.8%. The general expenditure of local governments in Manitoba in 1989 totaled $1.79 billion. The net general purpose public debt was $5.2 billion. The province has also guaranteed other debt of similar amount, most of it for Manitoba Hydro.

In 1990–91, the provincial personal income tax was 52% of the federal tax, with a surtax up to a maximum of about 4% on net income. The corporate income-tax rate of 17% for large corporations was the highest in Canada. For mining companies, the rate was 20%. The sales tax was 7% and the capital tax on financial institutions was 3%. Other taxes include a payroll tax on employers (with a minimum of $600,000), tobacco tax and gasoline tax.

Employment: In 1990, there were an average of 505,000 people employed in Manitoba and 39,000 unemployed, for an unemployment rate of 7.2%, lower than that of most provinces. The unemployment rate was 7.8% in 1988. About 67% of adult Manitobans were in the labor force in 1990, when weekly earnings averaged $462.74. There were 78,162 government employees in 1987: 17,955 federal, 19,004 provincial and 41,203 local. In October 1990, employment was 505,000. By sector, this total consisted of: services, 196,000; trade, 92,000; manufacturing, 60,000; transportation and utilities, 49,000; agriculture, 40,000; public administration, 35,000; finance, 30,000; construction, 25,000; and nonagricultural primary industries, 10,000. The Manitoba Federation of Labour had a membership of about 74,000 in 1985. The largest unions are in the public sector, followed by the United Food and Commercial Workers and the Steelworkers.

Prices: Consumer prices in Winnipeg increased 42% from 1982 through 1988, slightly below the national average. Between October 1988 and October 1989, they increased 4.1%, compared to 5.2% for all Canada, and between October 1989 and October 1990 5.0%, compared to 4.8% for all Canada.

SOCIAL SERVICES

Welfare: The Canada Assistance Plan, a joint federal-provincial program, spent $179.8 million on 60,600 Manitoban beneficiaries in fiscal 1987.

The federal government administers and funds old-age pensions and unemployment insurance. In addition, welfare recipients in Manitoba are given either provincial or municipal assistance, and each of the municipalities is allowed to establish its own rules. The Manitoba Department of Family Services operates provincial welfare programs and financial-support services for pensioners and low-income working families with children. The department also operates employment services for youth and students, a wide variety of training and employment-preparation programs, and settlement-assistance programs for immigrants. The Department of Family Services operates mental-retardation services, rehabilitation services and child and family services. The department licenses, inspects and sets care standards for group homes, other residential-care homes and day care centers. Financial support is available for a wide range of nongovernment social-service agencies and care providers such as day care centers.

Health: Manitobans receive prepaid hospital and physician's care, without premiums, through the Manitoba Health Services Commission. A pharmaceutical reimbursement program provides for payment of 80% of the cost of all prescription drugs in excess of a basic deductible incurred in each calendar year. The department's public-health programs include dental services, maternal and child health, hearing screening and diagnosis, public-health nursing, communicable-disease control, nutrition and home economics, home care, and environmental health. The department is also responsible for hospitals, personal-care homes and mental-health centers. The Alcoholism Foundation of Manitoba, which reports to the minister of health, operates residential and outpatient alcoholism and drug-abuse treatment programs.

In 1987, there were 17,438 live births in Manitoba (16.3 per thousand) and 8,782 deaths (8.2 per thousand). Both were above average for Canada. The abortion rate, 15.1 per hundred live births, was below the national average. Eighty-five hospitals had 6,447 beds in 1986–87; hospital expense per patient-day, $388.81, was well above the national average. There were 2,226 physicians in 1987, one per 486, slightly higher than the national average. There were 516 licensed dentists and 9,389 registered nurses. Health expenditures in the province came to $1.7 billion in 1985.

Housing: In 1986, 250,420 residences were owned and 126,250 rented; the ownership percentage of 63.6 was slightly above the national average. The average gross rent of $392 per month and average monthly home payment (with mortgage) of $673 were both below the national averages. There were 5,455 housing starts in 1988, of which 4,071 were in Winnipeg. The value of the 3,297 building permits for housing in 1990 was $394 million, of which Winnipeg permits were valued at $210 million. The maximum number of dwelling starts was 8,174, in 1987.

EDUCATION

School enrollment is compulsory between the ages of 7 and 16. Public elementary and secondary education can be either in English or French, and there is also a French-immersion program on which all subjects are taught in French for students whose mother tongue is not French. Some schools offer instruction in the majority of subjects in another minority tongue, such as German or Ukrainian. There were 47 school divisions in 1989, each administered by an elected school board under the Department of Education. There were also 10 school districts, of which four were financed mainly from sources other than provincial grants and taxes. School boards are responsible for maintaining and equipping schools, hiring teachers and support staff, and negotiating salaries. The Manitoba Teachers Federation negotiates with the boards. Public school enrollment in 1990–91 was 197,586. There are about 20,000 pupils in private or other schools. About 13,600 teachers were employed in the public school system in 1988–89.

There were 18,884 full-time and 15,476 part-time students in Manitoba's three institutions of university learning in 1989–90. The University of Manitoba, at Winnipeg, had 14,649 full-time students (in 1988–89) and about 8,729 part-time students. St. Boniface College is affiliated with the university and offers instruction in French. Brandon University had about 1,370 full-time and 1,700 part-time students in 1989–90. The University of Winnipeg had about 2,900 full-time and 4,700 part-time students. Three community colleges—Assiniboine in Brandon, Keewatin in The Pas and Red River in Winnipeg—offer programs to adults throughout the province, including in several regional centers and more than 120 Manitoba communities.

MASS MEDIA

Newspapers and periodicals: Of the five dailies in Manitoba in 1990, the largest were both in Winnipeg. *The Sun* had a 1990 daily circulation of 47,900 and a Sunday circulation of 54,800. The *Winnipeg Free Press* had a daily circulation of 167,900, a Saturday circulation of 234,000 and a Sunday circulation of 148,700. The other three were the *Brandon Sun, Portage la Prairie Graphic* and *Flin Flon Reminder.*

In 1988, there were 53 weekly newspapers, 8 other newspapers not publishing daily, and 32 periodicals. Among these were the weekly newspaper *La Liberté,* published in St. Boniface (circulation 11,800) and *Country Guide,* a Winnipeg farm monthly periodical (circulation 211,325).

Broadcasting: In 1989, there were 28 radio stations: 21 AM, and 7 FM. One broadcast in French, one in Native languages, and one was multilingual. There were also a large number of rebroadcasters. Of the seven originating television stations, one broadcast in French. There were also 11 rebroadcasting stations. There were 68 cable-television systems, most offering at least four Canadian and four American stations. Of the 382,000 households in Manitoba, 315,000 had access to cable television and 264,500 were subscribers.

BIOGRAPHICAL SKETCHES

Gary Albert Filmon.   Premier of Manitoba, president of the Executive Council and minister of federal-provincial relations. Born in Winnipeg on August 24, 1942, Filmon studied engineering at the University of Manitoba, receiving a bachelor's degree in 1964 and a master's degree in 1967. After serving as a consulting engineer from 1964 to 1969, he was president of Success/Angus Commercial College until 1980. He served as a Winnipeg city councillor, 1975–79, when he was elected to the Legislative Assembly as a Conservative. He was reelected in 1983, 1986, 1988, and 1990. Filmon was minister of consumer and corporate affairs and environment in 1981 and also assumed responsibility for the Manitoba Housing and Renewal Corp. In December 1983 he was named leader of the Conservative Party, and he became premier following his party's electoral plurality in May 1988.

Clayton Sidney Manness.   Minister of finance. Born in Winnipeg on January 23, 1947, Manness attended Sanford College and the University of Manitoba, from which he received a master's degree in agricultural economics. A resident of Domain, he has farmed in the area since 1968 and also worked in the areas of agricultural marketing, research and transportation for the Manitoba Department of Agriculture, the Canada Grains Council and the Cargill Grain Co. He was elected to the Legislative Assembly in 1981 and reelected in 1986, 1988, and 1990.

(Harry) John Enns.   Minister of natural resources. Born in Winnipeg on November 30, 1931, Enns attended St. John's Technical High School and became a rancher. In the Legislative Assembly since 1966, he was minister of agriculture, 1967–68; minister of mines and natural resources, 1968–69; minister of public works and highways, 1977–78; minister of highways and transportation, 1978–79; minister of government services, 1979–81; and minister of natural resources to November 1981. He was reappointed to the latter position after the Conservative electoral plurality of May 1988, and reelected in November 1990.

Harold Johan Neufeld.   Minister of energy and mines. Born in Altona, Manitoba on October 10, 1927. An accountant since 1954, Neufeld was elected to the Legislative Assembly in 1988, when he was appointed minister of energy and mines.

Gary Doer.   Leader of the opposition. Born March 31, 1948, in Winnipeg, he was educated at St. Paul's High School in Winnipeg. He was first elected to the Manitoba legislature in 1986 and was reelected in 1988 and 1990. He was appointed minister of urban affairs on April 17, 1986 and was reappointed September 22, 1987, and he also was appointed minister of crown investments and minister responsible for the administration of the Manitoba Telephone Act, the Crown Corporation Accountability Act and the Liquor Control Act. He was elected leader of the Manitoba New Democratic Party on March 30, 1988.

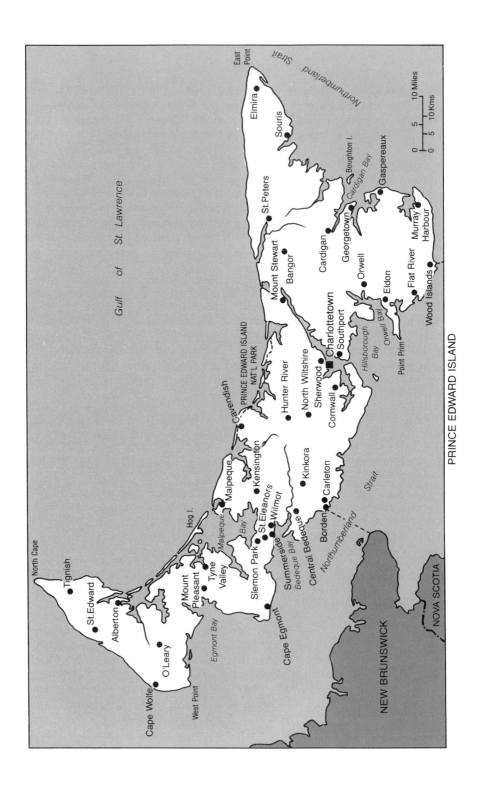

PRINCE EDWARD ISLAND

PRINCE EDWARD ISLAND

GEOGRAPHY

Features: Prince Edward Island, one of the four Atlantic Provinces, is Canada's smallest province in both size and population. The Island lies in the Gulf of St. Lawrence, separated from the mainland provinces of Nova Scotia and New Brunswick by the Northumberland Strait. Its crescent shape measures 139 mi./224 km. from tip to tip and from 3.7 mi./6 km. to 40 mi./ 64 km. across. From the highest elevation (466 ft./142 m.) in the central hilly region the land slopes down to gently rolling hills in the east and a nearly level plain to the west. The thick covering of fertile red soil is one of the Island's most striking features and, together with the sea, constitutes its most important resource.

Area: 2,184 sq. mi./5,660 sq. km. Makes up 0.1% of total area of Canada.

Mean maximum and minimum temperatures: Charlottetown: 65°F/18.3°C (July), 19°F/−7.2°C (January).

Relative humidity: 72%–86%.

Mean annual precipitation: 43 in./1,077 mm., of which there is 130 in./ 331 cm. of snow.

POPULATION

Total population (1986 census): 126,646. 1990 estimated population: 130,200.

Chief towns and populations (1986): Charlottetown (15,776) is the only city. Other municipalities include: Summerside (8,020), Sherwood (5,769), St. Eleanor's (3,743), Parkdale (2,035), Montague (1,994), Souris (1,379), Kensington (1,105) and Tignish (950), all towns.

Distribution: Although PEI has the densest population in Canada (22 people/sq. km.), it is also the most rural of the provinces, with only 38.1%

51

of its population classed as urban dwellers. Of the 61.9% rural population, 10% live on farms. Poor economic conditions have perpetuated high rates of emigration since the 1890s. Only in the past decade has a small net immigration gain, combined with natural increase, amounted to a population growth of 7.1%. However, the government has expressed concern over the fact that people over 65 years of age form a steadily increasing proportion of the population.

Ethnic composition (1986 census): The fairly homogeneous population consists of 73% British, 9% Acadians and 12% British and French. Dutch, Germans, Lebanese, Southeast Asians and Micmac together comprise a further 2%. The Micmac arrived on PEI approximately 2,000 years ago, but they are a branch of the Algonquians, traces of whose ancestors date back to 8,000 to 10,000 years ago on the Island. Today a small, vigorous population of 440 Micmac reside at Lennos Island on the north shore and at Scotchfort on the Hillsborough River. Highland Scots make up the majority of the British group, followed by Irish, English and Lowland Scots. A recent revival of Acadian culture is promoted by the very active St. Thomas Aquinas Society.

Language: In 1986 an overwhelming majority (94.1%) reported English as their mother tongue. Only 4.7 claimed French, although attempts are being made to revive the use of French, and one of the five regional school districts is French. Gaelic, the original language of the Highland Scots, has virtually vanished.

Religion (1981 census): The Islanders are almost equally divided between the Roman Catholic and Protestant churches. The 1981 census recorded 56,415 Catholics. The largest Protestant group was the United Church with 29,645, followed by the Presbyterian (12,620) and Anglican (6,850) churches.

CONSTITUTION AND GOVERNMENT

Executive: The Executive Council is the smallest in Canada, varying between 10 and 12 members, each of whom is responsible for one or more government departments. There were 12 members in July 1990, heading 13 departments. There were also 21 semi-independent agencies, boards, commissions or crown (public) corporations.

Legislature: The Legislative Assembly of PEI is unique in a number of respects. Its 32 representatives form the smallest such assembly in Canada. It elects two members, instead of the usual one, from each riding, an artefact of abolishing an earlier bicameral legislature by combining the two houses. One member is a councillor, the other an assembly-man. In addition, PEI is the only province that does not publish a Hansard record of proceedings. An interesting effect of the small size of the legislature is that one-third of its members, and the majority of members on the government side, sit in the cabinet, giving the legislature even less opportunity for independent action than in other provinces.

Political parties: The Conservatives and Liberals have regularly taken turns in office since 1873, when PEI joined Confederation. Only two other parties (the Patrons of Industry in 1886 and the Progressives in 1923) have ever succeeded in getting representatives elected. The Co-operative Commonwealth Federation ran unsuccessful candidates between 1943 and 1951. In the election of 1935, the Conservatives won every seat, a unique event in Canada until the Liberals did the same in New Brunswick in 1987. The provincial general election in May 1989 returned 29 Liberals and 2 Conservatives.

Local government: Because of PEI's small size, many local issues are handled at provincial level. The city of Charlottetown and the eight towns are governed by a mayor and councillors, elected for a two-year term. The 77 incorporated communities elect commissioners.

Federal representation: PEI is represented in the Senate by four members. Liberals hold its four seats in the House of Commons. On the basis of population, PEI is overrepresented in Parliament, but it protested so vehemently in 1911, when its entitlement fell to three members, that a constitutional amendment was passed guaranteeing a province at least as many members in the House of Commons as its constitutionally fixed number of senators.

Judicial system: The seven-member Supreme Court has estates, family and trial divisions and sits on appeals *en banco.* There are three provincial courts and a small claims court, but no county courts.

RECENT HISTORY

It was in the post World War II period that the first real modernization on Prince Edward Island began. Between 1953 and 1959, the Liberal party under Alexander Matheson initiated a program of rural electrification. However, problems in other areas led to a Conservative victory in the 1959 election and a period of much more radical changes. Premier Walter Shaw was much concerned with bureaucratic reform and economic diversification. The former resulted in the establishment in 1963 of the Civil Service Commission. Shaw's activities in the latter sphere included the creation of a department of tourism and securing provincial funding for the Georgetown project to provide new industrial development based on traditional activities.

After the 1966 election, the pace of modernization accelerated under the Liberals and their new leader, Alex Campbell. It was Campbell's government, in conjunction with Ottawa, that devised the Comprehensive Development Plan. Conceived to run for 15 years, its objectives were wide-ranging and far-reaching. It set out to strengthen and rationalize the provincial economy; improve public services; increase production levels; restructure the agriculture and fisheries industries; enhance education, training and management; and develop new markets for Island products. The plan relied on large injections of federal funds and required a new Department of Development manned almost entirely by outside experts.

Even in purely economic terms, the plan could not be judged an unqualified success. For instance, manufacturing attracted to new industrial estates has often been unable to compete with central Canadian firms. By the middle of the plan, the federal government gradually began to decrease its funding. The construction of shopping malls was halted by Angus Maclean, his Conservative Party having won the 1979 election on a platform of "rural renaissance." By the time Conservative premier James Lee signed the last phase of the Development Plan in 1981, Ottawa had stopped paying the salaries of the 200 Department of Development officials running the plan.

In about 1975 energy was added to transport as a recurring political issue. PEI's problem has always been to secure an adequate and economical supply of energy in the face of neither fossil fuel nor hydroelectric resources. The Island relied on oil generators fueled by imported oil until the rising price of oil from about 1973 made PEI electricity the most expensive in Canada. In 1975 Alex Campbell signed a long-term agreement with New Brunswick for the supply of nuclear-generated electricity through a new submarine cable which was laid between the two provinces. There are now 22 km of submarine cable, and the province receives over 85% of its power through it, generating the remainder thermally, in 1989 104,000 megawatt hours out of 727,000. During his term in office between 1981 and 1986, James Lee instituted a public inquiry into high electricity prices, but with little result. He did, however, secure agreement from Ottawa in 1985 to repay the debt on the underwater cable and to subsidize electricity rates to allow a 20% reduction in price to industrial and residential users.

The year before, Lee had launched his new development strategy entitled "Blending Tradition and Innovation," and had signed a new five-year, $120-million Economic Regional Development Agreement with the federal government.

Despite Conservative success in negotiations with Ottawa, problems continued on the economic front and the 1986 election brought a change of government, though not of political issues. The Liberals, under Joseph Ghiz, continue to grapple with problems of transportation and the high cost of electricity. The idea of a causeway as a permanent link to the mainland had been revived in Ottawa in the mid-1980s, when it was pointed out that the federal government was losing $40 million annually on subsidizing the ferry. In a provincial plebiscite on a causeway in 1988, 59% voted in favor. However the financial problems of the federal government have deferred any action in the early 1990s. In efforts to solve the energy problem, small-scale success has been achieved with wind, solar and wood-fired generators, but the cost of electricity remains uneconomically high.

ECONOMY

Attracted by its strong economy, Canada wooed PEI into Confederation, confident in its vision of a prosperous alliance. In fact, opportunities opened by the industrialization of central Canada and expansion at its western frontier enticed a continuous stream of people from the Island. Apart from a single success in the breeding of foxes for pelts during the first half of this century, PEI's economy declined steadily until by the early 1950s its per capita income had sunk to just over half the Canadian average.

Any attempts to promote prosperity on the Island must first acknowledge the many factors outside the control of government. First, any economy based on agriculture and fishing will fluctuate unpredictably according to the vagaries of weather, disease and external market prices. Second, a summer season of only eight to ten weeks puts a natural ceiling on tourism, PEI's second most important industry after agriculture, and tourism is also prey to poor weather. Third, the absence of coal and hydroelectric resources means that the price of electricity is under the control of outsiders with PEI in a weak negotiating position. The high price of power, coupled with high transportation costs, places manufacturing operations at an immediate disadvantage compared to mainland competitors. Fourth, the financial fuel for boosting the economy is not available from such a small, low-income population and must be secured from outside, primarily from the federal government. In 1987, federal transfers contributed 49% of provincial revenue. There is little the province can do to further its own development plans in the face of changed federal priorities.

These limitations notwithstanding, major attempts to strengthen Island economy have been made since the 1960s. Programs such as the Comprehensive Development Plan have aimed at improving agricultural productivity, developing manufacturing and expanding the tourist industry. The federal government moved the entire Department of Veterans' Affairs to Charlottetown in the early '80s, and later established the Goods and Services Tax offices in Summerside. Some measure of success might be noted in the fact that per capita income now hovers around 70% of the national average, though at $15,300 in 1989 it was the second lowest after Newfoundland and 23% consists of government transfers, such as unemployment insurance benefits and old age security payments. PEI economic growth has been erratic over the later 1980s, a period during which the national economy has expanded faster than in any other of the big seven industrial countries. The GDP of $200 billion (at market value) in 1990 represented a growth rate 30% higher than the Canadian average; in the previous year it had been 20% less. Combined public and private investment showed little increase, from $429.6 million in 1986 to $434.7 million in 1987. On the other hand, 1988 produced an encouraging growth rate of more than 5.3% based on large increases in lobster catches and construction activity, and a 12% increase in investment to $487.3 million. Investment increased again to $532.0 million in 1989 and $563.8 million in 1990. Strong growth was expected through increases in agricultural acreage and the construction of facilities for the 1990–91 Canadian Winter Games. It may be that two decades of development programs are beginning to bear fruit, but it is too early to tell what this augurs for the long-term prosperity of the Island.

Agriculture: Agriculture employs about 6,000 people and forms approximately 13% of the Island's GDP, compared to 5.2% nationally. Only in Saskatchewan is agriculture a more important component of a provincial economy. It was especially disappointing, therefore, that total farm cash receipts in 1988 declined by 2.9% to $206.3 million. This was largely due to weak hog prices and low prices for the 1987 potato crop marketed in 1988. However, cash receipts increased to $256.1 million in 1989 and $247.6 million in 1990. The soil and climate of PEI favor the cultivation of potatoes, which regularly contribute 30% to 40% of the value of farm cash receipts (47% in 1989). Seed potatoes make up three-quarters of the potato yield and are exported to more than 15 countries. Unfortunately in 1991 allegations that PEI seed potatoes were carriers of a virus damaging to the other crops led to restriction on imports by the United States. Table potatoes are either sold fresh in Canada and the United States or are processed into French fries and other products, thus contributing to the manufacturing sector. Of greater importance to the food industry are dairy products, which comprise the second most important farming sector, 14.6% of cash receipts in 1989. Only slightly lower contributions to cash receipts come from the sale of cattle and calves (10.4% in 1989) and hogs (8.5% in 1989). No other single crop is of particular significance except tobacco. It was introduced to PEI in 1959 and regularly contributed between 5% and 7% to cash receipts; this fell to 4.2% in 1989, and 2.5% in 1990.

Farming operations have altered dramatically in the postwar period from numerous small, unmechanized family farms to commercial-scale setups requiring heavy investment in machinery and equipment. Between 1951 and 1986 the number of farms dropped from 10,137 to 2,833 and average size increased from 109 acres/44 hectares to 237 acres/96 hectares. Over the same period, the area of farmland has contracted by 39% to 673,196 acres/272,433 hectares. Most of the recent decrease has been in pasture, with cropland remaining relatively steady and area seeded to potatoes actually increasing slightly.

Tourism: PEI attracts more than 600,000 visitors each year, making tourism one of the Island's most important industries. In 1989 nonresident tourists spent 98.3 million, approximately 4.9% of the GDP for that year. Ever since Premier Thane Campbell laid the foundations of the tourist industry just before World War II, successive PEI governments have viewed the expansion of tourism as one of the most promising ways of strengthening the Island economy. The short eight- to ten-week summer season places a natural limit on the numbers of people who can be enticed to the obvious attractions of sandy beaches and lobster suppers. Therefore, the government has assisted in promoting activities in other seasons and in developing the less visited eastern and western ends of the Island. Apart

56

from a dip in 1982 and 1983, the number of tourist parties (via auto vehicles) increases every year; 238,800 were counted in 1990.

Fishing: Compared to the other Atlantic Provinces, fishing in PEI contributes less to both employment and GDP. The total value of fish landings in 1990 was $66.8 million, down 8.0% from 1989, when it accounted for 3.8% of GDP. Its true importance in the economy only becomes clear when one takes into account the 18.5% of the value of manufacturing shipments that were fish products in 1988. The further addition of outfitting and vessel construction brought the total contribution of the fishery industry to over $140 million.

For the tourist industry, the lobster supper is an indispensable attraction of holidays in PEI. For Island fisherman, lobster is by far the most valuable species caught. While it made up only 15.3% (22.5 million lb/10,208 tonnes) of the total catch in 1990, it contributed 60.4% ($40.3 million) of total landed value. The rest of the shellfish industry, which includes scallops and oysters, suffered in mid-1988 from a temporary closure at the end of 1987 due to infection of the crop by a toxin harmful, even lethal, to humans. Much more important for the fishing industry are groundfish species, such as cod, hake, flounder and redfish, and pelagic and estuarial species, such as herring and mackerel. Both contribute significantly more weight than lobster to the annual catch but only about 10% to 15% of the dollar value. Preliminary figures for 1990 put groundfish at 43.4 million lb/19,700 tonnes, worth $6.5 million, and pelagic and estuarial at 33.3 million lb/15.100 tonnes, worth $4.3 million. Irish moss, a marine algae, is harvested at the western end of the Island. Its value in 1990 (preliminary) was $3.4 million. It is exported for the extraction of carrageenin, an emulsifying and stabilizing substance used in convenience foods.

The fishing industry employed approximately 3,200 people in 1985, and a further 2,000 in seasonal work in processing plants. Employment in the fishing industry typically tends to be part time. Even those who claim fishing as their principal source of income do not usually derive all their income from it. Whereas in the Pacific and central regions of Canada the balance often comes from other activities, in the Atlantic Provinces unemployment insurance benefits provide the main supplement.

Manufacturing: This is much less well developed in the Atlantic region generally than in the rest of the country. The Comprehensive Development Plan sought to rectify this imbalance in PEI, but many experiments in the manufacture of non-food products failed. New industries that have managed to gain a foothold include high-technology metalwork, precision components for the medical industry, high-fashion optical frames and stainless steel and aluminium pots and pans. But with the processing of food products making up approximately 68% of manufacturing in 1988, production remains closely tied to primary activities. The total value of manufactured shipments increased in 1988 to $391.7 million. Fish products represented 18.5%, and dairy products 19.5%. Employment in the sector averaged 5,000 per month, compared to 4,000 in 1987.

Services: The services sector employs the greatest number of people in the Island. In August 1990 27% (15,600) of the employed labor force came from the community, business and personal services sector, which includes education, health and welfare services, accommodations and restaurants. Two-thirds of the services employees were female. Government activities make a major contribution to the services sector; the labor force in public administration numbered 6,000 in August 1990.

Foreign trade: International exports contribute less than 10% of the Island GDP. In 1990 they totaled $167.6 million (preliminary). Vegetables (mainly potatoes) and fish and their processed products are the province's major exports, the former valued at $67.7 million and the latter at $64.3 million in 1987. In fact, at 81.8% of total exports, they were the only significant categories of exported products. The United States stands out among customers as the purchaser of 60.0% of all exports in 1990. Uruguay came second at only 5.5%, Venezuela third at 4.7%, France fourth at 4.6% and Trinidad and Tobago fifth at 3.3%.

Construction: The construction industry contributes approximately 8% of total GDP and employs a seasonal labor force of around 3,000. Strong growth was predicted for 1989–90 due to the construction of facilities for the 1990–91 Canadian Winter Games, and building construction in 1989 did remain higher than in the mid-1980s but fell off again in 1990.

Employment: In 1990 PEI's employed labor force averaged 55,000, the participation rate 6.5% and the unemployment rate 14%. Unemployment is one of the Island's most intractable problems. Over the last decade and a half it has worsened significantly from the 1975 level of 8.0%. The closure of the military base at Summerside, one of the largest employers on the Island, in April 1992 aroused fears of the addition of another 1,200 to 1,500 people to the those already unemployed. But the federal government is encouraging the development of the base into an industrial park and aerospace center, and is offering inducements to industry. The federal government also chose Summerside for the administrative center of its Goods and Services tax introduced in 1991, and the net impact of all these developments appears to be positive.

Prices: The exceptionally low increases in the consumer price indexes for Charlottetown-Summerside in 1986 (2.0%) and 1987 (3.5%) were due to a federal government subsidy to electricity prices, which resulted in a 14.1% overall drop in energy prices in 1986 and a 1.5% decrease in 1987. Energy prices began rising again in 1988, and the increase of 3.7% in the overall consumer price index approached the national rate of 4.1%.

SOCIAL SERVICES

Welfare: The Department of Health and Social Services is responsible for a wide range of welfare services which are offered through regional offices, public health centers and manors (residential care for the elderly) across the province, as well as the central office in Charlottetown. The department's programs are provided primarily to assist people to become capable of independent living and emphasize the role of local communities in meeting needs of the elderly, families and their children. Child welfare covers adoptions, protection, foster care, services for unmarried parents, early development and day care and free dental care. Means-tested financial assistance is offered under the Welfare Assistance Act to those in need. Individuals in receipt of financial assistance are also eligible for Employment Enhance services designed to help develop skills or experience that may improve chances of employment.

Health: A provincial health care plan, providing non-premium medical and hospital services, was introduced in the late 1960s. In 1988 there were 146 practicing physicians and a total bed capacity of 2,040 divided among nine hospitals plus a number of licensed nursing homes, residential homes for the elderly, Hillsborough Hospital for the mentally ill and other health care institutions. The largest of the hospitals is the Queen Elizabeth in Charlottetown, which was opened in 1982–83 and now houses the Provincial Laboratories Unit, Active Care Unit, Rehabilitation Unit and Cancer Unit. A prescription drug service is available to some chronically ill patients and to those receiving financial assistance. The Drug Cost Assistance Plan provides similar help to senior citizens. Community health programs include nursing, hygiene, mental health and home care and support.

Housing: PEI funds home ownership, rental and repair programs. Home ownership is assisted through a Rural Mortgage Lending Support Program, which ensures that adequate competitive funding is available to people in rural areas, and a Second Mortgage Loan program. The Home Rental Program is specifically for new construction. It forms part of the joint federal-provincial social housing construction scheme under which the federal government provides 75% of the costs and the province 25%. Beneficiaries include senior citizens, families and special needs groups (e.g., adolescents). The Home Repair Programs aim to assist senior citizens on low and modest incomes with emergency repairs and repairs carried out by approved job-creation project groups.

EDUCATION

Education is one aspect of Island life that has been most affected by changes under the Comprehensive Development Plan. At the end of the 1960s the educational system consisted of several hundred autonomous school districts, each offering classes from grades 1 to 10. Few students were able to attend the single high school in Charlottetown. Although the schools provided an important focus for community life, they fell far below the educational norm in the rest of the country. Starting in 1970 the entire system was reformed; the number of schools was drastically reduced while expenditure was equally dramatically increased.

Today the public school system in the province provides free education for students from grades 1 to 12. In 1988–89 there were 24,708 students in the elementary-to-secondary system. Of the 70 schools in operation, two are private schools; one is under the jurisdiction of the federal government; and one is operated by a recognized Indian band. Provincial public schools are organized into five regional administrative units, each with an elected school board composed of 15 trustees. Approximately 2% of the students receive their education in the French language, while an additional 10% are enrolled in French immersion programs.

The province has one university and one college of applied arts and technology. The University of Prince Edward Island offers undergraduate programs in arts, science, education, music and business administration to more than 2,000 full-time and 800 part-time students. An undergraduate course in veterinary medicine opened in September 1986 to provide a needed program in the Atlantic Provinces. The primary purpose of Holland College is to provide training for students seeking employment at semiprofessional levels in business, applied arts and technology. Each year 800 to 900 students register in postsecondary programs within the college. The college is also responsible for the operation of the vocational high school program, the vocational trade program and adult night classes.

Annual expenditures on education for the province totaled $124.8 million for the 1987–88 fiscal year.

MASS MEDIA

Newspapers and periodicals: PEI is served by three local daily newspapers: *The Guardian* and *The Evening Patriot* both serve Charlottetown and are owned by the Thomson Newspaper Company. The *Journal Pioneer,* in Summerside, is owned by Sterling Publishers.

There are two English-language weeklies. *The Eastern Graphic* and *The West Prince,* and one French-language publication, *La Voix Acadienne. Gulf Wings* appears bi-weekly.

Broadcasting: There are three AM stations and two FM stations on the Island. CBC Television maintains a studio in Charlottetown, while the programs of the CTV network come to the province via a repeater station fed from the ATV station in Moncton, New Brunswick. Radio-Canada offers French FM and UHF-TV from Moncton through repeater stations situated on the Island. Cablevision and pay TV are available in the more populated areas.

BIOGRAPHICAL SKETCHES

Hon. Joseph A. Ghiz, Q.C. Ghiz was first sworn in as premier and president of the Executive Council of PEI in May 1986 and was reelected in May 1989. He was born in Charlottetown in 1945 and received his early education there. He later studied at Dalhousie (B.Comm. 1966, LL.B. 1969) and Harvard (LL.M. 1981). Ghiz was a senior partner of Scales,

Ghiz, Jenkins and McQuaid and served as president of the PEI branch of the Canadian Bar Association. Having participated in the national and provincial Liberal Party since 1970, Ghiz was elected president of the PEI Liberals in 1977 and became their leader in 1981. His inexperience was partly responsible for the defeat of the Liberals in the 1982 election. As Member of the Legislative Assembly (MLA) for Sixth Queens, he developed into an effective opposition and party leader and led the Liberals to victory in 1986. In addition to his duties as premier, he also serves as minister of justice and attorney general.

Hon. Gilbert R. Clements. Minister of the environment and minister of finance. Born at Victoria Cross, PEI in 1928, Clements was educated at Montague Memorial School and Mount Allison Academy. He was first elected MLA in 1970 and served as minister of the departments of municipal affairs, environment and tourism, and parks and conservation from 1974 to 1978. From 1979 to 1986 he was opposition critic for the finance and energy portfolios. In 1986 he was appointed minister of finance and minister of community and cultural affairs. Following the election of May 1989, he became minister of the newly created Department of the Environment and was reappointed minister of finance.

Hon. Leonce Bernard. Minister of community and cultural affairs and minister of fisheries and aquaculture. Bernard was born in Abram Village in 1943. He graduated from Evangeline High School and continued his commerce training with courses in accounting and business management. In 1970 he became manager of Evangeline Credit Union, as well as serving as the executive director of Baie Acadienne Venture Capital Group. Bernard was first elected as Liberal MLA for Third Prince in a by-election in 1975. He was appointed to the cabinet as minister of industry in 1986 and was named chairman of the PEI Development Agency. In June 1989 he was appointed to his current cabinet positions.

Hon. Keith Milligan. Minister of agriculture, and minister responsible for the Liquor Control Commission. Milligan was born in 1950 in Inverness, PEI. Having received his early education at Inverness, in 1974 he graduated from the University of PEI with Bachelor of Arts and Bachelor of Education degrees. Before his election as MLA for Second Prince in 1981, Milligan worked as a teacher and served on the Advisory Board and then as coordinator of the West Prince Regional Services Centre. In the Legislative Assembly he has held the positions of leader of the official opposition and opposition critic for education. From June 1986 until June 1989 he held the portfolio of minister of health and social services. For several years Milligan has operated a silver fox ranch in Tyne Valley and has been active in promoting and rebuilding the silver fox industry in West Prince and in PEI generally.

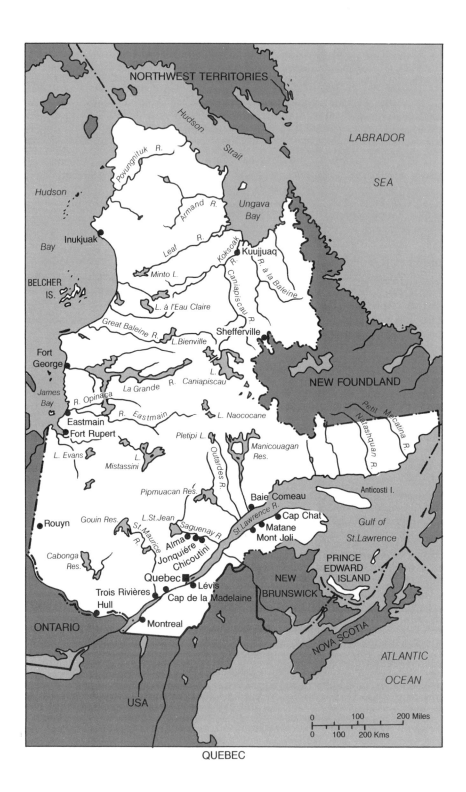

NORTHWEST TERRITORIES

Hudson

Strait

LABRADOR

SEA

Povungnituk R.

Hudson

Armand R.

Ungava Bay

Leaf R.

● Inukjuak

Minto L.

Koksoak R.

● Kuujjuaq

R. à la Baleine

Caniapiscau R.

Bay

BELCHER IS.

L. à l'Eau Claire

Great Baleine R.

L.Bienville

Shefferville

Fort George ●

L. Caniapiscau

NEW FOUNDLAND

La Grande R.

James Bay

R. Opinaca

R. Eastmain

L. Naococane

Eastmain ●
Fort Rupert ●

Pletipi L.

Manicouagan Res.

Petit Mecatina R.

Natashquan R.

L. Evans

L. Mistassini

Pipmuacan Res.

Outardes R.

Baie Comeau ●

St.Lawrence R.

Anticosti I.

● Rouyn

Gouin Res.

L.St.Jean

Saguenay R.

St. Lawrence R.

Cap Chat ●
Matane ●
Mont Joli

Gulf of St.Lawrence

St. Maurice R.

Alma ●
Jonquière ●
Chicoutini ●

Cabonga Res.

■ Quebec
● Lévis

PRINCE EDWARD ISLAND

Trois Rivières ●
Hull ●

Cap de la Madelaine

NEW BRUNSWICK

ONTARIO

● Montreal

NOVA SCOTIA

ATLANTIC

OCEAN

USA

| 0 | | 100 | | 200 Miles |
| 0 | 100 | | 200 Kms | |

QUEBEC

QUEBEC

Features: Quebec is Canada's largest province. It borders on Ontario to the west and Newfoundland and Labrador to the east. To the south are the province of New Brunswick and the U.S. states of Maine, New Hampshire, Vermont and New York. The Hudson, James and Ungava bays make up the remainder of its boundaries. Quebec is composed of three main geographical regions: the St. Lawrence River Valley, the Canadian Shield and the Appalachian region. The St. Lawrence River, one of the world's great waterways, is a dominant feature of Quebec's geography. Together with the St. Lawrence Seaway, upstream from Montreal, it provides a major artery for sea-going vessels to penetrate the 2,400 mi./3,600 km. distance from the Atlantic coast to the Great Lakes. The province's principal cities and most of its industries and farming are concentrated in the river valley and adjacent lowlands. To the north of the valley lies the Canadian Shield, covering 80% of the province. Finely dissected by many rivers and lakes and only sparsely populated, it is seen by all of Quebec's inhabitants as a major source of natural resources: coniferous forests for the pulp and paper industry; summer and winter resort areas for the tourist industry; salmon, deer, moose and caribou for the aboriginal people as well as sports fishermen and hunters; energy potential for hydroelectric development; gold, copper and zinc for the mining industry. The Appalachian region stretches from Quebec City to Lake Champlain along the south bank of the St. Lawrence River. Part of the ancient Appalachian mountain chain, its rounded rolling hills support a variety of uses, from ski resorts and fertile farmland to asbestos mining.

Area: 643,987 sq. mi./1,667,926 sq. km. including 70,981 sq. mi./ 183,889 sq. km. of fresh water. Makes up 15.5% of total area of Canada.

Mean maximum and minimum temperatures: St. Lawrence Valley: 72°F/22°C (July), 14°F/ − 10°C (January); Nouveau-Québec: 54°F/12°C (July), −8°F/ −22°C (January).

Relative humidity: 58%–80%.

Mean annual rainfall: Quebec City: 40 in./1,008 mm.; Montreal: 30 in./ 776 mm.; Nouveau-Québec: 16 in./408 mm..

POPULATION

Total population (1986 census): 6,532,461. Estimated population 1990: 6,797,800.

Chief towns and populations (1986 census): Montreal (1,015,420; metropolitan area estimated at 3,068,100, as of June 1990), Laval (284,164), Quebec City (164,580; metropolitan area estimated at 622,200 as of June 1990), Longueuil (125,441), Sherbrooke (74,438), Verdun (60,246), Hull (58,722) and Trois-Rivières (50,122).

Distribution: Since the early 1920s a majority of Quebec's population has been urban. Today 80% live in cities, giving Quebec the second largest urban population after Ontario. The region of Montreal alone accounts for 60% of total population. Only 3% of the entire population live on farms.

Ethnic composition (1986 census): Quebec is unique among the provinces in having a majority (79%) of people of French origin (5.1 million). Approximately 6.7% (435,500) of Quebecers are of British or partly British origin and 2.7% (174,250) are of mixed French and English origin. Italians (163,880) and Eastern Europeans (135,138) have constituted the other main ethnic groups, but since 1960 they have been joined by smaller numbers of Portuguese, Haitians, Greeks and various Southeast Asian groups. Approximately 81,000 Native peoples live in Quebec: nearly 6,500 Inuit, some 37,000 Indians given status under the Indian Act and 40,000 Métis and non-status Indians.

Language: In 1986 nearly 82% of Quebecers claimed French as their native tongue. The remainder are primarily English speaking, though only 11% claim English as their mother tongue. Since the adoption of Bill 101 in 1977, French has been the sole official language of Quebec. However, the anglophone minority is well served with its own complete school system, a number of newspapers, radio and television stations, hospitals and many cultural institutions.

Religion (1981 census): Until the 1960s the Roman Catholic church dominated every aspect of Quebec society. It still retains by far the largest number of adherents (87%), followed by the Anglican Church (3%), the United Church (3%) Judaism (2%) and the Greek Orthodox Church (1%).

CONSTITUTION AND GOVERNMENT

Executive: The executive branch of government is the Executive Council (Conseil executif), which is composed of the premier and 25 or more ministers appointed by the premier. The council determines executive policies and is responsible to the National Assembly. Since reforms in the 1970s, it is operating more and more through departmental standing committees, each headed by a minister. The treasury board, a cabinet committee headed by the president of the board and supported by its own staff, is responsible for formulating and supervising the implementing of the government's financial policies.

Legislature: The National Assembly (Assemblée nationale) consists of 125 members elected by universal suffrage. Each member represents a separate electoral riding and belongs to a political party. Elections must be held at least every five years but may be called more frequently if the governing party loses the confidence of the legislature through a defeat on a major vote or after dissolution of the legislature by the lieutenant governor upon the recommendation of the premier.

Political parties: In principle, Quebec has a multiparty system, but in practice a succession of two-party rivalries has fought elections and held seats in the Assembly. Up to 1936 it was the Conservatives and Liberals, then the Liberals and Union Nationale until 1970; since then the Liberals and the Parti Québécois have been the primary two parties. The provincial general election in 1989 returned 82 Liberals, 25 Parti Québécois, and 4 Equality Party, who represent a protest vote against the Liberals by an English-speaking minority in Montreal.

Local government: Quebec has 1,571 municipalities of various types, all of which come under the Municipal Code and the Towns and Cities Act. Each municipality is headed by an elected mayor and councillors. Since 1978, municipal tax reforms have provided a greater degree of financial autonomy, and the Agricultural Land Protection Act of 1978 increased the activities of municipal governments. Quebec also has two urban communities (Montreal and Quebec City) and one regional community (the Outaouais), each of which has jurisdiction over its assessment, development, public transportation, taxation and public safety. In addition, in 1966 Quebec divided its territory into six regions in order to pool certain community services outside urban centers and to decentralize some public administration.

Federal representation: Quebec is represented by 24 seats in the Senate. The number of seats in the House of Commons currently stands at 75, 63 of which are held by Conservatives and 12 by Liberals. Two additional Quebec senators were appointed in 1991 when Prime Minister Brian Mulroney invoked a section of the Constitution Act of 1867 to break the deadlock between the two houses regarding the Goods and Services Tax.

Judicial system: Quebec's mixed French and British past is reflected in its judicial system. The Civil Code derives its content from the Custom of Paris and its form from the influence of the French Code Napoléon, whereas the Criminal Code is based on English criminal law. The superior court is called the Superior Court of Quebec with 107 judges. The Court of Appeal has 22 judges. Judges of both courts are appointed by the federal government. The other components of the provincial court system are justices of the peace, municipal courts, juvenile courts (Social Welfare Court), courts of Sessions of the Peace and the Provincial Court, which among them handle civil and criminal cases at municipal and urban levels.

There is a great chronological divide in Quebec's history. Until 1960 the Roman Catholic church played a leading, often the only, role in education and social welfare, its aim being to perpetuate a traditional life-style and its own dominance in Quebec society. Since the Quiet Revolution of the 1960s the church has come to be depicted as a negative element in Quebec's development. Much of the thrust of the Quiet Revolution was aimed at improving the economic and social status of the francophone community by dismantling the power structures of the church and outside investors and replacing them with state institutions, which favored French-Canadian Quebecers.

This spirit of reform also swept away the prevailing political pattern of long, stable periods of single-party, single-leader domination. Since 1960 no party has enjoyed more than nine consecutive years in office.

The victory of Jean Lesage and the Liberal Party in June 1960 ushered in the period now known as the Quiet Revolution. Lesage and his ministers followed a new interventionist style of government. They initiated action in a number of areas. Especially important were health, education and welfare, the nationalization of private electricity companies and reforms in the political process itself.

Economic reform aimed at improving opportunities for French Canadians in upper levels of management. By setting up public enterprises, the government could ensure that recruiting policy favored French Canadians and that French became the language of the workplace. The most notable achievement was the nationalization in 1962 of Hydro-Québec.

At the election of 1966, the Liberals were accused of moving too far too fast. Their defeat, however, could not be taken by the victorious Union Nationale and its leader, Daniel Johnson, as a popular mandate to abandon the policies of the Quiet Revolution. With a majority of seats but only 41% of the vote compared to the Liberals' 47%, the Union Nationale merely slowed the rate of reform without abandoning it. The administration was more nationalistic than the Liberals but, as in the Duplessis era, less practical in satisfying the aspirations of the French Canadian community. The major clashes with Ottawa revolved around Quebec's increasing participation in international francophone affairs.

Johnson died in 1968 and was succeeded by Jean-Jacques Bertrand. His leadership was contested within his own party and he was criticized outside for taking neither a stand that was clearly federalist, accepting that Quebec was a Canadian province, albeit with some special powers, or a stand that was clearly separatist, advocating the creation of an independent nation state. Bertrand was defeated in 1970 by the Liberal Party under their new leader, Robert Bourassa. Bourassa was clearly antiseparatist. In 1967 he had rejected René Lévesque's sovereignty-association proposal—for a sovereign Quebec in close economic association with Canada—which resulted in Lévesque leaving the Liberal Party and ultimately joining with other separatist parties to form the Parti Québécois.

In October 1970 the new government faced a major political and social crisis when the Front de Libération du Québec kidnapped British trade commissioner James Cross and Quebec labor minister Pierre Laporte, and later killed Laporte. Prime Minister Pierre Elliott Trudeau invoked the War Measures Act and hundreds of Quebecers were imprisoned.

Much of Bourassa's economic policy was motivated by his election promise to create 100,000 jobs per year and his commitment to achieving this through private sector initiative. As in the decades before the Quiet Revolution, an economic and social climate conducive to private investment, especially American, had to be created and maintained.

The perceived need for private investment—especially American investment—also influenced the framing of social legislation and relations with Ottawa. In 1974 Language Bill 22 made French the official language of Quebec. It was an attempt to answer the demands of French-Canadian nationalists without offending the anglophone elite; however, it succeeded in enraging both and satisfying neither. The confidence of outside investors would have been undermined by a separatist stance, but without that weapon as an ultimate threat, Bourassa's bargaining power with Ottawa was severely diminished, particularly in the face of strong resistance from Trudeau.

A popular fear of independence had partly determined the results of the 1973 election. The separatist Parti Québécois had increased its share of the vote to 30% from 24% in 1970. As the only party strong enough to defeat the PQ, Liberals also increased their share of the vote to 55% and won 102 out of 110 seats in the legislature. By the mid-1970s rising unemployment, allegations of patronage and corruption, poor labor relations, the open contempt of Ottawa Liberals for Bourassa and internal party dissension over Bill 22 and constitutional policy weakened the Liberal position. In 1974 the Parti Québécois had diluted its stand on separatism and committed itself to a referendum prior to a declaration of sovereignty. It triumphed in the 1976 election, securing 41% of the vote and 71 seats.

The PQ under the leadership of René Lévesque did not hold the promised referendum for four years. In the interim it instituted a program of major reforms. Its most significant piece of legislation was the Charter of the French Language (Bill 101), which aimed to end the economic inferiority of French-speaking Quebecers and promote assimilation of immigrants into the francophone community.

By the time of the referendum in 1980, the sovereignty question had been moderated in order to gain maximum popular support. Sovereignty was only to be considered in conjunction with economic association with the rest of Canada. In addition, the referendum did not ask for approval of the principle of sovereignty-association, but only for a mandate to negotiate. Nevertheless the government position was defeated by 59.6% against to 40.4% in favor, with an 87% turnout. Confidence in the rest of PQ policy remained high; they carried on at the 1981 election with increased popular support, despite a total overhaul of the provincial Liberal Party.

In 1982 Prime Minister Trudeau amended the constitution of Canada by ending all participation of the British Parliament and made other changes, including addition of a bill of rights, all without the Quebec government's consent. Lévesque announced in November 1984 that he was shelving the sovereignty issue for the next campaign. Six ministers resigned immediately and others left later. The PQ parliamentary majority dwindled, especially as a result of the June 1985 by-elections. Shortly after, Lévesque resigned. Pierre Marc Johnson, son of the former Union Nationale premier, succeeded Lévesque and called an election for December 1985.

Robert Bourassa had left Quebec in disgrace after his 1976 defeat, but he returned and regained leadership of the Liberal Party in 1983. He then staged the most remarkable political comeback in Canadian history, leading the Liberals to victory with a majority of 99 seats (56% of the vote).

The second Bourassa regime witnessed unprecedented cooperation between Ottawa and Quebec. Anxious to consolidate surprising Conservative support in the 1984 and 1988 national elections Prime Minister Mulroney granted substantial federal aid for Quebec developments. Bourassa supported Mulroney's free trade initiative with the United States.

At the 1987 Meech Lake meeting of first ministers, an accord was reached in which Quebec agreed to sign the constitution it had rejected in 1982 in return for recognition as a "distinct society" and greater powers over immigration. But the agreement was reached only by making concessions to other provinces that were not universally acceptable, and the distinct society clause was widely resented, especially in the west. Although the legislatures of eight provinces had approved the accord by the deadline, the new Liberal majority in Newfoundland revoked a previous approval, and the Manitoba legislature failed to approve because of the opposition of a Native member to the failure of the accord to provide for Native rights. Constitutional matters moved into a complete state of flux.

ECONOMY

Quebec has had much to offer entrepreneurs. Abundant natural resources, notably hydroelectricity, forests and minerals, provided raw materials for development. An unusually high birthrate among French-Canadians ensured a prolific, if untrained, work force. Successive governments, whose express policy it was to create an atmosphere conducive to foreign investment, completed the trio of attractions.

It was not until the Quiet Revolution of the 1960s that the government began to take an active role in economic development. Its most effective intervention, from the point of view of providing new opportunities for French Canadians, was the nationalization in 1962 of private electricity companies and their incorporation into Hydro-Québec. This was also the period (1965) when the Caisse de Dépôt et Placement was set up to administer funds from public pension and insurance plans in the province. By December 1988 it had accumulated realizable investments of $18.5 billion and equity holdings in some of Canada's major corporations.

Although the Quiet Revolution set the trend toward greater government control of the economy, subsequent administrations have returned at least in part to a more conservative stance, favoring private enterprise and foreign investment as the engines of development. The Bourassa administration has concentrated on reducing the budgetary deficit and public investment has remained at around $5.0 billion per year. Private investment, on the other hand, rose dramatically in 1986 to more than double the 1982 figure. In 1987 the Quebec Chamber of Commerce extolled the "slowing down of the welfare state" and the rise of the "entrepreneurial spirit."

Quebec's gross domestic product of $136.6 billion is second only to Ontario, but its per capita GDP in 1989 ranked Quebec fourth among the provinces. Per capita personal income was estimated at $20,550, well below the national average. As a result, Quebec qualifies for large federal equalization payments, a point of contention with other provinces. In 1989–90, 18.3% of Quebec's provincial revenue came from federal transfers.

Through the mid-'80s, economic indicators looked reasonably good. In 1983, in the wake of a worldwide recession, the Parti Québécois launched an economic recovery plan. From a position of negative growth in 1982, real GDP grew 3.4% in 1983 and 5.4% in 1984. Although economic growth was down to 3.3% in 1986, it was slightly ahead of Canada as a whole, which surpassed the United States, Japan and Europe that year. Retail sales, manufacturers' shipments and housing starts all continued an upward trend between 1982 and 1986. Despite a sharp fall in housing starts, preliminary figures showed Quebec as one of the star performers in 1988. However, the '90s brought the Canada-wide and then North America-wide recession, and problems associated with the failure of the Meech Lake Accord. Native land claims and a rising demand for constitutional recognition threatened the government plans for development in the north and domestic harmony in the south, and threatened the United States market for Quebec exports of electric power. In view of Native objections to the Great Whale project, in March 1992 the state of New York announced cancellation of the contract for Quebec power that Great Whale was to supply.

Manufacturing: Quebec has the second largest manufacturing production in Canada, approximately half that of Ontario but three times that of British Columbia, which lies in third place. In 1990 manufacturing and construction together accounted for 24.5% of employment and 26.8% of GDP. The total value of manufacturers' shipments was $72.9 billion, representing 24.8% of total Canadian shipments.

Much of Quebec manufacturing still centers around the traditional industries of food and beverages, paper and related products and clothing and textiles. Quebec produces 16% of world output and about 50% of Canadian output of newsprint (46% in 1988), and is the second largest exporter of newsprint in Canada. The pulp and paper sector employs 31,400 workers. Increasingly, manufacturers in Quebec are moving into the production of durable goods: transportation equipment, metal products, electrical and electronic goods, as well as the processing of primary metals. Three of the world's six largest aluminum firms (Alcan, Reynolds and Péchiney) take advantage of Quebec's cheap hydroelectricity, which is required in large quantities for the processing of aluminum.

Services: The services sector generated about two-thirds of real GDP in 1986 and 71.0% of total employment. Community, business and personal services, including health and education, accounted for more than 20% of output. Consulting engineering firms, outgrowths of the development of Quebec's hydroelectricity, form an important component of the services sector. Research and development is encouraged by the government through tax incentives and assistance programs. In 1988 revenues of firms providing architectural engineering and scientific services totalled $1.8 billion from public and private sources. These included services to areas such as electrical products, chemicals, aeronautics and telecommunications. More than half the research conducted in Quebec is commissioned by private firms, increasingly in collaboration with universities. Total revenue for major business service industries in 1988 was $8.5 billion compared to $6.1 billion in 1986.

In 1991, the financial sector employed 189,000 people. The sector has enjoyed growth of 57% from 1976 to 1991. Despite the exodus from Montreal of several chartered banks and insurance companies (notably Sun Life) in reaction to the French language bill (Bill 101) of 1977, Montreal still houses the headquarters of three of the major Canadian banks and eight foreign banks established in Canada. The Mouvement Desjardins, a federation of credit and savings cooperatives, is a principal banking institution in terms of numbers of branches and employees. It is peculiarly French Canadian, having originally consisted of locally based *caisses populaires* (credit unions), and producers' cooperatives established throughout French Quebec. In the 1970s, following the developments of the Quiet Revolution, the Quebec-wide federation of the *caisses populaires* began engaging in some major economic ventures, thereby enhancing francophone economic power. Its assets amounted to more than $29 billion at the end of 1986. Other financial institutions active in the province are trust companies, insurance companies and brokerage firms. The importance of the Montreal Stock Exchange in the Canadian market has grown over the past few years. It is the second largest stock market in Canada after Toronto.

Energy: Hydroelectricity is Quebec's most abundant natural resource. It has favored the development of processing industries (pulp and paper, aluminum, chemicals) and manufacturing. A dramatic increase in hydroelectric potential came more recently from two massive developments. During the Quiet Revolution of the 1960s, the newly nationalized Hydro-Québec began the Manic-Outardes complex on the North Shore. Completed in 1976, it consists of seven hydroelectric power stations and reservoirs representing an installed capacity of 5,500 megawatt hours (mwh). In 1971 the Bourassa administration announced the James Bay Project, an even more ambitious scheme in northern Quebec on La Grande Rivière. The completion of Phase I in 1984 pushed Hydro-Québec's output up to double that of 1971. Total generation in 1990 was 135 million megawatt hours, over one-third of Canada's electricity production. A further 27 million mwh were imported from other provinces, most of it from the disputed Churchill Falls development in Labrador (26 million mwh in 1990). In 1992 the Quebec government announced that in spite of the New York cancellation of a $17 billion contract, Quebec would proceed with Great Whale to supply Quebec's expected needs. The price of electricity is among the lowest in the world: 20% less than elsewhere in Canada and 66% less than New York State in 1985. Quebec's electricity exports have virtually quadrupled since 1971, with New York State, Ontario and New Brunswick as its main customers.

One objective of hydroelectric development was to decrease dependence on imported petroleum products. In 1970 oil contributed 74.2% of Quebec's overall energy needs. By 1985 the proportion had dropped to 44.6%, while over the same period electricity rose from 18.9% to 39.0% and natural gas increased from 4.4% to 15.2%. Coal makes up the remaining 1.2%, half its 1970 value. The energy sector as a whole provides employment for 50,000 workers.

Agriculture: Agriculture forms only a small component of the provincial economy. In 1986 it contributed about 2% of the GDP and about 3% of total employment. Much of the province's territory is unsuitable for agriculture. The agricultural zone totals only about 5.3 million hectares, of which 3.6 million hectares were used by 41,448 farmers for livestock and crop production in 1986. Since the mid-1970s the Quebec government has succeeded, through a number of insurance plans and assistance programs, in reviving the agricultural sector. Self-sufficiency in food rose from 50% in 1973 to 73% in 1984, and farm cash receipts increased 63% since 1979 to $3.75 billion in 1990, accounting for 17.4% of Canadian production. Over much of this period Quebec's share of total Canadian agricultural production has averaged under 15%. Its primary contributions come from dairy herds, hogs, poultry and cattle, which together in 1990 amounted to 79% of agricultural revenues. Like forestry, the significance of agriculture in Quebec's economy is greatly enhanced by its supply of raw materials to the manufacturing sector. In 1930 dairy products, meat and poultry made up 29% of the value of deliveries for the food industry, which is itself the largest producer in the manufacturing sector.

Forestry: Forestry's importance lies in the processing industries it feeds: paper, pulp, timber and wood products, which in 1990 together made up 16% of Quebec's manufacturing shipments, and 22% of exports. These processing industries are one of the largest employers in the manufacturing sector. Half the territory of Quebec is covered by forest, 90% of which is owned by the provincial government. Approximately 116,000 sq. mi./ 300,000 sq. km. are accessible forests, estimated inventory is 150 billion cubic feet/4.2 billion cubic meters. The forests lie mainly in the regions of Saguenay-Lac Saint-Jean, Abitibi and North Shore, where forestry is one of the principal industries. The annual cut in 1989 was 39 million cubic meters, most of it conifer, and of this 4.2 billion board feet/11.2 million cubic meters were lumber. The provincial government runs a major refor-estation program and plans to increase the number of seedlings planted annually to 300 million.

Mining: Mining operations generated $2.5 billion in 1990, 60% of which came from gold, iron, asbestos, copper and titaniferous iron ore. With two-thirds of world reserves of asbestos, this was an early mainstay of the min-ing industry in Quebec. It now ranks 13th among Quebec's exports. Iron ore only became important in the 1950s when huge deposits were discov-ered in northern Quebec at a time when demand from the American steel industry was increasing. Today iron ore is the fifth most important export. Two St. Lawrence ports, Sept Îles and Port Cartier together handle almost 60% of tonnage at Quebec ports, consisting mainly of iron ore, concen-trates and scrap. Mining as a whole accounted for $1.4 billion of exports in 1987. In the same year, some $425 million was allocated to exploration, primarily in the precious metal sector.

Foreign trade: In 1990 Quebec's international exports reached nearly $24.8 billion. The United States, as Quebec's most important trading partner, received more than 74% of the total. Well behind in second and third place were the United Kingdom and the Netherlands, each of which took less than 5%. Almost three-fifths of the exports were composed of three main product groups: wood and paper products 21%; metals, metal prod-ucts and nonmetallic minerals 24.5%; and transportation equipment 12%. Newsprint, automobiles and chassis and aluminum and alloys together make up about 30% of exports. Other exported products include lumber, iron ore, electronic tubes and semiconductors, aircraft engines and parts, tele-communications equipment and electricity.

Imports in 1990 exceeded $26.4 billion, giving Quebec a trade deficit. Motor vehicles ($4.4 billion) and oil ($3.2 billion) headed the list of im-ports. The United States and the European Economic Community (EEC) were the province's main suppliers, accounting for 45.6% and 23.3% of imports respectively.

Employment: In 1990 the labor force numbered 3,399,000. Employment gradually increased during the 1980s, rising from 2,574,000 in 1982 to 3,055,000 in 1990. The unemployment rate dropped from 13.9% in 1983 to 9.3% in 1989, then rose to 10.1% in 1990, mirroring the average fall and then increase in all of Canada. Nevertheless, it remains higher than the Canadian average, 8.1% in 1990. The province suffers from major regional disparities with unemployment rates in regions such as Abitibi-Témiscamingue, the Lower St. Lawrence and Mauricie running as much as 20% above the Quebec average.

Prices: The Montreal consumer price index increased 4.4% in 1989 and 4.2% in 1990. This was below the 5.0% and 4.8% averages for the country as a whole. The index for the province for 1990 was 117.3 [1986 = 100] compared to 119.5 for Canada as a whole.

Trade: Wholesale trade in 1990 totaled $45.9 billion. Retail trade reached $45.7 billion.

SOCIAL SERVICES

Quebec's social services are distinctive in the degree of integration that exists between health care and other forms of social assistance. For 1987–88, 40.1% of government expenditure was earmarked for social services. The largest portion of this budget is allocated to health and social rehabilitation services and to the guaranteed income program.

Welfare: The guaranteed income program encompasses support and income replacement services, including social aid, unemployment insurance, pensions, guaranteed income supplements, old age pensions and family allowances. Social aid benefits single persons and heads of households who are unable to provide for their basic needs. The federal government administers the unemployment insurance fund, but both levels of government provide complementary assistance programs related to employment, training and job placement. The Quebec Pension Plan is compulsory for all citizens between the ages of 18 and 65, provided their annual income exceeds a minimum threshold. The plan provides minimal financial protection for wage earners and their dependents when they retire, are incapacitated or die. All citizens aged 65 or older are also entitled to the federal old age pension.

The government also contributes in a number of other areas. It subsidizes an extensive network of day care centers and manages a child care program in private homes. Through the Workmen's Compensation Board, the government participates in prevention and inspection programs and provides assistance and rehabilitation schemes for injured workers. There is a Quebec government consumer protection office, a legal aid service and an automobile insurance plan under which accident victims are compensated regardless of who is at fault.

Health: All Quebecers, regardless of their income, receive free health and hospital care under the provincial health insurance plan. Doctors are prohibited from demanding additional fees from patients. There are more than 900 health and social service establishments divided into four categories: 228 hospitals, 554 reception centers, 138 local community service centers and 14 social service centers. Some 13 regional health and social services councils (Conseils régionaux de la santé et des services sociaux), representing most of the administrative regions of Quebec, act as the intermediaries between Quebecers and the government. Of the 228 hospitals, about 30 have departments of community health, which are responsible for conducting epidemiological studies, providing immunization, monitoring infectious diseases and epidemics, maternal and infant health, the health and nutrition of school children, dental health, occupational hygiene and the health of the elderly. The reception centers provide rehabilitation treatment for individuals who are not wholly self-reliant. Local community service centers deal with preventive and curative health and social services, and support services related to the organization of social life. Social service centers are responsible for people of all ages who require rehabilitation or protection.

EDUCATION

School attendance is compulsory for children between the ages of 6 and 15. Preschool, elementary and secondary programs were provided in 2,906 public schools or specialized institutions in 1989–90. About 90% of these schools are administered by school boards under the aegis of the Quebec Department of Education, which finances them and establishes curricula. Slightly less than 10% of Quebec school children attend private schools, which are extensively subsidized by the government. In 1988–89 Quebec allocated 4.50% of its GDP to elementary and secondary education, compared to an average of 4.37% in the rest of Canada. In 1988–89 the budget for the preschool, elementary and secondary levels totaled $6.3 billion for a student enrollment of 1.14 million. Although the Charter of the French Language stipulates that French must be the language of instruction in Quebec from kindergarten to the end of secondary school, children with at least one parent a native-born Canadian whose mother tongue is English are entitled to be educated in English.

Collèges d'enseignement généraux et professionnels (CEGEPs) and universities are the responsibility of the Quebec Department of Higher Education and Science. There are 44 public CEGEPs and 47 private junior colleges with a total enrollment in 1989–90 of 154,290 full-time and 61,720 part time. The 1988–89 budget for CEGEPs was $1.36 billion. The six private universities include the French-language institutions of Université Laval, Université de Montréal and Université de Sherbrooke and the English-language institutions of McGill, Bishop's and Concordia. The Université du Québec is a public university with six university campuses, two research institutes and two training institutions. In 1989–90 university enrollment was 12,700 full-time and 122,400 part-time students. The budget for university training and research in 1988–89 totaled $2.16 billion.

The Quebec Department of Education also finances various adult education programs. In 1986–87 96,000 adults attended 350 training centers organized by 80 school boards.

MASS MEDIA

Newspapers and periodicals: Quebec has 10 French-language and two English-language daily newspapers. The major French papers include *La Presse, Le Devoir, Le Journal de Montréal, Le Soleil* and *Le Journal de Québec.* The two

English papers are the *Montreal Gazette* and *Montreal Daily News*. Regional dailies, such as *Le Nouvelliste de Trois Rivières* and *La Voix de L'Estrie*, serve local populations. While most of the papers are privately owned, there is a Press Council (Conseil de presse) that hears complaints from the public and those working in the media. It is made up of representatives of press agencies, journalists and members of the public. Its decisions carry moral weight only and are not binding.

There are some 185 weekly newspapers, more than 150 periodicals and 15 ethnic publications. *L'Actualité* is the most widely read magazine dealing with political and social matters.

Broadcasting: Radio Station XWA went on the air in 1919, making Montreal the first city in the world with a radio service. In 1987 the number of stations had grown to 51 AM and 26 FM stations plus hundreds of rebroadcasters across the province. Six networks, four of which come under the Canadian Broadcasting Corporation (CBC), operate nationally; the others, privately owned, are all local or regional. Five television networks are national and three are public services (Radio-Canada, the CBC and Radio-Quebec). All together Quebec is served by 175 television stations plus 176 cable networks. The latter are used by local and ethnic groups to produce community television programs. Cable also makes American channels available to Quebec viewers.

BIOGRAPHICAL SKETCHES

Robert Bourassa: Bourassa became premier of Quebec for the second time in 1985. Born into a middle-class, francophone family in Montreal on July 14, 1933, he studied at the universities of Montreal, Harvard and Oxford and holds degrees in law and economics. Between 1960 and 1966 he served as fiscal adviser to the Department of National Revenue, held the post of professor at the universities of Ottawa, Laval and Montreal and was research director for the Bélanger Commission on fiscal policy. Bourassa entered politics in 1966, and he won the Liberal leadership in 1970 and his first election the same year. At 37 he was the youngest-ever premier of Quebec. When the Liberals were defeated by the Parti Québécois in 1976, his political career appeared to be at an end. He left immediately for Belgium to study the EEC and later lectured in the United States. However, he retained his political connections in Montreal, and as the PQ government became bogged down in constitutional wrangling and the recession of the early '80s, Bourassa returned to the political stage. In 1983 he recaptured the Quebec Liberal leadership. His efforts to rebuild the party's electoral base and its image as the party of sound economic management were rewarded in the provincial elections of December 1985. The Liberals swept to power with 99 seats out of 122, winning a clear majority of both the anglophone and francophone vote. They were reelected in 1989 in spite of the desertion of many anglophone voters.

Claude Ryan. Minister of municipal affairs and public security and minister responsible for the administration of the French language. Born January 25, 1925 in Montreal, Ryan was educated at the University of Montreal and the University of Rome. He worked as a newspaper editor. He was first elected to the Quebec National Assembly at a by-election in 1979 and was reelected in 1981, 1985 and 1989. He was elected leader of the Quebec Liberal Party in 1978 and served as leader of the opposition from 1979 to 1982. He resigned as opposition leader and leader of the Liberal Party in 1982. Ryan served as minister of education and minister of higher education and science in 1985. He became minister responsible for the administration of the French Language Charter in 1989 and minister of municipal affairs and public security in 1990.

Gerard D. Lévesque. Minister of finance. Born May 2, 1926 in Port Daniel, Bonaventure, Quebec, Lévesque was educated at the University of Montreal and McGill University. He worked as a lawyer and he was first elected to the National Assembly of Quebec in 1956. He was reelected in 1960, 1962, 1966, 1970, 1973, 1976, 1981, 1985 and 1989. He served as minister of fisheries and game in 1960–62; minister of industry, trade and commerce in 1962–66 and 1970–72. He was minister of intergovernmental affairs in 1970–71 and 1972–75. From 1970 to 1976 he was government house leader. He was deputy premier and minister responsible for the Quebec Planning and Development Office in 1972–76, minister of justice in 1975–76, and leader of the opposition in 1976–79 and 1982–85. He was interim Liberal party leader in 1977–78 and 1982–83. From 1979 to 1982 and also in 1985 he served again as opposition House Leader; he was named minister of finance in 1985 and again in 1989.

Jacques Parizeau. Leader of the opposition. Born August 9, 1930 in Montreal, he was educated at the École des hautes études commerciales de Montréal, the Institute d'études politiques de Paris and the London School of Economics. He became a professor of economics. He was first elected to the Quebec National Assembly in 1976 and was reelected in 1981; he resigned in 1984 and then was reelected in 1989. He served as minister of finance and minister of revenue in 1976 and as president of the Treasury Board in 1976–81. He was named minister of finance and minister of financial and co-operative institutions in 1981. Parizeau resigned as minister in 1984; he was elected leader of the Parti Québécois in 1988 and leader of the official opposition in 1989.

BRITISH COLUMBIA

GEOGRAPHY

Features: British Columbia is the westernmost province of Canada. It is bounded on the north by the Yukon and Northwest territories; on the east by the province of Alberta; on the south by the U.S. states of Montana, Idaho and Washington; and on the west by the U.S. state of Alaska and the Pacific Ocean.

The Rocky Mountains form the southern half of the border with Alberta, with some peaks rising more than 10,000 ft./3,000 m. above sea level. To the immediate west of the Rockies is the narrow Rocky Mountain Trench, the longest valley in North America, running more than 900 mi./1,500 km. along the length of the province. In the southeasternmost part of British Columbia are cattle ranches, logging and timber processing plants, mines, smelters and a series of dams along the Columbia River. The northeastern corner of the province is a portion of the Canadian interior plains and is flat to gently hilly. This area is sparsely populated, but coal mines have recently been developed there, and there are farms and ranches, logging and energy development.

West of the Rocky Mountain Trench are more mountain systems. In southern British Columbia lie the Columbia Mountains, with peaks of 6,500–10,000 ft./2,000–3,000 m. Somewhat to the north and west is another high range, the Cariboo. In northern British Columbia are the Omineca and Cassiar ranges. Moving west into central and north-central British Columbia, the Interior and Stikine plateaus are gently rolling uplands at 2,000 to 4,000 ft./600 to 1,200 m. above sea level. Here are found farms, orchards, and ranches; mining; forestry; and pulp and paper production.

Farther west rise the Coast Mountains, reaching as high as 13,182 ft./4,019 m. at Mount Waddington. The so-called lower mainland in southwestern British Columbia, dominated by metropolitan Vancouver, contains more than half the province's total population. Farming, fishing, manufacturing and service industries all flourish there.

Vancouver Island and the Queen Charlotte Islands are formed out of the offshore Insular Mountains. In addition to the provincial capital, Victoria, and its metropolitan area, this subregion has important forest industries. The sparsely populated north coast includes the beautiful Queen Charlotte Islands; logging, fishing, fish processing, pulp and paper mills, mining, and aluminum smelting are found. In the far northwest of this area and of

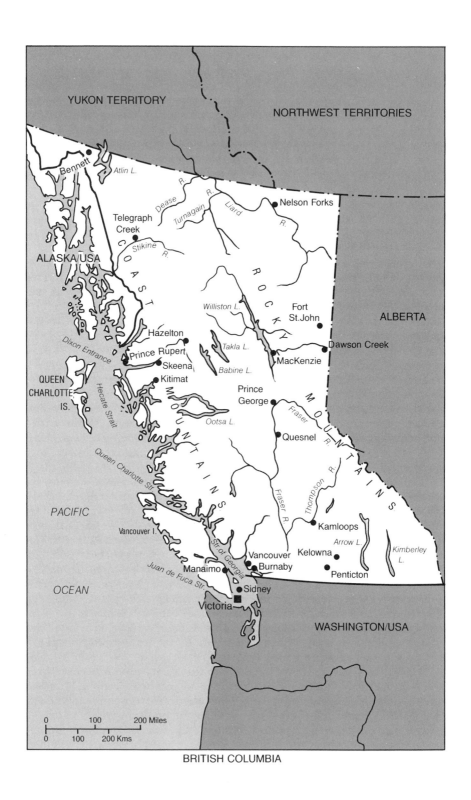

YUKON TERRITORY

NORTHWEST TERRITORIES

Bennett

Atlin L.

Dease R.

Turnagain R.

Liard R.

Nelson Forks

Telegraph Creek

ALASKA/USA

C O A S T

Stikine R.

Williston L.

Fort St.John

ALBERTA

Hazelton

Takla L.

Dawson Creek

Prince Rupert

Skeena

Babine L.

MacKenzie

QUEEN CHARLOTTE IS.

Dixon Entrance

Hecate Strait

Kitimat

M O U N T A I N S

Prince George

Fraser R.

R O C K Y   M O U N T A I N S

Ootsa L.

Quesnel

Queen Charlotte Str.

PACIFIC

Thompson R.

Vancouver I.

Fraser R.

Kamloops

Arrow L.

Kelowna

Kimberley L.

Str. of Georgia

Vancouver

Burnaby

Nanaimo

Juan de Fuca Str.

Sidney

Penticton

OCEAN

Victoria

WASHINGTON/USA

0   100   200 Miles

0   100   200 Kms

BRITISH COLUMBIA

the province along the border with Alaska, lie the St. Elias Mountains. Here rises Mount Fairweather (15,295 ft./4,663 m.), the highest point in British Columbia. Mining is the chief economic base of communities found in the sparsely settled northern interior.

River systems run through the valleys between the mountain ranges. The Fraser swings a giant arc from the Rockies, first northeast, then sharply south, finally west, emptying into the Strait of Georgia near Vancouver. The Columbia and Kootenay run south through southeastern British Columbia into the United States, but the Kootenay swings back north and meets the Columbia near Cranbrook, British Columbia. The Peace River, formed from the waters of the Findlay and Parsnip in central British Columbia, flows into Alberta. Large natural lakes are numerous in the valleys, and several high dams have backed-up long reservoirs, particularly on the Columbia and Peace.

Area: 366,253 sq. mi./948,596 sq. km., including 6,976 sq. mi./18,068 sq. km. of inland water. The province makes up 9.5% of the total area of Canada.

Mean maximum temperatures: Victoria 68°F/20°C (July), 43° F/6°C (January); Barkerville (in the Cariboo Mountains, east-central British Columbia), 54°F/12°C (July), 12°F/−11°C (January).

Mean annual precipitation: Victoria 25 in./647 mm., of which 13 in./33 cm. is snow; Barkerville 41 in./1,044 mm., of which 212 in./538 cm. is snow.

POPULATION

Total population (1986 census): 2,889,206. Population density averaged 7.9 per sq. mi./3 per sq. km. The population was estimated at 3,131,700 in 1990. British Columbia has a high rate of population increase (17%, 1977–87), of which migration from other provinces and countries forms a large share; in 1987, estimated net in-migration of 31,386 accounted for 61% of the estimated population increase of 51,142.

Chief towns and populations (1986 census): Vancouver (435,815, metropolitan area, 1,380,729; estimated at 1,547,000 in 1990, the third largest in Canada); Victoria, the capital (66,973 metropolitan area 255,547 estimated at 278,700 in 1990); Prince George (66,812), Kelowna (62,980), Kamloops (61,887) and Nanaimo (49,424).

Distribution: The lower mainland area, including metropolitan Vancouver, accounted for 55% of provincial population in 1988. Vancouver Island and the adjacent Strait of Georgia mainland coast accounted for another 19%. About 16% lived in other southern areas of the province, and about 7% in central British Columbia, including the Queen Charlotte Islands. The remaining 3% lived in the northern third of the province. The population of the province was 79% urban.

Ethnic composition: Taking into account both single and mixed ethnic origins, 60% of the provincial population was British or part British (including Irish) in 1986. On the same basis, 7% was French. About 5% was of German single origin and about 4%, Chinese. Those of Dutch, East Indian (including Pakistani), native Indian, Ukrainian, and Italian single origin each comprised about 2% of the population. Of the 66,585 registered Indians (status Indians) in 1986, about 40,000 lived on reservations. In the years 1986 to 1989 there were 598,000 immigrants to Canada and 13.4% of these have given British Columbia as their destination. However, of the 80,234 immigrants to Canada of Asian birth in those years, 62% have given British Columbia. Of these a significant proportion were from Hong Kong; many were encouraged by the federal government program favoring immigrants with capital and entrepreneurial skills.

Language: English was the mother tongue and home language of 82% and 91% of the population, respectively, in 1986. French was the mother tongue of 1.6% and the home language of 0.6%. Other languages accounted for the remaining 16% and 8%, respectively.

Religion: Although the largest single denomination in 1981 was Roman Catholic (20%), 55% of the population was Protestant. The largest Protestant denominations were the United and Anglican churches, followed by Baptists and Pentecostals. British Columbia led all provinces in the proportion of residents who professed no organized religion (21%).

CONSTITUTION AND GOVERNMENT

British Columbia, like the other provinces, has an executive headed by a lieutenant governor who represents the Queen, who is the sovereign of Great Britain and of Canada. Under the province's parliamentary system, the real executive leader is the premier, who appoints a cabinet composed of members of the legislature. The executive branch includes not only government departments (called ministries) but also a number of crown (public) corporations and semi-independent agencies and boards. The executive is responsible to the legislature and needs majority support in the legislature on major issues to stay in power.

Executive: The premier is president of an executive council, or cabinet, consisting, in November 1991, of 19 members. The civil service has the right of collective bargaining. There is an ombudsman.

Legislature: There is a single-chambered Legislative Assembly; it had 69 members in 1990. Although 35 represented single constituencies, 34 represented 17 constituencies that elected two members each. For the 1991 election six single-member constituencies were added to give 75 members.

Members are elected for a maximum five-year period, but elections for a new assembly can be called at any time by the lieutenant governor on the recommendation of the premier, and they are normally held every three or four years. Following elections, unless the governing party fails to retain confidence of the new legislature, the lieutenant governor calls on the leader of the majority party to become premier and form a government. Elected members of the largest minority party form the official opposition.

Political parties: The Liberals and Conservatives (since 1943 called the Progressive Conservatives) have been the traditional parties. But the Great Depression of the 1930s saw the advent of the socialist-oriented Co-operative Commonwealth Federation (CCF) and the Social Credit party. Under W. A. C. (Cecil) Bennett, the latter came to power in 1952 with the support of those looking for a conservative alternative to the Liberal-Conservative coalition that had governed the province in 1942–52. The Social Credit party remained in power until 1991 except during 1972–75, when the province was governed by the New Democratic party (successor to the CCF). In the election of 1991 the New Democrats defeated Social Credit to form their second government. On the provincial level, the Conservatives fell into insignificance with the rise of the Social Credit party, and until the 1991 election the Liberals had had no significant support since 1972. The Social Credit party has attracted those who favor unfettered development of the province's natural resources and fear socialism, including those who might otherwise have supported a traditional party. The New Democrats attract those who support the party's program of income redistribution and increased regulation and taxation of business, with some public ownership of industry.

Local government: There were 38 cities, 14 towns and 46 villages in 1989. There were also 48 districts, mostly rural, and one Indian government district. All cities, towns, villages, and districts are incorporated under the Municipal Act, which provides facilities such as roads, waterworks and sewers, as well as a wide range of social, recreation and protection services. All municipalities are governed by a council consisting of a mayor and aldermen. In 1989, there were also 29 regional districts, which combine municipal and other local-government areas to provide services efficiently over a large area. They are governed by boards.

Federal representation: British Columbia is represented in Parliament by six federally appointed senators and 32 elected members of the House of Commons. The 1988 federal elections sent 19 New Democrats, 12 Conservatives and one Liberal to the House of Commons.

Judicial system: The federally appointed Supreme Court, with a chief justice and 39 associate justices in 1988, has original jurisdiction in all civil actions not expressly excluded by statute. Also federally appointed is the Court of Appeals, with a chief justice and 17 associate justices. The Supreme Court of Canada hears appeals beyond this point. The County Court, sitting in 12 locations with a chief judge and 52 other judges in 1988, is federally appointed and hears most actions not exceeding $50,000 in value. The Provincial Court sat, in 1988, at six locations, with a chief judge, two associates and 24 other judges, all provincially appointed. It hears most small claims not exceeding $2,000 in value and may deal with family and youth matters.

RECENT HISTORY

Recent political history in British Columbia begins with the rise to power of the Social Credit party in the 1952 elections and the accession of its leader, W. A. C. Bennett, as premier, a position he held for the next 20 years. Investment (largely foreign) in the mining and forestry sectors was high when he took office, and the revenue was used for social and economic benefits. In 1961 Bennett abandoned his free-enterprise rhetoric to make the privately owned B.C. Electric utility a public corporation; this action enabled him to build a Peace River dam. Bennett also backed a U.S.-Canadian agreement in 1964 to build three storage dams on the British Columbia portion of the Columbia River.

By 1972 the economic situation was not so bright. The New Democratic Party, led by Dave Barrett, came to power. One of its first acts was a guaranteed income of $200 per month for senior citizens and free prescription drugs for this group. Welfare rates were substantially increased and day care was vastly expanded. Low-income housing was built and rent control was introduced. Corporate taxes and mineral royalty rates were increased. Several private forestry companies were taken over and merged into a public corporation. Automobile insurance was made a public monopoly.

In the 1975 elections, Liberal and Conservative voters swung to the Social Credit party. The new premier was W. A. C. Bennett's son William (Bill), who emphasized fiscal restraint. The government made it more difficult for workers to organize and limited the scope of strikes, by broadening the definition of essential services in which strikes were prohibited. Mining royalties were replaced by a profits tax. Most of the forest holdings acquired by the NDP were privatized.

The Social Credit party narrowly defeated the NDP in 1979 and 1983. Following the latter elections, it stressed a neo-conservative program of deregulation. Labor-code amendments limited or abolished many previous rights. Rent control was abolished, and medicare premiums and hospital user fees were raised. Spending was chopped in most fields, but funding on infrastructure development was raised in order to facilitate economic growth through the private sector. Corporate taxes were cut in 1985, and the government offered a four-year royalty holiday for companies drilling for oil.

Shortly before the 1986 elections, Bennett stepped down and was succeeded as premier by William Vander Zalm. In October 1986 the Social Credit party was reelected. The new premier continued on the same course as his predecessor. A new issue was abortion; Vander Zalm's attempts to restrict abortions and funding for abortions were overturned by the courts in 1988. The Vander Zalm government was plagued by internal controversy and ministerial resignations. Charges that Premier Vander Zalm had mixed private with public business and had thus been guilty of conflict of interest led to his resignation; the courts subsequently found him to be not guilty of any criminal wrongdoing. The new premier and leader of Social Credit, Rita Johnson, led the party to defeat in October 1991. The NDP formed the government under Premier Michael Harcourt and the Liberal Party under Gordon Wilson became the official opposition.

ECONOMY

Although only 6.3% of the employed population worked in agriculture, forestry, fishing or mining in 1988, these primary industries form the basis of the economy. The province's small population is unable to support local production of mass-produced consumer goods or provide a market for natural-resource products. As a result, the economy depends on extensive trading relationships with the rest of the world.

The gross provincial product of British Columbia at factor cost was $72.1 billion in 1990, ranking it third among Canadian provinces. Of this total, community, business and personal services accounted for 23.5% of GDP; finance, insurance and real estate, 17.1%, manufacturing, 13.6%; wholesale and retail trade, 12.3%; transportation, communication and storage, 10.8%; construction, 7.8%; public administration and defense, 5.2%; utilities, 3.0%; mining, 2.9%; forestry and logging, 2.1%; agriculture, 1%; and fishing and trapping, 0.6%. Per capita personal income was $22,437, second only to Ontario among the provinces, and higher than the national average of $22,184.

Agriculture: Only about 4% of the land area is considered arable or potentially arable. However, an estimated 18.3 million acres/7.4 million hectares are classed as open or forested grazing land utilized by the ranching industry. In 1990, farm cash receipts totaled $1.22 billion, and net farm income was $252 million. The only significant cash crops are fruits, vegetables, and floriculture and nursery products, which combined accounted for $217 million in cash receipts. The mild coastal climate of the lower Fraser River valley enables British Columbia to lead all provinces in the production of apples, sweet cherries, raspberries, blueberries and cranberries.

Dairy products provide the second biggest agricultural sector, accounting for more than $240 million in cash receipts in 1990. Large daily herds are concentrated in the lower Fraser River valley, southeastern Vancouver Island, and the North Okanagan-Shuswap area. Cattle and calves accounted for $190 million. Cattle ranching is carried out primarily on the rangelands of the southern and central interior, the Peace River district and southeastern British Columbia. Poultry and eggs receipts came to $200 million, and hogs to $45 million. Hog and poultry production are concentrated near the Vancouver and Victoria metropolitan areas.

Forestry: Forests cover about 65% of British Columbia's land area—148.9 million acres/60.3 million hectares—of which 96% is provincially owned and 92% consists of coniferous softwoods. The total timber volume available in 1986 was 313.1 billion cu. ft./8.9 billion cu. m. About 72% of this area (126 million acres/51 million hectares), with 90% of the timber, is considered productive forest land. British Columbia leads all provinces in timber production, which in 1988 totaled 3.1 billion cu. ft./86.8 million cu. m., of which 62% came from the interior and 38% from coastal regions, Lodgepole pine, spruce, hemlock, balsam, Douglas fir and cedar, in that order, all accounted for at least 10% of the timber volume. In all, the value of forestry and logging production was nearly $1.4 billion in 1988.

Fishing: With landed value of $457 million, British Columbia led all provinces in 1988 in the value of its seafood production. There were 20,613 valid commercial fishing licenses in 1988. Of the more than 20 species of fish and marine animals indigenous to provincial waters that are harvested and marketed, in 1988 the five species of Pacific salmon accounted for 57% of landed value; herring 19%; shellfish 8%; and halibut 5%. Salmon returning to rivers to spawn are caught by large, modern fishing vessels at the mouths of most coastal rivers, especially the Fraser and Skeena. In terms of quantity, the 1989 fishery catch totaled 225,400 tons/204.500 tonnes out of a Canadian total of 1.57 million tons/1.43 million tonnes.

Mining: Most of British Columbia lies within the Canadian Cordillera mountain system, a geological formation known to contain a wide variety of valuable minerals. In 1990, the province led all others in copper production (44% of the national total) and was the sole national source of molybdenum. The total value of metals in 1990 was $1.70 billion; industrial minerals and structural materials accounted for another $128 million and $313 million, respectively.

Copper mining, centered around large open-pit mines southwest of Kamloops, is of chief importance; production of 761.7 million lb./345.6 million kg. in 1990 was valued at $1.11 billion. Gold mining has been important since the Fraser gold rush of 1858; 1990 production of 35,500 lb./16,106 kg. was worth $232.2 million. Next in importance was zinc, with 1990 production of 130.3 million lb./59.1 million kg., valued at $113.9 million. Silver output of 1,373,000 lb./623,000 kg. was valued at $113.7 million, and molybdenum production of 29.7 million lb./13.5 million kg. at $98.9 million. Lead production of 45.2 million lb./20.5 million kg. was valued at $24.5 million. The Sullivan mine at Kimberley is one of the world's major sources of lead and zinc. Among industrial minerals, the most important were sulfur, at 480,000 tons worth $50.4 million, and asbestos, at 96,000 tons worth $52.6 million. Among structural materials, 52.5 million tons of sand and gravel were valued at $158.7 million and 1.5 million tons of cement at $106.1 million.

Energy: British Columbia is second to Alberta in coal production, accounting for 36% of all Canadian coal in 1990. Eight mines, the most important of which are in the southeastern part of the province, produced 27.3 million tons/24.8 million tonnes of bituminous coal in 1990, valued at more than $1 billion. The Peace River district in the northeast yields crude oil and natural gas. Reserves were estimated in 1988 at 600 million cu. ft./17 million cu. m. of oil and 9 trillion cu. ft./256 billion cu. m. of natural gas. There were 188 wells drilled in 1988. Production in 1990 was 74.1 million cu. ft./2.1 million cu. m. of oil, valued at $338 million, and 363.7 billion cu. ft./10.3 billion cu. m. of natural gas, valued at $509.1 million. Condensate, butane and propane are extracted from a gas-cleaning plant at Taylor (near Fort St. John), and sulfur is scrubbed from gas at plants at Chetwynd, Fort Nelson and Taylor. Natural gas by-products were worth $70.7 million in 1990. British Columbia had six oil refineries in 1987, with annual capacity of 342.6 million cu. ft./9.7 million cu. m.

With one-twelfth of the world's supply of fresh water, British Columbia is admirably suited for hydroelectric power generation. The province has 12.5 million kilowatts of generating capacity, of which 87% is hydroelectric and the rest thermal. Of British Columbia's five power plants with installed capacity of 700 or more megawatts, two are on the Peace River, two on the Columbia, and the remaining one, for an aluminum smelter, on the Nechako. Net generation in 1990 was 60.7 million kilowatt hours (96% hydroelectric), and consumption was 57.6 million kilowatt hours. British Columbia Hydro and Power Authority, a public utility, produced 84% of total power in the province; mining and forest-products companies produced most of the rest.

Manufacturing: British Columbia's manufacturing industries are largely based on its natural resources. The greater Vancouver area and Vancouver Island are the chief manufacturing sites. Total manufactured shipments in 1990 were valued at $24.5 billion, of which the wood and paper and allied products accounted for 47%. British Columbia ranks first among provinces in the wood and paper products sectors. Lumber production in 1988 was 1.3 billion cu. ft./36.7 million cu. m., and plywood production was 64.6 million cu. ft./1.83 million cu. m. Pulpwood, the first step in paper production, is produced in 24 mills, with total output in 1988 of 7.2 million tons. Newsprint, paper and paperboard production, at nine mills, was 2.9 million tons. In all, manufactured wood was valued at $6.4 billion in 1990, and paper and allied products at $5.1 billion. Food products are the third most important manufacturing sector, totaling $2.9 billion in shipments in 1990, followed by primary metals ($946 million). Lead, zinc and silver are refined at Trail. Nonmetallic mineral products came to $756 million.

Of secondary-manufacturing sectors, the most important, in terms of 1990 value of shipments, was metal fabricating ($1.23 billion). There is a large Alcan aluminum smelter at Kitimat.

Transportation: British Columbia had 29,242 mi./47,060 km. of provincial roads and rights-of-way in 1989, of which 13,821 mi./22,242 km.

were paved and 12,676 mi./20,400 km. graveled. The number of motor vehicle licenses in 1988 was about 2.3 million, of which 1.7 million were for passenger vehicles. Mainline railway track totaled 3,864 mi./6,219 km. in 1986. All three major railways are involved in extensive freight-hauling operations. The provincially run BC Rail provides passenger service from North Vancouver to Prince George. VIA Rail Canada Inc. provides passenger service on CN Rail Lines from Vancouver via Edmonton, Alberta to Prince Rupert. CP Rail has service from Vancouver to Calgary, Alberta (and farther east), and from Victoria to Courtenay on Vancouver Island. A 14-mi./22-km. commuter rapid-transit line between New Westminster and downtown Vancouver was completed in 1985; an extension to Surrey has been completed to Surrey North and the remaining section to Surrey Central is under construction (1992).

British Columbia ports were the busiest in Canada in 1986, handling 114.9 million tons of cargo. Vancouver was Canada's leading port in 1989, handling 70.2 million tons/63.7 million tonnes, mostly bulk commodities for export such as coal and grain. Prince Rupert handled 12.7 million tons/ 11.6 million tonnes, mostly coal for export. There are also deep-sea ports at New Westminster, Victoria, Nanaimo, Port Alberni, Campbell River and Powell River. Small coastal vessels and tug and barge services link small communities on the province's major islands and mainland coast, some of them quite isolated otherwise. The crown (public) British Columbia Ferry Corporation provides freight service and passenger service on major routes between the lower mainland region, Vancouver Island and other coastal points. Sixteen provincially run freshwater ferry routes carried nearly 3 million passengers and 2.7 million vehicles in 1988–89. There is also steamship passenger service between Vancouver and Seattle, Washington.

Major domestic and international air service is provided by Air Canada and Canadian Airlines. Many other major foreign airlines provide service through Vancouver International Airport, Canada's second busiest; the airport handled 9.1 million passengers in 1989.

Wholesale and retail trade: Wholesale trade totaled $23.5 billion in 1990. Retail sales totaled $24.5 billion.

Foreign trade: In 1988, exports accounted for 26% of British Columbia's gross provincial product. Exports of British Columbian origin reached $17.0 billion in 1990. Almost all coal mined in the province, more than 80% of fisheries production, and about 75% of the forest sector's production is destined for other countries. By commodity, the leading exports in 1988 were lumber, $3.9 million; pulp, $3.4 billion; coal, $1.5 billion; newsprint, $943 million; copper, $743 million; paper and paperboard, $576 million; and aluminum, $534 million. In 1990 the United States received 43% of British Columbia's exports; Japan, 27%; the European Economic Community, 15%; and Pacific Rim countries other than Japan, 11%. Imports totaled $14.2 billion, mostly consisting of manufactured goods. Of this total, 44% came from the United States and 31% from Japan.

Banking and finance: There were 803 bank branches in 1988. Business loans outstanding at the end of the year totaled $7.8 billion, and personal loans outstanding totaled $6.8 billion. The 118 credit unions had more than a million members and total assets of $8 billion. The Vancouver Stock Exchange is the second largest in Canada. Almost 3.5 million shares, with a value of $3.3 billion, were traded in 1.7 million transactions in 1988. Public and private investment in the province totaled $17.3 billion in 1988.

Services: Between 1978 and 1988, real output and employment in business services more than doubled, growing almost 50% faster than the economy as a whole. Personal services rose more than 30% in real output during the same period, and employment grew 72%. More than 50% of such businesses are operated by self-employed individuals.

Construction: Construction activity in 1990 totaled $14.5 billion, of which $10.0 billion was for the construction of buildings and $4.5 billion for engineering projects. In 1988, of the latter the largest sectors were highway and road construction and airport runways ($1,251 billion), oil and gas wells ($420 million) and underground mines ($378 million).

Tourism: Eight national parks offer spectacular scenery, and 387 provincial parks cover 20,603 sq. mi./53,363 sq. km. A new national park in the South Moresby region of the Queen Charlotte Islands was agreed upon in 1987. In 1988 there were 8.2 million nonresident visitors to the province (58% Americans), who spent nearly $2 billion. British Columbian travelers numbered 10.5 million and spent $1.5 billion. In 1990 2.7 million Americans and 700,000 other non-Canadians stayed in British Columbia for one or more nights.

Public finance: General Fund expenditure in 1990–91 was $15.3 billion, and total revenue was $14.4 billion. After transfers from the Budget Stabilization Fund, of $926 million the 1990–91 General Fund deficit was $15 million. The budget for 1991–92 called for spending at $16.45 billion and revenue of $16.15 billion. The government debt was $4.9 billion at the end of fiscal 1989; counting public corporations and agencies, the total debt was $11.5 billion. Trust funds under public administration totaled $18.2 billion. Of General Fund expenditures for 1990–91, 33% went to the ministry of health, 27.0% to the ministries of education and advanced education and job training, and 10.6% to the ministry of social services and housing. Municipalities, regional districts, and local school boards were expected to spend about $4.5 billion in 1989.

Of total revenue, 58.5% came from taxation, not including another 8% in revenue on natural resources, 13.5% from the federal government, 4% from government enterprises and 10% from fees and licenses. In 1990, the personal income tax was 51.5% of the basic federal tax. The corporation tax was 15% of taxable net income (9% for small businesses). The retail sales tax had a general rate of 6% and was 10% on liquor. There is a mining tax of 12.5% (15% for metallic minerals), and a logging tax of

10%, and also taxes on mineral land and production tracts and the cash flow from metal and coal mines.

Employment: In 1990 the provincial labor force averaged 1,601,000 of which 157,000 were unemployed, for an unemployment rate of 8.3%, higher than the Canadian average of 8.1% and the highest rate in western Canada. The participation rate of 66% of the potential labor force was below the national average of 67.0%. Average weekly earnings in 1990 were $515.91, higher than in any province except Ontario. By sector, 23.5% of those employed were in community, business and personal services; 12.3% in trade; 13.6% in manufacturing; 10.8% in transportation and communications; 9.7% in primary industries and utilities; 17.1% in finance, insurance, and real estate; 7.6% in construction; and 5.2% in public administration.

British Columbia is one of the most highly unionized provinces in Canada, and its labor movement has a history of militancy, particularly in the isolated resource communities.

Prices: The Vancouver consumer price index rose by 5.1% between October 1989 and October 1990, and the Victoria index rose by 4.9%. The national average was 5.3%. During 1982–89 the index rose 42.5% in Vancouver, compared to 48.8% for all of Canada

SOCIAL SERVICES

Welfare: The Canada Assistance Plan, a shared-cost federal-provincial welfare program, extends income assistance to residents unable to provide the necessities of life for themselves and their dependents. It served 229,982 people in March 1989, for example, providing $868 million. A supplement for senior citizens provided $21 million for 50,006 recipients. The Ministry of Social Services and Housing provides services for families and children, including adoption services, child protection, foster care and family support (such as homemakers to help care for children). In 1988–89, expenditure totaled $116 million. The ministry spent $118 million for rehabilitation and support services, including residential care, self-help skills training, achievement centers, supported work placement and professional services for mentally handicapped adults, subsidized and special-needs day care, infant-development programs, and senior-citizen counselors. Expenditure for special programs for the mentally handicapped, including operating institutions in Alder Lodge and Woodlands, totaled $42 million. Programs for senior citizens include rental assistance for those in financial need and subsidized bus passes. The federal government funds and administers old-age pensions and family allowances.

Health: British Columbia residents are covered by the Medical Services Plan, which provides comprehensive insurance coverage of medical care, including hospital stays, physician services, and continuing care such as home nursing and support and group homes for the handicapped. Approximately half of the cost of this service is paid for by premiums. The pharmacare program reimburses prescription drugs and eligible medical supplies and prosthetic appliances. Most residents, in 1989, were reimbursed 80% of expenses in excess of $325; prescription drugs were free for senior citizens except for 75% payment up to an annual maximum of $125. The province also offers mental-health and psychiatric services, services to the handicapped, and community and preventive health services. Facilities include a 1,200-bed psychiatric hospital, 55 other mental-health centers, a facility for mentally ill adolescents, and a facility for severely physically and mentally handicapped persons. Services for substance abuse included 101 outpatient clinics, eight detoxification centers, and 14 residential centers and recovery homes. Ambulance service and pre-hospital care were provided, in 1989, by 359 ambulances and 15 support vehicles based in 164 communities.

The birthrate of 14.6 and death rate of 7.4 per 1,000 people in 1986 were close to the national averages, while the abortion rate of 27.1 per 100 live births was the highest in Canada. There were 116 hospitals in the province in 1986–87, with 21,250 beds. The average hospital expense of $269.71 per patient-day was below the national average. In 1987, there were 6,420 physicians, 1,918 licensed dentists and 25,862 registered nurses.

Housing: In 1986, 62.2% of the province's 1,074,575 homes were owned rather than rented, about the same as the national average. The average gross rent of $460 per month and average home payment (with mortgage) of $753 per month were both above the national averages. Housing capital and repair expenditures totaled $4.1 billion in 1988, when there were 30,487 housing starts, of which 17,761 were single detached homes.

A public corporation owned, in 1988, 7,744 subsidized rental units, with tenants paying 30% of their incomes in rent. Rent supplements were also available for tenants of 14,122 nonprofit and designated private-sector housing units. A provincial home-purchase assistance program offered second mortgages of up to $10,000 to eligible purchasers of new or existing homes; in 1988–89, 9,593 mortgages were issued under this program, totaling $66 million.

EDUCATION

Education is compulsory between the ages of 7 and 15. Of a total school enrollment of 532,244 in 1987–88, 491,309 students were attending public schools. These schools (1,502 in 1989) were 82% provincially and 18% locally financed, with an expenditure of approximately $4,400 per pupil.

British Columbia had seven universities in 1987–88, with 37,350 full-time and 17,689 part-time students. The three largest were publicly funded: the University of British Columbia in Vancouver, with enrollment of 20,725; the University of Victoria in Victoria (7,590), and Simon Fraser University in Burnaby (7,426). There are also a variety of other postsecondary programs, administered through 15 community colleges and three institutes. During 1988–89 these centers were attended by about 150,000 students.

MASS MEDIA

Newspapers and periodicals: British Columbia had 20 daily newspapers in 1992. The largest were Vancouver's morning paper, *The Province* (daily circulation, 182,462; Sunday circulation, 222,178), and the evening *Vancouver Sun* (daily circulation, 254,908), and Victoria's *Times-Colonist* (daily circulation, 77,201; Sunday circulation 74,318).

Periodicals: There were 128 nondaily newspapers and 82 periodicals in 1988. The periodical with the largest paid circulation (261,000) was the *Vitamin Supplement Journal,* a monthly published in Vancouver.

Broadcasting: As of March 31, 1989, British Columbia had 91 originating radio stations, of which 62 were AM and 29 FM. One FM station broadcast in French. The Canadian Broadcasting Corp., a federal company, operated six stations; five more were CBC affiliates. In 1991 there were 147 stations, including rebroadcast stations. Of the 10 originating television stations, two were operated by the CBC, five were affiliates, and two were CTV network stations. One station broadcast in French. During 1988, cable television was available to more than 80% of the homes in the province through 134 cable television systems. In 1991 there were 12 stations, including rebroadcast stations.

BIOGRAPHICAL SKETCHES

Michael Franklin Harcourt. Premier of British Columbia. Harcourt was born in Edmonton, Alberta on January 6, 1943 and was educated at the University of British Columbia, after which he became a lawyer. He was elected alderman in 1972 and then mayor of Vancouver in 1980. He was first elected to the legislature in 1986, and he was elected leader of the B.C. New Democratic Party in April 1987. He was sworn in as premier of British Columbia on November 4, 1991.

Glen Clark. Minister of finance and corporate relations responsible for B.C. Ferries and B.C. Transit. Clark was born on November 22, 1959 in Nanaimo, British Columbia. He was educated at Simon Fraser University and the University of British Columbia and became a resource policy consultant. First elected to the legislature in 1986, he was shortly thereafter named finance critic. He was appointed minister of finance and corporate relations on November 5, 1991, the youngest finance minister in British Columbia history.

Anita Hagen. Deputy premier, minister of education and minister of multiculturalism and human rights. Hagen was born on May 6, 1931 in Sydney, Nova Scotia. She was educated at Dalhousie University and worked as a teacher and adult educator. First elected to the legislature in 1986, she became opposition critic for education and seniors. She was appointed minister of education and minister of multiculturalism and human rights on November 4, 1991.

Colin Gabelman. Attorney General. Gabelman, born February 11, 1944 in London, England, was educated at the University of British Columbia. He worked as labor union organizer and staff member. He was first elected to the legislature in 1972, was defeated 1975, and was reelected 1979, 1983 and 1986. He was appointed attorney general on November 4, 1991, becoming the second non-lawyer to hold that position in British Columbia.

Gordon Wilson. Leader of the opposition. Wilson was born in 1951 in Vancouver and was raised in Kenya. He was educated at the State University of New York and the University of British Columbia and worked as an instructor in resource management and economic geography at Capilano College, North Vancouver. In 1985 he became a director of the Sunshine Coast Regional District. He had been leader of the Liberal Party for four years when he was elected to the legislature in 1991, its first Liberal member since 1979.

Ungava
Bay

LABRADOR

SEA

Hebron

Nutak

Nain

QUEBEC

Rigolet

Smallwood Res.

Churchill Falls

L.
Melville

Labrador City

Churchill *R.*

Eagle R.

Cartwright

Wabush

Atikonak L.

Goose Bay

ATLANTIC

Little Mecatina

LABRADOR

R.

Port Hope Simpson

Battle Harbour

Str. of Belle Isle

Qirpon

St.Anthony

OCEAN

White Bay

GROS MORNE
NAT'L PARK

Twillingate

Island of

Stephenville

Grand
L.

Grand Falls

TERRA NOVA
NAT'L PARK

Newfoundland

Gulf

Stephenville
Crossing

Bay de Verde

Trinity Bay

of

St.George's Bay

St.Lawrence

ST.PIERRE &
MIQUELON
(To France)

St.Johns

Placentia

Bay

Burin

PRINCE
EDWARD
ISLAND

NEW
BRUNSWICK

NOVA SCOTIA

0	100	200 Miles
0	100	200 Kms

NEWFOUNDLAND

NEWFOUNDLAND

Features: Newfoundland is the easternmost province of Canada. It consists of (1) the island of Newfoundland and (2) Labrador, on the eastern end of the continent. The latter is bordered by Quebec on the north, west and south; is separated from Newfoundland on the southeast by the narrow Strait of Belle Isle; and faces the Atlantic Ocean to the east. The island of Newfoundland, part of the Appalachian Mountains system, consists of four geographic regions. The northeastern coast region, stretching from the Great Northern Peninsula to the Avalon Peninsula, faces the Atlantic Ocean. The region's numerous bays, coves, fjords and islands often provide excellent harbors and make it the focus of the province's fishing activity; and the region's Avalon Peninsula is the center of political, economic and cultural life in the province, with the preponderance of the province's manufacturing and service industries. The southern coast has a submerged shoreline with deep bays. A few fishing ports and processing plants are located here, as are the province's major shipyard and two mines. The western coast, unlike the others, faces the Gulf of St. Lawrence rather than the Atlantic Ocean; it has several deeply indented fjordlike bays. This region is dominated by the Long Range Mountains of the Great Northern Peninsula, reaching a maximum elevation of 2,670 ft./814 m. Economic activities include fishing, fish-processing plants, paper-products mills and the manufacture of fabricated metal products. The interior of the island is an extensively forested, well-watered, plateaulike region drained by the Exploits, Gander, Humber and Terra Nova rivers; lumbering is carried on here, and there is a paper mill. Soils are poor throughout Newfoundland, and very little of the island is farmed.

Labrador, the easternmost part of the ancient Precambrian Canadian Shield, consists of a ruggedly mountainous northern coastal region with sparse subarctic vegetation, a rugged, forested southern coastal region and a forested plateau in the vast interior. In the north, the Torngat Mountains rise to a maximum height of 5,320 ft./1,622 m. at Mount Caubvick, the highest point in Canada east of the Rocky Mountains. The chief economic activity in Labrador is iron-ore mining at the western end.

Area: 156,200 sq. mi./404,557 sq. km. (of which the island of Newfoundland is 42,031 sq. mi./108,860 sq. km. and Labrador 114,169 sq.

mi./295,697 sq. km.), including 13,140 sq. mi./34,032 sq. km. of inland water. The province makes up 4.1% of the area of Canada.

Mean maximum and minimum temperatures: St. John's, 68° F/20.1° C (July), 31° F/−0.6° C (January); Goose Bay, Labrador, 59° F/15° C (July), −5° F/−20.5° C (January).

Mean annual precipitation: St. John's 59.5 in./1,511 mm., of which 143 in./364 cm. is snow; Goose Bay, Labrador, 37 in./946 mm., of which 175 in./445 cm. is snow.

POPULATION

Total population (1986 census): 568,349, of which Labrador had 28,741. The population density was 1.4 per sq. mi./3.6 per sq. km. The population has almost doubled since 1935. Estimated population as of 1990 was 573,100.

Chief towns and populations (1986 census): St. John's, the capital (96,216, Metropolitan area 161,901; estimated at 163,900 in 1990), Corner Brook (22,719), Mount Pearl (20,293), Conception Bay South (15,531), Gander (10,207), Grand Falls (9,121), Labrador City (8,684) and Stephenville (7,994).

Distribution: All but 5% of the population lives on the island of New-foundland. In 1986, 59% of the population lived in incorporated towns.

Ethnic composition: The population is almost entirely of British Isles stock (96%) including 6% part British, of which about three-fifths are of English origin and two-fifths of Irish origin. The English tend to live on the western part of the island and the Irish on the eastern part. French make up 2%, although another 4% are part French, including those who are part British. There are small numbers of Inuit (Eskimos) and Innu (Montagnais-Naskapi) in Labrador and Micmac Indians on the island of Newfoundland.

Language: English is the mother tongue and language used at home by about 99% of the people in the province. Only about 0.5% reported French.

Religion: The main religious groups (1981 census) are Roman Catholic (36%), Anglican (27%) and United Church (19%). These denominations are followed by the Pentecostals (7%).

CONSTITUTION AND GOVERNMENT

Newfoundland's political evolution differed from that of the other Atlantic provinces—New Brunswick, Nova Scotia and Prince Edward Island—because, unlike them, it did not join the Canadian confederation during 1867–73. Indeed, it gained internal self-government but lost it in 1934, and was ruled by a six-member British-appointed commission until 1949. Another peculiarity is the absence of country or township government. Newfoundlanders generally lived in isolated coastal settlements, sought to avoid taxation, building codes, and other regulations, and were willing to forego the concomitant services. Until 1938 the capital, St. John's, was the only incorporated place in Newfoundland.

Executive: The executive council, or cabinet, is responsible for the functioning of the executive branch of government. The premier, who is the head of the political party that holds a majority of seats in the legislature, presides over the executive council and chooses the cabinet members from among members of the legislature. In 1991 there were 15 cabinet ministers, 14 of them heads of government departments or a central agency. There were seven cabinet committees in 1989, and there is a cabinet secretariat which had 34 officials in 1986. In addition to the regular government departments, the province has a number of semi-independent agencies, boards, commissions and crown (public) corporations. The civil service is entitled to collective bargaining, and the province has an ombudsman.

Legislature: The House of Assembly is the only legislative chamber. It has 52 members, each of them singly elected from a separate district. As is the case in all the provinces, the executive is responsible to the legislature and depends on majority support in that body.

Political parties: In the century after Newfoundland was granted representative government in 1832, there were Liberal, Conservative, Union, and People's parties, but these names did not reflect any particular ideology; rather, the parties were loose coalitions of individuals or social groups. More politicians have changed party in Newfoundland than in any other Canadian province. Protestants tended to vote Liberal and Catholics Conservative, and this tendency continues, despite the absence of religious issues in recent times.

In Newfoundland's first legislative election as a province in 1949, the Liberal party won 22 of the 28 seats. The Liberals remained in power until 1972, their candidates regularly polling nearly 60% or more of the more of the total vote in provincial elections. From 1972 to 1989, the Progressive Conservative party was in power, and in two provincial elections (1972 and 1982) its candidates collectively polled more than 60% of the total vote. In April 1989, the Liberals returned to power, winning 31 seats to 21 for the Conservatives. The New Democratic Party has not been an important factor in general elections, although in 1985 its candidates won 14% of the vote and it elected a member to the legislature for the first time. However in recent years it has won three by-elections.

Local government: Fewer than half of the more than 800 communities are incorporated. In 1988, there were only three cities, St. John's, Corner Brook and Mount Pearl, a metropolitan area bordering St. John's; 169 towns; 141 communities; and 146 quasi-municipal local service districts. Communities

95

and local service districts usually represent groups of settlements. Town and community governments typically provide a few local services, such as roads, water, sewage systems and fire protection. They have no role in health, welfare or the administration of justice. They have limited powers of taxation, and the real-property tax is an innovation in many localities. In general, major projects are mainly financed by the provincial Department of Municipal Affairs. Cities elect mayors; cities, towns and communities have elected councils; and local service districts have elected committees. The St. John's metropolitan area has appointed boards. Cities and towns are usually administered by appointed managers.

Federal representation: Newfoundland sends seven elected members to the House of Commons and six appointed members to the Senate. By custom, one of the Commons members serves in the federal cabinet. In the 1988 federal elections, five Liberals and two Progressive Conservatives were elected from the seven constituencies in the province.

Judicial system: The Supreme Court is divided into a Trial Division with a chief justice and 12 associate justices, and an Appeals Division with a chief justice and six associate justices. These are federal courts, and all of these justices are federally appointed. The six judicial centers are also federally administered, and the judges are appointed by the federal government. A Unified Family Court hears cases presided over by a single justice, who is also federally appointed. The 20 provincial courts, located in major communities and funded and administered by the provincial government, handle cases of lesser importance.

RECENT HISTORY

In 1948 Newfoundlanders, in a plebiscite, voted to join Canada, although the margin of approval was only 52% to 48%. The following year they elected the Liberal Party, which had favored confederation, to power under Joseph Smallwood, who began a 23-year reign as premier.

The province immediately benefited from federal social payments such as family allowances and old-age pensions, and Canada assumed Newfoundland's external debt. The creation of Memorial University in 1949 served to produce teachers for the province's schools. The 1950s saw many schools, roads and hospitals built, but Smallwood's search for industrial development yielded few benefits. During the 1960s two iron ore mines and a hydroelectric power plant opened in Labrador. However, the province received little revenue from these projects, while the fishing and forestry industries on the island were becoming increasingly mechanized. The closure of U.S. military bases, dating from World War II, added to unemployment. The Liberals lost the elections in October 1971, and Frank Moores replaced Smallwood as premier.

Moores's seven years in office as premier of a Conservative government saw administrative reform and a more businesslike approach to development. The establishment by Canada in 1977 of a 200-mi./320-km. offshore economic zone in which Canadians would have priority in catching fish, long demanded by Newfoundland, helped alleviate the problem of depletion by foreign fleets. Continuing economic problems included labor unrest and rising taxes.

Another Conservative, Brian Peckford, succeeded Moores in 1979. The main question in the 1980s was management of three vital natural resources: fish, hydroelectricity and offshore oil.

An Atlantic Ocean offshore oil and natural gas strike in 1979, perhaps even larger than the North Sea deposits, indicated the possibility of commercial production. The province lost a dispute in the courts with the federal government over ownership of these resources, but in 1985 a joint petroleum board was established and Newfoundland was given the right to collect revenues from undersea resources. Despite a preliminary agreement in 1989 with a consortium of oil companies, the way was not yet cleared to begin oil and gas production in the 1990s, as had been anticipated.

In March 1989 Peckford resigned office—a victim, ironically, of another ill-advised scheme for economic development. A hydroponics cucumber-growing project for which the government provided money and tax exemptions without consulting the legislature proved to be a costly disaster. Peckford was succeeded as premier by fisheries minister Thomas Rideout. In provincial elections a month later, the Liberals returned to power, winning 31 Assembly seats to 21 for the Conservatives, although candidates of each party collectively polled about 47% of the vote. The new government, headed by Clyde Wells, pledged to drive a harder bargain in exploiting the province's natural resources.

ECONOMY

Newfoundland is the poorest province in Canada, with the lowest annual income per capita and the highest unemployment rate. Its economy depends on primary commodities—lumber, fish and minerals—and these products face stiff competition in the international marketplace. Moreover, increasing mechanization of primary-resource industries offers little hope of employment for the province's young people.

The gross domestic product at factor cost was estimated at $7.9 billion in 1990. In real terms (excluding inflation), it increased by 3.3% in 1987, 3.8% in 1988 and 2.3% in 1989, and it decreased an estimated 0.4% in 1990. The service sector accounted for about 69% of GDP in 1989; of this sector, community, business and personal services accounted for 37.1%, followed by public administration, 14.8%; wholesale and retail trade, 19%; finance, insurance and real estate, 20.3%; and transportation, communication and other utilities, 8.9%. Of the estimated 31% of GDP in the goods-producing sector, manufacturing accounted for 26.6%; construction, 24.8%; mining (including quarries and oil), 20.7%; electric power and water utilities, 16.5%; fishing and trapping, 7.6%; forestry, 2.5%; and agriculture, 1.3%. The 1986 per-capita income of $11,181 was the lowest in Canada. In 1990 it had risen to $15,859, an increase of 42% in current dollars, but only about 19% in real terms.

97

Agriculture: There were a total of 651 farms in 1986, with about 12,044 acres/4,876 hectares cultivated for crops, and 9,438 acres/3,821 hectares in pasture. Total cash receipts came to $57.9 million in 1989, mostly for poultry, dairy products and eggs. Potatoes and other vegetables (mainly turnips and cabbages) accounted for about half of total crop receipts. Although the province is virtually self-sufficient in egg production, more than 80% of its meat, fruit and vegetables are imported. Aside from a small amount of furs sold from ranches, the only export is blueberries. The combined harvest of cultivated and wild blueberries came to 2,300 tons, valued at $2.9 million, in 1987.

Mining: Mining and quarrying employed 4,200 and the value of mineral production in Newfoundland and Labrador in 1990 totaled $862 million. Of this total the production from two iron ore mines in Labrador City and Wabush came to $696.0 million, or 81% of the total. Output, which is sent by rail to Quebec, was about 20 million tons, or almost half of Canada's total iron ore production. Most of the ore is exported to the United States or Europe. Employment at the two mines totaled 2,460 on average during 1990.

An asbestos mine at Baie Verte on the northern coast employed about 380 workers and in 1990 produced about 80,000 tons/72,600 tonnes. Exhaustion of reserves has been met by use of a 10–15-year supply of tailings. A zinc mine at Daniel's Harbour on Great Northern Peninsula employed about 150 workers and its 1990 production was valued at $36 million, although depletion of ore reserves caused shutdown in the third quarter. A gold mine near Cinq Cerf Brook on the south coast produced about 750 lb./340 kg. worth about $7.8 million, in 1987 after opening in September of that year. In 1990 its shipments were valued at $51.6 million. Other mines and quarries extract pyrophyllite, silica, fluorspar and structural materials such as cement, sand and gravel, clay products and stone.

Forestry; The total productive forest land of the island of Newfoundland is about 6.9 million acres/2.8 million hectares. About 56% of this land is controlled by provincial pulp and paper companies. In addition, there is a commercial timber concentration of 890,000 acres/360,000 hectares of productive forest in south-central Labrador, near Goose Bay.

A total of about 89.5 million cu. ft./2.5 million cu. m. of timber was harvested in the province during 1989, of which about 68% was used within the province for pulp and paper, another 12% for sawmilling, or construction timber and the remainder was mostly burned locally as fuel, although a small amount was exported. Pulpwood harvested for the province's pulp and paper mills amounted to 61 million cu. ft./1.72 million cu. m. in 1990. The spruce budworm has become a serious threat to the industry in recent years.

Fishing: In 1985, there were more than 26,000 registered fishermen in the province (including about 2,000 in Labrador), of which more than

13,000 were registered as full-time fishermen. Inshore fishermen—the vast majority—provide fish to seasonally operated inshore plants, while offshore trawler fleets supply integrated fish companies with raw material on a year-round basis. The offshore trawler catch usually amounts to about 40% of the total.

The total catch of fish and shellfish was estimated at 506,000 tons/459,000 tonnes in 1990. In 1988 it had been 615,000 tons/558,000 tonnes. The main fish taken is cod, which comes inshore during the summer to feed on capelin and other fish and moves offshore during the fall. Landings of codfish totaled 308,000 tons/279,984 tonnes in 1987. The value of the catch in 1990 was $240.6 million, of which cod accounted for $171.2 million. Recently the decline of stocks has led to severe cuts in fishing quotas by the Canadian government, which blames overfishing by foreign fleets. However, there are claims that the growth of the seal population or the Canadian use of offshore trawlers is the culprit. Depletion became so serious that in mid-1992 the Canadian government took the drastic step of imposing a two-year moratorium on the centuries-old cod fisheries. The moratorium, depriving fishing communities of their very rationale for being, was accompanied by a compensation package that provided a modest income to the fresh army of unemployed.

In return for an increased cod quota off the province's shores, France in 1989 had accepted referral to an international court of its long dispute over maritime boundaries and fishing rights around the islands of St. Pierre and Miquelon, a French territorial collectivity located south of Newfoundland. In June 1992 the international tribunal drew a boundary granting Canada control over most of the seas off southern Newfoundland but France was awarded 24 nautical miles around St. Pierre and Miquelon and a corridor 10.5 nautical miles wide stretching 200 nautical miles toward the Gulf of St. Lawrence.

Manufacturing: The total value of manufacturing shipments in 1990 was $1.43 billion. By GDP, fish processing accounted for 47.1% of total manufacturing value added; pulp and paper products, 19.8%; and other manufactured products, 33.1%. In 1986, 201 registered processing plants were active, providing employment to about 173 communities. The heaviest concentrations are on the northern coast, including the northern coast of the Avalon Peninsula; on the coasts of the Great Northern Peninsula; and on the southern coast of Labrador. Fishery Products International, a government business partnership, operated 16 processing plants, buying fish directly from about 2,500 fishermen, and employed nearly 8,000 people in the late 1980s. Although a few fishermen still prepare the traditional sun-cured salt cod, most production now is frozen fillets, blocks and sticks. The cutting of fish quotas has led to the closing of processing plants and severe unemployment in communities dependent on them; the moratorium is worsening this situation.

Newsprint is produced from the province's three pulp and paper mills, located at Corner Brook, Stephenville and Grand Falls. Production in 1990 was 680,244 tons/617,280 tonnes, valued at $397 million. There are also some 1,500 small sawmills. In 1986 about 6,000 people were employed in logging, wood manufacturing, sawmills and the pulp and paper industry.

Other manufactured goods are fabricated metal products, wood products (including furniture), ships and boats, chemicals and paints, foods and beverages, footwear, furs, clothing and asphalt. An oil refinery closed in 1983 but reopened in 1987 with an expected refining capacity of 100,000 bbl of crude oil a day by 1988.

Energy: Total electrical power production in 1990 was about 37 million megawatt hours. The Churchill Falls hydroelectric project in Labrador is about two-thirds owned by the province and one-third owned by Quebec. With an installed capacity of 5,403 megawatts, it is the ninth largest in the world, but less than 10% of the capacity (350 megawatts) is earmarked for consumption in Labrador; the rest is reserved for sending on a grid to Quebec under a long-term contract not due to expire until 2041. The contract is a sore point with Newfoundland, since under its provisions power is exported at a fixed price, now far under market value, that will actually decline over the term of the contract. On the island, installed capacity of about 1,800 megawatts, of which 70% is hydroelectric and 30% thermal, meets all needs. About 75% of production is by the province-owned utility and 25% by private producers. Industry accounted for 57% of provincial consumption of 9.7 million megawatt hours in 1986.

The Hibernia oil and gas field was discovered by Mobil Oil Canada in the Atlantic, about 200 mi./320 km. east of Newfoundland in 1979. Further exploration work revealed high-grade crude oil reserves estimated at between 500 million and 800 million bbl, plus reserves of 925 billion cu. ft./26 billion cu. m. of natural gas. By the end of 1987, 129 wells had been drilled off the coast of the province, resulting in 19 significant discoveries and cumulative total expenditures of about $3.5 billion. This activity has provided work for repair and maintenance services to oil rigs, especially at the Marystown shipyard on the south coast. In July 1988 the federal and provincial governments signed a preliminary agreement with a consortium of four oil companies, headed by Mobil Oil Canada, for a $5.3-billion project to begin production in the Hibernia field in 1996, with the federal government pledging $2.6 billion in grants and loan guarantees. The project called for building a mammoth concrete platform 180 mi./290 km. off the southeastern coast of Newfoundland, and it was expected to create 3,000 jobs. However, signing of the final agreement in March 1989 was postponed until 1991. Initial contracts had been let and the letting of subcontracts was proceeding when one of the major members of the consortium withdrew in early 1992, putting the project on hold for the foreseeable future.

On March 9, 1987 Petro-Canada announced its intention to develop the Terra Nova field, 25 mi./40 km. southeast of the Hibernia field. However this project was not under way by the spring of 1992.

Transportation: Marine Atlantic, a federal crown corporation, operates four vessels that carry passengers, motor vehicles and freight across the Gulf of

St. Lawrence, linking North Sydney, Nova Scotia with the Newfoundland ports of Port-aux-Basques and Argentia. It also operates 11 vessels that serve isolated communities on the Newfoundland and Labrador coasts. Transport Canada, a federal agency, runs three ferries, including one between St. Barbe, Newfoundland and Blanc Sablon, Quebec.

A federal corporation operated a freight rail line of about 550 mi./880 km. of track between St. John's and Port-aux-Basques until 1988, when it was closed. Generally parallel to this line is the Newfoundland sector of the Trans-Canada Highway. In Labrador, a provincial road runs between Happy Valley-Goose Bay and Labrador City, passing Churchill Falls at about midpoint. In 1986 there were 5,119 mi./8,238 km. of roads, of which 3,524 mi./5,671 km. were paved. There were 273,192 registered motor vehicles in the province in 1986, of which 176,351 were passenger cars. In 1987 there were 81,337 commercial vehicles in the province.

There are major airports at St. John's, Stephenville, Deer Lake and Gander, Newfoundland and at Goose Bay, Churchill Falls and Wabush, Labrador. Gander is the airport for international flights. The province is served by two major airlines: Air Canada and Canadian Airlines International. The number of air passengers in 1985 was 737,860.

Sea cargo loaded and unloaded totaled 5,093,300 tons in 1986. St. John's was the leading port, with 871,100 tons of cargo, followed by Holyrood, Long Harbour, Corner Brook and Botwood.

Wholesale and retail trade: The value of retail trade was $3.615 billion in 1990 and the value of wholesale trade was $1.99 billion.

Foreign trade: Of major commodity exports from the province to non-Canadian markets in 1986, the United States took 54.6%, Europe 24.2% and Asia 11.5%. Of mineral products, 49.1% went to the United States, 41.5% to Europe and 8.8% to Asia. Of newsprint, 37.7% went to the United States in 1987, 23.5% to Europe, 14.8% to Central America and the Caribbean, 12% to South America and 7.5% to Asia. In 1986, 75.9% of fish-product exports went to the United States, 11.9% to Asia and 8.2% to Europe.

Banking: In 1988, there were 136 bank branches in the province, including those of the Bank of Nova Scotia (61), Bank of Montreal (29), Royal Bank of Canada (21) and Canadian Imperial Bank of Commerce (17).

Construction: In 1990, the total value of building construction in the province was $1.06 billion, of which $670.6 million was residential. Engineering construction was valued at $609 million.

Tourism: Newfoundland has two national parks, Gros Morne and Terra Nova, and five national historic sites. One of the latter is at L'Anse aux Meadows on Great Northern Peninsula; this is the site of the only authenticated pre-Columbian settlement in America, a Viking encampment unquestionably Norse in character, dating from about 1000. The total number of visitors in 1989 was estimated at 1.5 million of which 312,000 were non-resident and expenditures estimated at $383 million. Provincial parks had 1,617,342 visitors in 1987.

Public finance: The provincial retail sales tax of 12% in 1990 was the highest in Canada. The personal income tax was also the highest in Canada, 62% of the federal tax. The corporation tax ranged from 10% for small businesses to 17% for large ones. There is a capital tax of 3% on banks and trusts and loan corporations. In 1990, the gasoline tax came to 13.7 cents per liter and the tobacco tax to 6.78 cents per cigarette. In 1986, 223,320 provincial taxpayers paid $475 million in federal income tax and $283.3 million in provincial income tax on personal income of $6.7 billion. Provincial corporation income tax was $65.4 million. In 1990 taxpayers paid $448 million in provincial personal income tax on personal income of $9.1 billion. Corporations paid $55.8 million in provincial income taxes.

The budget presented in June 1991 called for expenditures of $3.514 billion in fiscal 1991–92, projecting a deficit of $1.54 billion on current account. The provincial debt was expected to reach $5.35 billion. Education ($796.8 million), health ($841.2 million), debt service ($590.3 million) and social welfare ($259.0 million) had the largest shares of projected expenditures. The main sources of revenue were expected to be federal transfer payments and equalization grants (projected at $1.37 billion for 1990–91), retail sales tax ($586 million) and personal income tax ($468 million). In 1984, local-government revenue came to $228 million and expenditures to $243 million.

Employment: After reaching 21.3% in 1985, the unemployment rate dropped to a low of 15.8% in 1989, but it was still the highest of any province in Canada. In 1990 the average unemployment rate was 17.1%, and 201,000 of the province's labor force of 242,000 were employed. In 1989, by sector, community, business and personal service employment led with about 67,000, followed by trade, about 37,000; manufacturing, about 24,000; and public administration, about 19,000. In 1987–88, 27,071 people were employed by the province, 14,136 by the federal government and 2,498 by local governments. The minimum wage was $4 an hour in 1986, and the average weekly wage in 1987 was $423.64. In 1990 it was $484.48. The most important labor union in the province is the United Food and Commercial Workers Union, which represents fishermen and fish-plant workers and has about 28,000 members. The Newfoundland Federation of Labour has a membership of about 50,000.

Prices: Based on a standard of 100 in 1986, the consumer price index in St. John's was 109.2 in 1989 and 113.9 in 1990. The inflation rate was 4.3% in 1990, considerably lower than the Canadian rate of 5.0%.

SOCIAL SERVICES

Welfare: The federal government administers and funds old-age pensions, family allowances and unemployment insurance. The CAP, a joint federal-provincial general-assistance plan for the needy, provided benefits of $108 million for 50,500 recipients in the province in 1987. The provincial government, through the Department of Social Services, provides protection of children, adoption services, and services to disabled or disadvantaged persons as well as income support through CAP. Newfoundland had the highest proportion of low-income families of any province in Canada in 1986, at 21%.

Health: The Department of Health coordinates existing hospital and home services. Total health expenditures in the province, public and private, came to $745 million in 1985, of which $350 million was for hospitals. The per-capita health expenditure of $1,282 was the lowest in Canada except for Prince Edward Island.

There were 42 public provincial hospitals in 1986–87, with 3,624 beds. The number of physicians was 1,070 and of active licensed dentists, 135 (only one for 4,199 people—the highest ratio in Canada). There were 397 pharmacists and 4,590 nurses—one nurse for 123 persons, the highest provincial ratio in Canada. The 1986 birthrate of 14.6 and death rate of 6.2 per 1,000 were both low for Canadian provinces, as was the abortion rate of 4.9 per 100 live births.

Housing: There were 159,080 occupied dwellings in Newfoundland according to the 1986 census, of which 122,895 were single detached units. Eighty percent were owned rather than rented—the highest such percentage in Canada. The average owner's major payments, with mortgage, came to $614 a month in 1986, and the average gross rent was $408. Of the 2,682 dwelling starts in 1987, 2,530 were detached homes. The number of completions was 2,390, and the average number of units under construction was 3,631. The value of residential building permits in 1987 was $124.5 million. During that year, 41% of total housing sales in the St. John's area were accounted for by sales of houses costing $80,000 or more. The Newfoundland and Labrador Housing Corporation is a public agency that provides housing. Its 1987–88 fiscal-year gross expenditures were estimated at $7.3 million. In 1990 there were 3,245 dwelling starts, 1,884 in centers of 10,000 population or over, and 1,627 completions there. The average selling price of new single and semi-detached houses was just over $140,000.

EDUCATION

The departments of education and of career development and advanced studies develop and maintain the provincial education system. In 1983–84, $1,028 per capita was spent in the province on education, the highest proportion of personal income (11.9%) in any province. But studies have shown that the adult illiteracy rate is as high as 44%.

Beginning in 1843, education grants were divided between Catholic and Protestant school boards, with the Protestant grant eventually distributed among several Protestant denominations. This system survives and, excepting a few small private institutions, the province's 607 primary and secondary schools (in 1986) are administered by regional denominational school boards. In 1989–90 there were 7,994 teachers and 130,500 students in 546 schools from kindergarten through high school.

The Memorial University of Newfoundland, founded as a college in 1925, is the province's only university. The main campus is located on the northern outskirts of St. John's; Sir Wilfred Grenfell College, a two-year branch, is in Corner Brook. In 1989–90 the university had 11,634 full-time and 4,348 part-time students. Postsecondary vocational schools include the College of Fisheries, Navigation, Marine Engineering and Electronics and the College of Trades and Technology, both in St. John's. The Bay St. George Community College is on the west coast of Newfoundland.

MASS MEDIA

Newspapers and periodicals: The province had two daily newspapers in 1991: the St. John's *Evening Telegram* and the Corner Brook *Western Star.* Both are owned by the Thomson newspaper chain. Circulation in 1992 was 17,460 with 31,000 at the weekend, and 10,645, respectively.

Periodicals: Twelve weekly regional newspapers, a semiweekly newspaper, and a weekly periodical were published in 1988, all in English. The largest weekly was the *Newfoundland Herald,* circulation 39,704, published in St. John's.

Broadcasting: The Canadian Broadcasting Corporation has television stations in Corner Brook, Goose Bay, Labrador City-Wabush, and St. John's. The Canadian Television Network has stations in Corner Brook and St. John's. Cable television dates from 1977 and is available in 10 communities. There were 30 AM and 19 FM radio stations in 1988.

BIOGRAPHICAL SKETCHES

Clyde Kirby Wells.   Premier of Newfoundland after the Liberal Party electoral victory of April 1989. Wells was born in Buchans Junction, Newfoundland on November 9, 1937. He attended All Saints School in Stephenville Crossing and Memorial University of Newfoundland, from which he received a B.A. in 1959. He received a law degree from Dalhousie University Law School in Nova Scotia in 1962 and served in the Canadian army for the following two years. In private law practice from 1964, Wells was formerly chairman of the board of Newfoundland Light and Power Co. Ltd. Elected to the House of Assembly in 1966, he was appointed minister of labor, but he resigned from the cabinet in 1968 and from the legislature in 1971. He was chosen leader of the provincial Liberal Party in June 1987 and was again elected to the House of Assembly in December 1987. He became premier after the Liberals defeated the progressive conservative government of Thomas Rideout, who had followed Brian Peckford but had served as premier for only one month before the April 1989 provincial elections.

Winston Baker.   President of the Treasury Board, president of the Executive Council, government House leader, minister responsible for the status of women. Born December 17, 1939 in Grand Bank, Newfoundland, he was educated at Memorial University, the University of Toronto, Queen's University and Laurentian University. He was a teacher and became Deputy Mayor of Gander, Newfoundland. He was first elected to the Newfoundland legislature in 1985 and became opposition spokesman on Finance and the Newfoundland Hydro, and the Chairman of the Public Accounts Committee. He was reelected in 1989 and appointed to the cabinet.

Chris Decker.   Born in St. Anthony, Newfoundland, in 1948, he was educated at Memorial University, Newfoundland. He was a businessman, and was first elected to the Newfoundland legislature in 1985 and reelected in 1989. He was appointed minister of health in 1989.

Len Simms.   Leader of the opposition. Born October 23, 1943 in Howley, Newfoundland, Simms attended King's College School, Windsor, Nova Scotia and the University of New Brunswick. He was first elected to the Newfoundland legislature in 1979 and was reelected in 1982, 1985 and 1989. He served as speaker in 1979; minister of culture, recreation and youth in 1982–1984; and was named minister of forest resources and lands in 1984. He was appointed President of the Treasury Board, president of the Executive Council, and government House leader in January 1988; and he was also named minister of development in March 1988. In 1989 he became opposition House leader following defeat of the Progressive Conservatives, and he was elected leader of the Progressive Conservative Party and leader of the opposition in October 1991.

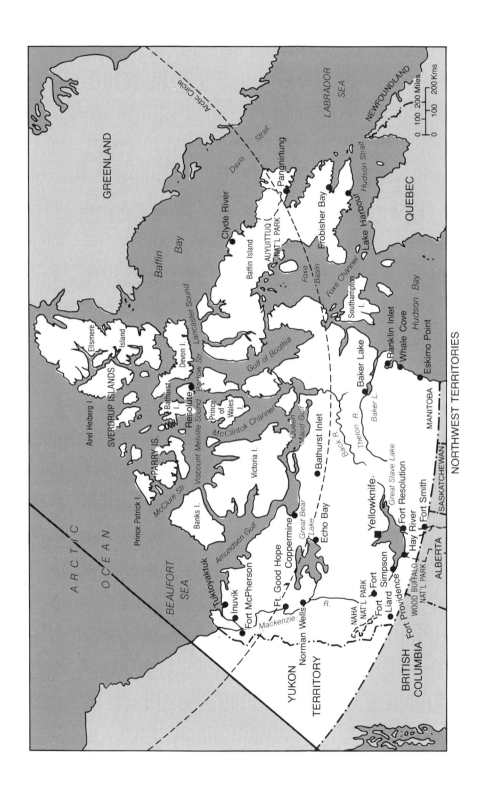

NORTHWEST TERRITORIES

NORTHWEST TERRITORIES

GEOGRAPHY

Features: The Northwest Territories forms more than one-third of the area of Canada. It is bordered on the north by the Arctic Ocean; on the east by Kane Basin, Smith Sound, Baffin Bay and Davis Strait, all of which separate the Arctic and Atlantic oceans and divide the Northwest Territories from Greenland; on the south by Hudson Strait, Hudson Bay, James Bay and the provinces of Manitoba, Saskatchewan, Alberta and British Columbia; and on the west by the Yukon Territory, Beaufort Sea and the Arctic Ocean.

The vast Northwest Territories can be divided into three main areas. The western mainland consists of the subarctic Mackenzie River valley, which is the most habitable and economically productive part. It is generally a lowland plain rising in the western part to the Mackenzie Mountains, where is found the territorial high point, an unnamed peak reaching 9,095 ft./2,773 m. above sea level. The Mackenzie River, which empties into Beaufort Sea, rises in Great Slave Lake, but its tributaries have their sources as far south as British Columbia and Alberta; the total drainage area (695,000 sq. mi./1.8 million sq. km.) and length (2,635 mi./4,241 km.) of the Mackenzie and its tributaries are the largest and longest in Canada. Also in this region are the two largest lakes wholly in Canada, Great Bear Lake (12,096 sq. mi./31,328 sq. km.) and Great Slave Lake (11,030 sq. mi./28,568 sq. km.). Only the northernmost part of the Mackenzie River valley is within the continuous permafrost zone; the rest has spruce, pine, birch, larch and poplar forests.

The eastern mainland consists of the Canadian Precambrian Shield, a gently undulating rocky lowland surface with numerous rivers and lakes. The climate is arctic, and vegetation is of the tundra type. The Native peoples are Inuit (Eskimo), who have traditionally relied either on the seal or have followed the migratory caribou herds. Most now live in permanent settlements and seek other sources of income.

Except for a few islands in Hudson Bay and James Bay, all of the Northwest Territories' many islands are north of 60°N latitude and form the arctic archipelago, which extends north to Cape Columbia of Ellesmere Island at 83° 07' N latitude, less than 500 mi./800 km. from the North

Pole. Baffin Island, 195,927 sq. mi./507,451 sq. km., is the largest of these islands, more than twice the size of Great Britain. Islands lying north of the straits west from Lancaster Sound (which is north of Baffin Island) are known as the Queen Elizabeth Islands. The eastern islands are mountainous and average 5,900 to 6,900 ft./1,800 to 2,100 m. in height, with Mt. Barbeau (8,580 ft./2,616 m.) on northern Ellesmere Island the highest peak in the archipelago. The central islands are plateau-like, while those in the west are mainly lowland plains. Vegetation is tundra, ranging from low bush to grass.

Area: 1,322,902 sq. mi./3,426,320 sq. km., of which 51,465 sq. mi./ 133,294 sq. km. are inland water. The Northwest Territories occupies 34.4% of the area of Canada.

Mean maximum and minimum temperatures: Yellowknife, 61° F/16° C (July), −28.6° F/−19.6° C (January); Inuvik, 57° F/14° C (July); −22° F/−30° C (January); Iqaluit (formerly Frobisher Bay), 46° F/8° C (July); −15° F/ −26° C (January).

Mean annual precipitation: Yellowknife, 10.5 in./267 mm., of which 53 in./135 cm. is snow; Inuvik, 10 in./266 mm., of which 70 in./177 cm. is snow; Iqaluit, 17 in./433 mm., of which 101 in./256 cm. is snow.

POPULATION

Total population (1986 census): 52,238. Population density averaged 0.04 per sq. mi./0.015 per sq. km. Estimated population in 1991, 53,700.

Chief towns and population (1986 census): Yellowknife, the capital (11,753, estimated at 12,600 in 1991); Inuvik (3,389), Hay River (2,964), Iqaluit (2,947) and Fort Smith (2,460).

Distribution: The Northwest Territories was 46% urban and 54% rural in 1986. Of the 66 communities, most of which consist of only a few hundred people, about half are in the Mackenzie River valley.

Ethnic composition: In 1986, 33% of the population was Inuit, 14.5% Dene (North American Indian) and 4% Métis (mixed European and Indian). Taking into account both single and multiple origin, 29.5% of the population was of British (including Irish) stock. On the same basis, 7% of the population was of French origin. Other European ethnic groups, by single origin only, included Germans, 2%.

Language: In 1986, English was the mother tongue of 55% of the population and the home language of 66%. French was the mother tongue of 3% and home language of 1.5%. Other languages, chiefly those spoken by Inuit and Dene, accounted for the remaining 42% and 32.5%, respectively.

Religion: According to the 1981 census, 40% of the population was Roman Catholic, 33% Anglican and 8% United Church of Canada.

CONSTITUTION AND GOVERNMENT

The government of the Northwest Territories generally resembles that of the provinces but there are important differences. Provincial constitutions, which define the powers of the legislative and executive branches of government as well as the division of the legislative power between the federal and provincial governments, are entrenched in the Constitution Act of 1982 and are not subject to unilateral change by the federal government. By contrast, the Northwest Territories Act, which serves as the territorial constitution, is a federal statute legally subject to change at the will of Parliament.

The Northwest Territories Act vests executive authority in a federally appointed commissioner who administers the government under instructions from the federal cabinet or the minister of Indian and northern affairs. The commissioner's function is similar to that of the lieutenant governor of a province, but a lieutenant governor is constitutionally bound to follow the advice of the provincial cabinet, which is in turn responsible to the provincial legislature. The commissioner is not constitutionally bound to follow the instructions of the territorial cabinet. Also, the jurisdiction of the legislature of the Northwest Territories is defined by federal legislation and can be overridden by contrary federal legislation.

In practice, the Northwest Territories has a considerable degree of self-government. Although the commissioner still takes an active part in the government of the territory, he has been directed to seek the advice of the executive council, or cabinet, and to give that advice the fullest possible consideration. The government leader, who is chosen by the legislature, now chairs the cabinet in place of the commissioner, and the minister of finance, also chosen by the legislature, chairs the Financial Management Board, instead of the commissioner.

The federal government is committed to establishing responsible government in the Northwest Territories—that is, making the executive fully responsible to the elected legislature. Responsibility for forests, fire management, health services, for the scientific resource centers at Iqaluit, Igloolik and Inuvik, and for the Northern Canada Power Commission have been transferred to the territorial government in recent years. Further transfers are under consideration, including the federal ministry's land-titles office and Transport Canada's responsibility for arctic airports. In 1991 there were 14 departments and five regional offices.

Executive: The executive council is composed of the commissioner, who is a federal civil servant, and eight members of the Legislative Assembly, each of whom is also minister of a department or departments. The first Native commissioner, a Métis, was appointed in 1991. Executive members are collectively responsible for decisions on policy and programs, for relations with federal and provincial governments, and for the general conduct of government in the Northwest Territories. The first Native government leader was elected in 1991.

Legislature: The Northwest Territories Council, popularly called the Legislative Assembly, consists of members elected singly from a minimum of 15 and a maximum of 25 districts. They serve for up to four years. In October 1991 the newly elected Assembly consisted of 24 members; among them were nine Inuit, nine Dene or Métis, and six non-Natives. Members of the executive council are elected by the Legislative Assembly. Proceedings in English or French are simultaneously translated, if necessary, into Inuktitut and the Dene languages. Two unilingual Native members were elected to the Council in 1991. There are a number of standing and special committees. In November 1987 the Ordinary Members' Committee was formed of those legislators who were not chosen to sit on the executive council. The committee acts as an informal organization to advise and counsel ministers in the territorial cabinet.

Political parties: In the 1987 legislative elections, 63 people sought to represent one or another of the 24 districts, but without party affiliation. The imperatives of partisan politics tend to clash with the imperatives of native political culture in the Northwest Territories. In the absence of party affiliations in the Legislative Assembly, alliances have developed along regional, ethnic or philosophical lines rather than on the basis of political party.

Local government: Of the Northwest Territories' 66 communities and mining settlements in 1988, there were one city, five towns, two villages and 30 hamlets. Eight unincorporated settlements also had elected councils. The others are administered directly by the Department of Municipal and Community Affairs, which also provides financial and technical assistance to the organized municipalities.

Federal representation: The Northwest Territories sends two elected representatives to the House of Commons. Both members chosen in the 1988 elections were Liberals. The territory is represented in the Senate by one federally appointed member.

Judicial system: The Supreme Court has original jurisdiction in all civil actions not expressly excluded by statute. In 1988 it consisted of three resident judges and 28 nonresident judges, all federally appointed. The appellate court is the Court of Appeal, which consists of the chief justice of Alberta, the judges of the Court of Appeal of Alberta, one or more designated judges of the Court of Appeal of Saskatchewan, the resident judges of the Northwest Territories, and the justice of appeal resident in the Yukon. Appeals beyond this level go to the Supreme Court of Canada. The Territorial Court has jurisdiction in civil actions not exceeding $5,000, excluding actions regarding title to land; the validity of any devise, bequest or limitation; malicious prosecution; false imprisonment; libel or slander.

In 1988 this court had a chief judge and four other judges, all territorially appointed.

RECENT HISTORY

Until 1951 the government of the Northwest Territories consisted of a commissioner and executive council composed entirely of federal civil servants based in Ottawa. Starting in 1951, elected members were slowly added to the council. In 1963, for the first time, the commissioner was relieved of other administrative responsibilities. In 1967 the seat of territorial government was moved to Yellowknife, and the commissioner moved there to head the beginnings of an in-place territorial service. In that year the council was expanded to 16 members.

The territorial council of 1975—the first fully elected one—resembled a legislative assembly and so styled itself. A speaker was chosen by the members, and three members were given executive portfolios. In 1979, the assembly was enlarged to 22 seats. This assembly lobbied successfully for including aboriginal rights in the Canadian constitution.

In 1982 a plebiscite endorsed dividing the Northwest Territories into an Inuit eastern half and a Dene-Métis western half. Negotiations foundered on the problem of establishing a boundary between the two parts. The east wanted a treeline boundary that would run northwest to southeast and would divide the potentially oil-rich Beaufort Sea. The west wanted a north-south boundary line, reflecting existing transportation and communications routes.

In a second plebescite in 1992, territorial voters supported division by a narrow margin, but there was a deep regional split. In the eastern half, Inuit voted overwhelmingly for a new territory to be called Nunavut, but Dene-Metis and non-native residents of the western half opposed the split. It is expected that Nunavut will be created as part of the final settlement of Inuit land claims.

Important land-claims settlements have been under negotiation in recent years. In 1984 the Inuvialuit of the north Mackenzie basin were granted $152 million in cash and title to 36,000 sq. mi./93,240 sq. km. of land. The Dene-Métis of the Mackenzie Valley initially signed an agreement—in principle—but then split along regional (and tribal) lines, with northern groups ratifying an agreement and others rejecting. There is an agreement—in principle—with the Inuit of the eastern and central Arctic.

ECONOMY

The gross product of the Northwest Territories was more than $2.0 billion in 1989, and real annual growth had averaged 13% between 1977 and 1989. The future appears even brighter because of the likely development of its oil and gas resources. Economic growth is needed to support a population that has grown sixfold since 1931, when there were only 9,316 people in the territory.

Agriculture: A few market gardens operate in the Hay River valley.

Forestry: The inventoried forest lies in the Mackenzie River valley and in 1986 covered 237,065 sq. mi./614,000 sq. km., nearly 20% of the territory's land area, with available wood volume of 15.75 billion cu. ft./446 million cu. m., all of it federally owned and consisting about 70% of softwoods. The total approved timber harvest during 1987–88 was 2,372,566 cu. ft./67,184 cu. m., or 13.4 million board feet. Sawmills converted more than 60% of this total to lumber, with almost all the remainder being used as fuel wood. Most lumber production comes from the Cameron Hills and the Slave River valley. The value of forest products in 1985–86 was $2.8 million.

Hunting and trapping: Many of the people in the smaller communities earn most of their living by hunting, trapping and fishing. The value of fur production of 41,000 pelts during the 1989–90 season was $2.9 million, of which the more than 22,800 marten taken accounted for $1.7 million. Other commercial fur animals are lynx, beaver, muskrat and fox. Polar-bear skins still provide some income for the Inuit.

Fishing: Commercial fishing is confined mainly to Great Slave Lake, where the catch is principally trout and whitefish. Arctic char supports some commercial fishing in Inuit areas. The Northwest Territories in 1989–1990 accounted for 2,115 tons/1,921 tonnes of fish landings, almost all freshwater, valued at $2,424,000.

Mining: Metal mines generated $704 million in value in 1990. Gold production of 17.1 tons/15.6 tonnes was worth $223.8 million. Lead and zinc mining, on Baffin and Little Cornwallis islands, yielded 240,500 tons/218,241 tonnes of zinc, worth $420.6 million, and 51,340 tons/46,588 tonnes of lead, worth $55.8 million. Silver, mined in the Great Bear Lake area, yielded 21 tons/19 tonnes valued at $3.5 million. Small amounts of antimony, cadmium and copper were also produced. Quarries produced 3.6 million tons/3.3 million tonnes of sand and gravel, valued at $13.9 million, and 1.65 million tons/1.5 million tonnes of stone, worth nearly $9.1 million. In addition, 19 tons/17 tonnes of sulfur, produced during smelting operations, was worth $2.7 million. Mining and exploration companies (including oil and gas companies) purchased some $168 million in goods and services in 1987.

Energy: Oil production, chiefly from Norman Wells in the Mackenzie River valley but also from Bent Horn on Cameron Island, was 55.44 million cu. ft./1.57 million cu. m. in 1987, worth $144.5 million. Some 5.9 billion cu. ft./166 million cu. m. of natural gas, valued at $8.5 million, was produced at Pointed Mountain, near the borders with the Yukon Territory and British Columbia. An oil refinery at Norman Wells, with capacity of 5.9 million cu. ft./168,000 cu. m., meets territorial needs, and the rest of the production from Norman Wells is transported by pipeline to Zama

Lake, Alberta. Natural gas is also piped south, while the Cameron Island oil is taken by tanker to Montreal.

Exploration activity is conducted at locations in the Mackenzie River delta, bordering the Beaufort Sea, and in the arctic archipelago. In 1987, 71 licenses for oil and gas exploration were held for more than 17.8 million acres/7.2 million hectares. The Amauligak oilfield in the Beaufort Sea has reserves estimated at 4.5 billion cu. ft./127 million cu. m., and there is major exploration in the northwest Queen Elizabeth Islands, Davis Strait and northwest Baffin Island. Negotiations are under way to export 325 trillion cu. ft./9.2 trillion cu. m. of natural gas from the Mackenzie River delta and Beaufort Sea to the United States by pipeline, beginning in 1996.

Installed electrical capacity was 210 megawatts in 1987, most of it belonging to the Northern Canada Power Commission, which was bought by the territorial government from the federal government for $53 million in 1988. The commission's facilities include three hydroelectric plants on rivers in the Great Slave Lake area. Electricity production in 1987 was about 542,000 megawatt-hours, of which 55% was hydropower and 45% thermal.

Transportation: Highways link northwestern Alberta to Hay River and Yellowknife, with an extension eastward from Hay River to Fort Smith and another west and north to Fort Simpson and Wrigley. The Liard Highway connects Fort Simpson to the Alaska Highway. The Dempster Highway links Inuvik and other Mackenzie River delta communities to Dawson City in the Yukon Territory. Winter roads over frozen lakes connect some isolated communities and towns. The total road length is about 1,365 mi./ 2,200 km., mainly gravel. In 1986 there were 20,231 registered motor vehicles in the Northwest Territories, of which 17,124 were passenger cars. Four river ferry crossings intersect with the highway system. A 432-mi./ 696-km. rail line links Hay River to Grimshaw, Alberta.

The Mackenzie River has commercial water transport during the summer. A tugboat and barge fleet is based at Hay River, with a secondary base at the mouth of the Mackenzie. Communities on the northern mainland coast east of the river delta are also served by tugboat and barge. Eastern Arctic communities are visited by vessels operating out of Churchill, Manitoba; Montreal; and Halifax, Nova Scotia. In 1985 the federal government announced it would build a $500-million icebreaker capable of year-round operations in the Arctic Ocean, and in 1988 Canada and the United States reached an agreement to permit U.S. icebreakers access to arctic waters on a case-by-case basis. Cargo handled in the territory totaled 239,900 tons in 1986.

Of the 184 airfields in the territory in 1987, serving most communities with populations over 100, 14 are operated by Transport Canada as licensed airports. These will eventually devolve to the territorial government. Scheduled airline service is available between southern Canadian cities and the larger Northwest Territories communities as far north as Resolute on Cornwallis Island. An east-west service links Yellowknife and Iqaluit, with stops along the way. Almost all communities now have local air service, and chartered bush plans will fly to almost any point. Yellowknife handled 97,622 incoming and outgoing passengers in 1987.

Arts and crafts: More than one-sixth of the native population is engaged seasonally in arts and crafts programs that generated $25 million in 1987. Inuit prints and sculpture, mostly handled through 46 local cooperatives, are a major source of employment in Cape Dorset, Holman Island, Baker Lake and other communities.

Banking and finance: The Yukon and Northwest Territories had 27 bank branches in 1987, of which the Canadian Imperial Bank of Commerce had 16. Private investment in the territories totaled $609.4 million in 1987; public investment totaled $505 million.

Tourism: Part of the Wood Buffalo National Park, which supports a herd of protected bison, is in the Northwest Territories. There are also three national-park nature reserves: Nahanni, Auyuittuq and Ellsmere Island. Nahanni has been declared a United Nations World Heritage Site. The Kekerten and Northwest Passage historic parks were officially opened in 1988. The Arctic Winter Games, held every two years, include a variety of traditional Native games. The Northwest Territories has fly-in sport fishing lodges and wilderness camps, and maritime settlements are sometimes stops for cruise ships. There were nearly 60,000 visitors in 1987. The travel sector generated some $120 million in revenues during 1988.

Public finance: Territorial expenditures totaled $972 million in 1989–90, of which education accounted for 17.6%; health 16.6%; transportation 14.8%; public works 10.9%; municipal and community affairs 9.7%; Northwest Territories Housing Corporation 8.5%; and social services 8%. The general expenditure of local governments was $143 million in 1990.

Revenue for 1989–90 totaled $1.013 billion: transfers from the federal government were $816 million, own source revenue amounted to $197 million. The personal income tax is 44% of the federal income tax. Corporations and small businesses pay 12% and 5% of net income, respectively. There is no retail sales tax, but there are fuel and tobacco taxes. Other revenue is raised from licenses, fees and permits. The deficit was $6.6 million. The public debt of the Northwest Territories Power Corporation and Northwest Territories Housing Corporation together amounted to $159 million in 1989. The public debt of the territorial government itself in 1986 was $119 million.

Employment: In 1986 small business accounted for 52% of employment and public administration for 29%. The number of Native people working in the public service was 1,496 (31%) in 1988. In 1989 the government replaced its Native employment policy with an affirmative action policy which gives preference in public employment to indigenous aboriginal persons and promotes training and promotion for women, disabled, and indigenous non-aborginals. Local cooperatives, which operate a variety of services, including hotels, restaurants and retail stores, are the largest employers of Native people in the northern areas. About 2,100 people were employed by operating mines during 1988. The unemployment rate was estimated at 17% in 1987, when weekly earnings averaged $609.53, highest in Canada. In 1990 the average weekly earnings reached $733.64 (industrial aggregate).

Prices: The consumer price index rose 5% in Yellowknife between October 1988 and October 1989, compared to 5.2% for all Canada. During 1982–88 the index rose 32.6% in Yellowknife, compared to 43.8% for all Canada. In early 1991 it was 121.8 (1986 = 100).

SOCIAL SERVICES

Welfare: The federal-territorial shared-cost Canada Assistance Plan provided $18 million to a monthly average of 3,050 persons and their dependents in 1988. The federal government also provides old-age pensions and family allowances. The territorial Department of Social Services provided a monthly average of 1,541 senior citizens with an $85-a-month supplement to their federal pension benefits in 1988; total expenditure for the year was $1.5 million. The department also operates child-care facilities, including group homes and foster homes, and homes and home-care programs for the handicapped and elderly requiring assistance. In addition, it provides support for community alcohol- and drug-abuse centers and community mental health services, and it operates correctional facilities at Yellowknife, Hay River, Iqaluit and Fort Smith. Safe-shelter programs for women who are the victims of family violence are in Hay River, Spence Bay and Cambridge Bay. A facility in Fort Smith provides care and treatment programs to teenagers.

Health: The territorial Department of Health provides and administers government health insurance programs and services for eligible residents, including medical care, hospital and physician insurance, medical travel, and supplementary health benefits, including insured outpatient care, chronic care and home nursing services. The pharmacare program provides coverage for prescription drugs to eligible residents. The department also provides dental services for the status Indian (those having the legal status of Indian under the Indian Act) and Inuit population and extended health benefits to eligible residents aged 60 or over. All health facilities are under the direction of eight regional health boards, which operated five hospitals (with 298 beds) and 47 community and public health centers in 1988.

The 1987 live birthrate of 28.1 per 1,000 was almost twice the Canadian average. The leading cause of death (27%) was accidents, injuries and violence. The abortion rate of 16.5 per 1,000 live births was about average for Canada. Hospital expense per patient-day of $567.34 was the highest in Canada. There were 46 physicians in 1987—1 per 1,120 persons, compared to 1 per 467 in all Canada. There were 40 active licensed dentists.

In 1987, community nurses saw 187,782 patients and performed 281,495 services.

Housing: The Northwest Territories Housing Corporation provides rental housing for families and individuals where alternative affordable housing is unavailable. Through local housing associations it managed, operated and maintained more than 4,200 public housing units in 1988, with rents based on income. It also provides materials packages to approved applicants who wish to build their own homes and provides financial assisstance for eligible homeowners to make repairs. The value of residential construction permits in the Northwest Territories was $22.9 million in 1987. In 1986, the average gross monthly rental was $360, below the national average, but the average monthly payment (with mortgage) of $1,014 was the highest in Canada.

EDUCATION

School enrollment is compulsory between the age of 6 and 15. Enrollment in elementary and secondary schools was 13,386 in 1987–88, all public. Schools in three of the territory's five administrative regions were run by divisional boards of education in 1988. The Arctic College had campuses at Fort Smith, Rankin Inlet, Inuvik and Iqaluit, offering the first year of university studies and adult education programs. An apprentice program had 431 enrollees. In addition, 950 territory sttudents were attending outside universities or technical institutions in 1988, 345 with financial assistance from the territorial government.

MASS MEDIA

Newspapers and periodicals: There are no daily newspapers in the Northwest Territories. There were six weekly newspapers in 1988, two in Yellowknife and one each in Fort Smith, Hay River, Inuvik and Iqaluit. The one with the largest paid circulation (5,977) was the *Yellowknifer,* published twice weekly. Also published in Yellowknife, six times a year, was *Up Here: Life in Canada's North,* with circulation of 16,000.

Broadcasting: In 1988 there were six AM and six FM radio stations. One of the latter broadcasts full-time, and five part-time, in Native languages. There were television stations in Inuvik and Yellowknife, both licensees of the Canadian Broadcasting Corporation. Yellowknife had a cable television system with 3,100 subscribers. Satellite channels now make it possible to transmit radio and television programs to even the most remote northern communities.

BIOGRAPHICAL SKETCHES

Nellie J. Cournoyea.   Government leader. Minister of energy, mines and petroleum resources and Northwest Territories Power Corporation. Born in

Aklavik in 1940, Cournoyea was station manager for CBC Northern Services and administrator of the Committee for Original People's Entitlement. She belongs to the Inuvialuit people and was first elected to the Legislative Assembly in 1979. She served as minister of renewable resources and minister of culture and communications, 1983–85. In 1987 she became minister of health and minister of energy, mines and resouces. The following year she was also chosen minister of public works and highways. In November 1991 she was elected government leader following her reelection to the Legislative Assembly in October.

Dennis Glen Patterson. Minister of justice, municipal and community affairs, safety and public services and Workers' Compensation Board. Born December 30, 1948 in Vancouver, Patterson was graduated from the University of Alberta in 1969 and received a law degree from Dalhousie University, Nova Scotia, in 1971. He was the first director of the Frobisher Bay (now Iqaluit) Legal Services Center, 1975–81. A member of the Legislative Assembly since 1979, Patterson was minister of education, 1981–88, and minister of aboriginal rights and constitutional development, 1984–87. He was elected government leader in 1987. In 1991 he was reelected to the Assembly and to the cabinet.

Stephen Kakfwi. Minister of intergovernmental and aboriginal affairs, and personnel. President of the Dene Nation, 1985–87, Kakfwi was elected to the Legislative Assembly in 1987 and was chosen minister of government services, minister of aboriginal rights and constitutional development, and minister responsible for the Northwest Territories Housing Corporation. In 1988 he was also named deputy government leader, Minister of safety and public services, minister responsible for the Workers' Compensation Boards and minister of education. In 1991 he was reelected to the Assembly and to the cabinet.

Titus Allooloo. Minister of education, culture and communications; minister of transportation. Born near Pond Inlet in 1953, Allooloo became mayor of Pond Inlet in 1975. He was elected to the Legislative Assembly in 1987 and was named minister of culture and communications and minister of renewable resources in the same year. In November 1991 he was reelected to the Assembly and cabinet.

117

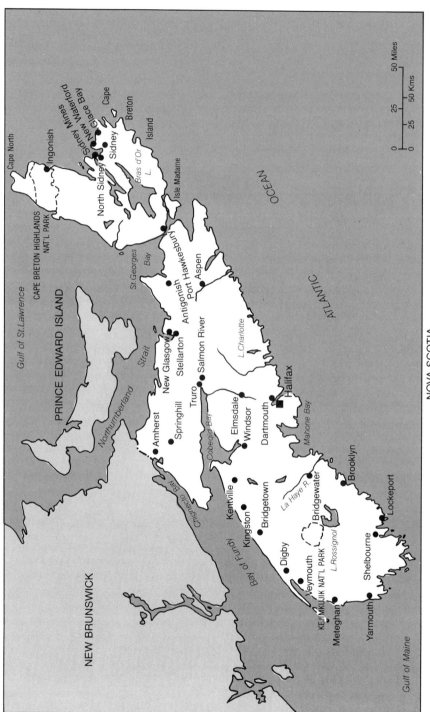

NOVA SCOTIA

NOVA SCOTIA

GEOGRAPHY

Features: Nova Scotia is bounded on the north by the Northumberland Strait, which separates it from Prince Edward Island, and by the Gulf of St. Lawrence; on the east and south by the Atlantic Ocean; and on the west by the Bay of Fundy and the province of New Brunswick. Discounting its 3,809 coastal islands, it consists of two parts: peninsular Nova Scotia, attached to New Brunswick by the narrow Chignecto Isthmus, and Cape Breton Island, which is separated from the peninsula by the narrow Strait of Canso. Both parts belong to the Atlantic Upland. On the peninsula, running parallel to the Bay of Fundy, are two parallel ranges of rocky headlands divided by the fertile Annapolis River valley. Another fertile region lies along the Northumberland Strait coast. South of this coast is the Cobequid Range, which extends into the Pictou-Cumberland area of the northeastern peninsula. The long Atlantic coastline is marked by numerous inlets, islands, bays and coves. Here is found Halifax, the province's capital and largest city, and the chief port of the Atlantic Provinces. Fishing is particularly important to the southwestern part of the peninsula, facing the Bay of Fundy.

The southern part of Cape Breton Island is mainly lowland, but the northern part is a wooded plateau that rises to the province's high point, 1,745 ft./532 m. The chief center of population and economic activity is Sydney, on the northeastern coast of the island.

Area: 21,425 sq. mi./55,491 sq. km., including 1,023 sq. mi./2,650 sq. km. of inland water. The province makes up only 0.6% of the total area of Canada.

Mean maximum and minimum temperatures: Halifax 64° F/18° C (July), 27° F/−3° C (January).

Mean annual precipitation: Halifax 50 in./1,282 mm., of which 85 in./216.5 cm. is snow.

POPULATION

Total population (1986 census): 873,176. Population density averaged 41 per sq. mile/16 per sq. km. The 1990 population was estimated at 895,700.

119

Chief towns and populations (1986 census): Halifax, the capital (113,577; metropolitan area 295,990; estimated at 312,000 in 1990); Dartmouth (65,243), Sydney (27,754), Glace Bay (20,467), Truro (12,124) and New Glasgow (10,022).

Distribution: The population was 54% urban in 1986. About one-third of the people lived in the Halifax metropolitan area. Another 20% lived on Cape Breton Island, which includes Sydney and Glace Bay.

Ethnic composition: Taking into account both single and multiple origin, in 1986 81% of the population was British (including Irish) in origin, and 10% French (Acadians). About 2% of the population was of German single origin, and 1% was of Dutch single origin. There were 5,575 North American Indians. There are also 8,000 blacks, descendants of those who came from the American colonies or the United States.

Language: In 1986, English was the mother tongue of 94% of the population and the home language of 96%. French was the mother tongue of 4% and the home language of 3%. Other languages accounted for the remaining 2% and 1%, respectively. Legislation enacted in 1981 provides for Acadian children, the descendants of the French colony in the Maritimes, to be taught in French wherever their numbers make it practicable.

Religion: In 1981, 37% of the population was Roman Catholic. Adherents of the United Church constituted 20%; Anglicans, 16%; Baptists, 12%; Presbyterians, 5%; and Lutherans, 1.5%

CONSTITUTION AND GOVERNMENT

One of the four original provinces of Canada, Nova Scotia, like the other provinces, has a government in theory headed by the lieutenant governor, representing the queen, who is sovereign of Canada and also sovereign of Great Britain. In practice, the chief executive is the premier, who heads an executive council, or cabinet. Cabinet ministers are selected from the elected representatives of the majority party in the legislature, and each is responsible for a government department. In addition to government departments, there are agencies, boards, commissions and crown (public) corporations. The civil service has the right of collective bargaining. There is also an ombudsman. As in the other Canadian provinces, the executive is responsible to the legislature and relies on the support of the majority of the legislature to remain in power. The minimum voting age is 18.

Executive: In early 1991 the executive council had 22 members, and there were 21 government departments. A new premier, Donald Cameron, elected by the party after the resignation of John Buchanan, reduced the cabinet to 17 members and combined some departments.

Legislature: There is a single-chamber General Assembly of 52 members, each representing a separate, single constituency. As in the other provinces, the party that commands majority support in the legislature forms the executive, and the next largest becomes the official opposition. Elections are usually held every three or four years but may be called earlier if the government loses a vote in the legislature on a major issue.

Political parties: The traditional Liberal and Conservative (since 1943 Progressive Conservative) parties continue to prevail in Nova Scotia. The Liberals ruled the province from 1867 to 1956 except for two short periods of Conservative power. The Conservatives came into office in 1956 and continued in power until 1970. The Liberals ruled again from 1970 to 1978, when the Conservatives were elected to office. They were returned to office in 1981, 1984 and 1988. In general, there have been no great ethnic, religious or class antagonisms in Nova Scotia, and both parties attempt to accommodate all interests. The New Democratic Party (before 1961 the Co-operative Commonwealth Federation) has contested every provincial election since 1941 and since 1974 has polled more than 19% of the popular vote, but it elects very few legislators. Farther left than the two mainstream parties, the NDP receives some support from the Cape Breton working class and the peninsular urban middle class.

Local government: Nova Scotia has 18 counties, of which 12 are rural municipalities and the other six are each divided into two districts, each a separate rural municipality. There were three cities and 36 towns in 1987. These are politically and administratively independent, while 26 incorporated villages (in 1988) are within the rural municipalities. There are also a number of boards and commissions, such as rural fire districts and local service commissions. More than 700 special-purpose bodies have the power to levy taxes. Local government is financed by the property tax, a number of variants such as the occupancy tax, and provincial and federal grants.

Federal representation: Nova Scotia is represented in Parliament by 10 federally appointed senators and 11 elected members of the House of Commons. The 1988 federal elections sent six Liberals and five Conservatives to the House of Commons.

Judicial system: The highest court in the province is the federally appointed Supreme Court of Nova Scotia, which is divided into trial and appeals divisions. The former had, in 1988, a chief justice and seven other judges; the latter had a chief justice and 12 other judges. Beyond this level, appeals go to the Supreme Court of Canada. The federally appointed County Court has original jurisdiction in actions not exceeding $50,000 and actions of replevin not exceeding $2,000; in 1988, this court sat in seven locations and had 10 judges. County Court judges also act as judges of Probate Court, which has jurisdiction over wills and estates. Below this level is Provincial Court, which in 1988 sat in 14 locations and had 28 judges, including a chief judge. Also provincially appointed are the judges of Small Claims Court, which has jurisdiction over most actions not exceeding $2,000. Finally, there is a Municipal Court with provincially appointed judges to hear matters regulated by municipal bylaws. It has jurisdiction over actions regarding debt, contract or tort where the amount does not exceed $500 and the title or right of possession of real property is not in dispute.

In April 1991, the legislature accepted a plan to merge the County and Supreme Courts, to create four judicial regions and to reduce the number of levels in the system to three and then two.

RECENT HISTORY

The accession to power of the Conservative Party in 1956 was a tribute to the leadership of Robert Stanfield, who was premier for the next 14 years. He delivered on a promise to improve roads, later established comprehensive secondary schools, and extended French-language education through secondary school. He also ended some of the worst aspects of party patronage in government appointments and contracts. A major revitalization of downtown Halifax was started, and the Halifax and Canso harbors were expanded. His major emphasis, however, was to attract outside industry. Among the achievements of his first term was the establishment of auto-assembly plants in Dartmouth and Sydney.

In 1967, Stanfield resigned to become the national Conservative Party leader and was succeeded by G. I. "Ike" Smith. To prevent the Sydney steel plant and Sydney-area coal mines from closing, the province took them over. But government support for two mismanaged private installations—a Glace Bay heavy-water plant and a Stellarton stereo and color television factory—proved financially disastrous. In 1970 the Conservatives were unseated and the Liberals, with Gerald Regan as premier, came to power.

The new government took over the privately owned light and power company and salvaged the Halifax shipyard. The government persistently incurred a deficit in spite of increased taxes. Unemployment and inflation both were on the rise, and there were frequent labor disputes in the public sector. In 1978, the electorate turned to the Conservatives again, and their leader, John Buchanan, became premier. Under Buchanan, the fishery industry was reorganized with federal and provincial support, two gold mines started production, and North America's first tidal-power generating station opened in Annapolis Royal. On the whole, the 1980s saw economic progress in the province, although Cape Breton's sick economy worsened. After easy victories in 1981 and 1984, the Conservatives were again returned to power in 1988, but by a reduced margin.

In 1990 the Royal Canadian Mounted Police was probing charges by a senior Nova Scotia civil servant of corruption, and there were allegations that Premier Buchanan had been receiving secret payments from the provincial party and a trust fund to supplement his salary. In September 1990 Buchanan resigned to take a senate seat and Roger Bacon became acting premier. In February 1991 Donald Cameron became leader and the premier. The loss of Buchanan's seat at a by-election in July reduced the party to 26 seats in the 52-member Legislative Assembly.

ECONOMY

Nova Scotia is the most prosperous of Canada's four Atlantic provinces, and Halifax is the region's leading port and financial and trade center; however, this region is the poorest in Canada, and the province suffers from its economic problems. Nova Scotia's natural resources are limited, its industries find it hard to compete with rivals, and it is distant from central Canadian and U.S. markets.

The gross provincial product was $14.9 billion in 1990, which, discounting inflation, was a 7.5% increase over 1988 and a 34% increase since 1985. By sector in 1990, community, business and personal services accounted for 25%; finance, insurance and real estate, 15.3%; wholesale and retail trade, 13% each; manufacturing, 12.4%; public administration and defense, 9.9%; transportation and communications, 8.5%; construction, 7.7%; utilities, 2.8%; fishing, 2.5%; agriculture, 1.2%; forestry, 0.8%; and mining, 0.6%. Per capita income averaged $18,151 in 1990, the highest in the Atlantic Provinces. Although only 82% of the national average of $22,184, this was a considerable increase over the 75% recorded in 1981.

Agriculture: Nova Scotia's agriculture is of only local importance, but subsistence living on family farms has been common throughout wide areas of the province. About 1,186,000 acres/538,000 hectares, or 10% of the land area, is farmed. The largest cultivated areas are found in the Annapolis River valley and in some parts of northern Nova Scotia. There were 4,283 farms in 1986, averaging 240 acres/97 hectares in size.

According to preliminary 1990 statistics, total farm cash receipts came to $313 million. (Net income from farming operations was $75.5 million in 1990.) Of 1988 cash receipts, livestock and products accounted for 72% and crops, 23%. Dairy products ($87 million) was the single largest sector, followed by poultry and cattle and calves. Among crops, fruits ($25 million) was the largest sector.

Forestry: Nova Scotia had 15,444 sq. mi./40,000 sq. km. (about 75% of the land area) in inventoried forests in 1986, with 8.6 billion cu. ft./244 million cu. m. of wood available. About 70% was privately owned and 28% provincially owned, and about 62% of the trees were softwoods. Forest production in 1987 was 145 million cu. ft./4.1 million cu. m., of which 91% consisted of softwoods. Pulpwood amounted to 74% of the total and logs to 26%. In 1990 lumber production was 15.8 million board feet. Forestry production was valued at $45.6 million in 1986.

Fishing: Nova Scotia ranks second to Newfoundland in fish (and shellfish) landings by quantity and second to British Columbia in landings by value. In 1986, there were nearly 15,000 fishermen and more than 6,100 fishing vessels in the province, the latter ranging from small inshore boats to large offshore trawlers. A total of 267 harbors are maintained specifically for the fishing industry. The most important species are cod, scallops, lobster, haddock and herring. By quantity, fish landings in 1989 came to 511,000 tons/463,603 tonnes, of which cod accounted for 26%, herring for 17.5% and scallops for 17%. Total value came to $411 million, of which lobster accounted for 30%, cod for 19% and scallops for 19%.

Mining: Nova Scotia is not well endowed in non-energy minerals. Two gold mines opened in 1987, a small lead-zinc mine recently opened at Gay's River, and a tin mine at East Kemptville began full operation in 1986—the only primary tin mine in North America. The value of metals production was $52 million in 1990. The chief minerals, however, are gypsum and cement. Gypsum, found largely in Hants and Cumberland counties, is quarried more extensively than anywhere else in Canada and is sent to the United States for processing. Production was 6.6 million tons/ 6.0 million tonnes worth $53 million, in 1990. Cement production was worth $58 million. Sand and gravel production of 7.6 million tons/6.9 million tonnes was worth $22.9 million, and stone production of 8.0 million tons/7.3 million tonnes was valued at $39.5 million. Salt production is worth about $30 million a year. The total value of all non-energy minerals in 1990 was $253 million; of all minerals, $453 million.

Energy: Nova Scotia is Canada's third-ranking coal producer. About 1 billion tons of the mineral are considered recoverable. Seven mines produced 3.7 million tons/3.35 million tonnes in 1990 (almost all of it in Cape Breton County), worth $199 million. There is a long history of mining disasters; on May 9, 1992, an explosion at the Westray mine in Plymouth killed 26 miners. Substantial reserves of natural gas and smaller reserves of oil have been found by the drilling of more than 100 exploratory offshore oil wells since 1967. Production is possible in the area of Sable Island, which is in the Atlantic Ocean about 180 mi./290 km. east of Halifax. A public corporation, Nova Scotia Resources Ltd., invests in energy exploration and production.

A public corporation, Nova Scotia Power Company, was responsible for 97% of all electricity generation in the province in 1988–89, which totaled 8.7 million megawatt hours, of which 89% was thermal and the rest hydroelectric, wind or tidal. Installed capacity was 2.2 million megawatts. In 1988–89, coal was the fuel for 61% of the province's electrical energy (10% lower than usual owing to a coal mine strike); oil made up 22% and hydro 11.9%. The public Tidal Power Corporation administers the Annapolis Royal tidal-power project on the Bay of Fundy. It started generating 20 megawatts of electric power in 1984, using the largest turbine ever built for hydroelectric development.

Manufacturing: More than 800 manufacturing establishments produced output that 1990 preliminary statistics valued at nearly $5.0 billion. Several hundred new manufacturing plants have located since the 1960s in the 40 industrial parks throughout the province. These parks are owned and operated by the public Nova Scotia Business Capital Corporation, which also offers loan financing and provides loan guarantees.

The steel industry, located in Sydney and Pictou, has a 100-year history of producing ships, boats, railcars and other fabricated-steel items. Three Michelin tire factories are in the province (at Granton, Bridgewater and Waterville), and Pratt & Whitney Canada produces aircraft engine components in Halifax County, at the same industrial park that houses Litton Industries' facility for aircraft navigational systems. Hermes Electronics Ltd. manufactures submarine-detection devices in Dartmouth. Magnus Aerospace Manufacturing Corporation has a supercomputer in Sydney, the first in Atlantic Canada. Two electronic navigational-equipment manufacturers (Intronav and Micronav) are also in Sydney.

Volvo Canada Ltd. has an auto-assembly plant on the outskirts of Halifax. Halifax and Dartmouth have shipbuilding facilities. Dominion Textile Inc. produces industrial fabric, fabric conveyer belts, and cotton and polyester yarns in Yarmouth. Moosehead Beer is brewed in Dartmouth. Two oil refineries in the province had in 1989 a combined capacity of 208 million cu. ft./5.9 million cu. m. a year.

Food products was the biggest manufacturing sector in 1990, with shipments valued at nearly $1.3 billion, of which slightly more than half consisted of fish products turned out at about 235 processing plants in the province. Next in importance was paper and allied products ($602 million), followed by transportation equipment ($150 million) and wood products ($171 million).

Transportation: Roads in 1987 totaled 16,031 mi./25,800 km., of which 8,333 mi./13,411 km. were unpaved. There were 505,116 registered motor vehicles in Nova Scotia in 1986, of which 337,120 were passenger cars. The Trans-Canada Highway runs between Amherst and North Sydney. There were 1,202 mi./747 km. of mainline railway track in 1986. Passenger train lines in 1987 ran from Halifax to Sydney, Halifax to Yarmouth, and Halifax to Montreal via Amherst. In 1987, Air Canada had service from Halifax to major Canadian and international centers; it also used regional airports at Yarmouth and Sydney. Eastern Provincial Airways acted as a regional carrier and also flew between Halifax and Toronto. Canadian Airlines International flew between Halifax and Montreal. Halifax International Airport handled a total of 2,035,150 arriving and departing passengers in 1987. Four seagoing car ferries connected Yarmouth, Digby, Caribou and North Sydney to Saint John, New Brunswick; Woods Islands, Prince Edward Island; and points in Maine and Newfoundland. Ferry passengers totaled 1,454,600 in 1988.

Halifax is Canada's busiest Atlantic port, a full day closer to Europe than other mainland ports. It has three containerized cargo terminals; Sydney and Port Tupper are also deepwater ports. Of 20.3 million tonnes of cargo handled in Nova Scotia ports in 1990, Halifax accounted for 18.5 million tons/16.8 million tonnes; Sydney accounted for nearly 1.3 million tons. Cargo tonnage reached 25.1 million tons/22.8 million tonnes in 1987, of which 73% was international cargo.

Wholesale and retail trade: Wholesale trade in 1990 amounted to more than 4.6 billion. Retail trade amounted to $6.1 billion.

Foreign trade; Nova Scotia foreign exports in 1990 totaled $2.35 billion, 66% to the United States. Fish and marine products accounted for 34% of the value of exports, followed by plastic and plastic articles, 17%; wood pulp, 13%; and paper and paperboard, 11%. Imports came to $3.2 billion, of which 43% came from the EEC, 21% from other OECD countries and 14% from the United States. Total re-exports amounted to $138.6 million.

Banking and finance: In 1988 Nova Scotia had 253 bank branches, of which the Royal Bank of Canada had 86 and the Bank of Nova Scotia had 70. Deposits totaled $3.6 billion in March 1988. Public and private investment totaled $3.7 billion in 1987.

Construction: The total value of construction in the province was nearly $2.8 billion in 1990. Of the total, $1.9 billion was for new and repair construction of buildings and $950,000 of this was residential.

Tourism: Nova Scotia has two national parks: Kejimkujik and Northern Cape Breton Island. Fortress Louisbourg National Historic Park is also there. Nova Scotia also has 122 provincial parks with a total area of 151 sq. mi./ 243 sq. km. In 1988 Nova Scotia had 1,222,000 tourist visitations, both Canadian and foreign. In 1990 there were 188,400 foreign tourist visits.

Public finance: Total expenditures of the provincial government for 1990–91 were estimated at $4.5 billion, of which health was expected to account for 27.2%, education for 22.8% and debt service for 17.2%. Total revenues were projected at $3.9 billion, of which income taxes were expected to account for 26%, the sales (health services) tax for 16% and federal payments for 39%. The personal income tax rate in Nova Scotia was 59.5% of the federal tax in 1990; the corporate-income tax rate was 15%. The sales tax was 10%. There was a capital tax of 3.0% on financial institutions.

Employment: In 1990, the labor force was 424,000, of which an average of 379,000 were employed. The 1989 average unemployment rate of 9.9% was the lowest in the province since 1981, but the rate was back up to 10.5% in 1990. In each year since 1986 the rate was the lowest for the Atlantic Provinces but also higher than the Canadian average rate. The 1990 participation rate of 62% of the potential labor force was below the Canadian average of 67%. By sector, 26% of those employed were in goods producing industries: 2.3% in agriculture, 5.5% in other primary industries, 11.4% in manufacturing, 6.8% in construction. Another 73% were in service producing industries: 6.8% in transportation, communication and other utilities; 18.4% in trade; 4.8% in finance, insurance or real estate; 34.3% in services; and 9.1% in public administration. Public-sector employment in Nova Scotia, including hospitals, schools, etc., was 95,578 in 1988: 37,894 federal, 27,514 provincial, and 30,350 local. Weekly earnings in Nova Scotia in 1990 averaged $458.42. The Nova Scotia Federation of Labour has a membership of about 65,000. Many of its affiliates are public-service unions, along with the Steelworkers and the United Food and Commercial Workers Union.

Prices: Consumer prices in Halifax increased 41% from 1982 through 1988, slightly below the national average. Between October 1988 and October 1989, they increased by 4.9%, compared to the national average of 5.2%, and by October 1990 they had risen a further 4.9% as compared to 4.8% for all Canada.

SOCIAL SERVICES

Welfare: The jointly funded federal-provincial Canada Assistance Plan, in fiscal 1987 spent $165.2 million to aid an average of 73,000 beneficiaries in Nova Scotia. The Department of Community Services provides financial assistance to individuals and families whose income is insufficient for basic needs and social services to individuals and families who cannot cope on their own. The department also provides child care, custody, protection, and adoption services, and foster homes. It operates a youth-training center, a center for young offenders, and four facilities for severely mentally retarded children. It also provides grants for day care.

Health: The federal and provincial governments share the costs of comprehensive hospital and medical-care insurance programs. These two plans were merged in 1973 under the Nova Scotia Health Services and Insurance Commission. To these free services have been added dental care for children and prescription drugs for those 65 years and over. Other provincial health programs include drug-dependency treatment services and subsidies to ambulance operators. The Department of Health and Fitness has divisions of dental health, nursing service, public-health engineering, nutrition, tuberculosis, hospitals and nursing homes, child and maternal health, communicable-disease control, industrial health and emergency health services. Both this department and the Department of Community Services have roles in subsidizing home-care services and aid to the disabled.

The 1988 birthrate of 14.0 per thousand people was below the Canadian average, while the death rate of 8.3 was above the national average. The abortion rate of 14.2 per hundred live births was below the national average. There were 49 hospitals in Nova Scotia in 1986–87, with 5,827 beds. The hospital expense of $414.95 per patient-day in 1987–88 was above the national average. In 1987, there were 1,912 physicians in the province, with one physician per 461 persons, about the national average. There were 397 active licensed dentists and 8,933 registered nurses in 1987.

Housing: Provincial rental subsidies and property-tax rebates are available for eligible senior citizens. The Department of Housing subsidized, in 1989–90, more than 10,700 public-housing units, 1,300 rural- and Native-housing units, and 326 rent-supplement units. More than 1,200 new housing units were expected to be constructed during 1989–90 as a result of government-sponsored programs. A further 3,200 units were expected to qualify for assistance under government repair and renovation programs.

There were 3,681 housing starts in Nova Scotia centers of over 10,000 in 1991, of which 1,593 were single or semi-detached homes. Eighty percent of the housing starts were in the Halifax metropolitan area but 67% of this total was for apartment units. The value of residential building permits was $479 million. The 1986 census found that of the 294,645 homes in the province, 72% were owned rather than rented, well above the national average. The average 1986 gross rent was $418 a month and the average home payment (with mortgage) was $638, both below the national averages.

EDUCATION

School enrollment in Nova Scotia is free and compulsory between the ages of 6 and 16. Enrollment in 1988–89 in elementary and secondary schools was 171,220; during 1987–88, when total enrollment was 172,959, public school enrollment was 169,478. Nova Scotia does not have separate Protestant and Catholic public school systems, but under a long-time arrangement certain public schools have been staffed with Catholic teachers and allowed to engage in religious instruction after regular hours. There were 14 regional vocational schools in 1987.

University enrollment in 1989–90 was 25,706 full-time and 8,282 part-time. Nova Scotia has 11 institutions of higher learning, of which the largest, Dalhousie University, in Halifax, had 8,843 students in 1987–88. The Université Sainte-Anne in Church Point is the only one that offers instruction in French. There is also a fisheries training center, a nautical institute, and a Canadian Coast Guard college. Three modern institutes of technology similar to community colleges also offered postsecondary education in 1987.

MASS MEDIA

Newspapers and periodicals: Nova Scotia has seven dailies, of which the largest are in Halifax and Sydney. Halifax's *Chronicle Herald,* a morning paper, and *Mail Star,* an evening paper, are under the same ownership; 1992 circulation was 86,932 and 51,957 respectively. Halifax's *Daily News,* a morning tabloid, has a daily circulation of 25,200 and a Sunday circulation of 36,200. Sydney's *Cape Breton Post* had daily circulation of 30,970. The province's other dailies are in Amherst, New Glasgow and Truro.

In 1988, there were 28 weekly and one monthly newspaper and 17 periodicals. The largest periodical was *Atlantic Co-operator* (circulation 74,000), a monthly on the cooperative movement published in Antigonish.

Broadcasting: In 1988, there were 18 AM and 15 FM radio stations. Of the 17 television stations, four broadcast in French and nine were rebroadcast stations. There were 48 operating cable television systems in the province in 1987, with 190,002 subscribers.

BIOGRAPHICAL SKETCHES

Donald William Cameron. Premier of Nova Scotia. Cameron was born on May 20, 1946 in Egerton, Pictou County, Nova Scotia. He attended McGill University and worked as a dairy farmer. He was first elected to the Nova Scotia Legislature in 1974 and was reelected in 1978, 1981, 1984 and 1988. He served as minister of fisheries and of education, 1978–1980 (resigned); minister of industry, trade and technology (1988); and minister responsible for the administration of the Nova Scotia Research Foundation Corp. Act and minister responsible for the Advisory Council on Applied Science and Technology (1988). He became leader of the Progressive Conservative Party on February 9, 1991 and premier of Nova Scotia on February 26, 1991.

Thomas Johnson McInnis. Deputy premier; minister of industry, trade and technology; chairman, Policy Board; minister for small business development. McInnis was born in 1945 in Sheet Harbour, Nova Scotia. He attended St. Mary's University and Dalhousie Law School, and then went to work as a lawyer. He was first elected to the Nova Scotia legislature in 1978 and was reelected in 1984 and 1988. He served as minister of transport (1978–81), municipal affairs (1981–85), education (1985–87) and community services (1987–88), and as attorney general (1988–91). He became deputy premier in 1991.

Vincent James Maclean. Leader of the Liberal Party. Maclean was born on December 8, 1944 at Sydney, Nova Scotia, and was educated at St. Francis Xavier University, the University of New Brunswick, and St. Mary's University and worked as a teacher. He was first elected to the Nova Scotia legislature in 1974 and was reelected in 1978, 1981 and 1988. He served as speaker in 1974–1976. He was appointed minister of lands and forests and minister responsible for administration of the Energy Measures Organization (Nova Scotia) Act and Regulations. He was elected leader of the Liberal Party and became leader of the opposition in February 1986. In the Liberal Party convention of February 1992 he received only a 51% vote of confidence, and on March 3, 1992 he was removed by the Liberal caucus as leader of the opposition and replaced by Dr. Bill Gillis. He remained leader of the party outside the legislature, pending election of a new leader.

129

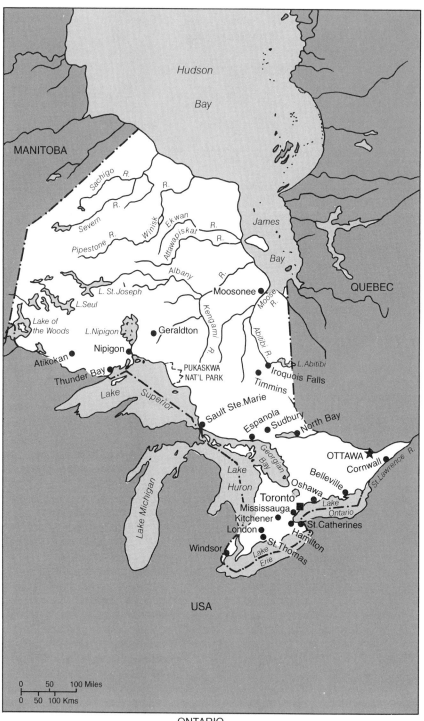

ONTARIO

ONTARIO

GEOGRAPHY

Features: The province of Ontario, second largest in Canada, is bounded on the north by Hudson Bay and James Bay; on the east by Quebec; on the south by the St. Lawrence River and lakes Ontario, Erie, Huron and Superior, which border the U.S. states of New York, Pennsylvania, Ohio and Michigan, and also by the U.S. state of Minnesota; and on the west by Manitoba.

The Canadian Precambrian Shield covers two-thirds of the province, including most of the north except the Hudson Bay lowland. The average elevation is about 1,000 ft./305 m., but the rugged area north and east of Sault Sainte Marie is higher, and Ishpatina Ridge, at 2,273 ft./693 m. the highest point in the province, is found there. Except for a few areas north of Georgian Bay and the Rainy River area in the west, this region is unsuitable for agriculture, but mining and forestry companies are active. The southeastern peninsula of the province, which touches lakes Ontario, Erie and Huron, consists mainly of rolling hills and plains. The extreme eastern corner, between the Ottawa and St. Lawrence rivers, is also a plain. These are the productive areas of the province, with most of its agriculture, industry and population. The Hudson Bay lowland is sparsely settled, and economic activity is limited to fur trapping.

In addition to parts of four Great Lakes, Ontario contains thousands of lakes, especially in the western part, which has the largest ones, Lake Nipigon and the Lake of the Woods. A number of major rivers, including the Albany, drain the Canadian Shield and Hudson Bay lowland, emptying into Hudson Bay or James Bay. Other rivers, including the Ottawa and the Thames, flow into the Great Lakes or the St. Lawrence River. The Niagara River, between lakes Erie and Ontario, flows over the Niagara Falls.

Area: 412,581 sq. mi./1,068,587 sq. km., including 68,490 sq. mi./ 177,389 sq. km. of inland water. The province comprises 10.7% of the area of Canada.

Mean maximum and minimum temperatures: Toronto 72°F/22°C (July), 23°F/ −5° (January); Ottawa 70°F/21°C (July), 12°F/−11°C (January); Thunder Bay 64°F/18°C (July); 5°F/−15°C (Jan.).

Mean annual precipitation: Toronto 32 in./801 mm., of which 55 in./139 cm. is snow; Ottawa 35 in./879 mm., of which 80 in./227 cm. is snow; Thunder Bay 28 in./712 mm., of which 84 in./213 cm. is snow.

POPULATION

Total population (1986 Census): 9,101,694. With 36% of the population, Ontario was Canada's most populous province and accounted for half the growth in the national population between the 1981 and 1986 censuses. Population density is 26.5 per sq. mi./10.2 per sq. km. The population was estimated as 9,803,400 in 1990. Ontario benefits from both interprovincial and international immigration. Between 1981 and 1986, the province had net in-migration of 99,350 from other provinces. Ontario was the intended destination of 84,807 foreign immigrants (56% of the Canadian total) in 1987.

Chief towns and populations (1986 census): Toronto, the capital (612,289; metropolitan area 3,427,168; estimated 1990 3,751,700, the largest in Canada); Ottawa, the federal capital (300,763; metropolitan area, which includes Hull, Quebec, 819,263; estimated 1990 863,900—Ontario part 651,900); Hamilton (307,690), London (274,981), Oshawa (203,543), Windsor (193,111), Sudbury (152,476), Kitchener (150,604), Thunder Bay (112,272) and Peterborough (105,056).

Distribution: Ontario is the most urbanized province in Canada, with 82% of the population classified as urban in 1986. Nearly half the population lives in the so-called Golden Horseshoe conurbation along the western end of Lake Ontario, which includes St. Catharines, Hamilton, Toronto and Oshawa. Northern Ontario, with nearly 90% of the land, contains only 10% of the population.

Ethnic composition: Taking into account both single and multiple background, 57% of the population was of British (including Irish) or partly British origin in 1986. On the same basis, 10% was French or partly French. By single origin only, ethnic Italians formed 5% of the population; Germans, 3%; Dutch, Chinese and Portuguese, 2% each; and Poles, Ukrainians, and East Indians (including Pakistanis), 1% each. North American Indians numbered 51,165.

Language: In 1986, English was the mother tongue of 78% of the population and the home language of 87%. French was the mother tongue of 5% and the home language of 4%. Other languages accounted for the remaining 17% and 9%, respectively. Legislation guarantees an education in French to any student in the province desiring it.

Religion: In 1981, 52% of the population was Protestant and 36% Roman or Ukrainian Catholic. The largest Protestant denominations were United Church (19%), Anglican (14%), Presbyterian (6%), Baptist (3%) and Lutheran (3%). Jews and Eastern Orthodox Christians comprised 2% each, and Muslims and Hindus, about 1% combined.

CONSTITUTION AND GOVERNMENT

Ontario is one of the four original provinces of the 1867 Canadian confederation. Like the other provinces, it has an executive headed by a lieutenant governor who represents the sovereign of Canada and the sovereign of Great Britain. In practice, the executive is headed by a premier who is the leader of the party that commands a majority in the legislature. The cabinet ministers are appointed by the premier from legislative members, and they head government departments. In Ontario, as in the other provinces, the executive is responsible to the legislature and cannot stay in office if defeated in the legislature on a vote concerning a major issue.

Executive: The premier heads an executive council consisting, in 1991, of 27 members. In addition to the 28 government departments, there are about 700 crown (public) corporations, agencies, boards and commissions. Some, of which Ontario Hydro is the most prominent, have a large measure of independence, while others are little more than ordinary departmental units. The province has an ombudsman.

Legislature: The single-chambered Legislative Assembly has 130 members, each of whom is elected by a single district for a maximum term of five years. Elections are customarily held before the completion of a five-year period, but the length of service can, in extraordinary circumstances, be extended by legislative action. All Canadian citizens over the age of 18 and resident in Ontario are eligible to vote. Following elections, the lieutenant governor calls on the leader of the party with the most legislative members to become premier and form a government. Members of the second-largest party in the legislature form the official opposition.

Political parties: Although the Liberal and Conservative (since 1943 Progressive Conservative) parties have historically commanded the most support, several third parties have elected members to the Legislative Assembly. Of these, the Co-operative Commonwealth Federation, formed in 1932–33, continues as the New Democratic Party; it became the government in Ontario for the first time in 1990. Conservative governments ruled the province continuously from 1943 to 1985, when the Liberals took office with New Democrat support. Since 1967, all three parties have won at least 20% of the vote in every election. On the provincial level, Eastern Ontario traditionally votes predominantly Conservative, while the rural southwest of the province is a Liberal stronghold. The Conservatives and New Democrats vie for dominance, and are stronger than the Liberals, in northern Ontario and the Toronto metropolitan area. The three parties have roughly equal support in the urban southwest. Traditionally, Anglo-Saxon Protestants tended to vote Conservative and Roman Catholics Liberal, but this may no longer be the case. The New Democrats are backed by organized labor, but many of their supporters are not working class, and the two other parties have significant working-class support.

Local government: In 1987–88 Ontario had 12 regional municipalities, 49 cities, 147 towns, 1 borough, 4 separated towns, 119 villages, 27 counties, 478 townships and 4 improvement districts. The first regional municipality (1954) was the Municipality of Metropolitan Toronto (Toronto Metro), a federation of the city of Toronto and its suburbs that is responsible for assessments, police, water, sewage, designated major (metro) roads and planning. There are six components within the Toronto regional municipality: the cities of Toronto, North York, Scarborough, Etobicoke, York and the Borough of East York. The other regional municipalities were established between 1969 and 1974.

Cities, towns and villages are incorporated urban municipalities. Cities usually have more than 15,000 people, towns 2,000 to 15,000, and villages less than 2,000. A county is an incorporated municipality that is a federation of towns, villages and townships within its borders. Townships exist within counties; most rural areas in southern Ontario are township municipalities. East York is the only remaining borough, which is a municipal corporation with the legal status of a township but resembling a city. Separated towns are separated from the county in which they are situated and are considered to have the same status as cities. Cities, towns, villages, counties and townships are governed by popularly elected councils usually headed by a mayor or reeve. Most cities and many towns, townships, counties and regional municipalities have an appointed permanent official who is the chief administrative officer. Unorganized territory in northern Ontario is directly served by the provincial government.

Federal representation: Ontario is represented in Parliament by 24 appointed senators and 99 elected members of the House of Commons. In the 1988 federal elections, 46 Conservatives, 43 Liberals and 10 New Democrats were sent to the House of Commons. Twelve residents of Ontario were serving in the federal cabinet in 1989.

Judicial system: The Supreme Court of Ontario consists of the High Court of Justice and the Court of Appeal. The High Court of Justice, with a chief justice and 58 other judges in 1988, has original jurisdiction in all civil actions not expressly excluded by statute. The Court of Appeal, with a chief justice and 18 other judges, has jurisdiction over administrative law matters, judicial review, and appeals other than final judgments for more than $25,000 or for relief other than the payment of money. Beyond this level, appeals go before the Supreme Court of Canada. These courts are federally appointed, as is the District Court, which in 1988 sat at 49 locations and had 151 judges. The District Court has jurisdiction that includes actions not exceeding $25,000 except on consent of the parties.

Surrogate Court has jurisdiction and authority for matters and causes testamentary and for granting or revoking of probate of wills and letters of administration. The judges are all District Court judges appointed by the province to act as Surrogate Court judges. The Provincial Court, which in 1988 sat at 51 locations, has provincially appointed judges and is divided into civil and criminal divisions. The civil division, or Small Claims Court, has jurisdiction over most matters not exceeding $1,000, except in metropolitan Toronto, where its jurisdiction extends to $3,000.

RECENT HISTORY

While Leslie Frost was the Conservative premier, in 1949–61, Ontario experienced an economic boom financed by heavy U.S. investment. The St. Lawrence Seaway, linking Great Lakes ports to Europe, was constructed in this period. A comprehensive hospital-insurance plan was adopted in 1959. Highway construction was a top priority, several new universities were in the process of being established, and continued improvements were made in agricultural, labor and welfare legislation. This record was marred by several corruption scandals, but Frost led his party to three electoral victories before turning over office, in 1961, to John Robarts. During the 1960s there was increased recognition of French-language rights, including the introduction of French-language public high schools. A system of community colleges was established, and local school boards were consolidated. Ontario entered the federal medicare program, and initiatives were taken in the areas of property-tax reform and pollution control.

Bill Davis succeeded Robarts as premier in 1971. Under his leadership, medicare premiums were abolished for senior citizens, the needy received free prescription drugs, and a new guaranteed-income plan for the elderly, blind and disabled was adopted. However, there were political scandals and a deficit problem. In the 1975 elections the Conservatives dropped to their lowest popular-vote percentage since 1919. They still elected more members than either of their rivals, however, and continued in office as a minority government. The late 1970s were difficult years for Ontario economically, with high unemployment and inflation. One government response was to establish a development fund that provided grants to companies as incentives to establish themselves in the province or to expand or modernize existing operations. Legislation was passed on several occasions to end strikes. A ceiling on rent increases was imposed. The Conservatives won a majority in the 1981 elections, but economic problems, especially high unemployment, continued over the next four years, and the government deficit continued to grow. Shortly before resigning office, Davis announced in 1984 that the government would fund the Roman Catholic secondary-school system to the same extent as the public system.

In the 1985 elections, 52 Conservatives, 48 Liberals and 25 New Democratics were elected, but the Liberals outpolled the Conservatives, 38% to 37%, while the New Democrats won 24%. Shortly after the voting, the Liberals and New Democrats agreed on a common legislative program, and David Peterson took office as premier of a Liberal government.

Full funding for Catholic schools was adopted in 1986. The following year, Ontario adopted the first measure in North America guaranteeing equal pay between the sexes for jobs of comparable worth. Aided by a strong economy, Peterson called new elections in 1987, making opposition to the federal government's proposal of free trade with the United States the centerpiece of his campaign. The Liberals won a landslide victory, electing 95 members to the legislature. The New Democrats won only 19 and the Conservatives only 16. Expecting an easy victory, Peterson called an election in September 1990, but his Liberals fell to second place with 36 seats. The Progressive Conservatives won 20. The New Democratic Party with 73 seats formed its first government in Ontario under Premier Robert (Bob) Rae.

ECONOMY

Ontario is the economic powerhouse of Canada. Its fortunate position astride eastern and western Canada also gives it easy access to the large industrial U.S. states of New York, Pennsylvania, Ohio and Michigan. The income of the average census-family—consisting of husband and wife, or single parent, plus any never-married children living with them—in Ontario of $55,286 in 1989 was the highest in Canada (the national average was $48,992) and the 1990 average unemployment rate of 6.3% was the lowest in Canada. Ontario was, however, hit hard by the recession of the early '90s, with unemployment ballooning to 11.5% in metropolitan Toronto (almost the same as the Canadian rate of 11.6%). Ontario ranks first among provinces in agriculture and metals mining, while its manufacturing output makes up more than half of the entire nation's total. Between 1985 and 1988, economic output, discounting inflation, grew by an average 5.5% per year—a higher rate of growth than that of any of the major industrialized countries.

The gross provincial product at factor cost was $241.3 billion in 1990, 40.5% of the national total. Of this amount, manufacturing accounted for 23.7%; community, business and personal services, 23.6%; finance, insurance and real estate, 16.9%; wholesale and retail trade, 11.3%; construction, 6.0%; public administration, 6.1%; transportation, storage and communication, 7.1%; other utilities, 2.6%; agriculture, forestry and fishing, 1.6%; and mines, quarries and oil wells, 1.1%.

Agriculture: There were 72,713 farms in Ontario (more than in any other province in 1986), but the average size was only 192 acres/78 hectares, and only 6% of the province's land area was in farms. Nevertheless, Ontario has the largest amount of Canada's best agricultural land, just over 50% of the Canadian total of Class 1 land. Farm cash receipts of $5.6 billion in 1990 were first among the provinces and amounted to 25.8% of the Canadian total. In crop production, Ontario ranked first in corn, carrots, cauliflower, cucumbers, onions, rutabagas, peaches, pears, sour cherries and tobacco. In livestock production, it ranked first in poultry and eggs, second to Quebec in hogs and dairy products and second to Alberta in cattle.

In 1990 crops accounted for more than $2 billion in cash payments, with the chief earners being vegetables ($424 million), floriculture and nursery crops ($358 million), corn ($331 million), tobacco ($249 million), soybeans ($247 million) and wheat ($146 million). Livestock products earned $3.3 billion, led by dairy products ($1.1 billion), cattle and calves ($950 million), hogs ($593 million), poultry ($428 million) and eggs ($167 million).

Forestry: Ontario had 180,000 sq. mi./466,000 sq. km. of inventoried forest land—52% of its land area—in 1986, with available wood volume of 123.6 billion cu. ft./3.5 billion cu. m. Ownership of forest land was 85% provincial, 14% private and 1% federal, and about 70% of the volume consists of softwoods. Forest production in 1988 was 1.03 billion cu. ft./29.3 million cu. m., of which 44% was logs and bolts and 48% timber converted to pulpwood. Forestry production is especially important in northwestern Ontario, where it accounts for two-thirds of the region's total employment in primary and manufacturing activities. In 1989 1,567 sq. mi/4,059 sq. km. were burned in forest fires.

Fishing: Landings of 23,254 tons, more than half the Canadian freshwater commercial catch, were worth $40.6 million as late as 1985. But overfishing and deterioration in Great Lakes water quality have continued to take their toll on the commercial harvesting of whitefish, pickerel and trout, and industrial pollution has caused contamination of the fish that have been a dietary staple of some Native communities. Sport fishing by tourists is of importance to parts of northern Ontario.

Mining: Ontario has the most diverse range of mineral production in Canada. It led all other provinces in 1990 in the production of barite, cadmium, cobalt, gold, nickel, salt, selenium, silver and zinc. In all, the province earned $6.3 billion from the production of non-energy minerals and structural materials. Of greatest value was gold, with production of 87.8 tons/79.6 tonnes (46% of national production), valued at $1.15 billion. Gold is mined in the Kirkland Lake-Timmins area, near Red Lake, and at the Hemlo mine near Marathon. Next in importance was nickel, which is mined chiefly at Sudbury. Production of 141,500 tons/128,402 tonnes (65% of Canadian output) was worth $1.3 billion. Copper, mined mainly at Sudbury and Timmins, yielded production of 305,300 tons/ 277,067 tonnes, valued at $887 million. Uranium production of 5,393 tons/4,894 tonnes, mainly from mines in Elliot Lake, was worth $635 million. Zinc production is chiefly from the Kidd Creek mine—the largest zinc mine in Canada—near Timmins. Production in 1987 came to 309,800 tons/281,131 tonnes, worth $542 million. Silver production of 404 tons/ 367 tonnes was valued at $67 million. Iron ore, mined at several locations in northern Ontario, came to 1.2 million tons/1.08 million tonnes. Salt production of 6.7 million tons/6.1 million tonnes (56% of national production) was valued at $115 million. Quarried products are also of importance. Sand and gravel production of 88.9 million tons/80.7 million tonnes was valued at $284 million, stone production of 59.0 million tons/53.4 million tonnes, at $273 million, and lime production of 1.5 million tons/ 1.4 million tonnes at $102 million. Cement production of 5.7 million tons/5.2 million tonnes was worth $402 million, and clay products were valued at $90 million.

Energy: Production of petroleum and natural gas is minor. In 1987, crude-oil production of 8.5 million cu. ft./240,000 cu. m. was worth only $44.3 million, and natural-gas production of 16.1 billion cu. ft./457 million cu. m. only $51.5 million. Ontario has coal deposits near James Bay, but it has not proved economical to exploit them.

About 95% of the province's electricity is produced by a public corporation, Ontario Hydro, which harnesses waterpower from Niagara Falls and the Ottawa and St. Lawrence river systems. It also has nuclear-power stations at Douglas Point, Pickering, Darlington and Bruce, and in addition uses imported coal as fuel for electricity generation. Installed peak capacity in the province was 31,150 megawatts in 1990. Of 135,698,439 megawatt hours of electricity production in 1990, nuclear power accounted for 48%, waterpower for 26%, and thermal power for the remaining 26%, almost all in the form of imported coal. Energy sales in 1990 amounted to 131,452,000 megawatt hours.

Manufacturing: In terms of value of manufacturing shipments ($152.9 billion in 1990), Ontario leads all provinces in every major category except wood and paper products. By far the largest sector is transportation equipment, worth $42.0 billion in 1990. Motor-vehicle assembly and parts accounts for 80% of the sector, with aerospace, bus and railway-equipment manufacturing comprising the remainder. About 90% of production is exported, almost all to the United States. Automobiles are produced in Brampton, St. Catharines, Oshawa, Oakville and Windsor.

The primary- and fabricated-metals sectors depend chiefly on Ontario's own mineral production and had a combined value of $20.8 billion in 1990. There are gold refineries at Brampton, Burlington, and the Royal Canadian Mint in Ottawa, and nickel refineries in Sudbury and Port Colborne. Zinc is refined at Timmins, silver at Cobalt, and copper is refined and smelted in Sudbury and Timmins. Ontario's steel plants, chiefly in Hamilton and Sault Sainte Marie, account for about 78% of Canadian production. Food-industry shipments had a value of $15.3 billion and included production from plants in Kitchener, London and Peterborough.

The value of shipments of chemicals and chemical products was $2.3 billion, and that of electrical and electronic products, $11.2 billion. Sarnia is a center for chemical production, and Hamilton produces wire, heavy machinery and electrical products. Ottawa has become a center for high-technology industries producing computers and computer-related products. The province's electronic-products industry has traditionally accounted for more than two-thirds of Canada's factory shipments in this sector. Northern Telecom, with headquarters in suburban Toronto, is the second largest telecommunications company in North America. In 1988, Lumonics Inc. was the world's third-largest laser company.

Sarnia is a center for petroleum refining as well as chemicals. In 1987 there were seven oil refineries with an annual capacity of 1.3 billion cu.

ft./36.8 million cu. m. In 1990 shipments of refined petroleum and coal products were valued at $5.6 billion. Paper products were worth $7.6 billion in shipments, printing and allied publishing, $6.9 billion, and wood products $2.4 billion. Toronto and Ottawa are centers for printing and publishing. More than 600 apparel manufacturers produced about $1.6 billion worth of goods in 1990.

Transportation: Ontario roads and highways total 25,661 mi./41,297 km. The province is well served south of the watershed between the Great Lakes and Hudson Bay; north of that point reliable transportation is by either air or water. The number of registered motor vehicles was 5,367,277 in 1986, of which 4,244,200 were passenger cars. Mainline railway track totaled 8,550 mi./13,760 km. in 1986, more than any other province. Ontario is served east-west by the Canadian National and Canadian Pacific rail lines. The province-owned Ontario Northland links North Bay on Lake Nipissing to James Bay. The Algona Central connects Sault Sainte Marie and Hearst. The provincial government has created a rail-and-road commuter service, called GO Transit, for the Hamilton-to-Oshawa corridor along Lake Ontario and aids municipal transport through its Urban Transit Development Corporation. Toronto's metropolitan government operates a subway line through the Toronto Transit Commission (TTC).

Ontario has the St. Lawrence Seaway along its southern frontier. The Welland Canal, an important part of the system, links lakes Ontario and Erie, and one of the 500 canals connects lakes Superior and Huron. The province's ports handled 40.8 million tons/37.7 million tonnes of cargo in 1989. Thunder Bay (14.7 million tons/13.3 million tonnes), on Lake Superior; Hamilton (13.8 million tons/12.5 million tonnes) on Lake Ontario; and Nanticoke (10.5 million tons/9.5 million tonnes), on Lake Erie were the busiest. Thunder Bay mostly ships coal and grain for domestic distribution, while Hamilton and Nanticoke mostly unload coal from abroad and domestic iron ore.

Toronto/Pearson International Airport was Canada's busiest in 1989, handling 20,263,574 passengers. Ottawa International Airport accommodated 2,636,178 passengers. The province is served by Air Canada, Canadian Airlines International and numerous foreign airlines.

Wholesale and retail trade: Ontario's wholesale trade came to $73.5 billion in 1990. Retail sales totaled $71.2 billion in 1990.

Foreign trade: Ontario alone ranks second to Japan in its share of U.S. trade. Of Ontario's $74.4 billion in 1990 exports (50% of the Canadian total), 86% went to the United States. Motor vehicles and automotive parts accounted for 51% of the total. Of the $79.1 billion in 1990 foreign imports, 76% came from the United States and 22% consisted of motor vehicles and automotive parts.

Banking and finance: Toronto's Bay Street area is the financial and banking capital of Canada; the five largest banks in Canada have their headquarters in Toronto, and 90% of all Canadian domestic chartered bank assets are headquartered there. Of the 59 foreign banks in Canada in 1987, 46 had their head offices in Ontario. Of the 2,830 bank branches in Ontario in 1988, 670 belonged to the Canadian Imperial Bank of Commerce, 581 to the Royal Bank of Canada and 522 to the Toronto-Dominion Bank.

From 1985 to 1987, Ontario received more than 61% of a total 2,251 foreign investments registered under the Investment Canada Act. Private investment in Ontario totaled $45.8 billion in 1987, when public investment was $9.6 billion. A total of 627 Ontario companies had $20.5 billion invested abroad in 1985. The Toronto Stock Exchange is by far the biggest in Canada. The average value of shares traded daily in December 1987—$5.8 billion—was 79% of the Canadian total.

Construction: Total construction in 1990 was valued at $37.5 billion. Of this, $29.7 billion was building construction, including $18 billion residential and $9.9 billion industrial or commercial. Engineering construction of $7.5 billion included $1.95 billion for roads and highways.

Tourism: Ontario had six national parks in 1987 and 270 provincial parks with a total area of 24,563 sq. mi./63,618 sq. km. Ontario's tourist sector accounts directly for about 4.2% of provincial employment. In 1990 Americans made more than 7 million visits of one or more night's stay and other non-Canadians more than 1.5 million.

Public finance: The 1991–92 budget called for spending $48.5 billion, of which 35.1% would be allotted for health; 21.6% for education, including postsecondary education; 17% for community and social services and 10.3% for public debt interest, as the largest components. Municipal spending was estimated at $14.5 billion. Revenue was projected at $43.0 billion, with personal income tax expected to account for 37.1%, sales tax for 18.5%, federal government payments, 12.4%, and corporate income tax, 7.4%. The government debt was $42.3 billion in 1990–91 and was projected as $51.7 billion for 1991–92. The total public-sector debt was $74 billion, including that of the Ontario Hydro-Electric Power Commission, one of the largest publicly owned electric utilities in North America.

The personal income-tax rate in 1990–91 was 53% of the federal tax. The general corporate income-tax rate was 15.5%, but the rate for manufacturing and processing operations, mining, logging, farming and fishing was 14.5%, and the rate for small businesses was 10%. All corporations in Ontario except insurance companies (which pay a premium tax) paid an 0.3% tax on paid-up capital. The general retail sales-tax rate was 8%. A payroll health tax ranging from 0.98% to 1.95% was imposed in 1990. The province also levies taxes on land transfers, alcoholic drinks, meals, accommodation, tobacco, and motive fuels such as gasoline.

Employment: The labor force in 1990 totaled 5,118,000, for a participation rate of 69.4% of the potential labor force, the highest rate in Canada. Of these, an average of 4,937,000 were employed and 256,000 unemployed during the year for an unemployment rate of 6.3%, the lowest in Canada. In October 1991, 34% of the labor force were in services; 19.29% in manufacturing; 16.2% in trade; 6.9% in transportation, communication and other utilities; 6.8% in finance, insurance and real estate; 6.6% in construction; 6.1% in public administration; 2.2% in agriculture; and 1.0% in other primary industries. In 1988 the service sector had accounted for 79% of all new jobs created since 1985. Revenue for 11 major business service industries in 1988 was $18.7 billion compared to $13.3 billion in 1986. Weekly earnings in Ontario averaged $535.79, including overtime, in 1990.

Organized labor in Ontario is strong, numbering more than a million members. The Ontario Federation of Labour has a membership of about 700,000. The largest individual unions are the autoworkers, the steelworkers, and two unions representing public employees. More than 1.1 million person-days were lost to strikes in 1987, 28% of the national total.

Prices:　Consumer prices rose 4.3% in Toronto, 4.3% in Ottawa and 4.5% in Thunder Bay between October 1989 and October 1990, compared to the Canadian average of 5.2%. During 1982–89, consumer prices rose 56.6% in Toronto, 49.5% in Ottawa and 47.6% in Thunder Bay, compared to the national average of 48.8%.

SOCIAL SERVICES

Welfare:　The federal-provincial shared-cost Canada Assistance Plan had 518,400 Ontario beneficiaries in fiscal 1987, receiving more than $1.6 billion in income support. The province has a supplementary-income system for the elderly and disabled, and offers an income supplement to general-assistance recipients who return to work. The Ministry of Community and Social Services funds centers and home-support services for senior citizens and has responsibility for a variety of children's programs. Ontario transfers to persons in 1989, excluding workers' compensation, employees' pensions and indirect payments, totaled almost $4 billion.

Health:　Ontario's health insurance system is consolidated in the Ontario Health Insurance Plan (OHIP), into which solvent residents paid premiums while those unable to pay full or partial premiums were subsidized. However, effective at the beginning of 1990, OHIP premiums were eliminated and replaced by the revenue from the new employer payroll tax. The Ministry of Health administers OHIP, a drug-benefit plan, public hospitals, and other programs. In 1988–89, Ontario's per-capita health-care spending was $1,416, about 12.5% above the average spent in the other provinces.

The 1988 birthrate of 14.5 and death rate of 7.4 per 1,000 people were about average for Canada. The abortion rate of 20.8 per 100 live births was above average. Hospital expense per patient-day of $367.18 in 1986–87 was also above average. In 1987 Ontario had 20,847 physicians, 5,496 active licensed dentists and 96,303 registered nurses.

Housing: Housing starts in 1987 totaled 105,213 in 1987, when the value of residential-construction permits was $9.4 billion. The average monthly gross rent in 1986 was $454, above the national average, and the average monthly home payment (with mortgage) was $776, also above the national average. In that year, 2,048,085 Ontario homes were owner-occupied and 1,166,160 were rented, for an average of 64% owned, above the national average. The average price of a home was $119,612 in Ontario in 1987, but the average in Toronto was $189,105. Vacancy rates in larger cities are very low, 1% or 2%. A new residential rent-regulation act was passed in 1986, and a replacement was put into place in 1991.

The public Ontario Housing Corporation provides subsidized housing to qualified lower-income families, senior citizens and the handicapped. The public Ontario Mortgage Corporation provides mortgage assistance aimed at making home ownership available to low- and moderate-income groups. Other provincial mortgage programs are intended to assist in providing rental and owner accommodations.

EDUCATION

School enrollment is compulsory between the ages of 6 and 16. School enrollment in 1989–90 was 1,976,617, of whom 1,911,918 were in public schools. These consist of nonsectarian and separate Roman Catholic public-school systems. The Catholic schools did not receive equal provincial financial support until 1986, however, when Ontario agreed to cover all the costs of separate school education into grades 11, 12 and 13. Grade 13 is gradually being phased out of the school system. Traditionally, boards could establish French-language schools "when numbers warrant." In 1984, the Ontario Court of Appeal ruled that every francophone (and anglophone) student in the province has a right to education in the other tongue. Linguistic minorities, the court also made clear, must be guaranteed representation on school boards and a say in minority-language education.

In 1989–90, enrollment in higher education was 208,527 full-time and 102,721 part-time. The largest of 21 institutions of higher learning was the University of Toronto, with 35,648 full-time students. Other major universities were the University of Western Ontario, York University, the University of Waterloo, Carleton University, the University of Ottawa, McMaster University and Queen's University. There were also 22 colleges of applied arts and technology, or community colleges, with full-time enrollment of about 93,337 and 75,884 part-time, and four colleges of agricultural technology, a school of horticulture, a chiropractic college and an institute of medical technology.

MASS MEDIA

Newspapers and periodicals: Of Ontario's 360 newspapers in 1992, 48 were dailies. The largest of these were Toronto's all-day *Star* (daily circulation 511,696; 763,193 for the Saturday weekend edition; Sunday circulation 526,975), and the morning *Toronto Sun* (daily circulation 257,610; Sunday circulation 444,181). *The Globe and Mail,* a national daily newspaper published in Toronto, had circulation of 325,113. *Le Droit,* published in Ottawa, is a French-language daily with weekday circulation of 36,000 and 42,300 on Saturday.

Toronto is also the home of the large majority of Canada's big magazines. *Maclean's,* a current-events weekly, had circulation of 615,000 in 1988 and is now being distributed free with their newspapers to many households. *Saturday Night,* a general monthly, had circulation of 110,000. Other monthlies include Toronto's *Flare* (circulation 224,000) and *Canadian Business* (95,908), and Ottawa's *Legion* (543,254), for veterans.

Broadcasting: In 1988, there were 102 AM and 81 FM radio stations, of which seven of the former and three of the latter broadcast in French. Two AM and one FM stations broadcast in North American Indian languages, and three AM stations were multilingual. Of the 36 originating television stations, five broadcast in French. The main English-language facilities of the Canadian Broadcasting Corporation and the private CTV network are in Toronto. There were 111 cable systems in Ontario in 1988.

BIOGRAPHICAL SKETCHES

Robert Keith (Bob) Rae. Premier of Ontario, president of the Executive Council and minister of intergovernmental affairs. Rae was born on August 2, 1948 in Ottawa and was educated at the University of Toronto and Oxford University, where he was a Rhodes Scholar, and at the University of Toronto Law School. He became a community worker and lawyer. He was elected to the House of Commons in a by-election in 1978 and was reelected in 1979 and 1980; he resigned in 1982. He was elected leader of the Ontario New Democratic Party in 1982. He was then elected to the Ontario Legislature in 1982, and won reelection in 1985, 1987 and 1990. He served as leader of the opposition in 1987–90 and was named premier of Ontario on October 1, 1990.

Floyd Laughren. Deputy premier, treasurer of Ontario and minister of economics. Born on October 3, 1935 in Shawville, Quebec, Laughren was educated at Ryerson Polytechnical Institute and York University. He was elected to the legislature in 1971 and was reelected in 1975, 1977, 1981, 1987 and 1990. He was appointed deputy premier and treasurer of Ontario and minister of economics on October 1, 1990.

Frances Lankin. Minister of Health. Lankin was born in London, Ontario and was educated at the University of Toronto. She worked as a public servant (correctional services officer) and a union negotiator. She was first elected to the Ontario Legislature in 1990 and was named minister of government services and chairman of the Management Board of the Cabinet in October 1990.

Ruth Anna Grier. Minister of the environment and minister responsible for the greater Toronto area. Grier was born on October 2, 1936 in Dublin. She served as an alderman in Etobicoke, a borough of metropolitan Toronto, from 1965 to 1985. She was first elected to the Ontario Legislature in 1985 and was reelected in 1987 and 1990. She was appointed minister of the environment and minister responsible for the greater Toronto area on October 1, 1990.

Lyn McLeod. Leader of the opposition. Born in 1942, she was educated at the University of Manitoba. In 1968 she was elected a trustee on the Lakehead Board of Education, where she served 17 years, 7 of them as chair. After receiving an M.A. in psychology from Lakehead University she worked with troubled youth in a Thunder Bay hospital and became a member of the Board of Governors of Lakehead. She was elected to the Ontario Legislature in 1987. She became minister of colleges and universities in 1987, and in 1989 minister of natural resources and minister of energy. She was reelected in 1990 and became opposition critic of community and social services. She was elected leader of the Liberal Party of Ontario at a convention in February 1992.

SASKATCHEWAN

GEOGRAPHY

Features: Saskatchewan is one of the Prairie Provinces of western Canada and is the only one with all man-made boundaries, forming a rectangle with the short ends at 49° and 60°N latitude. It is bounded on the north by the Northwest Territories, on the east by Manitoba, on the south by the U.S. states of North Dakota and Montana, and on the west by Alberta. Most of Saskatchewan consists of gently rolling plains characterized by the fertile soils that have made Saskatchewan Canada's leading wheat-producing province. On the western boundary and across the southwestern corner is another plains region, also with rolling terrain but generally with higher altitudes. Here is located the province's highest point, Cypress Hills, 4,815 ft./1,468 m. The natural vegetation of most of these two areas is prairie, but aspen parkland characterizes the northern part. The southern half of the province contains almost all the population, agriculture, and industry, and most of the mineral wealth. Sloping diagonally northeast to southwest along the northern third of the province, the Precambrian Canadian Shield consists of rugged rock exposures, thin soil, coniferous forest, swamps and many lakes. A band of subarctic forest tundra runs along the northern boundary. The northern third of Saskatchewan has gold, copper, uranium and zinc mines.

Saskatchewan's rivers generally run in an easterly direction and ultimately flow into Hudson Bay. The province is drained by parts of three major river basins: the Churchill in the north, and the Saskatchewan and Qu'Appelle-Assiniboine in the south. Both agricultural and industrial development require large amounts of water, but annual precipitation in the province varies greatly. Irrigation development has been minor, however. The largest lakes are in the north: Lake Athabasca (shared with Alberta), Reindeer Lake (shared with Manitoba), and Wollaston Lake.

Area: 251,865 sq. mi./652,300 sq. km., including 31,517 sq. mi./81,630 sq. km. of water. Saskatchewan comprises 6.5% of the total area of Canada.

Mean maximum and minimum temperatures: Regina 66 F/19°C (July), 0 F/ −18°C (January).

145

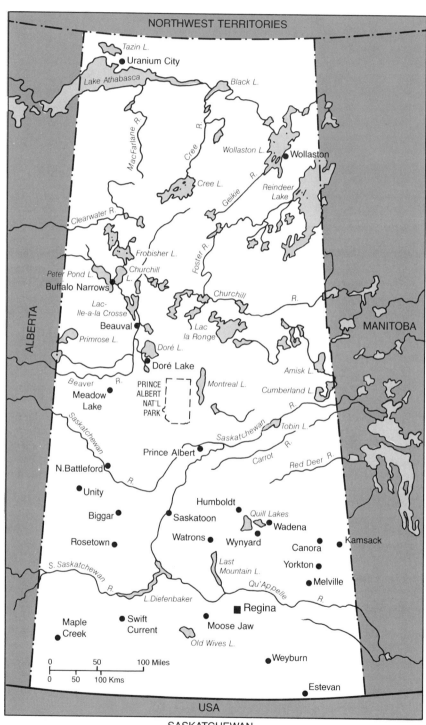

NORTHWEST TERRITORIES

Tazin L.
● Uranium City

Lake Athabasca

Black L.

MacFarlane R.

Cree R.

Wollaston L.
● Wollaston

Cree L.

Geikie R.

Reindeer Lake

Clearwater R.

ALBERTA

Foster R.

Frobisher L.

Churchill L.

Peter Pond L.
● Buffalo Narrows

Churchill R.

Lac-Ile-a-la Crosse

● Beauval

Lac la Ronge

Primrose L.

Doré L.

● Doré Lake

Amisk L.

Montreal L.

Cumberland L.

Beaver R.

● Meadow Lake

PRINCE ALBERT NAT'L PARK

Saskatchewan R.

Saskatchewan R.

Tobin L.

● Prince Albert

Carrot R.

Red Deer R.

● N.Battleford

● Unity

● Biggar

Humboldt ●

● Saskatoon

Quill Lakes

● Wadena

● Watrons

● Wynyard

● Canora

● Kamsack

● Rosetown

Yorkton ●

Last Mountain L.

● Melville

S. Saskatchewan R.

Qu'Appelle R.

L.Diefenbaker

■ Regina

Maple Creek ●

● Swift Current

● Moose Jaw

Old Wives L.

● Weyburn

0   50   100 Miles
0   50   100 Kms

● Estevan

USA

MANITOBA

SASKATCHEWAN

Mean annual precipitation: Regina 15.1 in./384 mm., including 45.7 in./ 116 cm. of snow.

POPULATION

Total population: (1986 Census): 1,009,613. Estimate, 1990: 1,000,300. Saskatchewan is the only province to lose population in the four years following the 1986 census. The population almost doubled between 1911 and 1931 but has not increased much from the 921,785 in 1931.

Chief towns and population (1986): Saskatoon (177,641), Regina, the capital (175,064), Moose Jaw (35,073), Prince Albert (33,686), Swift Current (15,666), Yorkton (15,574), North Battleford (14,876).

Distribution: The population was 61% urban and 39% rural in 1986. In 1990 the Saskatoon metropolitan area had an estimated population of 205,000 and the Regina metropolitan area, 190,600. All 12 of Saskatchewan's cities are in the southern half of the province.

Ethnic composition: According to the 1986 census, 49% of the population was, either solely or partly, of British (including Irish) origin. By the same criteria, the population was 9% of French origin. Other predominant European ethnic groups (single origin only) included Germans (13%), Ukrainians (6%), Scandinavians (2%), Poles (1%) and Dutch (1%). North American Indians numbered 43,385 (4%) and Métis (mixed white and Indian), 12,215 (1%). A total of 32,102 Indians were living on reservations in 1986.

Language: The 1986 census found that English was the mother tongue and home language of 82% and 94%, respectively, of Saskatchewan's people. French was the mother tongue and home language, respectively, of only 2% and 1% of the people. Other languages accounted for the remaining 16% and 5%, respectively. French was prohibited as a language of instruction in 1931, but public schools teaching the regular curriculum in French began to appear in the 1960s. In 1988, the use of French was made legal in the courts and legislature.

Religion: The 1981 census found that the United Church, the largest Protestant denomination in Saskatchewan, had the most adherents (32%), followed by the Roman Catholic Church (26%). Lutherans and Anglicans accounted for about 10% each, followed by the Ukrainian Catholic, Greek Orthodox, Mennonite, Presbyterian and Baptist churches, ranging from 4% down to less than 2% each. Jews comprised about 1% of the population. There is a separate publicly administered school system for Catholics.

CONSTITUTION AND GOVERNMENT

Saskatchewan became a province in 1905. The sovereign of Canada is Queen Elizabeth II and, as in the other Canadian provinces, she is represented by a lieutenant governor who is formally chief of the provincial executive. In practice, the premier heads an executive council, or cabinet, composed of members of the majority party or coalition. As in the other provinces, the executive needs the support of the majority of the legislature to stay in office. There is a leader of the opposition (the next largest party), who is paid as if a cabinet minister. The province has an ombudsman. The civil service has the right of collective bargaining.

Executive: The New Democratic Party cabinet sworn in on November 1, 1991 had only 11 members but the new premier predicted that six or seven more would be appointed to provide better geographical representation. In 1990 there were 17 departments and 21 semi-independent agencies. One of these, the Crown Management Board, is responsible for the administration of government policy as it relates to those corporations under its purview with respect to business efficiency and effective management.

Legislature: The Legislative Assembly consists of 68 members, each singly elected by a separate constituency. The essential role of the assembly is to consider all legislation, review the estimates of government spending, and debate issues of public importance. The bills and estimates, once approved by the legislature, require assent by the lieutenant governor before they are in effect. The assembly usually meets between February and seeding time and again after the harvest. It is also common for legislative committees to meet between sessions and conduct public hearings around the province. Elections are generally held every four years but may be held sooner if the governing party loses a major vote in the legislature or the premier recommends dissolution of the body by the lieutenant governor. In 1991 the election was called only as the legislature approached its maximum constitutional life of five years.

Political parties: The traditional parties are the Conservative (since 1943 Progressive Conservative) and Liberal parties. In the early years of the province, the Liberals were dominant and tended to receive solid support from the Catholic minority because of Conservative opposition to public support for Catholic schools. Beginning in 1921, the Conservatives were also overshadowed by a number of groups representing farmers and advocating socialist-oriented programs. The Co-operative Commonwealth Federation (CCF) proved to be the most effective organ for these views and came to power in 1944. They also benefited from the division of antisocialist votes between the Liberal, Conservative and Social Credit parties. The CCF (since 1967 the New Democratic party, or NDP) remained in office until 1982, except for 1964–71, when the Liberals were in power. The Conservatives replaced the Liberals as the official opposition in 1978 and swept into office in 1982. Saskatchewan tends now to have a two-party system on class/income lines, with professionals, business people, and well-off farmers favoring the Conservatives and the urban working class and marginal farmers supporting the NDP. The election of 1991 brought the NDP back into power, possibly

148

partly because of western dissatisfaction with the performance of the federal conservatives.

Local government: In 1990, Saskatchewan had 12 cities (including the city of Lloydminster on the Saskatchewan-Alberta boundary), 144 towns, 364 villages, and 298 rural municipalities averaging about 350 sq. mi./900 sq. km. each. Cities are governed by an elected council consisting of a mayor and an even number of aldermen. Towns are governed by a mayor and six aldermen elected at large. Villages are governed by a mayor and either two or four aldermen who are elected at large. The above elections are held every three years. Rural municipalities are governed by councils composed of a mayor, overseer, or reeve elected at large, and a councillor elected in each division, with the terms of office being two years. Local governments provide such services and facilities as streets, police, water, sewage disposal and hospitals in the urban areas; roads and problems of drainage and weed control in the rural areas. They also collect taxes for other local spending authorities, the largest of which are school districts. The northern half of the province is basically unorganized for municipal purposes, although there were 2 northern towns (Creighton and La Ronge), 12 northern villages, and 13 northern hamlets in 1990. General expenditure of local governments came to $1.6 billion in 1984. The province transfers a portion of its revenues to municipalities.

Federal representation: Saskatchewan is represented in Parliament by 6 appointed senators and 14 elected members of the House of Commons. In the 1988 federal elections, Saskatchewan sent 10 New Democrats and 4 Conservatives to the House of Commons.

Judicial system: The civil courts of Saskatchewan are the Court of Queen's Bench, the Surrogate Court and the Provincial Court. The Court of Queen's Bench, whose judges are federally appointed, has original jurisdiction over all civil actions not expressly excluded by statute. In 1988, this court had a chief justice and 31 judges in 18 judicial centers. The Surrogate Court, which is federally appointed, has authority over the probating of wills. There is a Unified Family Court of three judges. The Provincial Court, which has provincially appointed judges, hears small claims not exceeding $3,000. In 1988, there were 15 provincial courts, presided over by a chief justice and 41 judges. Routes of appeals are stipulated in the enabling legislation for each civil matter. The Court of Appeal, which is the highest appellate court in Saskatchewan, had a chief justice and six judges in 1990. Appeals go to the Supreme Court of Canada beyond this level.

RECENT HISTORY

Modern political history in Saskatchewan begins with the coming to power of the Co-operative Commonwealth Federation in 1944. Under the leadership of the new premier, T. C. (Tommy) Douglas, the CCF established public ownership of a brick-manufacturing plant, a shoe factory, a tannery,

149

a woolen mill, a sodium-sulfate mine and a box factory. These public enterprises were justified as a means of diversifying the economy, creating jobs and generating revenue. The government also established a printing company, a bus company, a northern airline and an automobile-insurance corporation, later extended to a full-scale insurance plan. It took over municipal telephone operations and private power companies, raised mining taxes and royalties, and allowed farmers to keep their land while paying off accumulated debts. A public hospital-insurance scheme necessitated much hospital construction and expansion. The province became a leader in the care of mental health, cancer and tuberculosis; established a college of medicine and an air ambulance service; and provided pensioners with free medical, dental and hospital services.

The CCF was returned to power in 1952, 1956 and 1960; the following year Douglas left the province to become national leader of the New Democratic party. With Woodrow Lloyd as premier, the government introduced a medicare plan in 1962 despite a three-week strike by doctors.

Despite a buoyant economy, the CCF was defeated in 1964. Under the new Liberal premier, Ross Thatcher, the government did not move far to the right, but it did emphasize exploiting the province's natural resources through private and usually foreign investment. Two large potash developments, a new sawmill, and a base-metal mine were soon announced, and a new pulp mill was built by U.S. interests. During their second term in office, the Liberals imposed an austerity government, cutting public spending and raising taxes.

The former CCF, renamed the New Democratic Party, returned to power in 1971 under Allan Blakeney. Many innovations were instituted, for example a commission that bought land from retiring farmers and leased it back to those wanting to get started in farming, with an option to buy. Cash supplements were introduced for the working poor, along with free preventive dental care for children and a plan to subsidize the cost of prescription drugs. The government took over 90% of the province's oil and gas reserves, for which companies were compensated. In an even more controversial move, the province imposed a surcharge to recover windfall profits arising from the sharp jump in world oil prices that began in 1973. A crown corporation was established to enter all phases of the industry. A public potash-mining corporation was created in 1975, and the government acquired 40% of the potash industry in the province. Rent control was imposed in 1977. The NDP, which had won the 1975 elections, won again in 1978, but this time the Conservatives became the official opposition.

In 1982 the Conservatives won a surprise landslide victory under Grant Devine, who implemented his party's campaign promises by abolishing the 20% provincial tax on gasoline and subsidizing all mortgages above 13.25% annual interest. He welcomed private investment in resource industries, and the oil industry expanded. In October 1986 the Conservatives won 38 seats to 25 for the NDP and one for the Liberals, even though NDP candidates polled the most total votes. Cutbacks in health care and education were imposed in 1987. A publicly owned pulp mill was sold in 1986, and shares of the provincially owned Saskatchewan Oil & Gas Corporation were offered to the public in 1986. The publicly owned Potash Corporation of Saskatchewan was partially privatized in 1989. In October 1991 the NDP defeated the Conservatives in a landslide election, winning 55 of 66 seats in a legislature enlarged from 64. The Progressive Conservatives won 10, including the seat at the former Conservative premier, and the Liberals one, that of their leader.

ECONOMY

In most recent years, Saskatchewan has been the least prosperous province in western Canada, slightly behind Manitoba in per capita income. Its economy is limited by low population, a small manufacturing base, and its considerable dependence on wheat farming, which is subject to fluctuations in world prices and the vagaries of weather. On the other hand, it ranks second only to Alberta in crude-oil production. Saskatchewan is unusual in the extent of the provincial government's role in the economy; indeed, socialism had been carried further in the province than anywhere else in the United States or Canada. Under the Conservative government of the late 1980s, however, privatization of public companies was pursued. Saskatchewan's penchant for socialist experimentation is based on its experience with the cooperative movement, through which citizens banded together to satisfy economic needs. The province contains nearly 20% of all the cooperative associations in Canada, which are found in virtually every segment of retailing and distribution and in many service industries. In 1986, 56% of the population belonged to 1,313 cooperative associations, the total assets of which amounted to more than $55 billion.

The gross provincial product at factor cost in 1988 was $18.3 billion. Services accounted for the largest share, 23%, followed by finance, insurance and real estate, 21%; trade and agriculture, 10% each; transportation, communication and storage, 9%; mining and public administration and defense, 7% each; manufacturing, 6%; construction, 4%; and utilities, 3%. In real terms, the gross provincial product fell 4.5% in 1988 because of a disastrous drought and harvest, but it rose 26% in the 1978–88 decade. In 1990 the GPP at factor cost reached $19.2 billion. The 1990 per-capita personal income of $17,784 was the lowest in western Canada and only 84% of the national average of $21,184; near-parity was achieved only in 1975 and, since 1956, has otherwise ranged between 72% (1961 and 1970) and 97% (1963).

Agriculture: With 63,431 farms (second to Ontario), averaging 1,036 acres/ 420 hectares (first in Canada), Saskatchewan had more land in farms than any other province in 1986—47% of the total land area of the province and 44% of Canada's cultivated farmland. With total farm cash receipts of $4.5 billion in 1989 and $4.05 billion in 1990—two years of drought— Saskatchewan ranked third among provinces and, in relation to the size of its population, agriculture was of greater importance than in any other province. Saskatchewan is the breadbasket of Canada, producing 54% of the nation's wheat in 1990 and 57% in 1991; in 1988, the crop came to

7.3 million tons/6.6 million tonnes (only 43% of the 1987 crop), earning the province's farmers $1.4 billion. Another $191 million came from Canadian Wheat Board payments for exports, and an additional $378 million in grain-stabilization payments. Canola (rapeseed) was the second most important crop ($412 million) in income, followed by barley ($152 million). Oats, rye and flax are other crops cultivated. Production was more than 2.2 million tons/2 million tonnes for barley, nearly 1.9 million tons/1.7 million tonnes for oats, 207,000 tons/188,000 tonnes for flax, and 98,000 tons/89,000 tonnes for rye. Saskatchewan farmers also earned $262 million in crop-insurance payments. In all, total income from crops came to $2.8 billion in 1988 but fell to $2.4 billion in 1989.

Income from livestock and animal products ($903 million in 1989) is of lesser importance, although Saskatchewan still ranks fourth among provinces. Cattle and calves accounted for $607 million in cash receipts, followed by hogs ($115 million) and dairy products ($96 million). In 1988 1,235,000 cattle and calves and 1,051,000 hogs were marketed.

Saskatchewan has many marketing boards for commodities. Made up largely of elected farmer representatives, they regulate production as well as marketing.

Forestry: Although Saskatchewan had 91,500 sq. mi./237,000 sq. km. of inventoried forest land—42% of the province—with available timber volume of 31.8 billion cu. ft./905 million cu. m., forestry accounted for only $51 million in gross domestic product at factor cost in 1990. In terms of volume, 1989 forest production was 124 million cu. ft./3.7 million cu. m. of timber, of which 41% was logs and 34% pulpwood. When counting sawn lumber, plywood, and particle-board production, however, as well as logs and pulpwood, the total value of forest production for 1988 was $259 million. Ninety-six percent of the province's forest land is provincially owned, and 60% of the timber consists of softwoods. A public corporation, the Saskatchewan Forest Products Corporation, conducts logging operations. Major softwoods are jack pine and black and white spruce; hardwoods are aspen, black poplar and white birch.

Fishing: Saskatchewan's lakes and rivers are of more value to sport than to commercial use. Commercial landings of 3,815 tons/3,553 tonnes in 1989–90, including whitefish, walleye, pike, lake trout, tullibee and buffalo fish, yielded only $3.2 million in value. For sport, anglers fish mainly for trout, walleye and pike.

Mining: Excluding energy products, Saskatchewan's most important minerals are potash and uranium. It is estimated that the province could have nearly two-thirds of the world's recoverable potash reserves, and it supplies 25% of world demand. All 10 Saskatchewan potash mines, (including four owned by the Potash Corporation of Saskatchewan, a public corporation partially privatized in 1989 that is the largest potash producer in the Western world), are in the southern part of the province. Potash production was about 7.0 million tons/6.4 million tonnes in 1987 (83% of Canadian production). In 1988 it rose to 7.8 million tons/7.1 million tonnes, worth $974 million, but it declined to just 7.5 million tons/6.6 million tonnes in 1990. The province is also the world's largest exporter of uranium, accounting for 22% of world shipments in 1987. Massive reserves in Athabasca Basin in northern Saskatchewan hold more than 662 million lb./300 million kg. of uranium metal, about 80% of the world's known recoverable reserves. The Key Lake mine is the world's largest uranium producer, and the Cigar Lake mine contains the world's richest uranium deposits. Production in 1988 came to 18.5 million lb./8.4 million kg., worth $463 million. The totals rose to 20.0 million lb./9.1 million kg. in 1989 and fell to 9 million lb./4.5 million kg. in 1990, when it was worth $233 million. Other valuable metals, also mined in northern Saskatchewan, are gold, copper and zinc. Gold production in 1990 was 7,262 lb./3,295 kg., worth about $47.5 million. Copper production in 1988 was 5.1 million lb./2.3 million kg., worth $6.1 million. Zinc, mined with copper, also came to 5.1 million lb./2.3 million kg., worth $2.9 million. Saskatchewan Mining and Development Corporation, a public company with holdings in uranium and gold, was undergoing reorganization in 1989. The chief nonmetals mined in 1990 were sand and gravel (11.4 million tons/10.3 million tonnes, worth $23.3 million), salt (444,000 tons/403,000 tonnes, worth $20.4 million), and sodium sulfate (331,000 tons/300,000 tonnes, worth $25.0 million).

Energy: Saskatchewan had recoverable crude-oil reserves in 1988 of 3.7 billion cu. ft./105.2 million cu. m., or 662.7 million bbl. Nearly 14,000 producing oil wells are in four areas of the province: Estevan-Weyburn in the southeast, Swift Current in the southwest, Kindersley in west-central Saskatchewan, and Lloydminster, farther north and west. Oil wells yielded 416 million cu. ft./11.8 million cu. m., or 76 million bbl. of crude oil in 1990, worth $1.69 billion. This production was 13% of Canada's total, ranking Saskatchewan second to Alberta's 82%. In 1985 production had been a little less, but sales had totaled more than $2.2 billion. One of the oil companies active in the province is Saskatchewan Oil and Gas Corporation, a previously all-public company that began selling shares in 1986 but remained about 50% government-owned as of 1989. The province has 2,437 billion cu. ft./69 billion cu. m. of recoverable natural-gas reserves, primarily in the southwest. Production in 1990 was 204.2 billion cu. ft./5.786 billion cu. m., worth $314.0 million.

Two oil refineries with combined capacity of 109.5 million cu. ft./3.1 million cu. m. in 1987 produce gasoline, diesel and bunker fuel, propane, and butane in Regina, and asphalt in Moose Jaw. Since some of Saskatchewan's reserves and production are in the form of hard-to-use heavy oil, Canada's first heavy-oil upgrader, a $700-million plant in Regina capable of accommodating 50,000 bbl. a day of crude oil, was opened in 1988. A $1.2-billion upgrader is under development in Lloydminster.

Saskatchewan has 8.4 billion tons/7.6 billion tonnes of lignite coal reserves. Lignite is strip-mined in areas of the province near the U.S. border, and production in 1990 was 9.5 million tons (third among provinces), worth $100 million.

Saskatchewan had an electrical-generating capacity of 2,846 megawatts at the end of 1989, mostly from three coal-fired plants and the remainder from four waterpower facilities. There are also smaller gas-fired plants throughout the province. Production in 1990 was 13.5 million megawatt hours, of which 69% was thermal and 31% hydro. The public Saskatchewan Power Corporation has a monopoly over power production and distribution and operates an integrated electrical grid that blankets the province. SaskEnergy, another public corporation, distributes natural gas to industry and homes through a pipeline network. Oil still heats many homes, however, particularly in rural areas.

Manufacturing: Among Canadian provinces Saskatchewan ranks near the bottom in manufacturing because of small population and great distance from markets. In 1990, the value of its manufacturing shipments was $3.6 billion, of which Regina accounted for 38% and Saskatoon for 29%. Manufacturing establishments, most of them employing fewer than 100 workers, numbered 810 in 1987 and employed 19,800 persons. Food processing, Saskatchewan's largest manufacturing industry (25% of total value of manufacturing shipments in 1990), serves local and export markets with meat products, pasta and noodles, oilseed products, animal feed, processed potatoes and other products. More than 40 agricultural-implement manufacturers were active in 1987. There is a well-established chemical industry, including plants producing industrial gases, fertilizers, paints, plastics, herbicides, insecticides, disinfectants, caustic soda, chlorine, fatty-acid nitrogen derivatives, and ammonium phosphate. Saskatchewan also has a steel mill and pipe plant in Regina and produces sheet-metal products and boilers. Other factories produce wood products and household, industrial, transportation and office equipment. The public Saskatchewan Economic Development Corporation (SEDCO) runs industrial parks and provides developed industrial property for sale, lease and lease-option.

Transportation: Because Saskatchewan specializes in the production of bulk commodities and is landlocked, rail and road transportation is essential to its economy. Saskatchewan had 15,842 mi./25,489 km. of highways and roads (23% gravel) in 1990, the longest maintained highway and road network of any province in Canada. There were 755,350 motor vehicles registered in 1988, of which 460,969 were passenger cars. An intermodal transportation facility recently opened in Saskatoon. It functions as a warehouse and distribution center for the transfer and storage of containers. Mainline railway track in Saskatchewan accounted for 2,495 mi./4,016 km. in 1987, 12% of the total in Canada; total track is about 8,700 mi./13,000 km. A public bus company, Saskatchewan Transportation, provided passenger and parcel service to 402 communities in 1985, traveling nearly 5.5 million mi./8.9 million km. Direct jet service connects Regina and Saskatoon with Toronto and major cities in western Canada. A provincial airline flies into nine Saskatchewan communities as well as Edmonton and Calgary in Alberta and Minneapolis-St. Paul, Minnesota. In 1989, Regina's airport handled 524,100 passengers, and Saskatoon's, 507,600. There are about 180 airports, aerodromes and landing strips in the province.

Wholesale and retail trade: Wholesale trade totaled $6.2 billion in 1990, and retail trade totaled $6.4 billion. More than 200 retail cooperative stores do more than $700 million in business annually.

Foreign trade: About 300 Saskatchewan firms export to more than 100 countries. Saskatchewan's exports came to $4.7 billion in 1990. The United States took 40%; China, nearly 20%; the Soviet Union, 11%; and Japan, 13%. Of 1990 exports, grains accounted for 35% of value; crude oil, 13%; potash, 12.4%; and uranium, 9%. Imports in 1990 came to nearly $1.4 billion, of which 90% was from the United States.

Banking and finance: In 1988, there were 386 bank branches, of which the Royal Bank of Canada had 118 and the Canadian Imperial Bank of Commerce 100. The province is served by nine major Canadian and international banks, 50 trust and savings corporations, and five credit unions with commercial-credit capabilities. There were more than 200 cooperative credit unions of the 1985 total of 272 chartered credit unions with 566,867 members and assets of $3.95 billion. Nonconventional lending sources include the provincially owned Saskatchewan Economic Development Corporation, offering equity financing, term loans, guarantees and mortgages. Private investment in the province in 1987 was $4.2 billion; public investment was $1.6 billion. Total investment in 1988 was nearly $6.2 billion and in 1989 was $6.0 billion. The Saskatchewan Government Insurance Company has a monopoly on auto insurance, which is compulsory for motorists, and handles most kinds of property/casualty insurance.

Construction: The net value of construction of all kinds in 1990 was $3.7 billion, of which $870 million was for residential construction. The value of building permits issued for 1990 was $454 million, of which Saskatoon accounted for 48% and Regina for 24.7%.

Tourism: Saskatchewan has two national parks: Prince Albert and Grasslands. The 31 provincial parks have a total area of 3,506 sq. mi./9,080 sq. km. In 1989 there were 4.2 million visitors to provincial parks and recreation areas. Tourism receipts from non-Saskatchewan Canadian residents and foreign visitors totaled $320 million in 1989. In 1990 almost 97,000 Americans and 1,580 other non-Canadians made tourist visits direct to Saskatchewan.

Public finance: The 1989–90 budget called for expenditures of $4.3 billion, of which the biggest items were health, $1.4 billion; education, $841 million; and social services, $381 million. It projected revenues of $4.1 billion, of which provincial taxes were projected at $2.0 billion and federal payments at $1.1 billion. The public debt was $10.3 billion in 1987.

In 1989, Saskatchewan's basic personal tax rate of 50% of the federal tax was the second lowest among Canadian provinces. There was also a flat levy of 2% on net income and a surtax of 12% in excess of $4,000. The basic corporate tax rate was 15% for large businesses and 10% for small ones. The retail sales tax was 7%. There was a capital tax of 3% on financial institutions.

Employment: Saskatchewan's labor force averaged 483,000 in 1990, of which 34,000 were unemployed, for a rate of 7.0%, below the Canadian average of 8.1%. In 1989, average weekly earnings were $426, the lowest in western Canada. In 1989, about 144,000 people were classed in service occupations; 79,000 in trade; 77,000 in agriculture; 31,000 in transportation, communication and other utilities; 33,000 in public administration; 24,000 in manufacturing; 22,000 in construction; 23,000 in finance, insurance and real estate; and 13,000 in nonagriculture primary industries. The Saskatchewan Federation of Labour, which has about 66,000 members, is closely linked to the New Democratic Party. The largest unions are in the public service. In the private sector, the Retail, Wholesale and Department Store Union; the United Food and Commercial Workers Union; and the Steelworkers are the largest labor organizations.

Prices: In both Regina and Saskatoon the consumer price index rose 5.7% between June 1990 and June 1991. This rate was lower than the Canadian increase of 6.1% during this period. During 1982–88 the index rose 40.3% in Regina and 41.8% in Saskatoon, lower than the Canadian average of 43.8%.

Services: There are more than 600 service cooperatives, including childcare centers, laundromats, local bus lines, recreation facilities and health clinics.

SOCIAL SERVICES

Welfare: In addition to the federal spending totaling $153 billion in 1989 on unemployment insurance, family allowances and old-age pension programs, and to the shared-cost federal-provincial Canada Assistance Plan (which alone spent $215.5 million on 62,100 Saskatchewan beneficiaries in fiscal 1987), the province provides extensive social services. The province spent $596 million on social service in 1989. The Saskatchewan Assistance Plan ensures that no person lacks the means to pay for basic necessities. The Department of Social Services administers a family-income plan to supplement the income of working families with children and the Saskatchewan Income Plan for senior citizens who have little or no income other than from the federal pension and supplement. The Saskatchewan Pension Plan is a voluntary one that makes it possible for every resident to contribute to a pension plan, regardless of income. The plan is the first such program in North America to provide a pension for homemakers, and it provides for government contributions for low- and moderate-income earners. The department makes available training and employment experience opportunities for social-assistance recipients who are considered employable. A network of nongovernment organizations receives funding from, and works in partnership with, the provincial government to deliver services to children and families throughout the province. Many of the children who become wards of the department are cared for in foster homes, group homes or special institutions. The department also administers community programs and custody facilities for youth offenders; provides, directly or indirectly, rehabilitation services; licenses day-care facilities and assists in their development; and administers funding for activity centers and organizations for senior citizens.

Health: In 1988, Saskatchewan had a birthrate of 16.6 and death rate of 7.7 per 1,000 people, both higher than the national average. The abortion rate of 7.7 per 100 live births in 1988 was far below the national average of 17. In 1986–87, there were 135 hospitals with 7,391 beds. Hospital expense per patient-day of $279.01 was below the national average. Saskatchewan had 1,700 physicians, 381 active licensed dentists, and 8,605 registered nurses in 1987. The province's health expenditure came to $1.6 billion in 1985.

The provincial government was the first in North America to implement universal hospital-care insurance, at the beginning of 1947. The Medical Care Insurance Plan provides coverage to residents for a wide range of services, without charge. The Saskatchewan Dental Plan covers a wide range of services to children. The Saskatchewan Prescription Drug Plan pays the cost of most prescription drugs and drug materials and subsidizes the dispensing fee. Community health services are offered throughout the province. A cancer foundation has clinics in Regina and Saskatoon, and an alcohol- and drug-abuse commission conducts rehabilitation programs and research.

Housing: In 1986, there were 250,970 owner-owned and 101,540 rented households in Saskatchewan; the 70%–30% ratio of owned to rented was higher than the national average. In 1986, Saskatchewan gross rent averaged $390 a month, while the average home payment with mortgage averaged $690, both lower than the national averages. Homes are cheaper than in most Canadian urban centers: the average selling prices of single-family detached homes was $67,750 in Regina and $77,250 in Saskatoon. The value of residential construction permits in the province was $302.3 million in 1987. In 1988, 3,856 dwelling units were started and 4,352 were completed; of those started, 2,246 were single dwellings, 140 were double dwellings, 381 were row houses and 1,089 were apartments. The Saskatchewan Housing Corporation offers programs for low- and moderate-income families, senior citizens and the disabled.

EDUCATION

School enrollment is free and compulsory between the ages of 7 and 16. In 1987–88, 215,334 students were attending primary and secondary schools;

CANADA

enrollment in the public schools was 203,499. The urban campuses of the Saskatchewan Institute of Applied Science and Technology in Saskatoon, Regina, Moose Jaw and Prince Albert offer 143 certificate and diploma vocational-training programs. Eight regional colleges and the Northlands Career College offer a variety of programs to upgrade skills in locations outside the major cities, in rural areas, and in northern Saskatchewan. Forty-seven private vocational schools offer training in specific disciplines.

Saskatchewan's four institutions of higher learning had 20,729 full-time and 9,001 part-time students in 1987–88. The University of Saskatchewan, at Saskatoon, had 14,250 full-time students, and the University of Regina had 6,024. The Canadian Bible College and Canadian Theological College are also in the province.

MASS MEDIA

Newspapers and periodicals: Of Saskatchewan's daily newspapers, the ones with the largest circulations are Regina's *Leader-Post* (67,900 in 1992) and Saskatoon's *Star-Phoenix* (60,259). The other dailies are the Moose Jaw *Times-Herald,* the *Prince Albert Daily Herald* and the *Lloydminster Daily Times.*

There were 74 weekly and five semiweekly newspapers in 1988 and 19 periodicals. Among these are Saskatoon's *Western Producer,* a weekly newspaper (133,500 circulation in 1988), and Regina's *Farm Light & Power,* a monthly periodical (188,715).

Broadcasting: There were 22 AM and 10 FM radio stations in 1988, including rebroadcasters. One AM and one FM station broadcast in French, and there were two remote community and Native radio stations. There were 34 television stations, of which 22 were rebroadcasters and five (four of them rebroadcasters) broadcast in French. The Canadian Broadcasting Company owns and operates three radio and three television stations in the province, and there are a number of affiliates. The province had 13 cable systems in 1988, serving about 100 communities.

BIOGRAPHICAL SKETCHES

Roy John Romanow. Premier of Saskatchewan. Educated at Bedford Road College and the University of Saskatchewan, Romanow is a barrister and solicitor who served in the Legislative Assembly, 1967–82. He was attorney general of the province, 1971–82, and also minister of intergovernment affairs, 1979–82. Defeated in 1982, he was reelected in 1986 and was chosen leader of the New Democratic Party in November 1987.

Edwin Lawrence Tchorzewski. Deputy premier and minister of finance. Tchorzewski was born on April 2, 1943 at Alvena, Saskatchewan. He was educated at the Hudson Bay School, the University of Saskatchewan and the University of Regina, and he became a teacher. He was first elected to the Saskatchewan Legislature in 1971 and was reelected in 1975 and 1978. Defeated in 1982, he was re-elected in a by-election in 1985, and won election again in 1986 and 1991. He served as minister of consumer affairs and provincial secretary from 1972 to 1975, minister of education in 1977, minister of continuing education in 1975–76, minister of health in 1977–1979 and minister of finance in 1979–82. He became deputy premier and minister of finance in 1991.

Dwain Matthew Lingenfelter.   Minister of economic diversification and trade, government house leader. Lingenfelter was born in Shaunavon, Saskatchewan and was educated at the University of Saskatchewan. He became a farmer and small businessman. He was elected to the Saskatchewan Legislature in 1978 and 1982, was defeated in 1986, won reelection in a by-election in 1988, and won again in 1991. He served as minister of social service in 1980–82 and became minister of economic diversification and trade in 1991.

Grant Devine.   Leader of the opposition. Born on July 5, 1944 in Regina, Devine holds a bachelor's degree in agricultural economics from the University of Saskatchewan, master's degrees in agricultural economics and in business administration from the University of Alberta, and a doctorate in agricultural economics from Ohio State University. He worked as a federal agricultural bureaucrat, 1970–72, and as a professor of agriculture at the University of Saskatchewan, 1975–79. In 1979 he was elected leader of the provincial Conservative party. In 1982 he was elected to the Legislative Assembly, his party won a majority, and he became premier. He won a second majority in 1986. He resigned as premier following the electoral defeat of his party on October 21, 1991, to become leader of the opposition.

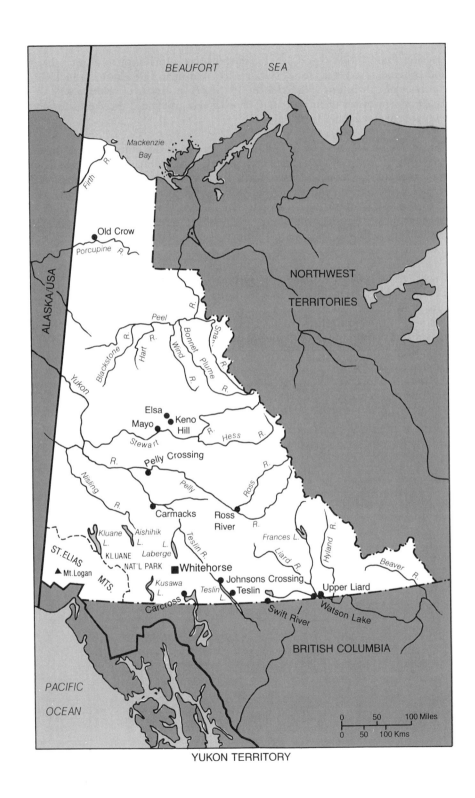

BEAUFORT   SEA

Mackenzie
Bay

Frith R.

ALASKA/USA

Old Crow

Porcupine R.

NORTHWEST

TERRITORIES

Peel R.

Blackstone R.

Hart R.

Wind R.

Bonnet Plume R.

Snake R.

Yukon

Elsa
Keno
Hill
Mayo

Stewart R.

Hess R.

Pelly Crossing

Nisling R.

Pelly R.

Ross R.

Carmacks

Ross
River

Frances L.

Liard R.

Hyland R.

Beaver R.

Kluane
L.

Aishihik
L.

ST. ELIAS

KLUANE

Laberge
L.

Teslin R.

▲ Mt. Logan

NAT'L PARK

■ Whitehorse

Johnsons Crossing

MTS.

Kusawa
L.

Teslin

Teslin
L.

Upper Liard

Carcross

Swift River

Watson Lake

BRITISH COLUMBIA

PACIFIC

OCEAN

0   50   100 Miles

0   50   100 Kms

YUKON TERRITORY

YUKON

Features: The Yukon Territory is bordered on the north by Mackenzie Bay of the Beaufort Sea, which is an arm of the Arctic Ocean; on the east by the Northwest Territories; on the south by British Columbia and the U.S. state of Alaska; and on the west by Alaska. The central Yukon Plateau, at an average elevation of 3,900 ft./1,200 m. is surrounded by, and interspersed with, mountain ranges. The mountains, and the deep valleys between them, run southeast-northwest and continue into Alaska. The Mackenzie and Selwyn mountains run along the border with the Northwest Territories. The Richardson Mountains continue north and are succeeded by the British Mountains, which stretch into Alaska and separate the northern coastline from the rest of the province. The Ogilvie Mountains, north of Dawson City in the west-central part of the Yukon, include Mt. Campbell, 7,400 ft./2,256 m. high. In the southwestern part of the territory, along the Alaskan border, are the St. Elias Mountains, the Yukon's highest range; here is found Mt. Logan, whose summit is the highest point in Canada, 19,524 ft./5,951 m. above sea level.

The main river system is the Yukon and its tributaries, which drain about 75% of the province. The Yukon rises in northern British Columbia, passes Whitehorse, and runs northwesterly past Dawson City into Alaska. There are several large glacial lakes, mostly in the southwestern part of the territory.

Area: 186,660 sq. mi./483,450 sq. km., of which 1,730 sq. mi./4,481 sq. km. are inland water. The territory makes up 4.8% of the total area of Canada.

Mean maximum and minimum temperatures: Whitehorse 57°F/14°C (July), −4°F/−20°C (January); Dawson City 61°F/16°C (July), −20°F/−29°C (January).

Mean annual precipitation: Whitehorse 10 in./261 mm., of which 54 in./137 cm. is snow; Dawson City 12 in./306 mm., of which 54 in./137 cm. is snow.

POPULATION

Total population (1986 Census): 23,504. Population density averaged 0.1 per sq. mi./0.05 per sq. km. The population was estimated at 29,607 in mid-1990.

Chief town and population (1986 Census): Whitehorse, the capital, 15,199. The biggest population centers, according to mid-1990 estimates, were Whitehorse (20,917), Dawson City (1,802) and Watson Lake (1,623).

Distribution: Whitehorse had 70% of the territorial population, according to mid-1989 estimates. The population was 65% urban in 1986. Although all the rest of the province is sparsely settled, the north is extremely so. Old Crow (population estimated at 265 in mid-1989) is the only settlement found north of Dawson City on a territorial transportation map.

Ethnic composition: Taking into account both single and multiple origin, 57% of the population was of British (including Irish) stock in 1986. On the same basis, 10% of the population was of French ethnic origin. Other European ethnic groups, by single origin only, included Germans, 4%; Scandinavians, 2%; and Dutch and Ukrainians, 1.5% each. The number of aboriginal people was 3,280 (13%), all but 115 Native North American.

Language: English was the mother tongue of 89% of the population and the home language of 97% in 1986. French was the mother tongue of 2.6% and the home language of 1.2%. Other languages accounted for the remaining 8.3% and 1.8%, respectively.

Religion: According to the 1981 census, 24% of the population was Roman Catholic, 20% Anglican, 14% United Church, 4% Lutheran and 3% Presbyterian.

CONSTITUTION AND GOVERNMENT

The Yukon Territory was established in 1898. As a result of administrative changes in recent years, its government closely resembles that of the provinces. However, provincial constitutions, which define the powers of the legislative and executive branches of government as well as the division of legislative power between the federal and provincial governments, are entrenched in the Constitution Act of 1982 and are not subject to change by the federal government. The Yukon Act of 1898, however, which serves as the territorial constitution, is a federal statute legally subject to change at the will of Parliament.

The Yukon Act vests executive authority in a federally appointed commissioner who administers the government under instructions from the federal cabinet or the minister of Indian and northern affairs. In theory, the commissioner's function is similar to that of the lieutenant governor of a province, but a lieutenant governor is legally bound to follow the advice of

the provincial cabinet, which is in turn responsible to the provincial legislature. The commissioner is not legally bound to follow the instructions of
the territorial cabinet. Also, the Yukon's legislature's jurisdiction is defined
by federal legislation and can be overridden by contrary federal legislation.

In practice, the Yukon has a considerable degree of self-government.
Responsible government, in which the executive is responsible to an elected
legislature, has been established in the Yukon, as in the provinces. The
executive council, or cabinet, now consists entirely of elected representatives, and it has entire control of the territorial budget. The commissioner
is bound by its advice in all areas except for matters of special federal
interest and responsibility. These are lands and resources (except wildlife)
and the power to change the Yukon Act.

Executive: The government leader, who is the leader of the majority party
in the legislature, heads a five-member executive council, or cabinet. The
premier appoints the other members of this body from fellow members of
the majority party in the legislature. The council has committees and sub-
committees to deal with social and economic policies and to help the council make decisions. There were nine government departments in 1988.

Legislature: The Yukon Council, popularly called the Legislative Assembly, is a single-chambered body with 16 members in 1989, seven of whom
represented Whitehorse districts. There were four standing committees: the
Members' Services Board; the Rules, Elections and Privileges Committee;
the Public Accounts Committee; and the Statutory Instruments Committee. There were also special committees on constitutional development and
privileges. The most recent election was in February 1989.

Political parties: Local party politics in the Yukon began in 1970, when a
slate of candidates ran in the territorial elections as Liberals. In the 1974
elections, candidates from the Liberal and New Democratic parties ran for
election, but most of those elected were independents. The 1978 Yukon
territorial elections were the first to have candidates from all three major
national parties. In these, and the 1982 elections, the Progressive Conservatives won a majority of seats. In the 1985 elections, New Democrats
won eight seats, Progressive Conservatives, six, and Liberals, two. The
New Democrats achieved a majority in 1987 when a New Democrat won
a by-election for a vacant opposition seat. In the 1989 elections, the New
Democrats retained power by winning nine seats to seven for the Conservatives. New Democrats polled 45% of the total vote, Conservatives, 44%,
and Liberals, 11%. In October 1991 the Progressive Conservative Party's
convention changed the party name to the Yukon Party to disassociate itself
from the federal Progressive Conservative Party, returning to the name it
first had when organized in 1978.

Local government: There is one city, Whitehorse; and there are three towns,
Dawson City, Faro and Watson Lake; four villages, Carmacks, Haines
Junction, Mayo and Teslin; and one hamlet, Elsa. The 10 unincorporated

communities include Beaver Creek, Burwash Landing, Carcross, Destruction Bay, Old Crow, Pelly Crossing, Ross River and Tagish. Cities, towns and villages have full municipal status and are responsible for their own taxation and administration. The territorial government provides municipal services to the unorganized communities.

Federal representation: The Yukon sends one elected representative to the House of Commons. A New Democrat was chosen in the 1988 election (and became national leader of the NDP in December 1989). The territory is represented in the Senate by one federally appointed member.

Judicial system: The Yukon has responsibility for the administration of justice except for criminal prosecutions. The Criminal Code specifies that the federal attorney general is also attorney general for the Yukon. The Supreme Court has original jurisdiction in all civil actions not expressly excluded by statute. In 1989 it consisted of a judge in Yukon and two in the Northwest Territories, all federally appointed. The Court of Appeal consisted of judges of the British Columbia Court of Appeal, the Supreme Court judge from the Yukon, and a Supreme Court judge from the Northwest Territories. Appeals beyond this court go to the Supreme Court of Canada.

The Territorial Court can hear small claims not exceeding $1,500, excluding actions regarding title to land; the validity of any devise, bequest or limitation; malicious prosecution; false imprisonment; libel; or slander. In 1988 it consisted of a chief judge, two puisne judges, and seven deputy judges, all territorially appointed. There were, in 1988, 34 justices of the peace in 16 communities. These are Yukon residents wherever possible and practical. The Council for Yukon Indians administers a Native court worker service. The Yukon justice department enforces court orders on spousal and child support through a maintenance-enforcement program and administers a victim-witness program to help people unaccustomed to appearing in court.

RECENT HISTORY

The Klondike gold strike of 1896, though spectacular for a time, petered out within a decade. In 1941 the population was only 4,914, but the construction of the Alaska Highway through the territory in World War II provided a lasting stimulus to development. In 1948 legal provision was made for the reappointment of a commissioner as chief executive officer of the Yukon. Territorial council elections were held in 1970. In 1971 the commissioner was instructed by the minister of Indian and northern affairs to establish an executive committee consisting of himself, two assistant commissioners (one a federal and the other a territorial civil servant), and two elected council members to be full-time executive officers paid from the Yukon consolidated revenue fund. Although the commissioner remained ultimately responsible for the administration of government, he was instructed to give the fullest possible consideration to the advice of the executive committee, particularly to that of the elected members, who were each to be assigned administrative responsibility for one or more departments. By 1978, the number of elected council members given executive responsibility had grown to five. In 1979, the executive committee was superseded by an executive council of five elected members. In time, the commissioner withdrew from an active role in the executive and was replaced by the leader of the majority party in the legislature. Resource-management programs, including those in forestry and mining, are gradually being transferred from the federal to the territorial government.

Economic development in recent years has included the completion of a road in 1978 through the territory to the Pacific at Skagway, Alaska, completion of a highway in 1979 between Dawson and Inuvik in the Mackenzie River delta of the Northwest Territories, and the opening of a lead-zinc mine. All major mines in the territory closed in the early 1980s, but mining activity rebounded in the latter half of the decade.

An important issue in the 1980s was the question of a federal settlement of Indian land claims. An agreement-in-principle of January 16, 1989 provided for Yukon Indians to receive $233 million over 15 years and retain ownership of some 16,000 sq. mi./41,500 sq. km. of land.

ECONOMY

Extraction of primary resources, especially minerals, has always been the mainstay of the territorial economy. Tourism is of increasing importance and is actually the Yukon's second largest industry.

Agriculture: Farming in the Yukon is negligible because of marginal soil, climatic and topographical restrictions, high costs and the availability of imported food. Permafrost is widespread through the territory. Nevertheless, there were 29 full-time and 75 part-time farmers in 1987, and the estimated value of agricultural production was $1.3 million.

Forestry: About 67.7 million acres/27.4 million hectares or 57% of the territory, is classified as forest land. All of it is federally owned, and more than 90% of the trees are softwoods. About 12% of the territory is considered productive forest, with the best stands in the moist eastern parts, especially the Liard River valley, where such trees as spruce, pine, aspen, poplar and birch are available. In 1986, nearly 17 billion cu. ft./480 million cu. m. of wood was available. Total production in 1989–90 was 5.5 million cu. ft./155,700 cu. m., of which 39% was lumber and 64% was fuelwood. The estimated value of forest products in 1987 was $7.2 million. With the reactivation in 1987 of a large sawmill by the newly formed Yukon Development Corporation, lumber production is expected to increase significantly.

Fishing and trapping: Fish are important to the diet of many Yukon Native people. Fish landings in the Yukon and Northwest Territories combined totaled 1,430 tons/1,298 tonnes in 1985, with a value of $1.5 million;

however, the latter accounted for most of this total, since the Yukon catch was worth only $294,000 in 1987. Salmon, lake trout and whitefish are of commercial value. Subsistence fishing (and hunting), primarily by Indians, is of importance, particularly in the smaller, rural communities. There is some fish and caviar processing and aquaculture. Trapping is also economically significant. The value of fur production was $1,067,916 in 1989, of which marten accounted for 63% and lynx for 31%. Pelts of bear, beaver, coyote, ermine, fisher, fox, mink, muskrat, otter, squirrel, wolf and wolverine were also sold.

Mining: A major lead-zinc mine at Faro reopened in 1986. Some 174,000 tons/158,000 tonnes of zinc (1989) and 129,000 tons/117,000 tonnes of lead (1988) were extracted, with a value of $341.6 million and $118.7 million, respectively. Two hard-rock gold mines went into production during 1987–88, and the 200 or so placer-gold operations set a 70-year production record in 1987. Gold production was about 13,000 lb./6,000 kg. in 1989, worth $80.5 million. Sharply increased silver production of 350,000 lb./159,000 kg. was valued at $42.5 million, but this fell to 141,000 lb./ 64,000 kg. ($13.4 million) in 1989. Small amounts of antimony, cadmium, copper, iron ore, molybdenum, nickel and sulfur are also mined. All told, metallic mineral output was valued at $486.8 million in 1988 and $534.4 million in 1989. In 1989 quarrying yielded 2.6 million tons/ 2.37 million tonnes of sand and gravel, worth $15.7 million, and in 1987 produced only 227,000 tons/206,000 tonnes of stone, worth $679,000.

Energy: There is no coal, petroleum, or natural-gas production in the Yukon. The Yukon assets of the federal Northern Canada Power Commission were transferred to the new publicly owned Yukon Energy Corporation in 1987. Installed electrical generating capacity was 107 megawatts in that year, 72% hydroelectric and the rest thermal. The major hydroelectric facilities are at Whitehorse, Aishihik and Mayo. Electricity generation in 1989 totaled 440,236 megawatt hours, of which 92% was hydroelectric and the rest thermal.

Manufacturing: Yukon-made goods include furniture, vinyl windows, trusses, printed materials, chocolates, clothing, handicrafts and gold-nugget jewelry. The value of manufactured shipments in the Yukon was estimated at $46 million in 1986.

Transportation: The Alaska Highway runs through Watson Lake and Whitehorse, continuing west to Fairbanks, Alaska. Two roads link the Yukon to Pacific outlets in Alaska: the Haines Highway, which meets the Alaska Highway at Haines Junction, and the Klondike Highway, which links Skagway, Alaska with Carcross, Carmacks, Mayo and Elsa. The Dempster Highway runs north from a point near Dawson to Inuvik in the Northwest Territories. In all, there are more than 3,040 mi./4,900 km. of roads in the territory, but only about 175 mi./280 km. are paved, and much of the road mileage is unusable in winter. In 1988–89, 27,080 road vehicles were registered, including 15,290 trucks and truck tractors, 9,030 passenger cars and 3,600 trailers. Most goods are hauled by truck. The Alaskan ports of Skagway and Haines provided a maritime outlet.

A 110-mi./177-km. narrow-gauge railway linking Skagway and Whitehorse, particularly important in exporting minerals, closed in 1982. A stretch of this railway has resumed service in order to carry cruise-ship tourists from Skagway to the summit of White Pass. The Whitehorse airport provides daily scheduled and charter links with Alaska, southern Canada via Vancouver and Edmonton, and the lower 48 U.S. states. In 1989, 49,997 passengers arrived at, and 51,587 departed from, Whitehorse airport by scheduled air carrier. Dawson City, Faro, Mayo, Old Crow, Ross River, Teslin and Watson Lake are also served by commercial air flights, and other settlements have airstrips.

Wholesale and retail trade: The combined volume of wholesale trade in the Yukon and Northwest territories was $152.6 million in 1986. Retail trade in the Yukon totaled $225.0 million in 1989.

Banking and finance: The Yukon and Northwest territories had 27 bank branches in 1987, of which the Canadian Imperial Bank of Commerce had 16. Private investment in the territories totaled $609.4 million in 1987; public investment totaled $505 million.

Construction: There were 1,172 building permits issued in 1989, valued at 49.6 million.

Tourism: Visitors are attracted to the Yukon Territory by its colorful gold-rush past and its Indians, hunting and fishing, scenery and wildlife. Kluane National Park has headquarters at Haines Junction, and the United States and Canada have jointly created the Klondike Gold Rush International Historical Park. The Northern Yukon National Park was established in 1984, and the first territorial park was established in 1987 on Herschel Island. Whitehorse has an annual winter festival, and the territory hosts the Arctic Winter Games every six years. In 1987, there were 498,000 visitors who spent an estimated $100 million. Almost half entered from Alaska.

Public finance: The 1990–91 territorial budget forecast $371.3 million in territorial spending and projected a deficit of $9.6 million. About 29% was expected to go to the Department of Community and Transportation Services, 19% to the Department of Education, and 17% to the Department of Health and Human Resources. Yukon Territory was expected to receive $204 million from the federal government during 1990–91, not counting the federal share of cost-shared programs. Most of the remaining funds come from taxes now levied directly by the legislature. The personal income-tax rate in 1990 was 45% of the federal tax. The corporate rate was the lowest in Canada, 2.5% for manufacturing and processing, 10% for other enterprises and 5% for small businesses. There are also taxes on alcoholic beverages, insurance, real property, gasoline, diesel fuel and tobacco. There is no retail sales tax. Other income is obtained from licenses and fees and the sale of government services.

Employment: In August 1990 there were 13,634 people employed and 1,321 in the labor force unemployed, for an unemployment rate of 8%, compared to the national average of 7.9%. By sector, government employed 4,706; accommodations and other services, 2,171; wholesale and retail trade, 2,161; mining and exploration, 1,829; transportation and communication, 1,547; finance and real estate, 439; business and educational services, 339; health and social services, 285; and agriculture, fishing and logging, 50. The average weekly earnings of $577.30 (August 1991) were well above the Canadian average of $501.86. Unemployment-insurance benefits paid out in June 1989 came to more than $1.5 million. The total number of claims in the peak month (February) of 1990 was 2,650.

Prices: In September 1990 the consumer price index was 15.6% higher in Whitehorse than in 1986 and 33.4% higher than it had been in March 1982. Although this rate indicated lower inflation than in Canada generally, the price level is higher. For example, in 1990 prices of all items were 12.3% higher in Whitehorse than in Vancouver, and 22.9% higher than in Edmonton. The weekly cost of a nutritious food basket for a family of four, $128.54 on an 18-city average, was $159.14 in Whitehorse. Prices are even higher in outlying communities.

SOCIAL SERVICES

Welfare: The Canada Assistance Plan extended benefits to 1,200 Yukon residents in fiscal 1987; expenditures were $2.2 million in fiscal 1986. Other federal programs provide old-age pensions and family allowances. The territory provides financial assistance, income supplements, home care, and utility grants for senior citizens. There are adoption services, foster homes, and care centers and subsidies for children.

Health: The territorial government shares responsibility for health service with the federal government and offers hospital and physician insurance. There are modern hospitals in Whitehorse, Dawson, Faro, Mayo and Watson Lake. One or more public-health nurses staffed two nursing stations, 12 health centers, and three health stations in 1987. Clinics, dental services and more specialized medical services are also available, and in emergency cases patients are evacuated by air to Vancouver or Edmonton. A detoxification facility for alcohol and drug-abuse treatment has opened in Whitehorse. The birthrate in 1986 was 20.6 per 1,000 people, higher than the national average, and the death rate was 4.8 per 1,000, lower than the national average. The abortion rate of 24.6 per 100 live births was higher than the national average. In 1987 there were 32 physicians and 16 active licensed dentists in the territory.

Housing: In 1989, 910 residential building permits were issued, with a value of $27.7 million. The average price of a single-family house sold in Whitehorse in 1989 was $89,800, and of a condominium, $62,800. There were 790 rental units in Whitehorse in September 1990, with a median rent of $525, higher than the national average. The vacancy rate was 40% in 1989, whereas in 1988 it had been only 0.5%. The 1986 average home payment (with mortgage) of $801 was also higher than the Canadian average. The territory offers home-improvement assistance, mortgage financing for do-it-yourself homebuilders, and funding for municipal and nonprofit-group housing projects. The Yukon Housing Corporation was expected to spend $14.9 million in 1990–91 on capital programs.

EDUCATION

Education is compulsory between the ages of 7 and 16. All school enrollment was public in 1987–88, when 25 elementary and secondary schools had 4,896 students. The curriculum is based on that of British Columbia, with modifications to reflect local interest. Native Indian-language programs are offered, as are French immersion, French first-language, and standard French courses. Yukon College, which is associated with the University of British Columbia, has a main campus in Whitehorse and 13 campuses in 12 communities, offering two years of university-level education. Specialized diploma and trade programs are also available. In 1988–89 the college had 736 full-time students and 2,831 in extension courses. Financial assistance is available for students who pursue postsecondary education in approved institutions outside the Yukon.

MASS MEDIA

Newspapers and periodicals: The *Whitehorse Star* (1992 circulation 4,337) is published weekday mornings.

Yukon News, published in Whitehorse, appears twice a week. Its 1988 circulation was 4,444. *Dan Sha News,* a monthly for Native Indians, is also published in Whitehorse.

Broadcasting: There are two AM and one FM radio stations, all in Whitehorse. Keno Hill and Whitehorse have television stations; both are licensees of the Canadian Broadcasting Corporation. A cable system in Whitehorse had 4,500 subscribers in 1991.

BIOGRAPHICAL SKETCHES

Antony (Tony) Penikett. Premier and minister responsible for executive council office and department of finance. Born November 14, 1945, Penikett was a union representative at the former Clinton Creek asbestos mine, 1967–70. He was an alderman in Whitehorse, 1977–79, and was first elected to the Legislative Assembly in 1978 as a New Democrat. From 1981 to 1985 he was leader of the opposition in the assembly and also national president of the New Democratic Party. Government leader since 1985, he also served as minister for finance, economic development, and health and human resources, 1985–89. In 1989 he relinquished these portfolios and became minister of mines and of small business.

Piers McDonald. Minister of education and government services, responsible for the Public Service Commission and Worker's Compensation Board. Born August 4, 1955 in Kingston, Ontario, McDonald was a miner who served as president of the United Steelworkers, Yukon, 1981–82. First elected to the Legislative Assembly in 1982, he was minister of education and of community and transportation services, 1985–89. He became house leader and minister of finance, economic development, and education in 1989, and in January 1991 he took over as minister of education and government services.

Margaret Muriel Joe. Minister of justice, responsible for the Women's Directorate and the Yukon Liquor Commission. Joe is a Yukon Indian who attended Vancouver Community College and was a practical nurse from 1963 to 1970. The first woman to hold a cabinet position in the Yukon, she has been a justice of the peace and has held many positions in organizations connected with the rights of women and of Indians. She was first elected to the Legislative Assembly in 1982 and served as minister of health and human resources from 1985 to 1989. In 1989 she was appointed minister of justice and minister responsible for the Public Service Commission and Workers' Compensation Board. In 1991 she was made responsible for the Women's Directorate and the Yukon Liquor Commission.

Arthur Victor Webster. Minister of renewable resources and of tourism. Born December 31, 1946, Webster received science degrees from the University of Waterloo in Ontario and Dalhousie University in Nova Scotia. He was executive director of the Yukon Sports Federation, 1976–79. Elected to the Legislative Assembly in 1985, he was deputy speaker from 1985 to 1989, when he was named minister of renewable resources and of tourism.

Daniel Lang. Leader of the opposition. Born in 1948 in Dawson Creek, British Columbia, Lang was educated in Whitehorse and at the University of Alaska. He worked as a real estate agent. He was first elected in 1974 and was reelected in 1978, 1982, 1985 and 1989. He served as minister of education, 1975–78, minister of highways and public works, municipal and community affairs, 1978–80; tourism and economic development, 1980–82; and education and social services, 1984–85. He was minister of tourism and small business briefly in 1985, until the Progressive Conservative Party was defeated. He became leader of the opposition in 1991, and when the party became the Yukon Party he declared he would run for its leadership at a 1991 convention. He withdrew at the last moment and John Ostashek, born 1935, who did not have a seat in the legislature, was acclaimed leader of the party at the November convention. Lang remained leader of the opposition in the legislature until the next general election.

170

COMPARATIVE STATISTICS

WILBUR GRASHAM

POPULATION[1]

	Population (thousands) 1989	Percent of Total	Percent Intercensal Increase 1981–86[2]	Density per sq. km. (sq. mi.) 1989	Percent Urban 1986[3] 1989	Percent Under 18 1989	Percent 65 or Over 1989	Median Age 1989
Newfoundland	570.0	2.2	0.1	1.5 (0.6)	58.9	29.6	9.3	29.5
Prince Edward Island	130.2	0.5	3.4	22.4 (8.7)	38.1	27.5	12.6	31.6
Nova Scotia	886.8	3.4	3.0	16.5 (6.4)	54.0	25.3	12.4	32.4
New Brunswick	718.5	2.7	2.0	9.9 (3.8)	49.4	26.5	11.8	32.0
Quebec	6,688.7	25.5	1.6	4.8 (1.9)	77.9	24.1	10.7	33.3
Ontario	9,569.5	36.5	5.7	9.9 (3.8)	82.1	24.4	11.5	33.1
Manitoba	1,084.2	4.2	4.4	2.0 (0.8)	72.1	26.5	13.1	32.2
Saskatchewan	1,007.0	3.8	4.3	1.8 (0.7)	61.4	28.7	13.4	31.3
Alberta	2,429.2	9.3	6.1	3.7 (1.4)	79.4	27.9	8.8	30.5
British Columbia	3,055.6	11.7	5.3	3.2 (1.2)	79.2	24.1	13.0	34.2
Yukon	25.4	0.1	1.5	0.04 (0.015)	—	30	3.9	29.4
Northwest Territories	53.4	0.2	14.2	0.01 (0.004)	—	38	2.8	24.4
Canada	26,218.5	100.0	4.2	2.8 (1.1)	76.5	24.9	11.1	32.8

[1] Statistics Canada, *Preliminary Postcensal Estimates 1989.*
[2] Statistics Canada, *Canada Year Book 1990.*
[3] 1986 Census, quoted in *The Canadian Encyclopedia.*

173

IMMIGRANT POPULATION BY PLACE OF BIRTH, 1986
(thousands)

	Total Immigrants	United States	Other North and Central America	South America	Europe	Africa	Asia	Oceania	Intended Destination Immigrants in 1987
Newfoundland	8.9	2.3	0.060	0.065	4.9	0.16	1.2	0.06	0.46
Prince Edward Island	4.3	1.6	0.060	0.060	2.1	0.075	0.38	0.030	0.16
Nova Scotia	40.5	9.9	0.49	0.32	22.9	0.68	4.6	0.20	1.23
New Brunswick	27.0	10.7	0.095	0.22	13.0	0.39	1.9	0.13	0.64
Quebec	527.1	34.8	7.5	16.9	298.0	35.0	83.9	0.95	26.8
Ontario	2,081.2	106.2	14.2	73.5	1,387.3	42.2	314.9	8.6	84.8
Manitoba	142.2	10.1	4.2	5.0	87.6	1.9	28.5	0.60	4.8
Saskatchewan	72.0	12.9	0.54	1.2	43.2	1.4	11.2	0.50	2.1
Alberta	368.8	36.4	3.5	8.3	209.4	13.0	84.5	4.7	12.0
British Columbia	630.7	56.3	3.7	7.9	363.2	15.5	161.5	18.3	18.9
Yukon	2.7	0.67	0.015	1.6	0.015	0.20	0.11	0.15	—
Northwest Territories	2.8	0.29	0.010	1.7	0.95	0.51	0.040	0.025	—
Canada	3,908.1	282.0	34.3	114.1	2345.1	114.4	692.6	34.28	152.1

Source: Statistics Canada, *Canada Year Book 1990, 1986 Census.*

VITAL STATISTICS

	Marriages Per 1,000 Population 1988	Divorces Per 1,000 Population 1988	Divorces Per 1,000 Married Women 15 and Older 1987	Births Per 1,000 Population 1988	Total* Fertility Rate 1988	Therapeutic Abortions Per 100 Live Births 1988	Infant Deaths Under One Year Per 1,000 Live Births 1988	Deaths Per 1,000 Population 1988	Life Expectancy at Birth 1986 m.	Life Expectancy at Birth 1986 f.
Newfoundland	5.9	1.6	7.6	14.2	n.a.	6.3	9.3	6.4	72.7	79.4
Prince Edward Island	7.4	2.0	8.1	15.3	1.9	3.5	7.1	8.9	72.6	80.4
Nova Scotia	7.6	2.8	12.4	14.0	1.6	14.2	6.5	8.3	72.2	79.4
New Brunswick	7.0	2.4	11.3	13.9	1.6	4.9	7.2	7.7	72.5	79.9
Quebec	5.0	3.0	12.2	12.7	1.5	14.7	6.5	7.4	72.0	79.6
Ontario	7.9	3.2	14.5	14.5	1.7	20.8	6.6	7.4	73.5	79.8
Manitoba	7.2	2.8	14.4	15.8	1.9	16.6	7.8	8.1	73.0	79.8
Saskatchewan	6.3	2.4	11.2	16.6	2.1	7.7	8.4	7.7	73.7	80.4
Alberta	7.8	4.0	15.9	17.5	1.9	15.0	8.3	5.6	73.5	80.0
British Columbia	7.6	3.6	15.7	14.4	1.8	25.5	8.4	7.4	74.0	80.4
Yukon	7.9	3.8		19.5	2.2	22.6	5.8	4.8	n.a.	n.a.
Northwest Territories	4.6	1.8	14.0	29.3	3.1	17.9	10.3	4.0	n.a.	n.a.
Canada	6.9	2.9	13.7	14.5	1.7	17.6	7.2	7.3	73.0	79.7

Sources: Statistics Canada, *Canada Year Book 1990*; *Health Reports*; *Report on the Demographic Situation in Canada, 1990*; *The Daily*, October 6, 1989.
*The number of children that would be produced by each woman throughout reproductive life assuming current age-specific birthrates. A value of 2.1 is required for replacement.

GEOGRAPHY AND CLIMATE[1]

	Land Area sq. km. (sq. mi.) 1000's	Fresh Water sq. km. (sq. mi.) 1000's	Total Area sq. km. (sq. mi.) 1000's	Greatest Elevation Meters (feet)	Major Urban Area	Elevation[2] Meters (feet)	Mean Daily[3] Temperature Jan. °C (°F)	July °C (°F)	Precipitation Total mm. (in.)	Snow cm. (in.)	Frost-free[4] Days
Newfoundland	371.7 (143.5)	34.0 (13.1)	405.7 (156.6)	1,622 (5,321)	St. John's	140 (439)	-3.9 (25.0)	15.5 (59.9)	1514 (60)	359 (141)	139
Prince Edward Island	5.7 (2.2)	0	5.7 (2.2)	142 (466)	Charlottetown	55 (180)	-7.1 (19.2)	18.3 (65.0)	1169 (46)	331 (130)	151
Nova Scotia	52.8 (20.4)	2.7 (1.0)	55.5 (21.4)	532 (1,745)	Halifax	32 (105)	-3.1 (26.4)	18.2 (64.8)	1282 (50)	217 (85)	155
New Brunswick	72.1 (27.8)	1.3 (0.5)	73.4 (28.3)	820 (2,690)	Saint John	109 (358)	-7.8 (18.0)	16.9 (62.4)	1444 (57)	293 (115)	139
Quebec	1,356.8 (523.9)	183.9 (71.0)	1,540.7 (594.9)	1,622 (5,321)	Montreal	36 (118)	-10.2 (13.6)	20.9 (69.6)	946 (37)	235 (93)	157
Ontario	891.2 (344.1)	177.4 (68.5)	1,068.6 (412.6)	693 (2,274)	Toronto	173 (568)	-6.7 (20.0)	20.6 (69.0)	762 (30)	131 (52)	149

Province/Territory					City						
Manitoba	548.4 (211.7)	101.6 (39.2)	650.0 (250.9)	832 (2,729)	Winnipeg	239 (784)	−19.3 (−2.7)	19.6 (67.3)	526 (21)	126 (50)	121
Saskatchewan	570.7 (220.4)	81.6 (31.3)	652.3 (251.9)	1,468 (4,816)	Saskatoon	501 (1,644)	−19.3 (−2.7)	18.5 (65.3)	349 (14)	113 (44)	117
Alberta	644.4 (248.8)	16.8 (6.5)	661.2 (255.3)	3,747 (12,293)	Edmonton	715 (2,346)	−16.5 (2.3)	15.8 (60.4)	467 (18)	138 (54)	105
British Columbia	929.7 (344.1)	18.1 (7.0)	947.8 (365.9)	4,663 (15,299)	Vancouver	3 (9)	2.5 (27.5)	17.3 (63.1)	1113 (44)	60 (24)	216
Yukon	479.0 (184.9)	4.5 (1.7)	483.4 (186.7)	5,951 (19,524)	Whitehorse	703 (2,306)	−20.7 (−5.3)	14.1 (57.4)	261 (10)	137 (54)	82
Northwest Territories	3,293.0 (1,271.5)	133.3 (51.5)	3,426.3 (1,322.9)	2,773 (9,098)	Yellowknife	205 (673)	−28.8 (−19.8)	16.3 (61.3)	267 (11)	135 (53)	111
Canada	9,215.0 (3,557.9)	755.2 (251.6)	9,970.6 (3,849.7)	5,951 (19,624)							

Sources: *Canada Year Book 1990*; Canada Climate Centre, *Canadian Climate Normals*

[1] Climate data are for the major urban area within each jurisdiction.

[2] Minimum elevation for all provinces and territories except Alberta and Saskatchewan is the sea level of their coasts.

[3] Elevations and climate are from airport weather stations, described as having climates compatible with those of suburban portions of the related urban areas.

[4] The average number of days between the last frost in spring and the first frost in autumn or winter.

177

DEATHS FROM SELECTED CAUSES
Rates per 100,000 of population in 1988

	All Cancers	Diseases of the Heart	Cerebro-vascular Diseases	Accidents Motor Vehicle	All Other Accidents	Suicide	Murder
Newfoundland	148	203	49	12	18	8	1.2*
Prince Edward Island	192	288	68	15*	27	10*	0.8*
Nova Scotia	222	260	57	17	23	12	1.5*
New Brunswick	188	250	53	23	21	15	1.0*
Quebec	197	223	47	16	20	16	1.6
Ontario	200	233	58	14	20	11	1.7
Manitoba	212	243	65	14	25	14	2.4*
Saskatchewan	196	256	64	21	27	14	2.0*
Alberta	144	164	43	20	21	17	2.8
British Columbia	200	211	62	18	23	13	2.2
Yukon[1]	186	123	32*	44*	55*	28*	3.9*
Northwest Territories[1]	96	60	14*	10*	64	40*	12*
Canada	196	223	54	16	21	13.5	1.9

Source: Statistics Canada, Health Reports, vol. 2.
[1] Rates for the Yukon and the Northwest Territories vary greatly from year to year because of their small populations.
* Rates marked with * are based on fewer than 30 items.

LANGUAGE

	English		French		Other	
	Percent Mother Tongue	Percent Home Language	Percent Mother Tongue	Percent Home Language	Percent Mother Tongue	Percent Home Language
Newfoundland	98.8	99.2	0.5	0.4	0.8	0.4
Prince Edward Island	94.1	96.8	4.7	2.8	1.2	0.4
Nova Scotia	93.8	96.0	4.1	2.9	2.1	1.1
New Brunswick	65.3	68.1	33.5	31.3	1.3	0.6
Quebec	10.4	12.3	82.8	82.8	6.8	4.9
Ontario	78.0	86.6	5.3	3.8	16.7	9.6
Manitoba	73.4	87.2	4.9	2.8	21.8	9.9
Saskatchewan	81.9	93.8	2.3	0.9	15.7	5.3
Alberta	82.3	92.0	2.4	1.1	15.3	6.9
British Columbia	82.1	91.4	1.6	0.6	16.3	8.0
Yukon	89.1	97.0	2.6	1.2	8.3	1.8
Northwest Territories	55.3	66.2	2.7	1.5	42.0	32.4
Canada	62.1	68.9	25.1	24.0	12.8	7.0

Source: Statistics Canada, *Canada Year Book, 1986 Census.*

ELEMENTARY AND SECONDARY EDUCATION

	Number Elementary and Secondary Schools 1988–89	Enrollment Elementary & Secondary Schools 1988–89		Pupil-Teacher Ratio Public Elementary and Secondary Schools 1988–89	Average Teacher Salary Including Administrators 1985–86	Expenditure Elementary/ Secondary Education 1987–88 (millions)
		Public (000)	Private (000)			
Newfoundland	558	133.0	0.30	15.8	31,222	529.4
Prince Edward Island	73	24.8	0.08	17.8	31,765	93.1
Nova Scotia	568	167.6	1.9	16.4	38,063	739.7
New Brunswick	464	136.5	0.95	17.4	33,349	647.2
Quebec	2,881	1,035.2	99.19	15.7	n.a.	6,491.8
Ontario	5,260	1,864.7	63.10	15.7	39,564	9,206.8
Manitoba	844	198.8	10.00	15.3	36,271	1,099.7
Saskatchewan	1,006	202.5	3.05	16.8	34,362	1,043.6
Alberta	1,694	461.2	14.46	17.7	36,413[1]	2,289.2
British Columbia	1,932	500.1	37.7	17.3	37,529	2,267.3
Yukon	26	0.5	—	14.6	44,242	40.7
Northwest Territories	72	13.4	—	15.7	44,219	127.8
Canada	15,387	4,742.8	230.8	16.1	37,912[2]	24,611.8

Source: Statistics Canada, *Education in Canada 1988–89. Characteristics of Teachers in Public Schools, 1985–86.*
[1] The Alberta salary is for 1984–85.
[2] This average excludes Alberta and Quebec.

MEDIA

	Daily Papers 1991	Other Papers[1,2] 1991	Thomson[3] Newspaper Corporation	Radio[4,5] Stations 1990	TV[4,5] Stations 1990	Operating Cable Systems 1990	Cable Business Organizations 1990
Newfoundland	2	19	2	48	7	245	35
Prince Edward Island	2	4	2	5	1	18	3
Nova Scotia	6	33	3	41	12	68	36
New Brunswick[6]	4	23	1	38	9	124	19
Quebec[6,7]	12	78	—	167	60	299	234
Ontario[6,7]	48	343	33	206	36	291	97
Manitoba	6	53	2	29	8	71	21
Saskatchewan	5	91	4	31	13	228	31
Alberta	10	136	1	82	15	159	33
British Columbia	20	152	5	146	12	142	98
Yukon and Northwest Territories[5,8]	—	8	—	14	3	—	—

Sources: Statistics Canada, *Communications Service Bulletin*; *Canadian Almanac and Directory*; *Matthews List*.

[1]Most weekly, some twice weekly and others monthly or twice monthly. Some papers publish editions under the same or different names for neighboring suburbs or communities.

[2]There are in addition to English and French newspapers enumerated here at least 127 "ethnic" newspapers. Most are weekly or even monthly but there are Chinese dailies in Vancouver and Toronto.

[3]Thomson Newspaper Corporation controls these 53 newspapers in Canada, including *The Globe and Mail* (Toronto) which also publishes a national edition, and the *Financial Times of Canada*. Southam Inc. controls 16 dailies and a number of weeklies. There are other small chains.

[4]All radio and television stations, public or private. These, together with all cable systems, must be licensed by the Canadian Radio Television Commission (CRTC).

[5]The Canadian Broadcasting Corporation owns and operates television and radio stations (in 1985, 31 television stations and 68 radio stations), providing services in both French and English through these and affiliated stations. The CBC Northern Service provides radio and television for the Yukon and the Northwest Territories in English and Native languages.

[6]There is one French-language daily in Ontario and one in New Brunswick, and there are three English-language dailies in Ontario.

[7]Provincial governments have the power to incorporate provincially financed agencies to provide educational broadcasts for all ages, not just for schoolchildren. TV Ontario, with 21 operating transmitters, provides services in English and French. Radio-Quebec, with 19 stations, provides services in French.

[8]Yukon and N.W.T. cable systems and cable business organizations are included under British Columbia.

181

POSTSECONDARY EDUCATION
(Universities and Colleges)

	Universities and Other Degree-Granting Institutions	Undergraduate Enrollment Full Time (Part Time) 1988–89 (000)	Graduate Enrollment Full Time (Part Time) 1988–89 (000)	Expenditure[1] Universities (Total) 1987–88 (millions)	Community Colleges	Enrollment[2] Community Colleges Full Time (Part Time) 1988–89 (000)	Expenditure Community Colleges 1987–88 (millions)
Newfoundland	1	10.7 (4.1)	0.68 (0.61)	172.9	12	3.2 (0.19)	32.6
Prince Edward Island	1	2.2 (0.8)	0.016 —	36.2	2	0.98	10.1
Nova Scotia	12	23.0 (6.5)	2.2 (1.4)	332.6	10	2.7 (0.35)	30.4
New Brunswick	5	14.9 (4.6)	0.80 (0.59)	207.9	8	2.5 (0.019)	38.9
Quebec	8	100.5 (107.3)	18.4 (17.0)	2,024.1	87	70.6 (11.2)	1,376.1

Ontario	22	178.2 (89.6)	22.9 (11.9)	2,813.1	31	94.5 (76.1)	967.8
Manitoba	6	17.5 (13.5)	2.3 (1.6)	321.1	10	3.8 (1.9)	61.1
Saskatchewan	3	18.9 (8.4)	1.4 (0.78)	302.3	1	3.2 (0.53)	58.3
Alberta	5	40.9 (17.3)	5.3 (2.2)	896.8	19	21.2 (7.7)	372.6
British Columbia	6	32.7 (16.4)	5.9 (1.6)	689.2	19	13.5 (19.1)	255.2
Yukon	0	—	—	0.90	1	0.053 (.51)	6.5
Northwest Territories	0	—	—	1.7	1	0.22 (.11)	17.1
Canada	69	439.4 (268.6)	59.8 (37.6)	7,911.1	201	216.6 (117.1)	3,228.8

Source: Statistics Canada, *Education in Canada 1988–89, 1989–90.*

[1]Funds from the government of Canada, provincial governments, local governments, fees and other sources.

[2]These numbers are for students in career-oriented programs, and exclude students in university transfer programs as follows: Quebec 85,537 full time and 51,032 part time; Alberta 3.408 full time and 856 part time; British Columbia 11,982 full time and 15,540 part time; Yukon 98 full time and 98 part time.

CRIME AND CRIMINAL JUSTICE [1]

	Criminal Offenses per 1,000 Population 1989	Persons Charged Adult (Young)[2] 1989	Average No. Persons in Provincial Custody Adult 1988–89	Average No. Probation & Provincial Parole Adult 1989–90	Police Officers All Forces[3] 1989	Total Policing Expenditures All Forces (millions) 1989	Staff Provincial Correctional Services Adult 1989–90	Per Capita Provincial Expenditure Adult Correctional Services 1989–90
Newfoundland	82	18,979 (5,394)	300	995	836	74.2	305	27.32
Prince Edward Island	104	5,146 (1,066)	76	593	178	14.1	109	31.94
Nova Scotia	107	33,714 (5,306)	367	3,043	1,492	108.8	427	25.44
New Brunswick	92	20,536 (5,071)	355	2,010	1,234	94.8	415	21.68
Quebec	80	141,755 (27,690)	2,837	8,238	14,338	1,237.4	2,543	20.73
Ontario	113	367,132 (89,921)	5,945	38,107	19,897	1,644.9	6,679	39.89
Manitoba	116	31,206 (11,693)	895	3,488	2,129	156.6	652	33.91

Saskatchewan	148	55,339 (13,472)	1,318	2,851	1,916	160.0	828	40.90
Alberta	143	95,724 (28,438)	2,185	5,576	4,303	367.2	1,717	38.14
British Columbia	166	81,535 (35,264)	1,817	9,798	5,649	467.6	1,521	29.02
Yukon	360	3,429 (675)	86	584	101	13.6	65	200.00
Northwest Territories	411	6,196 (1,776)	255	388	197	34.2	236	190.00
Canada	114	860,739 (225,766)	16,436	75,681	52,270	4,684.7	15,497	32.53

Sources: Statistics Canada, *Canadian Crime Statistics*; *Adult Correctional Services in Canada*; *Policing in Canada*; Canadian Centre for Justice Statistics, *Juristat*.

[1] Provinces have jurisdiction over the administration of justice including criminal justice in the province, and pay for the provincial court system apart from the salaries of the judge of the superior, district and county courts, who are appointed by the federal government. Offenders sentenced to two years or more are sent to federal prisons; those with two years less one day or shorter sentences are sent to provincial institutions. The Criminal Code is an act of the Parliament of Canada, but there are other federal statutes that carry criminal sanctions, as well as provincial statutes and some municipal bylaws. Three provinces have parole boards; the others are served by the federal board. In 1989–90 the average number of inmates in federal custody was about 11,400. The federal parole system served some 8,300 offenders from federal prisons and 8,900 from provincial. This included 2,500 released under statutory mandatory supervision or earned remission. It is not possible to allocate inmates and parolees in the federal system to provinces.

[2] Offenders under 18 and 12 or over are since 1984 dealt with under the Young Offenders Act. Apart from very serious cases, which may be taken to adult court, the correctional arrangements are more flexible with less reliance on confinement.

[3] Ontario and Quebec have provincial police forces and Newfoundland and New Brunswick have some provincial police services. These latter two and other provinces contract for policing services from the Royal Canadian Mounted Police, the federal police force, as do many municipalities. There are also railway and ports police included in the totals.

PROVINCIAL LEGISLATURES AND EXECUTIVES[1]
1987/1988

	Number of Members of Legislature	Member's Indemnity Plus Tax-free Allowance[2]	Average Sitting Days	Size of Executive Council (cabinet)[3]	Premier's Additional Indemnity	Minister's Additional Indemnity	Percentage of Members with Additional Indemnity[4]
Newfoundland	52	39,814	80	21	46,742	33,888	58
Prince Edward Island	32	27,000	40	11	43,000	33,000	44
Nova Scotia	52	38,410	85	21	42,510	32,950	100
New Brunswick	58	44,097	60	20	43,046	28,699	34
Quebec	122	61,968	90	28	55,427	39,951	76
Ontario	130	52,400	92	30	48,367	28,743	68
Manitoba	57	37,521	86	20	26,600	20,600	49
Saskatchewan	64	31,452	76	15	37,656	28,327	56
Alberta	83	35,649	80	26	50,157	40,841	38.5
British Columbia	69	40,047	79	17	45,000	39,000	58
Yukon	16	36,656	50	5	62,655	56,415	56
Northwest Territories	24	19,720	60	8	30,496	22,260	63

Source: Robert J. Fleming, *Canadian Legislatures 1987/1988*.

[1]The formal executive is the lieutenant governor advised by the Executive Council, the lieutenant governor in Council, the lieutenant governor advised by the Executive Council, members of which are drawn from the governing party in the Legislative Assembly and form the cabinet, where actual power lies. The lieutenant governor, representing the Queen, and the Legislative Assembly together form the legislature of the province. The lieutenant governor is appointed by the federal cabinet for a term of five years and is also an officer of the federal government. The Constitution Act prohibits amendment of the office by provincial legislatures. The lieutenant governor's salary, in 1990–91 $82,900, is an indexed statutory payment by the federal government, which also provides a pension. Both federal and provincial governments provide other expenses and allowances.

The title is pronounced in the British way: "leftenant."

[2]The tax-free allowance in 1988 varied from $7,883 in Alberta to $13,750 plus a new 8% raise in British Columbia.

[3]The premier nominates those who are sworn as ministers and members of the Executive Council and, although departmental ministers are provided for by statute, the size of the Executive Council is effectively at the discretion of the premier; e.g., a minister may be given several portfolios or a junior minister may be provided in a department. On September 11, 1990 the Manitoba government was returned with a reduced majority and on September 22 the revised Executive Council was sworn in with 18 members. In a 1990 cabinet shuffle the Quebec Executive Council was increased to 30. After the election of June 1990, the new premier of Ontario formed his new cabinet with 25 members.

[4]In most provinces the leader of the opposition received the same additional indemnity as a minister. Other members receiving additional indemnities included speakers and deputy speakers, third party leaders, parliamentary assistants, committee chairmen and party whips.

PROVINCIAL AND MUNICIPAL FINANCE AND EMPLOYMENT

	Provincial Government Own Revenues[1] 1988–89 (millions)	Transfers to Province From Other Governments[2] 1988–89 (millions)	Provincial Total Gross General Expenditure 1988–89 (millions)	Provincial Transfers to Local Governments[3] 1988 (millions)	Provincial Government Employment[4] 1989 (000)	Local Government Employment (General Service) 1989 (000)
Newfoundland	1,553	1,358	2,992	97	26	3.2
Prince Edward Island	352	285	642	101	5.4	0.52
Nova Scotia	2,292	1,475	4,104	876	28	8.2
New Brunswick	2,031	1,406	3,527	153	42	5.1
Quebec	30,053	6,537	37,155	5,649	147	72
Ontario	36,207	5,351	42,014	7,986	178	162
Manitoba	4,145	1,448	5,612	938	34	12
Saskatchewan	3,649	1,114	5,389	831	37[5]	14
Alberta	10,326	2,096	14,313	3,256	91	35
British Columbia	11,540	2,080	13,015	1,774	69	32
Yukon	67	239	316	14	2.9	0.29
Northwest Territories	171	749	933	62	6.4	1.4
Canada	102,385	24,139	130,013	21,738	629	345

Source: Canadian Tax Foundation, *Provincial and Municipal Finances, 1989.*
[1] Provincial taxation plus other own-source revenues.
[2] Primarily from the federal government.
[3] Forecast expenditures.
[4] General government employment plus government enterprises.
[5] Saskatchewan data for 1988.

SELECTED SOCIAL BENEFITS
1989

	Through the Federal Government (millions)					Through Provincial Governments (millions)		
	Family[1] & Youth Allowances	Old Age[2] Security	Unemployment Insurance[3]	Canada (or Quebec) Pension Plan[3]	Direct Relief	Worker's Compensation[4]	Pensions and Allowances[5]	Grants to Benevolent Associations
Newfoundland	67	362	818	185	108	52	—	568
Prince Edward Island	14	102	150	50	27	8	—	17
Nova Scotia	89	639	563	450	149	65	11	56
New Brunswick	76	509	624	309	221	40	61	139
Quebec	641	4,134	3,700	2,929	1,870	867	307	1,681
Ontario	939	5,415	2,453	4,769	1,534	1,554	581	1,200
Manitoba	115	759	378	512	177	67	9	75
Saskatchewan	114	735	313	455	224	68		281
Alberta	270	1,106	892	845	758	403	166	288
British Columbia	296	1,940	1,510	1,513	893	273	41	720
Yukon	3	6	22	5	2	3	—	4
Northwest Territories	8	11	20	5	23	11	—	16
Canada	2,632	15,718	11,445	12,027[6]	5,986	3,411	1,176	5,045

Source: Statistics Canada, *Provincial Economic Accounts*.

[1] There is also the Child Tax Credit through the Income Tax Program.

[2] In addition there are income-tested plans for old age pensioners with little or no additional income.

[3] Social insurance plans funded mainly by contributions from individuals and employers. The Quebec Pension Plan is an independent plan.

[4] Funded by contributions from employers.

[5] Benefits based on need, not provided by every province, and including old age pensions, blind pensions, and mothers' and disabled persons' allowances.

[6] The total includes the Quebec Pension Plan.

HEALTH PROVISION AND EXPENDITURES

	Physicians per 100,000 Population 1987	Dentists per 100,000 Population 1987	Number of Hospitals (all types) 1986–87	Gross Health Expenditures Provincial & Local Governments 1985 (millions)	Total Health Expenditures Public & Private 1985 (millions)	Health Expenditures per Capita Public & Private 1985
Newfoundland	189	24	42	493	745	1,305
Prince Edward Island	144	40	8	105	163	1,296
Nova Scotia	217	45	49	968	1,259	1,497
New Brunswick	136	32	35	649	975	1,373
Quebec	231	46	193	6,222	9,877	1,516
Ontario	222	59	226	10,495	14,539	1,612
Manitoba	206	48	85	1,263	1,730	1,628
Saskatchewan	169	38	135	1,310	1,551	1,537
Alberta	192	55	146	4,096	4,062	1,730
British Columbia	217	65	116	3,208	4,680	1,629
Yukon	129	65	—	23	213	—
Northwest Territories	89	78	5	72		2,816
Canada	214	52	1,040	29,904	39,793	1,580

Sources: Statistics Canada, *Canada Year Book, Provincial Government Finance, Local Government Finance*; Canadian Tax Foundation, *Provincial and Municipal Finance*, 1989.

BANKS AND NEAR BANKS

	Branches of Domestic Chartered Banks[1,4] 1988	Branches of Subsidiaries of Foreign Banks[1,4] 1988	Deposits Canadian Chartered Banks[4] (millions) 1990	Deposits Trust & Mortgage Companies[2,4] (millions) 1989	Deposits Local Credit Unions[3] (millions) 1989
Newfoundland	134	2	2,925	1,442	134
Prince Edward Island	29	1	826	772	106
Nova Scotia	248	5	5,958	5,400	324
New Brunswick	173	2	4,118	3,097	709
Quebec	1,246	53	46,356	31,608	32,786
Ontario	2,726	104	121,448	106,585	8,835
Manitoba	337	3	10,206	7,764	2,887
Saskatchewan	382	4	9,037	7,733	4,511
Alberta	718	11	25,749	17,426	2,825
British Columbia	718	85	37,388	24,658	8,633
Yukon and Northwest Territories	27	—	577	134	—
Canada	6,738	270	282,976	206,598	61,751

Sources: Statistics Canada, *Canada Year Book 1990, Financial Institutions; Bank of Canada Review.*

[1]Canadian chartered banks operate under the federal Bank Act, which is revised at approximately 10-year intervals. Of the domestic banks chartered by Parliament, two in 1988 were limited to one province but five had branches across Canada ranging in number from 954 to 1,489. Under the 1980 revision foreign banks are required to incorporate Canadian subsidiaries as Schedule B banks which have greater restrictions on ownership and lesser powers than those that qualify as Schedule A banks. In 1988 there were 57 such subsidiaries. Of these the Hong Kong Bank of Canada had the largest number of branches (57). Ontario operated branches of a provincial savings bank and Alberta Treasury savings offices under federal legislation. In 1987 the Montreal District and Savings Bank became a Schedule B bank as the Laurentian Bank of Canada.

[2]Trust companies and mortgage companies operate under the federal Trust Companies Act or Loan Companies Act or under the corresponding provincial legislation.

[3]Local Credit Unions operate under provincial legislation. In 1987 there were 2,975 chartered local credit unions, most belonging to a provincial central credit union, of which there were 14 in 1987.

[4]The federal government through the Canada Deposit Insurance Corporation (CDIC) insures deposits in all banks and in trust and mortgage loan companies, except in Quebec, where QDIB provides insurance for deposits in trust and loan companies incorporated there.

LABOR FORCE BY INDUSTRY[1]
1986 Census
(thousands)

	Agriculture and Related Industries	Fishing, Trapping[2]	Logging, Forestry	Mining, Milling, Quarrying, Oil Wells	Manufacture	Construction	Transport, Storage, Communication, Utilities	Wholesale & Retail Trade	Finance, Insurance, Real Estate, Services to Business	Government Services	Education & Health Services	Accommodation, Food, Personal & Other Services	Labor Force (total)
Newfoundland	1.5	11.6	4.1	4.4	36.1	15.0	19.0	38.7	12.3	29.2	36.6	28.2	236.7
Prince Edward Island	5.7	3.7	0.43	0.16	6.4	4.1	4.4	9.2	3.0	7.6	9.0	8.5	62.2
Nova Scotia	9.1	9.2	5.8	6.6	51.4	28.4	31.0	71.4	29.3	50.1	64.7	49.1	406.2
New Brunswick	8.2	4.5	9.0	4.1	46.4	21.6	27.9	54.8	19.4	32.2	48.8	40.4	317.3
Quebec	79.7	4.3	27.5	23.8	613.3	166.5	233.8	539.7	297.4	227.4	492.7	377.4	3,083.2
Ontario	139.7	2.7	17.7	32.7	1,069.6	278.4	335.4	833.1	553.6	335.5	668.5	593.6	4,860.4
Manitoba	45.4	1.1	1.7	4.9	65.8	31.0	51.2	90.6	44.7	45.4	86.7	64.4	533.1
Saskatchewan	93.4	0.48	1.7	12.7	28.0	29.7	37.1	83.0	34.9	36.9	76.6	59.0	493.2
Alberta	90.3	0.29	4.0	81.3	100.2	92.0	105.5	215.0	130.0	97.7	191.0	167.3	1,274.7
British Columbia	39.6	8.7	40.8	19.4	178.8	89.9	127.9	250.3	152.7	98.8	200.2	228.9	1,436.0
Yukon	0.14	0.04	0.15	0.91	0.33	0.97	1.2	3.2	0.76	2.8	1.4	2.3	13.6
Northwest Territories	0.06	0.25	0.16	2.13	0.34	1.6	2.8	2.7	1.4	5.7	3.3	2.9	23.6
Canada	512.7	46.8	113.0	193.3	2,196.7	759.2	977.6	2,190.8	1,279.6	969.3	1,879.5	1,622.0	12,740.2

Source: Census 1986 (reaggregated).
[1] Data are for the experienced labor force, including the currently unemployed but excluding long-term unemployed and those never employed, and includes self-employed and unpaid family members.
[2] Census data were not gathered for some Indian Reserves.

AGRICULTURE—FARMS AND LAND

	All Farms Census[1] 1986	Individual Family Farms	Percent Decline Census Farms 1981–86	Farm Area Thousands of Hectares (of acres)	Improved Land as % Farm Area	Farm Area as % Total Land Area	1989 Value[2] Per Acre Land and Buildings
Newfoundland	651	497	4.1	36.6 (90.3)	29.4	.10	868
Prince Edward Island	2,833	2,278	10.2	272.4 (673.2)	68.4	48.0	771
Nova Scotia	4,283	3,569	15.1	416.5 (1,029.2)	37.9	7.9	703
New Brunswick	3,554	2,898	12.5	408.9 (1,010.4)	41.3	5.7	494
Quebec	41,448	34,971	13.9	3,638.8 (8,991.7)	58.7	2.7	709
Ontario	72,713	56,708	11.8	5,646.6 (13,953.0)	72.5	6.2	1,688
Manitoba	27,336	22,869	7.2	7,740.2 (19,126.5)	69.8	14.1	312
Saskatchewan	63,431	54,478	5.8	26,599.4 (65,728.4)	75.4	46.6	259
Alberta	57,777	47,862	0.5	20,655.3 (51,040.5)	62.5	32.4	413
British Columbia	19,063	14,812	4.7	2,411.1 (5,957.9)	37.3	2.7	810
Yukon	—	—	—	—	—	—	—
Northwest Territories	—	—	—	—	—	—	—
Canada	293,089[3]	240,942	7.9	67,825.8 (167,601.1)	67.8	7.4	476

Source: 1986 census reported in *Canada Year Book 1990*.
[1] Census farms include farms under all forms of ownership. See note 3.
[2] Source: Statistics Canada, *The Daily*, May 31, 1990.
[3] In addition to 293,089 individual family farms, this total includes 12,147 written and 22,302 oral partnership arrangements, 15,091 family and 1,286 nonfamily legally constituted companies, plus 1,321 of other types.

SELECTED ECONOMIC INDICATORS 1989
(Values in millions of dollars)

	Manufac- turing Shipments	Mineral Production	Gross Domestic Product	Retail Sales	Building Construction	Engineering Construction	Housing Starts
Newfoundland	1,510	959	8,406	3,311	1,024	578	3,536
Prince Edward Island	391	2	1,897	784	254	96	815
Nova Scotia	4,784	443	16,019	6,336	1,836	748	5,359
New Brunswick	6,152	910	12,645	4,767	1,509	539	3,681
Quebec	74,921	2,812	151,801	47,560	16,450	5,547	49,058
Ontario	159,285	7,309	273,352	74,286	31,667	7,741	93,337
Manitoba	7,294	1,687	23,485	6,858	2,209	1,198	4,084
Saskatchewan	3,749	3,017	19,610	5,802	1,954	1,617	1,906
Alberta	18,612	16,207	64,415	19,542	5,253	6,541	14,712
British Columbia	25,872	4,091	76,332	23,465	9,119	4,184	38,894
Yukon	—	540	881	—	—	—	—
Northwest Territories	—	1,145	1,992	—	—	—	—
Canada	303,184	39,122	651,616	193,214	71,276	28,790	215,382

Source: Statistics Canada, *Provincial Economic Accounts and Estimates.*

PUBLIC LANDS: PROVINCIAL
(INCLUDING TERRITORIAL) AND FEDERAL[1]

	Provincial Forests sq. km. (sq. mi.) (000)	Provincial Parks sq. km. (sq. mi.) (000)	Other Provincial Lands sq. km. (sq. mi.) (000)	Private Land sq. km. (sq. mi.) (000)	Federal[2] Lands Including Fresh Water sq. km. (sq. mi.) (000)	Indian Reserves sq. km. (sq. mi.) (000)
Newfoundland	0.30 (0.12)	0.81 (0.32)	382.6 (147.7)	18.0 (6.9)	2.8 (1.1)	—
Prince Edward Island	0.21 (0.081)	0.032 (0.012)	0.44 (0.17)	4.9 (1.9)	0.037 (0.014)	0.008 (0.003)
Nova Scotia	13.7 (5.3)	0.13 (0.049)	2.7 (1.0)	37.4 (14.4)	1.5 (0.59)	0.11 (0.044)
New Brunswick	2.8 (1.1)	0.22 (0.083)	28.5 (11.0)	39.8 (15.3)	2.0 (0.77)	0.18 (0.065)
Quebec	613.7 (237.0)	130.0 (50.2)	674.8 (260.5)	119.4 (46.1)	2.0 (0.77)	0.75 (0.28)
Ontario	—	48.4	891.3	119.0	3.2	7.2

	—	(18.7)	(378.9)	(46.0)	(1.2)	(2.8)
Manitoba	14.0 (5.4)	10.7 (4.1)	482.0 (186.1)	138.1 (53.3)	3.2 (1.2)	2.2 (0.86)
Saskatchewan	348.9 (134.7)	4.9 (1.9)	35.5 (13.7)	247.0 (95.3)	9.3 (3.6)	6.2 (2.4)
Alberta	343.1 (132.5)	7.7 (3.0)	63.3 (24.4)	183.5 (70.9)	57.0 (22.0)	6.6 (2.5)
British Columbia	303.6 (117.2)	41.6 (16.0)	539.3 (208.2)	55.0 (21.3)	5.6 (2.2)	3.4 (1.3)
Yukon	—	—	0.94 (0.36)	0.17 (0.065)	535.2 (206.6)	0.032 (0.012)
Northwest Territories	—	—	2.9 (1.1)	0.073 (0.028)	3,376.5 (1,303.7)	0.135 (0.052)
Canada	1,640.4 (633.4)	244.5 (94.4)	3,104.2 (119.8)	962.3 (371.5)	3,998.4 (1,543.8)	26.5 (10.4)

Source: Department of Indian Affairs, Statistics Canada, *Canada Year Book 1980–81*.

[1] Indian Reserve areas are for 1987, other data for 1978.

[2] Including national parks and forest experimental stations but excluding Indian Reserves.

INDIVIDUAL AND FAMILY INCOMES 1989

	Personal Disposable Income per Person	Average Unemploy- ment Rate	Percent Families on Low Income[1]	Percent Unattached Individuals on Low Income	Percent Families Income $100,000 or Over	Percent Unattached Individuals $50,000 or Over
Newfoundland	12,520	15.8	12.9	34.9	2.2	4.2
Prince Edward Island	12,600	14.2	9.9	37.1	1.8	1.0
Nova Scotia	13,845	9.9	12.7	38.1	3.4	3.3
New Brunswick	13,078	12.5	12.3	38.3	2.2	1.4
Quebec	15,110	9.3	13.0	44.2	3.8	3.2
Ontario	18,810	5.1	8.1	28.4	9.3	6.9
Manitoba	15,033	7.6	13.4	36.4	4.6	2.2
Saskatchewan	14,071	7.5	12.7	32.8	3.4	3.9
Alberta	16,882	7.2	12.9	34.8	6.1	5.4
British Columbia	16,924	9.1	12.3	28.4	4.7	4.1
Yukon	19,723	—	—	—	—	—
Northwest Territories	18,630	—	—	—	—	—
Canada	16,660	7.5	11.1	34.4	6.0	4.8

Source: Statistics Canada, *Provincial Economic Accounts, Income Distribution by Size in Canada.*
[1]Low income is defined as a family or individual spending 20% more of total income than average on food, shelter and clothing (1986 base).

PART TWO

HISTORY

CANADA: A HISTORICAL OVERVIEW

KENNETH MCNAUGHT

The mere existence of Canada perplexes Europeans and Asians. More often than not Americans, too, are puzzled. Why is the vast, dimly perceived northern half of North America not a state or states of the American union? Why does a British queen still "rule" this great sprawling tract in a republican hemisphere? And, for the more knowledgeable, how is it that the Canadian cornucopia of natural resources and industry, clearly integrated in what the American Whig leader Henry Clay would instantly recognize as the American System, is politically independent of that system?

Canada has always been a monarchy—whether French or English, Louis XIV or Elizabeth II. Retention of a Canadianized crown as head of state remains the outward and visible sign of a sense of continuity that lies at the heart of the Canadian experience. Unlike the rest of the republican Americas, Canada waged no war of independence, no "democratic revolution." While the United States found legitimacy in a sharp break with Britain's mercantilist empire and then with the monarchs of Europe's Holy Alliance, the colonists to the north saw both benefits and legitimacy in the imperial political-economic system. American Tories became Canada's Loyalists; some 40,000 of them streamed north, voting with their feet against mobocracy. Requiring the establishment of two new provincial governments—New Brunswick and Upper Canada (now Ontario)—the loyalists strengthened the roots of conservatism in the already far-flung units of British North America.

Of equal potency in maintaining a conservative, evolutionary milieu was the survival of a vigorous French community along the banks of the St. Lawrence from Gaspé to the Ottawa River. When James Wolfe surprised the Marquis de Montcalm and captured Quebec in 1759, the 60,000 French Canadians were already a distinct community. For more than 150 years, as a colonial outpost of the French empire, les habitants had accommodated themselves to the climate and to the rivers and lakes draining the huge Precambrian Shield. They had carried the flag and the Catholic cross, along with their fur trade, to the mouth of the Mississippi, to Hudson's Bay and to within sight of the Rockies. If they often ignored or bent the rules of their bishops and their mercantilist overlords, they nevertheless were content with what their New England enemies regarded as an authoritarian polity. Moreover, in an effort to ensure the loyalty of these new Canadian subjects the British Quebec Act of 1775 granted them a special status. They could retain their modified feudal landholding system, their established church, their civil law, and use of their language in civil affairs; furthermore, the British ban against Roman Catholics holding public office was lifted in this one corner of the empire. Upon becoming "British" the French Canadians were already more of a nation than would the states of the Southern Cotton Kingdom be in the 1850s. La Survivance is the central concept of Quebec history; the official motto of today's Quebec is "Je me souviens"—I remember.

Continuity was thus the common basis of political-social assumptions in the origins of the Canadian states; a continuity, moreover, which recognized the rights of collectivités as equal to, sometimes more important than those of individuals. Cautious evolution, rather than dramatic declarations or doctrinal proclamations, has always marked the course of Canadian affairs. Some 90 years after Thomas Jefferson nailed "life, liberty and the pursuit of happiness" to the American masthead, Canada's goals were defined in the British North America Act (1867), which, with many amendments and a change of name, remains the country's basic constitutional law: the purpose of the Canadian federal government was to be maintenance of "peace, order and good government." How did these characteristics, more European than American, reveal themselves in social and political life?

Whether in francophone or anglophone[1] communities, the role of governmental authority—in policing, social-economic regulation or even economic enterprise—has been widely accepted. In Quebec[2] the role of the Roman Catholic Church reinforced a positive role for government. Down to the 1960s the clergy administered most educational, health and social service institutions[3] and more often than not gave influential advice on how to vote. In matters of morals the church was Jansenist, or puritanical. In matters of social purpose and structure the clergy carried the banner of survivance. Ultramontanist bishops, rejecting the rationalist revolution in France, demanded loyalty to the crown and its constituted authority—the surest way of sustaining French and Catholic civilization in an anglophone continent. French survival, in the eye of the church, required also a high birthrate and a stress upon agriculture, as opposed to the homogenizing effect of industry, as the true basis of survivance.

Respect for authority and social order, while stemming from different sources, remained equally evident in the anglophone provinces. Regard for the British connection, which appeared the surest defense against absorption into the leveling democracy to the south, was, however, a complex

---

[1] These two terms came into common use in the 1960s as being less cumbersome than "French-speaking" and "English-speaking."

[2] Named Lower Canada (1791), Canada East (1841), and Quebec (1867).

[3] With the exception of a Protestant school board for anglophone education.

matter. British institutions; administration of justice in the name of the monarch; conferring of titles (not ended until the 1930s); and the predominance of Britain as a source of capital, literature, political ideas and immigration all conditioned a basically conservative sense of identity. While many features of British (including Irish and Scottish) society were modified by experiences on various frontiers, the social standards and emphasis upon order as the true basis of liberty remained not only important; they were a source of confidence and pride. The Anglican church was disestablished by the mid-1850s, thereby losing state funding and privileged position in education. Protestant-oriented public education spread rapidly, modified by provision for separate (i.e., Catholic) schools increasingly funded by provincial governments.

Simultaneous regard for social order and community, together with the facts of geography and demography, governed Canada's frontier experiences. Unlike the United States, Canada's pattern of settlement was not an unbroken, westward-moving frontier. The Appalachians prevented the Maritime (Atlantic) Provinces from enjoying a "western reserve"; northwestern Ontario presented a thousand miles of Precambrian granite rather than a fertile midwestern bridge to the prairies. Leap-frogging, community-to-community settlement produced a continent-spanning island archipelago in which the roots of locality run very deep. The impact of geography, the survival of New France and a slender overall population base would combine to engender intense regard for provincial and local rights, ready acceptance of positive government—that is, government willing to take action and effect change—and suspicion of centralizing national governments.

In economic terms these patterns reinforced the effects of long experience with the garnering and marketing of staples, or natural resource products. From fish and furs to lumber, wheat and minerals, economic enterprise sought and received essential assistance from governments: tariffs, business-oriented regulations, monopoly grants, unending subsidization. The high economic costs imposed by vast internal distances, remote export markets and restricted local markets led also to early resort to public ownership initiatives, first in canals and railways, then in hydroelectric power, wheat marketing, airlines, broadcasting and even manufacturing. While geography and demography were crucial stimulants of a strong neo-mercantilist strand in Canadian policy, another influence was far from negligible. This was the somewhat un-American notion that governments should express and ensure collectively acceptable conditions of social equity.

The high costs of communication, transportation and marketing required large infusions of capital, often arranged and underwritten by governments. Throughout the 19th century the bulk of such capital came from Britain, which was also the major market for staple products. The imported capital was principally in the form of public bonds and government-guaranteed loans. Also, from mid-century, the economy was generating sufficient domestic capital to underpin a nascent manufacturing sector concentrated in Ontario and Quebec. Increasingly, American investors were attracted by the opportunities perceived not only in the exploitation of Canadian natural resources (especially pulp and paper) but also in manufacturing. More and more of them jumped the tariff wall to establish branch plants within the Canadian market, a procedure whose encouragement was a prime goal of the national policy of a high protective tariff.

As early as 1917, New York, Chicago and Boston had replaced London as providers of capital; the form of the inflow was, accordingly, shifting from bonds to equity or direct investment. World War I, in which Canada was a belligerent from the outset, expanded the country's industrial capacity markedly. The interwar years confirmed and deepened the shift from Britain to the United States as principal market and source of capital. Meshed with these economic facts were the ingredients of heavy immigration and westward settlement, encouraged by Prime Minister Sir Wilfrid Laurier, from 1897 to 1913. Adding some 2 million to a population that even by 1914 had reached only 8 million, this influx created a wheat-farming bonanza, known as the Laurier Wheat Boom, in the prairie west, provided the muscle for completing a transcontinental rail network and manned the growing manufacturing and natural resource industries. The majority of the pre-1914 immigrants were from the British Isles and the United States; some half-million came from eastern and southern Europe. Their social-political impact was as significant as the economic. Almost entirely non-francophone, the new arrivals pushed down the francophone percentage of the general population 3 points to 27.9. Throughout the 1920s and '30s, a period of more leisurely immigration, fears for la survivance deepened, laying a solid basis for nationaliste explosions after 1945.

At the same time the Protestant establishment in anglophone Canada reacted nervously to southern and eastern Europeans who, they believed, would eviscerate the superior qualities of Canada's "northern" peoples— and destabilize the growing workforce with syndicalist-bolshevik ideas from abroad. The red scare of 1919, occasioned by widespread militant unionism and a six-week general strike in Winnipeg, revealed, however, that virtually all the strike leaders, like these of the nascent socialist parties, were from Britain. Clearly, the continuing constitutional-emotional British connection underwrote not only orderly conservatism but also ideas about industrial unionism and democratic socialism. Unlike in the United States, where socialism was anathema because it was perceived to be European and un-American, in Canada its British origins were a positive assistance.

While anglophone Canada in the 1920s and '30s experienced contrapuntal aspects in its imperial relationships, francophones began to rediscover France. During the long church-imposed chill, ultramontanist Quebec clergy had sought to base French Canadian identity on the myth that Laurentia— the regions surrounding the St. Lawrence—was the true heir of pre-1789 France. In the 1920s and '30s young Québécois, returning from university studies in Paris, brought with them more secular notions of society. These included the impression that they could better survive if at least cultural links with France were strengthened; fashionable notions about corporatism as a break on the excesses of industrial capitalism also came to Quebec with the returning students. By 1939, then, although Canada had become closely interconnected with the American economy, its cultural-political outreach to Europe was substantial.

Political continuities have both expressed and affected cultural-economic evolution. An unbroken evolution in which constitutional statutes simply convert precedents into law, and major political parties retain British names (Reform, Liberal, Conservative, Tory), is the essence of Canadian political history. Instead of being fought for or declared, Canadian independence matured so gradually that it is not possible to date its arrival without sharp academic contention. At the end of the 1840s, after two minor, if traumatic, democratic rebellions, London acceded to Canadian demands for responsible government, whereby colonial cabinets would retain office only as long as they were supported by majorities in the elected legislatures. Adoption of this Westminster model of parliamentary government, in which British-appointed governors became, in effect, constitutional monarchs, coincided with the ending of the Navigation Acts, or imperial protective trade legislation. In 1859 the Canadian government[4] enacted a protective tariff from which British imports were not excluded. And this is about as close as Canadians have come to a declaration of independence.

For purposes of understanding Canadian political attitudes and methods, the term functionalism is most helpful.[5] The term itself came into use after 1945 to describe Canada's relationship to military alliances and other international organizations: the extent of Canadian participation, it was asserted, would depend upon assessment of functional utility, as well as Canada's capacity and self-interest in the particular circumstances. Precisely this approach, if not the word itself, lies behind the 1867 confederation of the British provinces and the gradual accretion of sovereignty thereafter.

British regular troops and sea power had been the mainstay against American invasion in 1812–14; that same power had been the bulwark against the Manifest Destiny that in the 1840s gobbled up half of Mexico and threatened British possessions on the Pacific coast. In the 1860s the American Civil War coincided with a temporary dominance in London of Manchester School thinking about empire: settlement colonies were an unnecessary financial burden and should be encouraged to move quickly toward independence. Particularly was this the case with the highly vulnerable Canadas. Thus it was with strong British endorsement that leaders of the provincial governments met in closed-door conferences to hammer out resolutions defining a federal union. Functional pragmatism remained the key political attitude as the colonial resolutions were passed into law at Westminster as the British North America Act on July 1, 1867.

Because major economic interests in central Canada (Ontario and Quebec) envisioned great benefits flowing from an integrated and protected

---

[4] I.e., the government of United Canada in which the provinces of Canada West and Canada East were legislatively combined from 1841 to 1867.

[5] In 1859 the British government still preserved the right to disallow Canadian legislation affecting external relations. However the Canadian government argued successfully that a revenue-raising tariff was a *function* of domestic government.

transcontinental market, the principal powers over trade and commerce, finance, transportation and taxation fell to the new central government at Ottawa. Yet the realities of cultural differentiation dictated strong protection of the component communities. Quebec retained its distinct civil law and use of the French language in legislatures and courts; all provinces retained control of education and "property and civil rights." While this basic federal statute created a more centralized federation than that delineated in the American constitution, historic conditions and assumptions were to lead through political compromises and court decisions to near reversal of the original positions. The future lay entrenched in a remark made by Sir John A. Macdonald (father of the British North America Act) during the confederation debates: "Thus we shall have a strong central government under which we can work out constitutional liberty as opposed to democracy, and be able to protect the minority . . ."

As the years following 1945 would demonstrate lucidly, both the methods and assumptions of Canadian democracy exhibit mistrust of simple majorities and conformist nationalism. Moreover, constitutional change continues to be regarded as a normal function of government rather than of plebiscites or constitutional conventions. Canadian national feeling has evolved slowly, yet with surprising confidence, out of its imperial chrysalis as the need to exercise new functions became apparent. Down to 1918 anglophone patriotism saw Canada as an "auxiliary kingdom" in the world's greatest empire—willingly shouldering more and more responsibility. By 1880 all the British possessions from Lake Superior to the Pacific, from the 49th parallel to the north pole, had been deeded to Ottawa; by 1905 these had been organized by federal statutes as provinces or territories. In 1914 Canada automatically entered the war upon Britain's declaration. Canada's economic contribution in food and munitions was crucial, as was its military. Some 500,000 men saw service, and Canada's 60,000 dead outnumbered those of the United States.

Acquisition of the west and the experience of World War I engendered conflicting forces that retain their strength, in altered guise, today. In the west, two small rebellions against federal authority (1870, 1885) were suppressed. Led by francophone Métis (French-Indian), these uprisings gained much sympathy in Quebec. When they were followed by anglophone endeavors to eliminate public support of French-language education in Ontario and the Prairie Provinces, francophones feared that their compatriots' imperialism was expressed in a plan to undermine la survivance. Such anxiety deepened as the anglophone majority compelled dispatch of a Canadian force to help Britain's suppression of the Boers in South Africa (1899). Francophones, thus, showed minimal enthusiasm for enlistment in what they saw as Britain's war in Europe after 1914. In 1917 a Tory-dominated coalition government secured a military conscription law; francophone resistance to conscription burst into rioting in Quebec. Francophone mistrust of the Conservative party cast a long shadow over Canadian politics throughout the interwar years and right down to the election of 1984.

For anglophone Canadians a very different set of attitudes evolved out of these events. As Canada's economic and military functions had expanded so, too, did its exercise of political authority. In the Paris Peace Conference and the League of Nations, Canada obtained seats in its own right; at several imperial conferences it led in securing for the self-governing British dominions the right to independent foreign policies, treaty-making and nonintervention by London in any domestic matters. This dominion status of virtual independence, arriving incrementally, was enshrined in the British Statute of Westminster (1931). Canadian disregard of legalities and constitutional logic revealed itself distinctly at the outbreak of war in 1939. Legally, as in 1914, Canada was at war by virtue of the British declaration of September 3. In a special session the Canadian parliament recognized an existing state of war but also authorized the government to ask George VI to declare war on behalf of Canada. This was done on September 10, thus confirming a sovereignty already existing functionally.

In both political and cultural affairs the interwar years sketched patterns that the war and postwar were to etch more deeply. A confident anglophone nationalism expressed itself in fiction, poetry and art. The Group of Seven painters adapted Scandinavian perceptions in portraying the stark, brilliant beauty of the lakes and forests of the Precambrian shield, creating a symbolic northern identity without severing the unbroken European linkage. The depression years, devastating Canada's export-oriented economy, brought a political response of a similar sort. In 1933 a convention of farm and labor organizations met with delegates from several tiny socialist parties to found the Co-operative Commonwealth Federation (CCF), a democratic socialist party modeled roughly on the British Labour party. While the CCF grew but slowly, its impact on Canadian politics was immediate; through its successor, the New Democratic Party (NDP), that impact would remain significant.

Establishment of the CCF ended the near monopoly of the political process by the Liberals and Conservatives. In effect the result was a European-style multiparty system, and this format was further entrenched by the appearance of provincially-based parties in the 1930s and after, such as Social Credit in Alberta and Union Nationale and the Parti Québécois in Quebec. The large influx of Europeans following World War II found the political context of a multiparty system and parliamentary-cabinet government comfortably familiar. Further, cabinet dependence upon majority support in the legislature meant that often a small number of seats gave quick influence to minor parties. In 1926, two socialist members of parliament had held the balance of power and forced the Liberal prime minister, Mackenzie King, to enact old-age pension legislation—the foundation of what was to become a comprehensive welfare state.

After 1933, continuance of a democratic socialist alternative to the predominately free enterprise Liberals and Conservatives reinforced traditional Canadian receptivity to positive government. Thus, from 1930 to 1935 the Conservative government of R.B. Bennett put on foot substantial public enterprise initiatives and proposed considerable state intervention in social-economic life such as unemployment insurance, hours and wages legislation and extension of state marketing of natural products. While much of this was declared by the courts to be beyond Ottawa's jurisdiction, some would soon be legislated by provincial governments, and much else federally, after empowering constitutional amendments. Moreover, the extensive public ownership[6] would remain and expand until challenged by a series of cutbacks and privatizations under neo-conservative auspices in the late 1980s: the Canadian Broadcasting Corporation, designed to ensure Canadian control of the airwaves, to promote native talent in drama and music and to ensure radio service to remote regions; the Bank of Canada; Trans-Canada Airlines (Air Canada), again to safeguard Canadian control of air transportation and provide service to nonprofitable areas. The question of whether growth of this mixed economy resulted from collectivist convictions or a perceived business interest in enlisting support services and inexpensive electric power is warmly debated by academics. Most likely it was a judicious mixture of both.

Anglophone nationalism in the interwar years led not only to a pronounced loosening of imperial ties and even to some minority, if very articulate, isolationism. It also deepened francophone suspicion that Ottawa's pan-Canadian policies imperiled, yet again, la survivance. In Quebec, rapid industrialization began to shake the agrarian foundations of the clerical nationaliste myth. Yet Quebec nationalisme grew in tandem with anglophone federalism. Because the direction, ownership and profits of economic life in the province remained in the hands of an anglophone elite, and because that Montreal-based society showed both pan-Canadian and imperial sentiments, the great majority of Québécois felt distinctly indifferent as war clouds gathered and another call to fight abroad for the Empire seemed imminent.

The Quebec political magician who rode astride this turbulent mix of "foreign" economic power, industrial strife and grass roots nationalism, Maurice Duplessis, had become premier in 1936. Supported by the bishops, who retained a directing influence in social-educational matters, and the corporate chieftains, Duplessis waged public (sometimes spurious) battles against Ottawa's authority, as well as against "communist" international unions[7] and "radicals." Despite an effective clerical-business entente that underlay the political power of his Union Nationale government, when war was declared, Duplessis bent his ear to Quebec's populist grass roots. In an election in October 1939, his government fell after he had accused Ottawa of infringing provincial rights with its suddenly implemented war measures. The defeat of Duplessis had been engineered by Ernest Lapointe,

---

[6] Most publicly-owned enterprises, provincial or federal, are called crown corporations, a term symbolizing nonpartisan public interest. Provinces and municipalities had pioneered before World War I with public ownership of hydroelectricity, regional railways, telephones and urban tramlines; by 1923 Ottawa had created the world's largest railway-hotel-telegraph-steamship organization, amalgamating several private and public lines as the Canadian National Railways.

[7] Branches of American unions that dominated organized labor in Canada until well after World War II.

chief francophone minister in the federal Liberal government of Mackenzie King. Lapointe had been able to rally francophone political support only after extracting a promise from King that Ottawa would not impose military conscription. The ghost of conscription would preside over wartime politics and was to remain as a symbol of Tory disregard for Quebec, haunting Quebec Conservatives down to 1984.[8]

By 1939 Mackenzie King was already a political legend. From then until his retirement in 1948 he further embellished that legend. Assessed by a critical academic admirer as "great, because he divided us least," King seemed to epitomize Canadian caution. Perhaps for that reason he was grudgingly admired, never loved. A colorless, excessively superstitious bachelor, he outmaneuvered one Tory leader after another, holding office for all but five years from 1922 to 1948. Unilingual, ostentatiously Protestant, sentimentally British, he nevertheless understood Quebec and the deep Canadian attachment to community—especially provincial community. Thus he had led the autonomists at imperial conferences, supported the first francophone prime minister, Sir Wilfrid Laurier, in opposing conscription in 1917, refused any prior commitment to war in the '30s, opposed R.B. Bennett's social-economic reform legislation as an unconstitutional invasion of provincial jurisdiction, and sidestepped foreign policy debate until the country was on a war footing, at which time he obtained a parliamentary resolution (seconded by a Quebec member of parliament) that Canada should "co-operate to a reasonable extent with France and England in the present conflict." He knew well that the war itself would resolve, temporarily, many political, economic and jurisdictional problems.

One nearly intractable problem, however, was created by the war: how to satisfy the country's increasingly heavy enlistment demands. Despite Hitler's conquest of France, a majority of Québécois remained indifferent to this second "British" war. As Quebec's recruiting figures fell farther and farther behind those in the other provinces, and as the United States imposed compulsory service after Pearl Harbor, anglophones pressed hard for "equality of sacrifice" through conscription. After firing a popular defense minister, King staved off crisis until the autumn of 1944. Finally, despite near mutiny among the thousands who had been conscripted for nonoverseas service, some 16,000 were dispatched to Europe. Political uproar in Quebec did not obscure francophone perception of King as Quebec's safest choice. In the euphoria following German capitulation, a June 1945 election confirmed the Liberals in power. Their slightly reduced majority would in no way diminish their enjoyment of Ottawa's war-enhanced authority.

Despite the quicksands of enlistment policy, King had managed Canada's war effort with extraordinary success. Both before and after American entry, Canada's contribution to Britain's survival and, therefore, to Hitler's defeat was crucial. In an explosion of industrial growth, Canadians turned out some 800,000 motor vehicles in addition to a steady stream of weapons, munitions, aircraft, ships and food. By 1945 more than a million

---

[8]Throughout the war, Conservatives had led in demands for conscription.

people had served in the armed forces, the Canadian-administered Commonwealth Air Training Plan had graduated thousands of airmen from Britain and the sister dominions, while the Royal Canadian Navy was escorting most convoys putting out from North America. Because accumulation of wealth in many forms surpassed by far the actual costs of war, Canada was able not only to subsidize British postwar recovery, but also to embark upon a marked expansion of social policies, partly modeled on those of Britain's Beveridge plan. Underlying postwar Liberal policies was a freshened sense of achievement, especially among the anglophone majority, who now looked with less suspicion upon Ottawa as the focal point of a Canadian identity.

Not all Canadians, however, agreed with the strongly business-oriented King policies. King believed himself a social reformer and was proud of having initiated Canada's first labor legislation. His remarkably voluminous diaries, however, together with the sequence of political events, indicate that most of his initiatives were responses to perceived political threats. Thus, early in the war, when the CCF was pressing for "conscription of wealth as well as manpower," and unions were restless, King told his diary, "What I fear is we will begin to have a defection from our own ranks in the House to the CCF." In 1940, having obtained an empowering amendment to the British North America Act, King instituted national unemployment insurance. In 1943 the CCF won sufficient seats to become the official opposition in Ontario and, in 1944, under T.C Douglas, the party won power in Saskatchewan—North America's first socialist government. It was in that year that King's government passed the Family Allowances Act by which parents received eight dollars a month for each child. As with old age pensions, the payments have been steadily augmented as an extensive social security system has evolved. The 1944 baby bonus had double merit from the federal Liberal point of view: for anglophones it suggested concern to build a social safety net and to provide mild income redistribution although, as with pensions and the later medicare system, there is no means test; for Quebec, whose steadily declining birthrate was augmenting fears for survivance, the political plus was clear enough.

Relying on budget buoyance and a war-management record that had included careful inflation control by a Wartime Prices and Trade Board, the Liberals further burnished a progressive image in the 1945 election with a platform pledging full training and re-establishment of veterans, a housing program, economic planning, and implementation of social programs such as public hospital insurance. Thus armed they won a clear majority. All but one constituency in Quebec went Liberal, while the CCF failed to make the substantial gains that nearly everyone expected. The 28 CCF seats were the most the party had yet won, but nearly all were in the west. While it would continue to sound its thunder-on-the-left, the CCF remained politically stymied at the federal level until a major structural change was undertaken at the end of the '50s. The Tories, also donning a reform image and the new name of Progressive-Conservative, failed to overcome the Liberal advantage of experience. With two ineffectual leaders in succession, John Bracken of Manitoba and George Drew of Ontario, they could do no more than split the vote in anglophone ridings and thus be swamped by a solidly Liberal Quebec. Only in 1957 would Tories interrupt the long Liberal hegemony in Ottawa, and then only because of Grit hubris.[9] In effect, the era of Mackenzie King was prolonged under Louis St. Laurent until that year.

If the Tories and the CCF were forced to mark time in these early postwar years, so, too, were the forces of change in Quebec. In 1944 Maurice Duplessis led his Union Nationale to electoral victory over Adélard Godbout, who had been eased into wartime office by the federal Liberal organization. Duplessis at once reactivated the unholy alliance of the church and anglophone business. Sallying forth in defense of provincial rights, the colorful, hard-living bachelor buttressed his power by showering tax and other favors upon the corporations, endowing loyal constituencies with roads, bridges and contracts, and endorsing church control of most education, hospitals and social services. Leaving rural constituencies over-represented in the legislature, he pursued his war against "foreign" international unions and radicals while encouraging a steady inflow of American investment. Under clerical ban as socialist–atheist, the CCF made no headway in Quebec. The Bloc Populaire, formed in 1942 to oppose conscription, found its nationaliste appeal undercut by Duplessis's populist, anti-Ottawa fist-shaking. Thus, the little magician's Union Nationale enjoyed an unbroken reign of 16 years.

Yet, if party opposition to this vestigal agrarian theocracy failed, the postwar maturation of industrialism, which reached far into the tributary communities of mining and pulp and paper, came under increasingly effective review. A new generation of liberal thought, enraged by massive political corruption as well as by the linguistic barrier to upward mobility in their society, made common cause with the embattled unions. Young professionals, many of whom held postgraduate degrees from French and American universities, detailed the crying need to revise church-state relations, electoral laws and an antiquated educational system. In newspapers such as André Laurendau's *Le Devoir* and the union-financed *Cité Libre* of Pierre Elliott Trudeau and Gérard Pelletier, muckraking combined with sophisticated analysis to create widespread demand for reform; especially to use a cleansed, secular democracy and progressive government action to modernize Quebec. Following the death of Duplessis in 1959, the Union Nationale fell into disarray. At the same time the secularist reformers captured the provincial Liberal party. Under a suave, popular leader, Jean Lesage, the Liberals swept into power in 1960. They launched what quickly became known as the Quiet Revolution.

For anglophone Canadians these postwar years saw a rediscovery of national identity. While sudden immigration from Europe would complicate their views, their assumption of normally fruitful cooperation with francophones at the federal level remained unchanged. What was happening in

---

[9] Like "Tory" for "Conservative," "Grit" is still frequently used as popular shorthand for "Liberal." The name was first applied to Upper Canadian reformers in the 1840s.

Quebec was largely unknown or misunderstood, and this would intensify the shocks that were to follow in the 1970s. Down to 1957 the political waters remained calm for the federal Liberals. When Mackenzie King retired in 1948 he easily secured the leadership succession for his minister of external affairs, Louis St. Laurent.[10] When Ernest Lapointe died in 1941 King had persuaded the elegant Quebec City lawyer to become his political chef in Quebec. St. Laurent, of Franco-Irish descent and fluently bilingual, stood in the tradition of Sir. G.-E. Cartier[11] and Sir Wilfrid Laurier: the survival and prosperity of French Canada would best be ensured within an independent, federal Canada. Uncle Louis to anglophones, St. Laurent had supported the war effort and his corporation law office did much work for the businessmen of Montreal and Toronto. Conservative by temperament (as, indeed, was King himself), St. Laurent was eminently suited to preside over a postwar affluence; he was automatically labeled by nationalistes *vendu,* one who had sold out to les anglais. Until the overthrow of the Union Nationale and the advent of a new Tory leadership in Ottawa, he remained the safest choice for both anglophone and francophone majorities.

A judicious policy mix in these last years of King Liberalism included extension of federal social insurance programs and enhancement of federal jurisdictions through tax-rental agreements with the provinces. These agreements underpinned Ottawa initiatives in support of cultural activities, higher education and developmental projects. A somewhat innocent anglophone confidence in what appeared to many francophones (and to some provincial rights anglophones) to be dangerous centralization, underwrote also the completion of confederation and an international role for Canada as a middle power.

In the 1860s the Maritime Provinces had been less than enthusiastic about the proposed confederation of Britain's North American colonies. Facing the Atlantic, geographically cut off from a western hinterland, their links with Britain, together with their own local identities, dictated caution. Prince Edward Island rejected union until Ottawa promised much-needed subsidies in 1873. Nova Scotia and New Brunswick accepted confederation in 1867 only after some very sharp political maneuvering and direct pressure from London. Newfoundland, intensely proud of being Britain's oldest colony, turned down successive offers from Ottawa until 1949. The depression of the 1930s had put "the Rock" into bankruptcy and forced a regression from dominion status to government by a London-appointed commission. During World War II the United States and Canada poured money into Newfoundland-Labrador to build and service defense facilities. As part of the destroyers-for-bases deal between Churchill and Roosevelt in 1940, the Americans obtained 99-year leases to several areas; Canada built crucial airports at Gander and Goose Bay. Canadian concern for controlling

---

[10] Canada's "foreign office," created in 1909, was named the department of external affairs and its head, secretary of state for external affairs—because the first representation abroad was to the United Kingdom, to which a high commissioner was dispatched as early as 1880 and which, of course, was not "foreign."

[11] Cartier was Sir John A. Macdonald's co-leader in securing the 1867 BNA Act.

the St. Lawrence approaches and for developing commercial air traffic deepened after 1945.

Despite Canadian and American spending in Newfoundland, however, standards of living in the fishing outposts and for employees of mining, lumbering, and fish-packing firms remained well below those of even the other Atlantic provinces. Many St. John businessmen, including the father of John Crosbie, a minister in the present Mulroney government and a vociferous advocate of the 1988 U.S.-Canada trade agreement, favored closer economic and political connection with the United States. However, in a 1949 referendum, a slender majority endorsed joining Canada as its 10th province. That the majority looked to the immediate benefit of Canada's social welfare and unemployment insurance programs as well as to Ottawa's future support of economic development seems incontestable. In this respect Newfoundland's choice heightened the image of an Atlantic region chronically dependent upon Ottawa's political patronage. A most interesting feature of Canadian thinking is the willingness to endow from general revenues communities that are perceived as possessing historic cultural worth quite apart from cost-benefit analysis. Around this value judgment political debate continues to swirl, especially with respect to the justice of competing regional equalization policies. Yet the mythic charms of Anne of Green Gables, of the sou'wester-clad dory fisherfolk, of the prairie farmer struggling from sod hut to bonanza wheat farm, of Maria Chapdelaine[12] and her habitant heritage, continue to nourish a nonmarket metropolitan notion of the social legitimacy of hinterland communities.

The symbols and policies of anglophone confidence abounded in the '50s. Despite the separate 1939 war declaration, some vestiges of the colonial constitutional tie had endured; all but one of these were ended. The right of appeal to the Judicial Committee of the Privy Council in London was abolished, leaving Canada's supreme court supreme. Changes were made in the laws defining the monarchy and the role of the governor-general, stressing Canadian independence. But because there was lack of agreement among Ottawa and the provinces, the British parliament (reluctantly) retained sole power to amend the British North America Act in matters affecting provincial jurisdiction or representation at Ottawa. The significance of custom as opposed to law was underlined in 1952 when St. Laurent advised George VI to appoint Vincent Massey as the first Canadian-born governor general. Previously only members of the British aristocracy had held the post of personal representative of the monarch. A wealthy art patron and diplomat who had been high commissioner in London during the war, Massey was an extreme anglophile who, at the same time, was intensely nationalist. While francophones were mildly dismayed, and some anglophones perceived a threat to egalitarian goals, Massey's major influence had already been exerted through his chairmanship of the Royal Commission on the Arts, Letters and Sciences, the report of which was published in 1951.

---

[12] *Maria Chapdelaine*, a 1914 novel by French-born Louis Hémon, romanticized early Quebec rural life.

The Massey Report, as it came to be known, became at once the flagship of anglophone nationalism. It argued forcibly a need to sustain and further develop a Canadian culture different from that of the United States. Massey's analysis underlined the themes of continuity and confidence and noted that his intention was not to define but to defend an imperilled identity— an identity resting upon "certain habits of mind and convictions which [Canadians] shared and would not surrender." The principal peril was the massive, easy penetration of the country by American giants in magazines, broadcasting and films, with their hefty cultural and ideological baggage. St. Laurent's government took the Massey Report to heart. A publicly funded Canada Council was established and directed to encourage Canadian talent by subsidizing scholars, writers, artists and a wide range of cultural organizations. The council has fulfilled its mandate; it was the starting point of what became a cultural flowering in the following years—in both languages.

Amid some allegations of navel-watching protectionism in cultural affairs, and continuing evidence of the strong appeal of American popular culture, Canadians have endorsed a competitive over a protective approach to their culture. Facing the explosion of American television, the CBC established a national television network and, in tune with mixed-economy thinking, private networks were also licensed, both public and private coming under regulation of the Canadian Radio-Television and Telecommunications Commission. On the assumption that the cultural-economic field of competition in North America is not level, but is tilted by about 10 to 1, Canadians have continued to accept the necessity of public subsidization of both cultural and economic activity. Production at the National Film Board, begun for wartime information, expanded steadily and has won international awards for documentary, animation and docudrama.

As the '50s gave way to the '60s, the example of the Canada Council led to creation of provincial and municipal arts councils, while private investors, often using people trained at public expense, began a feature film industry, set up dozens of small art galleries and lent support to a mushroom growth of legitimate theater. In many cultural activities the beginnings of an interpenetration of francophone and anglophone perceptions were evident. As the Quebec art historian François-Marc Gagnon puts it: "Federal institutions like the Canada Council, the Art Bank and the National Gallery have succeeded in creating among contemporary Canadian artists a sense of community that goes beyond the language barrier." Even so, Canadians had been parsimonious in budgeting education. Only when the requirements of the economy and rapid population growth became inescapable, and a brain-drain southward a perceived threat, did the purse strings loosen. From the end of the '50s and through the early '60s, budgets for universities expanded and many new ones were established. Federal funds for capital and salaries together with provincial student support programs proliferated. Yet the methods of funding and staffing the plethora of instant universities led to two problems that would plague political life for a decade. First, because Canadian universities had been slow to develop their own graduate programs, they were compelled to recruit faculty from abroad, mainly from the United States. This created a backlash of anglophone nationalist sentiment: "Americanization" of Canadian universities, claimed the critics, was the cultural counterpart of a startling increase of American direct investment and thus spelled cultural as well as economic dependence. Second, federal spending on education was seen in Quebec as a dangerous invasion of provincial rights—a glittering capstone in the edifice of centralization built by *les anglais*.

Comparable complexity also characterized the evolution of foreign-defense policy. The interwar years had seen completion of practical diplomatic-military independence. The Liberals had stressed that Canada had no prior commitments or, indeed, any responsibility for the diplomacy that might lead to war in Europe. In 1940, however, King had quietly reversed his "no commitments" policy. In that year he met with President Franklin Roosevelt at Ogdensburg, New York and signed an agreement to establish with the United States a Permanent Joint Board on Defense. The PJOB, with many later adjuncts, agreements and treaties, launched what was to become (outside the Warsaw pact) the tightest integration of military planning and procurement existing between any two nations. "In 1940," wrote a Canadian historian in the 1940s, "we passed from the British century of our history to the American century. We became dependent upon the United States for our security. We have, therefore, no choice but to follow American leadership." This inevitabilist conclusion, based plausibly upon the hard facts of a relative decline of British power, the nuclear age and the Cold War, nevertheless has been hotly contested down to the present. At the popular level a love-hate view of the United States supports resistance to continentalism; at the level of government this view has, somewhat spasmodically, received policy expression.

Postwar functionalism translated into a nonideological approach to international organizations while endorsing Cold War arguments about the need for nuclear deterrence. A founding member of the United Nations, Canada has contributed to every UN peacekeeping mission and voted against political tests for UN membership. Despite making the third-largest contribution to UN forces in Korea, however, Canada's defense reliance lay in a complex of bilateral and multilateral treaty arrangements—involving prior commitments beyond those ever made as a British colony. In 1948–49 St. Laurent was a prime mover in establishing the North Atlantic Treaty Organization. NATO was politically the most acceptable framework for an essentially European commitment in a progressively bipolar world: with both Canada's mother countries as well as the United States in the alliance, previous francophone suspicion of British imperialism was put to rest. Canada's military contribution to NATO would remain modest and has been justified on two principal grounds: first, as a commitment to the defense of the West, and second, as buying influence. The second has become the most weighty as Canada's rather inflated status in the immediate postwar arena declined with the recovery of the European powers and, later, of Japan.

If NATO represented a kind of membership fee in the executive of the Western club,[13] as well as a partial countervail to unavoidable entanglement with U.S. power, North America has dominated Canadian defense thinking. Following World War II, a series of executive agreements provided for joint construction of northern radar warning posts, defense production sharing and, in 1957, a North American Air Defense Command (NORAD). NORAD controls both Canadian and American intercepting planes and missiles; the commander is American, his deputy, Canadian. While critics alleged that NORAD is the military counterpart of economic integration with the United States—of "Liberal continentalism,"—the scheme, like the defense production agreement, was initiated by a Conservative government. In part to avoid the appearance of being merely an American satellite, Canada has resisted various pressures from Washington. Canada long rejected membership in the Organization of American States, while participating in most OAS functional agencies, but finally joined in 1989. Canada was on the point of recognizing China when the Korean War intervened. The Trudeau government recognized China in 1970 some months prior to the Kissinger-Nixon inauguration of détente. In both the United Nations and the Commonwealth, Canada sought a role, through quiet diplomacy, as mediator or honest broker. Thus, Lester Pearson successfully promoted peace-by-compromise in the Middle East and played a key role in resolving the Suez Crisis in 1956. The latter achievement was facilitated by Canada's record as leading advocate of a new Commonwealth to include ex-colonial nations in Asia and Africa. Yet the powerful facts of military-economic integration with the United States were constricting: when Canada became a member (with India and Poland) of the International Control Commission to invigilate the 1954 Geneva settlement in Vietnam, the Canadian role was clearly that of the Western member. Although Canada rejected a military contribution to the American intervention in Vietnam, a good deal of its military production found its way there, including bombsights for B-52 bombers.

In 1957 the postwar economic-population boom ended in a political upheaval the reverberations of which stretched through the following decade—puncturing the myth of a Liberal divine right to rule at Ottawa. Between 1945 and 1956 Canada had received some 2 million immigrants, mostly from Britain and the war-torn countries of Europe. Most of these new Canadians gravitated to the cities, enhancing an already marked urban-industrial evolution. Nativist rejection of the newcomers was less than in previous immigration surges; nor did post-1945 Canada press for immediate assimilation. While non-Anglo-Saxons began to breach establishment bulwarks in government, business and the professions, ethnic communities flourished in the cities. Anglophones spoke proudly of a mosaic as opposed to a melting pot. Postwar immigration from Europe, and increasingly from

---

[13] It is interesting that Lester Pearson, external affairs secretary in 1948, contributed Article II to the NATO treaty. This article stated that NATO should promote economic and cultural cooperation almost equally with military. Article II remained a dead letter, yet it perhaps anticipated the world of the 1980s, of GATT and the large trading blocs of Paul Kennedy's "decline of the great powers."

the West Indies and Asia in the later years, infused an invigorating variety displayed in street markets, vastly improved restaurants, expanded artistic and literary activity and even a growing interest in soccer. By 1989, according to a UN survey, Toronto had become, ethnically, the world's most cosmopolitan city. A contrapuntal note, however, was sounded in Quebec. There, fears for survivance deepened steadily. Most of the new Canadians opted for anglophone culture—not least because the doors of economic opportunity were less inviting for francophones. At the same time, francophone birthrates continued their sharp decline, setting the stage for a peaking of séparatisme in the '60s and '70s.

Population growth, together with a torrent of foreign investment, sustained a postwar economic growth interrupted only by recession in 1957–61. Urban building booms showered cities with industrial plants, high-rise commercial and apartment structures, multilane freeways. New capital explored and further developed the natural resource hinterlands from Ungava to northern Ontario and across the top of the prairies to the Arctic and the Pacific. To the staples of pulp and paper and lumber, and a widening range of industrial metals, were added uranium in Saskatchewan and Ontario and huge fields of oil and natural gas in Alberta. In 1952, with advice from the increasingly important National Research Council, Ottawa established Atomic Energy of Canada as a crown corporation. The corporation's efficient CANDU (Canada Deuterium–Uranium) nuclear power units enjoyed some export success and, by the '80s, were producing nearly half of the country's electric power. Even so, new megaprojects, publicly owned, were multiplying to harness still more of the turbulent water reserves of the Precambrian Shield. The new energy developments had many spinoffs: rail lines and air services, electricity transmission lines, and pipelines for both gas and oil, covered literally thousands of miles.

Symbolic of anglophone growth confidence was the 1959 opening of the St. Lawrence Seaway. Construction of a route to enable ocean ships to penetrate the continent's industrial heartland to the very head of the Great Lakes, with ancillary hydroelectric production, had been discussed by Canada and the United States since the 1930s. In 1954, following a Canadian threat to build the seaway without American participation, a treaty was signed providing for joint construction and operation of the waterways, with hydroelectric development to be undertaken jointly by Ontario and New York. Completed just as recession was deepening, however, the seaway sharpened previous shadowy concerns about the structure of postwar prosperity. Both by region and by occupation, disparities were emphasized by recession. In the Atlantic Provinces, employment to supplement incomes from fishing and farming evaporated quickly with shrinking export markets. St. John and Halifax were hit hard by the new seaway which bypassed their ports. Across the prairies, rural depopulation reflected the application of ever more costly machinery. The new agribusiness threatened family farms with the earlier fate of Scottish crofters who had been evicted by large-scale land enclosures. Similar marginalization of small farms emphasized pockets of poverty in Ontario and Quebec. Hovering in the wings was the anglophone specter of "continentalism."

Over 40% of the new seaway's traffic was generated by American-financed iron ore production in northern Quebec; electricity developed along the St. Lawrence entered a northeastern continental grid, while American investment throughout the rest of the economy grew apace. By 1960, well over half of Canadian manufacturing firms were owned by Americans while roughly three-quarters of imports and exports were from and to the United States. Throughout the '60s and '70s, debate would swirl around the question of "who owns Canada?" Analysts and politicians differed acrimoniously as to whether the country had become simply a province in the new American empire; over, for example, whether American head offices starved research and development and curbed marketing opportunities in their branch plants or were, in fact, good corporate citizens providing essential capital and know-how.

The shifting economic and demographic sands underlay an equally fluctuating political configuration. By 1957, King-St. Laurent Liberalism showed unmistakable signs of geriatric arrogance. As often happens in Canada, opposition strength had appeared first in the provinces; all but those in the Maritimes had fallen to a resurgent Conservatism. Yet, heedless of the warning signals, St. Laurent permitted his principal minister, C.D. Howe,[14] the economic czar of the war years, to bulldoze through the Commons a perilously contentious bill: to authorize Trans-Canada Pipelines to build a natural gas conduit from Alberta to the profitable markets of central Canada. Because the capital for this transportation route would be raised by an American-controlled company, both Tory and CCF members of parliament charged Howe with recklessly fueling the influence of American corporations in Canadian affairs. The bill passed, after too-brief debate, when the government imposed closure amid pandemonium in the House.

Chief beneficiary of the resulting political groundswell was John Diefenbaker. A skilled courtroom lawyer from Saskatchewan, Dief the Chief had won the Tory leadership in 1956. His old-fashioned populist rhetoric disconcerted many Conservative business leaders; his anglophilia and dramatic assertion of unhyphenated Canadianism, however, struck resonant chords across the country. When he won a very slim majority for his party in a 1957 election, business leaders loosened their purse strings. As an early second election seemed unavoidable, many Quebec voters suspended their traditional suspicion in favor of support for the party that was clearly about to gain power at Ottawa. The Diefenbaker electoral triumph, when it came in 1958, gave the Tories a record 208 seats. The Liberals were cut to 49, the CCF to 8 and Social Credit eliminated.[15] A startling 61% of Quebec's vote went to Diefenbaker.

---

[14] No neoconservative ideologue, Howe had created Polymer, a crown corporation, when private capital had failed to build a synthetic rubber industry during the war. Renamed Polysar, the corporation had expanded into a wide range of petrochemical products and was later to be privatized by the Mulroney government.
[15] The Social Credit party, originating in the west in the 1930s, and originally professing the funny money doctrine of Major C.H. Douglas, ruled Alberta from 1935 to 1971. While retaining a populist image the party became increasingly conservative and anti-socialist, with distinct touches of anti-Sem-

Disputatious assessments still envelop the Diefenbaker legend. Economic recession slowed temporarily the rate of American investment, which caused a balance of payments problem and unease among Tory businessmen. At the same time the government's success in securing large new sales of Canadian wheat in China and eastern Europe brought joy to western Canada. Suddenly the Tories' eastern business image gave way to one of rural and small-town values: defenders of the country's outsiders and ethnics. Business, anxious for resumption of the northward flow of American capital, viewed askance Diefenbaker's anti-American tenor, his flourishes as a Commonwealth spokesman against apartheid in South Africa, and an abortive proposal for a free trade agreement with the United Kingdom. Perhaps Diefenbaker's most damaging demerit was failure to find a strong Quebec lieutenant or to comprehend the significance of the Quiet Revolution. Yet, almost as costly to the Tories was his erratic course in defense-foreign policy. Having signed the NORAD agreement in 1957, Diefenbaker shortly asserted independence by refusing to accept nuclear warheads for Bomarc rockets positioned at NORAD bases in Canada. Confusion, indecision and inept administration continued to undermine Tory power; yet the image of a man dedicated to British parliamentary traditions remained.

Following the 1958 elections, the badly mauled Liberals and CCF worked diligently to regroup. Most dramatic in this process was the 1961 founding of the New Democratic Party (NDP). In the face of rising unemployment and deepening anti-union sentiment, the Canadian Labour Congress (CLC)[16] joined with the CCF to establish the new party. Direct union participation in a political party was antithetical to basic doctrine of the American headquarters of the internationals, whether CIO or AFL. The step was the first in a progression toward greater autonomy for Canadian unions. At the same time the NDP pushed further the moderation of socialist policy statements that had already begun within the CCF itself. Choosing as first leader T.C. Douglas, whose Saskatchewan government had just established a public medical insurance plan, the NDP, along with Social Credit and a sequence of provincial parties in Quebec and the west, confirmed the multiparty system. It would also reinforce, as it were, Canada's European ambience. The democratic socialism of the NDP was modeled upon the pragmatism of its British and European counterparts. Douglas once expressed his goal as "capitalism with a human face."

The Liberals, in 1957, had elected Lester Pearson as St. Laurent's successor. With no substantive policy changes they hoped that the quiet skills of an accomplished diplomat would be the best answer to Diefenbaker's bombast. In 1962 a federal election partially justified this analysis, leaving

---

itism. It governed British Columbia from 1952 to 1972 and, from its return to power in 1975, remained dominant until an NDP government was elected in 1991. In alliance with Réal Caouette's Ralliement des Créditistes, a Quebec rural populist grouping, Social Credit took 30 federal seats in 1962. For nearly 20 years thereafter it played a role at Ottawa in the calculations of several minority governments.

[16] The CLC itself had been formed in 1956 by amalgamation of the Trades and Labour Congress (mostly AFL affiliates) and the Canadian Council of Labour (mostly CIO affiliates).

the Tories in a minority situation. Early in 1963 Diefenbaker lost a confidence resolution in the House and called another election.

If Diefenbaker's painful pusillanimity was the decisive factor in the 1963 election, it was not the most colorful. The big emotional question was that of U.S. control of Canadian policies, especially foreign-defense policies. The issue split the Tory party and also called into question Pearson's integrity. Immediately preceding the campaign, General Lauris Norstad, the recently retired American commander of NATO, issued a well-publicized statement in Ottawa: Washington believed Canada must accept nuclear arming of the Bomarcs. Almost immediately Pearson reversed the existing Liberal opposition to the nuclear warheads, saying Canada's NORAD commitment, even if only implicit, must be honored. The Liberal about-face dismayed a growing antinuclear movement. On the other hand, three of Diefenbaker's cabinet resigned to protest their leader's position. A confused electorate returned another house of minorities with Pearson as prime minister.

Minority governments were becoming familiar at both the federal and provincial levels. Unlike the pattern in Europe, Canada's multiparty system has, with minor exceptions, eschewed the solution of formal coalitions. As it became evident that governments in constant danger of losing support in the legislature were not necessarily weak, appeals to elect stable majority governments lost much of their earlier force. Even though another federal election in 1965 simply renewed Pearson's minority position, the years 1963–68 were remarkably productive of legislation. Most analysts agree that pressure from the strategically situated opposition parties, particularly the NDP, accounted for much of that achievement. A few examples must suffice. By 1967 Ottawa was reimbursing the provinces for a full half of the burgeoning costs of education. In 1965 the Canada Assistance Plan restructured grants-in-aid to the provinces for the "further development and extension of welfare service programs." To this and other social-economic programs was added, in the same year, a full national insurance scheme for "all medically necessary services"—modeled on Saskatchewan's pioneer venture and operating on a federal-provincial shared-cost basis. While business pressure forced finance minister Walter Gordon to withdraw budget proposals for discriminatory taxation of American investments in Canada, the government secured approval of a Canadian flag. A measure that had intimidated previous majority governments, it occasioned emotional and protracted debate. The maple leaf emerged in triumphant compromise over the union jack and the fleur-de-lys. Capping a positive record, in 1965 a Canada-U.S. auto pact established free trade in automobiles and parts and included a guarantee that production in the American-owned automobile industry would equal sales in Canada. The pact clearly intensified continental economic integration; it gratified the unions while sharpening suspicion of Pearson's pliancy in the face of American clout.

The volatile '60s saw not only spreading fear about the Americanization of Canada. In Quebec, deeper and more poignant apprehension of anglophone Canadian nationalism led to serious social-political storms. In 1960 the Lesage government began the policy and structural changes that collectively would be dubbed the Quiet Revolution. The incubus of Duplessis corruption was largely removed by tough new electoral laws; clerical influence was minimized in education; a thorough, secular system of social welfare developed. A spirit of social democracy seemed to infuse Quebec society. The hydroelectric industry was placed under public ownership and other public enterprises were initiated. *Étatisme* was the term applied to this positive use of government to achieve social purposes. Foremost among those purposes was to make the Québécois, as they demanded, "maîtres chez nous"—that is, to make them their own masters. Unlike the bogus autonomism of Duplessis, the nationalisme of Lesage and his successors generated hard, specific demands for federal decentralization, demands that Ottawa tried hard to accommodate. The most significant federal concession was an opting out formula, that permitted any province to choose non-participation in shared-cost programs, such as medicare and the Canada Pension Plan. Opting out entitles a province to a federal payment equal to that of a participant's grant, but with no administrative strings attached. Quebec alone made use of the option.

Effective étatisme combined with avowedly flexible federalism to whet nationaliste appetites. After defeat of the Lesage government in 1966, René Lévesque, who had been Lesage's most forceful minister, resigned from the Liberal party to establish the Parti Québécois (PQ). The "Péquiste" goal was restructuring of Canada as two equal and independent states within a common market. Clearly secessionist, Lévesque described his aim as sovereignty-association. While the PQ remained committed to democratic constitutional change, others moved to extreme positions. Several séparatiste groupings (francophone separatists) advocated outright independence; some thought violence essential. Between 1963 and 1970 sporadic terrorist bombings, centering upon Montreal's wealthy Westmount community, shattered anglophone confidence.

Following the first bombings, Pearson appointed a Royal Commission on Bilingualism and Biculturalism, jointly chaired by André Laurendeau, editor of Montreal's *Le Devoir,* and Davidson Dunton, president of Carleton University. The "Bi-Bi" interim report in 1965 proclaimed that the country, "without being fully conscious of the fact, is passing through the greatest crisis in its history." The full report documented the disadvantaged position of francophones and the demographic threat to survivance. It talked of a compact between the two "races" and the urgent need of a more just accommodation. It recommended formal recognition of French and English as official languages at the federal level and in Quebec, Ontario and New Brunswick. The report stressed also the need to rectify under-representation of francophones at all levels of the public service, and for Ottawa to assist provinces to provide education and services in both languages wherever numbers warranted. Without endorsing the notion of two nations (deux nations), and with less enthusiasm in the west, anglophones supported the report's major recommendations. In 1969 an Official Languages Act implemented some of these recommendations. In policy, the Pearson and Trudeau governments spoke of cooperative federalism and promoted federal-provincial consultation. In succeeding years such consultation (both bilateral and general) has become so nearly continuous as to constitute almost a third level of government. The pace of cooperative federalism, however, was not sufficient to obviate the looming crisis of Quebec separatism.

Fearful that the insistent drive for a Quebec national state expressed dangerous introversion, even racism, a group of féderalistes (francophone federalists) propounded a different view of survivance. This was the view of Cartier, Laurier and the historic Quebec majority: full provincial rights within a Canadian federal state were the essential bulwark against extinction in an anglophone continent. A young Montreal lawyer, Pierre Elliott Trudeau, emerged as principal féderaliste spokesman. Trudeau and two close friends joined the federal Liberal party in 1965. Arguing that their own social democratic sympathies must be suspended in favor of a quicker route to office, the three were elected in that year. Pearson appointed Trudeau minister of justice, and at a constitutional conference in 1968, Trudeau argued passionately and persuasively for practical adjustments within the existing constitutional framework. Especially, Trudeau proposed an entrenched charter of rights to guarantee not only traditional individual liberties, but also collective rights, including those of language and education. Many anglophones, particularly in central Canada, were captivated by his pan-Canadianism. Later in 1968, having been selected by a Liberal convention to succeed Pearson, Trudeau became prime minister, and shortly thereafter he called an election.

The substantial majority won by the Liberals in 1968 had a double explanation. First, Trudeau's intellectually decisive manner and appeal as a communicator had brought euphoric response, especially among young voters; Trudeaumania entered the political language. Second, the Tories and the NDP had both wavered on the national question, proposing particular or special status for Quebec. The electoral majority, both anglophone and francophone, preferred the Liberals' "one Canada"—francophones not least because Trudeau seemed to be proving that French power in Ottawa was both possible and advantageous.

Despite enhancement of proportional employment policy and subsidized language training in the federal civil service, nationaliste opinion in Quebec remained strong. Showing doubt about Trudeau's goal of making all Canada a homeland of francophones, the Quebec government moved to make French the province's sole official language and to compel immigrants to have their children educated in that language. Continuing decline of the proportion of francophones in the Canadian population underlay this overt cultural protectionism. When Trudeau established a ministry of multiculturalism to preserve Canada's mosaic, séparatistes observed tartly that nonanglophone new Canadians generally opted for English rather than French as their second language.

A Quebec election in the spring of 1970 exacerbated radical séparatistes. Féderaliste Liberals, led by Robert Bourassa, had won handily; Lévesque's Parti Québécois, with 23% of the vote, captured only seven seats. Séparatistes found increasing support for their charge that anglophone money, Liberal support from Ottawa, and the electoral system posed a barrier that would only be breached by direct action. Such action was spreading. A

Montreal police strike, street marches, thefts of arms and dynamite, bombings, and bank robberies to finance such terrorist groups as the Front de Libération du Québec (FLQ) eroded public confidence in established authority. In the context of terrorism and secessionism around the world, of the theories of Fanon, Sartre and Che Guevara, Montreal seemed to many to be "next on the list."

In October 1970, crisis arrived. An FLQ cell kidnapped Richard Cross, the U.K. trade commissioner in Montreal, and issued demands for the release of imprisoned terrorists, $500,000 in cash, air transport to Cuba or Algeria for the released prisoners, and broadcasting of the FLQ revolutionary manifesto. Safe conduct abroad, alone, was promised by Ottawa to the kidnappers. During protracted negotiations, some labor leaders and intellectuals supported calls for student-worker demonstrations and further concessions to the kidnappers. Finally, with the captive Cross still under threat of execution, Bourassa requested Ottawa to send in the army. Trudeau at once proclaimed the War Measures Act,[17] and dispatched troops, declaring that "in this country laws are made and changed by elected representatives of all Canadians, not by a handful of self-styled dictators. Those who gain power through terror rule by terror." When the FLQ then murdered Pierre Laporte, the Quebec labor minister who had also been kidnapped, public opinion in Quebec and beyond hardened decisively. The Trudeau government submitted its policy, which included temporary arrest of several hundred suspects, for approval and continuing invigilation to the House of Commons. It was supported by all parties save the NDP, although four of that party's members broke party ranks to endorse the massive response to terrorism. Cross was finally located and freed in December. His captors were given free transport to Cuba.

The October Crisis shed considerable light on the nature of Canada. While many liberals were appalled by such drastic suspension of civil liberties, overwhelming majorities endorsed the government's action and, also, the distinct leniency shown subsequently to those who had been convicted. A tradition of quick suppression of political violence seemed to nourish a notable tolerance of political dissent. If terrorism did not reappear, however, séparatisme certainly did not die. Nor did the anglophone counterpart concern with "creeping continentalism." By the '70s American direct investment was being derived more from profits made in Canada on existing investment than from fresh capital inflow. The argument that Canada was being milked of the money that would complete an American takeover gained credibility. Demands to halt the process came from an influential nationalist pressure group, a left-wing caucus of the NDP and the country's largest newspaper, the *Toronto Star*.

Faced with such choppy crosscurrents, the Trudeau government was cautious in domestic policy. Despite rising unemployment, its tight budgets clearly favored the party's business supporters. While the prime minister

---

[17] Passed in 1914, the act gave nearly absolute powers to the federal government in time of war or insurrection "real or apprehended."

showed signs of nationalist sentiment (a sentiment that he had decried philosophically) and cut by 50% Canada's contribution to NATO's European forces, his government was open to criticism from the left. In a 1972 election Trudeau lost his majority in the Commons. Both the multiparty system and the vitality of minority government were reaffirmed. With 30 seats the NDP held a balance of power. As the prime minister remarked, "We are more forced to listen. . . . Probably as a result of that some of our legislation will be better." Progressive changes in tax and social legislation and a pronounced move toward economic nationalism were the immediate results; and these set the stage for a long regrouping of anti-Trudeau opinion both in provincial capitals and in the country's corporate boardrooms. That regrouping bore fruit only after a decade of almost constant constitutional and economic turmoil. When the elections of 1984 brought to Ottawa the firmly neoconservative government of Brian Mulroney, the contending forces of collectivism and noninterventionism, nationalism and continentalism, centralization and provincial rights would still be in play, but with a different tilt to the board. When an election in 1974 restored Trudeau's majority, the principal targets of his Conservative and provincialist opponents were in place: a national petroleum company (Petro-Canada) to counter American control of production and prices, and a Foreign Investment Review Board (FIRA) to screen future investment takeovers.

Behind the party fray lay not only some entrenched attitudes toward social equity, both by regions and class, but also a Canadianizing override to the ethnic mosaic. Despite the growing racial heterogeneity, long-established thinking about order, constitutional liberty and positive government retained its force. Special federal assistance for economic development in the less prosperous regions, and growing subsidization of agriculture, paralleled steady upgrading of social insurance schemes and welfare services. Most Canadians would still pick as favored national symbol the scarlet-coated Mountie. At the same time, structural changes in the economy and internal population movement spelled risk for political leaders. As the west, especially Alberta, entered a natural resources boom in the second half of the '70s, it began to draw people from the Maritimes and even from the industrial centers of Ontario and Quebec. Quebec's birthrate finally became lowest of all the provinces. With wheat selling well across the prairies, petroleum development fueling an explosive prosperity in Alberta, and the population shifting, the west restated firmly its historic political grievance: Canadian economic policies were controlled by central Canadian business in the interest of its own financial-manufacturing structure.

In the late '70s the Trudeau government's National Energy Policy (NEP) brought matters to a head. Designed to make the country self-sufficient in energy by using Petro-Canada and various developmental tax incentives, the NEP also set prices in an effort to guard against vagaries in OPEC pricing. Premier Peter Lougheed of Alberta led a bitter battle against Ottawa's centralizing intervention and in defense of total provincial control of natural resources. The accumulating alienation of the west coincided with a political-constitutional crisis that made allies, briefly, of the western provinces and Quebec. The crisis also illustrated the unique characteristics of Canada's federal democracy.

The curtain was raised by a surprise electoral triumph for Lévesque's Parti Québécois. Having played down the Péquiste goal of secession during the campaign, Lévesque's government pushed further the *étatisme* of the Quiet Revolution with giant hydroelectric development and expanded use of crown corporations. But passage of Bill 101 in 1977 pointed more clearly to the ultimate goal: it made French the sole language of debate in the legislature, banned English signs and required all businesses to establish programs of francization. In 1979, amid mounting public furor, a White Paper proclaimed the death of federalism and the need to choose "a free, proud and adult national existence." The wording of a referendum question, published in March 1980, while superficially nebulous, was nevertheless definite: the government would seek democratic authorization to secede from confederation and then to negotiate an "economic association" with Canada. Debate leading up to the referendum vote in May presaged no foregone conclusion. Even though secession was to be unilateral, anglophone political leaders stood, by and large, aside. The federalist case was eloquently argued by Trudeau and his minister of justice, Jean Chrétien, supported by other Liberal fédéraliste members of parliament. Stressing that Quebec had demonstrated that its existing powers were adequate,[18] the Trudeau team promised early patriation of the British North America Act and its amendment so as to further entrench francophone rights. When the voting results showed 59.5% "non" (including an estimated 52% of the francophone vote), few Canadians paused to reflect on the underlying significance: a democratic vote, with no accompanying violence, had decided whether a crucially important province should unilaterally secede. A similar event would have been unimaginable in the neighboring republic.

Other deep political currents were partly responsible for the comparatively calm anglophone contemplation of the Quebec referendum. Those currents, like the cyclical intensity of Québécois nationalisme, extended a historical pattern. Opposition to a federal government is often more effectively based in provincial capitals than across the floor of the Commons. In the late '70s, despite a general anglophone view that Trudeau was essential to averting Quebec secession, corporate leaders joined western premiers in vociferous criticism of Ottawa's "arrogant" economic nationalism. An election in May 1979 had revealed that Liberals had not heeded western claims of lack of influence in national policy-making. Under Joe Clark, a new and visibly indecisive leader from Alberta, the Tories unseated Trudeau without themselves gaining a majority. Dependent upon the NDP and Créditistes, Clark held office a scant nine months before being defeated on a vote of confidence—not least because of a pusillanimous attitude toward séparatisme and provincial rights. A month prior to Clark's defeat, Trudeau had

---

[18] In addition to the remarkable social-economic achievements of the preceding 20 years, francophones had fully penetrated management, both public and private, while the income gap between francophone and anglophones had virtually disappeared.

announced that he would step aside. With no time for a leadership convention, however, he acceded to caucus pressure and withdrew his resignation. Clearly one of the most significant, and bizarre, of Canada's political convolutions, this reestablished "French power" at Ottawa in time to defend fédéralisme against séparatisme. An election in February 1980 restored Trudeau's majority.

In the years following the 1980 election the reversal of Liberal and Conservative positions on federal relations and national policies would be firmly etched. The Tory legatees of Macdonald's National Policy of protectionism and centralization, and of Conservative-backed conscription, moved steadily toward extreme provincial rights, special status for Quebec, neoconservative "small government" and continental free trade. The Liberals, heirs to Laurier's provincial rights, free trade approaches to the United States and reluctant economic interventionism, emerged as proponents of economic nationalism, positive government and one Canada.

At the outset of the '80s Trudeau moved quickly to redeem his major pledge of the referendum campaign: patriation of the British North America Act and an entrenched Charter of Rights and Freedoms. The principal impediment to acquiring sole right of amending the basic constitutional law was the failure of preceding federal-provincial conferences to agree upon an amending formula: i.e., how many provinces must consent to an amendment affecting provincial jurisdictions? Despairing of unanimity, Trudeau presented to the Commons a series of resolutions incorporating an amending formula and a Charter of Rights. Opposition to this proposed "unilateral" action came strongly from Clark's Tories and from several provincial premiers led by Peter Lougheed of Alberta and René Lévesque. However, agreement between Ottawa and Alberta on a new division of oil-gas revenues moderated Lougheed's opposition, while support for the resolutions came from the Tory premiers of Ontario and New Brunswick as well as from the federal NDP. The procedural issue was referred to the Supreme Court, which issued an ambiguous decision about the constitutionality of Trudeau's proposal. Reasonably sure of the outcome, the prime minister threatened a referendum on the question. On November 6, 1981, after an all-night bargaining session, nine provincial premiers withdrew their opposition in return for minor concessions. These included an override clause empowering provinces to enact legislation contrary to a Charter provision, providing such law is reviewed by the provincial legislature within five years. This notwithstanding clause, used only by two provinces, has been employed by Quebec, to extend its prohibitions against the use of English, and remains a very hot issue. The general amending formula calls for endorsement of amendments by Ottawa and "at least two-thirds of the provinces that have . . . at least 50 percent of the population of all the provinces." The formula removed the possibility of any one province exercising a veto. Lévesque's consequent rejection of the agreement led to another constitutional accord in 1987 that failed to gain ratification in June of 1990.

Upon receiving a joint request from the Canadian parliament, Westminster automatically passed the Canadian resolutions in 1982. The British North America Act, thus amended and renamed the Constitution Act, remains the basic constitutional law, amendable only in Canada. The essential continuities in the whole process were evident as the Queen and the prime minister signed the Constitution Act on the steps of the Canadian parliament—even if that act was frequently referred to thereafter as the "new" constitution. The Charter clauses spell out customary individual rights as well as those of both official language groups. With characteristic Canadian caution about judicial review of parliamentary behavior, however, all rights (save the linguistic) were made subject to "such reasonable limits prescribed by law as can be demonstrably justified in a free and democratic society." Characteristically, also, this "renewed federalism" concerns itself as much with the rights of collectivités as with those of individuals: with provinces, women, native people, cultural groups. It became a constitutional requirement, moreover, for Ottawa to make "equalization payments to ensure that provincial governments have sufficient revenues to provide reasonable comparable levels of public services at reasonably comparable levels of taxation."

While the economy slumped severely in 1981–82, recovery was clearly evident by early 1984. Yet, politically, despite successful negotiation of constitutional and secession crises, the ground sloped steeply away from the Trudeau Liberals. Both unemployment and annual budget deficits were high; the western boom had collapsed with the 1981 fall in world oil prices. The service sector of the economy, expanding rapidly, nevertheless multiplied low-paid and part-time employment, especially for women. Business, nervous in the face of high deficits, demanded trimming of welfare, social security and unemployment benefits. A weary Trudeau resigned in February 1984.

Because of an unwritten Liberal rule that the party leadership should be alternately francophone and anglophone, the succession went not to the prominent and popular Jean Chrétien, but to an anti-Trudeau corporation lawyer, John Turner. Without waiting to paper over deep cracks in the party, Turner called an election for September. His mistake in timing proved disastrous. The Tories, after dumping Joe Clark unceremoniously in 1983, had replaced him with a fluently bilingual native of Quebec, Brian Mulroney. Tailor-made to capitalize on the Liberal disarray, Mulroney had risen from lowly beginnings in Quebec's north shore (of the St. Lawrence) to become president of the American-owned Iron Ore Company of Canada. Instinctively sympathetic to the idea of a continental economy, Mulroney enjoyed, also, a close friendship with Robert Bourassa, who had been re-elected Quebec premier in 1985. Almost excessively pragmatic, the new Tory leader would nevertheless complete the transformation of his party. Yet the neoconservative market-force notions of a Thatcher or a Reagan, to which Mulroney gives praise, a fulsome regard for provincial jurisdictions, and Quebec's special status would all be modified by Canada's attachment to its distinctive versions of collectivism and cultural independence.

Sweeping to an unprecedented majority in the 1984 election, Mulroney's Tories ended the federal Liberal hegemony in Quebec (so briefly interrupted by Diefenbaker, whom a young Mulroney had helped to remove), and all but eliminated the Liberals in the west. The damage suffered by the NDP was much less. This, again, confirmed multipartyism and also made the NDP the effective opposition in the Commons. Ed Broadbent, the NDP leader, was topping the opinion polls for leadership quality by 1986. This curious situation was to tempt the NDP to upset its traditional priorities. Stress upon leadership at the expense of issues would bring it sharp disappointment in the election of 1988.

During Mulroney's first term there was no dearth of openings for hostile criticism. By 1986 five ministers had been forced to resign; the prime minister's own credibility had been damaged by unreliable answers in question period in the House of Commons and by considerable vacillation in policy. Committed to budget reduction, the government reversed a decision to trim old age pensions when confronted by popular outcry. Pledged to privatize crown corporations and to promote deregulation, Mulroney also reneged. Apart from emasculating FIRA and dismantling the National Energy Policy (while giving the oil-gas industry substantial tax relief), Canada's mixed economy remained largely intact.

Yet neoconservatism had not simply capitulated. Nor had the rewarding Tory faith in Quebec's special status. In 1985 President Ronald Reagan met with Mulroney and the two agreed to have negotiations begin the following year for a Canada-U.S. free trade pact. In 1987, at a first ministers' meeting at Meech Lake, Mulroney gained the support of most premiers for constitutional amendments designed to enhance Quebec's special status. The amendments had been proposed to the prime minister by Premier Bourassa as constituting the minimum requirements for Quebec's endorsement on the 1982 Constitution Act. The Meech Lake Accord ensured Bourassa's support of the Tories in the 1988 federal election. The Free Trade Agreement (FTA) would similarly ensure support from most corporations when it became the central issue of 1988.

After lengthy negotiations, so acrimonious that the most contentious question of what constitutes a subsidy had to be set aside for future talks over a five- to seven-year period, the FTA was given executive approval in Washington and Ottawa. In press and parliament, and in the November 1988 election campaign, the government defended the agreement as the sine qua non of Canada's economic survival in the face of rising U.S. protectionism and division of the world into large trading blocs. Essential to the agreement was mutually free access for investors and business firms (especially in the financial and other service sectors), harmonization of policies concerning subsidies and standards, and progressive dismantling of tariffs. The government proclaimed that the FTA would create a level playing field for continental competition, producing efficiency, rationalization and mutual investment opportunities.

Recalling the Canadian rejection of free trade proposals—which had been major election issues in 1891 and 1911 and had been hashed out in secret cabinet discussions in 1948—the government endeavored to make the FTA but one of the issues in the election campaign. However, Liberals, the NDP and a broad coalition of unions, women's groups and cultural nationalists forced the issue to the forefront. As opinion polls showed a decline in support for free trade from 78% in 1984 to a bare majority in 1988, business poured money into a campaign that stressed the risk of being shut out of the American market and left at the mercy of other closed trading blocs. Financed largely by Canadian public service unions and the Canadian Auto Workers (who had recently become independent of the American United Auto Workers), the anti-FTA coalition argued that rationalization would mean lost jobs and debilitation of the Canadian economy. As the election campaign peaked, however, the issue of an independent way of life was clearly dominant. Harmonization and subsidies became central issues. There would be no level field, the opposition declared, because the partners themselves were so unequal. Subsidization of regions, of literature and the arts, together with the social security system and the network of crown corporations, would be imperiled. Canada's burgeoning unions would be undermined by harmonizing employment conditions with those in the United States, where union strength was steadily shrinking. The market forces of neoconservatism would spell the end of an independent Canadian identity.

While the November 1988 election results showed 52% voting for parties opposed to the agreement, constituency distribution gave Mulroney another, if reduced, majority. Quebec had been the linchpin of victory. Under Bourassa's business-oriented regime the province's newly empowered francophone managers, secure finally as "their own masters," looked with favor upon the FTA, at least partly because of their minimal interest in the rest of the country. At the same time, and for the same reason, they gave full marks to the Bourassa-Mulroney Meech Lake Accord. That accord, together with evolution of the FTA, a reinvigorated program of privatization, and severe cutbacks in cultural and regional subsidization,[19] remains at the center of Canadian political discourse.

The Meech Lake Accord, a product of what has been dubbed executive federalism, required endorsement by parliament and each provincial legislature before its clauses could become part of the Constitution Act. Parliament and eight provinces gave approval. Manitoba and New Brunswick held back, requesting modifications. Newfoundland revoked its endorsement; and opposition then grew in the other regions and among aboriginal people who felt they had been left out. Why did Meech Lake become a political time bomb?

The aborted accord proclaimed that "Quebec constitutes within Canada a distinct society" and that the government of Quebec enjoys power "to preserve and promote the distinct identity of Quebec." Other clauses provided that "reasonable compensation" be paid to any province that opted out of a shared-cost program if that province maintained a similar program "compatible with national objectives," and that unanimous provincial consent be required for a number of key constitutional changes in the future. Premier Bourassa, reiterating that the accord represented Quebec's mini-

---

[19] The CBC, the National Research Council, the NFB, the Via (passenger) rail system and many other subsidized social-economic activities received sharp revenue reductions in 1989 and thereafter.

mum constitutional demands, asserted that it would entrench Quebec's "right to self-determination" and give the province "a full veto over future constitutional change."

Critics of the accord focused on its vague terminology. Specifically, they charged that it would constrict Ottawa's power to institute new social programs, hamstring future constitutional change, and leave to the courts a dangerous leeway in interpretation. That leeway, they argued, could open sluice gates to expanded Quebec jurisdiction sufficient to achieve Lévesque's dream of sovereignty-association and then negate the proposition that Canada is more than the sum of its parts.

In the summer of 1990, the Meech Lake Accord went down to defeat and the Canadian political scene was thrown into a state of disarray. If anything appeared sure, it was that a perceived drift to continentalism and federal disintegration was deeply disturbing. Still, apparent confidence in the continuance of the Canadian experiment suggested that the twin storms of nationalism and nationalisme might once again be weathered.

FURTHER READING

Bercuson, D., J. Granatstein, and W. Young. *Sacred Trust?* Toronto: Doubleday Canada, 1986.

Bothwell, R., I. Drummond, and J. English. *Canada Since 1945.* Toronto: University of Toronto Press 1981.

Cook, R. *Canada, Quebec and the Uses of Nationalism.* Toronto: McClelland and Stewart, 1986.

Fox, P. *Politics: Canada.* Toronto: McGraw-Hill Canada, 1979.

Fraser, G. *René Lévesque and the Parti Québécois in Power.* Toronto: Macmillan of Canada, 1984.

Keith, W. J., and B. Z. Shek, eds. *The Arts in Canada: The Last Fifty Years.* Toronto: University of Toronto Press, 1980.

Klinck, C. F., ed. *Literary History of Canada.* Toronto: University of Toronto Press, 1976.

McCall-Newman, C. *Grits: An Intimate Portrait of the Liberal Party.* Toronto: Macmillan, 1982.

McCann, L. D., ed. *Heartland and Hinterland: A Geography of Canada.* Scarborough: Prentice-Hall Canada, 1982.

McNaught, K. *The Penguin History of Canada.* London: Penguin Books, 1988.

Marr, W. L., and D. G. Patterson. *Canada: An Economic History.* Toronto: Macmillan of Canada, 1980.

Rioux, M., and Y. Martin. *French Canadian Society.* Toronto: McClelland and Stewart, 1964.

Russell, P. ed. *Nationalism in Canada.* Toronto: McGraw-Hill Canada, 1979.

Saywell, J. T. *The Rise of the Parti Québécois.* Toronto: University of Toronto Press, 1977.

Smiley, D. V. *Canada in Question: Federalism in the Eighties.* Toronto: McGraw-Hill Canada, 1980.

Wade, M. *The French Canadians.* Toronto: Macmillan of Canada, 1968.

REGIONALISM AND THE REGIONS

R. DOUGLAS FRANCIS

Canada is a regional country. More so than in the United States—the other North American transcontinental nation with regions similar to, and co-terminous with, Canada's—regionalism has been a pervasive force. Regionalism is often the proverbial phrase juxtaposed to nationalism in debates over a Canadian identity, the participants in the debate arguing at length as to the pros and cons of regionalism in the development and nature of a Canadian nationalism. Regionalism in Canada can be questioned; it cannot be denied.

Despite such agreement as to the existence of Canadian regionalism, no consensus exists as to how to define it or what constitutes regions in Canada. Indeed, the concept of regionalism itself has gone through a historical evolution. The traditional approach defined the regions in geographical terms, as areas characterized by a common physical environment separated from other regions with different physical features. Goldwin Smith, a former Regius Professor of Modern History at Oxford and a renowned critic, first defined Canada's regions in those terms in 1891. In his popular book *Canada and the Canadian Question* he concluded that Canada consisted of five regions: the Atlantic, Quebec, Ontario, the Prairies and British Columbia. Today we would add the North to this list.

This classification Canadian geographers now label as "formal regions"—areas having distinct and common features. Initially, and to a great extent today still, those common features were topographical, although recently other distinguishing characteristics, such as climate, ethnicity or voting patterns, have been employed to differentiate one formal region from another.

A strong element of environmental determinism exists in this approach to regionalism, with its proponents arguing that a common physical environment creates a distinct political, social and cultural environment. This has led some political theorists to try and discover a unique political culture in each of the six formal regions of the country and to link that culture to environmental conditions. Similarly in literature a school of thought argues that regional literature is a product of the landscape. This interpretation has enjoyed greater popularity on the Prairies, a region with a unique and definite physical landscape. Henry Kreisel, a prairie literary critic, argues, for example, that "all discussions of literature produced in the Canadian West must of necessity begin with the impact of the landscape upon the mind." Similarly Laurence Ricou, another prairie literary critic, concludes that prairie fiction illustrates "the regional qualities which derive from the encounter with a specific distinctive landscape." In history, one theory of settlement contends that Canadian settlement occurred in "pockets," as opposed to the systematic east-west settlement pattern in the United States. Each "pocket of settlement" became a distinct regional entity with its own separate culture that "grew out of the land." These regional identities were clearly evident at the time of Confederation or nationhood in 1867 and have since remained, thus giving Canada its enduring regional character.

While the traditional approach to Canadian regionalism still holds great popularity, it has certain limitations. Regions become static entities, fixed in geological time. There is no provision for evolution and development, since geographical forms remain essentially unchanged over long periods of time. It also places too much emphasis on the regions over the nation. If regions are indeed clearly defined, distinct and rigid, with identities of their own, then how can one account for the existence of Canada itself? The country becomes a loose conglomerate of distinct regions held together only by political expediency. Furthermore, this theory fails to explain the interdependence of regions in Canada and their association over time; they have not remained isolated and separate entities. Finally, such an approach fails to account for the human element in shaping a region. Regions are more than a geographical form, a mere area of land; they are living entities, shaped by human experiences, direct and inherited, individual and social, over time. This historical dimension is absent.

A recent theory of regionalism, outlined by geographers (but heavily influenced by Canadian historical analysis), takes account of many of the deficiencies in the traditional regional approach. It sees a region in "functional" terms, as an area whose identity comes from its functional relationship with other regions through time. This is a dynamic view of regions, whose shape comes from the interaction of a people, politically, economically, socially and culturally, with other people having different needs and an alternative perspective. Because people's needs and perspective change according to whether they are concerned with economic, political, social or cultural issues, functional regions take on different configurations according to perspective. A political region might well be different from an economic or cultural region—and might itself also change as the historical context alters.

Within Canada, regions have tended to function as either heartlands (regions of dominance) or hinterlands (regions of subservience). The heartland-hinterland paradigm is an outgrowth of the metropolitan-hinterland interpretation of Canadian history first enunciated by historian J. M. S. Careless, and based on the earlier staple theory formulated by the Canadian economic historian Harold Innis. Innis argued that Canadian history could best be explained through an understanding of the exploitation of a series of staple products, such as fish, furs, timber, wheat and minerals. These staples were produced in hinterland regions for metropolitan centers elsewhere. Initially Canada itself was the hinterland, and either Paris (in the French regime) or London (in the British era) the metropolitan center. As Canada developed its own dominant metropolitan centers, chiefly Montreal and Toronto, the relationship partially shifted from external metropolitan centers to ones indigeneous to the country and the hinterlands became the regions of the Maritimes and the West. Careless went on to say that metropolitan centers dominated the political, social, and cultural, as well as the economic life of their hinterlands. He also noted that a series of metropolitan centers developed within the country, each with its own surrounding hinterland, moving in a centrifugal fashion from smaller to larger centers. Regions then are either hinterlands or heartlands, and neither one has any meaning except in its functional relation to the other.

This approach to Canadian regionalism has had a considerable following. The staple theory and its subsequent metropolitan-hinterland paradigm have become the new orthodoxy in Canadian historical writing. W. L. Morton, the distinguished western Canadian historian, accepted this interpretation as the most accurate reflection of Canadian history, even though the implication for his native region of the West was decidedly negative, relegating it to an inferior hinterland region serving the more powerful and wealthier region of central Canada. In literature, a new school of thought has challenged the traditionalist approach, which contends that literature is a product of the landscape. Its proponents argue that literature consists of external forms (shaped in the metropolitan centers of Europe, one might add) into which regional writers fit local content. That the landscape becomes a "landscape of the mind" and regions become "regions of the mind." They are shaped by, rather than shape, human perception. Regions become "mental constructs."

This new view of regions held in a heartland-hinterland relationship has a number of advantages as well as some disadvantages. It takes into account the way regions have interacted with one another and with the nation. There is also a creative process at work in this approach to regionalism. Rather than fixed entities sketched in stone for all time, regions become dynamic and fluid as historical circumstances change. Furthermore, the human element of regionalism is restored to its rightful place as a key component in the shaping of regions and the establishment of a regional identity. Finally, regions become internalized, where the creative power of the human mind can shape them into living entities. Yet it is precisely this openness, fluidity and level of abstraction that is the greatest weakness of this new view of regionalism. If, in essence, regions are what people perceive them to be, then the difficulty—and indeed impossibility—of defining regions in a meaningful way becomes evident.

The truth lies somewhere in the middle of these two somewhat extreme theoretical models. Regions in Canada do have an external reality based on geographical form, yet they are not only, nor simply, geographical entities.

Men and women transform them into living entities when they stamp their own political, economic, social and cultural institutions and beliefs on to the physical landscape.

The following brief historical overview of the regions of Canada will combine both views of regionalism discussed above. The country will be divided into its six formal regions—the Atlantic, Quebec, Ontario, the Prairies, British Columbia and the North—but the emphasis will be on the human element of regionalism by discussing the role that men and women have played throughout the history of the region in shaping that region's characteristics and hence its identity vis-à-vis other regions and the nation as a whole.

THE ATLANTIC REGION

This region, comprising the present-day province of Newfoundland and the three Maritime provinces of Nova Scotia, New Brunswick and Prince Edward Island, lacks the physical uniformity characteristic of some of the other Canadian regions. What has united it is its historical significance. Its proximity to the Atlantic Ocean and its location as the portal to the St. Lawrence River, an entrance into the heart of the North American continent, has given the region great strategic importance. Initially four European empires—the Portugese, Spanish, French and British—vied to claim the region, which had long been the homeland of the Beothuk (in Newfoundland) and the Micmac and Malecite Indians (in the Maritime provinces). In the end only the French and British remained to fight over the area. The Europeans came to the cod fisheries of the Grand Banks off the coast of Newfoundland, long one of the finest fishing areas in the world. Fish would be the first—and for some time the only—staple of export from the region. The French established the first permanent settlements, in what they called Acadia (present-day Nova Scotia), as a possible base for the fur trade. But the location proved less valuable than Quebec on the St. Lawrence, and France all but abandoned its interest in Acadia. Thus from the outset the Acadians developed as a distinct people—French, but unassociated with France and little interested in ties with the French Canadians in the St. Lawrence Valley. The Acadian French gave the region its initial cultural distinctiveness.

Britain acquired Acadia in the treaty of Utrecht in 1713, renamed it Nova Scotia, and established its own settlements, whose inhabitants came into conflict with the Acadians. Fearful of a potential fifth column in Nova Scotia on the eve of the Seven Years' War (1756–63), the British attempted to expel the entire Acadian population. The bitterness of the expulsion of roughly 10,000 people has since remained. During the American War of Independence (1775–83), the Nova Scotians, many of whom were "Americans" by birth or ancestry, preferred to remain neutral—"neutral Yankees"—although for a century afterward they continued close economic ties with the United States. American Loyalists wishing to remain under British rule came to the region in such large numbers in 1784 that it necessitated the creation of a new province, New Brunswick, and stamped on it the strong British imperial sentiment that has long been a hallmark of the province. The Atlantic colonies also benefited from British migration that peaked in the mid-19th century, reinforcing their British nature and providing their ethnically diverse population of Scottish, Irish (Protestant and Catholic) and English still evident today.

The mid-19th century was the golden age in the region's history based on an economy of wood, wind and water. As a major shipbuilding area, and exporter of timber and fish, the region shared in the triangular trade with Britain and the West Indies. Even when Britain abandoned its mercantile system of trade in the late 1840s, the Atlantic colonies continued to prosper, through free trade with the United States ushered in by the Reciprocity Treaty of 1854.

The termination of the Treaty in 1866 coincided with Confederation and a slow subsequent decline in the Maritime economy. To many Maritimers, Confederation and economic downturn went hand in hand. Stephen Leacock best expressed the feeling: "the shades of night were falling and the night was called Confederation." But there were other factors at play, including a slump in world demand for Maritime natural products, the replacing of sailing ships by steam ships, and the federal government's national policy of promoting railway building, western settlement and high tariffs that, in the end, benefited central and western Canada over eastern Canada. From 1890 on, the Atlantic colonies became a hinterland to central Canada, supplying the raw materials for the industrial centers of Montreal and Toronto and providing a market for the finished products. This metropolitan-hinterland relationship still prevails.

This hinterland status has contributed to the lower than average per-capita incomes, high unemployment, significant underemployment, and correspondingly lower wages in all four Atlantic provinces than elsewhere in southern Canada. Out-migration is a regular occurrence, resulting in the loss of skilled labor and the weakening of the region's political influence in the federal parliament. Yet there have been surprisingly few political protest movements and there is no history of significant third-party success in Atlantic Canada. Instead the region has remained remarkably loyal to the two national parties, the Liberals and the Conservatives. Even proposals for regional unity have gathered little support, bringing into question the existence of a regional identity. And yet the region is united in its belief that it has paid a higher price in Confederation than any other region. This gives Atlantic regionalism a negative emphasis.

The federal government, especially since 1945, has dealt with this feeling of injustice through economic and financial assistance. A federal Economic Development Board has funded local projects, particularly local manufacturing, and in 1969 the newly established federal Department of Regional Economic Expansion (DREE) offered incentives to encourage companies to locate in less-favored areas, such as the Atlantic provinces, to alleviate regional inequalities. Ottawa has also provided equalization grants and other subsidies. Federal transfer payments comprise about 50% of provincial revenues in the region, thus making the federal government the major employer in the region. This unhealthy situation simply perpetuates the region's feeling of loss of autonomy and makes the four provinces appear as "wards of the [federal] state."

Quebec is a region unlike any other, not because of geography but because of linguistic and cultural differences. Populated by a French-speaking people who have had to struggle to survive in what has become a predominantly English-speaking continent, the region has developed a strong regional identity which at times has expressed itself in national terms—as a distinct society whose destiny should be expressed in a separate sovereign state. This idea has been particularly popular since the late 1960s.

Quebec, or New France, began as a colony of France in 1608. As furs, particularly beaver furs, became a lucrative item of trade in the European courts, France was interested in having a North American colony. It established its base on the St. Lawrence River, which allowed for penetration into the interior of the continent and easy access to the Atlantic Ocean and the metropolitan centers of Europe. This area had become a no-man's land between the Algonquian Indian tribes to the north and east and their enemies, the Five Nations or Iroquois, to the southwest in present-day New York State. Permanent settlement grew slowly, the French preferring to explore inland for new sources of furs rather than to clear agricultural land. By the time of the British Conquest in 1760, a century and a half after the first permanent settlement was established at present-day Quebec City, New France had a population of only 65,000, although France lay claim to a North American empire that included large areas of present-day Maritimes, Quebec and Ontario, the Canadian West, and the American midwest extending down to the Gulf of Mexico. Most of this land was populated by Indians.

Farming in the St. Lawrence Valley was carried on by habitants who worked for seigneurs who in turn either owned the land or leased it from the French Crown. The land itself was divided into seigneuries on the long-lot system—long and narrow parcels of land on both sides of the St. Lawrence River to allow access to the river for a maximum number of settlers for purposes of transportation and communications. This unique long-lot system is still evident in rural Quebec today.

The vast French empire in North America was ceded to Britain in 1763 at the end of the Seven Years' War. The French Canadians, who had already developed a distinctive identity from that of the European French, became a conquered people, a cataclysmic event that has had a psychological impact ever since. The influx of thousands of American Loyalists during and after the American Revolution led to their domination of the political, economic and social life of the colony. This aggressive English Protestant minority gained control of the fur trade and bought up seigneurial land, the two economic activities that had been the basis of French Canadian livelihood, and also established businesses. The French Canadians receded into the background in the urban settlements, taking inferior economic positions. In the mid-19th century many began emigrating in large numbers to work in the New England sweatshops; others tried to farm the marginal land of the Precambrian Shield of northern Quebec, or moved into the professions. The Roman Catholic Church and this professional elite of doctors, lawyers and notaries perpetuated the myth that the French Canadians were a "chosen people" whose destiny was to preserve a French-speaking, rural, agricultural and Catholic society in the midst of an Anglo-American, urban, commercial and Protestant continent. French Canadians entered the urban and industrial society of the 20th century with this archaic and anachronistic view. The gap between myth and reality widened until the situation erupted in the Quiet Revolution of the 1960s, an attempt, in essence, by French Canadians to catch up to the rest of North America.

The roots of the Quiet Revolution lay in the post-World War II era. Maurice Duplessis and his Union Nationale (UN) party held continuous power in Quebec from 1944 to 1960. The Duplessis Era coincided with a time of dramatic change in Quebec, with a 30% increase in population, rapid economic growth chiefly through American investment, and increased urbanization. Yet the Union Nationale government failed to modernize the political and economic structures of the province, as was occurring, for example, in Ontario during the same time period. As workers went on strike for higher wages and better working conditions, Duplessis reacted with authoritarian measures designed to suppress the strikers rather than deal with their demands. The Asbestos Strike of 1949 and its brutal suppression by the provincial police contributed to the development of a Quebec working-class consciousness.

Opposition arose on other fronts as well. A number of university professors, trained in the new social sciences, criticized the authoritarian society, and worked for a more liberal and secular Quebec. The magazine *Cité libre* became an influential voice for change in Quebec. Many urban Quebeckers complained of the undue influence of rural voters in the government as a result of an outdated electoral map that blatantly favored rural areas, and of a distinct bias in government policies in favor of rural constituencies.

The forces of opposition galvanized around Jean Lesage, the new provincial Liberal leader who had been chosen in 1957. With the death of Duplessis on the eve of the provincial election of 1960, conditions seemed ripe for a dramatic change. The Liberal victory in the spring of 1960 has been seen as the beginning of the Quiet Revolution. Certainly the changes that the new government implemented during its first term in office were dramatic: a new provincial ministry of education along with a complete revamping of the Quebec school system; the nationalization of key public utilities including hydroelectric power through the creation of Hydro-Québec; public financial support to French-Canadian investors to offset foreign domination of Quebec industries; the liberalization of the labor code; improved social welfare measures including a provincial hospitalization insurance plan; and support for French-Canandian cultural expressions through a new ministry of cultural affairs.

These changes fueled national aspirations in the region, and heated up debate among French-Canadian nationalists as to whether Quebec's destiny

235

lay in federalism or separatism. The separatist forces gained momentum with the election in 1976 of the Parti Québécois, a party committed to an independent Quebec under its popular leader René Lévesque. Yet when the party attempted to achieve its objective democratically in a referendum in the spring of 1980, a majority of Quebeckers voted "non." The federalists had a strong and dynamic leader in Prime Minister Pierre Elliott Trudeau, the French-Canadian leader of the federal Liberal Party. Today the region faces serious economic problems while its future in Confederation remains uncertain.

ONTARIO

The region of Ontario lacks common and unique features to set it off from the other geographical regions of the country; it also contains within its political boundaries a variety of subregions. Equally the region lacks economic, ethnic, social or cultural unity, thus causing some regional analysts to conclude that "Ontario does not exist"—that it lacks a regional indentity. Yet regional unity has prevailed throughout its history.

Ontario came into existence as the political region of Upper Canada in 1791 and as an economic region in the early to mid-19th century. Before that time the southern area was part of the French Empire and its fur trading network, and the northern area was part of Rupert's Land, a vast territory controlled by the Hudson's Bay Company. But the great majority of the population was Indian. The coming of American Loyalists during and after the American Revolution was the first substantial non-Indian immigration into the region, and within a decade the Indian population was outnumbered. These ex-Americans, educated in democratic practices and accustomed to ruling themselves, resented being ruled by a distant and autocratic government in Quebec City. Britain agreed to divide the colony of Quebec along the Ottawa River, and the present province of Ontario (then known as Upper Canada to distinguish it from Quebec, renamed Lower Canada) came into existence through the Constitutional Act of 1791. John Graves Simcoe, the first governor, wanted to make Upper Canada a "truly British" colony, and thus fostered British practices and encouraged British immigration while playing down the American influence. The test to Simcoe's plan came in the War of 1812, when the United States made the capture of Upper Canada its foremost Canadian objective. This war, and the British success at fending off the American attackers, is seen as the beginning of a regional consciousness and an Upper Canadian identity.

With an abundance of good agricultural land and a sparse population, Upper Canada welcomed new settlers especially if they were British. The majority farmed, and wheat became the major staple of export from the colony by mid-century. To export wheat required a sophisticated transportation network of roads, railroads and canals. By the time of Confederation in 1867, a network of transportation lines crisscrossed the colony, resulting in the rise of centers to service the local hinterlands. The Great Lakes and the St. Lawrence system—"the Commercial Empire of the St. Lawrence"— linked the inland colony with Europe.

After Confederation, the industrial heartland of Ontario (renamed at the time it became a province) expanded transcontinentally to include the Maritimes and the West as its hinterlands. The national policy of high tariffs, set in place by the federal government in 1879, provided the protection that allowed central Canadian industries to develop. The Canadian Pacific Railway, completed in 1885, provided the means to tie heartland and hinterland together. The region of southern Ontario already had the financial institutions, wholesale and retail tradehouses, transportation network, and population necessary to make it the industrial heartland. As well it had easy access to the Pennsylvania coal fields, the hydroelectric power of Niagara Falls, and the mineral and timber wealth of its own northern hinterland area—coined "new Ontario" because of its great economic potential—to fuel the region's industrial expansion. This was the boom era, roughly from 1880 to 1920.

Ontario continued to solidify its position of regional dominance in the interwar years. Many American companies looked north to central Canada to establish branch plants to get around the tariff wall. Ontario experienced a second "boom era" in the post-1945 period. Postwar prosperity coupled with a rapidly growing population stimulated the demand for consumer goods—automobiles, televisions, refrigerators and stoves, for example—many of which were produced in their own province in the "Golden Horseshoe" area, the band of industrial sites stretching from Niagara Falls around the western end of Lake Ontario to Oshawa. Economic prosperity led to a demand for better social services, such as schools, universities and hospitals.

Energy for this new wave of prosperity came from three main sources: hydroelectric power from the St. Lawrence Seaway; uranium and nuclear power from the uranium mines of northern Ontario; and natural gas piped in from Alberta. After a brief lapse in the 1970s and early 1980s, when, momentarily, capital and people moved west and energy prices skyrocketed, Ontario resumed its position of economic dominance, though the province has been hit hard by the recession of the 1990s.

Along with prosperity came resentment from the other regions of Canada, which believed that the expansion occurred at their expense. Ontarians replied that their region has shouldered their share of the "burden of national unity" through increased taxation to support equalization grants, unemployment insurance, and industrial development projects that the federal government gives the poorer regions. This ongoing debate reinforces the inequality among the regions of the country and the fragile nature of regionalism itself.

THE PRAIRIE

The Prairie region appears to have the most uniform topography of any region in Canada, although geographers are quick to point out that there are three different landscapes in the region: the prairies to the south (and the area most commonly associated with the region as the name implies); the parkland further north; and the boreal forest where the Prairie region verges on the region of the North. The Prairie, which today comprises the provinces of Manitoba, Saskatchewan and Alberta, has, at least in the past, had a uniform economy and culture and a common history, although that appears to be changing now as the region diversifies.

With the coming of the white man, the northerly reaches of this region were of interest for their furs. Two empires vied to control the region: the British through the Hudson's Bay Company, a commercial company established in 1670 and trading out of Hudson Bay; and the French through their family-based companies located in Quebec after 1608. After the British Conquest of 1760, the French companies were taken over by British merchants, and a new dynamic North West Company was formed. These two companies, the Hudson's Bay and North West, were rivals despite their common British base, and they fiercely competed with one another to explore the region and establish fur trading posts.

Permanent settlement was discouraged in the region because of its threat to the fur trade. But in 1811 Thomas Douglas, fifth earl of Selkirk, bought a controlling interest in the Hudson's Bay Company to fulfill a dream of establishing a colony of Scottish crofters in the region. The Red River colony, as his settlement was called at the confluence of the Red and Assiniboine rivers (present-day Winnipeg), had a difficult beginning plagued as it was by floods, drought, grasshoppers, and raids by North West Company traders (until 1821 when the two companies were forced to amalgamate into a single Hudson's Bay Company). But the colonists persevered to become the first permanent European settlers in the region. Through intermarriage of the French fur traders with the Indians, a new people— the Métis—had emerged who had a sense of identity and saw themselves as constituting a "third nation." The Métis, under Louis Riel, their legendary leader, clashed with the Canadian government in 1866–70, when the latter purchased the region from the Hudson's Bay Company, and again in 1885, as the coming of white settlers threatened their livelihood.

Canadian control resulted in the shift from fur trade to agricultural settlement and the transformation of the region into a hinterland of central Canada. The Canadian government took direct control of the land and natural resources in the region (contrary to the practice established elsewhere) to be used "for the purpose of the Dominion." Within a decade, the land was surveyed into square townships, a Homestead Act was passed, law and order were established, the Indians were placed on reserves, and a rail link to central Canada was almost completed. Immigrants were slow to come at first, but by the turn of the century they were arriving in the hundreds of thousands. By 1914, the region boasted a polyglot population of over one million, engaged mainly in wheat farming, although towns and cities grew rapidly too to service all the needs of the settlers. This multicultural society and the predominantly rural agricultural economy were distinguishing characteristics of the region.

The aspirations of western farmers ran contrary to the needs and interest of the Canadian government and eastern businesses; as a result, third parties arose in the interwar years to represent western interests: the Progressives in the 1920s, and the Co-operative Commonwealth Federation (CCF) and Social Credit in the 1930s. Political protest has been another distinguishing characteristic of the region.

A "new west" has emerged since 1945, one more urbanized, economically diversified, and, as a result, more like the other regions of the country in its social and cultural composition. Wheat farming gave way to mixed farming, and agriculture in general took a back seat to natural resource production—potash, uranium, gas and oil in particular. Consolidation of farms has occurred, due to more efficient agricultural machinery. The people enjoyed a higher standard of living than ever before, participating in the consumer society, although to less an extent than central Canadians did. Not all western Canadians have enjoyed this prosperity, most notably the Indians and the Métis.

With the shift to a more homogenized, urban, and manufacturing-based society, distinctive Prairie politics declined in fervor. In all three Prairie provinces there was a shift back to the two mainline parties, the Liberals and the Conservatives. In the early '90s, however, the New Democratic Party (NDP)—the successor to the CCF—was elected provincially in Saskatchewan while the Reform Party was built from a Prairie base to become a new right-wing protest party in federal politics.

One distinguishing feature of the region prevails: the Prairie continues to be an economic hinterland of central Canada. Despite attempts to develop secondary manufacturing and tertiary industries in the region, the prairie west remains primarily a producer of natural resources for industrial centers outside its borders in central Canada and also in the United States. This hinterland-heartland relationship lies at the base of the current regional protest—expressed in terms of "western alienation." Add to this feeling of economic subordination a belief that in national politics the region's needs are not taken seriously because of underrepresentation in the federal parliament, and one can understand the persistency of a regional consciousness and a continued regional identity in Prairie Canada.

BRITISH COLUMBIA

Geography and history have combined to make British Columbia a unique region. Geographically, the region has a physical environment bound on the west by the Pacific Ocean and separated from the rest of Canada on the east by the Rocky Mountains but containing within at least two distinct areas: the coastal fringe of settlement, and the mountainous interior. Some claim that this range of mountains acts not only as a physical barrier but also as a cultural, and possibly psychological, barrier. British Columbians often appear to be in, but not of, Canada. Historically, this region, with its bountiful natural resources—fish, minerals and especially its forest resources—has served as a hinterland for metropolitan centers outside its borders.

In the early years of Pacific coastal exploration in the late 18th century, Spain, Russia and the United States sought to control the rich coastal fur trade with the Indians. In the end only Britain and the United States competed commercially for the area that now includes present-day British Columbia. In 1818 the two countries agreed to claim jointly the Oregon Territory, an area bounded by the Rocky Mountains to the east, the Pacific Ocean to the west, the Russian claims to the north (present-day Alaska) and Spanish territory to the south (roughly the northern tip of California). Meanwhile, European fur traders, from both the Hudson's Bay and the North West companies, arrived overland in the region, establishing a strong British presence on the Pacific. The United States was also active in the 1840s, and the two countries agreed in 1846 to divide the Oregon Territory along the 49th parallel to the coast and to include Vancouver Island as part of the British territory.

Britain pressured the Hudson's Bay Company to colonize the area, which was mainly populated by Indians until the late 19th century when disease greatly reduced their numbers. In 1851 James Douglas became governor of the Colony of Vancouver Island. Shortly afterward, in 1858, gold was discovered on the lower Fraser Valley on the mainland, and the British Columbian gold rush was on. Thousands of American gold diggers, many from the California gold fields, arrived, giving a strong American presence in the area. To prevent a possible American takeover in the mining fields, Britain claimed the mainland, including its mineral rights, and established a second colony there, which Queen Victoria named British Columbia.

Major economic problems, caused chiefly by the dramatic decline of the gold rush in the mid-1860s, forced the two colonies to unite in 1866. On the eve of Confederation in 1867, this united colony faced three options: join the United States, remain a British colony or join Canada. Of the three choices, the third seemed the least feasible given the fact that the colony was separated from the rest of Canada by 2,500 miles of wilderness.

When Canada purchased Rupert's Land in 1869, the situation changed. Anxious to create a transcontinental nation "from sea to sea," the Canadian government offered British Columbians generous terms to join Confederation, including the promise to complete a transcontinental railway to link British Columbia to the rest of Canada within 10 years. On July 20, 1871 British Columbia joined Confederation.

The completion of the Canadian Pacific Railway in 1885 dramatically shifted the British Columbian economy from its traditional maritime to a continental orientation. British Columbia became an economic hinterland for central Canada, supplying raw materials for industrial expansion and providing a market for the finished products. This hinterland-heartland relationship resulted in rapid growth in the southwestern coastal area of the province, especially in the port of Vancouver, which became the local metropolitan center of the region. After World War I, British Columbia became more closely integrated into the world economy through export of its resources to the United States, Japan and the United Kingdom.

In the post-1945 period this trend toward continental and world integration continued at a faster pace partly as a result of provincial government intervention. The government encouraged multinational corporations to locate in the region, searched out international sources of financial investment, and built an elaborate infrastructure of railways, roads and power lines to open up isolated resource-rich areas, and to integrate and consolidate the provincial economy. Vancouver grew as the economic center of this expansion. The strategy worked in that British Columbia prospered in the 1950s, '60s, and '70s, but it further entrenched the region into its traditional role as a staple-extracting hinterland. The question that remains for the future is what will happen to this region when the natural resources are exhausted?

The hinterland-heartland relationship has resulted in two unique cultural traditions in the region. Politically, British Columbians have distinguished themselves from the rest of Canada at least in the post-World War II era by electing Social Credit and CCF-NDP provincial governments. The two mainline Canadian parties, the Liberals and the Conservatives, are weak. This is indicative of British Columbia's indifference to, and disillusionment with, the federal political process, and reflective of the tension that has existed between Victoria and Ottawa over resource, fiscal and constitutional questions. British Columbia is also known for its bitter labor-management feuds and a resulting series of labor strikes in the province. The vulnerability of resource-extracted primary industries to economic instability, and the importance of labor in processing those resources, has left the region open to labor unrest. This tension has been a part of the province's regional consciousness and has contributed to British Columbia's separate and distinct regional identity.

THE NORTH

To define the region of the North is difficult. In some respects, it constitutes all that area not included in the other regions of the country. This definition by elimination, however, is hardly satisfactory. Politically, the North is the area north of the 60° parallel, constituting two territories: the Yukon Territory and the Northwest Territories. These territories, over 40% of the country in geographical size, still lack provincial status and are therefore "colonies" of the federal government in Ottawa. Economically, the North is a hinterland to the metropolitan centers to the south. The federal government, dominated by the populated southern provinces, essentially owns, and dictates policy for, these northern resources. Geographically, the North is the region containing two environmental areas: the Arctic and the Subarctic. The Arctic is treeless (the area north of the 10° isotherm for July), while the Subarctic contains the northern forest zone, including the boreal forests in the northern parts of all the southern provinces except the Maritimes. Culturally, the North is the region that gives Canada its distinctive identity. From the time of Confederation, a popular myth has prevailed that Canada is a northern nation, inhabited by northern "races" and dominated by a northern climate and a northern topography that has molded a unique people—particularly differentiating Canadians from the Americans who live in "the South." By any one of these definitions, the North is a region that is sparsely populated (predominantly by Native people), isolated from the southern areas of dominant settlement, and heavily depen-

241

dent on natural resources (initially animals for furs, oil, baleen, and ivory, and more recently minerals, oil and gas) for an exacting livelihood.

Three main native groups live in the North: the Inuit (previously known as the Eskimos) in the Arctic; the Dene throughout the Yukon and the Mackenzie River Valley; and the Métis in the Mackenzie Valley. All three groups originally depended on fish and game for their livelihood. Early contact with the white man came initially in the eastern Arctic as a result of European interest in a North West Passage to the Orient, followed by their interest in whaling and in fur trading. The Hudson's Bay Company in the 19th century established fur trade posts. Anglican and Roman Catholic mission stations followed. During the fur trading era (which lasted essentially up to the mid-20th century due to the extreme isolation of the area), the native people continued their traditional hunting and fishing occupations, though no longer solely for the purpose of subsistence but also for an external market. They exchanged their furs for material goods. This initial metropolitan-hinterland relationship made them reliant on the white man.

In 1869 the Canadian Government purchased Rupert's Land from the Hudson's Bay Company, and in 1880 Britain transferred its claim over the Arctic Archipelago to Canada, thus giving this newly founded nation a vast territory that stretched from the 49° parallel to the Arctic Circle. Canadian acquisition had little impact on the region, however, since Canada had no interest in this "northern wasteland." It did, though, send the Royal North West Mounted Police to the Yukon during the Klondike gold rush in 1896 and it established police posts in the Northwest Territories in the early 20th century. Discovery of oil in the Mackenzie River Valley at Norman Wells in the 1920s heightened Canadian interest in the region, but the real turning point in Canadian interest came in World War II. The Americans built two major projects, the Alaska Highway and the CANOL oil pipeline from Norman Wells to Whitehorse, as well as a series of airfields used to ferry airplanes to the war fronts in Europe.

The North after 1945 became of strategic and economic importance. Strategically it became a "buffer zone" between the two superpowers of Russia and the United States. In the 1950s a series of radar stations were built along the 70° parallel (the DEW line; i.e., the Distant Early Warning line) financed and manned by Americans. The fur trade declined in the post-1945 era, thus making the native population ever more reliant on the Canadian government. The government responded by extending the social welfare measures implemented for all Canadian citizens in the 1940s to the Inuit and northern Indian population. At the same time large corporations—especially the multinational corporations—became interested in extracting the region's hydrocarbon and mineral resources. This has led to a heightened crisis for the Native population, but also to a growing regional consciousness that they need their own political power so as to direct, and to benefit from, this economic growth in their region. As well, concern has been raised as to the ecological impact that intense oil and gas exploration and development will have on the region. The Mackenzie Valley Pipeline Inquiry, better know as the Berger Inquiry after then British Columbia

Justice Thomas Berger who headed the inquiry, recommended in its report, *Northern Frontier, Northern Homeland* in 1977 that no pipeline be built along the valley for at least 10 years. The report coincided with a downturn in the oil and gas economy, and only as Canada entered the 1990s has renewed economic interest in the North resurfaced.

Along with new interest comes the Native people's concern for aboriginal rights. Some Native groups in the Northwest Territories and the Yukon have signed agreements-in-principle with the federal government settling outstanding land claims. As well the Canadian government has agreed to negotiate the transfer of responsibility for offshore oil and gas, plus a share of royalties, to the territorial governments. The larger questions of Native self-government and division of the sprawling Northwest Territories still remain unresolved; the Northwest Territories is the only political jurisdiction in Canada in which a majority of the members are Natives and the Inuit want their own territory.

Today the region of the North, more than any of the other regions, is on the threshold of development. As Canada's last frontier, the region remains a test of the nation's ability to accommodate local regional needs while serving national interests.

Regionalism has been a pervasive force throughout Canadian history. The nation began as a country of regions and has remained so since. The nature of these regions change and their relations to one another and to the nation as a whole is in constant flux, yet a core of consistency remains to distinguish one region from another and to give each region of the country a strong identity. One of the challenges Canadians have faced and continue to face is how best to recognize and preserve these regional differences and characteristics while also maintaining the unity of the nation as a whole. This is the heart of the Canadian dilemma—and its most rewarding challenge.

FURTHER READING

Bercuson, David J., ed. *Canada and the Burden of Unity*. Toronto: Macmillan, 1977.

Careless, Maurice. "Limited Identities," *Canadian Historical Review*. (March 1969.)

Francis, R. Douglas, Richard Jones, and Donald B. Smith. *Destinies: Canadian History Since Confederation*. Toronto: Holt, Rinehart and Winston, 1988.

Journal of Canadian Studies. 15, 2 (Summer 1980). Special issue on "Regionalism/ Le régionalisme."

McCann, L. D., ed. *Heartland and Hinterland: A Geography of Canada*. Scarborough: Prentice-Hall Canada Inc., 1982.

Mandel, Eli, and David Taras, eds. *A Passion for Identity: An Introduction to Canadian Studies*. Toronto: Methuen, 1987.

Phillips, Paul. *Regional Disparities*. Toronto: James Lorimer and Co., 1982.

Putnam, Donald F. and Robert G. Putnam. *Canada: A Regional Analysis*. Toronto: J. M. Dent and Sons Ltd., 1970.

Westfall, William, ed. *Perspectives on Regions and Regionalism in Canada*. Ottawa: Association for Canadian Studies, 1983.

Woodcock, George. *The Meeting of Time and Space: Regionalism in Canadian Literature*. Edmonton: New West Institute for Western Canadian Studies, 1981.

PART THREE

POLITICS

FEDERALISM

DONALD V. SMILEY

The late J. A. Corry, a distinguished Canadian political scientist, wrote more than a decade ago that Canada is an "incorrigibly federal country." In a similar vein the American scholar of federal systems Daniel Elazar has pointed out that Canada is the only nation in the world in which a book on federalism may be bought in any major airport. Canadians are preoccupied, even obsessed, with federalism and almost every important question of Canadian public policy has a federal dimension.

A federal *society* is one in which the most salient aspects of human association, identification and conflict are linked to specific territories. A federal *governmental system* may be defined in these terms:

1. There is a constitution which distributes the powers of state between central and regional governments and which provides some protection for the people and/or the governments of the regions in the composition and operations of the central government.
2. The elements of the constitution defining the respective powers of the center and the regions are not alterable by the unilateral action of the central or the regional governments.
3. Individual citizens and private groups are subject to the laws and other authoritative exercises of state power by both the central and regional governments. The interactions between federal societies and federal governments are exceedingly complex. Territorially bounded social diversities based on language and/or ethnicity buttress federal organization within governmental systems, as is the case of the division between francophone Quebec and the rest of Canada. Yet once federal arrangements in government are put in place, they sustain important interests even when such interests in their origins at least appear not to be undergirded by important social or economic cleavages. For example, the Canadian provinces of Alberta and Saskatchewan were established as such in 1905 and the boundary between them did not reflect either geographical features or important social and economic differentiation at that time. However, each of these provinces subsequently developed distinctive political cultures as well as important interest groups operating within their respective territorial boundaries.

Let us examine Canadian federalism in terms of (1) the interactions between three sets of territorially based cleavages and (2) the Canadian constitutional combination of federalism with the inherited Westminster model of parliamentary government.

CLEAVAGE I: FRANCOPHONES AND ANGLOPHONES

The Dominion of Canada came into being as a federation in 1867 because the French-speaking politicians of Lower Canada (Quebec) would not enter a new political union on other terms. Most of the English-speaking leaders of British North America would clearly have preferred a unitary system in which whatever sub-national units of government existed held and exercised their powers at the discretion of the central authorities. The compromise between these conflicting pressures was embodied in the British North America Act enacted by the Parliament of the United Kingdom. The Act conferred on the provinces power over those matters deemed most essential to the preservation of a distinctive French-speaking culture in Quebec, where of course francophones were a majority. The most important of these powers related to education, the private law system based on Roman law rather than as elsewhere in British North America on the English common law, and what we would now call health and welfare services, which at the time and for nearly a century afterward were for the most part controlled by the Roman Catholic Church. On the other side, the new Dominion government received jurisdiction over matters deemed essential to establishing and sustaining a second national economic community in North America, separate from the United States. This gave the Dominion powers over interprovincial transportation and communication, over tariffs and excise and the power to raise money by "any Mode or System" of taxation; power over banking; and paramountcy over immigration and agriculture.

The French-English compromises effected at Confederation provided a high degree of stability in relations between the two communities for over a century. Although Quebec was a resolute defender of provincial autonomy, the most bitter conflicts between anglophones and francophones did not involve the federal distribution of powers at all but rather the treatment of French and Catholic minorities in education by certain of the provinces and Canada's foreign commitments as a member of the British Empire/Commonwealth.

The stability in the relations between Canada's two historic communities was challenged by the coming of the Quiet Revolution in Quebec from about 1960 onward. The Quiet Revolution was essentially a rather abrupt transition from a traditional to a modernized society. There were several interrelated changes:

• A dramatic decline in the francophone birthrate disturbed the French-English demographic balance both within Quebec and within Canada as a whole. From Confederation to the 1960s the francophone part of the population had remained at about 30% of the Canadian total, with the assimilation of most immigrants to the anglophone community being balanced by the higher rate of natural increase among francophones. This latter changed from the late 1950s onward, and even within Quebec the disposition of immigrants to opt for English rather than French provided a challenge to the majority community.

• The Quebec majority redefined itself. There was a transition here from being French Canadian, a definition implying a minority status within Canada, to being Québécois as a nation within the boundaries of Quebec.

• There was a vast expansion of the role of the Quebec state in the affirmation of Québécois nationhood.

Although the francophones of Quebec had asserted provincial autonomy in the past, until the Quiet Revolution the Quebec government had not acted as a positive instrument of this community. All this changed in the 1960s. A large and competent provincial bureaucracy was rapidly created, and the provincial state intervened in areas of activity hitherto under the control of the Church and private businesses.

There were two broad responses to readjust the Canadian system of government to the circumstances of a modernized and modernizing Quebec.

First, there was the affirmation of Québécois nationalism. I have already outlined briefly the nature of this development within Quebec. Outside the province, those who were supportive of this thrust had a generalized tolerance for those nationalist currents and a willingness to see Quebec attain a "special status" within the federal system, a de jure or de facto range of powers broader than that of the other provinces.

Second, there was the pan-Canadian alternative. This alternative was most clearly and forcefully elaborated by Pierre Elliott Trudeau, prime minister of Canada from 1968 to 1984 except for nine months in 1979–80. The basic affirmation here was that the francophone and anglophone communities were both Canada-wide communities. The federal authorities could legitimately speak for both communities, a special status for Quebec was denied and there was emphasis on securing the rights of the francophone minorities outside Quebec. Along with all this was a vast enhancement of the influence and numbers of francophones in the central government at both the elected and senior appointed levels.

The nationalist and pan-Canadian alternatives were clearly juxtaposed in the Quebec referendum of May 1980. The Quebec election of November 1976 had brought to power a Parti Québécois government pledged to Quebec independence with some kind of continuing economic association with Canada. The 1980 referendum asked the provincial electorate to give the government a "mandate to negotiate" such an arrangement. The government was denied such a mandate by a 60–40 margin and this was followed by a radical weakening of Quebec popular support for sovereignty.

With the decline of the Quebec movement for independence, the conflicts between the anglophone and francophone communities of Canada related largely to the constitutional and legal regulation of the two languages. Interestingly, prior to the 1960s there was almost no such regulation, apart from the very limited constitutional protection of English and French in parliament and courts of Quebec contained in Section 133 of the British North America Act of 1867. All this has now changed. In 1969 Parliament enacted the Official Languages Act, which explicitly conferred on citizens the right to deal with the federal government in either English or French when this was at all practical. Amendments to the constitution which came into effect in 1982 extended and strengthened these rights and included certain rights to education in the minority official languages. By way of these changes New Brunswick became officially bilingual, and Ontario has enacted comprehensive legislation related to the French language. All these constitutional and legal changes have been specifically directed toward enhancing the position of francophones outside Quebec and in the operations of the central government.

A countermovement has reaffirmed the primacy of the French language within Quebec, both in the operations of provincial and local governments and, so far as these matters are within provincial jurisdiction, in the private business sector. Such legislation was enacted by the Quebec National Assembly as Bill 22 in 1974 and with much more extensive protection for French in Bill 101 of 1977. In early 1989 the Assembly used its powers under the Constitution Act of 1982 to override a decision of the Supreme Court of Canada which invalidated a section of Bill 101 prohibiting the use of other languages than French in commercial signs. This decision by the Quebec legislature was very unpopular in English-speaking Canada and gave impetus to the demand for the elimination of the override provisions of the constitution which made it possible. The failure of the Meech Lake Constitutional Accord in 1990 (see below) angered Quebec and pushed support for Quebec independence to unprecedented levels.

CLEAVAGE II: HAVE AND HAVE-NOT AREAS

Canada is a large and regionally diverse country and its various areas have different economic foundations undergirded by the dominance of different kinds of economic activity. Thus much of the more overt economic conflict does not involve the struggle of classes defined in a Marxist sense but rather that of areas with differing kinds of material enhancements. These areas do not always follow the boundaries of the provinces. There are important subnational regions such as Northwestern Ontario and, until the last generation, the three Prairie Provinces of Manitoba, Saskatchewan and Alberta had a dominant common regional interest in their overwhelming dependence on the wheat economy.

The government of Canada has come to play an important role in redistributing resources to the residents and governments of poorer areas. Ottawa is committed to fiscal transfers which benefit the less prosperous provinces more than the others. This responsibility is embodied in Section 36(2) of the Constitution Act, 1982, "Parliament and the government of Canada are committed to the principle of making equalization payments to ensure that provincial governments have sufficient revenues to provide reasonably comparable levels of public services at reasonably comparable levels of taxation." The bulk of these transfers are made according to a complex formula related to the fiscal capacity of the various provinces to raise moneys from the revenue sources available to them. Other transfers to the provinces from Ottawa are on behalf of post-secondary education, welfare, and hospital and medical insurance services. Some of these latter benefit the poorer provinces less than the more prosperous ones in per capita terms but constitute a higher proportion of the former's expenditure on the aided function.

Federal programs to support the income of individuals benefit the poorer areas more than the more prosperous ones in a relative sense. Because per capita personal incomes are lower in these areas, such transfers are a higher proportion of Gross Provincial Product. In such areas there are higher than proportionate numbers of senior citizens receiving supplementary federal assistance in addition to the Old Age Security payments made to all Canadian residents 65 and over. There are also higher rates of unemployment and higher than proportionate unemployment insurance payments from Ottawa. In general, the Canadian welfare state is a significant instrument of inter-regional equalization.

There are diverse federal programs to support economic activity in the less prosperous areas. Some of this involves activities of the federal government itself in its civilian and military roles. There is also a complex of programs to stimulate private economic activity in the less prosperous areas by way of tax incentives, subsidies and so on and cooperation with the provinces toward the same end. Despite different kinds of public policies, regional economic differences persist and some specialists in these matters believe such policies have been ineffective in establishing a sound economic base in the poorer areas of Canada.

CLEAVAGE III: CANADA AND THE UNITED STATES

A major impulse to the establishment of the Dominion of Canada in 1867 was the desire to establish and sustain a second transcontinental nation in North America independent of the United States. Confederation and the National Policy adapted by the government of Canada in 1879, which was its fulfillment, had three major economic elements: by way of a high customs tariff to create a flourishing industrial base in the central heartland of Ontario and Quebec, to people and develop the Canadian West and to build a transcontinental railway wholly on Canadian territory. The federal government rather than the provinces would assume the dominant role in these nation-building enterprises. In general, the other cleavages mentioned—those between French and English and between have and have-not areas of Canada—have been and continue to be powerfully influenced by the Canadian-American dimension.

On January 2, 1988 Prime Minister Brian Mulroney and President Ronald Reagan signed a Free Trade Agreement on behalf of their respective nations to come into effect at the beginning of 1989. Canadian adherence to the FTA was in a sense given political ratification by the results of the Canadian general election of November 1988, in which free trade was the dominant issue and which returned the Mulroney Conservatives to power with a majority. The major Canadian impulses behind a liberalized trading regime with the United States were fears of a rising American protectionism and a generalized ideological preference within the government and among Canadian business for market forces as against governmental decisions in the allocation of economic resources. The terms of the FTA relate for the most part to matters within federal jurisdiction rather than provincial, although it would seem to limit certain powers of the provinces in respect to controls over investment and energy development, and its general thrust is anti-interventionist.

It is wise to be very tentative about the impact of the Free Trade Agreement on the domestic dimensions of the Canadian federal system, but the following suggestions can be made:

- The agreement may enhance the scope of federal jurisdiction over economic matters. In broad terms, the courts have tended to give a relatively restricted scope to parliament's powers over "Trade and Commerce," certainly compared with judicial interpretation of congressional authority over interstate commerce under the U.S. Constitution. Competent legal scholars suggest that the existence of the FTA may influence the Canadian courts to expand federal jurisdiction over trade and commerce.
- The FTA may be an influence against federal policies encouraging economic activity in the less prosperous areas of Canada. The FTA does not define what are acceptable kinds of subsidies by the state and these are to be negotiated in a seven-year period. The American authorities clearly believe that some of the Canadian policies related to inter-regional distribution are contrary to the conditions of what has come to be called "a level playing field."
- The agreement has at least the potentiality of creating new kinds of cleavages between francophone Quebec and the rest of the Canadian community. From the early 1980s onward there was a weakening disposition among Québécois to look to positive action by the Quebec state as an instrument of national affirmation. During the 1988 Canadian federal election there was little support for the anti-free-trade position in Quebec, and the leader of the separatist Parti Québécois has declared that free trade works toward Quebec sovereignty by decreasing the economic dependence between Quebec and other parts of Canada. On the other hand, opponents of free trade outside Quebec oppose the market philosophy inherent in the agreement and associate the preservation of Canadian nationhood with inverventionist policies of federal and provincial governments which are, it is claimed, put at risk by the agreement. As in the past, Quebec and pan-Canadian nationalisms are pulling in opposite directions.

THE INSTITUTIONAL AND CONSTITUTIONAL DIMENSION

Institutional structures are never neutral in determining how demands on a political system are converted into laws, government regulations, judicial divisions and other "outputs" of that system. The American political scientist C. E. Schattschneider put it well: "All forms of political organization have a bias in favor of the exploitation of some kinds of conflict and the suppression of others . . . Some issues are organized into politics while others are organized out."

Canada was the first political community to combine federalism, a form of government invented at Philadelphia in 1787, with the British system of responsible parliamentary rule. This combination was subsequently repeated in other parts of the British Empire Commonwealth—Australia, India, Malaysia and Nigeria. What has been called the "Westminster model" involves the final powers of government being vested in a collective executive (cabinet), most of whose members are drawn from and who are accountable to a chamber of persons popularly elected from the various districts into which the jurisdiction is divided for such purposes. In Canada, as in other federations operating under this model, the parliamentary form prevails in both the central and regional governments. The British North American "fathers" of Confederation in 1864–67 deliberately chose the Westminster model because in their views it represented what one scholar has called "strength, order and authority" and rejected the American system of checks and balances, which were perceived to result in governmental weakness.

From the 1960s there has been an enormous emphasis on constitutional reform on the part of governments in Canada and of politically aware elements of the population. The initial impetus of this movement was a modernized and modernizing Quebec, and relations between anglophones and francophones have been crucial to its development. However, as affairs evolved many other groupings which have felt themselves disadvantaged have pressed for one kind or other of constitutional reform. These groupings include women, aboriginals, persons whose ethnic backgrounds are neither anglophone nor francophone, persons who have mental and physical handicaps, and so on. Further, pressures arose in western Canada for constitutional reform to weaken the majoritarian disposition of the parliamentary system in the workings of the federal government. It is hardly too much to say that by the late 1980s almost every ailment in the Canadian body politic was diagnosed by some influential grouping in the country to be susceptible to cure by constitutional change.

Although intergovernmental discussions of comprehensive constitutional reform began in 1968, it was only after the Quebec referendum of 1980 that such discussions resulted in important reforms. During the referendum campaign Prime Minister Trudeau had promised the Quebec electorate that if they voted against the Parti Québécois proposal for sovereignty association, decisive moves would be taken toward what was designated as "renewed federalism." Immediately after such a negative response was given by Quebec voters, intensive constitutional discussions began between the federal and provincial governments about constitutional change. In November 1981 the governments of Canada and of all the provinces but Quebec agreed to a series of important constitutional reforms, which were enacted by the Parliament of the United Kingdom and became the law of Canada by the Constitution Act, 1982.

The 1982 changes contained two important elements: First, there were procedures by which the Constitution might be amended without recourse to Britain. The federal elements of the constitution distributing legislative powers between the Canadian parliament and the provinces were to be amendable by actions of parliament and seven of the provinces having at least half the population of all the provinces. Prior to 1982 the most important parts of the constitution were subject to amendment by the Parliament of the United Kingdom—not because the British wanted it that way but because in spite of several attempts from 1927 onward, the Canadians had not been able to agree on a domestic amending formula.

Secondly, a very broad range of individual and group rights was given constitutional recognition and protection. Prior to 1982 such rights as Canadians had were for the most part subject to the actions of Parliament and the provincial legislatures respectively, although the British North America Act of 1867 had contained protection of a very limited nature for the English and French languages in national affairs and those of Quebec and for Protestant and Roman Catholic minorities in education. The 1982 Canadian Charter of Rights and Freedoms gives constitutional recognition not only to traditional liberal rights related to speech, association, etc. and to regularized procedures for those charged with committing offenses under the law, but also for the rights of certain defined groups, such as aboriginals, denominational minorities in education, and official language minorities. There are also provisions related to the rights of all citizens to vote for candidates for federal and provincial public office and antidiscrimination rights related to equality on the basis of sex, religion, national origin and so on, with provisions that safeguard affirmative action programs on behalf of disadvantaged individuals or groups. The charter vastly expands the role of the courts in the constitutional process despite the presence of controversial Section 33, which permits Parliament and the provincial legislatures to override parts of the charter as interpreted by the judiciary.

The government of Quebec did not assent to the terms of the 1981 intergovernmental settlement or the procedures by which that settlement was reached. Although the separatist Parti Québécois government was displaced by the Bourassa Liberals as a result of the provincial general election of 1985, the Quebec authorities continued to boycott the ongoing process of intergovernmental consultations on the constitution.

In order to give the 1982 constitutional settlement legitimacy in Quebec, the Mulroney government (elected to federal office in 1985) took the initiative in getting the assent of all 10 provincial governments for the Meech Lake Accord of 1987. Had it been implemented, the Accord would have incorporated into the Canadian constitution provisions:

- recognizing Quebec as a "distinct society."
- providing financial compensation from Ottawa for provinces that wish to opt out of national programs with national standards.

- requiring the federal government to choose members of the Senate and Supreme Court of Canada from lists submitted by the provinces.
- making certain aspects of the constitution more difficult to amend by requiring unanimous provincial consent for amendments which now require the consent of only seven provinces containing together at least half the population of all the provinces; this gave Quebec the veto it wanted but gave it to all the other provinces too.

To become part of the constitution the Meech Lake Accord required the assent of Parliament and all 10 provincial legislatures. Except for the provinces of Manitoba and New Brunswick that condition was met. However, after 1987 there were changes in government in those provinces and the new administrations made important changes in the accord a condition of their supporting it. In addition, a newly elected government of Newfoundland withdrew its assent formerly given by its provincial legislature. Popular support for Meech Lake outside Quebec dwindled. Opponents of the accord focused their objections on the "distinct society" clause, which they claimed could be used by Quebec authorities to justify restrictions on the rights guaranteed by the charter to persons in that province and on the provincializing thrust of Meech Lake more generally. In the summer of 1990, the accord failed for want of approval by Newfoundland and Manitoba.

The Meech Lake Accord also raised the contentious issue of the procedure by which the Northwest Territories and the Yukon might become provinces. Under the existing constitution this would require the consent of Parliament and the legislatures of at least seven provinces having together at least half the Canadian population. Meech Lake would have changed this by requiring unanimous provincial consent. These northern areas, which cover a vast land area but have only a sparse and scattered population, have attained an increasing range of self-government. Because of the requirement of provincial consent and Ottawa's reluctance to confer on these jurisdictions ownership of their natural resources, provincial status in the foreseeable future for these territories is unlikely.

The impetus for constitutional reform in Canada during the past generation has come from Quebec and from attempts to adjust to the circumstances of modernizing changes in that province. However, since the mid-1970s another strain of reform has arisen. This latter suggests that the Canadian political system is deficient in that regional values and interests are given inadequate representation in the composition and operation of the central government. There is here the double effect of denying the federal authorities the legitimacy they need and of making the provincial governments the almost exclusive channels through which regional interests are expressed. The Westminster model of parliamentary government is essentially majoritarian, and, it is claimed, these majoritarian dispositions of Ottawa are incompatible with the continuing territorial diversities of Canada.

Prior to the 1980s there was a long period in which governments in power in Ottawa almost never contained representatives from all regions of the country. Thus when the Liberals were in office there were few members from Western Canada and under the Conservatives there was little representation from Quebec. This circumstance led many observers of federalism from the mid-1970s onward to demand changes which would ensure, it was hoped, the effective representation of all regions in the operations of the government of Canada. The federal general elections of 1984 and 1988 gave the Mulroney Conservatives a significant number of seats in the House of Commons from all the regions. However, pressure for an elected Senate continues.

The "Triple E Senate" movement—the movement for a Senate that would be Elected, Effective and Equal—has been vigorously promoted by the government of Alberta and has had its most concentrated support from within that province. Under the latest version of that proposal, the present appointed Senate would be replaced by a body consisting of eight members from each province and two each from the Yukon and the Northwest Territories (and a small number of aboriginal representatives). These persons would be elected by proportional representation at the same time as federal elections took place. The Triple E Senate would be able to obstruct the government of the day with its control of the House of Commons but would require in some instances a 70% vote to do so.

Although the attempts to reform the constitution in the 1960 and 1970s had their origins in the circumstances of Quebec, the process of reform has led to many other groupings being impelled into making demands for constitutional change. During the period leading up to the Charter of Rights and Freedoms, such groups as those representing aboriginals, women, official-language minorities, persons whose ethnic origins were neither anglophone nor francophone and the physically handicapped demanded constitutional guarantees to meet their respective needs. In particular, there is widespread recogniton among the Canadian public that aboriginal people have been badly treated in the past and that redress may require entrenching the aboriginal right to self-government in the constitution. There are continuing influences to make the composition and operations of the government of Canada more responsive to regional needs.

For a number of reasons, then, constitutional reform is likely in the immediate future to be more prominent on the Canadian political agenda than that of other developed nations. In spite of a wounding recession and pervasive voter dissatisfaction with the state of the economy, Canada's political leaders spent a disproportionate amount of time in the early 1990s in one more major effort to rewrite the constitution.

CANADA: CENTRALIZED OR DECENTRALIZED

In Canada as in other federations there is considerable debate about how centralized or decentralized the federal system is or should be. For example, in the early 1980s Prime Minister Trudeau and his supporters argued that Canada was the most decentralized federation in the world and that further provincializing influences should be resisted.

Careful students of federalism have pointed out the almost insurmountable problems in defining a useful index of centralization/decentralization to measure the development of a particular nation in this dimension over time or to compare different federations. It is the problem of adding apples and oranges. For example, it is often said that the United States is more centralized than Canada. However, the Americans have no national criminal law, while in Canada the federal Parliament has exclusive legislative jurisdiction over the Criminal Code. In the United States the state legislatures have important roles in determining how the president and members of the Congress are elected, while in Canada members of the House of Commons are elected by processes regulated by national law.

Despite the difficulties in measuring how centralized or decentralized the Canadian federation is, it can be said with some confidence that the provinces are strong. This strength has several aspects:

1. *Jurisdictional.* The provinces have exclusive legislative jurisdiction over many important matters. These include health, welfare and education, although the central government controls several programs of financial assistance to individuals, such as family allowances, unemployment insurance, old age pensions and contributory public retirement pensions outside Quebec. The provinces own their natural resources within their respective boundaries. The provinces also legislate in relation to private law matters. In the early formative years of judicial review of the constitution, the tendency was to expand provincial powers and restrict those of Ottawa, and, unlike its American counterpart, the Supreme Court of Canada continues to police the jurisdictional boundaries between the two orders of government.

2. *Financial.* The provinces have access to major sources of taxation: taxes on personal and corporate incomes and on retail sales, and royalties from the development of provincially-owned natural resources. Furthermore and in very general terms, financial transfers from the federal to the provincial governments do not substantially restrict the latter's powers. Fiscal equalization payments do not impose conditions on the provinces, and even those transfers paid on behalf of particular services such as public welfare and education in the minority official languages do not carry detailed conditions.

3. *Organizational.* The Westminster model of parliamentary government which prevails in the provinces as well as in Ottawa permits the coherent expression of jurisdictional powers through unified cabinets. Within the past generation the larger provinces and some of the smaller ones have developed sophisticated appointed bureaucracies.

4. *Partisan-political.* More than in other federations there is in Canada a relatively clear-cut separation between the federal and provincial organizations of the political parties. Characteristically, politicians choose either federal or provincial careers rather than switching from one to the other. Nominations to elective office whether that of party leader or of candidates in electoral district are made under the separate auspices of federal and provincial organizations. A very high proportion

of the electorate is disposed to vote for different parties federally and provincially.

5. *Political Identity.* National identity in Canada is relatively weak. Thus in conflicts with the federal government the provinces can draw on strong popular loyalties. These loyalties are particularly strong in Quebec with its French-speaking majority and sense of a common history.

For these and other reasons the Canadian provinces remain strong, and the largest two contain more than 60% of the Canadian population. Federalism thus remains a Canadian preoccupation and from time to time an obsession.

FURTHER READING

Banting, Keith G. *The Welfare State and Canadian Federalism.* 2d edition. Kingston and Montreal: McGill-Queen's University Press, 1987.

Cairns, Alan C. *Constitution, Government and Society in Canada.* Edited by Douglas E. Williams. Toronto: McClelland and Stewart, 1988.

Gibbins, Roger. *Regionalism: Territorial Politics in Canada and the United States.* Toronto: Butterworths, 1982.

Leslie, Peter. *Federal State, National Economy.* Toronto: University of Toronto Press, 1987.

McRoberts, Kenneth. *Quebec: Social Change and Political Crisis.* 3d edition. Toronto: McClelland and Stewart, 1988.

Milne, David. *Tug of War: Ottawa and the Provinces under Trudeau and Mulroney.* Toronto: James Lorimer, 1986.

Shugarman, David, and Reg Whitaker, eds. *Federalism and Political Community, Essays in Honour of Donald Smiley.* Peterborough, Ont.: Broadview Press, 1989.

Smiley, Donald. *The Federal Condition in Canada.* Toronto: McGraw-Hill Ryerson, 1987.

Stevenson, Garth. *Unfulfilled Union: Canadian Federalism and National Unity.* 3d edition. Toronto: Gage, 1989.

QUEBEC

PIERRE FOURNIER

An understanding of contemporary Quebec politics must begin with an analysis of the institutional, political and ideological changes which took place in the province in the 1960s. These changes have been described as a Quiet Revolution. While profound, the reforms introduced during that period are very similar to those which were introduced in most other Canadian provinces or the rest of the Western world during the postwar era. If observers have talked of a "revolution," it is mainly because of the rapid pace at which political modernization occurred.

The Quiet Revolution can be viewed essentially as an adaptation of Quebec social and political structures to those of an industrial society. Indeed, the rapid industrialization, urbanization and rural decline which followed World War II were not accompanied by corresponding structural and ideological changes. During the 1940s and 1950s, the province continued to be ruled by a rural elite, made up of an influential clergy, small business and the traditional professions (lawyers, doctors and notaries). Throughout the period, the Union Nationale, the party in power, defended conservative values, including a laissez-faire vision of the state, a clerical society and an exclusively cultural nationalism.

In 1960, a year following the death of Premier Maurice Duplessis, and with the election to power of the Liberal Party of Premier Jean Lesage, a new urban elite, made up mainly of businessmen, teachers, civil servants and various professionals came to power. The most striking political change was the rapid increase in the role of the state. Between 1960 and 1965, public expenditures rose by more than 20% annually. In the 1960 to 1970 period, the number of civil servants increased by 53%, and 27 top level administrative bodies were created.

In the areas of education and social services, the church gradually yielded its leadership. Within 10 years, universities, colleges, hospitals, social assistance institutions, labor unions and many other organizations lost their denominational character. By 1970, Quebec society had become almost completely secular. After two years of consultation, a Department of Education was created in 1964. Free public schooling was introduced up to the university level. Schools programs were given a more scientific, technical and professional orientation. Between 1960 and 1970, the education budget increased from $218 million to over $1 billion. Enrollment was 101% higher at the high school level, 82% at the college level and 169% in the universities.

The state also took over health services. In 1961, a hospital insurance scheme was introduced, followed in 1970 by a comprehensive and universal health insurance scheme. In 1964, a state-run pension plan was set up and administered by the Regie des rentes (Quebec Pension Plan). Its considerable resources were invested by the Quebec Deposit and Investment Fund, which rapidly became a powerful investment arm of the Quebec government. In the civil service, a merit system was introduced, replacing the appointments based on political partisanship and patronage. Salaries were increased and unionization was encouraged. At the end of the 1960s, the Quebec civil service was very similar in composition and effectiveness to the Canadian civil service.

The influence and legitimacy of labor unions, who fully supported the objectives of the Quiet Revolution, increased sharply during the 1960s. A new Labour Code extended the right of association, eliminated many of the repressive aspects of previous labor laws and provided a larger role for the state in mediation. Membership in the Confederation of National Trade Unions (CNTU), which was close to the Liberal Party and succeeded in unionizing large numbers of civil servants, passed from 94,114 in 1960 to 204,361 in 1966, whereas union membership as a whole increased from 28% to 33% of the work force. At the end of the 1960s, however, the unions were increasingly disillusioned with the government, and they began to adopt a more socialist perspective, which included a strong critique of the inequalities generated by capitalism.

In the area of economic policy, as other industrial states had done, the government began, with mitigated success, to experiment with planning, as evidenced by the creation of a *Conseil d'orientation économique* (Economic Advisory Board) in 1962 and an *Office de planification du Québec* (Quebec Planning Bureau) in 1969. The state also intervened in the economy by financing technological innovation, nationalizing weak or risky sectors, building and improving the communications and highway system, and offering systematic assistance programs for private industry.

Another important objective of the Quiet Revolution was to give the Québécois more control over their economy. To this end, the state was to become a crucial instrument for the creation of an economic power base for Quebec business. Indeed, in the early 1960s, foreign capital, mainly American, controlled 41.8% of the value added in the manufacturing industry and was dominant in the production of machinery, petroleum, chemical products, and mineral and metal products, among others. Canadian capital, on the other hand, was responsible for 42.8% of the value added and was in a strong position in industries such as textiles, food processing and pulp paper. English Canadian business was also very strong in the areas of financial institutions, services and telecommunications. French Canadian capital, finally, despite the fact that the French element represented over 80% of the total Quebec population, controlled only 15.4% of the value added in manufacturing. Also, companies owned by French Canadians were concentrated in the traditional, low productivity, and labor-intensive sectors such as woodcutting, leather and furniture.

In the manufacturing sector, Quebec production was mainly concentrated in light industry: foods, textiles, wood, furniture and leather, for example. These sectors were generally labor-intensive and low on the value-added scale, which implied not only below-average salaries but also intense international competition, as in the textile industry. Ontario, on the other hand, occupied a more favorable position in heavy industry, such as metal products, transport equipment and machinery, for example, which tended to be high-productivity sectors and which used a more specialized work force with above-average salaries. Thus, 52% of Ontario industrial production was concentrated in heavy industry, compared to 31% for Quebec, whereas light industry in Quebec accounted for 45% of production compared to 28% in Ontario.

One of the key elements in the policy of economic nationalism was the creation in the 1960s and early 1970s of a very important network of state enterprises in Quebec. Despite limited resources, the state intervened in a large number of economic sectors, including steel, mining, electricity, pulp and paper, agriculture, petroleum, and finance, through state corporations. As a result of the nationalization of electricity, Hydro-Québec became a giant corporation controlled by the government, and hence by a majority of francophones. In itself the event was not spectacular; Ontario and other provinces had nationalized hydropower some time earlier. But for francophone Quebecers, nationalization had a special symbolic and structural importance. Quebec hydropower resources were enormous; for the first time in French Canadian history, a major corporation was owned and managed by francophones. As Premier Jean Lesage liked to point out, nationalization and government intervention in the economy were not ideological choices, a form of socialism, but rather a concrete way for French-speaking Quebecers to find a place in the sun.

Other important governmental initiatives in the area of state enterprises included the setting up of a General Investment Corporation in 1963, the creation of the Quebec Deposit and Investment Fund in 1965 and the development of a state-owned steel complex. It should be stressed that, as a result of these policies, Quebec came to control a much larger share of overall economic activity than any other Canadian province.

In order to understand the political evolution of modern Quebec, it must be understood that a great majority of Quebecers have consistently regarded themselves collectively as a "nation." If nation is defined as a group of people living in a well-defined geographical area, speaking a common language, possessing a literature in which their aspirations have been expressed, attached to common traditions and common customs, venerating their own heroes, and, in some cases, having a common religion, there is little doubt that francophone Quebecers are a nation. Thus, nationalism, in the sense of the struggle for survival and recognition, has been, for the last two centuries, at the heart of the Québécois' collective existence, and most of the time an essential ingredient of their political life.

With the Quiet Revolution, nationalism legitimized state intervention. By the mid-1960s, a widespread popular consensus had developed among Quebec francophones that their society had become the only effective embodiment of their language and culture on the North American continent and the sole French-speaking culture with the essential institutions to make it viable over the long term. And only if such a base existed in Quebec could francophones elsewhere in Canada hope to see their minority rights accorded serious attention by the anglophone society and political system surrounding them. Francophone Quebecers also increasingly agreed that anglophones and immigrant groups with native languages other than English and French should be brought to realize that they must learn French to pursue satisfying careers and lives in Quebec. French Canadian nationalism, with its mainly cultural character, did not seriously threaten the federal government of Canada in its increasing interventionism. Québécois nationalism, by contrast, called for a new distribution of power in the Canadian federation; and its separatist version called for the outright political independence of the province.

The 1961 census and various demographic studies stimulated the insecurity of francophones in Quebec and the development of nationalism. Francophone births per thousand between 1921 and 1971 fell from by far the highest in Canada, and one of the highest in the industrialized world, to well below both the Canadian and U.S. national averages. The fertility rate dropped from four children in 1960 to 1.46 in 1984, the third lowest in the world. New immigrants to Quebec also massively integrated into the English community.

These trends have been reinforced by the continuing decline in the population of Quebec relative to that of the rest of Canada, and the accelerating assimilation of offspring of francophones outside Quebec. Whereas members from Quebec represented 30% of all members in the Canadian House of Commons when the British North America Act was adopted in 1867, they are expected to number only 20% by 2000. The proportion of the Canadian population outside the province who spoke French at home declined from 5.3% in 1931 to 4.2% in 1981. The corresponding projection for 2000 is between 2.2% and 3.5%. While Canadians outside Quebec increased by 12% between 1971 and 1981, those whose mother tongue was French (many of whom no longer spoke that language) declined by 5%.

Under these circumstances, it should come as no surprise that francophone Quebecers tend to identify more with Quebec and its governments, which they have controlled to a growing degree, than with Canada and the federal government, in which their long-term political influence will decline further. It is also understandable that they have become more and more concerned about their ability to protect their language, culture and way of life in the face of the steadily growing anglophone majority.

Thus, the joint impact of modernization and nationalism strained the distribution of powers between Canada and the provinces which had been agreed upon in 1867. Various proposals were put forward to redefine Quebec's place within Confederation. The province felt that it needed more extensive powers and more resources to achieve its social and "national" objectives. Special status and associate statehood were the two main positions defended in the 1960s. Between 1960 and 1966, the government of Jean Lesage argued that Quebec was the only province where there was a French majority, and that it should have special powers (over language, social policy, immigration and communications, for example) to assume its role as leader of one of the two nations. The associate-state concept was defended by Daniel Johnson, who led a rejuvenated Union Nationale to power in 1966. He believed that each nation should have its own state, and that they should be associated in a loose confederal structure. Throughout the 1960s, there also existed a significant separatist movement, which became embodied in two main political parties, the RIN (Rassemblement pour l'indépendance nationale) and the RN (Ralliement national). But it remained a minority movement, never reaching more than 10% of the population. These parties were hampered by contradictions between social and national objectives; while some were simply attempting to create a national bourgeoisie in Quebec, others were pursuing social-democratic or socialist ideals. Other movements, including the Front de libération du Québec (FLQ), who felt that a violent revolution was the only effective means of achieving independence and socialism, became active in the late 1960s, culminating in October 1970 with the kidnappings of a British cultural attaché and a Liberal cabinet minister, and the eventual death of the latter.

Disappointed with the failure of Quebec to obtain a new status in the Canadian Federation, former cabinet minister René Lévesque left the PLQ (Quebec Liberal Party) after he failed to rally the party to a strong nationalist platform. In the fall of 1967, he founded the MSA (Mouvement souveraineté-association), with the intention of obtaining political sovereignty for the province and an economic association with the rest of Canada. The MSA became the Parti Québécois (PQ) a year later, with the RIN and RN members joining the new party. In 1970, the Union Nationale won enough seats to remain the official opposition, but, with 23% of the popular vote, the PQ became the second most powerful party in Quebec. From then on, the political spectrum became polarized between the advocates of sovereignty and the federalists.

In the mid-1960s, the federal government began to organize a counteroffensive to halt the progress of "autonomist forces" in Quebec. This culminated in the election of orthodox federalist Pierre Elliott Trudeau as head of the Liberal Party of Canada and prime minister. The stage was set for what turned out to be the major political confrontation of the 1970s, the struggle between Quebec *indépendantistes* and federalist forces.

The election of the PLQ in 1970 was not based on nationalism. Yet during his six years at the helm, Premier Robert Bourassa was more than once pressed into a nationalist stance by events and provincial majority opinion. In 1971, at an important federal-provincial conference in Victoria, British Columbia, Prime Minister Trudeau offered the provinces a scheme for patriating the Constitution from London (the British North America Act was still a law passed by Westminster). The amending formula would give a veto to a province representing 25% or more of the Canadian population, which was the case for Quebec. Bourassa was ready to accept, provided Ottawa would yield its right to dispense funds for unemployment insurance, family allowances and old-age pensions. As Ottawa refused, and as pressure against the agreement mounted among nationalists inside and outside the PLQ, the premier decided to reject the formula.

By the early 1970s it had become apparent to most Québécois and the Liberal Bourassa government that effective action must be taken to stem the decline of the French-language population. Given freedom of choice in the language of education, immigrants' children were being assimilated into anglophone society in large numbers. There were also widespread demands for more effective action to open jobs in anglophone-controlled private enterprises to the growing number of francophones emerging from the universities. The Liberal leadership also felt that it must act to prevent further shifts of francophone voters toward the PQ, which had achieved 30% of the vote in 1973. On the other hand, Premier Bourassa also had to deal with his anglophone electorate and financial supporters. Some 90% of anglophone votes had gone Liberal in 1970 and 1973.

In 1974, Premier Bourassa enacted Bill 22, which made French the official language of Quebec, made it compulsory on all signs (without prohibiting English), and provided incentives for the use of French in private corporations. Bill 22 satisfied neither the nationalists, who thought it was too weak, nor the English-speaking community, who felt it unfairly jeopardized their position.

In the social and economic sphere, the Bourassa government pursued, during the 1970–76 period, policies based less on government intervention and more on private economic forces. The government was primarily concerned with creating a social, economic, and political climate that would attract U.S. investment. Nonetheless some major steps continued to be taken in the direction of greater governmental support for Quebec state enterprises. Robert Bourassa initiated the hydroelectric development at James Bay, a multibillion-dollar project which was by far the most important economic initiative of any Quebec government. He also reinforced several key state corporations, including the Société générale de financement (General Investment Corporation) and the Société de développement industriel (Industrial Development Corporation).

On November 15, 1976, the Parti Québécois, with 41% of the popular vote, obtained a clear majority of seats in the National Assembly. It must be emphasized, however, that the PQ fought the campaign on the promise to be a "good government" and on the commitment to submit the issue of sovereignty-association to a special referendum. The PQ's promise to enact stricter language requirements was a significant factor in its election. In 1977, it passed Bill 101, a piece of legislation which has come to symbolize political nationalism in Quebec as well as the deep rift between the francophone and anglophone communities in the province.

Bill 101 limited English primary and secondary school attendance to children at least one of whose parents had been educated in Quebec English schools. However, exceptions even in the original version of the law were relatively liberal. Immigrants' children who had already begun in English schools, their younger siblings, and children whose parents lived in Quebec when the law was passed, but had received their primary schooling in English elsewhere, could also attend English public schools. Fluency in English would no longer be a criterion for hiring; but Bill 101 permitted several years for the transition. All businesses with fewer than 50 employees, as well as larger ones serving primarily non-francophones, were excepted. Labels and instructions for goods sold in Quebec had to include French versions, and commercial signs (other than very small ones) had to be in French only.

Interpretations and enforcement were relatively flexible. From the outset, anglophones temporarily employed in Quebec were permitted to send their children to English schools for three years, with the likelihood of extension for another three. In 1984, the Lévesque government further liberalized the law. The children of anglophone parents, regardless of citizenship, who came to Quebec to work or study could now attend English schools for five years. In July of the same year, the Canadian Supreme Court struck down the "Quebec Clause" of Bill 101 in favor of a "Canada Clause" opening Quebec English schools to children of all Canadians who had themselves attended English schools anywhere in Canada.

With regard to French as the language of work, compromises were also worked out. For example, English would remain the working language of research and technology-intensive units and headquarters dealing with the rest of Canada, the United States, and other anglophone countries, provided progress in hiring francophones was demonstrated.

Even if Bill 101 shifted much of the burden of bilingualism from francophones to anglophones, the overall position of the latter within Quebec is not that of an oppressed minority. Its survival is not seriously in doubt. It can rely on a complete set of institutions (such as schools, media and hospitals), a favorable economic situation and a supportive Canadian and American environment. The English community was slow to react to the rapid developments in the province in the 1960s and 1970s. It also failed to play a positive role in attempting to improve relations between Quebec francophones and the rest of Canada.

In 1981, 17.6% of Quebecers were non-francophone, including 10.9% whose native longue was English and 6.7% whose native language was neither French nor English. An overwhelming majority of this latter group, often called allophones, chose to integrate into the anglophone community and shared the same political perspectives. Whereas francophones identified more with Quebec and its government than with Canada and the federal government, non-francophones regarded a strengthened central government as their principal counterbalance to actions by the Quebec government. During the 1976–81 period, net anglophone emigration was the highest in recorded history: 133,000. Those who spoke little or no French were the most likely to leave. One of the results was to open more managerial and technical jobs to trained francophones.

At the economic level, the policies adopted by the PQ government are closely in line with those of the Quiet Revolution. A series of measures were introduced to support local francophone business in the private, public and cooperative sectors. These include the creation of a Cooperative Development Corporation, a preferential buying policy, the SOQUEM (a state-owned mining company) project at Iles-de-la-Madeleine, the setting up of a state-controlled Asbestos Corporation, and a program of financial assistance for small local companies. The buying policy seeks to systematically use the purchasing power of the public sector to favor the expansion of Quebec-based companies. It is an attempt to stimulate the development of small and medium-sized Quebec firms, and to follow, for all practical purposes, the example of Hydro-Québec's buying policy, which has contributed to the creation of at least 31 companies in Quebec.

On the whole, the initiatives of the PQ government did not constitute the radical departure one would have expected from a social-democratic party dedicated to sovereignty. The moderation of the Lévesque administration can be traced to fiscal constraints facing all governments in North America: the mounting pressure against increased taxation and the spiraling costs of public borrowing. It can also be explained by the fact that the PQ concentrated most of its efforts in the 1976–80 period on the preparation of the referendum on sovereignty-association.

Given that most opinion polls throughout the 1970s clearly demonstrated that a majority of Québécois were not prepared to support separatism or outright independence, the PQ proposed that an economic association with the rest of Canada should be an integral part of sovereignty. In addition, the referendum question in 1980 only asked for a mandate to negotiate sovereignty-association. While it is unlikely that any other strategy would have met with more success, the promise of an economic association with the rest of Canada weakened the position and credibility of the PQ during the debates. Indeed, the federal government and the other Canadian provinces made it clear during the campaign that they would never accept such an association. In general, the PQ failed to convince the majority of Québécois that sovereignty would not bring about economic hardship. This insecurity turned out to be stronger than the desire for an autonomous Quebec nation-state. It must also be added that the federal government of Pierre Trudeau had worked long and hard throughout the 1970s to make the Canadian option more appealing to the Québécois. Thus, in May 1980, the PQ lost its referendum by a 60/40 margin.

During the referendum campaign, the federal government and the provincial Liberals promised that federalism would be renewed substantially in the event of a defeat of sovereignty, and that Quebec would obtain more leeway in building up its own security within Confederation. It is largely for this reason that the Canada Act or the new constitution brought down by Prime Minister Trudeau in 1981 was perceived as a humiliation and betrayal, not just by the Parti Québécois, but by all Quebec nationalists, and was opposed by most political forces in the province, including the provincial Liberals. Indeed, the new constitutional package did not even attempt to respond to the demands put forward by the various Quebec premiers since 1960. The episode provoked the reelection of the Parti Québécois in 1981, and more importantly, built up resentment toward English Canada.

The second term of the Parti Québécois government was relatively un-eventful. The quest for sovereignty appeared more and more irrelevant and unproductive in the wake of the referendum defeat. The deep economic recession not only prevented significant initiatives in the social or economic areas, but led the government to a series of spending and wage cuts which severely alienated unionized labor, particularly in the public sector.

With the return to power of the Bourassa Liberals in 1985, there were strong reasons to expect that the Quebec state, and its role in Quebec society, would undergo fundamental changes. Given the PLQ's close links with the business community and English-speaking Quebec, it was pre-sumed that the role of the state would be reduced, that Quebec's position within the federal system would be reinforced, and that language legisla-tion would be relaxed. While the government pursued all three objectives, it rapidly confronted major obstacles and constraints, and its achievements were mixed at best. Important elements within Quebec society were strongly committed to the social and economic roles the Quebec state had assumed over the last 25 years. Nationalist feelings also remained strong during the period, preventing major changes in language legislation.

Shortly after its election, the Bourassa government produced its own proposal for constitutional revision. The proposal was rather modest in scope, reflecting the government's desire to reach an accord despite Quebec's weak bargaining position. The election of the Mulroney Conservatives in Ottawa opened the door to an agreement. Eager to dissociate itself from the "rigid" approach to federalism of the Trudeau years and anxious to solidify support of the Québécois for the Canadian federal order, the Conservatives were determined to secure Quebec's official inclusion in the constitution. In the spring of 1987, Prime Minister Brian Mulroney and the provincial pre-miers reached a constitutional agreement, which became known as the Meech Lake Accord, and which was intended to form the basis of the reintegration of Quebec in the Constitution.

The accord represented a compromise achieved on the basis of Quebec's initial demands, and was originally supported unanimously by the federal government and the provincial premiers. It included the following major points: recognition of Quebec as a "distinct society" within Canada; the right, in areas of exclusive provincial jurisdiction, for provinces to opt out of national shared-cost programs with "reasonable compensation"; broader provincial powers over immigration, provided national standards were re-spected; participation of the Government of Quebec in the nomination of three of Canada's nine Supreme Court judges; and the extension, in the amending formula, of the number of items which required the unanimous consent of the provinces, including the powers of the Senate, the creation of new provinces and representation in the House of Commons.

The accord needed the unanimous approval of the 10 provincial legisla-tures before June 1990. Quebec was the first province, in June 1987, to vote in favor of the Meech Lake agreement. The Parti Québécois and other groups in the province strongly criticized the accord. They claimed that the concept of a "distinct society" was too vague, and that Quebec's exclusive jurisdiction over language matters was not sufficiently recognized. They also argued that the province gained no explicit new powers, except in the field of immigration. Finally, they pointed out that, by recognizing Ottawa's spending power in fields of exclusive provincial jurisdiction, the constitutional accord conferred legality on federal invasion of areas of provincial power. It was feared that the provincial obligation to conform to national standards would eventually nullify Quebec's right to opt out of a federal shared-cost program.

Despite the criticism of the more nationalist Québécois, the Meech Lake Accord came to acquire substantial symbolic significance within the province. Quebec was to "rejoin Confederation" after the 1982 constitutional fiasco. For the first time in more than 25 years of modern nationalism, some of Quebec's fundamental demands were met: a government in Ottawa and the anglophone provinces recognized the province's specificity. In June 1990, the provinces of Manitoba and Newfoundland failed to ratify the accord, provoking a major constitutional crisis. The Quebec government responded by boycotting the federal-provincial process and setting up a commission, which recommended that a referendum on sovereignty be held in October 1992 if satisfactory constitutional "offers" were not received by the province by that deadline. At the federal level, the demise of Meech Lake led to the creation of the Bloc Québécois, a pro-sovereignty parliamentary group, led by former Conservative cabinet minister Lucien Bouchard, and composed of seven Conservative and two Liberal members of the parliament who quit their respective parties after the failure of the accord.

With regard to the economic and social role of the state, the most significant achievements of the 1960s and '70s were not overturned. The government of Robert Bourassa did reduce the tax rate for upper-income groups and it sought to curtail expenditure growth. It privatized several state enterprises, including Québecair, Donohue, Madelipêche and the Raffinerie de sucre (Quebec Sugar Refinery). By and large, however, the most important state enterprises were left untouched. In the social arena, the government did launch a highly publicized campaign to uncover instances of cheating and fraud among social assistance recipients, but existing social policies were left in place. And despite strong business pressure to modify existing labor relations laws, the government undertook no major changes in that area.

Contrary to promises made by the Bourassa government to the English community during the 1985 electoral campaign, and even though Bill 178 allowed a degree of bilingualism in commercial signs, Bill 101 was not significantly modified. So strong was the rallying of nationalist forces around Bill 101 that the government abandoned most of the projected changes to the law.

On September 25, 1989, the government of Premier Bourassa was reelected, obtaining 92 of the National Assembly's 125 seats. The Parti Québécois, which appeared headed for virtual extinction a few months before the election, gained a half dozen seats and over 40% of the popular vote, despite an explicit pro-sovereignty platform. The election of four members of the Equality Party, an English rights group formed a few months earlier, also proved a major surprise.

Nationalism has always been a factor in the political history of the province, and it will likely continue as a political force in the forseeable future. It will remain a means for a small francophone society existing in the midst of an overwhelming anglophone North America to express its inevitable insecurity. By the year 2000, close to 95% of Canada's francophone population will live in Quebec. By the same token, Quebec itself is expected to become even more heavily francophone, perhaps by over 84% in the year 2000. Thus, if the nation should continue to be defined primarily in terms of language, it will become more and more congruent with the boundaries of Quebec. In addition, the drop in Quebec's demographic weight within Canada will provoke a corresponding decline in the province's influence within Canadian political institutions.

The Canada-U.S. free trade agreement could also become an important factor in the province's political evolution. Quebec strongly supported free trade, while most of the other provinces, fearing for their political and cultural survival, expressed considerable opposition. From the perspective of the Parti Québécois, in the long run free trade could minimize the economic uncertainties of Quebec sovereignty, which were held responsible for the 1980 referendum defeat. At the same time, however, closer economic integration with the United States and American cultural influences could severely weaken the Québécois sense of identity.

FURTHER READING

Balthazar, Louis, and Alfred O. Hero. *Contemporary Quebec and the United States.* Boston: University Press of America, 1988.

Bernard, André. *La politique au Canada et au Québec.* Montréal: Presses de l'Université du Québec, 1976.

Fournier, Pierre. *A Meech Lake Post Mortem: Is Québec Sovereignty Inevitable?* Montreal: McGill-Queen's University Press, 1991.

Gagnon, Alain G., ed. *Quebec State and Society.* Toronto: Methuen Publications, 1984.

Holloway, Kaye. *Le Canada, pourquoi l'impasse?* Montréal: Editions Nouvelle Optique, 1983.

McRoberts, Kenneth. *Quebec: Social Change and Political Crisis.* Toronto: McClelland and Stewart, 1988.

Moniere, Denis. *Le développement des idéologies au Québec.* Montréal: Editions Québec/ Amérique, 1977.

Pelletier, Réjean. *Partis politiques et société québécoise.* Montréal: Editions Québec/ Amérique, 1989.

THE NORTH

EDWARD R. WEICK

The Canadian north is vast, diverse and complex. The focus of what follows is on political change, and deals mainly with the Northwest Territories, the Yukon and northern Quebec—regions in which some of the most significant political changes in the recent history of Canada have taken place.

Four ethnic populations currently occupy these regions: Indians (including the Dene of the Mackenzie Valley and the Cree of Northern Quebec); Inuit;[1] Métis, who are of mixed Native and European origin; and non-Native people who are mainly of European origin. Regardless of how one defines the region, the population of the Canadian north is small. The Yukon Territory has a population of some 25,000, of which about 6,000 are Native people. In the Northwest Territories, Native Indians, Inuit and Métis comprise a majority of the population, numbering about 30,000 in a total population of about 55,000. In that part of northern Quebec under consideration here, there are approximately 12,000 people, of whom about 10,000 are Indians and Inuit.

This discussion of northern political development focuses on the two processes which have dominated the political development on the frontier during much of Canada's history, namely, the development of public government institutions and the assertion by northern Native people of their rights to land (land claims) and self-determination. Since almost the beginnings of Canada, no less in the north than in other regions, these dual processes have stood in opposition to each other. The greater the pressure to include Native people within the ambit of public government and assimilate them into the general population, the more these people have pushed back to preserve and assert their identity and institutions. Historically, each process has been determined, indeed driven, by a third, essentially economic, process, the westward and northward thrusts of the industrial frontier. This process has now been largely completed in the populous Canadian south, but it is still in its beginnings in the north.

---

[1] Though they are known by a variety of names (for example, Eskimos, Inupiat or Inupiak, Inuvialuit, Greenlanders), the Eskimoan people of the Arctic now generally refer to themselves as "Inuit," the term used in this essay except when specific Eskimoan groups are referred to.

THE RESOURCE FRONTIER AND THE DEVELOPMENT OF
GOVERNMENT INSTITUTIONS

The Industrial Frontier

For much of the postwar period, a vision of the northward spread of the industrial frontier has dominated northern development policies in Canada. It was expected by government and corporate officials, and by the growing non-Native population of northern Canada, that the development of oil, gas, minerals and hydroelectric power would lead to sustained economic development, transforming the northern wilderness into a more productive and ultimately economically viable part of Canada. Encouraged by federal policies, government agencies and private interests in the Canadian south have invested many billions of dollars in the resource potential of the north.

Initial postwar industrial forays into the northern frontier were small and marginal, an extension of the kind of development witnessed by the commencement of oil production at Norman Wells on the Mackenzie River in the 1920s and gold and base metal mining in the northern parts of the provinces and at Yellowknife in the Northwest Territories (NWT). However, by the late 1960s and early 1970s, the scale of industrial projects had increased significantly. Large mines were developed in both the Yukon and NWT. Massive machinery had begun to exploit the oil sands of northern Alberta. Large hydroelectric power projects were undertaken in northern Quebec and Manitoba. Extensive oil and gas exploration, and in some cases production, occurred in the northern part of the western provinces, the Mackenzie Valley of the Northwest Territories, the Yukon Territory, the Beaufort Sea, the coast of Labrador and the Arctic Archipelago. Mines were developed in the more northerly reaches of the Canadian Shield and in the high Arctic. Pulp, paper and lumber production was expanded in the boreal and coastal forests of Ontario and the western provinces. A number of projects, such as large-diameter pipelines which would connect the oil and gas reserves of northern Alaska, the Mackenzie Delta and the Beaufort Sea with the continental economy, were planned though not built. Nevertheless, even their planning phases created boom conditions in much of the western Arctic.

The northern policies of the federal and provincial governments have both encouraged the development of frontier resources and provided a suitably benign institutional environment for such development. Paving the path for industry has led to the imposition of a variety of new institutions on the largely Native populations of frontier regions. For example, in northern Quebec, regional self-government arrangements of an essentially municipal kind have followed from the James Bay and Northern Quebec Agreement, the instrument which settled Native land claims and enabled large-scale hydroelectric power development to proceed. In the two federal territories, the Northwest Territories and the Yukon, the new political arrangements were modeled along the lines of political institutions in the provinces. While such arrangements have given the people of the north a measure of control over inevitable development, and some benefits, one of their most important functions has been to bring about the "order" needed for the orderly development of the resource frontier.

Public Government in the Northwest Territories
Historically, the Northwest Territories (originally known as the North Western Territories) existed over much of what is now western Canada, and was the region from which the Yukon Territory and the grain and oil producing provinces of Manitoba, Saskatchewan and Alberta were carved. This earlier region saw the crushing of Native resistance and rebellions, the signing of Indian treaties, the construction of railways, the establishment of lands for agriculture, the confinement of Native people on reservations and of their children in residential schools, and the creation of provinces, all to enable the orderly development of non-Native society and its economy to proceed.

The development of public government in the Northwest Territories as the region now exists began in earnest in 1967 when the federal government moved its appointed commissioner and his staff from Ottawa to Yellowknife and expanded the ratio of elected to appointed members of the territorial council (the territorial legislature). However, such measures, even though quickly followed by the transfer of programs such as education, social services and local development from Ottawa to Yellowknife, did not result in an early regional acceptance of the new institutions. Given the barriers of language, culture and isolation, it is probable that many Native people did not really understand what they were expected to accept. Others undoubtedly saw what was happening as the business of non-Native people, not theirs. Misconceptions and misunderstandings worked both ways. The new government of the Northwest Territories (GNWT) and its bureaucracy had little understanding of the economy, culture and aspirations of Native people, and strongly aligned itself with industrial forms of development which Native people opposed.

As well, the GNWT made some serious errors in dealing with its Native constituents. It attempted to promote the notion that, regardless of their ethnicity, culture and history, all of the people living in the NWT were first and foremost "northerners," putting the interests of Native people on an approximate parity with those of the Chamber of Commerce. Programs normally administered to Indians under a regional Indian Affairs office elsewhere in Canada were placed under the administration of the GNWT, and it was suspected that funds which were transferred by Ottawa to meet federal obligations to Native people were used for general budgetary purposes. As well, municipal government institutions created by the territorial government challenged the authority of Native institutions which had been established earlier under the Federal Indian Act. (This statute, first enacted in 1876, has been amended many times, most recently in 1985). All of this angered Native people, who soon came to regard the new government as little more than a new colonial form replacing the earlier federal one.

A variety of other issues also promoted political change. Among the most important was the nature of industrial development itself, which, by the early 1970s, had evolved to a "megaproject" scale. Uncertainty about the effects of such development greatly troubled the small Native communities of the Mackenzie Valley and western Arctic. The industrial centerpiece was to have been the large-diameter Mackenzie Valley natural gas pipeline which would run from the Arctic coast to the mid-continent, traversing many areas of environmental and social sensitivity. The pipeline issue escalated to a cathartic national debate about the values placed by Canadians on industrial development, the rights of Native people and the environment. At its center was a commission of inquiry under Justice Thomas Berger of the Supreme Court of British Columbia. After three years of hearings, Judge Berger concluded that no pipeline should be built until fundamental issues, particularly Native land claims, had been resolved. However, by this time, the Mackenzie Valley pipeline had become a dead issue, superseded by a proposal to build a pipeline from the Alaskan north slope to the continental United States via the Yukon, with a Yukon connection to the gas reserves of the Mackenzie Delta.

Since the debate over the Mackenzie Valley pipeline laid bare the deep divisions which existed in the Northwest Territories in the 1970s, the GNWT has matured, and it has gradually achieved credibility as a regional government. It has aligned itself with Native people on a variety of issues and by taking an increasingly pro-northern stance independent of the federal government, to which it is still bound by Canadian law. It has succeeded in attracting Native people as candidates for political office: a majority of elected representatives are now Native people, and two Native people have served in the post of Government Leader. In its deliberations, it continues to operate out of an essentially Native "consensus" model, in which decisions are taken by the government as a whole, and not by a particular political party in power. The non-Native population, which continues to make up the majority of the population of the larger communities of the territories, has grown in its understanding of Native culture and values, providing an improved basis for the development of government institutions able to represent both Native and non-Native people. Moreover, both in pursuing their claims and in their work in a variety of national and international organizations, northern Native people have gained increasing political recognition outside of the context of their dealings with the territorial government.

The Yukon
Resident public government in the Yukon began in the late 19th century, when the influx of thousands of goldseekers required the establishment of basic law, order and government services. The Yukon became a judicial district in 1897 and was carved out of the Northwest Territories as a separate territory in 1898. By 1908, it had a fully elected legislature. However, these beginnings were cut short. By 1910, the peak of the Klondike gold rush had passed, and the number of people in the territory had gone into a long decline. Little further political development occurred for several decades.

The next economic boom came during World War II. This occurred because of the territory's strategic inland location between the continental

273

United States and Alaska, where the Aleutian Islands were under attack by Japan. This period witnessed the construction of the Alaska Highway, a series of airports to permit the ferrying of aircraft to the Alaskan war zone, pipelines, and other facilities. Reminiscent of the gold rush, it witnessed the sudden influx of many thousands of people, with Whitehorse alone quickly growing from a small village of 700 to a large encampment of some 40,000 people. The Alaska Highway opened up much of the western Yukon and led to the development of a number of permanent communities along its right of way.

Both the gold rush and the wartime boom had drastic effects on the Yukon Indian population, which had probably never numbered much more than a few thousand. During the gold rush, Native people were still highly vulnerable to diseases of non-Native origin, and available data suggest a substantial decline in the Native population to about 1910, when it stabilized. The wartime boom and the construction of the Alaska Highway brought more disease, alcohol and social turmoil. Subsistence harvesting of wildlife and trapping were abandoned for short-lived jobs in road construction. People moved from traditional lands to the growing Native slums of Whitehorse, though some later returned to their lands. Until quite recently, Native people played virtually no role in the administration of the territory.

The period since World War II has included the development of mining, the extension of transportation facilities, and the growth of the resident government bureaucracy. Much of this period was economically buoyant. Successes in mining during the 1960s and 1970s, and the growing dependence of the territory on a mineral-based economy, fostered the notion, widely prevalent in the non-Native community, that all of the purposes of the territory must be subservient to the extraction and export of minerals. For a time, this boom outlook was fed further by the expectation that major gas pipelines from Alaska and the Mackenzie Delta would soon traverse the territory.

Since the early 1980s, boom attitudes have softened, in part because no major pipelines have as yet been built and because the territory has had to weather an economic crisis based on the near collapse of base metal mining and the closure of the territory's only railway. There has been something of a political convergence between Native and non-Native people, with the government of the Yukon recently making significant strides in recognizing and accommodating the interests of its Native constituents. This will almost certainly be followed by an economic convergence following the completion of the Yukon Indian land claim and the investment dollars it will generate. As in the Northwest Territories, Native people have in recent years played an important role in the territorial legislature. While important distinctions between the interests of Native and non-Native northerners remain, common interests are nonetheless acknowledged, as they were in Yukon 2000, a recent landmark public planning exercise.

The Current Situation

By means of a major policy statement by the minister of Indian and Northern Affairs in June 1988, the federal government is on record as favoring a rapid development of autonomous government, including the transfer of all remaining programs which would normally be administered by a Canadian province to the territorial governments, the early settlement of Native land claims, and a full debate on the division of the Northwest Territories into an eastern and western territory.

In the years immediately preceding this policy statement, the federal government had increased the fiscal autonomy of the territories by means of agreements which gave the territorial governments guaranteed annual funding by formula instead of negotiation, thus ending a long era in which territorial officials had to come to Ottawa for money each year "caps in hand." The federal government had greatly restricted the role of the commissioner, its top territorially resident official, and had enhanced the role and visibility of elected territorial officials. Instead of being part of the federal delegation, the territories can now participate on their own behalf at most federal-provincial conferences. The territorial post of Government Leader has become roughly comparable to a provincial premier in status, and members of the executive committees of the territorial councils carry the title of "Minister."

Despite such changes, the territorial governments still fall well short of having either the powers or the credibility of the provinces. They have no constitutionally defined position in Canadian Confederation, and they continue to exist as creatures of federal legislation, formally responsible to a federal minister, the minister of Indian and Northern Affairs. The prospects for change in this situation are not bright because of the difficulty of obtaining provincial cooperation with regard to the constitutional amendment it would require.

Nor is the federal government likely to want to fully release the territories from their subordinate status, even though recent agreements in principle on energy resources and revenues (the Northern Accords) may be viewed as concrete demonstrations of federal sympathy to territorial aspirations. Though it will probably continue to extend management powers over lands and resources to the territorial governments, how far it will go in transferring ownership is unclear. To transfer such ownership would greatly diminish the federal land and resource base, and could weaken federal leverage with the provinces. It is also quite likely that longstanding federal aspirations concerning an industrialized north based on major resource development, with large royalties flowing into the federal treasury, are not dead but merely asleep, ready to awaken when oil, gas and mineral prices rise significantly.

Compounding the territorial government's lack of credibility is the fact that they have only a small revenue base of their own, and are heavily dependent on the federal government for their financial resources. The small revenue base may, on first impression, be surprising in light of the very large corporations which have been active in the north during recent decades. However, these corporations and many of their employees are not resident in the territories and therefore contribute little to taxation there. Moreover, with the exception of mining, very little profitable production has actually taken place in the north. Despite several decades of federal promotion, the fiscal independence of the territories seems as far away as it was shortly after World War II.

While governments have tried to use the process of building public government institutions to encourage private capital and industrial development, it is ironic that, in many parts of the north, it is the development of the public institutions themselves that has provided the major impetus to growth. Government has been the most rapidly growing sector of the economy of the territories during the past two decades. It is the territories' largest purchaser of goods and services. Government employees make up about a third of the labor force.

Even much of the investment that has gone into industrial development has come from government rather than the private sector. Government has provided much of the transportation infrastructure on which private development is based. Recovering only a small fraction of the costs, it has built railways, harbors and townsites for mines, and has provided ice-breaking services to northern resource-based shipping. It has trained the resident labor force to work in industrial jobs. And it has invested directly in private ventures. In the 1977 to 1986 decade, government paid out roughly $5 billion (1989 dollars) in subsidies and capital assistance to industry, about 6.5 times as much as it transferred to persons. Payments to large oil and gas exploration companies under the petroleum incentives provisions of the National Energy Program alone amounted to nearly $4 billion

THE DEVELOPMENT OF NATIVE INSTITUTIONS

The Assertion of the Native Interest
Though northern Native people now live in what has been termed a "mixed" economy, hunting, trapping and fishing remain at the heart of their culture. While they use modern technology and methods, the Native people of today continue to harvest northern lands and waters much as their forebears did to produce food ("country food") and a variety of other products for both domestic consumption and sale. Yet, with the ever increasing presence of industry in the north, Native people have become concerned about protecting and maintaining their harvesting lands and subsistence economy in future. This is why the resolution of their claims to land has been one of the most important concerns of recent decades.

Prior to the 1970s, the nature of the Native claim was unclear, though it had been asserted and argued by generations of Native leaders. In the Mackenzie Valley and several other parts of the north, land claims were believed to have been extinguished by Treaties 8 and 11, signed in 1899 and 1921 respectively. Where there had been no formal extinguishment of Native title, as was the case in the Yukon, much of northern British Columbia, northern Quebec and the eastern Arctic, the issue of aboriginal land rights was not, by the middle of the 20th century, believed by governments to be important. It was regarded as something of the historic past, not the present.

The reasons for official unwillingness or inability to focus on Native claims were complex. Prior to World War II, governments and the Canadian public were, at best, indifferent to the northern regions in which Native title had not been formally extinguished. Following World War II, prosperity and the need for strategic materials arising out of the Cold War greatly increased the demand for minerals which the North was believed to contain. Governments began to see the potential of resource development in the northern hinterlands. Some government officials may have felt Canada had much to gain by denying or ignoring Native claims and maintaining that the lands which Native people inhabited belonged to the Crown. Others were simply unaware of the issue and proceeded with programs of development as though it did not exist.

As well, many officials felt that while the issue of title might have to be dealt with at some stage, northern Native people raised more pressing and immediate problems. The federal northern development policies which prevailed between the mid-1950s and early 1970s were in part founded on the notion that the very survival of Native people depended on a rapid industrialization of the north and the rapid acculturation and assimilation of Native people into industrial society. Federal officials of the period expressed alarm at the prospect of social disintegration among northern Native people and the emergence of a permanent welfare population.

There was cause for such concern. From about the middle of the 19th century through to about the 1950s, northern Native groups had suffered greatly from diseases such as influenza and smallpox and from the depletion of the animal populations which comprised their resource base. By the early 1950s, the fur and subsistence economy of many Native groups had become severely eroded, fur prices had fallen to historic lows, and starvation occurred in some locations. Tuberculosis and venereal diseases, compounded by poor shelter and alcohol abuse, had become endemic in northern Native societies.

As though conscience-stricken by duties it had neglected for too long, the federal government responded by mounting a widespread, intensive program of relief and rescue in which the cure may at times have been worse than the disease. Native people were moved into badly designed, hastily constructed housing. The longstanding practice of separating children from their parents and sending them off to distant church-operated residential schools was expanded. Tubercular parents and children were sent to sanatoriums in the provinces, in many cases never to return.

As disruptive as such measures were at the time, their results were positive in the longer term. There was an improvement in health, with mortality and morbidity rates declining markedly, particularly among infants and children. The hold of some endemic diseases was broken or greatly weakened. Despite the trauma of the residential schools, educational attainment increased. Moreover, after the initial intensive phase, government social programs became more humane: houses became larger; health stations were put into the Native communities; regional hospitals were built; and young children were able to go to school in their communities.

By the late 1960s, Native people had acquired an expanded awareness of the industrial and bureaucratic world which had moved in on them, and were less inclined to be patient with non-Native politicians and bureaucrats. In the spirit of the growing militancy which was moving Native people to political action throughout North America, northern Native leaders had become determined that their people should regain control of their lives.

Since the beginning of the 1970s, several events have brought about important changes in relations between Native and non-Native people throughout Canada, and perhaps most visibly in the North. One of the most important of these was official recognition that Native people had land rights in the form of "aboriginal title." That such title existed was affirmed by the Supreme Court of Canada in 1973 in a ruling concerning the Nishga of northern British Columbia, and was further affirmed by other legal judgements. It was underscored by the report of the Mackenzie Valley Pipeline Inquiry, which not only emphasized the validity of Native title but insisted that no major development take place in the western Arctic until the matter of Native claims to the lands of the region had been settled.

Claims and Native Self-Government
The recognition of a Native interest in land led to the creation of organizations to research the nature of comprehensive land claims, and to negotiate them into rights which were legally binding on governments. The process of negotiating land claims has now been underway for almost two decades. Its length and complexity has been partly due to variations in pressures on government and the Native people to get on with the business of settling claims. The James Bay and Northern Quebec Agreement was negotiated quickly because hydroelectric development was underway in northern Quebec. The Native people felt themselves to be faced with a situation of settling speedily or losing everything. The Inuvialuit (Inuit of the Beaufort Sea region) also settled within a relatively short period after they had experienced several years of large-scale oil and gas exploration. Other claims in the territories have proceeded much more slowly because resource development did not come as expected during the 1970s and 1980s.

Three comprehensive land claims have been completed to date: the James Bay and Northern Quebec Agreement, the Northeastern Quebec Agreement, and the Inuvialuit Final Agreement. The claim of the Council for Yukon Indians, representing 14 bands, is reaching its final stages, as is the claim of the Inuit of the eastern Arctic. Another claim, the Dene/Métis claim of the western Arctic, fell through at an advanced stage, though claims in the western Arctic are now moving forward on a regional basis.

The settlement of comprehensive claims has resulted in Native rights to tracts of land in the form of fee simple title and harvesting or management rights. But these lands are far smaller than the lands which the Native claimants once occupied and harvested—and indeed have needed to harvest, given the low biological productivity of the land. Under the James Bay Agreement, the class of lands which are held in fee simple surface title amounts to about one to two square kilometers, per individual claimant (0.39 to 0.77 square miles). A second class of lands, which the Cree and Inuit do not own, but on which they have exclusive rights to hunt, fish and trap, are more extensive. However, industrial development is not excluded from such lands; the only protection the Native people have is that, if it occurs, they are to be compensated in land or money. The Inuvialuit of the Beaufort Sea region, the only other aboriginal group which has completed its comprehensive claim, was able to negotiate sub-surface rights which the Cree and Inuit of Quebec do not have. Sub-surface title is also a feature of other claims which are reaching final negotiations and ratification.

Generally, under claims completed to date, Native people have attained a variety of harvesting rights and environmental and wildlife management powers. However, where such powers extend beyond the boundaries of settlement lands to which Native people hold title, they are usually of an advisory or administrative nature, and are exercised jointly with government authorities.

Money Native people obtained via the claims process has brought the Native claimants into closer integration with the economic mainstream. The Dene and Métis invested in an oil and gas exploration company. The Inuvialuit signed a long-term exploration agreement with a major oil company. The Inuvialuit and Inuit of the eastern Arctic own a large northern tug and barge company. Makivik, the Inuit development corporation of northern Quebec, owns airlines and construction companies. Having taken these steps, Native people can no longer claim to be little more than hunters and trappers, and indeed few would still do so. While they can continue to take political positions against major resource development, as the Cree have in the case of the further development of northern Quebec's power resources, they may now have become economically dependent on such development.

Other measures in the claims support traditional economic practices. The Cree harvester income security program under the James Bay Agreement is a notable case in point. This program, which is funded by the government of Quebec, is designed to provide an adequate monetary income for full-time hunters, and has encouraged the Cree to pursue life on the land as an alternative to wage employment. The program has put a considerable amount of money into the Cree communities, money which has put people back on the land where they can produce food.

Native people have argued that self-government should be an aspect of their claims, but the federal government has resisted this, and has kept the negotiation and legislation of self-government arrangements in a separate process. There are two instances of the enactment of self-government legislation specifically for Native people to date: the Cree-Naskapi (of Quebec) Act and the Sechelt Indian Band Self-Government Act (the latter affects a band in southern British Columbia, however). Other northern Natives, such as the bands of the Yukon, are currently negotiating self-government arrangements. Along with land claims settlement agreements, such arrangements are expected to give Native people greater control over their own lives. It could enable them to operate their own municipal, social and educational services, their own system of laws and enforcement, and their own political systems based on their traditions. This is of inestimable importance to peoples who continue to comprise a large part of the prison population, and who for decades have suffered from poor access to health services, sub-standard education, and a high incidence of welfare dependence.

The Quality of the Environment
In addition to the variety of issues which the claims and self-government processes will continue to raise, another matter has appeared on the horizon: the fish and game resources that native people use may become unfit for human consumption. The north is under threat both from activities which occur within the region and from activities in industrial heartlands far outside it. That no major oil spill took place in oil exploration regions such as the Beaufort Sea in the late 1970s and early 1980s was due both to good luck and the fact that high oil prices and abundant government support made the use of state-of-the-art drilling and support technology possible. Other regions appear to have been less fortunate: In northern Quebec and Manitoba, widespread environmental damage may already exist because hydroelectric development has increased the level of methyl mercury in lakes and rivers, greatly increasing the concentrations of mercury in fish.

Yet, a major part of the threat to the northern environment comes not from activities which take place in the north but from industrial activity which occurs much further south. The circumpolar Arctic is a depository for contaminants and hazardous wastes from the industrial world. Dangerous levels of toxins, including PCBs, dioxins, pesticides and heavy metals, are found in the Arctic food chain. The Canadian North alone contains over 800 sites in which there are hazardous or dangerous materials. There is mounting concern over industrial development in northern watersheds and offshore areas.

In response, in 1991, the government announced its Arctic Environmental Strategy, a five-year initiative which, according to Canada's Green Plan, is intended to achieve sustainable development in the Canadian Arctic. The major elements of the Strategy include dealing with Arctic contaminants, managing waste in the North, improving northern water quality, expanding research and information services, integrating environmental and economic issues, and protecting Arctic ecosystems.

Internationally, Canada along with the other circumpolar countries, is an active participant in working toward an Arctic Environmental Protection Strategy, a process initiated by Finland. Priority items for international consideration and possible action include heavy metals, chlorinated organics, radioactivity, oil pollution, acidification of Arctic regions, underwater noise, and monitoring.

The government of the Northwest Territories has recently shown leadership among Canadian jurisdictions in legislating an Environmental Rights Act (1990), which grants "every person the right to protect the environment . . . from the release of contaminants by commencing an action in the Supreme Court." The Yukon Territory is in the process of considering a Yukon Environment Act, which will cover such sectoral fields as: waste management; hazardous substances; pesticides; air; water; land use, conservation and reclamation; forests; protection of wilderness; and spills; and such functions as: approvals; development assessment; enforcement; and dispute resolution. It proposes a "Yukon Conservation Strategy" to guide the planning, assessment and regulatory decision of the Yukon Territorial government by the inclusion of measurable objectives and performance goals.

THE POLITICAL FUTURE

It is unlikely that the two territories will become provinces in the foreseeable future. Granting them provincial status would require constitutional amendments which the existing provinces are not likely to favor, and provincial status may also not be perceived to be in the federal interest. Nevertheless, the trend of enabling the territories to govern themselves in much the same manner as provinces, with all of the forms if not all of the substance of provincial powers, is likely to continue. Management arrangements giving the territories legislative authority, though not ownership, over lands and inland waters, and onshore oil, gas and mineral resources, will probably be worked out between the territorial and federal governments after the settlement of Native land claims. Some form of constitutional entrenchment may be possible. Gordon Robertson, onetime commissioner of the NWT, has suggested that entrenchment might be realized by attaching the legislative basis for the territories to the constitution as schedules, giving them the status of "autonomous federal territories."

Insofar as the territories' fiscal dependence on the federal government is an obstacle to political development, the hope is that an improvement to the situation may eventually result from the Northern Accords, which include provisions for federal-territorial sharing of oil and gas revenues. In turn, the territories are to negotiate sharing arrangements with Native claimant groups. But the realization of such revenues will depend on whether and when northern oil and gas resources are actually developed and moved to markets.

The concept of dividing the Northwest Territories into an eastern and western territory is not new, but it has recently been driven by the desire of the Inuit for an eastern Arctic homeland. In 1982, a territory-wide plebiscite supported the notion of division. Though this support was lukewarm in the territories as a whole, it was overwhelming in the eastern Arctic. Subsequently, the GNWT established a "Constitutional Alliance," representing the major Native organizations and the territorial government, in order to reach a consensus on territorial boundaries and develop proposals for new territorial constitutions. Failure to reach agreement on overlapping territorial claims stalled the process of division.

The question of dividing the Northwest Territories into an eastern (Nunavut) territory and a western territory was discussed at an Ottawa workshop in November 1990. Prior to the workshop the government leader of the government of the Northwest Territories and the president of the Tungavik Federation of Nunavut, the political body representing Inuit of the eastern and central Arctic, had jointly written the prime minister urging the government of Canada to proceed with the creation of Nunavut on or before the time Nunavut land claims ratification legislation is expected to be introduced. By way of response, the senior federal representative reminded the workshop of conditions first outlined by the federal government in 1982: that a majority of northerners continue to support division; that there be an agreement on the boundary between the two territories; that land claims be settled; and that there be agreement on the distribution of powers between the territorial level of government and the regional level of government. In a second plebiscite in 1992, territorial voters supported division by a narrow margin. The Inuit in the eastern half again voted overwhelmingly for division but Dene-Métis and non-Native residents of the western half now opposed.

In the territories, where the two territorial governments still exist by virtue of federal legislation and not constitutional entrenchment, the issue of Native self-government raises the symbolic and practical question of whether Native first nations are to be equal in status to the territorial governments, or whether they are to be subordinate governments. From public positions they have taken during the past two decades, it is probable that Native people have equality in mind, but this may raise problems for federal and territorial policymakers.

Native self-government will have to be well funded if it is to succeed. Given the need for a bureaucracy, the development of programs, and the recruitment and training of staff, it will probably be significantly more costly than the funding which is now available through Indian Affairs. If the concept of raising standards is built into self-government, substantially larger sums of money than Ottawa appears willing to make available will be needed. If these are not forthcoming from the federal government, the provinces and territories might well be concerned that Native people will turn to them to keep essential programming going.

Where the claims process will take the North is uncertain, though it would seem that, after the current initial round of negotiations is completed, claims will proceed slowly, perhaps taking a century to resolve, if indeed many are ever resolved. The issues are simply too complex for a fast-track process. The current claims occur mainly in the territories, where the federal government has sole jurisdiction and can therefore strike a bargain. Following their completion, the claims process will move fully into the provinces, where the federal government will not only have to compensate Native people but perhaps also the provincial governments if it is to persuade them to relinquish lands and powers to Native people. An indication of the levels of compensation which may be required was given by the case of South Moresby Island, where the creation of a national park required the payment of over $100 million to the province of British Columbia for potential losses of revenue.

But wherever the claims may lead, the most important fact is that the recognition of Native rights and the negotiation of claims have blunted the cutting edge of the frontier to a degree that no previous obstacles to development have ever been able to do. Because they have been able to use the courts effectively and have proven themselves astute politicians, Native people have been able to require a new and higher standard of morality from governments. They had never been able to do this before, at least not in the industrial era, because those in authority never thought it necessary to take their claims seriously. In a very real sense, the recognition of Native claims represents a maturing of the Canadian judicial and political system, and the forced maturation of governments, as much as it represents a political coming of age of the Native people themselves.

FURTHER READING

Abele, Frances. "Canadian Contradictions: Forty Years of Northern Political Development." *Arctic* 40, 4 (1989).

Berger, Thomas R. *Northern Frontier, Northern Homeland.* The Report of the Mackenzie Valley Pipeline Inquiry: Volume One, Supply and Services Canada. Ottawa, 1977.

Brody, H. *The People's Land: Eskimos and Whites in the Canadian Arctic.* London: Penquin Books, 1975.

Dacks, G. *A Choice of Futures: Politics in the Canadian North.* Toronto: Methuen, 1981.

Fumoleau, Rene. *As Long as This Land Shall Last.* Toronto: McClelland and Stewart, n.d.

Inuit Committee on National Issues. *Completing Canada: Inuit Approaches to Self-Government.* Aboriginal Peoples and Constitutional Reform, Position Paper, Institute of Intergovernmental Relations, Queen's University, Kingston, Ontario, 1987.

MacGregor, R. *Chief: The Fearless Vision of Billy Diamond.* Markham, Ont.: Viking, 1989.

Richardson, Boyce, ed. *Drumbeat: Anger and Renewal in Indian Country.* Toronto: Summerhill Press, 1975.

Richardson, Boyce. *Strangers Devour the Land.* Toronto: Macmillan of Canada, 1975.

Watkins, M., ed. *Dene Nation: The Colony Within.* Toronto: University of Toronto Press, 1977.

A GLOBAL PARTNERSHIP: THE CANADA- UNITED STATES POLITICAL RELATIONSHIP IN THE 1990s

JOHN KIRTON

For most of the 20th century, practitioners and observers of international politics on the North American continent have considered the Canada-United States relationship to be truly special in world affairs. This specialness stemmed firstly from the achievement of the two countries over the past two centuries in eliminating the use or even threat of force in relations between them, and in substituting a shared respect and even altruism for the normal emphasis of sovereign states on maximizing short-term, narrowly defined national interests. The specialness arose secondly from their cumulative and ongoing success during this century in coping with the uniquely rich and dense flow of transactions between two of the most open, interconnected societies in the world, and in jointly constructing the economic, defense, transportation, communication, energy and environmental protection infrastructure of their common continent. And specialness was grounded thirdly in the construction over the past half century of a political regime of "partnership" to govern the interaction between their two national governments.

This regime of partnership took as a given the overwhelming disparity in overall capability between a United States that is at least 10 times as large as Canada on most standard factors of national power. However, to prevent this profound inequality from producing outcomes which overwhelmingly favored the United States, the two countries dealt with each other on the premise that common values and interests dominated their relationship both within North America and especially in their activities in the wider world. Moreover they sought to institutionalize their relationship in bilateral and multilateral organizations, groups and processes that provided symbolic, formal and operational equality to each party. And they organized their national governments to deal with each other not as "foreign" powers subject to a highly politicized, coordinated "foreign" policy aimed at winning competitive negotiations, but as special neighbors deserving easy access to the individual expert responsible for a particular problem and best able to solve it with speed and satisfaction. Together these "special" elements of common values, joint institutions, and open national decisionmaking produced agreements distinguished by their mutual benefit and overall balance, as each country favored solutions in which both benefited, and each won those disputes it cared about and needed the most.

Despite its apparent longevity and inevitability, however, this special partnership was really a direct result of World War II and the ensuing Cold War. During the quarter century from 1940 to 1965, America's preeminent global position allowed it to be generous with its continental neighbor, while its overwhelming sense of extra-continental threat induced it to subordinate local differences to larger common concerns. Subsequently, after America's self-imposed defeat in Vietnam in the late 1960s, the relative decline of the United States as a globally dominant power and the emergence of superpower détente led to the demise of this "special partnership," to the point where even the new Cold War of the early 1980s was unable to revive it. Since 1985, however, political forces in the larger global system have given rise to a third, more complex, and still evolving era in the Canada-United States relationship, based on a much more equal, expansive and globally effective partnership than had ever prevailed before.

Propelling this new partnership is the continuing relative decline of the United States, to the point where it can no longer afford its post-World War II generosity or post-Vietnam War unilateralism, and must now depend for its international well-being on concerted action with the principal powers of the West. At the same time, the disappearance of the Soviet Union and the emergence of Europe and Japan as potential rivals in the post-Cold War era have underlined the American need for Canada, both as a partner in building a continental and hemisphere-wide bastion to compete with other regional blocs and as a colleague in meeting the challenges of a new global economy, ecosystem and political order. And although Canada itself faces substantial threats to its international competitiveness and internal political cohesiveness, its continuing ability to mount a global foreign policy focused on priorities distinctly different from, but fundamentally compatible with, those of the United States renders its cooperation particularly valuable in the new world the United States confronts.

The emergence of a new order in the Canada-U.S. relationship as the 1980s ended was signaled most dramatically in the rapidity with which arrangements long considered beyond the realm of political possibility became accomplished facts. In October 1987 the United States and Canada signed an Arctic Cooperation Treaty in which the United States, for the first time ever, acknowledged Canada's de facto sovereignty over the ice-covered waters of the Northwest Passage. In December 1988 the two countries concluded a comprehensive free trade agreement, containing a sweeping continental energy policy and innovative bilateral dispute settlement mechanism. In February 1989, on his first visit to Canada as president, George Bush promised to sign an accord with Canada controlling acid rain emissions and to introduce beforehand the congressional legislation required to render this international obligation effective. And in October 1989, Canadian prime minister Brian Mulroney joined President Bush and several Central American and Latin American leaders for a hemisphere-wide summit in San José, Costa Rica, where he announced Canada's decision to join the Organization of American States. As the 1990s opened, the pace quickened. Canada and the United States moved to extend their free trade agreement to Mexico, forged an intimate partnership at the Houston summit of major industrial democracies in July 1990, and over the following eight months went to war together to liberate Kuwait.

Behind this cascade of historic initiatives lie three emerging patterns which define the structure of the Canada-United States relationship in the 1990s. Traditional assumptions of commonality, based on principles of political democracy which other "like-minded" and above all Anglo-Saxon countries share, have been replaced by a conception of the two North American countries as uniquely open, pluralist polities, multi-ethnic societies, and market-driven economies unencumbered by the heavy statist inheritance of Europe and Japan. The old network of specialized joint institutions has been superseded by a new array of high-level, politically driven, personally intimate and much more authoritative institutions of both bilateral and plurilateral scope. And the old preference for reactive, ad hoc problem solving focused on continental concerns has given way to a more integrated effort within both governments to mobilize the bilateral relationship to shape the new global order in ways compatible to both countries. What the contemporary Canadian-American relationship is witnessing is thus not a revival of the old special relationship but the birth of a new and more powerful partnership to meet the demands of a transformed world.

THE RISE OF THE SPECIAL RELATIONSHIP, 1940–1965

The fundamental structure and novel character of the contemporary Canada-United States political relationship is seen most clearly against the backdrop of the traditional special relationship of the post-World War II era, and the very different post-Vietnam War order which succeeded it. The traditional special relationship had its deepest roots in the post-1870 decline of the United Kingdom as the dominant actor in world politics and in Canadian external relations, a transition reflected in the Treaty of Washington of 1871. It was furthered by the emergence of the United States as a major international actor before and during World War I (which Canada entered in 1914 and the United States in 1917). And it was reinforced by the need for Canada and the United States to manage bilaterally the natural resource base of their continent in the face of the increasing demands of 20th-century industrialization. It was this need that inaugurated the tradition of creating intergovernmental institutions to jointly and rationally manage the continent to mutual benefit, in the form of the International Waterways Commission/International Joint Commission of 1905, the International Boundary Commission of 1908, the International Joint Fisheries Commission/International Pacific Halibut Commission of 1923, the Pacific Salmon Commission of 1930 and the Trail Smelter Arbitration of 1928–41.

It was, however, the onset of the totalitarian threat from Germany, the shock of the fall of France in 1940, and the attack on Pearl Harbor in 1941 that produced four years of unprecedented military coordination, economic integration, policy harmonization and sense of solidarity between the two North American countries. This externally engendered spirit of oneness rapidly extended the array of joint institutions into the defense and economic fields, through the Permanent Joint Board of Defense of 1940, the Hyde Park Agreement of 1941, and the five temporary bilateral committees and several Combined Boards involving the United Kingdom created from 1941 onward. Although much of this structure was dismantled at the end of the war, the cold war shocks of the Czechoslovakian coup of 1948 and the outbreak of the Korean War in June 1950 rapidly revived the special relationship of the wartime era. The subsequent shocks of the launch of Sputnik in October 1957, the Berlin crisis and the Cuban Missile Crisis of October 1962 reinforced, and seemed to render permanent, the pattern.

The profound sense of commonality between the two countries during this period was well captured in Canadian prime minister Louis St. Laurent's famous "Gray Lecture" of January 13, 1947, when he said: "We have travelled so much of the road together in close agreement that by comparison the occasions on which our paths may have diverged seem insignificant." This feeling of togetherness provided an incentive to engage in joint action for the common welfare of the continent, most ambitiously in the St. Lawrence Seaway of 1954 and the Columbia River Treaty of 1964, and in the construction of radar lines (the 1951 Pinetree Line and the 1954 Distant Early Warning Line) to aid in the air defense of the continent against the looming Soviet threat over the North Pole in the air-atomic age.

The drive toward commonality and integration was reflected in an outburst of joint institution-building: the 1949 Military Cooperation Committee, the (now defunct) 1949 Canadian-U.S. Industrialization Mobilization Committee, the 1950 Regional Planning Group of NATO, the 1951 Civil Defense Committee/Civil Emergency Planning Committee, the 1953 Ministerial Committee on Trade and Economic Affairs, and the 1955 Great Lakes Fisheries Commission. In 1958 alone four bodies were added: the Senior Committee on Defense Production-Development Sharing, the North American Air/Aerospace Defense Command, the Ministerial Committee on Joint Defense, and the Canadian-U.S. Inter-parliamentary Group. The ensuing decade added the 1963 Balance of Payments Committee and the 1964 Roosevelt Campobello Park Commission.

The emphasis on joint problem solving embodied in these organizations rendered unnecessary the need for coherent national strategies or procedures for conducting the bilateral relationship in each capital. As St. Laurent put it in his Gray Lecture: "It is not customary in this country for us to think in terms of having a policy in regard to the United States. Like farmers whose lands have a common concession line, we think of ourselves as settling, from day to day, questions that arise between us, without dignifying the process by the word 'policy.' " In practice, the lack of internal coherence was seen in the easy access, information sharing, consultation and decision-making power which individual departments had with functional counterparts in the other government, and the inability and unwillingness of the foreign offices of either side to even monitor the flow.

These processes of national decision making and international interaction operated to reduce the level of political conflict in the relationship, to produce solutions of joint benefit, and to give to each country, in a relationship of overall balance, victories in those disputes it cared most about. Indeed, the American scholar Joseph Nye has calculated that in the 39 conflicts between the two countries important enough to receive the attention of the U.S. president from 1920 to 1970, Canada and the United States each won exactly an equal number of times. This convergence was facilitated by the ability of Canada to claim and receive special treatment from the United States on economic matters, as in its exemptions from the United States 1959 oil import program and 1963, 1965 and 1968 balance of payments control measures, and in its unique attainment of the defense production sharing agreements of 1958 and 1963, and the automotive pact of 1965. Conversely, the United States was able to prevail in the end on its core security concerns, most notably in overcoming Prime Minister John Diefenbaker's reluctance to provide full support during the 1962 Cuban Missile Crisis, and to accept American nuclear weapons on Canadian soil.

Perhaps the greatest testament to the spirit of the special relationship came in a special report the two governments commissioned from their former two-time ambassadors to each other as a guide to the successful management of the relationship. Entitled "Principles for Partnership," the July 1965 report by American Livingston Merchant and Canadian Arnold Heeney suggested that to make their unique and growing interdependence "as mutually rewarding as it is inevitable," the two countries should create joint bodies and integrative arrangements in additional fields. It also affirmed the classic precept of "quiet diplomacy" by advising that "wherever possible, divergent views between the two governments should be expressed and if possible resolved in private, thought diplomatic channels."

THE DEMISE OF THE SPECIAL RELATIONSHIP, 1965–1985

The Merchant-Heeney Report had provided the most clear and eloquent expression of rules of the regime of "special partnership" that Canada and the United States had enjoyed for a quarter of a century. But the reality of that regime was decaying even as the document was issued. For three months earlier, in April of 1965, Prime Minister Lester Pearson himself had traveled to Temple University in Philadelphia to voice publicly, on American soil, his dissent from the United States' conduct of the war in Vietnam.

The hostile response Pearson's gesture evoked from President Lyndon Johnson, and the ensuing intensification of, and America's eventual defeat in, the war in Vietnam, destroyed the special relationship. Vietnam was the first major war in the century in which the two countries had not eventually fought together. Moreover America's ultimate humiliation in the conflict confirmed, in both English and French Canada, a growing and at times anti-American nationalism, and strong belief in the wisdom of pursuing a different, more "independent" foreign policy path. At the same time, the material and psychological costs of the war for the United States meant it was less able and willing to give generous or special treatment to even the closest of its traditional friends. Moreover the war generated in turn French president Charles de Gaulle's assault on what he saw as Anglo-American domination of the western alliance, his attempt to liberate Quebec from this domination by encouraging its separation from Canada, and the need for Canada's federal government to affirm its francophone rather than Anglo-American identity in world affairs. Finally, the macroeconomic prosperity induced by exports to feed America's war effort, and to fuel America's energy and commodity needs in the resource-scarce 1970s, gave Canadians a growing confidence that they had the national capability to sustain a more independent course. Indeed, the American scholar Charles Doran has calculated that Canada, which had only 6% of the overall national power of the United States in 1950, had doubled its proportion to 10% by 1970 and 13% by 1975.

The move to separateness rather than specialness began with Canada's Gaullist-like unilateral recognition of the People's Republic of China in 1969, the withdrawal of half its forces from the European theater of NATO in 1969, and its assertion of national jurisdiction over the ice-covered waters of the Northwest Passage in 1970. It was accomplished on August 15, 1971 when the United States unilaterally suspended the convertibility of gold into dollars pending an upward revaluation of foreign currencies, imposed a 10% surcharge on imports into the United States to enforce its demand, and refused a Canadian request to be exempted from these measures. Canada's refusal to accede to the demands placed on it, and its ultimate success in having the surcharge removed without adjustments on its part, gave the Canadian government a new confidence that their country was sufficiently strong to flourish without special exemptions or even ever increasing integration with the United States. The quadrupling of oil prices in 1973 and the subsequent rise in the world value of resources in general fueled a feeling that Canada was emerging as a major rather than merely a middle power in the world, even as the election of the separatist Parti Québécois in the Quebec elections of November 15, 1976 revived the imperative of focusing on foreign policy concerns quite distinct from those of the United States.

The end of commonality as the dominant concept in the Canada-U.S. relationship was first signaled by Prime Minister Pierre Trudeau in a May 1971 visit to the Soviet Union, when, at a news conference in Moscow, he described the United States as a cultural, economic and perhaps even military threat to Canada's national identity. It was formally proclaimed by

President Richard Nixon in his statement to the House of Commons during his visit in April 1972. He declared: "It is time for Canadians and Americans to move beyond the sentimental rhetoric of the past. It is time for us to recognize that we have very separate identities; that we have significant differences; and that nobody's interests are furthered when these realities are obscured." Canadian officials readily concurred, and soon jointly agreed that the relationship was no longer special, but at best merely unique. The election of the Parti Québécois in 1976 did lead Pierre Trudeau to search for American support for a united Canada, and thus in his speech to the U.S. Congress in February 1977 to stress the similarities between the two countries. But this stress on commonality was merely tactical, and it disappeared when the separatist threat died with the defeat of a pro-independence referendum in Quebec in 1980.

In keeping with the emphasis on separateness, the 1970s saw an atrophy of the existing array of joint institutions, a lack of interest in creating new ones, and an unwillingness even to engage in regular interaction at the highest level. After Nixon's April 1972 visit there was no meeting between the leaders of the two countries for two and a half years, an unprecedentedly long period of summit isolation in the post-World War II period. Moreover President Nixon's anger at a Canadian House of Commons condemnation of his bombing of Vietnam in December 1973 led him to impose a series of punitive measures against Canada, including an embargo on contacts between middle and senior level U.S. government officials and Canadian representatives. While the December 1974 summit between President Gerald Ford and Pierre Trudeau ended the long divorce, and produced an agreement to provide advance warning of each side's unilateral initiatives affecting the other, the summit-level relationship never recaptured its historic intimacy. Indeed, the well disposed but increasingly beleaguered President Jimmy Carter became the first post-World War II U.S. president never to visit Canada. Presidential management of the relationship with Canada was delegated to the vice-presidential level, where Walter Mondale maintained a close and privileged relationship with Canadian ambassador Peter Towe. At lower levels, despite some efforts to create joint commissions to manage East Coast fisheries and maritime boundaries, and consultative committees to discuss the growing array of bilateral energy disputes, no new joint institutions of any significance were created during the 1970s.

With separate rather than common interests ascendant, and the joint management mechanisms atrophied, both countries came to rely on nationally coherent policies, and nationally coordinated decision-making processes, for dealing with each other. In Washington Henry Kissinger asked the National Security Council apparatus to produce a comprehensive country study of Canada, a paper that he finally succeeded in getting once the prospect of Quebec's separation endowed Canada with the status of a national security threat to the United States. In Canada, the shock of the Nixon surcharge led the federal government to produce a comprehensive policy toward the United States. In its public version, released in September of 1972, Secretary of State for External Affairs Mitchell Sharp signaled that thenceforth Canada would pursue a "comprehensive long-term strategy to develop and strengthen the Canadian economy and other aspects of its national life and . . . reduce the present Canadian vulnerability." Within the executive branch in Ottawa, this "third option" policy was enforced by new procedures for maintaining an overview of the multifaceted Canada-U.S. relationship, in an effort to fashion an overall balance to Canada's advantage. These efforts ended the old conviction that issues should not be linked, but should be treated on their individual merits for a speedy resolution.

Thus as the 1970s progressed, even as U.S. presidents became increasingly well disposed toward Canada, the level of conflict in the relationship increased. And, in a reversal of what many thought was the traditional pattern, such agreements as were reached seemed to come increasingly from the United States adjusting to Canada's priorities and interests. In the field of energy, from the oil shocks of 1973 to those of 1979, Canada raised the price and reduced the supply of its oil and gas exports to a United States increasingly afflicted by serious energy shortages. President Carter concluded agreements favorable to Canada to define the boundary and manage the resources off the East Coast, and to facilitate the construction of a massive pipeline across Canada to bring Alaskan and Canadian Arctic gas to markets in the "lower forty-eight" United States. In the multilateral arena, President Ford successfully sponsored Canada's membership into the exclusive club of major industrial democracies at the Puerto Rico summit in 1976, while President Carter followed with far more accommodating support for Canadian initiatives in nuclear non-proliferation, the north-south dialogue, and the United Nations Treaty on the Law of the Sea. Reciprocally Canada lent support to an increasingly beleaguered America by agreeing with its NATO allies in 1978 to an annual 3% real increase in defense expenditures, by rescuing trapped American diplomats in Iran following the 1979 Iranian revolution, and by joining in a partial grain embargo and boycott of the Olympic games in Moscow in response to the Soviet Union's invasion of Afghanistan in 1980.

The first half of the 1980s saw a new and deeper round of divergence and disagreement between the two countries. With his third parliamentary majority mandate in the federal election of February 1980, his convincing defeat of the separatist "sovereignty-association" option in the Quebec referendum of May 20, 1980, and his country still enjoying the strong prosperity of commodity and energy producers in the resource-scarce '70s, Pierre Trudeau was free to pursue with unparalleled vigor his favored policies of state intervention in the domestic economy, an arm's-length relationship with the United States, the development of ties with Europe and Japan, arms control and cooperation with the Soviet Union, and north-south dialogue and redistribution. On almost every count these policies were directly at odds with those favored by President Ronald Reagan, who was elected in November 1980 with a strong mandate to shift the United States sharply rightward by reducing government regulation of the economy, rebuilding America's military might to counter the "evil empire" of the Soviet Union, forcefully countering communist incursions in the Third World, and unilaterally asserting America's interests in such multilateral forums as the United Nations and its conference on the law of the sea.

The results of such divergent philosophies on the part of two determined and self-confident leaders were soon apparent. Soon after entering office President Reagan withdrew from Senate consideration the East Coast fisheries and maritime boundary treaties that had been negotiated in good faith between the executive branches of the two governments. He began a bitter campaign to alter or remove critical provisions of Canada's new National Energy Program and its strengthened Foreign Investment Review Agency. He flatly refused to take any action to reduce the American emissions of acid rain that Canadians saw drifting northward to destroy their ecosystems.

Beyond North America the conflicts were equally intense. President Reagan initiated a year-long review of, and ultimately repudiated, the United Nations Law of the Sea Treaty that represented a model of Canada's multilateralist approach and successful international leadership in pursuit of its own national interests and values. Further assaults followed on such favored Canadian international institutions as UNESCO and the International Development Agency. A similar chill soon emerged in the field of international security. Pierre Trudeau responded with stony silence when the United States invaded the Commonwealth Caribbean state of Grenada. And while he reluctantly allowed the United States to test its cruise missiles in Canada, he reacted to President Reagan's escalating rhetoric against the Soviet Union by launching a "peace initiative" designed to restore communication, confidence, and common principles across the east-west divide.

THE EMERGENCE OF GLOBAL PARTNERSHIP, 1985–1991

By 1985, however, the two increasingly distinct countries of North America began a new process of coming together, in a way that was fundamentally different from the special partnership of the past. The catalyst for this new era was a recognition on the part of the Reagan presidency that it could no longer sustain its first-term efforts unilaterally to rebuild American power by mounting the largest peacetime defense buildup in American history and by maintaining a high exchange rate for the U.S. dollar. At the same time the advent of the Gorbachev era in the Soviet Union, and the increasing diminution of Soviet power and assertiveness, provided a freedom and incentive to redirect attention to the new economic threats from the rapidly integrating Europe (of the Single European Act of 1985) and the rapidly growing and more assertive Japan under the prime ministership of Yasuhiro Nakasone from 1983 to 1987. After 1989, the increased continental preoccupations and self-confidence of Europe generated a growing common concern on the part of the United States and Canada that they might be marginalized or even left out of the new European-centered institutions such as the Bank for European Reconstruction and Development and the Conference on Security and Cooperation in Europe. And while the United States pledged to be "partners in leadership" with Europe's principal powers, as its traditional special relationships with once defeated and rebuilt and now fully restored Germany, Japan, and Italy and even allied Britain eroded, its remaining relationship with Canada—the last country of consequence on which it could count—acquired a scarcity value of increasingly significant proportions.

As a result, starting in 1985, the United States, led by the increasingly influential vice president George Bush, and treasury secretary James Baker, looked toward Canada as a central partner in shaping a new international economic order. And a patient President Reagan, more conscious of his legacy as the end of his presidency approached, and with his exceptional fondness for Canada intact, mobilized to bring into being his longstanding vision of a North American accord. That vision, which dated back to Reagan's campaign for the Republican presidential nomination in 1976, had reappeared at the opening of his 1980 presidential campaign, and at the outset of his presidency, until knowledgeable professionals informed him that public pushing for such an accord inspired Canadian resistance, and thus delayed the day of its realization. But while the theme itself disappeared from the presidential rhetoric, an inherently optimistic President Reagan continued to accord Canada a larger place in his foreign policy than any of his postwar predecessors, to value its stability as a firm northern front against the Communist expansion that was causing him such discomfort on the United States' southern borders, and to feel inherently comfortable with a country that was, he thought, so like his own California.

His path was eased considerably by the election in Canada in September 1984 of a majority Progressive Conservative government under Brian Mulroney. Never before had Canada had a prime minister so close to and impressed with things American, so firmly pledged to make "good relations, super relations" with the United States the foundation of his foreign policy, and so willing to give the United States "the benefit of the doubt." Because Mulroney's Conservatives substantially shared Reagan's emphasis on limiting the role of government in the economy, and, at least rhetorically, on the need for a strong national defense, the ideologically based divergences of the early 1980s largely disappeared. Thus Canada eliminated the contentious National Energy Program and Foreign Investment Review Agency, joined with the United States to construct a North Warning System for continental air defense, and dispatched additional forces to the European theater of NATO. Although Canada sharply diverged from American policy in declaring full sovereignty over its Artic waters, declining an American invitation for government-to-government participation in the Strategic Defense Initiative, and mounting an aggressive campaign of sanctions against the apartheid regime in South Africa, from September 1985 to January 1989 it negotiated and ratified a comprehensive bilateral free trade agreement with the United States. Partly by seeking and successfully producing the first component of the North American Accord, Brian Mulroney became one of Ronald Reagan's favorite foreign leaders, enjoying a close personal relationship that Reagan otherwise reserved only for Britain's Margaret Thatcher, Japan's Yasuhiro Nakasone, and, at a lesser level, with such bona fide leaders of the English-speaking democracies as Australia's Bob Hawke.

With the accession of George Bush to the presidency, and James Baker to the secretaryship of state in January 1989, and Brian Mulroney's success in securing a second majority government in the Canadian federal election of 1988, this new partnership took on greater strength and broader dimensions. While the rapid retreat and reduction in Soviet power evident in 1989 eroded the external security threat that had helped glue Canada and the United States together since 1940, it also gave rise to a newly self-confident Europe preoccupied with its continental challenges, eager to organize its security on a continental basis, and quite willing to lessen its transatlantic identity and loosen its ties to North America. At the same time the end of the Soviet Empire, and the democratic and market revolution underway elsewhere in the world, presented the United States and Canada, more than a continentally absorbed Western Europe, with an opportunity and self-confidence to rebuild an international order now freed from the 40-year freeze of the Cold War. While neither George Bush nor Brian Mulroney offered a vision of what this rapidly changing international system meant for their relationship, it quickly carried them into a tighter partnership in ventures to build a stronger, more institutionalized order, first on their home continent, and then in the world beyond.

This global partnership rested on a new conception of shared values. The common values that had underpinned the traditional special relationship had been based on a view of the United States and Canada, as descendants of the British empire, as two English-speaking societies governed by a common law tradition, regulated market economy, and multiparty democracy, flourishing together in the unencumbered environment of frontier lands. They were thus truly exceptional countries, with a historical path shared by no others save possibly the junior distant British offshoots of Australia, New Zealand and South Africa. Although Ronald Reagan took seriously the notion of a fraternity of English-speaking countries, and while George Bush shares the liberal internationalist perspectives of the Northeastern establishment of the Republican Party, the new sense of shared identity is far less Anglo-Saxon, transatlantic and exclusively North American and far more multicultural, southward and westward oriented and hemispheric. It embraces in a serious way Canada's distinct francophone society with its civil law tradition, the United States' burgeoning Hispanic population, and a rich array of new North Americans from all corners of the globe. And in a world in which American power is retreating from its dominance in open global regimes toward regional blocs closer to home, its focus is less transatlantic and transoceanic and more on the southward possibilities in the western hemisphere, and perhaps westward toward the Pacific. Inspired by the global movement toward economic and political liberalization launched during the Reagan presidency, it rejects the more closed, homogenous societies and statist governments in Europe and Japan and one-party or one-person systems in much of the rest of the world. It sees the United States and Canada sharing common problems of economic renewal in the face of a rapidly growing Japan and newly self-confident Europe and finding the solution, for themselves and others, in well-managed market mechanisms nationally and internationally.

A central embodiment of the new common identity is the vision of a North American Accord developed by President Reagan and his fellow Californians, which accorded equal value to Mexico as well as Canada and integrally linked both with the United States. And the aspiration of "Enterprise for the Americas" prompted by President Bush and his close, fellow Texan cabinet colleagues (notably Secretary of State James Baker and Treasury Secretary Nicholas Brady) has extended the vision further southward to embrace the western hemisphere as a whole. Prime Minister Mulroney's decision to attend the San José summit of Central American leaders in October 1989, to join the Organization of American States, and to take up the United States' cause of waging the drug war in the hemisphere have taken Canada well beyond its historic Commonwealth Caribbean bastion and made it a full player in the hemisphere as a whole.

A new shared identity has been accompanied by a closer, more institutionalized, and much higher-level set of mechanisms for managing the Canada-U.S. relationship. The rise of what American scholar Joseph Jockel has called the "semi-institutionalized management of the relationship" began as early as 1982 when the United States and Canada both acquired new foreign ministers, in the person of George Shultz and Allan MacEachen respectively. Both brought to their positions long ministerial-level service in their governments in several portfolios, a personal acquaintance with each other, and a determination to end two years of harsh rhetoric and conflict in the relationship. At their first meeting as foreign ministers in October 1982 they agreed to meet bilaterally four times a year, two meetings of which would be full-scale reviews of bilateral relations. These foreign minister "quarterlies" continued even as Allan MacEachen was replaced by Jean Chrétien and then Joe Clark in 1984, and as George Shultz was replaced by James Baker. By ensuring that all potential disputes in the relationship will receive regular and if necessary detailed review at the political levels, these quarterly (or more recently thrice-yearly) meetings reduce the need for "public diplomacy" by either partner, induce both national bureaucracies to develop coordinated, long-term approaches more resistant to short-term parochial pressures at home, and permit reasonable compromises to be reached before problems develop into major conflicts. They also give Canada a larger prominence in the consciousness of those conducting America's global foreign policy, and with it an expanded understanding of Canada's growing importance in these larger pursuits. It is a measure of their efficacy that the example of regular bilateral ministerial-level meetings was copied, beginning in 1985, by ministers in a host of other portfolios, and by the heads themselves.

At the presidential and prime ministerial level, the process was launched in September 1984 when, at their first summit in Washington (held immediately after Prime Minister Mulroney assumed office), President Reagan and Prime Minister Mulroney agreed to meet at least once a year. At their next summit, held in Quebec City in March 1985, President Reagan asked the prime minister to telephone him on urgent issues, and launched an ambitious work program containing integrative ventures in several key fields. Despite formidable distractions on both sides of the border over the ensuing years, they maintained personal oversight of the program in their annual summits, and succeeded in largely realizing the goals of the program by the end of the Reagan presidency.

With the advent of President Bush, the joint management became intense and intimate as well as institutionalized. President Bush and Secretary of State Baker not only agreed to continue the annual springtime summits and quarterly foreign minister meetings. They also used their opening gatherings to give Canada the long-awaited acid rain accord that President Reagan had denied them. Moreover the annual springtime, structured "Shamrock Summits" have been supplemented by the much more informal August "working holiday" summits at the president's vacation home in Kennebunkport, Maine. Finally, there has arisen a pattern of ad hoc "working dinner" summits, as the president, taking advantage of Ottawa's proximity, has invited Prime Minister Mulroney to fly to Washington for an evening to discuss such major global security issues as American-Soviet relations and the Iraqi invasion of Kuwait. When added to the president's penchant for "direct-dial diplomacy" with Prime Minister Mulroney (among others) and the more dense web of plurilateral and multilateral summits discussed below, the result has been an unparalleled frequency of face-to-face encounters between prime minister and president. In 1989, Bush and Mulroney met on seven occasions, four in a bilateral and three in the wider context of the Seven-Power Summit, the San José Summit of the Americas, and NATO. In 1990 there were eight such encounters, four on a bilateral basis and four in the broader context of NATO, the Seven-Power Summit, the United Nations World Summit on Children, and the Conference on Security and Cooperation in Europe (CSCE). With the president meeting the Canadian prime minister an average of every six weeks, and more than any other foreign leader, it is easy for the two not only to manage much more vigorously and comprehensively their continental relationship, but to jointly consider ways to shape global issues as well.

Such intense, political-level management has reduced the need for creating the formal joint committees and commissions featured by the old special relationship or the supranational continental institutions emerging in the European Community. Rather, the new partnership has relied on a plethora of "consultative mechanisms," under which senior officials in each country regularly meet to discuss bilateral issues and prospective national initiatives in such fields as energy and transportation. The one major institutional innovation has been the creation of the multi-layered bilateral dispute settlement mechanism of the Canada-U.S. Free Trade Agreement, which promises to put the entire trade relationship under the de facto influence, rather than the formal final authority, of a joint rather than national center of decision. The apparent failure of the Uruguay Round negotiations for multilateral trade liberalization enhanced the value of the bilateral dispute settlement mechanism, despite some predictable disappointment in various quarters with its early decisions. In 1991, trilateral talks began to bring Mexico into the Free Trade Area. In mid-1992, a North American Free Trade Agreement (NAFTA) was successfully negotiated, to come into effect after ratification by the legislatures of all these countries.

A further feature of the new partnership has been the eagerness of each party to participate in the domestic political process of the other, with the tacit or explicit consent of the other's executive branch. Canada was the first and most active participant in penetrating the thin wall of sovereignty between the two countries, with extensive efforts at public diplomacy, and lobbying Congress and American interest groups, on a host of trade issues and, most ambitiously, acid rain. More recently, in an extension of President Carter's public comments following the election of the Parti Qúebécois, President Bush has spoken out with increasing vigor on his visits to Canada in favor of a united Canada.

As impressive as this new degree of continental institutionalization, intimacy and interpenetration is, a more significant development has been the extension of the exceptionally close Canada-U.S. relationship into the broader multilateral arena. While the old special relationship had seen common global threats breed continental cooperation, in the actual conduct of global diplomacy the United States had tended to maintain privileged relationships with its European great power associates (notably Britain), while Canada had looked to its fellow middle powers (particularly in the Commonwealth) as its key partners in building the coalitions that might constrain a unilaterally predisposed United States. In contrast, the new partnership is a fully global one, as the United States and Canada increasingly look to each other as the poles of the coalition through which global order can be shaped.

The Canada-U.S. partnership at the annual summit of the major industrial democracies dates back to 1976 when the United States, over French opposition, successfully secured Canada's entry into the club at its second meeting. The partnership strengthened in the early 1980s when the new Reagan administration included Canada in the even more exclusive subsidiary trade ministers' quadrilateral (composed of the United States, the European Community and Japan) despite the acute disagreements raging at the time between the two North American countries over energy and investment. It took a major step forward in 1986 when James Baker as U.S. treasury secretary enlarged the Group of Five (the United States, Japan, Germany, Britain, France) into a new and ultimately more consequential Group of Seven which included Canada (and Italy). Ensuing summits saw further collaboration in new groups at the subministerial level on missile technology control and money laundering, and a new role for the participants' "political directors" in the annual cycle of summit preparation. In the first summit that President Bush hosted (in Houston in July 1990), the assistance which Prime Minister Mulroney's personal representative, Derek Burney, gave his American colleagues in preparing the summit, and the visible Canada-United States cooperation at the event itself, indicated that this summit-ensconced partnership has reached a new height and expanded relevance in multilateral as well as bilateral affairs.

This intense, intimate, and institutionalized senior-level interaction has inevitably changed the way decisions affecting the other country are made in both the United States and Canada. Organizationally, the old special relationship resided in career civil servants, specialists in their particular functional area and lifelong professional colleagues with their Canadian counterparts. In contrast, the new partnership rests with political leaders, with the long experience needed to manage the relationship more directly and ambitiously than ever before. In both capitals the leaders and, until the Canadian cabinet shuffle of April 21, 1991, their foreign and other senior ministers had an unusually long tenure in senior government positions involving the other country, and thus had the experience and self-confidence to manage the relationship personally. Supporting their ability to do so has been the emergence during the 1980s of organizational innovations that increase the constant, coherent, influential attention each country's affairs receive in the other's capital. In September 1983 the U.S. Department of State (returning to a short-lived innovation of 1973) established a deputy assistant secretary of state for Canada, making Canada the only country within the State Department apparatus to receive such singular, senior-level attention. In January 1985, through a formal National Security Study directive, the president also launched a comprehensive review of the Canadian relationship at the National Security Council level. Within Canada, a reorganization of the Department of External Affairs a year earlier created a new branch for U.S. affairs, headed by an assistant deputy minister with no other responsibilities. The incumbent, Derek Burney, went on to become Prime Minister Mulroney's chief of staff during the free trade negotiations, and he became Canada's ambassador to the United States in 1989. Because he continues to be a close advisor to the prime minister on domestic Canadian issues, and while in Washington has acquired the role of the prime minister's personal representative in preparing the Seven-Power Summit, he is especially well positioned to ensure that Canadian decisions are well tuned to the current priorities in Washington, and to keep the U.S. government apprised of Canadian needs.

Such organizational changes have brought a new process of Canada-U.S. decision making. When the same senior politicians deal with the panoply of issues there is far less chance that the other country will be "taken for granted" (as Canada was in Washington's balance of payment's programs in the 1960s and as the United States was in Ottawa's National Energy Program of 1980) or suffer from malign neglect (as when President Nixon banned senior government contacts with Canadians in 1973). It also makes it normal that issues in the relationship will be linked, not as direct threats or bribes but as part of an overall effort to maintain a balance and overall harmony in the relationship. Moreover, the direct ongoing access afforded to those conducting each country's general foreign policy means there is a far greater chance each partner will understand the other's global relevance, aspirations and constraints. Finally, there is also an enhanced opportunity to form proactive partnerships to design and secure a more desirable global order, rather than merely react to the other's complaints about unilateral, bilateral or multilateral affairs. This new integration of continental and global concerns has overcome traditional tendencies to conduct an isolationist retreat into building a better continent as a sanctuary or passive model for a less fortunate world, to let Canada focus on extracting continental advantages from a United States preoccupied with global dilemmas, or to vent divergent national ideologies on global issues. It has substituted far more genuine advance consultation about goals and strategies for achieving global order, and has produced harmonized approaches to which each party has substantially contributed.

This global, proactive partnership has been evident, in the hemisphere, in Canada's support for American initiatives to control the inflow of narcotics to the United States, to assist major Latin American debtors under the Brady Plan, to develop the OAS, to launch an "Enterprise for the Americas", and to embrace Mexico in an expanded regional free trade area. They have also been seen, in the global arena, in the United States' support for Canadian initiatives to provide debt relief to the world's least developed countries, to mount santions against South African apartheid, and to energize the United Nations to assist the world's children. At the same time, the two countries have acted closely together to direct the West's attempt to modernize NATO, to build a stronger CSCE and pan-European security structure, to found the new Bank for European Reconstruction and Development, and to devise workable programs to sustain the fragile global environment.

The new pattern of partnership was most clearly expressed during the conduct of the Gulf War from August 1990 to March 1991. Apart from Margaret Thatcher, who was visiting President Bush when Iraq invaded Kuwait, Prime Minister Mulroney was the first foreign leader with whom the president met to discuss what the international response should be. Partly as a result of such close consultation, Canada became one of only three other western countries that joined the United States in providing the air power the offensive operations of which proved decisive in liberating Kuwait. And partly due to Canadian urging, the United States resisted pressure for a unilateral military response in favor of acting with the approval of the United Nations, as Canada has traditionally preferred.

FURTHER READING

Bothwell, Robert. *Canada and the United States: The Politics of Partnership.* New York: Twayne Publishers, 1992.

"Canada and the U.S. in a Changing Global Context." *International Journal* 46 (Winter 1990–1991).

Clarkson, Stephen. *Canada and the Reagan Challenge.* Updated edition. Toronto: James Lorimer, 1985.

Doran, Charles. *Forgotten Partnership?: U.S.-Canadian Relations in the 1980's.* Baltimore, Md.: The Johns Hopkins Press, 1983.

Fox, William T. R. *A Continent Apart: The United States and Canada in World Politics.* Toronto: University of Toronto Press, 1985.

Holmes, John. *Life With Uncle: The Canadian-American Relationship.* Toronto: University of Toronto Press, 1981.

Jockel, Joseph. "Canada-U.S. Relations in the Bush Era." *Canadian-American Public Policy* 1 (April 1990): 1–27.

Lipset, Seymour Martin. *Continental Divide: The Values and Institutions of the United States and Canada.* Toronto: C. D. Howe Institute, 1989.

Lisée, Jean-François. *In the Eye of the Eagle.* Toronto: HarperCollins, 1990.

Swanson, Roger Frank, ed., *Canadian-American Summit Diplomacy, 1923-1973.* Toronto: McClelland and Stewart, 1975.

Swanson, Roger Frank. *Intergovernmental Perspectives on the Canada-U.S. Relationship.* New York: New York University Press, 1978.

CANADA,
THE COMMONWEALTH
AND LA FRANCOPHONIE

PETER LYON

The Commonwealth and La Francophonie: each is a highly individualistic, postcolonial international organization which has evolved out of imperial experience and arrangements, principally those of Britain and France, respectively. They are much more postcolonial than many casual commentators seem to appreciate. In both organizations Canada has played a prominent part in transforming these associations and in shaping them into their present condition.

The contemporary character of these two associations and Canada's prominent role in each of them was most evidently demonstrated in 1987 when, within two months, Canada was the host country for two summit meetings: La Francophonie in Quebec City, September 2–4, and the Commonwealth, in Vancouver, October 13–17, 1987.

AN EVER-EVOLVING COMMONWEALTH

The gradual transformation of the erstwhile British Empire into the contemporary Commonwealth began in Canada in the 19th century. Many historians have regarded Lord Durham's famous report of 1839, with its advocacy both of parliamentary government and of anglicization (the spread of British "culture" in its broadest sense), as a seminal starting point. The British North America Act of 1867 undoubtedly made Canada the first dominion. This was a condition of self-government combined with a somewhat ambiguous international status, but one which eventually came to connote complete independence from and equality with Britain. Australia achieved dominion status in 1900, New Zealand in 1907, South Africa in 1910, and Newfoundland in 1919 (although it lost this status early in the 1930s during the great depression and reverted de facto to being a colony until 1949, when it joined Canada as the 10th province). The Irish Free State became a somewhat reluctant dominion when launched as an independent state in 1921, as the island was partitioned, and remained a dominion until 1949—when its withdrawal underlined the voluntary, unforced nature of the Commonwealth association. India's willingness in 1949 to remain in the Commonwealth (taken just after the former exclusively "white man's" Commonwealth had become South Asianized by accepting the membership of Pakistan in 1947 and of Ceylon in 1948) was made possible by a new formula which no longer required allegiance to the Crown but accepted the British monarch of the day as "Head of the Commonwealth," a mostly titular post. The British Commonwealth of Nations, as it was often popularly called between 1919 and 1947, was not only led by Britain, and strongly monarchical in its symbolism—it was also small, with a membership of only between six and nine countries throughout these years. From the late 1950s and early 1960s the Commonwealth expanded rapidly in membership as decolonization proceeded apace. Its multiracial character became pronounced as countries in the Caribbean, the Pacific, the Indian Ocean, and the Mediterranean joined others from Africa and Asia. A membership of eight in 1949 had risen to 21 by 1965 when the Commonwealth Secretariat (ComSec) was launched with a Canadian as its executive head. By 1992 the membership was 50.

The overall record of comings and goings of membership is generally one of expansion, but with a few withdrawals—notably Ireland in 1949; South Africa in 1961; Pakistan in 1972 (though in October 1989, Pakistan rejoined the Commonwealth); and Fiji, whose membership was deemed (by the Commonwealth Heads of Government Meeting in British Columbia, Canada, in October 1987) to have "lapsed," basically because of the policies pursued by the new, post-coup regime in that country. Informed expectations were that further decolonization (notably Namibia, which joined in March 1989, and a few others, such as Bermuda) would in the 1990s take the membership to more than 50 countries but was unlikely to extend to many more.

The establishment of the ComSec in London, England in 1965, with an experienced Canadian diplomat, Arnold Smith, as the first secretary general, was a major landmark in the evolution of the modern Commonwealth. This came just after the British government's first attempt to secure U.K. membership of the European Economic Community (the EEC) had been rebuffed by French president Charles de Gaulle's veto and when a number of newly independent members of the Commonwealth were increasingly irritated by Britain's assumption of permanent managerial and chairman functions in pan-Commonwealth affairs. Together these factors encouraged the British to adopt a lower profile in the Commonwealth and also to accept, though not to enthuse over, the inception of the ComSec.

Smith did much in his 10 years of office, 1965–75, to establish the ComSec on firm foundations and to build up its reputation. In this task he was much aided by the discreet but firm support and help he received from successive Canadian governments. The ComSec was set up to facilitate coordination and consultation in all intergovernmental areas of Commonwealth joint endeavor. The secretariat was instrumental in organizing the cooperative efforts of Commonwealth members to assist with economic and social development, especially of smaller member countries (27 out of the

48 members in mid-1949 had populations of only about one million or less, in several cases much less). Arnold Smith published, in 1981, an engaging account of the foundation of the ComSec and indeed of the role of the Commonwealth in world affairs in the years 1965 to 1975, which he entitled *Stitches in Time*. His successor as secretary general, Shridath Ramphal from Guyana, retired from his post in June 1990, so there were only two secretaries general in the first 25 years of the ComSec. Member countries staff the secretariat according to merit and experience, and with some attention to reflecting the geographic diversity of the Commonwealth. English is the common, working language. Canadians have been prominent among the senior staff of the ComSec since its launching.

One of the most innovative, certainly most high profile, of the coordinating practices pioneered by the Commonwealth is the holding of regular Commonwealth Heads of Government Meetings (nowadays acronymically abbreviated as CHOGM). These biennial meetings have been able to retain a high degree of informality and genuine discussion rarely seen at other large international gatherings The routines of a CHOGM derive very considerably from practices commended or proposed by Canadian spokesmen, and notably by the then prime minister, Pierre Elliott Trudeau, when a CHOGM convened in Ottawa in August 1973. Difficult issues to be dealt with at a CHOGM are often left for a mid-conference (usually a weekend) retreat where the top leaders are able to benefit from an atmosphere of informality and small group meetings.

CHOGMs have produced a number of diplomatic deals and declarations over the years. These include the 1971 Singapore Declaration of Commonwealth Principles; the Gleneagles Agreement against sporting contacts with South Africa (1977); the Lusaka Accord (1979), which facilitated the transition to independence of Zimbabwe; and the Vancouver agreement of 1987 which led to the setting up of the Commonwealth of Learning. CHOGMs also provide the highest level of consultation and guidance for functional cooperation. Additionally, there are periodic meetings of Commonwealth ministers responsible for finance, law, industry, health, employment, agriculture, women's affairs and education.

Commonwealth countries make assessed or voluntary financial contributions to various intergovernmental Commonwealth organizations and activities. Ever since its launching, Canada has been the second largest contributor, after Britain, to the budget of the ComSec, in 1986–87 paying $1,995,098 or 15.84% of its total budget of $12.598m (Britain paying 30% of this sum). The ComSec provides information and assistance to governments, as in the drafting of legislation and the handling of international trade negotiations. It also services the Commonwealth's expert study groups and provides a variety of other aids to member countries, and especially their governments.

The Commonwealth Fund for Technical Co-operation (CFTC) is the largest Commonwealth development program and has been ever since its launching in 1971 as a multilateral development fund. It is an undertaking in mutual self-help, designed to meet the technical assistance needs of developing member countries, associated states, dependent territories, and

Commonwealth intergovernmental organizations and agencies. The CFTC provides assistance through five programs, in each of which Canada is a contributing participant: General Technical Assistance, Fellowships and Training, the Technical Assistance Group, the Industrial Development Unit and the Export Market Development Division. Throughout the existence of CFTC, Canada has been one of its foremost contributors and supporters, and in 1986–87 Canada pledged $16.434 million, much the largest single sum (Britain, the second, pledging $12.54 million in the same year) out of a total budget of $38.62 million—which is, however, itself a small amount relative to Canada's total aid budget.

CANADA'S PROMINENT ROLES
IN THE COMMONWEALTH

From the time of its pioneer role as the first self-governing dominion, Canada invariably has been one of the strongest supporters of and active participants in Commonwealth endeavors. Following World War I, it was prominent in pressing for equal status for the dominions with Britain and therefore in setting an example which other colonies were to follow, albeit often somewhat faster, on their roads to full formal independence.

John Diefenbaker, while prime minister in 1957–63, became one of the leading politicians in the condemnation of South Africa's policy of apartheid. This led to the departure of that country from the Commonwealth in 1961 and to a reaffirmation and reemphasis of principles of racial equality. When Arnold Smith was appointed first secretary general and head of the ComSec, this inaugurated a new era in Commonwealth relations.

Robert Stanfield, former premier of Nova Scotia and leader of the federal opposition, was in 1987 appointed as chairman of the Commonwealth Foundation, a pan-Commonwealth body set up in 1966 to promote professional contacts and cooperation in the widest sense in the Commonwealth. Canada's secretary of state for external affairs, Joe Clark, became chairman of the Commonwealth Committee of Foreign Ministers, which was set up at the Vancouver CHOGM in 1987 to monitor, spearhead and make further proposals in the Commonwealth's campaign against apartheid.

Canada has been responsible for a number of significant Commonwealth initiatives: the present style and format of CHOGMs, the Commonwealth Scholarship and Fellowship program, the concept of an annual Commonwealth Day (from 1975 onward), in the work of the CFTC, and the practice of complementing the quadrennial Commonwealth Games with an arts festival—all these matters were pioneered by Canada. It has lately been in the forefront in introducing women's issues directly into the political process through ministerial meetings (1983), in calling for an equal ratio between men and women in scholarship awards (1984), and in the launching in 1987 of the Commonwealth of Learning (with its headquarters in Vancouver) to utilize modern technology and long-distance learning techniques in the sciences, education and the arts.

As well as the official organization and its agencies, there is the "unofficial" Commonwealth, with about 300 nongovernmental organizations and arrangements. Canada is widely and prominently involved in the activities of virtually all of this unofficial "people's" Commonwealth whereby thousands of individuals are linked across the association by extensive international networks of professional and interest groups. In 1987, for instance, a very well organized and instructive young persons' replica of a CHOGM was held in Ottawa, with wide Commonwealth youth participation.

LA FRANCOPHONIE

La Francophonie is a term which first acquired general currency in the 1950s and now has two main meanings. Primarily, it denotes those peoples and societies throughout the world for whom French is their mother tongue or preferred first language. The main groups of francophones outside France are to be found in Canada, Belgium, Switzerland, the Caribbean, Vietnam, and north and west Africa. It is, however, the second main sense of the term which relates most directly to Canada's external relations, where it signifies an interlinked set or sets of private and public arrangements and organizations designed to promote friendly ties among francophones.

With the exception of those international associations formed and directed by France, such as Alliance Française (founded in 1883), La Francophonie as an international factor is a product of the age of rapid decolonization of the west Europeans' overseas empires which accelerated so markedly in the 1960s and encouraged the formation or expansion of post-imperial arrangements.

Some genuinely multilateral associations formed to promote closer ties between francophone groups began to emerge shortly after the Second World War, e.g., La Fédération internationale de la presse de langue française (Paris, 1948) and L'Institut international de droit d'expression française (1964). These were all, however, private bodies even though many of them have become recipients of government subsidies. In the 1970s and 1980s this private, or nongovernmental, dimension of La Francophonie expanded considerably. By the mid-1980s there were about 50 international French-language federations, academies, associations and institutes seeking to increase their impact in various fields.

The intergovernmental dimension of La Francophonie dates, however, only from the late 1960s and, contrary to a frequent misconception, did not stem from initiatives taken by the government of France. In 1967, members from some 20 national parliaments met in Luxembourg and set up L'Association internationale des parlementaires de langue française. Two years later an international conference held in Zaire in central Africa brought together a similarly wide group of ministers of education and this led the following year, when 21 countries were represented in Niamey, Niger, to the founding of L'Agence de coopération culturelle et technique (ACCT), an international francophone organization devoted to the mutual promotion of cultural and technical cooperation. Jean-Marc Léger, a Canadian journalist and then secretary general of the Association of Partly or Wholly French-Language Universities (AUPELF), became the first secretary general of ACCT—at a time, it is worth recalling, when another Canadian, Arnold

Smith, was Commonwealth secretary general. The ACCT has come to be widely regarded as the most important of several francophone institutions.

The ACCT comprises a general conference which directs its activities and approves the program (meeting at the ministerial level every two years); the board of directors, which approves and monitors the development of the proposals submitted to it by the members (meeting every year); the consultative council, which is responsible for cooperation between the agency and the many nongovernmental francophone agencies; and, finally, the secretariat, which is in charge of preparing and implementing the program and producing the budgetary and financial reports.

Canada has participated, and still participates, in all ACCT programs and assists prominently in the scientific and technical fields by promoting methods for circulating information rapidly among the members. Canada, seeking to maintain a balance between the cultural and technical aspects of the agency, and inspired by the Commonwealth Fund for Technical Cooperation (CFTC), successfully proposed the creation of the Special Development Programme (PSD) in 1975, which, supported by voluntary contributions, studies and carries out modest technical assistance programs, mainly in three sectors: technical assistance, training and up-grading, and technical and feasibility studies. Canada's aim in promoting the PSD was to give ACCT a new momentum and to respond to needs expressed by developing countries. In the late 1970s and 1980s the ACCT also became a forum for sectoral ministerial meetings—of ministers of science and technology, of justice, and of culture, for example.

From the late 1960s and early 1970s the policy of the Trudeau government toward the francophone world took on both markedly external and internal features. The external aspect sought to gain greater influence with francophone states in Africa and to signify to them Canada's determination to assume a major role, or roles, in francophone organizations. Domestically, the Ottawa government sought to resolve the tricky question of Quebec's quest for an international role by federal-provincial negotiations rather than through representational matters involving foreign governments. The primary objective was to convince the government of Quebec that all its major aspirations could be met within a Canadian framework. A second objective was to convince Quebecers that the threat to Canadian unity of a divided international presence was genuine and not just a specter conjured up by the federal government to justify and perpetuate its intervention in provincial affairs while denying Quebec the benefits of international activity.

A further objective of the federal government, which was made all the more important because of the difficulties with Quebec, was to enlist the support of the three other provinces with sizable francophone populations: Ontario, New Brunswick and Manitoba. Their active and apparently willing participation with the federal government would demonstrate that "French Canada" and "Quebec" were not exact synonyms and therefore that only the Canadian government could truly represent all French Canadians. The Federal government sought also, therefore, to remind foreign governments of Quebec's status as a province and to ensure that no uniquely special status was conceded to Quebec in external any more than in domestic affairs.

Thus, as proposals to create institutions for La Francophonie built up pace from the late 1960s onwards, Canadian government policy had three main objectives: (1) to present and project an undivided international personality for Canada; (2) to demonstrate that the Canadian government represented French Canadians from all provinces, including Quebec; and (3) to give substance to the declaratory policy of strengthening relations with the French-speaking world. These objectives were certainly not entirely new; what had changed was that they were now invested with more importance and a sense of practical urgency.

CANADA HOSTS TWO SUMMITS IN 1987

Representatives of 37 countries using French as a common language came together in Quebec City, on September 2–4, 1987 to discuss a wide range of subjects, from education and cultural exchanges to improved means of promoting high technology through the diffusion of scientific information. Despite much discussion of the matter, the meeting failed to agree as to whether the organization should take on a markedly more political role, as in the Commonwealth.

The 28th Commonwealth heads of government meeting (since 1944) was held in Vancouver from October 13 to 17. Queen Elizabeth II, as head of the Commonwealth, was present in Vancouver during the meeting and gave audiences to each head of government as well as holding receptions and hosting a dinner while, as is customary, playing no part at all in the formal proceedings. An active but rather unproductive discussion on South Africa (with Britain's prime minister, Margaret Thatcher, being opposed to further sanctions being imposed) led to Canada's Joe Clark being made chairman of a Committee of Foreign Ministers on South Africa. The CHOGM having decided to set up a long-distance educational network, using video and satellite technology, especially to meet the needs of developing countries, Canada agreed to provide half the initial costs.

AN ACCORD BETWEEN ACCT AND CFTC, 1988

A Protocole d'Accord was signed in Paris in October 1988 whereby the ACCT and the CFTC agreed to finance French-language training for Namibians and South African nominees of the nationalist movements. The secretary general of the ACCT, Paul Okumba d'Okwatesgue, and the managing director of CFTC, William H. Montgomery, a Canadian, were the signatories. In this accord, the ACCT agreed to provide the CFTC with approximately $200,000 toward the training of up to 25 Namibians and South Africans at the Village du Benin in Lomé, West Africa. This stemmed from a decision of heads of government of the francophone countries in 1987 to provide training awards for victims of apartheid. The CFTC undertook to match the ACCT contribution and to ensure that the funds are used to maximum advantage.

In his address at the ceremony, delivered in French and English, Montgomery stressed the common aim of the ACCT and the CFTC to work toward many goals, one of the greatest of which was "to abolish completely the perfidious system of apartheid."

DAKAR, 1989

At the third francophone summit held in Dakar, Senegal in May 1989, the Canadian government played a prominent part in ensuring that problems of human rights would be tackled directly for the first time at the summit. Once again, the premiers of Quebec and of New Brunswick enjoyed participatory status at this gathering of French-speaking "countries."

In a report published before the Dakar meeting, Amnesty International had accused more than 30 francophone countries of violating human rights. In its 1989 report, it claimed that the governments of four countries— Chad, Haiti, Madagascar and Burundi—kill people outside the law and that 11 nations practice torture. Joe Clark said that the previous summit in Quebec City in 1987 avoided dealing with abuses of human rights in member countries because their association was too young and fragile. Instead, leaders criticized South African apartheid. This time, however, Canadian officials lobbied the francophone leaders about abuses of human rights.

COMPLEMENTARITIES

It is a sobering reflection on the barriers which different languages still constitute that little is known of La Francophonie in the anglophone world and little of the Commonwealth in the francophone world. Arguably, this mutual indifference or incomprehension has lessened in recent years, but not dramatically.

Canada is something of a notable exception to this prevailing public ignorance. A few—very few—top officials in the small secretariat of these two international associations know of the work the other body does, and there are even some small programs of cooperation between these two international bureaucracies, as has been briefly indicated above. Yet the record suggests that both of these bodies are eminently useful, rather inexpensive, albeit secondary, instruments for the conduct of multilateral diplomacy. They are of some value to Canada and to the world at large.

Finally, it seems appropriate to endorse a judgement of the late John Wendell Holmes, who wrote that "any suggestions that Canada might take over (active) leadership roles from Britain and France . . . get little encouragement in Ottawa. Canadians are anti-imperialist not so much by conviction as by laziness—and a surfeit of territory. They prefer to be a supplementary rather than a leading power." This is how the value of the Commonwealth and La Francophonie should be adjudged for Canada in the 1990s: useful forums for multilateral, mostly conference diplomacy. They are useful secondary rather than major instruments in Canada's continuing international concerns. They are also broadly acceptable, relatively uncontroversial instrumentalities for most of the Canadian public.

In short, membership of the Commonwealth and of La Francophonie chimes with certain prevailing dispositions in the Canadian public mind:

- a distaste for imperial dominances and a refusal of Canada and Canadians to assume imperial or neo-colonial roles;
- a determination to maintain a distinctive Canadian identity and contribution to international affairs despite Canada's relative juniority in some of its more onerous and important associations, such as NATO and the Group of Seven, and the dominance of the United States, the colossus to the south, in Canada's economy and in many other aspects of Canada's nationhood;
- a preference for gradual rather than radical change; and
- a pragmatic, practical approach to diplomacy.

FURTHER READING

Annuaire de la Francphonie. Paris, yearly.

Delvoie, Louis. "The Commonwealth in Canadian Foreign Policy." *The Round Table* 310 (April 1989):137–43.

Doxey, Margaret. *Canada and the Evolution of the Modern Commonwealth.* Canadian Institute of International Affairs, Behind the Headlines. Toronto: November 1982.

———. *The Commonwealth Secretariat and the Contemporary Commonwealth.* Cambridge Commonwealth Series. London: Macmillan, 1989.

Deniau, Xavier. *La Francophonie.* Paris: Presses Universitaries de France, 1983.

Groom, A. J. R., and Paul Taylor, eds. *The Commonwealth in the 1980s.* London: Macmillan, 1983.

Painchaud, Paul, ed. *From Mackenzie King to Pierre Trudeau. Forty Years of Canadian Diplomacy 1945–1985.* Quebec: Les Presses de L'Université Laval, 1989. Especially chapter 10 by Gilles Lalande, "La francophonie et la politique étrangère du Canada", pp. 217–248.

Smith, Arnold, with Clyde Sanger. *Stitches in Time. The Commonwealth in World Politics.* London: André Deutsch Ltd, 1981. The Commonwealth and La Francophonie are compared especially at pp. 177–82.

Tetu, Michel. *La Francophonie: Histoire, Problématique, Perspectives.* (Montréal: Guérin Littérature, 1987.

Viatte, Auguste. *La Francohonie.* Paris: Librairie Larousse, 1969.

The Commonwealth Yearbook. Her Majesty's Stationery Office, London, annual.

DEFENSE AND DISARMAMENT

THOMAS S. AXWORTHY

Fashioning a security policy appropriate for a world of competing sovereign nations, ideological passion, big power rivalry, technological change and nuclear threat is never easy for any state. In Canada's case, the task is made even more difficult because the national territory to be defined is the size of a continent. As military historian Desmond Morton has asked succinctly: how can a coherent defense policy emerge in a country that is simultaneously indefensible and invulnerable?

In area, Canada is the second largest country in the world and, lapped by three oceans, it has the longest coast line. But with a population of only 27 million, Canada is one of the most sparsely settled nations on earth and each of its neighbors—the United States and the states of the former Soviet Union—has roughly 10 times the population, greater economic strength and vastly more powerful militaries. With over a third of its gross national product dependent upon trade—one of the highest percentages in the world— Canada has more than a passing interest in securing a safe and cooperative international environment. Because of this, and due to its historic ties with Britain, France and the United States, Canada is the only member of NATO, apart from the United States, that contributes to the defense of North America, the North Atlantic and Western Europe. For a thinly populated state with a vast territory to defend, the scope of Canada's international obligations is quite striking.

Canada is also wealthy, but not wealthy enough to meet all its foreign and domestic commitments. With a 1991–1992 GDP of $683 billion, Canadian per capita income is among the highest in the world. Canadians have used this wealth to create a highly developed welfare state. But Canada has also been living beyond its means. Since the late 1960s the federal government has run a persistent annual deficit that exploded in the 1980s to the $30 billion level. In 1991–92, for example, the federal government has again projected a deficit of $30.5 billion, similar in proportion to a U.S. deficit of $300 billion.

Among the most basic decisions of any state is how much of the national treasure to allocate to security, consumption or investment. For the past

25 years, Canada has consciously decided to favor priorities other than military spending. The Trudeau government is usually blamed or praised, depending on one's point of view, for this decision, but in fact it was the Pearson government that began the trend in 1964.

Arriving in office with an ambitious program for social reform, the Pearson government immediately cut the defense budget by 11.6% in real terms, put the Department of National Defense on a fixed formula of spending increases less than inflation, and initiated the radical restructuring of the three services into a single unified structure. Unification was supposed to reduce overhead costs so that the defense department would still have an adequate budget for equipment purchases. In 1969 the new Trudeau government froze the defense budget for an additional three years, so that by 1975, when a modest program of rearmament began, the defense budget had been squeezed for a decade. Since 1975 the Department of National Defense has received real increases greater than inflation almost every year, and by the early 1980s, the capital portion of the budget had been restored to 25% of the total defense expenditure—the original goal of the Pearson unification reform. But despite recent increases, the percentage of federal government expenditure dedicated to defense has declined from 21% in 1964–65 to 8.3% in 1988–89. Defense expenditure as a percentage of GNP declined a full percentage point over the same period from 3.1% in 1965 to 2.1% in 1988.

Canada's decision over the past quarter century to favor social security spending and economic investment rather than defense has naturally shrunk the size of the defense establishment: military manpower has declined from 120,412 in 1964 to 85,627 in 1987. By way of comparison, the Netherlands with a population of 15 million spends about 3% of its GNP to maintain a force of 103,000. Although Canada's defense budget is the sixth largest within NATO, at 2%, Canada's proportion of GNP allocated to defense is well below the NATO average of 3.8%.

Canada, then, is caught on the horns of a dilemma. For a host of historical and foreign policy reasons, it has agreed to entertain an impressive number of international obligations; for equally valid financial and domestic reasons, it has limited defense spending and reduced the capabilities required to carry out its commitments. It is firmly ensnared in what Professor Samuel P. Huntington of Harvard University has termed "the Lippmann Gap."

CANADA'S LIPPMANN GAP

Writing in 1943, Walter Lippmann judged that "foreign policy consists in bringing into balance, with a comfortable surplus of power in reserve, the nation's commitments and the nation's power." If a balance exists, and the public supports the objectives of the commitments, the policy will command support. "If commitments exceed power," writes Huntington, "insolvency results which generates deep political dissension."

In Canada, in recent years, there has been dissension aplenty. An impressive number of analysts and parliamentary reports have castigated Canada's defense policy for overpromising and under-delivering. Reputable scholars such as Joseph Jockel and Joel Sokolsky have even recommended that the United States take the extraordinary step of urging the NATO Alliance to restrict Canada's participation in NATO-related activities such as the Defense Planning Committee. Canada's most powerful business lobby, the Business Council on National Issues, has also argued for increased military spending while recommending equally strongly that the government reduce the deficit. In a series of reports issued throughout the 1980s, the Special Committee of the Senate on National Defense totaled up the equipment needs of the forces and recommended that an additional $2.2 billion of defense spending a year for 10 years was the minimum necessary if Canada was to retain all its commitments and build a military equal to the task. John G. H. Halstead, a respected former Canadian ambassador to NATO, captures well the essence of the problem: "The chickens are now coming home to roost all at once. The gap between existing defense commitments and in-place capabilities has become dangerous just at a time when urgent action is called for to reduce the budget deficit and restore the economy."

Missing from most of these lamentations about Canada's defense record, however, is a broad conception of power. Military might is a traditional way of acquiring power but armed prowess ultimately depends upon an economic base. If the productive core of an economy declines, in time there will not be sufficient resources to pay for armaments. Indeed, devoting too much of a society's capital to nonproductive military spending is a sure way to weaken the economy. The Soviet Union was a military colossus but an economic weakling, while Japan is the opposite. Unlike military power, economic power also has the advantage that it can be more readily used. Plentiful resources allow a state to invest abroad, purchase resources, contribute to multilevel agencies, and give foreign aid bilaterally. Military power is still a significant attribute but economic power is a far more supple resource in the interdependent world of the late 20th century.

Without real sacrifices from its citizens, Canada cannot afford to be *both* a significant economic and military power. Critics are correct that Canada can afford to pay for more defense: in the 1950s at the height of the Cold War, nearly 8% of the GNP was devoted to the military. But if Canada doubled its defense spending to the NATO average of 3.8% of GNP, or even met the Canadian Senate target of 2.34% of GNP, that money would have to come from somewhere—from either a multi-billion-dollar increase in the deficit, higher taxes, or less spending on social and economic infrastructure. In assessing Canada's overall power and influence, what would be gained from such a switch in priority? While maintaining only a modest military, Canada's economic strength has made it an important player in multilateral agencies such as the World Bank and the United Nations. It is a leading nation in the Commonwealth and La Francophonie. It devotes considerable sums to foreign aid. With only half of the population of Britain, for example, Canada has an economy two-thirds the size of the former "mother country," large enough to become a member of the Economic Summit and the Group of Seven monetary powers. As its critics are forever pointing out, Canada's percentage of defense outlay may rank only with Luxembourg and Iceland, but on issues of the world economy, Canada sits at the table with the United States, Germany and Japan.

In advocating a switch from economic and social investment to the military, defense analysts ignore another reality: there is *no* significant domestic constituency in Canada for sustained defense spending and there never has been. The Conservative Sir John A. Macdonald, Canada's founding prime minister, began the new dominion's defense policy by cutting militia estimates by two-thirds between 1871 and 1876. Showing a bipartisan devotion to low defense estimates, Sir Wilfrid Laurier, Macdonald's Liberal successor as prime minister, attacked the jingoism of his turn-of-the-century contemporaries: "There is a school in England and in Canada, a school which is perhaps represented on the floor of Parliament, a school which wants to bring Canada into the vortex of militarism which is the curse and blight of Europe. I am not prepared to endorse any such policy." Laurier was true to his word. On the eve of the Great War, Canada's regular forces numbered only 3,000 men. William Lyon Mackenzie King, Canada's longest-serving prime minister, followed the Macdonald-Laurier tradition of low military spending. In 1920, for example, during a debate on the militia, King put the question that Canadians have had difficulty in answering ever since: "The Minister says this expenditure is needed for the defense of Canada—defense against whom? There is no answer; there is no answer to be made."

Mackenzie King's pertinent question illustrates the paradox posed by Desmond Morton. Both Canada's indefensibility and invulnerability militate against military power. Ever since Europeans first settled Canada in the 1600s, there has been a lot of Canadian geography and relatively few Canadians. Whenever a real threat emerged, the rational response has been to seek allies. The few hundred French settlers of Quebec needed an alliance with the Huron nation to match the strength of the Iroquois in the Indian wars of 1630–80. Contemplating the threat from Manifest Destiny and 30 million Americans in the 1860s, the Fathers of Confederation knew that only the deterrent of the British Navy could provide security for the 2.5 million inhabitants of the Province of Canada. To meet the Cold War threat of a nuclear armed Soviet Union of 265 million, Canada joined in an alliance with the United States and Western Europe. Because there has always been too much territory, with too few people, in times of trouble Canada has always followed the sensible course of seeking out allies. As with any non-superpower, diplomacy rather than force is our first line of defense.

But if indefensibility operates on one level to reduce the viability of a military option—Canada could spend its entire budget on defense but still not have a margin of safety—a sense of invulnerability also lessens anxiety among Canadians. Who threatens Canada? Once the United States matured sufficiently so that forceful annexation of British North America was no longer a possibility, Canada was in the happy position of being a state without enemies. In the modern age, like anyone else, Canada is threatened by international instability, and a nuclear attack on the United States would destroy Canada too, but the threat is general, not directed toward Canada alone. Since the War of 1812, when Canada fought with Britain against the United States, Canadians have fought abroad. To Canadians, military force is a power to be used to help friends in peril such as Britain or France, to uphold a principle such as collective security in Korea, or to stop other countries from fighting in operations such as the United Nations Emergency Force in the Gaza Strip. Force is not something that has been necessary to defend Canada's territory. "Canadians have come to consider war as an aberration," writes Desmond Morton, "beyond their control and, happily, beyond their shores."

In addition to the ideas on power, commitment and balance quoted earlier, Walter Lippman wrote in *U.S. Foreign Policy: Shield of the Republic* that a nation is secure to the extent to which it is not in danger of having to sacrifice core values. Security, then, can be measured in an objective sense by assessing the strength of threats to acquired values and in a subjective sense, by the absence of fear that such values will be attacked. Objectively, Canada faces no direct threat to its security, and subjectively, Canadians have no fears about invasions from abroad. Put simply, Canada is one of the most secure places on earth. This too works against those who seek a greater military role.

THE 1987 WHITE PAPER ON DEFENSE

In June 1987, the Conservative government of Brian Mulroney responded to the commitments-capability gap with a new White Paper on Defense, Canada's first since 1971. The document was a bold one. By recommending the acquisition of a fleet of 10 to 12 nuclear-powered attack submarines, the White Paper sought to transform in one stroke the cautious and modest traditions of Canadian defense policy. Uncharacteristically for Canada, it was a "call to arms." Four years after the White Paper, however, it is evident that no one has answered the call. The rationale of the White Paper has been shredded and Canada is more deeply ensnared than ever in the commitments-capability gap.

The underlying rationale of the White Paper was firmly rooted in a Pentagon-like assessment of the malign designs of the Soviet Union. Criticizing the 1971 White Paper of the Trudeau government for its unrealistic hopes for détente, the White Paper states that "the realities of the present, however, call for a more sober approach to international relations and the needs of security policy." Complete with pictures of the Berlin Wall, and maps filled with Soviet red, the White Paper asserts that "the new Soviet leadership continues to view the world as divided into two antagonistic camps . . . it continues to seek to translate military power into political gain." Seeking to jolt Canadians from their traditional benign view of the world, the White Paper's declaratory tone was the most hawkish in Canada's postwar history.

313

The timing of the White Paper, however, was not conducive to its theme. Soon after its release, the Soviet Union and the United States concluded an agreement on the abolition of intermediate missiles in Europe. One year later, President Ronald Reagan concluded an amiable summit in Moscow, with kind words about the Soviet leader Mikhail Gorbachev. The odds on the Canadian public ever accepting the White Paper's Manichean view of the world were long but *glasnost* and *perestroika* made the paper's geo-strategic assessment look spectacularly outdated only months after its conception.

The White Paper may have been spectacularly overtaken by events but it did attempt, at least, to rationalize commitments and resources. First, Canada's obligations were reduced: Canada's commitment to supply Norway with a brigade in times of crisis was dropped in favor of a consolidation of forces in southern Germany. But the real emphasis of the White Paper was on building up, not cutting back. Every element of the armed forces was promised new equipment. The highlights included:

- Creating a three-ocean navy by acquiring 10–12 nuclear-powered submarines, construction of six new frigates, the acquisition of new minesweepers, and the purchase of modern helicopters.
- Reinforcing surveillance by participation in the North Warning System (replacing the Distant Early Warning Line) and new aircraft purchases of six long-range patrol aircraft, and additional CF-18s.
- Strengthening territorial defenses and the NATO contribution with a Total Force concept of 180,000 made up of 90,000 regulars and 90,000 reserves (an increase from the existing level of 20,000), the purchase of new tanks, and by consolidating Canada's existing efforts in southern Germany.

The White Paper, however, did not really offer a "new" policy. With the exception of the abandonment of Canada's Air-Sea Transportable Combat Group (CAST) commitment to Norway, existing defense obligations were confirmed. But something was promised to everyone—the Canadian Forces (navy, air force, army and reserves), as well as both the Europeans and the United States.

But underneath the sizzle of the White Paper, there was an important catch. The White Paper was to be financed out of minimum annual budget increases of 2% over a 15-year period, with major equipment purchases to be funded on a case-by-case basis. Yet, the Department of National Defense estimated that it would need on average a 5% annual budget increase after inflation to finance the re-equipment package. After all, it was the 2% formula introduced by a Liberal government in 1964 that has been blamed for starting the process of "rust out" of the Canadian Armed Forces.

Canada's traditional reluctance to spend money on defense was never addressed by the Conservative document. Its authors simply hoped that the money would eventually be found. While praising the White Paper as "artful and innovative," Charles Doran of the Johns Hopkins School for Advanced International Studies made the point that:

> . . . if Canada really is going to buy a Class 8 Icebreaker, finance new frigates, update Tribal Class destroyers, provide replacement for lost CF-18s, assume its share of the costs of the North Warning System, properly equip its European forces, increase the reserves to 90,000, all on a budgeted two per cent annual increase in defense spending after inflation, magic will have to be performed.

Financial magic, however, was in short supply. In 1988 the Conservative government of Brian Mulroney was returned to office and the prime minister campaigned, in part, on his promise of new defense rearmament. But in April 1989 the financial underpinnings of the White Paper collapsed. The minister of finance announced that while "the basic parameters of the White Paper remain the defense policy of the government," the planned spending increases of the defense budget would be cut by $2.7 billion over the next five years. Instead of expansion, 14 military bases would be closed instead. The centerpiece of the White Paper—the acquisition of nuclear submarines—was shelved. More bad news followed. A year after the 1989 budget tore a gaping hole in the spending assumptions of the White Paper, the 1990 budget announced that defense spending would be subjected to additional cuts of over $600 million from 1990 to 1994. The construction of a Polar 8 Icebreaker project was also canceled, leaving the Arctic with neither nuclear submarines nor the surface capability to ensure sovereignty. In the 1991 budget the Mulroney government restored the 1990 cuts by increasing defense spending by $600 million to pay for the Gulf War, but the equipment assumptions of the White Paper are still in tatters. In the spring of 1991 Vice Admiral Chuck Thomas resigned from the Canadian armed forces in protest against the funding cutbacks and the lack of policy, a move which "confirms the confusion and utter lack of political direction on defense policy from the Mulroney government," according to Jeffrey Simpson of the *Globe and Mail,* one of Canada's leading journalists. Canada's commitments-capability gap is alive and well.

Breaking with tradition in its strong denunciation of the Soviets, boldly promising an unprecedented peacetime rearmament program, the 1987 White Paper was nonetheless entirely conventional in the roles and priorities it assigned to the armed forces. In April 1969, for example, the first Trudeau government announced that Canada's four defense priorities were (1) the surveillance of Canadian territory and coastlines to protect national sovereignty; (2) the defense of North America in cooperation with U.S. forces; (3) the fulfillment of such NATO commitments as may be agreed upon; and (4) the performance of such international peacekeeping roles as Canada may assume. In the 1987 White Paper the same roles re-emerge: (1) maintenance of strategic deterrence; (2) credible conventional defence (NATO); (3) protection of Canadian sovereignty; (4) peaceful settlement of international disputes; and (5) effective arms control. Governments may change but strategic realities, it seems, endure.

THE WESTERN ALLIANCE

In 1991–92, the $12.7 billion budget of the Department of National De-fense supports a modest, all-volunteer armed force of 85,627, which in-cludes the army, navy and air force. Maritime Command has an operational force of 20 destroyer-frigates, three submarines, various support vessels and 18 long-range patrol aircraft. Mobile Command, the land element of the armed services, has a force of 22,500 located in three brigades across Can-ada (18,400 regulars) and the four Canadian Mechanized Brigade Groups situated in southern Germany (4,100 soldiers are stationed in Germany, with plans for a further 1,400 to be flown over from Canada in a crisis). The army has 114 main battle tanks. The air force has seven air groups, six based in Canada under Air Command and one based in Europe under Canadian Forces Europe: the main weapon of the air force is 138 modern CF-18 fighters, with 44 aircraft assigned to the three tactical fighter squad-rons of the 1st Canadian Air Group in Germany.

This force, like its predecessors, is committed to four major defense re-sponsibilities: to contribute to collective defense within NATO, to defend the North American continent in partnership with the United States, to protect Canada's sovereignty and to contribute to the peacekeeping opera-tions of the United Nations. Although their significance has varied with time and changing circumstances, these four responsibilities, in one form or another, have been outlined in the 1959 and 1987 Conservative Defense White Papers and the 1964 and 1971 Liberal White Papers. This consen-sus is challenged by Canada's social democratic New Democratic Party, which announced in April 1988 that if the NDP formed a government, it would not renew the NORAD agreement and would begin to work toward withdrawal from NATO. These positions, however, are not widely sup-ported by public opinion and the NDP again placed a poor third in the 1988 election.

NATO has been the cornerstone of Canada's security policy since 1949, so much so that Prime Minister Trudeau once declared that "we had no defense policy . . . except that of NATO. And our defense policy had determined all our foreign policy." In 1948, Canada was the first western nation to advocate explicitly a formal European-North American alliance to deter the Soviet Union and during the NATO negotiations, Canada won acceptance of Article II, which pledged that the nations in alliance would strengthen free institutions, encourage economic collaboration and work toward developing an Atlantic community. The fears arising from the Ko-rean War turned NATO from a loose guarantee pact into an integrated theater army. Canada contributed an armored brigade and 11 fighter squad-rons. By 1956, the annual report of the Department of National Defense stated that "almost everything Canada is now doing in the military field relates quite naturally to our participation in NATO."

This "heyday of the alliance," as John Gellner has described it, lasted from NATO's founding until the early 1960s. For the past 20 years, how-ever, the prevailing mood has been one of skepticism. NATO's appeal to Canadians has waned because of excesses of the Canadian military, a changing perception of the Soviet threat, and the transformation of European power. During the period of John Diefenbaker's Conservative Government (1957–63), the Canadian military orchestrated a campaign in favor of the acquisition of nuclear weapons. By 1963, Canada had purchased three weapons systems with a nuclear capability, and when Diefenbaker balked at the final step of arming these platforms with nuclear warheads, both the Supreme Allied Commander of NATO, General Lauris Norstad, and the Kennedy administration issued statements critical of the Canadian government. The Conservatives disintegrated over the defense issue, and, following the victory of Lester Pearson's Liberals in 1963, Canada acquired tactical nuclear weapons under a "two key" arrangement with the United States.

But if the Department of National Defense won the battle over nuclear weapons, it also lost the war. Canada's military had endorsed without question the 1957 NATO doctrine of limited nuclear war. This mute acceptance of alliance priorities over Canadian needs typified the absence of independent strategic thinking. In time, many Canadians came to resent the subservient stance of the department and the strong-arm tactics of the Americans. Détente further reduced the salience of NATO. And as Western Europe's recovery restored the wealth and power of that region, a good many Canadians began to ask why Canadian troops should be in Germany when there was so much of Canada to defend? The troops after all were only sent to NATO as a temporary gesture when Europe was weak. Acting on this logic, in 1969 the first Trudeau government cut Canada's NATO contribution in half.

The new Mulroney government assumed office in 1984 much more convinced about the virtues of collective security and NATO than the departing Trudeau administration. One of the first defense decisions of the Conservatives was to augment the Canadian forces in Europe by 1,200 men, bringing the brigade closer to war strength. And the rhetoric of the White Paper is certainly ringing enough with declarations such as "the Soviet conventional threat to Canada and Canadian interests is often overlooked in the face of the nuclear menace."

But doubts persist. There are reports that an earlier version of the Defense White Paper proposed to withdraw Canadian forces from Central Europe, pre-position heavy equipment in Norway, build a transit base in Scotland, and air transport the entire brigade to Europe in time of crisis with a strengthened commitment to Norway. Subjected to severe criticism by the German and British governments, the minister of national defense, Perrin Beatty, decided on the alternate course of dropping the northern commitment to Norway in favor of a consolidation in Germany. With a brigade already in Germany, troops in Canada formerly committed to Norway will now reinforce the Central Front, meaning that army planners intend to provide a full division of 16,500 men to Europe in time of crisis.

To be effective in this enhanced role, however, the army requires new tanks, and therein lies the rub. In 1976, the Trudeau government approved the purchase of 128 Leopard 1 main battle tanks. Advances in Soviet armor and firepower, however, made this relatively new equipment obsolete. The army hopes to acquire 250 new tanks at a cost of $2.5 billion. But the 2%

spending commitment mentioned in the White Paper will not cover such a large purchase, so like the navy, which hopes to replace its nuclear submarine program with conventional submarines, and the air force, which has requested billions for new long-range patrol aircraft and additional CF-18's, the army must stand in line and pray that a future cabinet will make the money available. It is unlikely that such prayers will ever be answered: indeed, even the 2% spending commitment of the White Paper was shattered with the $2.7 billion worth of cuts announced in the 1989 budget. Unrealistic, even in the heady days of 1987, the equipment dreams of the armed forces have now turned into a nightmare.

NATO and the Warsaw Pact have recently signed a treaty reducing conventional armies in Europe. If the present entente between the United States and the former Soviet Union continues, mutual and balanced force reductions in Europe will proceed at the same time as deep cuts in American and former Soviet strategic nuclear arsenals. If the United States is able to reduce the size of its ground forces in Europe as part of a general reduction, there will be intense pressure in Canada to do the same. The White Paper commitment for a European division and the army's dream of new tanks will literally fall victim to a new era of arms limitations. But reducing forces in Europe is not the same as "withdrawing from NATO," despite the claims of the Europeans. NATO is the *North Atlantic* Treaty Organization, not the Western European Treaty Organization. If Canada does decide at some future date to reduce its commitment in Europe—and tanks in Germany certainly have less public appeal than ships or aircraft in the Arctic—then Canada would be well advised to argue that it is simply transferring forces from one area of NATO concern to another.

DEFENDING NORTH AMERICA

Canada's second major commitment—Canadian-U.S. cooperation for continental defense—dates from the Ogdensburg Agreement of 1940 and the creation of the Permanent Joint Board of Defense. Since 1957, Canada has contributed to strategic deterrence by agreeing to integrate its air defense forces with those of the United States in the North American Aerospace Defense Command. Historically, Canada's armies in World Wars I and II were under the control of the British, and today in NORAD, an American general commands Canada's air defense, and the American Supreme Allied Commander of NATO commands Canada's forces in Europe. Canada may be the only country in the world never to have had a national commander ultimately responsible for the conduct of its armed forces.

Technology has driven the relative importance of Canadian territory to American deterrence. In the 1950s, Canada's North was a critically important piece of real estate occupying the most direct bomber route between what was then the Soviet Union and the United States. Canada and the United States built the Distant Early Warning Line (DEW Line) of northern radars and the NORAD agreement was consummated in 1957. In the 1960s, ballistic missiles replaced the bomber as the primary threat and active antibomber defense atrophied. In the 1980s, the cruise missile suddenly elevated the bomber threat and the possibility of massive U.S. investment in antiballistic missile (ABM) defense through the Strategic Defense Initiative ("Star Wars") heightened fears that Canada's North would once again become the front line in the Soviet-American rivalry.

Amid controversy, in 1985 the Mulroney government approved Canadian participation in the North Warning System, to replace the Distant Early Warning Line, and in 1986, NORAD was again renewed for a five-year term. Critics made much of the potential linkage between NORAD and the Strategic Defense Initiative. For its part, the White Paper on Defense blandly announced that "should the results of our studies and those of the Unites States show that space-based radar is feasible, practical and affordable, the Department will have to devote, over the next 15 years, significant resources to the establishment of a space-based surveillance system for North American air defense." In fact, if a future American administration decides to deploy an antiballistic missile defense system, it is certain that the United States will have to request the use of Canadian territory for the basing of ABM components. Acceptance would mean a greater U.S. presence in the North: rejection might entail a crisis in Canadian-American relations. The Strategic Defense Initiative is the spectre that haunts Canadian defense.

SOVEREIGNTY

In July 1985, the U.S. Coast Guard icebreaker *Polar Sea* passed through Canada's Northwest Passage without acknowledging Canada's claim to jurisdiction over the area. The resulting outcry focused attention on the surveillance and control responsibility of the armed forces over Canada's 44,375 miles (71,000 kilometers) of coastline, and 2.5 million square miles (6.3 million square kilometers) of Arctic archipelago. The voyage of the *Polar Sea* may have been the determinant factor leading to the White Paper's dramatic announcement that Canada would spend $8 billion to acquire a fleet of 10–12 nuclear-powered submarines.

In 1971 the Trudeau White Paper on Defense made sovereignty the number one priority of the armed forces. Long-range patrol aircraft were purchased and NORAD's air zones were re-allocated to ensure that Canadian fighters had the sole responsibility for peacetime control and identification of aircraft over Canadian airspace. The 1987 White Paper continued this thrust with the announcement that five new air bases would be constructed in the North and that a Northern training center would be established in the 1990s.

But it was the government's plans for a three-ocean navy that provoked the most debate. Declaring that the Artic has "become an operating area for submarines," the White Paper made a case that nuclear-powered submarines were "the only proven vehicle, today or for the foreseeable future, capable of sustained operations under the ice" and that "through their mere presence, nuclear-powered submarines can deny an opponent the use of sea areas."

319

Opponents immediately attacked the costs of the submarine option as being exorbitant, inappropriate for a country that has signed the Non-Proliferation Treaty, and ultimately futile against any possible foe. B. J. Danson, a former minister of national defense in the Trudeau government, argued that "we shouldn't pretend that the Arctic threat alone is justification for acquiring nuclear subs while bleeding a maritime budget expected to go in two directions at once." Both opposition parties opposed the initiative and public opinion polls were very negative about the project, and soon after the 1988 election the government announced the cancellation of the program.

Ironically, the Mulroney government proposed a closer integration of the American and Canadian economies through the 1988 Free Trade Agreement at the same time as it was promoting a vast naval expansion to protect Canada's Arctic claims from those same Americans. Canada's partner in Arctic air defense is its opponent in Arctic jurisprudence. As defense analyst Nils Orvik has written, Canada's sovereignty policy is really "defense against help."

PEACEKEEPING

In 1956, external affairs minister Lester Pearson persuaded the United Nations to send a peacekeeping force to Suez and the Gaza Strip to end the British and French occupation of the Canal Zone. Pearson received a Nobel Prize for his efforts and a Canadian tradition was born. In 1964, Prime Minister Pearson made peacekeeping a central focus of the 1964 White Paper on Defense. Peacekeeping may be the only activity of the Canadian military with a significant defense constituency. Since the founding of the United Nations in 1945, 77,000 Canadians have participated in 18 different operations around the world. Peacekeeping commitments flow from an established policy whereby up to 2,000 Canadian Forces members can be called on for peacekeeping duties at any one time. The continued vitality of the peacekeeping mission was demonstrated in 1988, when the Mulroney government agreed to send 500 Canadians to Iran and Iraq to police a cease-fire in the Gulf War, in 1989, when 237 Canadian personnel were assigned to the UN Transition Group in Namibia, and in 1992, when Canada agreed to send a large force to Yugoslavia. "Warriors for Peace" is a role Canadians relish.

ARMS CONTROL AND DISARMAMENT

The 1987 White Paper declared that "arms control, like defense, is one of the pillars of Canadian security policy." The first postwar Canadian action in supporting this principle was also the most significant. In 1942, a British-Canadian team of scientists began to research urgently the problem of nuclear power. Canadian uranium from Great Bear Lake became a source for the first American atomic bomb. In September 1945, Canada's reactor at Chalk River went critical; if possession of reactors is a fair criterion, only the United States and Canada were atomic powers immediately after the war. But the Canadian government never considered making atomic weapons; in November 1945, Prime Minister King explicitly announced Canada's support of international control of atomic weapons and the peaceful uses of nuclear power. Canada's early example of restraint is a hopeful sign that the proliferation of nuclear weapons is not an inevitability.

Since the 1940s, Canadian governments have adopted an active role in multilateral arms-limitation talks. Howard Green, the minister of external affairs during most of John Diefenbaker's tenure as prime minister, was a passionate supporter of nuclear disarmament and vigorously opposed the efforts of the Department of National Defense to acquire tactical nuclear weapons. In Canada's postwar history, however, it is the figure of Pierre Elliott Trudeau who is most identified with the effort to persuade the superpowers to end the arms race. Proponents of arms control believe that the real threat facing Canadian security is not the malicious intentions of the former Soviets, but the dynamics of the arms race itself. To slow that arms race, non-superpowers such as Canada can lead through example, by declaratory support for bilateral or multilateral talks, and through attempts to influence the political environment. During his 16 years in power (1968–84), Trudeau tried all three routes.

First, the force of example: as a private citizen, Trudeau was passionately opposed to the Canadian military's program to acquire tactical nuclear weapons. Upon becoming prime minister, he dropped any Canadian nuclear roles within NATO and replaced nuclear weapon systems with conventional ones. By his retirement in 1984, Canada once more had a non-nuclear military. Second, the power of ideas: In 1978, at the UN Special Session on Disarmament, he outlined a "strategy of suffocation" to control and limit nuclear weapons before the virus of the arms race took hold. Canada supported measures such as the Comprehensive Test Ban, a prohibition on the production of all fissionable material for weapons purposes; and stringent controls on the export of nuclear reactors. Third, attempts to influence the conduct of East-West relations: In 1983, following the Soviet destruction of a Korean airliner, and the deterioration this caused in Soviet-American relations, Trudeau personally visited leaders around the globe arguing for restraint in the rhetoric of the Cold War and attempting to inject some political will into the languishing arms limitations talks. The Trudeau Peace Initiative was the most ambitious (though not particularly successful) Canadian effort to influence the strategic environment since Pearson's Suez initiative in 1956.

There has been a large and vocal domestic peace movement in Canada for some time. Like the mass movements in Europe opposed to NATO's nuclear policy, thousands of Canadians took to the streets in 1982–83 to protest Canadian permission for American testing of unarmed cruise missiles over Canadian territory. Most Canadians agreed that it was the politics and weaponry of both superpowers, not just the Soviet Union, which was at the heart of East-West tension. In late 1987, a survey sponsored by the Canadian Institute for International Peace and Security demonstrated that the public did not share the assumptions of the White Paper on Defense that "the principal direct threat to Canada continues to be a nuclear attack on North America by the Soviet Union." Only 5% believed the Soviets to be the greatest threat, while 8% thought our ally the United States posed even *more* of a problem. Most thought that either the spread of nuclear weapons to smaller countries (29%) or the superpower arms race (25%) was the greatest threat. Further, only 29% supported the idea that the best way to prevent wars is for the West to increase its military strength so as to be more powerful than the Soviets, while 71% were opposed. These findings represent a significant change since 1962, when a similar survey revealed that Canadians thought that the West should seek military superiority over the U.S.S.R. Canadians favor arms control, not arms build-up. Given these findings, the government's difficulty in selling the rationale of the White Paper becomes more understandable.

The primary objective of arms control is to pursue military stability at lower force levels in order to enhance security. Canada has a vital and an *independent* stake in the outcome of the superpowers' arms discussions. While supporting general arms reductions, Canadian security policy requires the elimination of certain *kinds* of weapons. In the present strategic arms reduction talks (START), for example, the superpowers are discussing reducing their stockpiles to 6,000 warheads but excluding cruise missiles from any possible agreement. Yet, more than any other weapon, the cruise missile affects Canadian security because if ballistic missiles are controlled but air- or sea-launched cruise missiles are not, Canadian territory again becomes vital to North American security. Defenses would certainly be built to overcome the cruise threat and Canada would either have to invest billions in active defense or let the Americans do it. Either option is unpalatable. There are specific Canadian arms-limitations priorities which must be incorporated into the superpower agenda. The future of Canadian security may depend more on this factor than any other element of its defense posture.

Conclusion
Canada is one of the most secure places on earth. This is wonderful for Canadians but difficult for defense planners. Providing for an adequate military force is a question of policy in Canada, not a necessity. The Canadian armed forces contributed to Western deterrence, they maintain national sovereignty, aid the civil powers and help promote the aims of our foreign policy. But Canadians are reluctant to pay for the military when the basic rationale—defending the country—seems so remote.

This is readily apparent when one evaluates the most important Canadian contributions to international security in the postwar era. Foregoing the nuclear weapons option in 1945 is Canada's most significant contribution to arms control; peacekeeping—a non-military use of the military—is Canada's most notable contribution to stopping the spread of international violence; while unification of the armed forces to reduce costs and interservice rivalries may be its most distinctive—if controversial—contribution to military science.

Recent events have especially highlighted the contradictions inherent in Canada's defense posture. On the one hand, Canada's record in the two world wars, when its contribution was out of all proportion to its size, demonstrates that Canadians are hardly pacifists. Canadians recognize that force is an ever-present element in human affairs. In the summer of 1990 this lesson was vividly driven home by crises at home and abroad. Domestically, Mohawk land rights (a matter of federal responsibility) were challenged by a municipal government backed by the Sûreté de Québec (the provincial police force). Mohawk warriors at the reserves of Oka and Kahnaweke blockaded bridges, and a police officer was killed. To restore order the government of Quebec had to request the Canadian army to intervene. After a tense standoff, Canada's soldiers were able to defuse the crisis without the loss of additional lives. Little credit accrued to anyone in this affair, except the Canadian army. Experienced in keeping the peace, the army cooly discharged a potentially explosive mission.

Canada's military were barely off the front pages after the resolution of the Oka and Kahnawake crisis when Iraq invaded Kuwait in August 1990. Military issues again leapt to prominence. Canada went to war for the first time since Korea. While hardly a major player in the coalition effort, Canada contributed three warships to patrol the Persian Gulf, and a squadron of F-18s was sent to defend coalition positions. Defense turned to offense when on February 20, 1991, in the last days of the war, the F-18 squadron began to bomb Iraqi ground targets. Mercifully, Canadian forces suffered no casualties from this action, but the efficient and quiet way that the Canadian armed forces went about their tasks proved once again Canada's military was a critical foreign policy asset.

Yet, while basking in rare public acclaim for their performance at Oka and in the Gulf War, Canada's military entered the 1990s still facing a yawning commitments-capability gap. Decisions could not be avoided. In September 1991 the government announced that Canada's NATO forces would be reduced and in February 1992 the government shocked many by announcing that all of Canada's troops in Europe would be coming home. Revealingly the decision was announced in the budget, not in a defense White Paper.

A rapidly changing international environment further complicates defense planning. Mikhail Gorbachev's efforts to end the Cold War undermined the assumptions of the 1987 White Paper only months after it was published. Spending cutbacks followed in 1989 and 1990. In 1991 the pendulum swung back when the Department of Defense's budget was increased by $600 million to pay for the Gulf War. And just as conventional wisdom began to accept that the Cold War was finally over, and respected think tanks such as the Canadian Institute for International Peace and Security sponsored studies recommending large cuts in Canada's ground forces and radical changes in the NATO contribution, civil unrest in Yugoslavia demonstrated that Canadian troops still have a useful peacekeeping role to play in Europe. In late summer 1991, Gorbachev was overthrown in a coup by conservative forces, and then returned to power, only to resign a few months later. The world continues to be in turmoil and Canada's military may not be out of business just yet.

"The study of war," wrote Karl von Clausewitz, the German philosopher of force, "is paradoxical." Never more so than when applied to the indefensible and invulnerable peaceable kingdom of Canada.

FURTHER READING

Business Council on National Issues. *Canada's Defense Policy: Capabilities versus Commitments.* Ottawa: September 1984.

Byers, R.B. *Canadian Security and Defense: The Legacy and the Challenges.* Adelphi Paper 214. London: The International Institute for Strategic Studies, 1986.

Canada. The Department of National Defence. *Challenge and Commitment: A Defense Policy for Canada.* Ottawa: Department of National Defence, 1987.

Canada. Senate Subcommittee on National Defence. *Manpower in Canada's Armed Forces.* Ottawa: January, 1982, Senate Subcommittee on National Defence. *Canada's Maritime Defence.* Ottawa: May 1983; Senate Special Committee on National Defence. *Canada's Territorial Air Defence.* Ottawa: January 1985; and Senate Special Committee on National Defence. *Military Air Transport.* Ottawa: February 1986; Senate Special Committee on National Defence. *Canada's Land Forces.* Ottawa: October 1989.

Cox, David. "Arms Control Magic . . . Less is More." *Peace and Security* 3 (Summer 1988).

Dosman, Edgar J. "The Department of National Defence: The Steady Drummer." In *How Ottawa Spends: 1988/89 The Conservatives Heading into the Stretch,* edited by Katherine A. Graham. Ottawa: Carleton University Press, 1988.

Doran, Charles F. "Sovereignty Does Not Equal Security." *Peace and Security* 2 (Autumn 1987).

Gellner, John. *Canada in NATO.* Toronto: The Ryerson Press, 1970, p. 19.

Hampson, Fen Osler. "Call to Arms: Canadian National Security Policy." In *Canada Among Nations: A World of Conflict 1987,* edited by Maureen Appel Molot and Brian W. Tomlin. Toronto: James Lorimer and Co., 1988, p. 68.

Hasek, John. *The Disarming of Canada.* Toronto: Key Porter Books, 1987.

Huntington, Samuel P. "Coping with the Lippman Gap." *Foreign Affairs* 66 (1987/88): 453–77.

Ignatieff, George. *The Making of a Peacemonger.* Markham, Ontario: Penguin Books Canada Ltd., 1987.

Jockel, Joseph T., and Joel J. Sokolsky. *Canada and Collective Security: Odd Man Out.* New York: Praeger, 1986, p. 5.

Lippman, Walter. *U.S. Foreign Policy: Shield of the Republic.* Boston: Little, Brown and Co., 1943.

McLin, Jon. B. *Canada's Defence Policy, 1957–1963: The Problems of a Middle Power in Alliance.* Baltimore, The Johns Hopkins Press, 1967.

Morton, Desmond. *A Military History of Canada.* Edmonton: Hurtig Publishers, 1985.

Munton, Don. "Superpowers and National Security." *Peace and Security* 2 (Winter 1987–1988).

Newman, Peter C. *True North Not Strong and Free: Defending the Peaceful Kingdom in the Nuclear Age.* Toronto: McClelland and Stewart, 1983.

Orvik, Nils. "Defence Against Help." *Survival* 15 (September/October 1973): 228–32.

Porter, Gerald. *In Retreat: The Canadian Forces in the Trudeau Years.* Toronto: Deneau and Greenberg, 1979.

Simpson, Jeffrey. "Admiral Thomas' Departure Raises Issues." *Globe and Mail,* April 30, 1991.

York, Geoffrey. "Large Reductions Urged to Canadian Land Forces." *Globe and Mail,* June 25, 1991.

POLITICAL PARTIES

WILLIAM CHRISTIAN

Canada inherited the British parliamentary tradition, and with it acquired a party system in broad outlines like that in the United Kingdom. All the major parties are unquestionably committed to vie with one another by peaceful means for sufficient seats to entitle them to form the government. With the exception of the provincial Parti Québécois in Quebec, none envisages major constitutional changes within either Canada's parliamentary or federal system. In general, each party is dominated by its leader and his elected followers, who tend to be white, male, middle-aged, from either French or English ethnic backgrounds, and most of whom possess at least one university degree. Ideologically, Canadian politics is dominated by liberalism, although other beliefs such as socialism and democratic Toryism are held by substantial minorities.

CURRENT CHARACTER

When the Liberal party met in its first leadership convention to choose Sir Wilfrid Laurier's successor in 1919, it also adopted a comprehensive policy statement which outlined the main lines of the welfare state which the Liberal party would cautiously construct over the succeeding half century. However, during the leadership of Mackenzie King from 1919 to 1948, the business elements within the party consistently fought the extension of controls over industrial and financial activity and the transfer of wealth to poorer sectors of society. By the time Pierre Elliott Trudeau had seized the leadership in 1968, however, the welfare or reform wing of the party was in secure control, and his successor, corporate lawyer John Turner, found that he was so dependent on these forces that he could not lead the party in the more business-oriented direction he previously had preferred.

In foreign affairs, the Liberals considered themselves consistently nationalistic. In the first instance, in the 1920s, '30s and '40s their concern was directed to freeing Canada from the remaining vestiges of colonialism. Subsequently, prodded by Walter Gordon who was Liberal finance minister in the mid-'60s, the Liberal party began increasingly to worry about the impact of American ownership of Canadian natural resources and manufacturing capacity. Under Lester Pearson and increasingly under Trudeau, Liberal governments adopted measures such as the Foreign Investment Review Act (FIRA), which sought to reclaim important sectors of the Canadian economy from foreign control. In 1988 John Turner chose to make the Free Trade Agreement (FTA) with the United States virtually the only theme in his campaign. He branded it the "Sale of Canada Act" and openly suggested that his party would abrogate the treaty should it come to power.

Historically the Progressive Conservative Party has been the pro-British party concerned with maintaining the imperial connection both for its own sake and as a counterweight to the influence of the United States. In both 1891 and 1911 the Conservatives won election on a platform opposing closer trade ties with the United States; and as late as the 1958 Conservative government of John Diefenbaker, the Conservatives sought to forge closer links with the United Kingdom. During the 1970s the Conservatives came increasingly under the influence of the business wing of their party and, partly in response to what was seen as Trudeau's increasing anti-Americanism, began to argue for a closer and more sympathetic understanding with the United States. When the Royal Commission on the Economic Union and Development Prospects for Canada under the direction of former Liberal finance minister Donald Macdonald reported in favor of a Free Trade Agreement with the United States, Prime Minister Brian Mulroney quickly made this policy the central thrust of his government's first period in office, and won the 1988 election on precisely this theme.

Both of Canada's major political parties share a long-standing commitment to membership in and support for international institutions such as the United Nations. They are committed to continued Canadian memberships in NATO and NORAD and will likely continue to make substantial contributions to United Nations peacekeeping forces.

In terms of domestic politics, the Conservatives historically have favored what former Conservative leader Robert Stanfield called "strong government, but government limited in extent." The effect of this has been that, particularly from 1957 when John Diefenbaker assumed the leadership, the Conservatives have not been uniformly hostile to extensions of the welfare state. During the 1970s as the business wing gained in influence, the Conservatives, worried by the size of the budget deficit, sought ways to pare down the role of government. The minority government of Prime Minister Joe Clark in 1979 proposed to sell the state-owned oil company Petro-Canada, and this became the major issue of the 1980 campaign which led to its defeat. The Mulroney government, which came to office in 1984, believed in the importance of privatization, but, worried by the Clark experience, it moved cautiously to implement its policies. The government also lowered personal income tax rates, especially for wealthier taxpayers, and moved in 1989 to implement a Goods and Services Tax (GST) to lower the budget deficit.

The formation of the New Democratic Party marked a decision by the mainstream of the Canadian trade union movement that it needed close institutional ties with a major Canadian political party if it were to achieve many of the social and economic goals it sought for its members. In general the NDP has supported the extensions of the welfare state undertaken by

Liberal governments, and has pressed for a more comprehensive transfer of wealth to those groups it considers socially and economically underprivileged. It has been in the forefront of most women's issues. In foreign affairs it is the most radical of the three major parties. It supports Canadian withdrawal from both NORAD and NATO, although its current policy is that an NDP government would not leave NATO during its first term in office.

ORIGINS

When Lord Durham published his report on the causes of the 1837 rebellions in Upper and Lower Canada (now Ontario and Quebec, respectively), he noted the presence already of two parties. The one, the French, had "been viewed as a democratic party, contending for reform." The other, the English, was a "conservative minority, protecting the menaced connexion with the British Crown and the supreme authority of the Empire."

Like most things Canadian, Canada's political parties originated when European ideas were put to the test of explaining the new world of North America. The settlers who came to the virgin forests of British North America brought with them not only their household furnishings, clothes and tools; they also came with settled beliefs about the relationship of man to God, the state and his fellows.

The American scholar Louis Hartz, in his celebrated book *The Founding of New Societies* (1964), argued that one of the distinguishing features of the United States was that it was a "fragment society." Those who had settled it were overwhelmingly liberal in their ideological outlook, and its ideological purity had been enhanced first with the expulsion and flight of the Tories after the victorious revolution, and then with the defeat of the southern planter aristocracy in the Civil War.

The arrival of the Loyalist Tories strengthened the conservative ideological strain in the colonies of British North America, and established it as a powerful voice in the ideological conversation of the territory that would eventually unite to form the Dominion of Canada in 1867. Although these Tories by no means rejected outright the Lockean principles of the Whig Settlement of 1689 which formed the intellectual core of the American Republic, they were also sensitive to the claims of hierarchy and privilege, especially with respect to the monarchy, and to the importance of maintaining the social order against the perceived ravages of lawless democratic individualism.

The other important difference was the presence in Lower Canada of a French-speaking, Catholic majority. Most of the French settlement had occurred before 1763 when France ceded New France to the British Crown. Quebec had refused to join the rebellion of the American colonies, and had repulsed the expeditionary force sent to take it. After the French Revolution of 1789, most Quebecers saw themselves completely cut off from their original homeland. The revolution's anticlericalism persuaded many that it was Quebec's destiny to nourish true Catholicism in the face of its secular rejection in Europe.

327

Although parties existed in the various colonies before Confederation, it was the formation of the new dominion which created the new units. The Liberal-Conservative party under the leadership of Sir John A. Macdonald was the direct ancestor of the current Progressive Conservative party. It was formed as an alliance between the conservative *Bleus* of Quebec, the Tories of Ontario and those, especially in English Canada, who admired British Conservative leader Benjamin Disraeli and wished to imitate his policies in the new country.

The Liberal party was a more disparate grouping in its origins. It consisted of the anticlerical *Rouges* from Quebec, the Reformers from Ontario and generally all those who opposed Confederation itself, or were wary of either the integrity or the policies of Prime Minister Macdonald. It would take the leadership of Sir Wilfrid Laurier, who presided over the Liberal party's destinies from 1887 until 1919, to weave its strands into a more cohesive force.

Although throughout Canada's history it has been the Liberals and the Conservatives who have taken turns in forming the national government, one of the most striking differences between Canada and the United States has been the presence north of the border of an enduring social democratic party. Socialism drew on three factors. First, the presence of the Tory strain in Canada meant that there was already a commitment to collectivism which socialism could adapt, and a belief in privilege which it could oppose. Second, Canada's continuing ties with Great Britain as part of the British Empire kept it open to ideological developments there, especially the rise of the Labour party. The third element was Christianity, especially the Social Gospel movement that was so important in Western Canada in the first two decades of this century.

It was not until 1932 that socialism established a major institutional presence with the founding of the Co-operative Commonwealth Federation (CCF). In 1933 the new party adopted its celebrated Regina Manifesto, which, although it was on the whole a moderate social democratic document, ended with a call for the eradication of capitalism. From 1935 to the present the CCF or its successor the New Democratic Party (NPD), founded in 1961, has elected members to the federal parliament and has on several occasions held the balance of power during minority governments.

STRUCTURE

Canadian parties are dominated by their national leaders. Before 1919 these leaders were chosen by the parliamentary party, but since that date they have been selected at a leadership convention. About one third of the delegates at a leadership convention are ex officio, federal Members of Parliament (MPs) and senators, provincial Members of the Legislative Assembly (MLAs, also called MHAs and MPPs), elected party officials and the like. The remaining two thirds are elected by the local constituency parties, usually six from each constituency with the additional requirement that at least two must be women and at least two must be under 30 years of age.

The leaders of the Liberals and the Conservatives hold office until after a defeat in a general election, at which time there is provision for a vote on whether to hold a leadership convention. The New Democrats make provision for a leadership election at each of the party's biennial meetings, but in practice the leader is rarely challenged and holds office until he or she decides to step down.

Each party also has a president and unpaid national executive. The president will be remunerated if he or she is not an MP or senator. The president presides over the party's national headquarters, all of which are in Ottawa, and generally supervises fundraising and organizational activities. Although in theory responsible to the extra-parliamentary party as a whole, the party president in fact works directly with and in support of the national leader, to whom deference is normally given. Membership on the national executive is not normally a matter of much importance except when the executive is charged with the responsibility of organizing a leadership convention. In that case the executive will make decisions about the timing, location and other details of the meeting, and its activities will be closely followed by the partisans of the various leadership aspirants.

The national leadership of the three main parties is usually an unpaid position, though the national leader will have a substantial support staff and office, provided in part by the party and in part by the federal government. In choosing the prime minister, if such becomes necessary, the governor general will, in normal circumstances, first approach the national leader of the party which obtained the largest number of seats at the preceding general election. The national leader automatically becomes leader of his party in the House of Commons, though if he is not a member an acting leader is appointed until he secures a seat.

The rules of the House of Commons give the leader extensive powers all the way from assigning the location where each of his followers sits to the appointment of spokesmen for various policy areas. The leader is responsible for appointing the party whips, who also receive an additional parliamentary stipend. It is the responsibility of the whips to organize the day-to-day business of the Commons, ensuring that sufficient party members are present to attend to the various tasks at hand. The chief whip is also responsible for appointing members to the various parliamentary committees. The leader also appoints another MP as House Leader, whose responsibility it is to negotiate with the other House Leaders on such important matters as the allocation of parliamentary time to different legislative matters, deciding which matters will come to a vote, and so on. All these subordinate officials hold their offices at the pleasure of the leader and can be replaced by him at any time.

When they are present, the party leaders usually dominate Question Period, the hour that is set aside each day for MPs to question members of the government. The leader of the opposition leads off, followed by the leaders of the other recognized parties. The speaker of the House by custom accords the party leaders a rather more generous latitude than he does to other members of the House when it comes to the length and the argumentative quality of the questions.

An institution which reinforces the power of the party leadership is the caucus. Every Wednesday morning when parliament is in session, all the party's MPs and senators are invited to a meeting at which they discuss a wide range of strategic and tactical partisan matters. The proceedings of caucus are supposed to be confidential, but the press usually find out fairly quickly about any noteworthy developments. British MPs who are familiar with the Canadian system say that they would not like to see it adopted at Westminster because it dramatically enhances the power of the leadership, which is in a position to argue that dissidents have had their opportunity to put their views privately, and now should toe the party line publicly.

Public opposition especially by government backbenchers is only very narrowly tolerated, and those who persist in their views are likely to be asked to withdraw from caucus until they can see their way clear to accept party policy. The leader also has the power under the Canada Elections Act to deny to any candidate the right to have the party label above his name on the ballot. Those without a letter from the leader of a registered party must run as independents, and their chances of election are extremely low. In government the leader can also dismiss parliamentary secretaries who oppose government policy, and the leader of the opposition can reassign the party's critics. Cabinet ministers are also bound by the concept of collective responsibility, and are required in almost all cases to give active support to the government's position or to resign.

Outside the House it is usually the party leader around whom the scrum of reporters gathers. It is the leaders who hold frequent press conferences on the important matters of the day. They are also entitled by law to equal media time to reply when the prime minister has made a statement on nationwide radio and television.

POLICY FORMATION

Canadian parties play only a small role in policy formation, since most policy initiatives either originate with the civil service or are significantly altered by it in the process of implementation. The Liberals and the Conservatives hold biennial policy conventions, but these are often managed affairs, especially when the party is in government. They usually consist of policy workshops, dominated by senior members of the party, and which, in any event, rarely end in a vote. The New Democratic Party is more serious about its policy conferences, and these are often spirited affairs as the various factions within the party jockey for ideological advantage. Even here, however, the leadership takes the view that an NDP government would not be absolutely bound by conference resolutions. Regardless of content, the leadership reserves full rights to decide the appropriate time to implement any policies.

From time to time, and usually in opposition, the Liberals and the Conservatives have summoned "thinkers' conferences." To these they have invited not only political partisans, but also businessmen and academics, with a view to infusing new thought into the party. The most influential of these was the Port Hope Conference of 1942, which committed the Conservative party to the welfare state. The general problem with these events is that they adopt policies that are intellectually interesting but are often politically naive. A more recent innovation, used with great effect by the Conservatives when they were in opposition, was the adoption of task forces on particular policy areas. These were funded by the party, and staffed exclusively with the party's MPs and senators. They traveled from coast to coast and held public hearings. The most successful was the task force on Revenue Canada, which probed the organizational difficulties of the government's taxation arm. The task force came up with extensive recommendations for change, many of which were adopted when the Conservatives formed the government in 1984. It is likely that the more serious abuses highlighted by the task force would have been quietly corrected by the Liberal Government if it had held on to office.

ELECTORAL BEHAVIOR

It is by no means possible to explain voter support for parties on the basis of ideology alone, if for no other reason than that the ideologies overlap between the three main political parties. Although there is no single demographic factor that dominates the basis of party support, there are a number with a significant impact.

Perhaps the most important is region. Since the 1950s, the Conservatives have been the party of western Canada, while the Liberals dominated Quebec from 1896 until 1984. This leaves Atlantic Canada and Ontario, which has the largest single number of seats, to determine the outcome of an election. The NDP is usually in the curious position that it draws its largest number of votes in Ontario, but secures the majority of its seats from the West. This factor is enhanced when one considers ethnic origins as well. The most significant cleavage is between English Canadians and French Canadians, with French Canadians, both inside Quebec and out, historically supporting the Liberals, and those of British ancestry preferring the Conservatives. Canadians of neither British nor French background on balance have preferred the Liberals, though more recently the Conservatives have been making progress with those who originally came from the Indian subcontinent.

These same factors are reinforced once again by considerations of language. Most francophones in Canada come from a Roman Catholic tradition, and most Roman Catholics support the Liberal party. Conversely, the Conservatives and the New Democrats are strong among Protestants. Although religion continues to be a reasonably significant demographic indicator, it no longer features as a important political issue, and it is unlikely that the voters pay much attention to the denominational loyalties of candidates.

Regardless of whether one measures class in an objective or subjective way, it does not appear to be a significant factor outside of British Columbia. Neither does sex, although there is a slight tendency for women to vote Liberal or NDP and men to support the Conservatives.

If it were necessary to identify one single factor that affected voting, it would probably be the party's national leader, though even here one cannot speak with confidence since Ed Broadbent, the NDP leader from 1975 to 1989, in his later years consistently led in terms of popular support, though his party came third in elections. In the 1988 election, Brian Mulroney led his party to a second consecutive election victory in spite of the fact that he was neither much liked nor respected by the general public.

PARTY FINANCES

Until the adoption of the Election Expenses Act in 1974, the Liberals and Conservatives received most of their financial contributions from corporations, although the large corporations often donated funds to both parties, as many still do. One of the reasons for the creation of the NDP out of the CCF was to secure a more stable financial base through union contributions, and affiliated unions often impose a levy on their members which is passed on to the NDP.

It was the intention of the Election Expenses Act to lessen the parties' dependency on a relatively small number of generous donors and to make the election financing process more open and democratic. It did this by creating a generous system of tax credits, whereby those who gave to registered political parties would receive back 75% of the first $100; the proportion fell after that, and the maximum contribution that was eligible for reimbursement was $1,150.

This system has proved a moderate success and the parties have exploited it with unequal skill. The Conservatives were the first and the most eager to adopt the direct-mail and telephone techniques which had been pioneered in the United States, and because of the Canadian tax credit system they score a higher percentage of donors and a larger gift per donation than do the American parties. The New Democrats have the largest number of individual contributors, but over the past five years the Conservatives have come close to doubling the total contributions of their two rivals. Indeed the Liberals entered the 1988 election campaign deeply in debt, and even now their financial position is far from secure. This situation arose in part because of the business community's distrust of Liberal leader Turner, a situation that was exacerbated by his opposition to the Free Trade Agreement, the implementation of which the business community generally favored. To avoid overdependence on any one funding source, the Liberals and Conservatives impose a limit of about $25,000 on any single contributor, and the NDP as a matter of principle refuses to accept corporate donations.

As well as an incentive to broaden the base for contributions, there is also a limit imposed on election expenses. This is determined by a formula, and depends on the number of voters. It affects the local candidate as well as the national parties. To be eligible for contributions, parties must be registered with the chief electoral officer, and to achieve this status they need to have had either 12 MPs in the preceding parliament, or to run candidates in 50 constituencies. Candidates who receive 15% of the vote have a portion of their election expenses refunded by the government. Although the act purported to limit expenditures other than by candidates or registered parties it was decided by the Canadian Supreme Court in the National Citizens' Coalition Case (1984) that this provision ran counter to the freedom of expression provisions of the Charter of Rights and Freedoms. As long as these expenditures are at arm's length from candidates, they do not appear to be subject to the limitations on election expenses imposed on parties and candidates. In 1989 the Conservative government appointed a Royal Commission to study the whole area of election reform and party financing and to make general recommendations.

ROLES OF CANADIAN PARTIES

At the local level it would only be a slight exaggeration to describe political parties as phoenixes, rising every four years from the ashes to run the next campaign. In the period between elections, active membership plummets and, except for some of the stronger NDP areas, it is the rare local party that does more than raise a little money and hold one or two primarily social gatherings in addition to a sparsely attended annual general meeting. The federal party, however, maintains its national office intact and it carries out organizational work, takes public opinion surveys and generally keeps the machinery oiled in preparation for the next election.

When an election is called or expected, the parties move into high gear. One of their main tasks is the recruitment of candidates. Securing nomination by one of the three main parties is a virtual prerequisite for victory for any candidate. Although the parties prefer candidates with local ties, it is not uncommon for the national party to attempt to "parachute" a strong candidate into a constitutency where the party has a good chance of winning. The national party, however, has no right to insist on its choice, and acceptability to the local constituency organization is the ultimate criterion.

The local party is responsible for local election organization. Under the guidance of a campaign manager and an official agent, through whom all financial transactions must pass, the party takes charge of the campaign appearances of the candidate, organizes media contacts, prepares and distributes literature, and, on election day, divides its time between getting out the vote and scrutinizing the election itself to ensure fairness.

The main job of the national party during the election process is to supervise the leader's tour, on which media attention primarily focuses. This involves the scheduling of press conferences, large party meetings, media events and photo opportunities and the like. The national party will also run the party's advertising campaign, prepare campaign literature for national and local distribution and track public opinion through various sorts of public opinion surveys.

MINOR PARTIES

Other than the big three parties that regularly elect MPs, Canadian elections are contested by a variety of other parties. Sometimes, like Social

Credit in 1962, they will burst upon the national scene and secure substantial parliamentary representation. For the most part, however, they must be content with garnering somewhere between a handful and a few thousand votes. Few of these parties' candidates secure the 15% of the local vote required for reimbursement of election expenses, but many of them qualify, according to federal rules, for free television and radio time.

Most of the minor parties such as the Communist Party and the Libertarian Party receive only a negligible number of votes, but there are four which deserve slightly more attention. The first is the Reform Party, whose leader is Preston Manning, son of the former Alberta premier. Conservative in its principles and Western in its focus, its candidates fed on dissatisfaction with the performance of the Mulroney government and made a strong showing in many Alberta ridings in the 1988 election. After the rejection of the Meech Lake Constitutional Accord and the selection of Jean Chrétien as Liberal party leader, there were defections by both Liberal and Conservative MPs from Quebec, who chose to form a new parliamentary party called the Bloc Québécois under the leadership of former Conservative cabinet minister Lucien Bouchard. Along with the Reform Party it looks well placed to elect a substantial number of MPs in any forthcoming general election. The Christian Heritage Party ran well in many rural ridings, particularly in Ontario. It is opposed to abortion and in favor of capital punishment. The final party worth noting is the Greens, the environmentalist party. Loosely, even chaotically organized, the Green Party attracts thoughtful and articulate candidates who are sometimes effective in pressing local, national or international environmental questions.

QUEBEC

Quebec deserves a special treatment in any discussion of Canadian politics. Its original settlers came from a France that had been little penetrated by liberal ideas. It first encountered liberalism in the van of the conquering British army, and then renewed the acquaintance with the anticlerical violence of the French Revolution. As late as the 1880s liberalism was a proscribed doctrine in the eyes of the Catholic clergy of Quebec.

Its political parties have reflected this different ideological and social composition. In 1935 Maurice Duplessis formed the Union Nationale, which held the government of Quebec until 1960, interrupted only by a period in opposition during World War II. "Le Chef," as Duplessis was known, promoted a conservative kind of nationalism, held together with a generous use of patronage and a brilliant tactical political sense. The party fell into a decline in 1959 with Duplessis's death, and now is virtually extinct.

In 1960 the Liberals came to power under Jean Lesage and began what they called the Quiet Revolution, which entailed, among other things, the secularization of education and health care. As the Union Nationale declined in strength, a new party rose to fill the void, the Parti Québécois (PQ). Formed in 1969 as a coalition of three separatist groups, the PQ was led by René Lévesque, a passionate and articulate proponent of what he called sovereignty association. He sought political independence for Quebec within the context of a continuing economic relationship with English Canada. The high point of the separatist movement was the 1980 referendum on sovereignty association in which 40% supported the idea. Defeated in 1985 by the Liberals under Robert Bourassa, the PQ continued to press for political independence.

Federally, Quebec was virtually a fiefdom of the Liberal Party from the death of Sir John A. Macdonald in 1891 until the 1984 election. Macdonald's decision to execute the French Canadian rebel Louis Riel in 1885 is often taken as the turning point. Other important factors were the leadership of Sir Wilfrid Laurier, who made political liberalism acceptable in Quebec, and the imposition of compulsory military service by the Borden government during the First World War. However, when the Conservatives chose Brian Mulroney, a Quebecer who speaks fluent colloquial French, as their leader, they set themselves up to make a dramatic breakthrough in the 1984 general election, one which they were able to consolidate in 1988.

PROVINCIAL PARTIES

Although it would be most accurate to say that each province forms a distinctive political culture and deserves individual treatment, it is possible to make some generalizations.

In the four provinces of Atlantic Canada (Newfoundland, Prince Edward Island, New Brunswick and Nova Scotia) only the Liberals or the Conservatives have ever formed the government, and generally only candidates from one or the other of the parties are electorally successful. Although partisan affiliation is probably more important here than in other regions, Atlantic Canadian politics is rarely ideological. Regional and administrative concerns are usually important factors influencing cooperation among the four provinces, as is the desire to take a united stand against the central government.

In Quebec, as we have seen, the Liberals vie for power with the separatist Parti Québécois. In Ontario, the Progressive Conservatives formed the government for 42 years, from 1943 until 1985. They were succeeded by the Liberal Party, whose government differed little in either style or substance from that of its predecessors. The New Democratic Party has always enjoyed strong support but did not form its first government until 1990.

West of Ontario, the situation becomes more complex. In Manitoba and Saskatchewan, the Conservatives and the New Democrats are the leading parties, although the Liberals have made significant recent gains in Manitoba. The CCF became the first democratically elected Canadian socialist government in Saskatchewan in 1944 and developed an impressive reputation for innovative social policies. In Alberta, the Social Credit Party formed the government from 1935 until 1970, at which point it yielded to the Conservatives, who have held power ever since. Other than Quebec, the most distinctive political culture is found in British Columbia. There a right-wing Social Credit party has tried, generally successfully, since 1952 to fight off the socialist challenge first of the CCF and then of the NDP; in 1991, however, an NDP government was elected. British Columbia politics are more polarized in ideological and class terms than politics anywhere else in English Canada. In the two northern territories, the partisan structure is more fluid; ethnic background and regional problems take precedence, although all three parties are active in the area.

Even where a provincial and federal political party bear the same names, there is no guarantee that the relationship between these two will be close, though it is often the case that activists at one level will also support the party at another. However there have been many notable examples of premiers placing provincial interests ahead of party loyalties. William Davis' Conservatives in Ontario were at best lukewarm supporters of their federal counterparts in the 1980 election, and Robert Bourassa gave covert support to Mulroney's federal Conservatives in 1984 and 1988 as did some PQ supporters. By contrast there have traditionally been relatively close ties between the British Columbia Social Credit party and the federal Conservatives. Even with the NDP, where a greater ideological commitment generates more consistency between federal and provincial levels, there are often conflicts between the national party and its provincial counterparts. In most cases, for all three parties, there is a separate national and provincial membership, and each level organizes on the basis of the territory marked out by the relevant electoral unit.

FURTHER READING

Christian, William, and Colin Campbell. *Political Parties and Ideologies in Canada.* 3rd edition. Toronto: McGraw-Hill/Ryerson, 1990.

Clarke, Harold, et al. *Absent Mandate.* Toronto: Gage, 1984.

Frizzell, Alan, and Anthony Westell. *The Canadian General Election of 1984.* Ottawa: Carleton University Press, 1985.

Goldfarb, Martin, and Thomas Axworthy. *Marching to a Different Drummer.* Toronto: Stoddart, 1988.

Graham, Roger. *One-Eyed Kings: Promise and Illusion in Canadian Politics.* Toronto: Collins, 1986.

Martin, Patrick, Allan Gregg, and George Perlin. *Contenders: The Tory Quest for Power.* Toronto: Prentice-Hall, 1983.

Morton, Desmond. *The New Democrats 1961–1986.* Toronto: Copp Clark Pitman, 1986.

Perlin, George, ed. *Party Democracy in Canada.* Toronto: Prentice-Hall, 1988.

Perlin, George. *The Tory Syndrome.* Montreal: McGill-Queen's University Press, 1980.

Wearing, Joseph. *Strained Relations.* Toronto: McClelland and Stewart, 1988.

Wearing, Joseph. *The L-Shaped Party: The Liberal Party of Canada 1958–1980.* Toronto: McGraw-Hill/Ryerson, 1980.

THE CANADIAN CONSTITUTION AND LEGAL SYSTEM

GERALD L. GALL

Canada is a free and democratic society with a parliamentary system of government. The Canadian legal system reflects that reality.

Under the major written component of the Canadian constitution, namely, the Constitution Act of 1982 (incorporating, among other things, the former British North America Act of 1867), 11 sovereign legislative bodies in Canada are established: the Parliament of Canada, and the 10 provincial legislatures. By the provisions of the Constitution Act, each is granted legislative authority to enact statutes, but the legislative competence of each is specifically limited to certain classes of matters. These bodies constitute the Canadian federation.

THE CANADIAN CONSTITUTIONAL SYSTEM AND THE BRITISH LEGAL TRADITION

The British influence on the Canadian legal system is very significant. British statutes serve as the underpinning of the Canadian constitutional system. Apart from the constitution, the private law in nine of the provinces of Canada is governed by a common law system, while, in the province of Quebec, private law is governed by a civil law system. A common law system emphasizes the importance of precedent. On the other hand, the system of law in Quebec is based upon the French and Roman traditions of codification.

The major written portions of the Canadian constitution are the Constitution Acts of 1867 (the old British North America, or B.N.A., Act) and 1982. Under the Canadian constitution, executive power vests in the Crown in Great Britain. However, the queen now acts only through her representatives in Canada. As a result, executive authority at the federal level vests in the governor general of Canada. Provincially, executive power vests in the various lieutenant governors of the respective provinces. Many of these executive powers are set out specifically in the Constitution Act of 1867.

Traditionally, the Crown's representatives in Canada have had their authority defined and communicated to them by way of letters of instruction and letters patent issued in 1947, with the result, essentially, that the queen's representatives in Canada now have plenary executive authority, as the queen does herself in the United Kingdom.

Notwithstanding the fundamental nature of the link between the exercise of executive authority in Canada and the Crown in Great Britain, the above is not a representative description of the constitutional and de facto exercise of executive power in Canada. In reality, under the conventional rules of Canadian constitutional law, the governor general acts only upon the advice and consent of the prime minister and his cabinet. Also, for example, under the Constitution Act of 1867, the Crown has a legislative role, namely, to assent to legislation (or, alternatively, to refuse to assent to or to reserve assent of legislation). However, under the conventional rules of constitutional law, the power to refuse to assent or to reserve assent will, most likely, no longer be exercised. In short, executive power in Canada, with some limited exceptions, lies in the hands of the prime minister and the cabinet and, provincially, with the various premiers and their cabinets.

There are other components of the Canadian legal system which share a British legal tradition: the historical evolution of Canadian courts along British lines, including, inter alia, the independence of the judiciary and the use of the jury trial in Canada; and the British influence on the development of the legal profession in Canada, including legal education and the admission to practice. In addition, Canada has inherited through the operation of the doctrine of stare decisis a rich body of jurisprudence containing centuries of decision making by English courts.

In 1982, the enactment of the Canada Act by the U.K. Parliament provided Canadians with the so-called "new" constitution. The new constitution contains, among other things, the Canadian Charter of Rights and Freedoms and a domestic amending formula. The Canada Act, which incorporates both the old B.N.A. Act of 1867 and the new instrument (including the Charter and the amending formula), states:

> No Act of the Parliament of the United Kingdom passed after the Constitution Act, 1982, comes into force shall extend to Canada as part of its law.

Notwithstanding the above provision, the Canadian constitution, at least until it is dramatically amended in Canada, is embodied in a British statute. That in itself is a commentary on the importance of the British legal tradition in the Canadian legal system.

THE CANADIAN CONSTITUTION, GENERALLY

Prior to April 17, 1982, the Canadian constitution could be reduced to two major components: a written component and an unwritten component. The written component consisted primarily of three British statutes enacted by the Parliament of Great Britain. In order of enactment, those statutes were the Colonial Laws Validity Act of 1865, the British North America Act of 1867 and the Statute of Westminster of 1931. When taken together these three statutes provided the basic framework of the Canadian constitution and enshrined in the constitutional system the doctrine of ultra vires. Under the doctrine of ultra vires, the B.N.A. Act possessed a supremacy over all statutes enacted by the Parliament of Canada and by the legislatures of the 10 provinces. The result of this was that any act passed by Parliament or a legislature had to conform to the jurisdictional constraints set out in sections 91 and 92 of the B.N.A. Act.

However, even then (i.e., prior to April 17, 1982) it was simplistic and incorrect to regard the B.N.A. Act as the total embodiment of the Canadian constitution. It was far more accurate to regard it instead as the main element of the written component of the constitution. In addition to the above, there were (and are) other elements of the written component of the Canadian constitution. For example, existing laws at Confederation are also elements of the written component in that they continue in force by virtue of Section 129 of the B.N.A. Act. Legislation creating the provinces of Alberta, Saskatchewan and Manitoba must necessarily be regarded as an important element in the constitution. In addition, every statute and every regulation of Parliament and of the provincial legislatures is also regarded as a part of the written constitution.

Some persons argue that some regular statutes possess, by their very nature, a special status. These so-called quasi-constitutional statutes include the Canadian Bill of Rights, the Supreme Court Act, provincial bills of rights and like statutes. Although these statutes are not entrenched in the constitution and, strictly speaking could be repealed at any time, they intrinsically occupy a special status for reason that their subject matters fall within the constitutional realm. Some statutes, such as the Canadian Bill of Rights, contain primacy provisions which, in effect, require that all other statutes of the same legislative jurisdiction conform to the substantive provisions contained in the statute possessing primacy, unless those other statutes specifically state that they shall operate notwithstanding the statute containing the primacy provision.

Still, the B.N.A. Act was the most important component of the written constitution.

Canada's receipt of a so-called new constitution on April 17, 1982 followed a somewhat tumultuous series of events during the preceding three years. After this series of events, there was a breakthrough in which the federal government and all provinces except Quebec agreed to patriation of a package, including a new amending formula and a Canadian Charter of Rights and Freedoms. The entire package was finally approved by the Parliament of Canada in December 1981. More specifically, a joint resolution of the House of Commons and the Senate was enacted in December 1981, after the consent of nine provinces was obtained. The joint resolution requested Her Majesty the Queen to place before the Parliament of the United Kingdom an act called the Canada Act of 1982. The Canada Act was passed by the U.K. Parliament and was proclaimed in Ottawa on April 17, 1982 by Her Majesty the Queen.

Quebec's failure to accept the patriation package made it feel like the "odd man out" in the Canadian "constitutional family." This led to renewed constitutional discussions, starting around 1985, during which the government of Quebec made a series of proposals that, if accepted by all, would lead to Quebec's return to the "constitutional family." In the interim, of course, Quebec was as legally bound as all of the provinces by the provisions of the Canada Act of 1982 and of its Schedule B, the Constitution Act of 1982. So, the Quebec proposals, although substantively important, also assumed a great symbolic significance.

Essentially, the Quebec proposals could be divided into two components. The first dealt with the distinctiveness of Quebec in the Canadian federation, and the second, although not entirely unrelated to the first, dealt with a potpourri of other matters. These other matters arguably tended to enhance the role of the provinces in their relationship with the federal government. Not surprisingly, then, when Quebec proposed this package, all of the provinces initially agreed to it under a principle of so-called "juridical equality." This package became known as the Meech Lake Constitutional Accord.

The Accord recognized the province of Quebec as constituting a distinct society within Canada. At the same time, it recognized, as a fundamental characteristic of Canada, that there is an anglophone minority in Quebec and a francophone minority elsewhere in Canada.

The provinces were, for the first time, given a formal role nominating persons to sit on certain federal institutions (namely, the Senate and the Supreme Court of Canada) and were given greater jurisdiction over social programs and immigration. In addition the Accord changed the 1982 amending formula.

The Accord was not unanimously approved by all provinces, and it died in June of 1990. Since the collapse of the Accord, there have been sustained constitutional discussions and negotiations dealing with the future of Quebec within confederation together with related discussion concerning the existing alignment of federal/provincial jurisdiction over legislation; aboriginal rights and Senate reform have also been major preoccupations.

The Constitution Act of 1982 contains numerous parts. Part I is the Canadian Charter of Rights and Freedoms; Part 2 is concerned with the rights of the aboriginal peoples of Canada; Part 3 deals with equalization and regional disparities; Part 4 is more or less a transitional provision dealing with a constitutional conference; Part 5 contains the new domestic procedure for amending the Constitution of Canada; Part 6 provides for a specific amendment to the B.N.A. Act of 1867, now cited as the Constitution Act of 1867; and Part 7 contains some important general provisions. Finally, the Constitution Act contains a Schedule, which is by virtue of Section 52(2) an integral part of the Act.

More specifically, Section 52(1) provides that the Constitution of Canada is the supreme law of Canada. Section 52(2) goes on to specify what constitutes the Constitution of Canada. It points out that the Constitution includes the Canada Act and its Schedule (namely, the Constitution Act of 1982 in its English and French texts and its Schedule) and any amendments to any of those instruments. The Schedule to the Constitution Act is therefore an integral part of the Constitution. It contains all of the British North America Acts passed since 1867. They have, however, been renamed as the various "Constitution Acts." The B.N.A. Act of 1867 is therefore brought forward as part of the Constitution as Item I in the Schedule to the Constitution Act of 1982. Accordingly, all the jurisprudence to date dealing with the division of legislative powers in sections 91 and 92, as well as the other sections of the B.N.A. Act, is brought forward and remains as relevant now as it always has been.

This raises the question as to what is, in fact and in law, "new" about the so-called new Constitution. Since all the old provisions, as well as all the attendant jurisprudence, are brought forward, what is new is, essentially, the Canadian Charter of Rights and Freedoms. It is now an entrenched instrument forming an integral part of the Constitution and occupying a constitutional status amendable only by formal constitutional amendment. The second major "new" aspect of the Constitution is the domestic amending formula. There are some other "new" matters but they are not quite as important.

THE PROVISIONS OF THE CHARTER

Essentially, the structure of the Charter follows a categorization scheme of civil liberties that has been widely accepted.

1. The Canadian Charter of Rights and Freedoms guarantees the rights and freedoms set out in it subject only to such reasonable limits prescribed by law as can be demonstrably justified in a free and democratic society.

Structurally, the Charter begins in Section 1, with the so-called "limitations clause" to which most other sections are referable. The theory behind having a limitations clause is that no right is absolute, and therefore the clause provides a court with a basis for placing limits on the exercise of particular rights.

The meaning of the words of Section 1 was the subject of several early cases under the Charter. However, the issue was fully and definitively explored by the Supreme Court of Canada in *R.* v. *Oakes* [1986] 1 S.C.R. 103. The so-called Oakes test may be summarized as follows: A limit is reasonable and demonstably justified in a free and democratic society if the limit is a rational, non-disproportionate, minimally intrusive means of achieving a pressing and substantial state objective.

2. Everyone has the following fundamental freedoms:
   (a) freedom of conscience and religion;
   (b) freedom of thought, belief, opinion and expression, including freedom of the press and other media of communication;
   (c) freedom of peaceful assembly; and
   (d) freedom of association.

Section 2 of the Charter, which is broken down into four subsections, is concerned with the fundamental freedoms.

3. Every citizen of Canada has the right to vote in an election of members of the House of Commons or of a legislative assembly and to be qualified for membership therein.
4. (1) No House of Commons and no legislative assembly shall continue for longer than five years from the date fixed for the return of the writs at a general election of its members.
   (2) In time of real or apprehended war, invasion or insurrection, a House of Commons may be continued by Parliament and a legislative assembly may be continued by the legislature beyond five years if such continuation is not opposed by the votes of more than one-third of the members of the House of Commons or the legislative assembly, as the case may be.
5. There shall be a sitting of Parliament and of each legislature at least once every twelve months.

Sections 3 to 5 deal with the so-called democratic rights and those rights are concerned with the matters previously contained in sections 91(1) and 92(1) of the former B.N.A. Act of 1867.

6. (1) Every citizen of Canada has the right to enter, remain in and leave Canada.
   (2) Every citizen of Canada and every person who has the status of a permanent resident of Canada has the right
       (a) to move to and take up residence in any province; and
       (b) to pursue the gaining of a livelihood in any province.
   (3) The rights specified in subsection (2) are subject to
       (a) any laws or practices of general application in force in a province other than those that discriminate among persons primarily on the basis of province of present or previous residence; and
       (b) any laws providing for reasonable residency requirements as a qualification for the receipt of publicly provided social services.
   (4) Subsections (2) and (3) do not preclude any law, program or activity that has as its object the amelioration in a province of conditions of individuals in that province who are socially or economically disadvantaged if the rate of employment in that province is below the rate of employment in Canada.

Section 6 deals with a relatively new category of civil liberties, namely mobility rights.

7. Everyone has the right to life, liberty and security of the person and the right not to be deprived thereof except in accordance with the principles of fundamental justice.
8. Everyone has the right to be secure against unreasonable search or seizure.
9. Everyone has the right not to be arbitrarily detained or imprisoned.
10. Everyone has the right on arrest or detention
    (a) to be informed promptly of the reasons therefor;

      (b) to retain and instruct counsel without delay and to be informed of that right; and

      (c) to have the validity of the detention determined by way of habeas corpus and to be released if the detention is not lawful.

11. Any person charged with an offence has the right

      (a) to be informed without reasonable delay of the specific offence;

      (b) to be tried within a reasonable time;

      (c) not to be compelled to be a witness in proceedings against that person in respect of the offence;

      (d) to be presumed innocent until proven guilty according to law in a fair and public hearing by an independent and impartial tribunal;

      (e) not to be denied reasonable bail without just cause;

      (f) except in the case of an offence under military law tried before a military tribunal, to the benefit of trial by jury where the maximum punishment for the offence is imprisonment for five years or a more severe punishment;

      (g) not to be found guilty on account of any act or omission unless, at the time of the act or omission, it constituted an offence under Canadian or international law or was criminal according to the general principles of law recognized by the community of nations;

      (h) if finally acquitted of the offence, not to be tried for it again and, if finally found guilty and punished for the offence, not to be tried or punished for it again; and

      (i) if found guilty of the offence and if the punishment for the offence has been varied between the time of commission and the time of sentencing, to the benefit of the lesser punishment.

12. Everyone has the right not to be subjected to any cruel and unusual treatment or punishment.

13. A witness who testifies in any proceedings has the right not to have any incriminating evidence so given used to incriminate that witness in any other proceedings, except in a prosecution for perjury or for the giving of contradictory evidence.

14. A party or witness in any proceedings who does not understand or speak the language in which the proceedings are conducted or who is deaf has the right to the assistance of an interpreter.

Sections 7 to 14 are concerned with the legal rights or the various protections afforded to those persons in contact with the criminal justice system. These legal rights constitute one of the most important parts of the Charter and are deserving of significant attention. Section 7, however, has proven to be extremely important in and of itself. The term "fundamental justice" in Section 7 has both procedural and substantive significance.

15. (1) Every individual is equal before and under the law and has the right to the equal protection and equal benefit of the law without discrimination and, in particular, without discrimination based on race, national or ethnic origin, colour, religion, sex, age or mental or physical disability.

    (2) Subsection (1) does not preclude any law, program or activity that has as its object amelioration of conditions of disadvantaged indi-

viduals or groups including those that are disadvantaged because of race, national or ethnic origin, colour, religion, sex, age or mental or physical disability.

28. Notwithstanding anything in this Charter, the rights and freedoms referred to in it are guaranteed equally to male and female persons.

Section 15 deals with equality rights and probably should be read together with Section 28. Section 15(1) provides for equal protection and equal benefit of the law and equality before and under the law, while Section 15(2) provides for the legality of affirmative action programs. Section 28 provides that, notwithstanding anything in the Charter, the rights and freedoms referred to in it are guaranteed equally to male and female persons.

16. (1) English and French are the official languages of Canada and have equality of status and equal rights and privileges as to their use in all institutions of the Parliament and government of Canada.

    (2) English and French are the official languages of New Brunswick and have equality of status and equal rights and privileges as to their use in all institutions of the legislature and government of New Brunswick.

    (3) Nothing in this Charter limits the authority of Parliament or a legislature to advance the equality of status or use of English and French.

17. (1) Everyone has the right to use English or French in any debates and other proceedings of Parliament.

    (2) Everyone has the right to use English or French in any debates and other proceedings of the legislature of New Brunswick.

18. (1) The statutes, records and journals of Parliament shall be printed and published in English and French and both language versions are equally authoritative.

    (2) The statutes, records and journals of the legislature of New Brunswick shall be printed and published in English and French and both language versions are equally authoritative.

19. (1) Either English or French may be used by any person in, or in any pleading in or process issuing from any court established by Parliament.

    (2) Either English or French may be used by any person in, or in any pleading in or process issuing from, any court of New Brunswick.

20. (1) Any member of the public in Canada has the right to communicate with, and to receive available services from, any head or central office of an institution of the Parliament or government of Canada in English or French, and has the same right with respect to any other office of any such institution where

    (a) there is a significant demand for communication with and services from that office in such language; and

    (b) due to the nature of the office, it is reasonable that communications with and services from that office be available in both English and French.

    (2) Any member of the public in New Brunswick has the right to communicate with, and to receive available services from, any office of an institution of the legislature or government of New Brunswick in English or French.

21. Nothing in sections 16 to 20 abrogates or derogates from any right, privilege or obligation with respect to the English and French languages, or either of them, that exists or is contained by virtue of any other provision of the Constitution of Canada.

22. Nothing in sections 16 to 20 abrogates or derogates from any legal or customary right or privilege acquired or enjoyed either before or after the coming into force of this Charter with respect to any language that is not English or French.

23. (1) Citizens of Canada
    (a) whose first language learned and still understood is that of the English or French linguistic minority population of the province in which they reside, or
    (b) who have received their primary school instruction in Canada in English or French and reside in a province where the language in which they received that instruction is the language of the English or French linguistic minority population of the province, have the right to have their children receive primary and secondary school instruction in the same language.
    (2) Citizens of Canada of whom any child has received or is receiving primary or secondary school instruction in English or French in Canada, have the right to have all their children receive primary and secondary school instruction in the same language.

Linguistic rights are contained in two separate categories. The first category, dealing with the official languages of Canada and New Brunswick, is contained in sections 16 to 22, while the second category, dealing with the controversial issue of minority language education rights, is contained in Section 23. After Section 23, the substantive protections of the Charter are more or less completed, and the balance of the Charter is concerned with applicability and procedural matters.

25. The guarantee in this Charter of certain rights and freedoms shall not be construed so as to abrogate or derogate from any aboriginal treaty or other rights or freedoms that pertain to the aboriginal peoples of Canada including
    (a) any rights or freedoms that have been recognized by the Royal Proclamation of October 7, 1763; and
    (b) any rights or freedoms that now exist by way of land claims agreements or may be so acquired.

27. This Charter shall be interpreted in a manner consistent with the preservation and enhancement of the multicultural heritage of Canadians.

There are, however, other sections, interpretative in nature, which deal with such matters as aboriginal rights in Section 25 and multicultural rights in Section 27, but the main human rights package is contained in sections 2 through 23 inclusive.

24. (1) Anyone whose rights or freedoms, as guaranteed by this Charter, have been infringed or denied may apply to a court of competent juris-

diction to obtain such remedy as the court considers appropriate and just in the circumstances.

(2) Where, in proceedings under subsection (1), a court concludes that evidence was obtained in a manner that infringed or denied any rights or freedoms guaranteed by this Charter, the evidence shall be excluded if it is established that, having regard to all the circumstances, the admission of it in the proceedings would bring the administration of justice into disrepute.

Section 24 deals with enforcement, inasmuch as Section 24(1) provides a mechanism for an application to a court for a remedy in the event of a breach of a substantive right, while Section 24(2) deals with the exclusion of evidence obtained through a breach of a substantive right. The other procedural section that is of considerable importance is Section 52(1).

52. (1) the Constitution of Canada is the supreme law of Canada, and any law that is inconsistent with the provisions of the Constitution is, to the extent of the inconsistency, of no force or effect.

(2) The Constitution of Canada includes

(a) the Canada Act, including this Act;

(b) the Act and orders referred to in Schedule I; and

(c) any amendment to any Act or order referred to in paragraph (a) or (b).

(3) Amendments to the Constitution of Canada shall be made only in accordance with the authority contained in the Constitution of Canada.

32. (1) This Charter applies

(a) to the Parliament and government of Canada in respect of all matters within the authority of Parliament including all matters relating to the Yukon Territory and Northwest Territories; and

(b) to the legislature and government of each province in respect of all matters within the authority of the legislature of each province.

(2) Notwithstanding subsection (1), section 15 shall not have effect until three years after this section comes into force.

33. (1) Parliament or the legislature of a province may expressly declare in an Act of Parliament or of the legislature, as the case may be, that the Act or a provision thereof shall operate notwithstanding a provision included in section 2 or sections 7 to 15 of this Charter.

(2) An Act or a provision of an Act in respect of which a declaration made under this section is in effect shall have such operation as it would have but for the provision of this Charter referred to in the declaration.

(3) A declaration made under subsection (1) shall cease to have effect five years after it comes into force or on such earlier date as may be specified in the declaration.

(4) Parliament or a legislature of a province may re-enact a declaration made under subsection (1).

(5) Subsection (3) applies in respect of a re-enactment made under subsection (4).

The entrenchment of various provisions in a constitution is significant because of the legal status those provisions occupy after entrenchment. Section 52(1) states that the Constitution of Canada is the supreme law of Canada and that any law that is inconsistent with the provisions of the Constitution is, to the extent of the inconsistency, of no force or effect. The result of this is that a constitutional challenge can now be based not only on whether a legislative body has exceeded its power under sections 91 and 92, but also on whether it has violated substantive rights. This changes our constitutional orientation in Canada to one somewhat akin to that of the United States. In Canada, to date, we have only been concerned, by and large, with jurisdictional questions, namely, who has jurisdiction to pass what laws. However, we are now also concerned with the issue of whether those laws, in terms of their content or substance, conform to the Charter of Rights and Freedom, which now forms an integral part of the Constitution. Thus, our orientation has changed from one of jurisdiction to one of jurisdiction and content. At the same time, the doctrine of parliamentary sovereignty has been preserved by virtue of the non obstante provision contained in Section 33 of the Charter, which provides the Parliament or a legislature may expressly declare that an Act of Parliament or the legislature shall operate notwithstanding the Charter of Rights and Freedoms. Two things ought to be said about this provision. First, the notwithstanding clause applies only to certain sections of the Charter, namely, Section 2 and sections 7 to 15, and to no other sections. Secondly, the political experience in Canada today indicates that it is not politically expedient to exercise this override option. For example, the human rights legislation of Alberta and Saskatchewan has contained similar such opting out provisions which have never been used in either of those two provinces. Federally, a similar provision exists in the Canadian Bill of Rights, but it has been used only once (and this was in respect of the federal statute passed in 1971 replacing the application of the War Measures Act by temporary measures legislation imposed at the time). It is true that an opting, out provision has been used a number of times in Quebec with respect to Quebec's human rights legislation. It has also been used recently in Quebec to authorize a law respecting the use of the French language in outdoor commercial signs after the original law was held by the Supreme Court of Canada to be unconstitutional. But Quebec ranks as an exception to the general experience elsewhere, which strongly suggests that it is politically inexpedient to use an opting out provision.

26. The guarantee in the Charter of certain rights and freedoms shall not be construed as denying the existence of any other rights or freedoms that exist in Canada.

Notwithstanding the entrenchment of the Charter of Rights and Freedoms in the Constitution, there are rights that continue to exist under various federal and provincial laws. Indeed, this is anticipated in Section 26 of the Charter, which provides the rights and freedoms guaranteed in the Charter shall not be construed as denying the existence of any other rights and freedoms that exist in Canada. Accordingly, federally, the Canadian Bill of Rights continues in force, at least to the extent that any of the provisions of the Canadian Bill of Rights do not conflict with the rights contained in the Charter. The same is true of the various provincial bills of rights and antidiscrimination statutes. This is significant in that some rights contained in these various provincial and federal enactments are not contained in the Charter, and some rights contained in the Charter are not contained in the various other human rights enactments.

Essentially, there are three types of applications that can be made under the Charter. The first is an application under Section 24(1) for a remedy by an aggrieved party whose rights have been infringed.

The second type of application that may be made under the Charter is an application to exclude evidence under Section 24(2). The test that is applied is whether the use of such evidence (which was obtained in a manner that infringed or denied any rights or freedoms guaranteed by the Charter) "would bring the administration of justice into disrepute."

The third type of application is provided for in Section 52(1), which provides that the Constitution of Canada is the supreme law of Canada and that any law that is inconsistent with the provisions of the Constitution is, to the extent of the inconsistency, of no force or effect. This invites the courts, upon application, to overturn legislation on the basis of the position of primacy occupied by the Constitution of Canada in the country's legal system.

Clearly a major change in the Canadian legal system relates to the role of the judiciary. Previously judges were largely responsible for the interpretation of laws. Although that responsibility has not changed in and of itself, what has occurred is a usurpation of the doctrine of parliamentary sovereignty by a regime under which the final say on legislative policy rests with the judiciary pursuant to the power given judges under Section 52 of the Constitution Act. Plainly and simply there has been a shift from a regime of parliamentary sovereignty to a system whereby the ultimate power rests in the Constitution as interpreted by a judge with powers under Section 24 to fashion new remedies in appropriate circumstances.

THE PROVISIONS OF THE CONSTITUTION ACT OF 1867

The British North America Act of 1867 (now renamed the Constitution Act of 1867) was primarily concerned with jurisdiction, but it was also concerned with questions relating to the establishment of a body politic for the new nation created at Confederation. This Act continues in force as the Constitution Act of 1867 by virtue of its inclusion, with all of its amendments, in the Schedule to the Constitution Act of 1982.

The principal features of the Constitution Act of 1867 are as follows:

(1) The preamble, which states essentially that our constitution is similar in principle to that of the United Kingdom;
(2) The provisions relating to the union of the four provinces of Nova Scotia, New Brunswick, Ontario and Quebec in 1867;

(3) The establishment of a federal executive;
(4) The establishment of a federal legislative body; this includes the Senate and the House of Commons;
(5) The establishment of provincial executives;
(6) The establishment of provincial legislatures;
(7) The distribution of legislative powers;
(8) Miscellaneous provisions relating to such matters as education, language rights, courts, agricultural marketing, etc.

The essential values which are promoted by the Constitution Act of 1867 relate, primarily, to a desire on the part of the drafters of our constitution to achieve a strong central government. It is interesting to note that the opposite notion was promoted in the drafting of the U.S. Constitution, a document that emphasized strong states' rights. Ironically, one might argue that the original American desire for strong states' rights has, throughout the nation's history, been transformed, de facto, into a strong central government, while the original Canadian notion of a strong central government has been transformed into an increase in provincial power. However, it is clear that a strong central government was one of the initial concerns arising from such practical considerations as, for example, the achievement of efficiency in expanding trade and commercial enterprises and the creation of a strong defense against the United States.

In addition, one can imply certain values promoted by the Constitution Act of 1867 from a reading of the preamble to the Act, which contains what has been termed "the implied Bill of Rights." The preamble states, essentially, that the drafters of our constitution desired to establish a constitution similar in principle to that of the United Kingdom, which has been interpreted as importing into the Canadian constitutional system certain values contained in the British system. These values include the principles enunciated in the Magna Carta, the British Bill of Rights, and the Petition of Rights, and refer to such notions as freedom of speech, freedom of association and assembly, freedom of the press, and fair play. However, more importantly, and more specifically, this implied Bill of Rights has imported into our constitutional system the British doctrines of parliamentary sovereignty, the rule of law and responsible government.

The most important provisions in the Constitution Act of 1867 are those provisions distributing legislative jurisdiction between the Parliament of Canada on one hand and the provincial legislatures on the other. The two main sections of the Constitution Act of 1867 concerned with the division of powers are sections 91 and 92, although there are other sections dealing with this as well.

Section 91 reserves exclusively to the Parliament of Canada a general grant of legislative authority, together with exclusive legislative jurisdiction in respect of various matters contained in the 29 enumerations following the general grant. Similarly, Section 92 reserves to the provincial legislatures exclusive legislative authority in respect of those matters falling within the 16 enumerations contained in Section 92. There is one exception, however, in Section 92 and that relates to Section 92(10) (a), (b) and

(c) which, by operation of Section 91 (29), bring certain matters within federal jurisdiction.

Powers of the Parliament

91. It shall be lawful for the Queen, by and with the Advice and Consent of the Senate and House of Commons, to make Laws for the Peace, Order, and good Government of Canada, in relation to all Matters not coming within the Classes of Subjects by this Act assigned exclusively to the Legislatures of the Provinces; and for greater Certainty, but not so as to restrict the Generality of the foregoing Terms of the Section, it is hereby declared that (notwithstanding anything in this Act) the exclusive Legislative Authority of the Parliament of Canada extends to all Matters coming within the Classes of Subjects next herein-after enumerated; that is to say, . . .

1A. The Public Debt and Property.
2. The Regulation of Trade and Commerce.
2A. Unemployment insurance.
3. The raising of Money by any Mode or System of Taxation.
4. The borrowing of Money on the Public Credit.
5. Postal Service.
6. The Census and Statistics.
7. Militia, Military and Naval Service, and Defence.
8. The fixing of and providing for the Salaries and Allowances of Civil and other Officers of the Government of Canada.
9. Beacons, Buoys, Lighthouses, and Sable Island.
10. Navigation and Shipping.
11. Quarantine and the Establishment and Maintenance of Marine Hospitals.
12. Sea Coast and Inland Fisheries.
13. Ferries between a Province and any British or Foreign Country or between Two Provinces.
14. Currency and Coinage.
15. Banking, Incorporation of Banks, and the Issue of Paper Money.
16. Savings Banks.
17. Weights and Measures.
18. Bills of Exchange and Promissory Notes.
19. Interest.
20. Legal Tender.
21. Bankruptcy and Insolvency.
22. Patents of Invention and Discovery.
23. Copyrights.
24. Indians, and Lands reserved for the Indians.
25. Naturalization and Aliens.
26. Marriage and Divorce.
27. The Criminal Law, except the Constitution of Courts of Criminal Jurisdiction, but including the Procedure in Criminal Matters.
28. The Establishment, Maintenance, and Management of Penitentiaries.
29. Such Classes of Subjects as are expressly excepted in the Enumeration of the Classes of Subjects by this Act assigned exclusively to the Legislatures of the Provinces.

And any Matter coming within any of the Classes of Subjects enumerated in this Section shall not be deemed to come within the Class of Matters of a local or private Nature comprised in the Enumeration of the Classes of Subjects by this Act assigned exclusively to the Legislatures of the Provinces.

Exclusive Powers of Provincial Legislatures

92. In each Province the Legislature may exclusively make Laws in relation to Matters coming within the Classes of Subject next herein-after enumerated; that is to say,
   1. The Amendment from time to time, notwithstanding anything in this Act, of the Constitution of the Province, except as regards the Office of the Lieutenant Governor.
   2. Direct Taxation within the Province in order to the raising of a Revenue for Provincial Purposes.
   3. The borrowing of Money on the sole Credit of the Province.
   4. The Establishment and Tenure of Provincial Offices and the Appointment and Payment of Provincial Officers.
   5. The Management and Sale of the Public Lands belonging to the Province and of the Timber and Wood thereon.
   6. The Establishment, Maintenance, and Management of Public and Reformatory Prisons in and for the Province.
   7. The Establishment, Maintenance, and Management of Hospitals, Asylums, Charities, and Eleemosynary Institutions in and for the Province, other than Marine Hospitals.
   8. Municipal Institutions in the Province.
   9. Shop, Saloon, Tavern, Auctioneer, and other Licences in order to the raising of a Revenue for Provincial, Local, or Municipal Purposes.
   10. Local Works and Undertakings other than such as are of the following Classes:
       a. Lines of Steam or other Ships, Railways, Canals, Telegraphs, and other Works and Undertakings connecting the Province with any other or others of the Provinces, or extending beyond the Limits of the Province.
       b. Lines of Steam Ships between the Province and any British or Foreign Country.
       c. Such Works as, although wholly situate within the Province, are before or after their Execution declared by the Parliament of Canada to be for the general Advantage of Canada or for the Advantage of Two or more of the Provinces.
   11. The Incorporation of Companies with Provincial Objects.
   12. The Solemnization of Marriage in the Province.
   13. Property and Civil Rights in the Province.
   14. The Administration of Justice in the Province, including the Constitution, Maintenance, and Organization of Provincial Courts, both of Civil and of Criminal Jurisdiction, and including Procedure in Civil Matters in those Courts.
   15. The Imposition of Punishment by Fine, Penalty, or Imprisonment for enforcing any Law of the Province made in relation to any Matter coming within any of the Classes of Subjects enumerated in this Section.

16. Generally all Matters of a merely local or private Nature in the Province.

Old Age Pensions

94A. The Parliament of Canada may make laws in relation to old age pensions and supplementary benefits, including survivors' and disability benefits irrespective of age, but no such law shall affect the operation of any law present or future of a provincial legislature in relation to any such matter.

Agriculture and Immigration

95. In each Province the Legislature may make Laws in relation to Agriculture in the Province, and to Immigration into the Province; and it is hereby declared that the Parliament of Canada may from Time to Time make Laws in relation to Agriculture in all or any of the Provinces, and to Immigration into all or any of the Provinces; and any Laws of the Legislature of a Province relative to Agriculture or to Immigration shall have effect in and for the Province as long and as far only as it is not repugnant to any Act of the Parliament of Canada . . .

Under the general power of Parliament, contained in Section 91 of the Constitution Act of 1867, the Parliament of Canada is given exclusive legislative authority to enact laws in respect of the peace, order and good government of Canada. The peace, order and good government clause, however, has met with various interpretations over the years. Under the emergency doctrine, Parliament may legislate, under the peace, order and good government clause, in respect of emergency situations arising out of war or famine. As a result of a case in the mid-1970s, it was held that certain types of economic emergencies might give rise to appropriate federal legislation. In effect, upon the application of the emergency doctrine, Parliament may encroach upon those matters falling within provincial legislative authority under the provisions contained in Section 92 of the Constitution Act of 1867.

Under the "national dimensions" doctrine, Parliament is given authority to legislate, under the peace, order and good government clause, in respect of those matters which affect Canada as a whole. It is difficult to rationalize the list of ad hoc matters which have been held to be within federal jurisdiction under this doctrine, but they include such matters as nuclear energy, aeronautics and the national capital region. Under this doctrine Parliament may again encroach upon those matters falling within provincial jurisdiction.

Finally, the peace, order and good government clause has been regarded as a residuary power in respect of those matters not falling within any of the specific enumerations in either section 91 or 92.

Generally speaking, under Section 91(2) of the Constitution Act of 1867, the Parliament of Canada has exclusive legislative jurisdiction over the regulation of international and extraprovincial trade. The provinces, on the other hand, possess exclusive jurisdiction over purely intraprovincial trade. However, this distinction has become somewhat blurred in recent cases as a result of an application by the courts of a "functional" or "flow of trade" analysis. Under a functional analysis, the courts often ask to what extent it is possible to sever an apparently intraprovincial operation, functionally speaking, from the whole of an extraprovincial operation. Recent cases leave some doubt as to what truly remains "intraprovincial trade" in view of the modern, highly interrelated economics of the various trading jurisdictions. The Supreme Court of Canada has also recently explored the notion of a general trade and commerce power.

The Parliament of Canada, under Section 91(27) of the Constitution Act of 1867, is granted exclusive legislative jurisdiction in respect of criminal law and procedure, although not in respect of the constitution of courts of criminal jurisdiction. A key issue, therefore, is the domain of criminal law. Criminal law has been defined in many ways and most often in a very wide sense to include subject matters which, by their very nature, fall within the domain of criminal jurisprudence. These matters, generally are contained in legislation promoting public peace, order, security, health or morality. In other words, the court examines an impugned statute and asks, in terms of its operational effects, whether that statute was enacted with a view to a public purpose which can support it as being in relation to criminal law. To support the legislation as a valid exercise of criminal law, the ordinary, though not exclusive, object of that law must be directed at public peace, order, security, health or morality.

On the other hand, the provinces can legislate in respect of purely regulatory matters as well as those matters referred to as "quasi-criminal" in nature. A quasi-criminal matter is one which is enacted with a view to suppressing conditions which are calculated to foster the development of crime. A quasi-criminal provincial statute is constitutionally permissible. However, a province cannot, under the guise or color of quasi-criminal legislation, legislate matters which are truly criminal in nature and thus fall under Section 91(27).

Federal jurisdiction over radio, television, cable and pay television and other similar forms of communication, including satellite communication, as well as federal jurisdiction over interprovincial railway and trucking operations, are derived from the exceptions contained in Section 92(10)(a) of the Constitution Act of 1867.

The Parliament of Canada has jurisdiction in respect of both direct and indirect taxation, while the provincial jurisdiction is limited to direct taxation within the province for provincial purposes. One major difficulty is the categorization of taxes as either direct or indirect.

The division of legislative jurisdiction in sections 91 and 92 of the Constitution Act of 1867 has given rise to what has been referred to as the "watertight compartment theory." By this theory, the doctrine of exclusivity has created two watertight legislative compartments. Accordingly there is a certain constitutional rigidity in Canada which must be surmounted by various means. First, the courts have allowed the notion of permissible interdelegation. While it is not constitutionally permissible for Parliament, for example, to pass a law delegating its exclusive legislative jurisdiction in respect of a given matter to the legislative assembly of a province, it can, nonetheless, delegate part of its exclusive legislative jurisdiction to a subordinate agency of a provincial legislature. Secondly, flexibility has been achieved through agreements reached at federal-provincial conferences which subsequently form the basis of a mutually agreed-upon legislative scheme. These agreements include conditional grants or grants-in-aid which tie certain conditions to the provision of funds from the federal government to the province. These conditions usually relate to how these funds are to be spent. Thus, even though the money is to be spent with respect to a matter within provincial jurisdiction, the tying of conditions gives the federal government some say as to the exercise of a matter normally within provincial jurisdiction. In recent years, equalization payments have played a major role in federal/provincial fiscal arrangements. Indeed, equalization has become constitutionally entrenched as a separate part of the Canada Act of 1982.

Since 1982, the Constitution now contains a comprehensive amending formula. The general rule is that a matter which directly affects federal/provincial relations can be amended by consent of the federal government and two-thirds of the provinces, provided those provinces constituting the two-thirds contain 50% of the population of Canada. There are special amendment procedures relating to special matters, some of which require unanimity for amendment. Interestingly, one of those special matters relates to the Supreme Court of Canada. In effect, the Supreme Court of Canada is given constitutional status, notwithstanding the fact that the Supreme Court is constituted under an ordinary statute of Parliament.

The devices of federal/provincial negotiations (and the resulting agreements), interdelegation, and amendment have provided for some flexibility in our constitution.

The main heads of legislative jurisdiction in sections 91 and 92 have been subject to various interpretations at various stages of our history. Generally, the notion of a strong central government was emasculated by interpretations of the Judicial Committee of the Privy Council in the 1920s and 1930s. However, stronger federal legislative authority has been restored by the Supreme Court of Canada since it became the final court of appeal for all criminal and civil matters in 1949.

THE CONSTITUTIONAL BASIS OF JUDICIAL AUTHORITY

The constitutional basis of judicial authority in Canada is provided for in sections 96 to 101 of the Constitution Act of 1867. The Parliament of Canada is granted legislative competence to enact laws providing for the establishment of certain courts and tribunals under the provisions of Section 101 of the Constitution Act of 1867. The various provincial legislatures are given authority to enact laws to provide for the establishment of certain provincial courts and tribunals under the provisions of Section 92(14) of the Constitution Act of 1867 (read together with the exclusion of federal jurisdiction to do so in Section 91(27) of the Constitution Act of 1867).

There are essentially three provisions of the Constitution Act of 1867 providing for the appointment of judges. First, Section 101 gives Parliament authority to enact laws establishing certain federal courts and tribunals and, by implication, also gives Parliament authority to pass legislation respecting the appointment of judges to these courts, the salaries of these judges, their tenure of office and their removal. Secondly, sections 96 to 100 provide for, among other things, the federal appointment of judges to serve on county or district, and superior courts established by the province under the provisions of Section 92(14). And thirdly, Section 92(14) provides for, by implication, the appointment of judges at the provincial level to serve on provincial courts established under Section 92(14). In summary then, the Constitution Act of 1867 provides for:

(1) Federal courts constituted under federal legislation enacted pursuant to legislative authority granted Parliament under Section 101 of the Constitution Act of 1867, with federally appointed judges pursuant to this same section.

(2) Provincial courts constituted under provincial legislation enacted pursuant to legislative authority granted under Section 92(14) of the Constitution Act of 1867, with federally appointed judges pursuant to the provisions contained in sections 96 to 100 of the Constitution Act of 1867.

(3) Provincial courts constituted under provincial legislation enacted pursuant to legislative authority granted under Section 92(14) of the Constitution Act of 1867, with provincially appointed judges pursuant to the provisions contained in this same section.

CANADIAN COURTS

Set out as follows is a diagrammatic representation of all the major courts within the Canadian judicial hierarchy. It is not exhaustive in that some minor courts at the municipal level, for example, are not included, and there is no mention of administrative tribunals at either the federal or provincial levels. The chart is intended to apply to all of the provinces of Canada, but there are, in reality, significant differences from province to province, some of which are noted in the chart. The reader should appreciate that the court system within a particular province may differ from the general model described below.

THE SYSTEM OF COURTS IN CANADA GENERALLY

A. *Federal Courts—Courts constituted under federal statutes with judges federally appointed.*

Supreme Court of Canada

- The Chief Justice of the Supreme Court is also the Chief Justice of Canada
- Eight Puisne Justices

Federal Court of Canada

- Appellate Division
- Trial Division

Tax Court of Canada

- Replaces Tax Review Board[3]

---

[3] In 1983, the Tax Review Board was replaced by the Tax Court of Canada. See S.C. 1980–81–82–83, c. 158.

B. *Provincial Courts—Courts constituted under provincial statutes with judges federally appointed.*

Courts of Superior Jurisdiction of a Province
or the
Supreme Court of a Province

Appellate Division

- This court is often referred to as the Court of Appeal of the province
- The Chief Justice of the Appellate Division is also the Chief Justice of the province

Trial Division

- In some provinces, such as Manitoba, for example, the two divisions here are separate courts constituted by separate statutes, with the trial court known as the Court of Queen's Bench. In turn, the Court of Queen's Bench of Manitoba is itself subdivided into three divisions—the general division, the family division and the surrogate division.
- Often this court is simply referred to as the Supreme Court of the province
- The Chief Justice of this court is properly referred to as the Chief Justice of the Trial Division

NOTE: In the province of Ontario, there is a further subdivision with the creation of the Divisional Court. The Divisional Court has an administrative law jurisdiction in respect of the granting of prerogative remedies. In addition, in December of 1976, the Supreme Court of Ontario was further subdivided to create a family law division. All of this is expected to change in 1990 and beyond as the province of Ontario embarks on major court reform. This dramatic initiative will be discussed later in this chapter.

County or District Courts

- In certain circumstances, the District or County Court judges exercise the jurisdiction of local judges of the Supreme Court of a province

Surrogate Courts

- Usually, judges of the County or District Court serve in the capacity of Surrogate Court Judges

NOTE: As indicated elsewhere, most of the provinces have or are about to merge their county or district courts with their superior courts. The result of such an amalgamation is the elimination of an intermediate court of trial jurisdiction with judges who are federally appointed.[4]

C. *Provincial Courts—Courts constituted under provincial statutes with judges provincially appointed.*

Youth Court	Family Court	Provincial Court (Criminal Jurisdiction)	Small Claims Court or Civil Division of Provincial Court

---

[4] When this occurs, judges of the newly amalgamated court of superior jurisdiction assume the surrogate court responsibilities.

NOTE: In some provinces, by the operation of various enabling statutes, two or more of the above courts are combined into a single court, with various divisions. For example, in Ontario the Provincial Court is divided into Family, Criminal and Civil Divisions. Alternatively, some provinces provide concurrent jurisdiction for judges serving on one or more of the above courts to deal with matters arising in another of the above courts. For example, in Alberta, under the Provincial Court Act, R.S.A. 1980, c. P-20, a judge of the Provincial Court has jurisdiction to sit in either, some or all of the criminal, small claims, family or youth divisions.

The Quebec court system differs somewhat from the other provincial court systems in Canada. Set out below is a diagrammatic representation of the Quebec court system.

QUEBEC COURT SYSTEM

Court of Appeal
• Provincial court constituted under provincial statutes • Judges federally appointed • This court has jurisdiction to hear both civil and criminal cases on appeal
Superior Court
• Provincial court constituted under provincial statutes • Judges federally appointed • This court has some civil jurisdiction • Adjudicates appeals under Pt. XXVII of the Criminal Code
PROVINCIAL COURTS
Court of Quebec
• Comprising what was formerly known as Provincial Court, Court of the Sessions of the Peace, Small Claims Court and Youth Court • Judges provincially appointed • Divided into Montreal regional section for the western part of the province and Quebec regional section for the eastern part of the province • Each regional section consists of three divisions: Civil Division; Criminal and Penal Division; and Youth Division • There is also an Expropriation Division set up under the Expropriation Act • Civil Division hears cases where amount in dispute is less than $15,000, but not applications for support or those reserved for the Federal Court of Canada • Small Claims Division of Civil Division deals with claims for $1,000 or less. Parties are to appear without representation of a lawyer unless case is complex and representation is authorized • Criminal and Penal Division deals with criminal offenses reserved for jurisdiction of Court of Quebec and offences which are not within exclusive jurisdiction of the Superior Court where the accused has elected the matter to be heard in the Criminal and Penal Division. Also has jurisdiction in penal matters for offences against provincial and federal statutes • Youth Division adjudicates in adoption cases and under the Youth Protection Act and hears cases in first instance in criminal and penal matters where accused is under 18 years of age
Municipal Courts
• Provincial courts constituted under provincial statutes • Judges provincially appointed

THE SUPREME COURT OF CANADA

The legislative jurisdiction of Parliament to establish a supreme court is set out in Section 101 of the Constitution Act of 1867. Pursuant to that jurisdiction, Parliament established the Supreme Court of Canada in 1875.

The Supreme Court has nine judges: one chief justice and eight puisne justices. It sits only in Ottawa. It hears, with some exceptions, only the cases it wishes to hear. Application is made for leave or permission to appeal to a panel of three judges. Leave is granted if the subject matter of the appeal is concerned with an important issue of law and/or a matter of public importance. One of the exceptions to the "leave" system relates to a particularly unique Canadian phenomenon: the "reference" case, in which governments may refer matters, constitutional and otherwise, to the courts for an opinion.

THE CANADIAN JUDICIARY, GENERALLY

The reader should consult the earlier section on the "Constitutional Basis of Judicial Authority."

With respect to the appointment of judges, essentially, there are 11, not one, processes of appointment. First, there is the federal processes of appointment of justices to the Supreme Court of Canada, to the Federal Court of Canada, to the Tax Court of Canada, to courts of superior jurisdiction in the provinces and to county and district courts in the provinces. In addition, each of the 10 provinces has its own process of appointment of provincial judges to the provincial courts. As a result, there may be no uniformity in these processes.

Federally appointed judges may remain in office until the age of retirement. That age, for judges serving on the Supreme Court of Canada and the Federal Court of Canada, is 75 years, pursuant to provisions contained, respectively, in the Supreme Court Act and the Federal Court Act. For judges serving on courts of superior jurisdiction in the provinces, the age of compulsory retirement is 75 years. Judges serving on the county or district court benches are compulsorily retired at the age of 75 years. Finally, judges serving on provincial court benches are compulsorily retired in accordance with the provisions contained in the enabling provincial statutes establishing those courts. Usually, these statutes provide for compulsory retirement at age 70.

Aside from mandatory retirement, the only other limitation on a judge's tenure of office is the requirement that he or she must conduct himself or herself in such a manner as to constitute good behavior. There is no test common to all courts as to what constitutes good behavior and, therefore, it is necessary to consult various statutes.

For example, the Federal Judges Act sets out those matters which are contraindicative of "good behavior"; namely, . . . the judge . . . has become incapacitated or disabled from the due execution of his office by reason of

(a)   age or infirmity,
(b)   having been guilty of misconduct,
(c)   having failed in the due execution of his office, or
(d)   having been placed, by his conduct or otherwise, in a position incompatible with the due execution of his office.

This provision is probably not exhaustive in delimiting the bounds of what does not constitute "good behavior," but it does provide at least some guidelines in applying this broadly worded standard. The effect of such narrow removal provisions is to provide the judiciary with security of tenure and this in turn is directed at achieving an independent judiciary.

In general, the Canadian legal system may be viewed as providing an opportunity to achieve domestic tranquillity and major advancements in the quality of life. Canadians, to borrow the words of Section 1 of our Charter of Rights and Freedoms, have the opportunity and the responsibility to preserve and protect the "free and democratic society" that Canadians cherish. In so doing, the Canadian Constitution and the Canadian legal system will continue to endure as cornerstones of liberty and democracy in Canada.

FURTHER READING

Beaudoin, G. A., and E. Ratushny. *The Canadian Charter of Rights and Freedoms.* 2nd ed. Toronto: Carswell, 1989.

Dawson, R. M., and W. F. Dawson. *Democratic Government in Canada.* 4th ed. rev. by N. M. Ward. Toronto: University of Toronto Press, 1971.

Gall, G. L. *The Canadian Legal System.* 3rd ed. Calgary: Carswell, 1990.

Gibson, D. *The Law of the Charter: General Principles.* Calgary: Carswell, 1986.

Hogg, P. W. *Constitutional Law of Canada.* 2nd ed. Toronto: Carswell, 1985.

Strayer, B. L. *On the Canadian Constitution and the Courts: The Function and Scope of Judicial Review.* 3rd ed. Toronto: Butterworths, 1987.

PART FOUR

ECONOMICS

CANADA-U.S. TRADE

CARL E. BEIGIE

To many Canadians, proximity to the United States colossus has been not merely the dominant but the determining factor in the country's economic evolution. It is indeed true that a large majority of the people of Canada live but a relatively short distance from the U.S. border. Large numbers of Canadians each year travel to the United States on business and/or pleasure (including the pleasure of being warmer in the winter); even larger numbers watch television, read magazines, and receive other visual stimuli originating in the United States that profoundly shape the tastes and preferences that impact directly into demand patterns among Canadians. In general, the people of Canada want what the people of the United States can have, or they feel cheated.

The dominance of the United States on Canadian preferences is not really surprising in the face of general U.S. influences on tastes that have been expanding around the world with the growing ease and scope of global communications. What is more surprising is a failure to find an internally generated alternative focus to moderate this dominance so as to prevent it from becoming the determining influence on the path Canadians, individually and in their government-institutionalized policy-making, are traveling. As the nation moves through the final decade of the 20th century, however, Canada is being confronted by conflict between the Canada-United States Free Trade Agreement of 1988 (FTA), the culmination of integrative forces judged by many to be inevitably victorious over Canadian nationalism, and the unleashing both of internally generated economic threats and policy challenges from within and without that are forcing Canadians in growing numbers to think through what they really believe.

THE CANADIAN ECONOMY BEFORE WORLD WAR II

Prior to, and in the early years after, becoming a nation in 1867, the territory of Canada was primarily a producer of staple commodities—furs, fish, forest products, grains, and so on. This staples economy generated a certain level of wealth, but that wealth was largely a function of external trade. This trade was a source of economic volatility.

In 1879, Canada's first prime minister, John A. Macdonald, launched what has become known in modern times as a national economic plan: the National Policy. This policy served both to force the axis of Canadian economic development from north-south to east-west through restrictive trade rules and to encourage its growth through transportation and other incentives (such as subsidies and tax breaks).

Canada's huge landmass, combined with a very limited population, gave the country a clear advantage in trade in natural resources. It was able to export these resources for wealth. It employed its export proceeds to help fund the development of a modern, effective infrastructure and to pay for imports of products of more finished manufactured goods than the nation, in general, produced.

The logic behind the National Policy was sound; the implementation was far less so. A combination of small, widely dispersed population centers; relative ease of access to externally produced manufactured products; and the impact of a reasonably strong staples base on wage rates and the value of the currency meant that it was difficult for a broad-based domestic manufacturing sector to be launched. The National Policy sought to "force-feed" Canadian manufacturing development through trade impediments.

Externally based firms producing goods Canadians desired were faced with a choice following introduction of the National Policy. They could continue to produce outside Canada and to export over the Canadian tariff barrier. Or, they could establish facilities for production in Canada known as "tariff factories." Not all firms followed the same course, but as the Canadian market grew in size, the pressures mounted to be located there or to be placed at serious competitive disadvantage.

A serious problem with the National Policy lay in overanxiousness to have as many firms as possible set up shop in Canada. The tariff established an opportunity for inefficiency that was, unfortunately, overused. Foreign (increasingly U.S. home-based) firms would locate a plant in Canada, the output of which could generally be sold at prices equal to (roughly) the U.S. price (adjusted for the exchange rate) plus the Canadian tariff.

An economist might ask why a tariff-induced firm operating in Canada would not try to capture a larger share of the host market by lowering price below the protected "limit." Some did, but most competed far more on the basis of using the opportunity for inefficiency to engage in product differentiation to allow Canadians a broadly similar choice (although at higher prices) as consumers in the firms' home markets.

If Canada had restrained the number of firms locating in the country or limited the proliferation of product choices they offered, a more generally efficient manufacturing sector possibly would have evolved. As it turned out, too many of these firms produced too many product variants for too small and spread-out a market. The National Policy was not successful in generating highly efficient, export-oriented (or at least export-sensitive) general manufactures. High tariffs served mainly to induce import substitution at relatively high cost—too high to be competitive outside the country.

Canada's net merchandise trade balance was positive in most years in the period prior to World War II, but this surplus was in unprocessed or thinly processed raw materials; adding value to natural resources was not a source of Canadian trading strength. Meanwhile, Canada experienced a fairly steady deficit on its current account, a development that tended to feed on itself.

A nation's current account is the summation of its goods trade, its services trade, and its transactions on interest and dividend payments. While Canada generally recorded a goods surplus in most years, it also recorded deficits on services trade (in other than financial payments). The major and steadily growing deficits, however, were recorded in financial payments. Foreign ownership of Canadian productive assets gave rise to dividend outflows (and other service payments for items such as management fees) that greatly outpaced dividend inflows. The current account deficits must be financed, assuming a relatively stable currency value is maintained; this financing—in either debt or equity form—makes it progressively more difficult to achieve an improved current account balance, at least in gross nominal amounts.

Over a period of time, steady current account deficits add to a nation's net international indebtedness position. Long before developed countries (such as the United States) became concerned about their international net financial positions, Canada accumulated a fairly large foreign indebtedness posture. But since this indebtedness was held by foreigners largely in equity form and the desire to do so seemed to be fairly secure, the Canadian attitude toward its international posture was rather relaxed at about the time of World War II.

THE CANADIAN ECONOMY SINCE WORLD WAR II

The impact of the U.S. economy on Canada strengthened in the first 20 years or so following World War II. Japan and much of Europe had been devastated by military conflict, and the north-south pull on Canada was accentuated. Canada's economic performance was strengthened in absolute terms, but its relative performance was judged internally in comparison with the badly weakened (but soon to be much improving) "losers" and with the currently strong (but soon to be challenged) economy of the main "winner." Natural resource-based production generally continued to prosper in Canada, as did a few indigenously developed and fostered value-adding producers. But the bulk of employment growth came from foreign-owned subsidiary companies operating within a sheltered (by tariffs) cocoon and by the steadily growing service sector.

Prior to the mid-1960s, Canada was not able to close noticeably the productivity gap that existed relative to U.S. manufacturing. This gap amounted to approximately a quarter less output per worker compared to what was achieved by U.S. employees. Moreover, Canada not only used more labor per unit of manufacturing output; it also used more capital. The outcome was that workers were generally paid fewer dollars in Canada than in the United States and the Canadian dollar traded at a discount relative to the U.S. dollar through much of this period. In short, Canadian workers were at a noticeable real income disadvantage, especially in the manufacturing segment of the economy.

In the late 1950s, a Royal Commission, chaired by a future finance minister of the Federal Liberal Party, Walter Gordon, examined Canada's economic prospects. The conclusions reached were generally optimistic, but the Gordon Commission signaled that foreign ownership had become clearly worrisome, if not excessive, in Canada. The steps that were proposed (in the report and later by Minister Gordon) were looked upon as too extreme by at least the business community in Canada. The negative assessment of the role of foreign-owned asset base in Canada was picked up later, but before turning to this there was a major development that occurred in the early 1960s in the automobile industry to consider.

The Automotive Industry
That portion of Canada manufacturing originating in the automobile sector represents a clear illustration of the way much Canadian manufacturing value added evolved. Dating to quite early years in the industry's history, Canadian inventors and entrepreneurs were present and not at all ineffective. As the industry evolved, a fairly rapid movement toward mergers and consolidations occurred. Canada's small, moderately successful pioneers quickly became part of fast-growing U.S.-based survivor firms.

The automotive industry is a prime example of one with very substantial economies of scale: unit costs drop as volume expands. Growth in North America originated largely in the vicinity of Detroit, Michigan. Canadian operations, even though they could be located virtually right next door (across the river) in Windsor and, more broadly, southern Ontario, were at much too small a market scale for efficiency if production was confined for the Canada consumer alone.

Canada maintained an early—albeit highly inefficient—automobile assembly operation by a clever use of tariff protection. Automotive parts could be imported without duty being payable if sufficient Canadian content (value added) was employed in assembling vehicles within the country (60% for cars and 50% for trucks). This led to effective protection for Canadian automotive production being approximately twice the nominal level. In short, the decision to locate assembly operations in Canada was determined not be efficiency but by tariff protection augmented by duty forgiveness provisions tied to Canadian content.

So long as Canada received a trade bonus relative to the United States under Commonwealth Preference provisions, relatively inefficient Canadian automotive production was not too great a burden for the country to be willing to bear. When that Preference was eliminated however, the full problems facing Canada's automotive industry became apparent.

In the late 1950s, Canada appointed Dean Vincent Bladen as a one-man Royal Commission to investigate the prospects of the industry. The resulting study revealed the serious difficulties facing Canadian automobile output. Since every car or truck bought by a Canadian involved not merely a higher price than in the United States but also a substantial import bill for parts brought in duty free, Canada's automotive manufacturing trade prospects were bleak.

Dean Bladen recommended that an "extended content" provision be substituted for the existing content provision, which applied only to value added to vehicles bought by Canadians. Although the government did not adopt Bladen's exact proposal, a variant figured in a unilateral series of initiatives that led to the adoption of the United States-Canada Automotive Agreement of 1965.

Canada acted in 1962 to allow automotive firms to achieve the remission of duties paid on increased imports into Canada conditional on the expansion of exports from Canada. The next year the previously suspended duties on key automotive parts imports were actually levied, but the range of automotive exports allowable for duty remission was expanded.

These duty remission schemes (which were later applied to certain European and Asian automotive firms operating in Canada) represented an interesting effort by Canada to circumvent the inefficiencies caused by Canada's small market combined with too many producers and products. The problem was that the duty remission provisions were subject to claims for countervailing duties by U.S. producers who could charge (not without reason) that they were being subjected to competition receiving an "unfair bounty or grant" from the Government of Canada.

Such changes were being made formally in 1964, but before a decision was announced the 1965 auto pact was signed. This agreement represents by far the largest bilateral sectoral accord ever reached. The specifics of this accord brought larger and surer gains for Canada than would have been possible from unilateral initiatives alone, but Canada insisted on certain "safeguards" that have been the source of bilateral controversy ever since.

These "safeguards" consisted of two components. One set was in the written agreement itself and served mainly to protect vehicle assembly operations (permanently) and, much more temporarily, existing automotive parts production in Canada. The second set lifted the absolute amount and guaranteed continued growth in Canadian automotive output as Canadian purchases of North American cars and trucks expanded. This set is not in the formal agreement but was in the nature of a "side deal" between the government of Canada and the automotive firms. U.S. congressmen, when learning of the "deal," expressed charges of deception by President Lyndon Johnson and claimed they had no choice but to accept a fait accompli.

It is unlikely that the "safeguards" were ever needed, as such, but Canada has retained them from fear of "worst case" contingencies occurring. In fact, however, efficiency in Canadian automotive production rose sharply to a point where output per worker is generally at least on a par with U.S. experience. Furthermore, Canadian automotive workers' wages have moved up much closer to what they are for unionized U.S. automotive workers, although in the 1980s the Canadian Automotive Workers (CAW) split off from the U.S.-based United Automotive Workers (UAW) and pursued their own bargaining priorities (including increased wages as opposed to the U.S. profit-sharing objective).

Canada has done quite well under the auto pact. Prices for vehicles made in the rest of North America are much closer (adjusting for exchange rate and tax differences) to those in the United States than was the case earlier.

Canada has a higher share of North American assembly and employment than it has of consumption, leading to a surplus in automotive trade with the United States that, while varying, grew to be upward of $5 billion in the mid-to-late-1980s. It is little wonder, therefore, that many business leaders as well as a majority (at least at the time) of Canadians saw considerable economic promise in the Canada-U.S. FTA.

The automotive industry received special attention in the FTA. Furthermore, emerging rapid expansion in trade between the United States and Mexico has caused mounting concerns in Canada. Before considering the industry in this broader context, events in the 1970s and early 1980s created an environment of tension and some not inconsiderable bitterness in the Canada-United States relationship that first merits attention.

Mounting Tensions

The mid-1960s also marked the beginning of a new era for the United States in world affairs and in a relationship between Canada and the United States that had come to be called "special" by many observers.

The year 1965 might be characterized as an economic success story for the United States (and, in a parallel manner, for Canada). Unemployment fell to just below 4.0%, inflation was roughly 2.0%, growth in real output was expanding at or above 3.0% a year, the government's budget was roughly in balance, the nation had a current account surplus in its balance of payments, and a rising percentage of the population was being brought above the so-called poverty-line.

By 1966, however, the U.S. economy was driven to excess by a sharp increase in military spending (related to Vietnam) that was not financed by higher taxes or reduced non-military spending, but rather by borrowing. Taxes were raised later, but the inflationary genie was let out of the bottle. In subsequent years, a modest slowdown was followed by a global upturn, sparked in no small part by rapid U.S. spending growth; an end of the pegged foreign exchange rate regime of the International Monetary Fund (IMF); a surge in world commodity demand that created an environment conducive to the 1973–74 petroleum price shock; and, "finally," the 1974–75 recession.

These were years in which Canada began "feeling its oats," in effect. Pierre Elliott Trudeau became the "new breed" prime minister of Canada in 1968; Canada, which had earlier allowed its currency to "float" relative to the U.S. dollar, returned to a flexible currency ahead of others in 1970; it sought to isolate domestic oil prices from OPEC's "shock" by imposing an export tax on shipments to the United States; the secretary of external affairs, Mitchell Sharp, authored an article exploring a "Third Option," geared toward developing broader trading relations with Europe and Japan and a stronger domestic economic policy performance; and it enacted the Foreign Investment Review Act (FIRA) that "screened" foreign takeovers and expansions by foreign-owned firms into new "unrelated" lines of activity.

Canada was only moderately affected by the 1974–75 recession in terms of unemployment and growth, but wage demands accelerated sharply and led, ultimately, to the imposition of wage and price controls in late 1975. These were reasonably "effective" in that inflationary pressures did not worsen (although they also did not improve much), but they indicated a proclivity for government intervention in yet another form that contributed to a sense of a strong "socialistic" slant to Canadian political life that was growing in the United States.

The second half of the 1970s produced years of major political change and challenge in Canada, highlighted by the election of the independentist Parti Québécois in the 1976 Quebec election. The United States in this period was under the ineffective leadership of the Democratic president Jimmy Carter. Economic performance rebounded from the impact of the first OPEC oil shock in terms of a restoration of growth, but unemployment remained high, budgetary deficits were emerging as a mounting concern, and serious inflationary forces persisted, exacerbated by the second oil shock in 1978–79.

The government of Pierre Elliott Trudeau held off an election until late into its third mandate, and when one was called in 1979 the Liberals lost their majority to a shaky Progressive Conservative minority led by Joe Clark. Clark's finance minister, John Crosbie, brought down a budget late in the year making a moderate effort to halt the deterioration in federal finances, but the moves went further than the public was prepared to support. The budget and the government were defeated and an election was called for early in 1980. Trudeau agreed to stay on to lead the Liberals, and they swept back into a majority position. That same year, 1980, Quebec held a referendum on the issue of allowing the provincial government to enter into negotiations for more independent status. The proposition was defeated, allowing the rest of the nation to breathe easier (at least for a while).

Return to office of the Liberal Party brought deepening problems in Canada-United States relations. During the campaign, Trudeau's advisors had convinced him to play up a sense that Canada should and would take firm steps to gain control over the deteriorating political economy. His speeches had included pledges to toughen up markedly on the administration of FIRA, which had become widely referred to as a "toothless tiger" and was not greatly at issue in the United States by the late 1970s. His pledges extended to ensuring that upon return to office his government would act to obtain majority Canadian ownership of development of the country's energy and other natural resources.

Budgets brought down by the federal government in 1980 and 1981 confirmed both to internal and to external business leaders that the newly reelected Trudeau Liberals were going to take a highly "interventionist" track. In the fall of 1980 the budget served mainly to launch the National Energy Program (NEP), probably the legislation most hated by the western provinces and the general business community of any ever passed in the country. Details of the NEP, looking back, made considerable technical sense. But the moves by the federal government to reposition itself—and the *national* economy—so as to more evenly spread the gains from an assumed further increase in world oil prices struck many as an unforgivable "power grab."

The budget presented early in 1981 turned out to be a disaster in timing and direction. Canada's economy was moving toward a major recession, the worst in the post-World War II era. By then, however, the federal budgetary position had deteriorated so badly that room for stimulative fiscal maneuver was quite limited. So the government focused on making the Canadian taxation and expenditure system "fair" but succeeded mainly in ensuring its massive defeat when another election was finally held in late 1984. For the foreign business community, this result could not have happened quickly enough.

Before turning to what happened next, it is worthwhile to pause to reflect on the Canadian experience of the early 1980s in the context of the historical predicament of the national economy sketched earlier.

Policy Incapacitation
As noted earlier, Canada had an abundance of natural resources, but its value adding manufacturing sector was small, excessively diversified and generally inefficient, not only relative to the United States but increasingly in relation to the disciplined economies of Asia. Canada was not competitive in export markets for non-resource goods, and its reliance on trade with the United States continued to increase because it was the only major market in which Canadian production was broadly capable of meeting the competitive challenge. Largely accounting for the success of Canadian manufactured products in the United States was the 1965 auto pact.

Several initiatives were taken by the Trudeau government in the early 1980s in an effort to upgrade Canada's productivity prospects. Chief among these was a so-called "mega-project" scheme that would have built upon the country's diversity in natural resource-based project potential. This diversity existed both in types of resources—such as hydroelectric projects, forestry projects and oil and gas projects—and in terms of locations; all provinces and virtually all regions had candidate projects judged worthy of support. The logic of this approach was founded in part on the ideas of Jay Forrester, intellectual godfather of the Club of Rome's *Limits to Growth* (1972), who had a meaningful impact on Trudeau. It also built upon the simple observation that Canada had developed largely through "mega-project" initiatives throughout its history.

Irrespective of the logic, the "mega-project" initiative failed both because capital costs had risen so high and because Canadian resources faced increasing external pressures from alternative sources of supply. Reliance on this approach in future will occur, as in the past, but on a far more selective basis than was implied by some who had visions of it being a new national economic strategy.

A second initiative that was explored would have built upon the widely acknowledged success for Canada in the 1965 auto pact. Preliminary efforts were made to seek out sectoral extensions of this bilateral approach, but it was clear rather early that the United States lacked interest both because it would not agree to Canada's concerns for some sort of "safeguards" and because there was little enthusiasm for taking such deals to the General

Agreement on Tariffs and Trade (GATT)—the multilateral trading body— to gain a waiver of the most-favored-nation principle. (The United States had had to seek such a waiver under the auto pact: Canada did not because it was prepared to sign a similarly "safeguarded" agreement with any taker.)

A third and final major exploratory initiative taken by the Trudeau government elected in 1980 was the appointment of a massive new Royal Commission chaired by a former senior cabinet official, Donald Macdonald. This commission, set up to investigate Canada's economic, social and constitutional future, released a report that figured prominently in the case made by the subsequent Progressive Conservative government to support its endorsement of the FTA.

A NEW LAUNCHING

When other candidates sought the leadership of the Progressive Conservative Party in 1983, they literally fell over each other distancing themselves from candidate John Crosbie's proposal to seek a free trade arrangement with the United States. Yet when the party was dramatically victorious in the September 1984 election, one of the highest priority items on an early caucus agenda was such an initiative. This is important because the leader, Brain Mulroney, had campaigned both for the leadership of the party and for the government of the country on a platform plank—i.e., no free trade with the United States—that he quickly discarded. This apparent opportunism has been a long-lingering criticism of him and of his leadership.

More important, however, the apparent turnaround reflected commitment with only limited analysis. Free trade with the United States constitutes, in effect, a new national economic policy. But it is an initiative that will be a victory of economic efficiency over political economy logic. Canada is different from the United States, but the description of the difference could not be captured by subtle shadings to an essentially "free market" document. The FTA is still being instituted in terms of phased tariff reductions. There have already been claims (undoubtedly exaggerated) that the FTA has resulted in massive net job losses among Canadians, and the possibility cannot be dismissed that the people of Canada might elect a party that had campaigned on the pledge to rescind the country's participation in the FTA as soon as practicable.

Details of the FTA
The so-called fast-track approach given by the U.S. Congress to the administration figured prominently in the evolution of the FTA. Wisely recognizing its own weakness in debating on a line-by-line basis, Congress had agreed to a format that would involve straight "up or down" voting with limited opportunity for item-by-item haggling so long as the administration would inform it in good time of its intention to enter into such a trade negotiation and allow timely generalized hearings on which to judge U.S. national interests. This suited Canada's experience and instincts, shaped by years of dealing with United States officials, quite well.

Broad goals. Canada entered into the negotiations of the FTA primarily, but not exclusively, for defensive reasons. There was growing concern in the business community that U.S. "contingency protection" (through such devices as countervailing and anti-dumping duties) and other forms of non-tariff barriers (NTBs) were being applied with increasing determination by the United States.

Back in August 1971, the so-called Nixon shock leading to an imposition of a 10% duty surcharge on dutiable imports into the United States, had caught Canada off guard. It caused such severe concern in Ottawa that a delegation—led by Simon Reisman who later became chief Canadian trade negotiator of the FTA—went to Washington seeking exemption because of Canada's assumed "special relationship." The delegation was promptly turned down. Canadian business wanted to ensure this would not happen again. In effect, Canada sought to ensure that if, as more and more commentators were thinking was possible, the United States retreated behind progressively higher trade barriers, Canada would not be outside longing to get inside.

It is interesting to note that Canada, which had used trade barriers (tariffs) to help launch its manufacturing sector with the National Policy, was now threatened by actions of Canadian firms seeking to protect themselves against the use of trade barriers (non-tariff) by the United States. These firms, taking job opportunities with them, were moving down to U.S. facilities. This was occurring at a time when falling tariffs, because of earlier GATT negotiations, and rising Canadian wages and currency levels had begun to erode seriously the effectiveness of Canada's policy of protection.

From the U.S. perspective, the principal goal sought from the FTA was to demonstrate in a concrete way what it was seeking in the broader GATT negotiations. Therefore, while Canada sought to halt the use of U.S. protection in relation to Canadian output, the United States wanted to move beyond merely freer trade in goods to encompass more open trade in agriculture and services, security of access to supplies, freer and fairer foreign direction investment, and greater limits on the use of subsidies, among other objectives.

Key aspects of agreement regarding trade in goods. The FTA entered into effect beginning January 1, 1989. Tariffs will be eliminated by January 1, 1998, or earlier for a number of products. Agricultural products will become subject to reduced tariffs over time, although provisions for emergency measures are made in the event of serious market disruption. Canada and the United States have relatively few (although by no means zero) bilateral agricultural issues, but both share growing concern about agricultural policies in Europe and Japan. Agriculture is not covered at all extensively under GATT, and Canada and the United States agreed to revisit this sector following whatever emerges from the Uruguay Round.

In the resources area, and in particular the energy sector, Canada has agreed not to restrict access to supplies from Canada unless Canada is forced to cut output for a number of accepted reasons. But in such a case, the United States would have the right to obtain a percentage of Canadian output to be determined by U.S. purchases over the past 36 months. Canada need not sell to U.S. customers, but once it does it cannot cut back access arbitrarily and must share any production cutback in terms of its own consumption. This provision has been criticized as involving a loss of Canadian sovereignty, but it basically establishes that if it wishes the United States to be a fair buyer, Canada must be a fair seller.

The automotive sector was the source both of conflicting imperatives and the realities of the existing auto pact. Canada had been using duty-remission incentives to induce foreign (particularly Asian) firms to locate assembly operations in the country. This created a source of inducement that the United States was finding increasingly objectionable. Furthermore, Canada was unwilling to bear the political heat associated with giving up the "safeguard" provisions described earlier. This, too, was a source of mounting U.S. frustration and irritation.

An innovative approach was adopted in this sector; it was not perfectly compatible with most other elements regarding trade in the FTA, but it was not a "bad" compromise. Over time, Canada will be able to retain the safeguard protection, but as the bilateral automotive tariff falls, the penalty for failing to meet the provision falls, with one significant caveat. Because U.S.-owned firms can, under the auto pact, ship goods (mainly parts) from "offshore" into Canada duty free, an incentive amounting to several hundred million dollars will persist as an enticement to the firms to keep Canadian value added above safeguard levels. In addition, Canada's ability to encourage offshore producers to locate in Canada with incentives that would (or could) impact negatively on production in the United States is sharply curtailed. Canada may not grant any additional foreign firms auto pact status and it must phase out duty-remission provisions.

These measures do restrict Canada's policy mobility, but these limits seem not unreasonable given what the bilaterally agreed auto pact has brought in terms of relative benefits for Canada. The option existed, but in reality a long time ago, to foster a Canadian-owned car company, but the (maybe only temporary?) limit on Canadian consumer sovereignty was a cost that politicians did not have the courage to impose then; now the country has little practical alternative to what it was able to elicit from the auto pact and the FTA.

Canada was able to keep beer out of the FTA, although challenges through the GATT to Canada's beer pricing and marketing policies appear to place very real deadlines on how much longer these policies can continue. Again, the problem is largely internal to Canada, since provincial laws require firms selling beer to produce it in the province (except in Prince Edward Island). For Canadian breweries to survive competition from outside, these provincial constraints on achieving scale economies must be phased out. By mid-1992, the two countries were involved in a "beer war" as each put punitive tariffs on the other's beer.

There are U.S.-induced constraints on full free trade, but these lie primarily in services (mainly transportation). Some limits persist on certain forest and steel products as a result of countervailing duties and the threat of so-called "injurious" imports of highly politically sensitive products.

Trade in services. A strong U.S. trade policy objective has been for some time to open up services to freer and fairer trade. The FTA moves beyond GATT in the services area (hardly a major accomplishment), but the achievement might be better described as setting a framework for future action than as breaking significant new ground.

The FTA distinguishes "covered" from "uncovered" services. Those that are "covered" by agreement are substantial, but far from all-inclusive. In most respects, existing policies are "grandfathered," meaning that practices in place can generally continue. The key aspect of the services agreement provides for "national treatment" of firms of one country by the policies and practices of the other. This does not mean the services policies of the two countries must be the same; rather, policies cannot be applied in a discriminatory manner varying with the nationality of ownership of the firm.

Financial services provide a good case in point. Canadian banks are allowed to engage in securities activities that U.S. banks are generally forbidden from engaging in by legislation passed during the years of the Great Depression (the Glass-Steagall law). For this and other reasons, it might fairly be argued that U.S. financial institutions receive a "better deal" from Canada than Canadian financial institutions did from the United States in the FTA. Quite probably true, but Canadian banks are basically as well-positioned as U.S. banks in the United States, in terms of U.S. law, and once the legislation changes, Canadian banks will be treated in a fully parallel manner to U.S. banks by those changes.

On Canada's insistence, cultural services generally were "left out" of the FTA, although many products related to what Canada calls "culture" will experience tariff reductions over time. Moreover, while existing policies may be exempted, subsequent actions judged to be at variance with the "spirit" of the FTA will permit disciplinary action (mainly by the United States, in all probability) having "equivalent commercial effect" in areas not confined to culture. On U.S. insistence, transportation services were "left out" of the FTA, mainly because there was very little prospect Congress would rescind the Jones Act, which requires commerce within and between U.S. locations to be transported by U.S. vessels.

Some limited progress toward freer and fairer services trade has indeed been made by the FTA. Nevertheless, more than enough remains to be done to keep interested bilateral negotiations busy for years to match the level of progress achieved in goods trade.

Investment policies. Following Canada's passage of FIRA and the threatened tightening of its provisions by the reelected Liberal government in 1980, tough economic realities imposed themselves. Canada began moving away from the threatened action quite quickly, apart from the energy sector, and the general policy stance toward foreign direct investment moved toward positive encouragement from apparent hostility. Canada had already moved to rename the agency Investment Canada, and while its approach was by no means passive, it severely curtailed its constraining actions and turned increasingly toward selling the virtues of the country to outside sources of funding, technology and managerial talent.

The United States probably received the most visible response by Canada to its overall objectives on this investment front. Canada agreed to limit, to the point virtually of eliminating, trade-related limits on U.S. investment in most (but not all—e.g., energy) sectors. Canada's ability to "screen" investments was subjected to limits that were raised to $150 million by 1992 (meaning in non-excluded sectors the acquisition would not be reviewed unless it exceeded $150 million in size). Furthermore, by the same date Canada agreed to do away with the review of *any* indirect acquisitions by foreigners. This concept related to the review of takeovers by foreign firms of other foreign firms with facilities in Canada. The United States had referred to this as an extraterritorial application of a Canadian law. Although possibly true, the use of such extraterritoriality was much more widespread and intentional on the part of the United States over the years.

Dispute settlement. A major disappointment from the FTA for Canada relates to one of the country's primary initial objectives: limitations on the use of anti-dumping, countervailing duties, etc., by the United States. The two countries did move beyond the GATT with respect to dispute settlement, but the gains have been mainly in the area of administrative procedures, e.g., regarding timing for reviews, bilateral oversight on adherence to national trade laws, etc. Although the progress was not inconsequential, it fell far short of what the Canadian government had insisted was its bottom line. A lingering notion in Canada is that their negotiators were bested by the U.S. negotiators, but this view rests largely on a narrow focus about legalisms and not enough on the greatly improved environment for an improved efficiency performance in the Canadian economy.

LINGERING PROBLEMS

There are serious problems facing Canada as it seeks to implement its new national policy, which is strongly focused on seeking greater reliance on market forces and less on government involvement. A brief commentary on the philosophical issue of whether or not this policy shift will prove acceptable to the people of Canada will conclude the essay. First, there are two fundamentally important practical issues that will influence strongly the degree of sustained political tolerance for this reversal, in effect, to the direction of national policy: macroeconomic policies in response to Canada's adjustment needs; and uncertainties as to the ultimate boundaries to the FTA.

Macroeconomic Policies: Non-complementary
Those who support the freeing of trade have long recognized the need for aid to the process of adjustment. Participating nations in trade-liberalizing efforts all stand to gain as units, but it can be expected that many individuals will suffer losses from the removal, or at least the reduction, of protection.

Because the Conservative government had very limited intellectual underpinning to its support for free trade with the United States, it had not thought through at all clearly its approach to the adjustment assistance issue. Confident that aggregate national growth would be sustained with only minor interruption under its leadership, the federal government did not think through the appropriate macroeconomic policy mix.

It must be recognized that during the second half of the 1980s, the Canadian federal (and overall national) deficit had become increasingly widely acknowledged as a problem of serious dimensions. Therefore, there was felt to be very little room (and probably little "need") for major fiscal initiatives to support adjustment. This constraint hampered a positive response to the need for enhancing displaced workers' skills, but once a sharp overall economic slowdown began in early 1990, means were found to assist the labor-retraining effort.

In some respects fiscal actions were taken that were not popular, but they will help Canada compete more efficiently in international markets. A case in point is determination in forcing passage of the Goods and Services Tax, a VAT-type tax that is far less regressive than its critics claim and that will replace a trade-distorting manufacturers' sales tax. Moreover, Canada's new approach to competition policy will encourage merger activity that is appropriate for the competitive environment the country now faces.

A far more serious problem lies in the fact that the Bank of Canada has decided to pursue a fundamentally different monetary policy stance than has characterized its stated objectives throughout the post-World War II era. Apparently no longer satisfied with the goal of doing no worse on inflation than its trading partners (read the United States, which accounts for upward of 75% of Canada's trade), the bank has now set the goal of "zero" inflation as an absolute objective. (Absolute zero is almost certainly tighter than the bank would settle for, but it appears to want *low* inflation, independent of U.S. and other major country inflation performances.)

In pursuit of this objective, the bank has allowed (encouraged?) short-term interest rates to rise to an exceptionally high premium relative to comparable U.S. rates. The result was a sharp upward move in the Canadian relative to the U.S. dollar. This has encouraged Canadian imports to expand and depressed Canadian exports and the profitability of U.S. dollar-dominated Canadian export earnings.

There is no doubt about the demand growth excesses that surged in Canada, particularly in southern Ontario, in the second half of the 1980s. To counsel the Bank of Canada not to resist the surge would have been exceptionally short-sighted. But something more than monetary policy was needed to supplement the response by the bank. In its absence, Canada's ability to adjust to the new opportunities created by the FTA has been severely limited. Were the government not so committed to "market" solutions, therefore eschewing any income policy initiatives, and yet preserving social policies the country was no longer willing to fund, an approach less disruptive to Canada's adjustment to the FTA would have been more feasible.

Uncertain Future FTA Boundaries
Canada had originally seen the FTA as a parallel approach to the GATT. Following assumed successful completion of the Uruguay Round, which it felt would be helped, not hindered, by the FTA, Canada thought several difficult problems in the bilateral negotiations (most important being subsidies) could be cleared up.

The Uruguay Round is in jeopardy, as may be the GATT itself. Partially in a defense movement with respect to the emergence of "blocs," the United States entered into another bilateral initiative with Mexico that Canada had little choice but to join. In the summer of 1992, a North American Free Trade Agreement (NAFTA) was successfully negotiated; it requires approval by the legislatures of all these countries. And if, as is increasingly speculated, a deal with Mexico expands to encompass other Latin American countries, Canada will be faced with a far more difficult set of adjustments than had originally been anticipated and, very importantly, an increasingly marginalized role for political identity in a U.S.-dominated Americas "bloc."

AN INCREASINGLY UNCLEAR FUTURE

Canada began the 1990s on a very uncertain note. It was in a recession with rapidly rising unemployment, sharply falling profitability, interest rates at the short-term end that were exceptionally high relative to U.S. rates, a dollar that was much above the Purchasing Power Parity level vis-à-vis the U.S. dollar, a very large budgetary deficit, and a quite weak current account in its balance of payments. Wages were too high at the current value of the currency, yet the unionized sector (at twice the percentage of the labor force observed in the United States) had a deeply held sense of being worth more than it earned.

On the political front, Quebec's relationship with the rest of Canada appeared destined to undergo major alterations, Ontario was governed by a bright and effective premier heading a "socialistic" party holding a majority, and federally it appeared almost inevitable that the next election (in late 1992 or early 1993) would be a five-way contest with no popular national leader emerging.

Clearly, Canada needs to rethink both its economic and its political future. If it decides to stay highly focused on FTA as its new national policy, its political options will be significantly more restrained than the nation yet realizes. Is there a credible alternative?

REASSESSING THE CASE FOR CANADA

The Canada-United States FTA is an imperfect agreement for Canada. No comprehensive accord with the largest economy in the world could be otherwise. Having agreed to it, however, Canada has no credible option involving its abandonment. Transitional costs have been high, but the magnitude of the displacements caused by Canada pulling out now would be horrendous, irrespective of the dreams of pro-Canadians that it would be otherwise. Nevertheless, Canada's betting on sustained forward momentum within the GATT to blunt the sacrifice of its effective sovereignty appears to be in serious jeopardy. Now, the United States wants to help fill the emerging global trade policy vacuum by leading its own "bloc." If Canada is to moderate the impact of this development upon its own policy options, some form of unilateral initiative appears increasingly imperative.

Given the very nature of Canada, and especially that factor that uniquely differentiates Canada and the United States, namely the "French fact" of Quebec, the shift away from the National Policy toward the more "right-wing" or "hands-off" approach of the Mulroney government has been excessive. Canada must determine carefully its priorities for efficient and effective support for well-defined national objectives and argue forcefully to maintain its policy prerogatives in the forthcoming negotiations with the United States regarding subsidies and countervailing duties.

On the trading front, the point has been reached at which Canada must think seriously about applying the FTA's reduction of tariffs to zero across the board to all countries through unilateral action. It might launch this initiative now to take effect over a sufficient period—say 10 years—so that its own producers have the necessary time to prepare and other countries have time to consider an appropriate response. For countries prepared to match the Canadian action, Canadian tariff eliminations could be formally "bound." For countries not so prepared, Canada would leave the tariff cuts "unbound" (meaning they could be raised again, selectively, at the country's discretion to the formally agreed GATT level).

Such trade action by Canada would go a long way toward avoiding an excessive degree of reliance upon U.S. initiatives toward a "bloc." It could create some new hardships on Canadian industry, but these hardships appear increasingly to be inevitable and would be reduced at least somewhat by the probability of a noticeable (and, it is hoped, temporary) drop in the Canadian dollar.

Another initiative that Canada might seek to investigate would be to support the achievement of well-thought-through "core" objectives for the Canadian economic development process. The principle would be to ensure that Canada works to be as efficient and effective as possible in pursuing goals it must achieve if it is to remain at the high end of the development scale. These goals might include the optimal development of its massive land and natural wealth and the maintenance of the leading-edge telecommunication service capability, among others. Foreign involvement would be encouraged broadly, but the purpose of this involvement would be set by Canada.

The United States, being so close and so powerful, has long provided a convenient excuse for Canada failing to develop to its potential. Now that the country has entered into the FTA with the United States, Canada may have set on a course that will involve a progressive diminution of its economic, political and cultural sovereignty. If so, the choice will have meant too many Canadians could no longer make for themselves a continuing credible case for Canada.

FURTHER READING

Cameron, Duncan, ed. *The Free Trade Deal.* Toronto: Lorimer, 1988.

The Canada–U.S. Free Trade Agreement. Ottawa: Minister of Supply and Service, 1988.

Crispo, John, ed. *Free Trade: The Real Story.* Toronto: Gage, 1988.

Gold, Marc and David Leyton-Brown, eds. *Trade-offs on Free Trade: The Canada– U.S. Free Trade Agreement.* Toronto: Carswell, 1988.

CANADIAN AGRICULTURE

BOB STIRLING

Canadian agriculture helped to spawn a commercial and industrial society. However, the foundation of market agriculture in Canada has often been tenuous and its future uncertain, a condition that remains today. The farm sector has experienced external market pressures from agribusiness, but it also has shown an internal dynamic characteristic of family farming systems. The combination of these forces has produced a changing agricultural structure heading toward the 21st century.

PHYSICAL RESOURCES

Canada's agriculture must contend with meager soil resources, awkward geography and severe climatic conditions. Most of Canadian farm production takes place in a narrow belt, generally within 500 kilometers of the U.S. border. Eighty-eight percent of Canada's land is entirely unsuitable for agriculture. Only part of Nova Scotia, and Southern Ontario, lie below the 45th parallel of latitude, while production in Western Canada takes place north of the 49th parallel. An agriculture so far north must contend with relatively short growing seasons and must provide added protection against the cold for livestock, poultry and the storage and transportation of perishable commodities. For example, spring wheat, which is Saskatchewan's main crop, usually takes at least 100 days to mature, but three of the province's 10 regional weather stations recorded average growing seasons of 100 or fewer days since World War II. As well, the Prairies are a long distance from major metropolitan areas or seaports. Consequently agricultural commodities produced there for either domestic demand or international sale must make long rail hauls to the St. Lawrence Seaway or over the mountains to the Pacific coast. Factors such as these become added costs which Canadian agriculture must counterbalance with either cost efficiencies for other inputs, or reduced incomes, if it is to remain competitive with other international suppliers.

Canada's soils are graded into seven classes based upon fertility, permeability, topography, erosion potential, stoniness, climate and so forth; Classes

I to III are suitable for crops, IV and V are suitable for pasture, VI is marginal and VII is unsuitable for agriculture. Sixty percent of Classes I to VI is currently used, the unused portion being mostly Class V and VI soils. There are about 114.9 million acres of cropland (Classes I to III) or 5 percent of Canadian soils, and only 10.1 million acres (0.5%) of Class I soil. Half of the Class I soil is in Ontario and under heavy pressure from urban expansion, while most of the rest is in the Prairies. Production is hampered by low rainfall in the Canadian Prairies, which are a dry, northward extension of the American Plains; only 7 to 12 inches of precipitation fall during the growing season and 12 to 18 inches yearly.

FARM PRODUCTION

Clearly these physical resources limit yields and total production, but they also restrict the range of field crops that can be profitably grown. In some regions, the combinations of these factors serve to limit beef, hogs, dairy and poultry output as well. But the historical development of Canadian agriculture as an engine of growth within the industrializing Canadian economy has also helped to form the structure of regional specialization. Table 2 shows the broad outlines of that structure. The Prairies are characterized by large farms and ranches specializing in the production of wheat and cattle. This region accounts for about 51% of Canada's farms and 49% of total farm receipts. Prairie feed grains are shipped to the other regions to sustain their livestock and poultry production. The federal policy that sustains these feed shipments, the Feed Freight Assistance Programme, was introduced as an emergency measure during World War II, but it has turned out to be a durable policy. Its effect has been to enhance regional specialization and hence help to mold a regional structure to Canadian agriculture. The Prairies have become heavily oriented toward cereals, oilseed and feeder cattle, while a great deal of livestock and poultry production has developed in the other regions. More than three-fourths of Canada's dairy farms, two-thirds of hog farms and one-half of poultry farms were in Ontario and Quebec in 1981. To cite the extremes, one-half of Quebec farms were dairy farms and almost two-thirds of Saskatchewan farms were wheat farms. Ontario, with one-fourth of Canada's farms and 26% of total farm receipts, specializes in beef, dairy, hogs and poultry products on farms that are about one-fifth as large as those in the Prairies. Quebec, with 14% of Canada's farms and 16% of total receipts, makes its major contribution in dairy and hog production. Similarly the Atlantic provinces have important livestock and poultry sectors with New Brunswick and Prince Edward Island also noted for potato production. British Columbia also emphasizes livestock and poultry production. Fruits and vegetables, while limited, appear in specific localities that have favorable growing conditions and/or have been heavily bonused by provincial and federal governments, such as orchard and field production in the Lower Mainland of British Columbia, the Niagara Peninsula in Ontario, parts of Quebec, and the Annapolis Valley in Nova Scotia, and greenhouse production in Newfoundland and most other provinces.

The structure of Canadian agriculture shows adaptation to these physical, economic and political constraints. In the export markets, Canada appears to have done best when it could supply fairly unique products and not try to compete head to head against countries with more favorable resources. Hence, Canada is historically best known for supplying high-protein wheat to European millers who could blend it with lower-quality wheats to upgrade the baking quality of their flour, and more recently for shipping grain to Communist countries when cold war politics hampered competitive U.S. sales. Similar examples, although in far less volume, include export of lean bacon and pork products to Britain when its normal supplies were cut off during World War II and recently to California and eastern U.S. metropolitan markets; export of flax with qualities particularly suited for the manufacture of oil-based paints; and export of canola (used for edible oils) and oats for the increasingly diet-conscious American urban consumer and of live feeder calves to be fattened at lower-cost U.S. feedlots near metropolitan markets.

In the past, agricultural exports have been crucial to the Canadian economy, making up one-half of total exports after World War I and 40% after World War II. But by the mid-1980s they had dropped to less than 10% of total exports. At the same time, in the domestic markets, Canada is not self-sufficient in food. Although it is not clear that Canada's physical resources are the most serious constraint here, foreign imports of fruits, nuts and vegetables, dressed beef and poultry, and increasingly of dairy products have seriously challenged Canadian production. For the past decade Canada's food imports have been about 7% of total imports and about one-half of the value of agricultural and food exports. Although the ratio of agricultural and food imports to exports has declined slightly since the 1970s and some of the imports such as certain fruits and nuts cannot be grown in Canada, it is clear that Canadian agriculture has also had to cope with international competition in its domestic markets. In general, Canada's historical adaptation to its physical resources, specialized export orientation and international competition has introduced a unique type of risk, an emphasis on "orderly" marketing of some commodities, and a partial or incomplete structure to Canadian commercial agriculture.

The declining importance of agricultural exports together with the significance of imports is indicative of the fact that agriculture no longer plays the major role within the Canadian economy that it once did. Almost one-fifth of GNP came from agriculture after World War I, but it was down to one tenth after World War II and it is now well below 5%, having been eclipsed by other resource export industries, specific manufactures and, of course, the enormous rise in the commercial and services sector. While agriculture is certainly not marginal to the Canadian economy, its reduced significance may be accompanied by a growing impatience with farm "problems" among Canadians and policymakers, and a reluctance to arrest its decline.

FARMS AND FARM FAMILIES

Fewer Farms

The number of farms in Canada has been steadily declining since World War II so that by 1986 there were less than half the number of farms that existed in 1951 (see Table 1). The rate of decline from 1971 to 1981 (13.0%) slowed considerably compared to the previous two decades, perhaps partly due to the improved farm economy toward the end of the 1970s and partly because there were simply fewer farms to disappear given that the rationalization process had been going on for more than three decades. But the higher rate of decline from 1981 to 1986 (7.9%) is indicative of the more depressed conditions for much of Canadian agriculture during the 1980s and perhaps a new wave of rationalization.

Farm Size

Since the amount of farmland scarcely changed from 1951 to 1986, and given the declining number of farms, the average area of farms more than doubled to 572 acres. But the average capital value (of land, livestock, machinery and buildings) increased almost 24-fold in current dollars (or 4.77 times in constant 1971 dollars) from about $15,000 to $375,000. The value of farm capital, particularly land, in part reflects the general financial health of agriculture. Hence the decline in average capital value from 1981 to 1986 illustrates the serious farm depression that set in during the early 1980s. There is great variation between regions; the average capital value of Prairie farms in 1986 was double that of farms in Quebec or the Atlantic Provinces (see Table 2). Also, there is a lot of variation between farms; farms with annual gross sales over $250,000 had average capital values approaching $2 million ($2.5 million in the Prairies), while farms with sales under $25,000 were, consistently, about one-tenth as large.

Farm Ownership

Overwhelmingly, Canadian farms are family farms where families own or rent their land, machinery and livestock, and provide most of the farm labor themselves. Between 1971 and 1986 these family businesses accounted for more than 99% of all farms in Canada while nonfamily corporate farms increased only marginally from 0.2% to 0.4% (although the corporate farms tended to be larger and to account for a disproportionately large measure of total production). But there has been a tendency for the distinction between corporate and family farms to become blurred: from 1971 to 1986 the proportion of family farms that had formed corporations or had set up written partnerships increased 5% to 12.7%. For many years the call has been for policy that would "defend the family farm," but it has become increasingly difficult to know precisely what this call refers to since it is now clear that the "family farm" structure is very malleable and quite capable of changing itself into a family-owned corporate structure with a much stricter business orientation than seems to have been the Canadian family farm heritage. It appears that these family-owned farm businesses will be the predominant element of the farm structure in the future with nonfamily corporate farms continuing to play a numerically small but, in some circumstances, strategic role in primary production.

Enthusiasm for owning land has certainly been a strong tendency among Canadian family farms (see Table 1). Only 6.5% of farm operations rented all of their land in 1986. However, the tendency for farmers to own all of their land has been dropping since the 1950s (from 77% in 1951 to about 60% in 1986). Increasingly farmers appear to have been augmenting their farm size by renting additional land. This may not mean that a class of nonfarm landlords has developed, since it appears that they include the state (through crown leases), relatives and estates, as well as the banks, credit unions and the Farm Credit Corporation (a federal lending agency), and a few agribusiness and real estate corporations. Typically provincial legislation and Canadian tax laws make it either illegal or seldom profitable for those not engaged in farming to own much farm real estate.

Since the vast majority of Canadian farms are family farms with fairly high capital investments, it is necessary for their property to be successfully transferred between generations if the structure is to reproduce itself over time. Of course, the declining number of farms since World War II means that many farm families have not accomplished generational transfers. Many of these farms were not financially viable under existing market conditions, but the family organization of these small businesses introduces a number of economically unusual factors to the transfer process. For example, there may be generational conflict, the family may have no sons (patrilineage and patriarchal authority patterns have predominated within the Canadian farm family and are eroding only very slowly), the members of the next generation may have preferred to find employment in the nonfarm sector, the rural community may no longer offer an adequate quality of life, the potential network of local support and extended family ties may have eroded, and so forth. Factors such as these are also present when people choose paid employment, and when wealth is inherited in the nonfarm sectors, but the fact that farm families both own the farm capital and provide most of the farm labor coupled with the fact that these "family" considerations are present in many thousands of transfer decisions, gives the farm sector a fairly high level of fluidity and a distinct potential for change.

This fluidity is also indicated by the age distribution of farm operators (from which we can infer the families' life cycles). Thirty-four percent were 55 years or over in 1986. Most of these operators (and their spouses) could be expected to retire during the ensuing decade. Indeed, this has been the typical pattern; about one-third have been in this age bracket for the previous two decades. However, fewer than 20% were under 35 years in 1986 (the average for farm operators was 48). In other words, the stock of replacement farmers was smaller than the number of retirees and the replacement farmers typically were in their middle years before they actually became farm operators. This also reflects a characteristic of generational transfer on Canadian farms. As we will see, annual farm income is not so high as to allow the average farm family to build up adequate retirement savings. Instead, their retirement "savings" lie in their farm investment, which, as we have seen above, can be substantial. But to realize these savings it is necessary for the next generation to buy out the previous generation's assets. Few young people are able to accumulate the funds necessary to make such a sizable purchase. Consequently, they must wait until their late twenties or thirties before taking over the farm can be feasible. The banks and credit unions have been heavily involved in this transfer process. The Farm Credit Corporation (FCC) was also created, in part, for this reason. One province, Saskatchewan, attempted to reduce the financial constraints on generational transfer by implementing a "Land Bank" which would purchase the farm from the retiring generation and lease it back to a family member from the next generation. Although the program initially worked well, it fell victim to partisan political criticism and was terminated. Many provinces have implemented alternate programs that augment the private lending agencies by guaranteeing loans or reducing the interest rates to beginning farm families. But these programs can be a serious drain on provincial revenues. They can also encourage farm families to take on levels of debt that are beyond the capacities of their farms to service, leading ultimately to bankruptcies, family hardship and abrupt rationalization in the farm industry. The facilitation of generational transfer remains one of the more vexing policy problems for Canadian agriculture.

Farm Family Labor
The fact that Canadian agriculture is overwhelmingly family agriculture accounts for the components of Canadian farm labor, that is, the farm operator (self-employed, usually the husband in the farm family), unpaid labor (most often the wife and older children, both male and female), and paid labor (the traditional "hired man," and seasonal or part-time workers). But there have been some interesting changes since World War II. In 1951, 96% of the farm labor force was male, but by 1981 more than 21% was female, including more than 10% of self-employed farmers, almost one-fourth of paid farm labor and more than two-thirds of unpaid family workers. The proportion of farm labor that is self-employed has been dropping while the proportion that is paid labor has been increasing (in 1981, 48% were self-employed while 44% were paid labor). Does this mean that we have been witnessing the "industrialization" of Canadian agriculture? Indeed, it does, but one must be cautious in interpreting this trend. Many of the new paid "employees" appear, in fact, to be family members, relatives and neighbors who were previously "unpaid labour." The dramatic rise in women's paid farm employment from 1951 to 1981 (754%) illustrates the point. While not all were wives or daughters, a number of provincial employment enhancement programs and a very slow but noticeable erosion of the traditional patriarchal approach to income taxation and matrimonial property surely account for some of this growth. Nevertheless, once wages are built into the farm budget, the logic of farm production changes a bit, traditional family relationships are potentially modified, and, one might argue, the stage is set for a new form of family farming.

Canadian farm families are closely integrated with the rural and urban nonfarm sectors of the Canadian economy and culture. During each five-year period from 1966 to 1981 roughly 30–35% of farm operators moved out of farming while some 25–30% moved in. Again we see the importance of the family cycle in this data. Some of the operators leaving farming are indeed the victims of financial crises and bankruptcies, but most of the consolidation of Canadian agriculture results from retiring farm families not being replaced, their land and productive capital going to the remaining established producers. Some Saskatchewan data illustrates this general characteristic. From 1971 to 1976, a net balance of 43,590 people moved out of the Saskatchewan rural farm sector (21,100 males and 22,490 females). Of these, 66% were age 15 to 29 and most would have moved to urban areas in search of further education, jobs, better quality of life, marriage partners, and so forth. At age 30 to 34 for men and 25 to 34 for women, the pattern reversed briefly; about 4.5% moved back into the farm sector having accumulated enough wealth, occupational experience and credit rating to be able to take over a farm unit. (Out-migration increased again during the retirement years of the family circle). Clearly, most farm people have a thorough experience of urban jobs and urban culture by the time they take up farming.

However, Canadian farm people are also heavily involved in nonfarm labor markets as part of their ongoing farm life. Canadian farm operators have always been involved in off-farm work. While the proportion fluctuated from 28 to 39% between 1951 and 1981, the average number of days they spent at off-farm work increased 128% (from 75 to 171 days). But the allocation of farm family labor extends beyond the operator's labor and is, no doubt, the result of complex family politics and decision-making structures. Fifty-three percent of farms operated by individual families had one or more family members working off the farm in 1981. By 1986 only 26% of individual family farms had no family members working off the farm. On average in 1981, the operator (usually the husband) contributed 68% of the family's total paid labor (three-fourths of his work going to the farm) while the spouse (usually the wife) contributed 18% (one-half of her work going to off-farm employment), and the children contributed 14% (one-half of their work going to off-farm employment, with daughters much more heavily involved in off-farm employment than sons). The decision to work off the farm may involve a family member's personal interest in a nonfarm job or career, or the pursuit of specific family values (for example attempting to ensure that the children receive an adequate life-style and education and are successful or financially secure as adults), but often it appears to be a way to enhance the viability of the farm as a family endeavor. More than one-third of farm family income came from off-farm work by family members in 1981, but for large farms (with gross sales of $56,000 or more) it contributed only one-eighth, while for small farms it contributed 45% (and almost 90% when both the operator and spouse worked off the small farm). By 1986, more than one-half of the family income of small farms and about one-sixth of large farm families' incomes came from off-farm employment. Of course the large farms produce the lion's share of total Canadian farm output (about three-fourths), so, on the one hand, we can observe that the management of most of farm production is not immediately integrated with off-farm work. On the other hand, small farms are more numerous and crucial to the maintenance of a farm population as well as the reproduction of the family farm sector. Even large farms typically started out small and off-farm work was often essential to their growth and financial stability.

Concentration and Differentiation
So far, we have the impression of a Canadian farm sector with several hundreds of thousands of families operating small businesses. But they are not all equal. Indeed, the farm sector displays a structure of concentration with many thousands of farms producing very little and relatively few farms producing a lot. For example in 1981, the smallest one-half of farms produced only 7% of Canadian gross farm sales (the same was true for 1986). The largest one-fourth of farms in 1981 produced three-fourths of total Canadian sales. Of course this does not begin to approach the level of concentration in some nonfarm industries, but it does identify a basis of differentiation within the farm sector itself.

Farm Income
Table 1 shows that average farm net income increased almost six-fold from 1951 to 1986, but if we compare farm income to the rise in the cost of living we find that 1986 farm incomes were 25% above 1951 levels but actually 13% below 1961 levels. Low and variable farm incomes have long been recognized as a characteristic problem of family agriculture. Average net farm incomes for both 1981 and 1986 were below the respective Canadian poverty levels for a rural family of four. Obviously many farm families had to look beyond the farm for sources of income to sustain their standard of living.

About 18.5% of farm families had total family incomes (from all sources, both farm and nonfarm) below the poverty line in 1986. However only 13% of families operating very small farms (below the 25th percentile in the distribution of gross farm sales) were below the poverty line, whereas 23% of families with middle-sized farms (between the 50th to 74th percentiles) were in poverty. The incidence of farm family poverty was fairly general across the regions (slightly higher in the Prairies), but it appeared to hit hog and beef (except feedlot) operations the hardest where the poverty rate for mid-sized farms ran from 28% to 35%. It was also more serious for younger farm families, particularly in the 25–34 year age group where one-fourth were in poverty. Typically, poor families had negative agricultural incomes and nonagricultural incomes in the $6,000–$10,000 range—not enough to bring them over the poverty line. But other families with negative or very low farm incomes managed to escape poverty by having substantial nonagricultural income—in the $30,000–$43,000 range. In fact 75% of the families with farms in the bottom half of the gross sales distribution, along with 33% in the top half, followed this pattern. Surprisingly, only 9% of the smallest half of the distribution and 47% of the top half had both adequate farm incomes coupled with adequate family incomes.

It seems clear that Canadian agriculture does not provide a basis for adequate family income for most of its practitioners. In other words, if as a family you want to farm in Canada, you must find a way to "connect" your family to the nonagricultural economy, not only in order to prepare yourself for getting into the business, but also as a way of stabilizing and sustaining the family farm. The majority of families with smaller farms appear to have approached farming from this perspective. On the one hand, there is a tendency among farm organizations and policy makers not to see them as bona fide farmers at all. On the other hand, this fairly well established pattern among small farm families may indicate a more pervasive trend that is affecting larger farms as well. Indeed there is some evidence to support this view if we examine mid-sized family farms, those in the upper half of the gross sales distribution but below the very large (less than the 95th percentile). These are the farms that produce most of Canada's total farm production and they are of a size that requires a serious commitment of family labor, capital and management. Clearly these are as close as we can come, with aggregate statistics, to the ideal-typical full-time family farmers in Canada. More than 55% did not receive an adequate agricultural income from their farms. For 35%, nonagricultural sources of income raised their total family incomes over the poverty line. But more than 21% of these farm families remained in poverty in 1986 (recall that only 13% of families on the very smallest farms were in poverty).

Survival Strategies
It appears that integration with the nonfarm labor markets is a common "survival strategy" for Canadian farm families. But it is not simply a strategy of survival in the short term or immediate sense. Indeed, family farms have several strategies of adaptation which make the logic or rationality of their farm production more like that of other small business sectors and less like textbook management or the logic of corporate firms. It's not uncommon for farm neighbors to trade labor services in order to help each other overcome crises or deal with peaks in the farm work cycle. Perhaps more important is the way that many farm families seem to be "extended" when it comes to assisting those who are on the farm. Assistance can come in the form of labor, machinery, land, direct financial help and help arranging loans, help in the farm home or with raising children, management advice and providing special skills. Often parents help their children get started farming, but children also tend to return home to supply labor at critical periods. These patterns of assistance can be essential for the stability of a family farm. Some 1986 Saskatchewan data suggests that almost half of farms currently receive some form of familial and community assistance and it is likely that the vast majority of farms benefit from these patterns of help at some point in the family cycle. Canadian family farms probably should not be seen as isolated and economically independent business. It may be that when a family farm goes bankrupt it often takes down a network of contributors with it.

AGRIBUSINESS

In the modern vernacular, "agribusiness" has come to mean large industrial farms or, indeed, any large family farm with a strict business orientation. This usage is of questionable analytical value, however, since it blurs the distinction between the farm and nonfarm sectors and masks a range of important questions about the relationship between the two, particularly the ways in which family farming adapts to the penetration of nonfarm interests and structures. Consequently we will follow the more traditional usage of the Canadian Task Force on Agriculture, where "agribusiness" refers to the industrial and commercial firms, usually organized as medium to large corporations, that interface with the farm sector on both its inputs and outputs sides. The relationship is based upon markets but it involves technological and political as well as economic power. At times and on some issues, the farm and agribusiness sectors have common interests, but often they are opposed. Increasingly the farm sector has not coalesced around a common "farm" interest, and there appear to be important, although less visible, divisions within agribusiness as well.

Industry Structure

There are two characteristics that appear to be generally true of agribusiness in Canada: high levels of concentration and high levels of domination by American branch plants. In the food and beverage industries by the 1970s, the largest eight firms controlled from 42% (in baking) to 100% (in each of vegetables oils, sugar and beer) of the industries' total Canadian shipments. Within the regions in Canada, however, the levels of concentration tended to be much higher (from 55% to 100%) since specific firms tended to hold regional market dominance. The structure of agribusiness on the farm inputs side appears to be similarly concentrated with a few dominant firms in industries such as petroleum products, fertilizers, chemicals, machinery, financial services and, to a lesser extent, livestock and poultry feed and building supplies. Generally the large oligopolistic firms have had higher profit rates than smaller competitive firms, although the collapse of the only Canadian farm machinery multinational in the 1970s illustrates that agribusiness firms on the farm inputs side are not immune to a downturn in the agricultural economy. The same may not be as true for the outputs side since the population must continue to eat and the typical response of family farms to reduced prices and low incomes is to try to produce more rather than less, although droughts and other natural disasters can have a serious effect. Certainly the retail food industry has been strong in Canada; indeed it may be the predominant power among industries on the farm outputs side. During the 1950s its profits ran 7% to 10% higher than the manufacturing or wholesale food industries. From the early 1950s to the mid-1970s the proportion of the retail food market controlled by the large food chains doubled to 60%.

Each agribusiness industry has large foreign firms, usually American branch plants, present. With a few exceptions their presence dates back to the World War I era or even earlier, and they appear to see the Canadian market as simply a northward extension of the farm and consumer markets in the United States, advancing continentalist policies for the Canadian food system, as well as for petroleum, fertilizer, chemicals and other farm inputs. Canadian food processing has mostly concentrated on the domestic market (the milling industry was the primary exception until the 1970s, when flour exports dwindled). Consequently, the presence of major U.S. firms in the Canadian food processing industries has reduced the chances of Canada approaching self-sufficiency in food. Still the Canadian food and agribusiness systems are not always identical to their U.S. counterparts.

Cooperatives and Marketing Boards

Canadian and American agriculture share a tradition of progressive farm organizations and cooperative businesses. Certainly after World War II cooperatives were firmly established. In both countries, farmers organized large cooperatives on their inputs side in an attempt to cut costs through buying in volume, "cutting out the middlemen," eliminating the "sharp" practices of the more ruthless suppliers, and so forth. But Canadian farmers were also successful in organizing large cooperatives in two industries on their outputs side: the grain trade on the Prairies and the diary industry in Central Canada, especially in Quebec. For example, by the 1970s, the Prairie Wheat Pools controlled more than two-thirds of the country elevator grain collection system and they had kept the "private" trade, including foreign branch plants, at bay for half a century. The importance of these successes in organizing large cooperatives in Canada, however, does not lie particularly in their own market practices, since they ultimately have tended to become profit-oriented and management-controlled agribusiness corporations similar to their private competitors. Rather, unlike their U.S. counterparts, they have been important because they organized and focused a very large block of farm people, to become a strong political force for the creation of systems of "orderly" marketing of farm commodities.

The federal system in Canada, with its division of powers between the national and provincial levels of government, has made state involvement in marketing structures constitutionally difficult. But by 1956, complimentary provincial and federal legislation was in place and marketing boards were rapidly organized. The Canadian Wheat Board, permanently established in 1943, was joined by some 80 provincial boards by 1970 in dairy, poultry, hogs, fruits and vegetables. Some boards merely promote their commodities or at most negotiate prices without any control over supplies. Other boards control supply by issuing quotas to farm producers, which enhances their power when they negotiate prices with food processors, and presumably allows farmers to receive at least a portion of the productivity gains that they have been able to achieve in commodity production. Since the 1970s, marketing "agencies" have also been created; they have the power to physically handle the commodities as they move from the farm gate to processors, allowing them to warehouse excess supply in an attempt to increase the price and/or smooth out price fluctuations. By 1975, marketing boards accounting for 64% of farm cash receipts (up from 41% a decade earlier) including 100% of dairy, 90% of poultry, 77% of egg and more than 80% of grain and oilseed receipts.

The implications of marketing boards are a heavily debated topic and the jury may still be out. In some cases they may contribute to higher food prices in the short run while evening out food price fluctuations and reducing the likelihood of sharp price increases in the longer term. As well, they probably have contributed to the gradual restructuring of the farm sector toward increasing specialization. But perhaps more importantly, they make the Canadian food and agriculture markets a bit unique, and tend to stand in the way of agribusiness firms that could benefit from a more thorough-going continentalization of the North American economy. Consequently, Canadian marketing boards have come under heavy political pressure during the 1980s with the advent of free trade.

Farm Inputs
World War II ushered in dramatic changes for Canadian agriculture, although it was several decades before the effects were fully realized. The war brought improved technology along with wartime companies anxious to spread this technology to civilian uses at the war's end. Farmers were willing consumers of these labor-saving and production-enhancing innovations. Mechanization was the first wave of change. The number of tractors per 100 farms increased 300% between 1941 and 1951; there were about two tractors per farm in 1976 and 2.8 tractors 10 years later. Electric motor use mushroomed as reliable power grids extended to rural communities. Machinery and equipment made up about one-fifth of total farm capital in 1986. Machinery capital per farm had more than doubled (in constant dollars) since 1971.

The subsequent waves of change were equally important. The herbicide 2,4-D was introduced in the 1940s, but it was not until after the 1970s that many new chemicals appeared on the market and chemical use dramatically increased. Some 42 million acres were sprayed for weeds or insects in 1981, representing 36.6% of improved land, up from 22% in 1971. By 1986 the area sprayed increased to 68 million acres or 60% of improved land. The input cost of herbicides and pesticides increased by 283% from 1971 to 1986 (in 1971 dollars). This firm demand by farmers no doubt helped the chemical companies to increase the price of these farm chemicals by 450%. Fertilizer use also increased. Farm expenses for fertilizers (in 1971 dollars) increased about 150% in the 1950s, 210% in the 1960s and 192% in the 1970s. By 1986, one-half of all improved land was fertilized, up from 16% in 1971.

The generation that farmed during the Great Depression had lasting memories of the negative side of farm debt, and it appears that this collective farm consciousness prevailed as a management style until the 1970s. Subsequently, outstanding farm debt increased from about $5 billion in 1973 to $22 billion by 1987. Although this was a marginal increase in constant dollars, and represented a declining proportion of total farm capital value, interest on indebtedness was the third most important farm cost

390

item in 1988, estimated at 13% of total operating expenses or more than 35% of net farm income.

Clearly, Canadian farmers have become increasingly dependent upon nonfarm inputs during the last three decades. The trend is illustrated in Table 1. In the early 1950s farmers could expect on average to net about one-half of their gross farm income. But by 1986, 82% of gross farm income went to expenses and depreciation, leaving only 18% as net income. Table 2 shows some regional differences in this pattern of expenses and incomes for 1986. The Atlantic Provinces and British Columbia have a somewhat lower-cost agriculture, but it is not reflected in better net-to-gross income ratios. In contrast, Quebec has a marginally higher-cost agriculture but its net-to-gross income ratio is better than for the other regions. Perhaps this reflects the importance of marketing boards and strong government encouragement in maintaining prices for the principal commodities that contribute to Quebec farmers' gross incomes. Table 2 also shows the relative insignificance of farm self-sufficiency; on average only 5% of farm net income came from the farm's own produce in 1986.

The Income Squeeze and Productivity
Prices for farm inputs have tended to rise faster than farm product prices, generating a "cost-price" or income squeeze for farmers. For example, from 1971 to 1986 the index of farm costs rose by 333 while the index of farm prices rose by 314. This squeeze accounts for low incomes and farm consolidation but it also tends to produce gains in farm productivity, an influence common to many industries. Farm population has dropped, farm labor being replaced by increasing levels of mechanization. Crop yields have increased (although wheat yields appear to have hit a plateau). Livestock and poultry productivity gains have been the most impressive: since before World War II, milk production per cow has almost doubled to more than 8,000 pounds, while egg production per layer increased by one-half to more than 200 eggs. A good deal of current thinking worries that Canadian agriculture is not sufficiently responsive to market forces. But these considerable and fairly rapid changes—decreasing the farm labor force and increasing the rate of commodity production—seem to challenge that view.

FARM CRISIS IN THE 1980s

Agrarian populism typically identified external forces as the main culprits bringing about change in the farm structure, but looking back from the early 1990s, one sees that there was an important internal dynamic to commercial farming as well. Farm families seek higher incomes. That translates into larger farms with higher capital values. It also means fewer farms.

Canadian agriculture experienced this interaction in the 1980s in a wave of farm bankruptcies. Product prices had started an upturn in the '70s; by 1981 they were 200% higher than in 1971. Flush with gross income, farm families bid up the price of land and other farm capital. Banks increased their farm loans based on these inflated equity values, which soon bore no reasonable relationship to the farms' productive capacities. But interest rates also rose—650% from 1971 to 1981. Finally, farm commodity prices tapered off and in some cases, such as wheat and other grains, they plummeted drastically by the mid-'80s.

Wheat and grain prices fell because of a concerted effort on the part of the United States to use these commodities as a vehicle for foreign policy. The international grain trade has long been dominated by large trading firms. Currently there are five. The two largest are headquartered in the United States and have had a significant impact on U.S. grain and agriculture policy. During the interwar period the United States held 16% of world exports of wheat and flour (during the depression and the two world wars it had been a net importer), with Canada holding more than 35%. After World War II the United States forced its share up to highs of 50% in 1973–74 and 48% in 1981–82, using Public Law 480 and other cold war policy vehicles to enhance its position in world trade and to defend its balance of payments. But by 1985 its share had again dropped to 29%, being challenged by the "orderly" state marketing system in Canada, and especially by state subsidy-induced increases in production and exports in the EEC. Announcing that it intended to regain its "traditional" market share, the United States initiated an Export Enhancement Program of subsidized exports combined with a complicated set of domestic support policies in the 1985 Farm Bill. Other exporting countries tried to meet this competition. The price for Red Spring (Canadian) wheat dropped from over $6.00 a bushel in 1981 to about $3.00 by 1987, well below its cost of production. The Canadian government tried to counter declining farm incomes with a range of special subsidy programs. By 1986–87, government subsidies accounted for almost 90% of net farm income on the Prairies, rising to more than 100% the following year compared to zero in 1980–81.

The farm bankruptcy rate mushroomed. By 1987, the Farm Credit Corporation (FCC) estimated that 8% of commercial farms were insolvent (carrying $1.7 billion in debt), and another 23.2% were experiencing cash flow difficulties (carrying $10.3 billion in debt). The FCC held more than 200,000 acres as a result of foreclosures. The banks held 284,000 acres and claimed to have lost $261 million on bad farm loans. Bracing for the fallout, the federal government introduced the Rural Transition Programme in 1986 to encourage farm families to leave farming and retrain for other occupations. The program helped only a fraction of the thousands that left.

There has been increasing specialization by farmers and this has led them to identify their interests more with the specific commodity they produced than with farmers as a community. In the 1970s and '80s, "commodity groups" sprang up, often opposing each other. Further, regional specialization sometimes pitted farmers against each other. Wages pitted farm owners against farm workers especially in the fruit and vegetable sectors. And several court challenges, the tragic suicide of a farm woman, and new property rights legislation demonstrated the inequalities inherent in the law and patriarchal farm structures, awakening a renewed interest in farm women's rights.

Table 1

SELECTED CHARACTERISTICS OF CANADIAN
FARMS, 1951–1986

	1951	1961	1971	1981	1986
Number of Farms	623,091	480,903	366,128	318,361	293,089
Tenure:					
Rent only	8.4%	6.3%	5.2%	6.2%	6.5%
Own only	77.3%	72.9%	68.6%	63.3%	59.5%
Both own and rent	14.3%	20.8%	26.2%	30.4%	34.0%
Organization:					
Family	—	—	92.1%	86.9%	82.7%
Partnership—informal				3.6%	4.2%
Partnership—written	—	—	5.8%	5.7%	7.5%
Family corporation	—	—	1.9%	3.4%	5.2%
Nonfamily corporation	—	—	0.2%	0.4%	0.4%
Average size:					
Acres per farm	279	359	463	511	572
Total capital per farm	$15,200	$27,388	$65,736	$409,297	$374,206
Realized net income/farm	$2,213	$3,639	$3,615	$10,180	$12,759
As a % of gross income	53.4%	36.4%	27.8%	17.3%	18.1%
Expenses and depreciation					
as a percent of gross	46.6%	63.6%	72.2%	82.7%	81.9%

Source: *Census of Canada.* Statistics Canada Cat. 21-603.

The influence of farm people even became diluted within the "farm" community. In 1941, 3.1 million (27.1%) of the Canadian population were farm people; in 1986, only 890,000 (3.5%). By 1986, three-fourths of Canadians lived in urban areas. Even though rural Canada was declining relatively, it actually increased numerically (from 5.2 million in 1941 to 6 million in 1986). In 1941, two-thirds of the rural population were farm people; in 1986 only 15% were. In fact, at the turn of the 1980s, urban to rural migration actually was greater than the traditional rural to urban migration. But many of these new rural dwellers do not depend on farmers for their livelihood or see their interests as tied directly to agriculture.

Collectively these forces led to a disintegration of the farm "class," the eclipse of agrarian populism and the breakdown of its organizational and political forms. Several "general" farm organizations disbanded in the 1980s, while others experienced financial crises. The farm cooperatives, having grown into large corporations serving the needs of ever larger, market-oriented farmers, and faced with renewed competition from the private sector, increasingly imitated their competition and forsook their previous role of populist leadership.

AGRICULTURE AT CENTURY'S END

The family farm has been dominant in Canadian agriculture and its "survival strategies" seem to give it a superior ability to undertake risk and

Table 2
REGIONAL VARIATION IN CANADIAN
FARMS, 1986

	Atlantic Provinces	Quebec	Ontario	Prairies	British Columbia	Canada
Number of Farms	11,321	41,448	72,713	148,544	19,063	293,089
Average size:						
Acres	248	217	192	915	313	572
Capital	$226,194	$228,086	$326,066	$453,470	$340,148	$373,840
Cash receipts	$64,124	$78,499	$74,323	$67,232	$56,382	$69,758
Percentage of total Canadian receipts	3.6%	15.9%	26.4%	48.8%	5.3%	100.0%
Percentage of each region's total sales deriving from:						
Cattle & Calves	12.2%	10.0%	21.0%	23.4%	18.3%	20.1%
Wheat & Durum	0.3%	0.5%	2.3%	33.0%	1.1%	15.7%
Dairy Products	25.1%	35.1%	18.4%	5.2%	23.4%	15.6%
Hogs	12.4%	23.2%	13.0%	7.8%	5.5%	11.8%
Poultry & Eggs	16.1%	12.3%	10.1%	3.3%	16.7%	8.0%
Fruit & Vegetables	7.8%	4.6%	8.8%	0.6%	19.2%	4.9%
Small Grains	0.8%	1.3%	0.3%	9.7%	0.9%	4.8%
Potatoes	15.3%	1.4%	0.9%	0.8%	2.4%	1.6%
Operating and depreciation expenses/farm	$53,813	$58,016	$59,912	$57,939	$48,653	$57,676
As a percentage of cash receipts	83.9%	73.9%	80.6%	86.2%	86.3%	82.7%
Realized net income/farm	$11,246	$21,972	$15,230	$9,675	$8,231	$12,759
Income in kind per farm	$936	$1,489	$819	$382	$501	$677
As a percentage of net income	8.3%	6.8%	5.4%	3.9%	6.1%	5.3%

Sources: *Census of Canada.* Statistics Canada Cat. 21-603.
Note: Receipts include supplementary or deficiency payments, whereas "total sales" refer to commodity sales only.

accommodate economic hardship. This will ensure that it continues to dominate farm production. But "family farm" is a broad category: it has changed, increasing in size and productivity, relying on off-farm employment and income, becoming more divided. The technological and managerial potential now exists in some commodity sectors (for example, eggs and poultry) for a few dozen very large, vertically integrated, family farms to produce most of Canada's output. Obviously these will not be the family farms that have been familiar to the Canadian landscape. But the potential is clearly there for far fewer farms to produce almost all of Canada's agricultural production in a much more concentrated industrial structure. These family farms will be specialized, closely integrated with agribusiness, and organized economically and politically around their commodity production. Their fortunes will depend heavily upon their success at overcoming the productive limitations of Canada's climate and geography so as to be able to meet international competition.

Canada's unique agricultural marketing system will also change. The divisions between farmers, the eclipse of agrarian populism and cooperative leadership, and the rise of agribusiness firms with a continentalist orientation has already begun to erode the "orderly marketing" system. The Canadian Wheat Board has progressively seen its powers eroded over the past three decades. Freight rates favorable to grain export have been reduced, enhancing the potential for non-board commodities. But the greatest challenge has come from the Free Trade Agreement signed with the United States in 1988, and from the General Agreement on Tariffs and Trade (GATT). Curiously seen as unfair subsidies to Canadian exporters, virtually all of the marketing boards are potentially on the chopping block since an open Canadian border will make their system of quotas unworkable. Fruits and vegetables, dairy products, poultry and eggs are likely to be the first and largest losers. Indeed, many British Columbia fruit farmers have already been displaced, and marketing of oats was removed from the jurisdiction of the Wheat Board in 1989.

But there are some ecological glitches in this scenario. Postwar, high-energy farm technology may not provide a sustainable agriculture. If we include food processing and retailing, the food system actually produces less energy than it consumes. And this energy efficiency ratio appears to be getting worse. When prices for energy (i.e., petroleum, electricity) rise as they did in the 1970s, modern farm inputs become prohibitively costly. The soil is also suffering. In the Prairies, up to 50% of soil organic matter has been lost in the eight decades since settlement. There are doubts about whether the productivity gains, which are essential for a specialized, high-cost farming system, can be continued, particularly in crop production. High-energy farm technology can present difficult environmental problems as well as occupational and consumer health problems. And global warming will have serious but as yet unclear effects on Canadian agriculture. Dry southern areas such as the Prairies will lose productivity while some northern regions with questionable soil fertility will become arable.

There are also some market glitches. Increasingly, food consumers are demanding higher-quality food, free from the chemical residues of herbicides, pesticides, antibiotics, growth hormones and other typical inputs of a specialized, large-scale farming system. It is not clear whether large, market-oriented family farms of the future will be able to accommodate the reduced income levels currently associated with organic production. A complementary but more serious challenge will come from a growing environmental movement that may demand a form of agricultural production that is ecologically and socially sustainable. The current trends in agriculture are not compatible with such a demand.

FURTHER READING

Agriculture Canada. *Growing Together: A Vision for Canada's Agri-Food Industry.* Ottawa: Agriculture Canada, 1989.

————. *Proceedings of the Canadian Agricultural Outlook Conference.* Ottawa: Agriculture Canada (published in December of each year).

————. *Challenge for Growth: An Agri-Food Strategy for Canada.* Ottawa: Agriculture Canada, 1981.

Fulton, Murray, Ken Rosaasen, and Andrew Schmitz. *Canadian Agricultural Policy and Prairie Agriculture.* Ottawa: Economic Council of Canada, 1989.

Morissette, Diane. *Growing Strong: Women in Agriculture.* Ottawa: Canadian Advisory Council on the Status of Women, 1987.

Sparrow, Hon. H. O. *Soil at Risk: Canada's Eroding Future.* Ottawa: Senate Standing Committee on Agriculture, Fisheries and Forestry, 1984.

INDUSTRY AND TECHNOLOGY

ANTHONY C. MASI

Canada occupies an interesting and unique position among the world's most advanced industrial democracies. It has a varied industrial structure, yet depends heavily on the export of resource-extracted products to balance imports of manufactured goods. Further, it stands alone among the prestigious "Group of Seven" (G7) nations (United States, Japan, Germany, France, United Kingdom, Italy and Canada), whose yearly economic summits make headlines throughout the world, by having a very large proportion of its industrial base either owned or controlled by foreigners, mostly Americans. In fact, while taking remarkably different positions on the implications of this structure for the country's economic prospects, most observers have agreed that Canada has the highest degree of foreign ownership of any industrial country. However, this dependency has not kept Canada from being among the nations of the world with the highest standards of living. This combination of factors in the historical evolution of Canada's industrial and overall economic structures (high degree of dependency on raw materials or semifinished products, high proportion of industrial assets owned by foreigners, relatively high standard of living) has given rise to an impressive, and quite original, body of literature on "Canadian political economy."

In discussing the evolution of the country, the central argument of the Canadian political economy tradition is that by having its productive capacities and market access controlled and/or dominated first by the United Kingdom (earlier for the Province of Quebec by France) and subsequently by the United States, Canada has relied so heavily on the export of raw materials or semifinished goods that its industrial development has been, and some would argue continues to be, both significantly slowed and perceptibly distorted. This approach has been labeled the "staple" theory of economic development. Staples, in this theory, are defined as extracted raw materials or cultivated agricultural products that are destined primarily, if not exclusively, for export markets (fur, timber, wheat, metals). As a consequence, these staples have in the past dominated and continue to dominate regional markets and, indeed, even the Canadian national economy as a whole.

Two very interesting and important reports were produced in the late 1960s and early 1970s that dealt with the extent and impact of foreign influence, mostly through the direct ownership of productive assets or by having a controlling equity share through investment, on Canada's industrial structure and the country's prospects for economic development. In 1968 the Watkins Report on the foreign ownership of Canadian industrial assets argued that the staple theory could effectively be transformed into a theory of investments. Two stages were involved in this process. First, the profits from the exports of raw materials and semiprocessed goods were directed to infrastructural developments. Second, in turn, the well-developed infrastructure itself then encouraged the diversification of the domestic economy, but in a truncated and distorted fashion since foreign firms were also encouraged to penetrate these markets as well as the staples production sectors themselves.

It should be remembered that Canada also encouraged settlement on the vast prairie regions at just the time (late 1800s and early 1900s) that industrialization was reaching maturity in North America. As a consequence, the attraction of self-employment in agriculture brought immigrants to the Canadian West and may have been a factor in inhibiting the expansion of industrial capital since it reduced the available labor supply in the cities of central Canada and thus may have operated to increase the wages that were offered to factory workers.

Historically, however, Canada had considerable industrial output as early as the late 19th century, and the presence of foreign ownership was already abundantly evident. Some commentators have seen a problem with subsequent developments, namely that, by having a large proportion of its industrial output controlled by foreigners, Canada was unable to develop a managerial class or entrepreneurs able to make autonomous decisions on product innovation and technological process adaptations. So, the very fact of having an extremely favorable balance of trade in staples led to a decidedly negative outcome in the terms of trade for manufactured goods for Canada even though the industrial base was evolving and fairly widely dispersed.

A second study, the 1972 Gray Report, documented that more than half of all manufacturing and mining was in the hands of foreigners, mostly American corporations. Further, at that time, these foreigners controlled nearly all of the production taking place at the high value-added end of the market.

In Canada, then, the historical record and the contemporary situation show a low percentage of finished manufactured goods in the total of exports and, further, when Canada is compared to the other industrial democracies, it has a lower level of manufactured products as a percentage of gross domestic product than its level of living would predict. Again, this difference is one of the features that makes Canada so unique—the high degree of dependency is associated with one of the world's highest standards of living!

While Canada is a vast country in terms of its geographic scope, at just over 27 million inhabitants (Statistics Canada estimate for mid-year 1991), it is the smallest of the G7 in population size. This means that it has a relatively modest internal market and must look to exports for the development of its industrial structure. But Canada has had some success in controlling its economic destiny even in light of the massive proportion of its productive apparatus that has been in the hands of foreigners and notwithstanding its reliance on the export of staples. In particular, Canada has maintained control of its financial institutions, and, limited only by the constraints that a small country bordering on a larger one faces, has been able to maintain a relatively autonomous set of macroeconomic policies.

INDUSTRIAL STRUCTURE

The general practice in discussions of the structure of a national economy is to divide it into three sectors: primary, secondary, and tertiary. *Primary* industries are resource-based, and, in addition to agriculture, fishing and forestry, include coal mining and other extractive industries. *Secondary* industries are involved in transforming primary products, that is, they are an economy's manufacturing sector ranging from petroleum refining, iron and steel, and pulp and paper to textiles, clothing, footwear, furniture and other consumer goods, plus equipment manufacturing, shipbuilding and other capital goods products. Finally, the *Tertiary* (or services) sector includes services from restaurants and bakeries to banks and insurance companies, and, of course, public administration. The focus of much of the remainder of this essay will deal with the secondary sector.

Table 1 provides percentage distributions for broad industrial sectors in terms of their contributions to Canada's gross domestic product (GDP), at factor costs. During the decade of the 1980s, the primary sector's share was less the one-tenth of Canada's total GDP, while manufacturing's share fell from just over to just under one-fifth, and services contributed about three-fifths. It should be noted at this point that Canada's gross domestic product for 1990 was approximately $510 billion. Table 2 gives data on the distribution of employment by roughly the same broad industrial sectors (with differences due to the way in which these data are reported in the various publications of Statistics Canada). There have been considerable shifts in employment shares over the decade of the 1980s. The services sector increased from 58.7% to 64.7% of total employment, while manufacturing fell from 19.7% to 15.9% over the same period. By 1990, there were over 11.3 million employed persons in the Canadian labor force of nearly 12.6 million individuals (with unemployment, at that time, running at about 9.5%).

In the manufacturing sector, by the end of the 1980s, Canada had nearly 37,000 establishments, covering more than 170 different industries or trades. Table 3 provides a summary of the number of establishments, the number of employees, a calculated average size of establishment, the total wage fund and a calculated average annual salary per employee, the total value added and a computed ratio of value added per employee for 22 industry

CANADA

TABLE 1
Percentage Distributions of Gross Domestic Product at Factor Costs, for
Canada, by Economic Sectors, 1980, 1985 and 1990

	1980	1985	1990
PRIMARY SECTOR			
Agriculture	2.4%	3.1%	2.3%
Forestry, fishing	0.8%	1.0%	0.8%
Mining	3.0%	6.1%	3.9%
SECONDARY FACTOR			
Manufacturing	21.9%	19.3%	17.9%
Construction	5.7%	6.9%	6.5%
Transportation	6.3%	5.1%	4.8%
Communications	4.3%	2.8%	3.6%
Utilities	3.2%	3.1%	3.2%
TERTIARY SECTOR			
Trade	12.6%	11.5%	11.2%
Finance	13.1%	14.3%	16.0%
Services	25.7%	20.4%	23.2%
Public administration	6.9%	6.6%	6.5%
TOTALS	100.0%	100.0%	100.0%

Source: Statistics Canada, Cat. 13-201, *Canadian Statistical Review;* National income and
expenditure accounts, annual estimates.

TABLE 2
Percentage Distributions of Employment, for Canada, by Economic Sectors,
1970, 1980, 1985 and 1990

	1970	1980	1985	1990
PRIMARY SECTOR				
Agriculture	6.5%	4.5%	4.2%	3.4%
Other primary industries	2.7%	2.8%	2.6%	2.3%
SECONDARY SECTOR				
Manufacturing	22.3%	19.7%	17.5%	15.9%
Construction	5.9%	5.8%	5.2%	6.2%
Transportation, communications and utilities	8.8%	8.5%	7.8%	7.6%
TERTIARY SECTOR				
Trade	16.8%	17.2%	17.7%	17.9%
Finance	4.8%	5.7%	5.6%	6.0%
Services	25.8%	28.9%	32.4%	34.2%
Public administration	6.4%	6.9%	7.1%	6.6%
TOTAL	100.0%	100.0%	100.0%	100.0%

Source: Statistics Canada, Cat. 71-001: The Labour Force.

TABLE 3

Manufacturing Establishments, Employees, Wage Funds, and Value-Added, by Industry Groups, Canada, 1987

Industry Group	No. of Plants	Number Employed	Average Size	Total Wage Fund	Average Wage	Value Added	Value Added per Employee
Food	3,144	197,167	63	4,926,656	24,987	12,810,156	64.97
Beverages	296	31,361	106	1,067,716	34,046	3,167,452	101.00
Tobacco	25	5,948	238	242,665	40,798	983,533	165.36
Rubber	164	24,238	148	715,058	29,502	1,421,586	58.65
Plastics	1,127	44,650	40	1,002,024	22,442	2,349,376	52.62
Leather	384	21,782	57	375,030	17,217	660,054	30.30
Primary textiles	219	25,935	118	663,653	25,589	1,450,794	55.94
Textiles	858	34,769	41	702,020	20,191	1,417,577	40.77
Clothing	2,390	112,002	47	1,846,275	16,484	3,380,610	30.18
Wood	3,424	121,655	36	3,304,256	27,161	6,547,852	53.82
Furniture	1,822	61,584	34	1,227,471	19,932	2,219,035	36.03
Paper	694	119,346	172	4,185,229	35,068	10,959,182	91.83
Printing	5,276	127,543	24	3,539,542	27,752	7,091,433	55.60
Primary metals	427	104,088	244	3,838,613	36,879	8,398,472	80.69
Fabricated metals	5,498	156,951	29	3,954,291	25,194	8,132,919	51.82
Machinery	1,908	82,422	43	2,183,235	26,488	4,224,339	51.25
Transportation equipment	1,514	218,368	144	7,065,819	32,357	14,855,210	68.03
Electrical	1,439	143,837	100	4,067,818	28,281	8,701,383	60.49
Non-metal minerals	1,547	56,822	37	1,668,869	29,370	4,163,025	73.26
Refined petroleum	126	15,148	120	708,309	46,759	2,066,515	136.42
Chemicals	1,306	89,030	68	3,003,188	33,732	10,153,268	114.04
Other	3,202	69,372	22	1,544,511	22,264	3,138,802	45.25
TOTALS	36,790	1,864,018	51	51,832,248	27,807	118,292,573	63.46

Source: Statistics Canada, Cat. 31-203: Manufacturing Industries of Canada, National and Provincial Areas.

groups in Canada for 1987. The industry groups with the largest number of establishments were fabricated metals, printing, wood, food, and the residual "other manufacturing" sectors. In terms of employment, the largest groups were transportation equipment (nearly 12% of the employed labor force in manufacturing), food (over 10%), fabricated metals (8%), electrical and electronics (just under 8%) and printing (just under 7%). The five groups with the largest average establishment size were primary metals (244), tobacco (238), paper and allied products (172), rubber (148) and transportation equipment (144). The five smallest on that criterion were other manufacturing sectors (a residual; 22), nonmetallic minerals (37), printing (24), fabricated metals (29) and the furniture industry (34).

The highest average annual wages were paid in petroleum refining ($46,759), tobacco ($40,798) and primary metals ($36,879), and the lowest in clothing ($16,484), leather ($17,217) and furniture ($19,932). Four sectors had ratios of value added per employee that exceeded 100: refined petroleum, chemicals, tobacco and beverages; while clothing, leather and furniture all had ratios below 40. The value added approach avoids double counting by subtracting expenditure in intermediate goals bought from other firms, i.e., only finished goods are considered.

Now, there is also considerable regional variation in the structure of Canadian industry. In the western regions Canada depends on agriculture, fishing and the forestry industry, mining and resource processing (which includes wood products, paper and allied products, primary metal extraction, nonmetallic minerals, petroleum and coal). Ontario and Quebec make up Canada's core central region and depend on some low-technology industries such as food and beverages and tobacco; labor-intensive secondary manufacturing in metal fabricating; transport and electrical machinery and equipment; communications and industrial equipment; and high-technology manufacturing industries such as aircraft, chemicals, scientific precision equipment and the like. The Atlantic region is low-technology with much of the activity concentrated on primary resource processing of fish and some mining.

These differences in the context of a relatively decentralized governmental structure make it difficult for Canada to formulate a coherent and consistent national policy today. In fact, the state of the economic union in Canada is a question of national debate and an issue of proposed constitutional change. Each of the three major regions has a different list of items for the national agenda or wishes to change the rank order of its presentation in the development of policy: in essence the resource-dependent regions want policies that encourage exports while the manufacturing sectors seek assistance in learning how to become, or remain, competitive in the global market place.

Canada's top 15 industrial corporations can be ranked on the basis of sales and asset figures. Three of the top 10 are American automobile manufactures: General Motors (1), Ford (3) and Chrysler (8). However, the single largest employer, with close to 120,000 individuals working for it, was the telecommunications giant BCE (formerly Bell Canada Enterprises, which includes Northern Telecom), and that company's stock has wide distribution with less than 10% in the hands of foreigners. Two provincially owned crown corporations in the energy sector, Hydro-Quebec and Ontario Hydro, as well as two federal crown corporations, Canadian National Railways and Petro-Canada, were also among the top 15 industrials in the country. What makes these facets of Canadian industrial structure interesting is, on the one hand, the significantly larger role played by the state in actually running productive enterprises in Canada when compared to its large neighbor to the south, and, on the other hand, the role of protection in helping develop the telecommunications industry, both in the delivery of services and in manufacturing components. The remainder of the top 15 industrials includes other energy companies, a world-class aluminum producer, mining and resource interests, and some diversified manufacturing holdings.

Table 4 provides data on the percentage distributions for foreign-controlled assets for the years 1976 and 1986. The overwhelming first impression is indeed the strong presence of foreign ownership in the Canadian context. At the same time, over the decade between the mid-1970s and the mid-1980s, the trend has been downward, and significantly so, for nearly every sector of economic activity. By way of illustration, the metal mining sector, which had 40% of its assets controlled by foreign interests in 1976, by 1986 only had 18% so dominated. In the manufacturing sector, textile mills in the hand of foreigners fell from 58 to 46%, paper and allied products from 40 to 23%, machinery from 65 to 47% and electrical products from 69 to 52%. The only major industry group to witness an increase in foreign ownership was primary metals, which includes smelting operations (which went from 15 to 20% foreign-owned). Little or no change was recorded for tobacco products (all foreign in both periods), chemicals (7 out of 10 in foreign hands) and transportation equipment (3 out of 4 dollar value assets controlled by non-Canadians).

By most standards of classification, Canada's is an open economy that by the end of the 1980s was exporting over one-quarter of its gross domestic product (GDP). However, 70% of its trade in the decade of the 1980s, and continuing into the 1990s, was with a single partner, the United States. Canada has a considerable merchandise trade surplus in its current account balance. Table 5 provides percentage distributions of merchandise exports and imports for Canada for 1990.

Canada in 1990 exported more agricultural products, energy and forest products than it imported, had a relatively equal balance in importing and exporting industrial goods and automobile products, but was a much heavier importer than exporter of consumer goods and machinery and equipment. This composition of trade corresponds roughly to the expectations of a staples economy perspective, modified according to the insights gained from having a branch-plant industrial system. In addition, and due in part to an important bilateral, sectoral-specific Automotive Products Agreement signed with the United States in 1965, Canada has a relatively favorable trade balance in automotive products. Canada has now embarked on a ma-

403

TABLE 4
Foreign Control of Canadian Economic Activities by Sector and
Industry Group, 1976 and 1986

	Percentage Foreign-Controlled Assets	
	1976	1986
Sector or Industry Group		
Agriculture	8	3
Metal mining	40	18
Other (non-metal) mining	56	25
Mineral fuels production	61	37
Manufacturing		
Food	38	34
Tobacco products	100	100
Textile mills	58	46
Clothing industry	16	12
Wood industries	21	16
Furniture industries	25	16
Rubber products	93	89
Paper and allied products	40	23
Primary metals (including smelting)	15	20
Metal fabricating	40	25
Transportation equipment	77	75
Machinery	65	47
Electrical products	69	52
Chemicals and chemical products	73	72
Petroleum and coal products	92	53
Transportation	12	4
Communications	15	12
Public utilities	2	0
Retail trade	16	13
Services	16	16

Sources: For 1976, Christopher Green, Canadian Industrial Organization and Policy (Toronto: McGraw-Hill Ryerson Limited, 1990, third edition), Tables 1–11, p. 20; for 1986, Statistics Canada, Cat. 61-210. Annual report of the Minister of Supply and Services Canada under the Corporations and Labour Unions Returns Act (CALURA). Part I, Corporations.

jor free trade agreement (FTA) with the United States. But Canada clearly imports considerably more products in the other highly manufactured goods sector than it is able to export.

There has been considerable debate in Canada concerning the transition from an industrial to a service-based economy. As noted above, there has been a noticeable decline in the proportion of GDP originating in the manufacturing sector, and employment in those segments of the economy has been significantly reduced. Further, the trade deficit in fully manufactured goods rose in current dollars from around 3 billion in the 1970s to over 20 billion by the 1980s, while investments in manufacturing industries have

TABLE 5
Distribution of Merchandise Exports and Imports
for Canada, 1990
(in millions of dollars)

	Exports	Imports
Agriculture and fish products	12,834	8,742
Energy	14,739	8,240
Forest products	20,866	1,324
Industry goods	30,018	26,109
Machinery and equipment	28,573	42,605
Automobile products	33,874	30,618
Consumer goods	2,792	15,861
Total	143,696	133,499
Agriculture and fish products	8.9%	6.5%
Energy	10.3%	6.2%
Forest products	14.5%	1.0%
Industrial goods	20.9%	19.6%
Machinery and equipment	19.9%	31.9%
Automobile products	23.6%	22.9%
Consumer goods	1.9%	11.9%
Total	100.0%	100.0%

Sources: Statistics Canada, Cat. 65-001. *Summary of Canadian International Trade.*

tended to decline over time. These factors are sometimes referred to as "deindustrialization".

Over the last few decades, Canada has had better than average growth rates when compared to the other major industrial democracies. It was negatively affected by the two oil shocks of 1973 and 1979 and had a much worse recession in both the early 1980s and the early 1990s than most other countries. The relative decline in the importance of the industrial sector has not been accompanied by absolute declines in the number of jobs nor in actual productive capacity in most sectors. Unemployment in Canada has been relatively high, notwithstanding the relative success of the economy in creating new jobs; prospects in the 1990s are bleak in this regard. Canada has a relatively large foreign-born population, and women have been entering the labor force in increasing numbers over the past 30 years.

INDUSTRIALIZATION AND TECHNOLOGY USE

The National Policy of 1879 represented a comprehensive plan for Canadian economic development. The policy had three principal parts. First, the plan called for the establishment of *protective tariffs* that would encourage location of firms within the country for nationals or foreigners who wished to sell their products on the Canadian market. Second, it hoped to

CANADA

use *immigration* as a mechanism for expanding the agricultural production of the Western regions. The immigration policy was also meant to aid in the creation of a large internal or domestic market. Third, by finishing the transcontinental railway, the policymakers hoped to provide the *infrastructure* necessary for the integration of the national economy—with central Canada (Ontario and Quebec) as the manufacturing base, with some steel (in Nova Scotia) and shipbuilding in the Atlantic provinces, and with the prairies and the west coast providing the bulk of agricultural goods and other raw materials. Governments would oversee the provision of services and regulate the financial institutions that would provide the up-front capital to the manufacturing and resource sectors.

Up until that time, Canada seems to have been simply a source of raw and semifinished products extracted from its natural resource base to be forwarded to the larger and more mature and dominant markets in the United Kingdom and then the United States. But the expansion of the manufacturing base of the Canadian economy required massive capital investments. With the tariff barriers firmly in place, the only alternative available for foreign capital was direct investment and the establishment of branch plants. The latter would, indeed, serve the Canadian market and do so by avoiding the tariffs, but the implications for technology and research and development were not as favorable. In any case, by the early 1920s, one estimate places U.S. capital at 50% of all foreign investment in Canada.

Prior to World War II, Canada seems to have depended largely on imported technology. Not surprisingly, several scholars and commentators have noted that Canada did somewhat better in innovative technological breakthroughs in the primary sectors of agriculture, mining, and pulp and paper. But in other manufacturing areas Canada has been characterized as a "competent user of technology," responsible for minor innovations but certainly not among the world leaders in any field.

Canada has, nonetheless, had some successes in several areas of technological innovation in the post-World War II period. In the development of its heavy-water (or CANDU) nuclear reactor, Canada efficiently modified its plutonium extraction reactor from military efforts on behalf of the Allied atomic bomb project to significant civilian use. Hydro-Ontario has managed (to date) some of the world's securest and most reliable nuclear electrical generating stations. The size and scope of hydroelectric projects, particularly in Quebec, have also been important areas of local research and development, although there is some growing concern for the potential ecological damage these developments might cause to Canada's pristine wilderness areas and/or traditional native hunting and fishing grounds. Extractive industries, particularly those having to work in Canada's cold northern climate, have also made significant contributions to research and development efforts and technology use in Canada.

Canada has made significant innovations in the aerospace industry from short-take-off-and-landing aircraft (STOL), to executive jets, to a robotic remote manipulator (or space arm) employed by the Americans on their space shuttles. In the 1950s and 1960s, however, an advanced military fighter jet, the Avro-Arrow, was canceled before it reached its final prototype. The Canadian telecommunications industry is among the world leaders in the development of computer-aided switching devices and digital phone systems.

The conclusions that some people have drawn from the history of Canadian efforts at industrial research and development is that governments have not provided the kind of support needed to foster innovations and to break into new markets, that Canada's domestically owned financial institutions have been too conservative in providing capital, and that Canada lacks the entrepreneurship and managerial skills that are to be found in the other advanced industrial nations. Yet Canada has the human, educational, and research resources to be among the world's leaders in industrial research and development. In fact, given the imperative of global competition, an accelerating rate of industrial innovation would appear to be absolutely essential for companies (and countries) that hope not to slip in the international rank-order in terms of standard of living.

A study by P. J. Wylie which examined technological adaptations in Canadian manufacturing firms during the first three decades of this century concluded that "there was a measurable element of indigenous technological adaptation to domestic factor prices . . . that differed from that of the United States. . . . The results suggest that the history of Canadian manufacturing development must be rewritten to give more emphasis to indigenous problem solving and technical advance embodying local knowledge."

RESEARCH AND DEVELOPMENT

Research and development spending as a percentage of gross domestic product in Canada has been generally at a much lower level than in the other major industrial democracies. Canada ranks in the middle levels of the Organization for Economic Cooperation and Development member nations, but at less than 1% of industrial domestic product being spent on in-house R&D it is well behind the world leaders (Germany, Japan and the United States). There is also little consistency in the way in which observers score Canada's performance on technology-use. Canada has been praised for the way it adapts technology in specific sectors and criticized for its low ranking in "making the most of technology." Canada is well behind world leader Japan in robotization, and the Economic Council of Canada has noted that Canadian firms in general are slow to introduce new technologies. Canada imports a considerable amount of its technology, which may reflect a lack of support for science and technology in general. In its trade with other countries, Canada has a deficit in high-technology products, but Canadian exports have a relatively high "technology intensity," probably because of inputs from parent companies in the United States or due to transfers of technology from them to their Canadian subsidiaries.

In recent times Canada has spent about 1.3% of its GDP on research and development, but about one-half of that was in publicly funded institutions, most in the Ottawa area. As is the case with other industrial nations, government involvement in R&D was most probably where there

TABLE 6
Extent of Foreign Control Among Canada's Leading Firms,
1980 and 1990

	Number of Firms 50% or More Foreign Owned		Number of Firms 100% Foreign Owned	
	1980	1990	1980	1990
Top 50	17	16	6	8
51–100	19	20	8	14
101–150	25	20	17	18
151–200	24	16	22	11
201–250	27	22	20	13
251–300	24	16	18	10
301–350	22	17	12	14
351–400	30	16	23	14
Totals:				
top 300	136	112	91	74
top 400	188	145	126	102

Sources: For 1980, Christopher Green, Canadian Industrial Organization and Policy (Toronto: McGraw-Hill Ryerson Limited), Tables 1–12, p. 21; for 1990, Financial Post 500, 1991.

was high risk (for example in Arctic oil exploration and techniques), where promising technologies failed to find a market in time for private investments to yield profit (short-take-off-and-landing and executive jet aircraft), or when the market system was not likely to produce outcomes considered to be in the national or provincial interests (energy "mega-projects").

Expenditures on research and development in Canada increased considerably over the decade of the 1980s and gross domestic expenditures on R&D now measure nearly $10 billion (current) per annum (government plus intramural). Nearly three-quarters of industrial R&D still takes place in the manufacturing sector, but interestingly it has been increasing in the tertiary sector since the mid-1980s.

It tends to be the case that the largest corporations do the most industrial R&D. In the Canadian context, however, a significant portion of the largest firms have historically been foreign-owned and thus have not been as predisposed to engage in intramural research and development activities as large, domestically owned firms. This situation is now changing. Table 6 provides journalistic data on the extent of foreign control of Canada's leading firms for the years 1980 and 1990, showing that over the decade of the 1980s, the percentage of top-300 firms in which foreigners had at least half the ownership dropped from 45% to 37%. Over the same time period, wholly owned foreign corporations among Canada's top 300 firms fell from 30% to 25% of the total. In fact, between 1965 and 1987, the share of industrial assets in the hands of Canadian nationals rose from 69.3% to 75.4%, with the American share falling from 23.7% to 16.6%. Similar trends can be noted for equity and sales figures as well. Finally, from 1965 to 1987, the Canadian share of profits rose from 56.7% to 68.3% among the top 300 firms in the national economy.

It has been said that it is difficult to assess Canada's R&D performance because "so many Canadian manufacturing firms, especially those in research-intensive industries, are subsidiaries of foreign-owned firms" (C. Green). While this undoubtedly reduces the amount of research and development in which a branch-plant engages, it does not necessarily limit the amount of technology available to such operations, since the parent company often simply transfers it there. In other words, technology use is not necessarily restricted because technology is not developed in-house. The leading sectors in R&D in Canada are the aircraft, telecommunications equipment, electronics, and business machine industries. It is certainly true that additional attention should be given to the impact of tax legislation on technology use as well as on research and development directly. For example, the tax policies of the federal government, by allowing depreciation of capital expenses over only a two-year period, made reinvestment, modernization, and new entry into the iron and steel industry relatively easy. The primary iron and steel industry in Canada, until very recently, was characterized by the use of the "best" technology, most of which was imported.

On an annual basis Statistics Canada surveys those firms that perform R&D on an "intramural" (in-house) basis. For the year 1987, the total number of responding R&D units was 2,685; they spent 3.2 billion current Canadian dollars and employed 23,031 scientists and engineers. While fully 22% of the units reported spending funds on "basic" research and development, their expenditures on that item represented only 7% of the total. The major sectors on basic intramural R&D were wood-based industries (which have considerable investments in research institutes) and the technology-pushed electrical and electronic industries. Some 72% of the expenditures for 1987 were for product development. Only the mining and petroleum industries spent significantly on process engineering.

A recent special survey by Statistics Canada indicated that significant numbers of firms in three high-technology sectors were engaging in important industrial research and development initiatives. The areas of interest covered by the survey were microelectronics, biotechnology and advanced industrial materials. This special set of questions was asked only of the larger intramural research and development spenders—587 R&D units from 485 firms, which spent a total of $2.8 billion current Canadian dollars (88% of intramural R&D for 1987) and that employed 19,070 scientists and engineers (83% of the total). Data from the survey are reproduced in Table 7. Since these firms represent the larger intramural R&D spenders in Canada, it is important to note that significant numbers were conducting basic research in one or more of these areas which are not traditional to the Canadian scene.

TABLE 7
Industrial Research and Development and Key Technologies, 1987

	Basic Research	New Products	Existing Products	New Process	Existing Process	New Technical Services	Existing Technical Services
Microelectronics							
Computer hardware	35	101	92	33	39	38	39
Software and systems	59	166	146	43	52	74	76
Artificial intelligence	18	35	22	9	15	11	8
Transmission carrier	20	52	42	7	11	15	17
Other	11	31	26	10	7	5	6
Biotechnology							
Biomass	5	12	6	10	6	1	1
Enzyme	9	17	11	6	6	5	3
Fermentation	7	16	9	10	4	5	4
Other	13	29	24	10	8	9	6
Advanced industrial materials							
Ceramics	11	22	12	10	5	4	3
Composites	14	29	23	13	14	5	6
Metals	17	46	43	29	40	11	12
Polymers	14	36	32	20	22	4	3
Other	10	24	18	14	14	9	8
Totals*	164	481	416	197	202	167	172

Source: Statistics Canada, Cat. No. 88-001, Science Statistics vol. 13, no. 4 (Survey of Manufacturing Technology) (July 1989).
* A unit could report that it was carrying out research in any or every technology.
A total of 587 units from 485 firms reported data.

INDUSTRIAL STRUCTURE, TECHNOLOGY USE AND R&D:
IMPLICATIONS FOR INDIVIDUAL POLICY

With regard to these aspects of economic development—industrial structure, research and development and technology utilization—governments throughout the world have turned their attention to policies designed to help their nations' firms compete better and smarter. Of course, the two opposing ideological approaches, direct interventionist and free market laissez-faire, are ever present in these debates.

Historically, as pointed out above, in the late 19th century Canada did have a National Policy that attempted to use protective tariffs, immigration and agricultural settlements, and infrastructural initiatives to develop and integrate Canada's industrial structure. After World War II, with the General Agreement on Tariffs and Trade (GATT), and more recently with the controversial Canada–U.S. Free Trade Agreement (FTA) and the pending North American Free Trade Agreement (NAFTA) that adds Mexico to the FTA, Canada has had to withdraw from these interventionist positions and take a more free-market approach.

In principle, industrial policies usually include some consideration of finances via investment banks, the active allocation of capital and other resources directly to the manufacturing sector, and foreign investors. Most are very short-sighted since the long-term consequences are not important to the immediate political situations out of which most industrial policies emerge.

Even after the National Policy period, Canadian governments have been engaged in a variety of programs designed to assist economic and industrial developments. These efforts have included the Canada Development Corporation, the Foreign Investment Review Agency, an export development corporation, and a myriad of smaller industrial assistance programs and projects. In general, the aim of these government policy initiatives has been to encourage investment, improve the marketing capacities of firms, increase corporate intramural research and development, and provide a modest level of industrial consultation processes which would foster sectoral competition and, therefore, international competitiveness. In addition, at various times in recent years, Canadian governments have established employment and immigration policies designed to retain highly qualified Canadians and to attract individuals from abroad who possess skills that are in short supply in the domestic economy. These policies too have been oriented to improve Canada's international competitiveness.

Canada has distinctive geography and population structure among the G7 advanced industrialized nations. It has developed a resource-based economy that is dependent on foreign markets, and that has relied, and continues to rely, on an inflow of people and capital funds from abroad. However, the economy now has a varied industrial structure, and, in many ways, is well poised to benefit from adapting technologies as well as actively innovating them. Canada is capable of adjusting rapidly to international changes and new technologies with a greater reliance on market mechanisms as opposed to government interventionism. While the overall scope of Canada's version of the welfare state is under some scrutiny, strong efforts will be made to maintain it, probably with reforms designed to strike a balance between economic efficiency and social equity.

The Foreign Investment Review Agency has been transformed into Investment Canada. The latter tries to uncover the "intentions" of interested foreign investors and then attempts to strike a deal which will get the maximum benefit for Canada in any agreement allowing foreign capital to operate in the national economy. At the same time, Canada has, on paper, redesigned its trade and industry ministries along the lines of Japan's MITI (Ministry of International Trade and Industry). In 1992, surprisingly, the federal government abolished both the Economic Council of Canada and the Science Council of Canada.

Internally, and, perhaps most strikingly for those who are used to strong centralized control over the flow of goods and services within a country, there are still a series of internal trade barriers—for example, beer produced in Nova Scotia cannot be sold in Ontario!—between Canadian provinces that current discussions on constitution reform are addressing.

The classic objection to the potential for R&D in Canada's "branch plant" industrial structure—namely, that branch plants do not contain all of the components and functions that an autonomous firm would have—still remains valid today, albeit in somewhat attenuated form given recent trends in "Canadianization." But Canada has taken strides over the last 15 or 20 years to gain more control over its productive assets (and profits), and its government-funded research and development activities have been increasing significantly.

FURTHER READING

Britton, J. N. H., and J. M. Gilmour. *The Weakest Link: A Technological Perspective on Canadian Industrial Underdevelopment.* Ottawa: Science Council of Canada, 1978.

Canada. *Foreign Ownership and the Structure of Canadian Industry* (Watkins Report). Ottawa: Queen's Printer, 1968.

———. *Foreign Direct Investment in Canada* (Gray Report). Ottawa: Information Canada, 1972.

Drache, D., and M. S. Gertler, eds. *The New Era of Global Competition: State Policy and Market Power.* Montreal: McGill-Queen's University Press, 1991.

Economic Council of Canada. *The Bottom Line: Technology, Trade and Income Growth.* Ottawa: Supply and Services Canada, 1983.

Green, C. *Canadian Industrial Organization and Policy.* 3rd ed. Toronto: McGraw-Hill Ryerson Limited, 1990.

Harris, R. G., and D. Cox. *Trade, Industrial Policy, and Canadian Manufacturing.* Toronto: Ontario Economic Council, 1984.

McFetridge, D. G., ed. *Canadian Industry in Transition.* Toronto: University of Toronto Press, 1986.

Masi, A. C., "Structural Adjustment and Technological Change in the Canadian Steel Industry, 1970–1986," in D. Drache and M. S. Gertler (eds.), *The New Era of Global Competition: State Policy and Market Power.* Montreal: McGill-Queen's University Press, 1991.

Science Council of Canada. *Canadian Industrial Development: Some Policy Directions.* 1984.

Smucker, J., *Industrialization in Canada.* Scarborough, Ontario: Prentice-Hall, 1980.

Solandt, O., and W. R. Stadelman. "Industrial Research and Development." In *The Canadian Encyclopedia.* Edmonton, Alberta: Hurtig Publishers Ltd., 1988, pp. 1061–62.

Wylie, P. J., "Technological Adaptation in Canadian Manufacturing, 1900–1929." *The Journal of Economic History* 49, 3 (September 1989): 569–91.

NATURAL RESOURCES AND PRIMARY MANUFACTURING INDUSTRIES

THOMAS I. GUNTON

NATURAL RESOURCES IN CANADA

From the beginning of the fur trade in the 18th century to the current development of energy and mineral resources, the development of Canada has been highly dependent on the extraction and export of natural resources. Although the relative significance of natural resource industries has declined somewhat in the postwar period, they remain an important component of the economy, accounting for almost one-half of Canadian exports and one-quarter of Canadian employment (see Tables 1 and 2).

On a regional level, the significance of resource industries is even greater. In the Prairie Provinces (Alberta, Saskatchewan and Manitoba) almost four out of 10 jobs and 100% of exports depend on the resource sector. In British Columbia, three out of 10 jobs and over 90% of exports are resource based. The Maritime Provinces, northern Quebec, and northern Ontario are similarly dependent on resource-based industries. It is not surprising, therefore, that much of Canadians' attention is on natural resource issues.

ROLE OF NATURAL RESOURCES IN CANADIAN DEVELOPMENT

The role of natural resources in development has been analyzed in terms of the "staple theory," one of Canada's contributions to the world development literature. According to the staple theory, external demand for natural resource products generates economic activity through "spread effects" including the further processing of natural resources prior to export (forward linkages), the production of imports such as resource machinery necessary for resource extraction (backward linkages) and the provision of goods and services to support needs of the domestic population employed in the

414

TABLE 1

Distribution of Labor Force, by Resource-Based Employment,
by Selected Regions, 1981 (percentage)

	Prairie Provinces	British Columbia	Canada
Direct resource-based employment [1]	18.5	16.7	13.8
Total, resource dependent employment [2]	37.0	33.4	27.6
Other	63.0	66.6	72.4
Total	100.0	100.0	100.0

Source: Gunton and Richards, 1987, 21.

[1] Includes agriculture; forestry; fishing and trapping; mines (including milling), quarries, and oil wells; electrical-driven, gas and water utilities; food and beverage (including food processing, flour milling); wood (including sawmills); paper and allied products; smelting and refining; petroleum and fuel products (including refining).

[2] Includes direct plus multiplier effects based on a multiplier of 2 applied to direct employment. This multiplier value is a conservative estimate drawn from a survey of the literature.

staple industry (final demand or consumer linkages). The development of these linkages is enhanced by the ability of natural resources to generate rent, a return to the resource above normal returns to the factors of production. As the domestic market expands, more specialized industries become viable, and the economy diversifies away from its initial reliance on resource industries.

While resource development can provide an important advantage in the development process, the Canadian experience demonstrates that it poses numerous challenges. First, the inevitable fluctuations in international

TABLE 2

Canadian Exports by Commodity Class, 1986

Commodity	Percentage of Total Merchandise Exports
Natural resource and primary industry exports	
Agricultural products	8
Ores, concentrates and semiprocessed minerals	11
Petroleum, natural gas and coal	7
Wood and paper products	15
Other crude products	4
Sub-total	41
Other exports	59
Total	100

Source: Statistics Canada, various publications.

415

commodity prices generate boom/bust cycles in the resource-based economy. The resource-based economy is particularly vulnerable to these cycles because it often has large debt obligations incurred to finance capital-intensive resource industries. These debts must be paid regardless of the state of the export market. The pattern of development, then, is usually commodity booms, accompanied by unrealistic expectations and excessive investment, followed by busts, characterized by surplus capacity and a legacy of public and private debts.

Development is also constrained by the natural limits of the resource base. Nonrenewable resources ultimately run out, while extraction of renewable resources has an upper limit, related to biological productivity. When the limits are reached, the staple economy can go into decline.

Because staple industries are capital intensive, export oriented and risky, their development is often in the hands of large multinational corporations. These corporations locate the higher-order activities—such as research and development, management and processing—outside of the resource region, thereby inhibiting the diversification of the economy away from its excessive reliance on a narrow export base.

These problems associated with resource development have been all too evident in Canada. Despite its stature as one of the world's largest exporters of many natural resource products such as potash, nickel, lumber, pulp and paper and zinc, Canada remains a large net importer of resource machinery and has not developed high-level processing industries related to natural resources. About one-half of Canada's base metals, for example, are exported as concentrate instead of being smelted and refined in Canada. Transformation of base metals into manufactured products such as wire, cable and stainless steel is almost nonexistent. Value added in the forest industry per unit of timber harvested is less than half that achieved in other forestry nations, such as Sweden. Research and development spending is about one-half the normal level for industrialized economies, even in Canada's resource sector.

Although Canada's major metropolitan regions have reduced their dependence on natural resources, the rest of Canada remains highly susceptible to the problems of resource-based economies. About one-quarter of Canadians, for example, live in communities based on a single resource industry. These towns are subject to unstable economies and can face ultimate extinction as the resource base is exhausted.

Natural resources, then, provide both a challenge and an opportunity. Clearly, public policy should focus on how to maximize the benefits and mitigate the problems associated with resource development.

THE ISSUE OF CONTROL

A leading issue in resource development in Canada has been the conflict over ownership and control of natural resources. This conflict has been intensified by the generation of sizable windfall rents resulting from successive commodity booms, particularly in energy and minerals.

One level of conflict is between the national government and the provinces, both of which have constitutional claims for managing various aspects of Canadian resource development. Section 109 of the Constitution Act gives the provinces actual ownership of federal government lands and resources within their respective borders. Given that most natural resources in Canada are still owned by the federal government, this is a significant power indeed. The national government, however, has sole jurisdiction over trade and commerce and the right to levy any tax. Because most resources are exported from the producing province, the federal control of trade and commerce is a powerful constraint on provincial jurisdiction.

The ambiguity in jurisdiction results in intense conflict as each side has used sections of the Constitution Act to support its claim for a share of resource rents or the right to regulate production. Saskatchewan, for example, was involved in two lengthy court battles, one dealing with its right to regulate the rate of production of its potash industry, and the other dealing with its right to impose royalties to collect a share of mineral rents. These legal challenges were a primary factor in Saskatchewan's decision to purchase one-half of the privately owned potash mines in the mid-1970s. Similar federal/provincial conflicts have occurred in other Canadian provinces. Alberta and the federal government, for example, have had lengthy battles over the share of oil and gas rents. Although some of this legal ambiguity has been removed by amendments to the Constitution in 1982 (Section 92A), both the federal and provincial governments retain powerful roles which will continue to necessitate delicate bargaining over the management of Canadian resources.

A second conflict is between the private sector and the public sector. The public sector in Canada retains outright ownership of most of Canadian natural resources. Most of the production of resources, however, is undertaken by private companies operating under various lease arrangements with the public owner. For much of the postwar period, the public sector was content to provide private resource companies with substantial tax concessions and subsidized infrastructure. Needless to say, the private sector was not displeased and the relationship between the two was rather benign.

Several major government reviews of the taxation system in the late 1960s, however, were highly critical of the concessions to the resource sector. Mining, for example, enjoyed an effective tax rate about one-half that of manufacturing. This critique, combined with the commodity boom in the early 1970s, broke decades of regulatory inertia and prompted Canadian governments to pursue policies to collect a share of the windfall profits for the public owner. During the 1970s, both the national and provincial governments enacted new royalty regimes, made lease conditions more onerous, and purchased some of the producing assets of private companies, particularly in the mining and energy sectors. Regulations were also implemented by the national government to control foreign investment.

Government actions to strengthen public control were reinforced by a growing concern over the high degree of foreign control and corporate concentration in the resource sector. Fewer than eight firms, for example, control all of the uranium, asbestos, and potash industries; more than 90% of

TABLE 3
Corporate Concentration in Resource Industries in Canada, 1980

Industry	Value of Shipments Accounted For by 8 Largest Firms (Percentage)	Total Number of Enterprises	Total Value of Shipments (millions of $)
Gold quartz mines	94	16	696.7
Uranium	100	6	722.5
Iron mines	98	9	1,872.7
Nickel-copper-gold-silver	91	18	4,572.1
Silver-lead-zinc mines	94	17	1,007.9
Coal mines	97	17	913.3
Asbestos mines	100	6	655.6
Potash mines	100	6	1,046.3
Iron and steel mills	90	39	6,431.5
Smelting and refining	93	17	3,273.2
Aluminum rolling and casting	93	59	1,049.3
Petroleum refining	85	16	14,255.8
Logging	34	3,073	4,559.3
Sawmill and planing mills	30	1,180	5,278.2
Pulp and paper mills	49	60	10,907.6

Source: Gunton and Richards, 1987, 17.

base metals, iron and steel, coal, and aluminum and petroleum refining; more than 50% of the pulp and paper industry; and one-third of the lumber industry (see Table 3). According to recent statistics (1987), foreign firms control 41% of the mining industry, 26% of the paper industry and 18% of the metal fabricating industry. This high degree of corporate concentration and foreign control was cited in several government reports as a factor inhibiting increased processing of Canadian resources prior to export and contributing to a leakage of rents from the public owner.

The private sector reacted to the changes in government policies by aggressive lobbying, threatened investment strikes and court actions. The private sector response, combined with downturns in commodity markets in the 1980s, encouraged the public sector to withdraw many of the more contentious policies, and to begin to privatize some of the publicly owned resource companies. Saskatchewan, for example, has privatized its crown potash and its crown oil and gas company.

Overall, the relationship between the public and private sectors can be understood as a pendulum swinging back and forth with swings in commodity markets. When prices are high, the public sector is more aggressive and the private sector somewhat less resistant. When markets weaken, the public sector becomes more supportive and the private sector more demanding. Given that government will remain heavily involved by virtue of its ownership of the in situ natural resource, the relative role of the public and private sectors will continue to be a major issue in Canadian resource policy.

Another area of potential conflict is between Canada and foreign governments, most notably the United States. The United States and Canada have a striking interdependence: Canada has a large supply of natural resources available for export and the United States has a large deficit. The relationship necessitates delicate negotiations to satisfy the interests of both parties. During the 1970s, Canada implemented policies restricting the export of some natural resources to satisfy domestic requirements. In the 1980s, the United States imposed restrictions on some resource imports from Canada, such as lumber and potash, to protect its domestic industry during the downturn in commodity prices. These disputes over resource trade provided much of the motivation for the negotiation of the Canada-United States Free Trade Agreement (FTA), which was ratified in 1988. In addition to reducing tariffs, the FTA prohibits regulations which restrict the ability of either the Canadian or U.S. government to interfere with trade. The Canadian government, for example, is prohibited from any action reducing the American share of Canadian production below the level enjoyed during the previous three-year period. Canada is also prohibited from imposing export taxes or taking any other action which raises the export price of a natural resource relative to the domestic price. Given the interdependence of the U.S. and Canadian economies in natural resources and the ambiguity of various provisions, natural resource disputes will continue to play a central role in Canada's international relations.

Another level of conflict which is becoming increasingly significant is the dispute between Native and non-Native communities over ownership and control. Resource development often occurs in the hinterland regions of Canada which are the ancestral home of Canada's Native population. The development can be highly disruptive to the Native economy. Hunting and fishing resources can be damaged and social health can be jeopardized by the influx of transient construction workers. Mercury from the pulp and paper industry, contaminants from mines, and flooding associated with large hydroelectric projects have all wreaked havoc on Native communities. The conflict is intensified by disputes over the ownership of lands between Natives and the government. In British Columbia, for example, there are a number of court cases in process which will set precedents affecting ownership of a large part of British Columbia's land base.

Conflict between development and the environment is another key issue in Canada. Resource industries, in particular, are being closely monitored because of the significant impact that they have on the environment: Logging jeopardizes scenic views, soil stability, and fish spawning areas. The pulp and paper and mining industries are a major source of air and water contaminants. Mining is responsible for about one-half of sulfur dioxide emissions—which cause acid rain—in Canada and is a major source of arsenic, cadmium, lead and mercury contaminants in water. Canadian governments are currently reviewing environmental regulations in the resource sector to reduce the environmental impacts.

THE SECTORS

Forestry

Forestry accounts for about 13% of total Canadian manufacturing shipments and 15% of total Canadian exports. The three principal products are newsprint, lumber and pulp, each accounting for about 30% of total forest product output. The industry is heavily concentrated in British Columbia, which supports about one-third of the Canadian forest products output, and Northern Ontario and Quebec, which support about one-quarter each. British Columbia's production is heavily oriented toward lumber, producing about one-half of Canada's lumber output, and Ontario and Quebec are more heavily oriented toward pulp and paper. Forestry comprises a much greater share of British Columbia's (22%) than in Ontario and Quebec (4% and 8% respectively). The smaller province of New Brunswick is also heavily dependent on forestry (22% of gross provincial product, or GPP) even though it contributes only a small portion of Canada's total forest products production (5%).

Canada is a significant player in the world industry, accounting for about 14% of world lumber production, 15% of wood pulp and 31% of world newsprint production. Its shares of world exports of lumber, pulp and newsprint are 50%, 33% and 61% respectively, with most of the exports going to the United States. In 1986, Canada provided about one-third of U.S. lumber demand and 57% of U.S. newsprint demand. Over the last several decades, Canada's share of world lumber production has been increasing and its share of newsprint has been declining.

About 95% of Canadian forests are owned by the provincial and federal governments. Production of forest products, however, is undertaken almost exclusively by private companies who obtain access to crown timber by various lease agreements. The nature of the lease arrangements and the charges for timber have been the subject of considerable debate. Most timber is provided to private firms under long-term leases for a nominal annual rental. The firms are charged a stumpage fee when the timber is harvested. U.S. lumber producers recently alleged that the stumpage fees, which were based on the difference between the market price for timber and the imputed costs of harvesting, were artificially low.

After several attempts, the U.S. industry successfully petitioned the U.S. government to impose duties on Canadian lumber imports until the Canadian governments agreed to alter the stumpage system to collect what the Americans estimated was a fair price. This was done in the form of a special agreement in 1986 in which Canada agreed to impose the equivalent of a 15% ad valorem tax on Canadian lumber producers. As a consequence, Canadian governments are now benefiting from a substantial increase in revenue for the forestry sector, thanks to American action. Stumpage calculation, however, is now arbitrary and is the subject of continuing conflicts and negotiations between Canadian governments, the U.S. government and private forest companies.

Another issue is the ability of the forest base to support higher levels of production. The various provinces regulate the rate of harvest on a sustained yield basis, which attempts to ensure that the volume of wood cut is roughly equivalent to the volume grown. Theoretically, the same rate of harvest can be sustained indefinitely. In the past, it was easy to increase the output of the industry because the volume harvested was below the sustained yield. Recently the sustained yield has been reached, and future growth will depend on increasing the productivity of existing sites, reducing the waste in production and increasing the value added by producing higher-order forest products. This will require a significant change in orientation. Canada will have to spend more on intensive silviculture, research and development and modernize its processing operations. Canada, for example, spends about one-third of what Sweden spends on silviculture per unit of forest land and achieves about one-half of the value added. Even with improved management, Canada will face a difficult challenge maintaining its competitive advantage over countries such as the southern United States and Brazil, where trees reach maturity in 15–20 years compared to over 80 years in Canada. The need for improved management will also strain relations between the public owners and private producers who will jointly bear the increased costs.

Forestry is also at the center of environmental conflicts. There is increasing concern in Ontario and British Columbia that the few remaining old-growth wilderness areas will be destroyed by logging. Logging companies, meanwhile, allege that preservation of old-growth and wilderness preserves will jeopardize jobs in the industry. The loss of jobs is a major concern since the dramatic loss of jobs between 1982 and 1984, when the industry restructured during the recession by reducing employment per unit of output by over 25%.

Although the debate between environmentalists and the forestry industry is intense, the amount of timber affected by wilderness preservation proposals is relatively small, representing under 5% of the existing harvest in British Columbia. In fact, the land area proposed for wilderness preservation is less than the area that has been harvested and not replanted by the forest industry. This dispute, then, should be easily resolved.

Another issue with broader ramifications is land claim disputes in which Natives are claiming ownership to a large portion of land, particularly in British Columbia. Logging in several areas is currently being held up by court injunctions as the protagonists await the outcome of cases that could set a dramatic precedent affecting ownership of much of the forest land base. The outcome will likely entail the negotiation of co-management arrangements between Natives and governments similar to the one currently being negotiated between the Haida and the federal government involving management of the Queen Charlotte Islands off the coast of northern British Columbia.

Minerals

Canada is the western world's largest producer of nickel, zinc and potash, and the second largest producer of gold, asbestos, sulfur and aluminum (see Table 4). Overall, minerals account for 11% of total Canadian exports.

421

TABLE 4
Canadian Share and Rank in Western World Mineral
Production, 1988

Commodity	Percentage of Western World Production	Rank
Copper	11	3
Nickel	23	1
Aluminum	12	2
Iron ore	6	6
Lead	9	3
Zinc	23	1
Gold	6	2
Potash	47	1

Source: World Bank, *Price Prospects for Primary Commodities, 1988.*

Except for two small mines in New Brunswick, Canada's potash production is located in Saskatchewan. Asbestos production is based in Quebec, nickel production in the Sudbury basin in northern Ontario and in Thompson, Manitoba, and aluminum in Quebec and British Columbia. Copper, zinc and precious metals are more dispersed.

Much of the debate on resource taxation discussed earlier has focused on minerals. The federal government's Carter Commission on taxation in 1969 launched the first salvo, attacking concessions to the mineral industry which resulted in tax rates less than one-half those paid by other sectors. The attack was repeated in a study for the Manitoba government in 1973, which showed that minerals generated substantial rents captured by the private sector as excess profits instead of by the public owner as a return on its natural resource. By 1975 most of the concessions were removed as governments attempted to collect a larger share of mineral rents. Provincial governments also got actively involved in mineral production by setting up crown corporations. Saskatchewan, for example, acquired 50% of its potash industry, in part to protect itself from legal challenges jeopardizing its right to tax and regulate production.

By 1982, however, the atmosphere had changed as the collapse in commodity prices led to large-scale shutdowns in the industry and threatened the viability of several of Canada's major mining companies such as Inco, Falconbridge, Sherritt Gordon and Hudson Bay Mining and Smelting. The concern was how to restructure the industry to improve productivity and ensure survival. The plight of the industry was also jeopardized by United States protectionist threats in copper and potash. In potash, Canadian producers were threatened with punitive import duties unless they agreed to reduce production to maintain the viability of high-cost United States producers in New Mexico. Ironically, the United States forced Canada to take action to raise prices and increase its return for the industry at the expense of United States farmers who had to pay higher prices for potash, an essential fertilizer.

The recent recovery in commodity prices combined with dramatic productivity improvements in mineral production has again changed the atmosphere. The Canadian mineral industry is booming, financial performance is robust and corporate takeovers are in process. The mineral industry pays about the same tax rates as other sectors, and governments are in the process of privatizing some of the producing assets acquired in the 1970s.

A recurring issue in the mineral industry is the debate on an industrial strategy to maximize its contribution to the Canadian economy. One component of a strategy is to develop linkages involving increased processing of mineral products prior to export and production of mineral equipment. About one-half of Canada's nickel and one-third of its zinc and lead production is exported as concentrate. Given that further processing is energy intensive, it is clearly an activity which could be undertaken in Canada. A second proposal is to increase research to develop new uses for minerals and improve production methods. Research and development in base metal industries is less than .1% of sales, substantially below industries such as transportation, electronics and chemical, which spend 3–4% of their revenue on research and development. A final area of discussion is whether to create cartels to raise prices by supply management. Canada clearly has market power in potash and nickel. In other commodities, such as coal and zinc, cooperation with one or two other producing countries could result in effective supply management.

Fisheries

Despite its position as only the 16th largest producer of fish, Canada is the largest exporter, accounting for about 10% of total world fish exports. As is the case with most Canadian resource products, the United States is the largest market, consuming about 60% of Canadian production.

About two-thirds of Canada's fishing industry is located on the Atlantic coast, about one-quarter on the Pacific coast and the remainder on freshwater lakes. Although the industry is a small component of Canada's economy, it accounts for about 15% of GPP in the three Atlantic provinces of Newfoundland, Prince Edward Island and Nova Scotia.

Unfortunately, the fishing industry suffers from the problems associated with a common property resource: surplus capacity and overfishing. Governments have attempted to reduce capacity by various measures over the years, including the purchase of fishing vessels and the restriction of types of gear. Despite these efforts, there is at least twice as much fishing capacity as required. Recently, this problem has been aggravated by a dramatic reduction in the allowable catch necessary to preserve the stocks in Atlantic Canada, culminating in a two-year moratorium on cod fishing in 1992. Trade action has added to the problems. The United States recently imposed an import duty on groundfish exports from Atlantic Canada to the United States. Canada's policy of requiring fish caught in Canadian waters to be processed in Canada has also been recently struck down by the United States-Canada trade dispute panel, jeopardizing processing jobs in both the Maritimes and British Columbia. The fisheries, it appears, will continue to face major restructuring during the coming decade. This may be mitigated somewhat by expansion of Canada's new aquaculture industry.

Future Directions in Resource Policy
Although Canada will remain a world leader in natural resource production, a concerted effort will have to be made to strengthen Canada's resource industries to maximize their contribution to the nation's welfare.

A first priority is to properly manage the natural resource base. In forestry, the large backlog of logged areas that have not been replanted must be reduced. Intensive silviculture is necessary to improve site productivity, and regulations are required to ensure that logging does not damage the soil. In fisheries, efforts will have to be made to protect fisheries habitat and eliminate overfishing.

A second priority is to maximize resource rents. One way of doing this is to reduce costs of production. Government regulations which attempt to achieve ill-defined objectives by forgoing rent should be removed. Recent studies, for example, have criticized regulations in the forestry industry restricting log exports and regulating harvest techniques. While there is justification for regulating resource industries to realize social goals, such goals should be pursued through explicit public policy, not implicit policies that hide costs.

A second way of reducing costs is to discourage the development of surplus capacity. This has been a characteristic problem of the resource sector because of the capital intensity of the projects and poor forecasting. In general, public subsidies of resource investment should be eliminated. More indicative planning would be useful. Such planning involves government influencing the decisions of individual producers by comprehensively assessing supply and demand, and seeking to reconcile producers' expectations of one another's intentions. This could be complemented by public investment funds whereby the resource corporations are encouraged to put profits into a fund during booms in order to discourage them from their seemingly inexorable propensity to invest during booms, only to have the new capacity come on stream during downturns. The funds would be released to encourage better timing of investment decisions.

Policies to increase revenue have received less attention than policies to reduce costs, despite evidence that prices can be influenced by producers or consumers. Producers such as OPEC, for example, have been successful in increasing petroleum rents by restricting output to realize market power. Resource producers should be encouraged to act collectively. Joint private/public marketing boards for major commodities could undertake indicative planning to prevent surplus capacity as well as regulate production and marketing.

Another priority is to ensure that rents be retained by the public owner to be distributed equitably as opposed to being retained by resource producers in the form of surplus profits. Although it is often alleged that attempts by the public owner to collect rents reduce efficiency by encouraging practices such as high grading, recent studies suggest that collection of rents actually increases efficiency by forcing resource firms to compete

Figure 1
COMPARISON OF NET EXPORT RELIANCE AND NET IMPORT
RELIANCE OF SELECTED CANADA AND U.S. RESOURCES

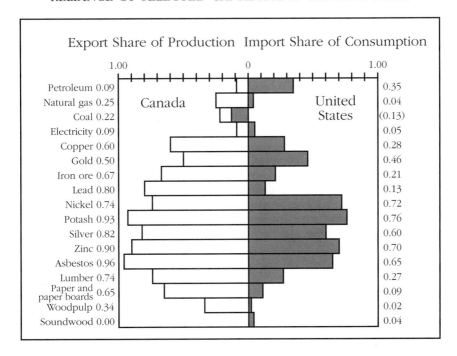

for access to resources. Failure to collect rents acts as a subsidy which distorts investment decisions and allows firms to earn adequate returns without due regard for costs.

Another priority is to develop linkages such as increased processing where economically justified. Research and development are also necessary to improve production techniques and product development.

A final priority is to ensure full public participation in resource decision making. This includes involvement by employees in the management of their firms and involvement by local communities in the allocation of natural resources.

Canada is clearly a world leader in the production of natural resources. Its institutions, internal conflicts, treatment of aboriginal people, spatial patterns and relationship with foreign governments have all been shaped by the demands of producing and exporting resources to foreign industrial powers, most notably the United States.

The nature of resource development in Canada represents both opportunity and challenge. Specialization in resources generates rapid growth, but at the cost of economic instability and potential decline as resources are exhausted. Some Canadians recommend continued reliance on natural resource development to realize Canada's comparative advantage, albeit with better public policies to collect rent, develop linkages and stabilize market fluctuations. Others recommend restructuring the Canadian economy away from its perceived excessive reliance on a narrow export base. One thing is certain. Canadians will continue to debate the merits of resource-based development and seek policies to mitigate its undesirable aspects, policies which, it is hoped, will be a model for other countries facing similar development problems.

FURTHER READING

Gunton, Thomas, and John Richards. *Resource Rents and Public Policy*. Halifax: Institute for Research on Public Policy, 1987.

Kierans, Eric. *Report on Natural Resources Policy in Manitoba*. Winnipeg: Government of Manitoba, 1973.

Whalley, John. *Canada's Resource Industries and Water Export Policy*. Toronto: University of Toronto Press, 1986.

Watkins, Mel. "A Staple Theory of Economic Growth." In W. T. Easterbrook and M. H. Watkins, eds. *Approaches to Canadian Economic History*. Ottawa: Carleton University Press, 1967.

THE SERVICE SECTOR

M. PATRICIA MARCHAK

Canada, like other industrial countries in the 1990s, has more of its population providing services than goods. Two-thirds of Canadians in the labor force are now classified as service workers and only one-third as goods producers. The proportion of the gross domestic product attributable to the service sector is nearly as high in Canada as in all industrial countries. A Canadian study recently pointed out that in Ontario, the manufacturing heartland of Canada, a considerably larger number of people are employed in hospitals than in the auto manufacturing and auto parts industries combined, and more are employed in universities and colleges than in iron and steel mills.

A gradual growth in services employment occurred over the first half of this century, as employment in agriculture declined and demand for consumer goods, with their attendant services, increased. The expansion of the services sector was more rapid after 1950, with growth especially marked in public administration, transportation, trade, finance, insurance, education and health services. This growth was partly due to the introduction of new social services and expansion of existing government services on a universal basis; and partly due to the development of computer technology and improved transportation technologies. Computers and satellite technologies have spawned a new range of "knowledge-intensive" services. Air transportation in particular, but containerized shipping and other transport developments as well, have facilitated the growth in world trade and tourism.

DEFINITIONS AND COMPOSITION

Services are intangible for the most part, but often are embedded in more tangible goods. The precise line between the "thing" and the "service component" in many products is not obvious, and national accounts differ in their inclusion rules, because of the diverse methods employed by countries to count services.

The Service Industries Journal (January 1987) includes retail and wholesale distribution, hotels and catering, tourism, business services (marketing, advertising, information systems), financial services (insurance, banking), professional and scientific services (accounting, law and medicine, research and development), leisure, recreation and entertainment. Engineering, architecture, construction, legal, publishing, and consulting businesses would be included by others. Transportation and all supporting and incidental services, machinery and equipment rentals and leasing should be added to the list. The public services, especially education, health care, justice, and social welfare, are major components.

With reference to international trade in services, Canada's official statistical agency, Statistics Canada, has chosen to include travel, freight and shipping, business services, and government transactions. The category "business services" comprises consulting and professional, insurance and financial, research and development and other such services, as well as services to manufacturing such as tooling done for automotive companies.

A definitional difficulty results from industrial restructuring. Services provided "in house" have traditionally been included in "value-added" calculations—which refer to value added to goods through processing—whereas those provided externally have been recognized as services. Since the mid-1970s, both public agencies and private corporations have restructured their operations, now contracting out many services previously performed "in house." As well, some services formerly performed by public agencies have been privatized, and as commercial operations, their functions are now separately measured and defined as services.

Both transportation and communications technologies have contributed to a changing definition as well as the overall growth of services. Numerous services that were once regionally stationary, in construction, medicine, education, oil, engineering and other sectors, are now physically mobile; the entire range of workers from unskilled to professional can be transported to the customer anywhere in the world. A considerable range of information services has become similarly "mobile" such as computerized banking, "on-line" financial and business data, and specialized news-gathering services, which might instantly serve subscribers located anywhere in the world. Some labor-intensive functions formerly performed in direct contact between the customer and the seller, such as travel bookings or customer billing, can now be performed in a place thousands of miles away from both without much loss of time. Such changes require new modes of compiling trade statistics, and have resulted in more precise definitions of the service component.

CHANGES IN GOVERNMENT SERVICES

The General Agreement on Tariffs and Trade (GATT) Code on Government Procurement for goods, established in 1981, promoted principles of nondiscrimination and national treatment between domestic producers and suppliers of other participating countries, but included services only where these were incidental to goods and of lower value than the goods being traded. The Canada-U.S. Free Trade Agreement, which came into effect on January 1, 1989, became a precedent for expanding GATT agreements to include services, most particularly by reducing state barriers to establishment, and for including services in the North America Free Trade Agreement that was negotiated in 1992 to bring in Mexico.

The FTA states:

> Trade in services represents the frontier of international commercial policy in the 1980s. Dynamic economies are increasingly dependent on the wealth generated by service transactions . . .
>
> It is no longer possible to talk about free trade in goods without talking about free trade in services because trade in services is increasingly mingled with the production, sale, distribution and service of goods . . .

Both within the FTA and in GATT, Canada is among the industrial nations calling for liberalization of trade in services, for deregulation, and for the "right to establish" branches and "the right to national treatment."

The "right to establish," now embedded in the Free Trade Agreement, means that no restrictions can be imposed on commercial firms by reason of nationality, and firms of either national origin have the right to establish branches in either country. Similarly, "the right to national treatment" means that government procurement policies, subsidies, insurance, financing, taxing, shipping, labor or other legislation must not discriminate in favor of citizens or nationally-based firms. All such restrictions are deemed to be non-tariff barriers to the complete liberalization of trade in services.

As this suggests, the changes introduced through this agreement, and also on the agenda of the Single European Market, have substantial implications for the operations of national governments. Many of the services under debate are presently performed or regulated by governments.

A major vehicle for restriction of foreign investment prior to the agreement was the Foreign Investment Review Agency (FIRA). Service sector applications between 1974, when FIRA was established, and 1982, before it was dismantled, exceeded those in the manufacturing and resource industries combined. In the last two years of its existence, FIRA disallowed some 15% of American service firm applications. Foreign ownership, under the new agreement, will encounter no appraisals that are not similarly applied to national firms.

Other regulatory controls included banking and insurance restrictions, such as limitations on the production of foreign ownership, requirements for Canadian participation in ownership, directorships, and management; limits on overall proportion of foreign participation in these industries; requirements on reserves relative to loans outstanding; and specifications on the nature of transactions for diverse financial component industries. Many of these regulations are now dismantled, and the Free Trade Agreement will facilitate further deregulation.

Further non-tariff barriers have included immigration laws inhibiting the employment of non-nationals, encouraging government procurement from national firms, and a vast range of legal restrictions governing social welfare, health and safety standards, consumer protection, labor, employment, shipping, and regional development. Some of these were designed to ensure the employment or participation of Canadians; others emerged within the general social policies of Canadian governments and were not intentionally linked to foreign investment controls. However, the Free Trade Agreement can be used to dismantle many of these where an argument may be made that existing government services, government procurement policies, or government programs operate in such a fashion as to restrict foreign investment or expansion.

Services identified in the agreement include agricultural and forestry services; mining, construction, and distributive trade services; insurance and real estate services; most commercial services; telecommunications, computer, and tourism services. The commercial services include, specifically, management services for hospitals, educational institutions, and other institutions presently within the public sector. Not surprisingly, the agreement is controversial because of these changes.

A 1982 Canadian task force on services looked at the public sector as a means of generating export funds. Education and health were highlighted: both were heavily regulated and in their current forms were not easily brought into the market. Education could become a commodity through sales to foreign students in Canada, and through exported programs and personnel. It recommended expansion of these. With reference to health care, the task force observed:

> The largely public nature of the sector has generally precluded trade. The complete health care packages available from companies in the U.S., Europe or Japan would not find a market in Canada unless there was a major change in policy to privatize the system.

Exports to the Third World were suggested as a potential growth area. Political pressure to remove barriers elsewhere, however, would raise questions about barriers to commercial services in Canada, and, as the quotation implies, privatization within Canada would facilitate the growth of services by foreign as well as domestic firms. American and Japanese commercial health care services are already available. Because no internal market has existed, there are few Canadian firms now serving non-Canadians in Canada or in export markets.

The subsequent inclusion of management services for health care and education in the Free Trade Agreement suggests that the government anticipates a gradual privatization of these public services.

PRIVATIZATION, COMMERCIALIZATION AND UNIVERSALITY

Privatization of public services and properties was already under way at both provincial and national levels prior to the signing of the Free Trade Agreement. The process has been accompanied by a distinct ideological shift away from the Keynesian model of interventionary government toward a more rigorous market-oriented economy. The commercial applications of new technologies and the changing composition and profitability of services are pertinent to that shift.

Governments in all industrialized countries increased their level of services to both business and individual citizens throughout the postwar period.

Postal services were everywhere under state control. In all member countries in the Organization for Economic Cooperation and Development, or OECD, except the United States, governments formally controlled large sectors of the utilities and business service sectors. Telecommunications were wholly controlled in all countries except the United States, Spain and Canada; in Spain and Canada, this industry was partially under government ownership and otherwise was regulated by government. Ideological persuasions of parties in power played a part in the differences by country, but probably a smaller part than is popularly supposed. A social democratic government initiated socialized medicine in Canada, but once it had been established in Saskatchewan, the model was adopted throughout the country by governments of other persuasions.

The stronger explanation for nationalization of business properties after the war, and for incremental state participation during the 1960s and 1970s, is a combination of necessity (businesses required the service on a universal, low-cost basis) and high risk or variable profitability. Prior to the introduction of electronic telecommunications, these services were unlikely to generate profits under private auspices, and yet their presence was essential for private accumulation to take place.

The support from private capital for state participation was evident in resource sectors. Where the state provided a professional service, such as agrology, forestry, and numerous information services, companies had equal access to it and were saved the cost of investment in high-skilled technicians. In some cases, as in the nationalization of hydroelectric power, the cost assumed by the state for engineering services was typically great, while the industries benefited from low-cost energy supplies on a guaranteed basis.

The privatization of some of these services is a direct consequence of changing technologies and new possibilities for commercial development. FAX and electronic mail have made postal services profitable as private businesses; hence a pressure on the state to withdraw or reduce its level of service. In airlines, the maturing of the industry reduced the incentives for government ownership and regulation. Parts of obsolete industries, such as shipbuilding, now become profitable in a new form. The substitute industries spawn new service affiliates: prepackaged food services for travelers, tourist agencies, or installation and repairs of materials supplanting steel-based products, for examples.

In other sectors the pressures to privatize are more complex. Public sector bureaucracies developed a momentum to grow irrespective of services demand. New service industries in consulting, energy conservation, and waste disposal were waiting in the wings.

Underlying these conditions were the internationalization of services and increased mobility of capital. A national or provincial government has very little control over economic development in its territory when transfers of money and information can take place rapidly, when there are tax havens in other countries, and when investment in fixed plant is lower than was the case when "smokestack" industries were dominant. National governments, charged with the task of protecting the property rights of citizens in a bounded territory, are disabled where those properties are intangible and are directed by transnational units. Tariffs, non-tariff barriers, and all other protective measures for physically located properties have become obsolete in the new global economy.

By the same token, the provision of universal social services becomes problematic because the relevant universe ceases to be a viable economic unit. A national government might equalize the costs of energy or medicine throughout a relatively small territory where both capital and labor were identifiably resident; but it becomes difficult to do this where capital is neither national nor necessarily resident, labor is obliged to be increasingly mobile, and national boundaries are disintegrating within larger multinational associations.

With a declining or unpredictable corporate tax base, governments may be caught in a fiscal squeeze. Taxes for individual citizens rose steadily throughout the 1970s and 1980s, while corporate taxes as a proportion of total government revenues from taxation declined. This trend encouraged governments to consider reductions in expenditures on social welfare programs. It also coincided with the unionization of public sector workers, and their growing capacity to negotiate higher wages and greater job security. The ideological shift away from Keynesian economics to greater reliance on market forces might be understood, then, in the context of the increasing reliance on individual taxpayers and the improved collective bargaining capacities of public sector labor, as well as the technological changes and internationalization of the service industries.

The specifics of current privatization and contracting out programs vary from province to province, but generally included in the transfer to the private sector are management, custodial, janitorial, food, and some professional and computing services for health care, educational, and social welfare facilities. Attempts have been made to turn over care facilities for the elderly and handicapped to private owners, but these have not met with much success since they are not high revenue-producing services.

Tourist facilities and services have been more successfully transferred to the private sector. In some regions, highway construction and maintenance services have been privatized. In the resource and agricultural provinces, there are moves to privatize crown lands, but business has not shown enthusiasm for these where private-sector commercial services are not able to profitably displace public-sector infrastructural services, or where government monopolies and regulation continue to benefit the larger corporate actors.

DIRECT INVESTMENT AND TRADE IN SERVICES

Although Canada has joined the United States in pushing for liberalization of the services sector, Canada is not well situated to capture downstream benefits from the sale of manufactured products. The service industries follow the goods-producing industries, and the capture of service benefits depends in large part on linkages between internationalized goods-producing companies and service firms. There are few internationalized Canadian manufacturing firms, and few of the essential linkages for the services trade. The paucity of Canadian international firms is linked to the high level of foreign, primarily American, direct investment in Canadian industries.

Two kinds of commercial services are identified in international statistics: tradable and non-tradable. The tradable services are defined as discrete sales through export from one country to another, such as medical services contracted out to foreign governments, news services originating in one country and sold in another, or consulting services provided across borders. Although these exported services have expanded, they are much less important to international trade than non-tradable services.

The non-tradable services are those resulting from direct foreign investment, such as a non-Canadian hotel chain or bank opening a branch in Canada and selling services in the host country. The services of the foreign-owned unit are accounted for in international data, with management fees, dividends, and other financial returns to the parent firm being treated as costs against the host country's service trade balance. The sales by foreign-owned affiliates are vastly more profitable than simple exports, and it is such sales that account for a positive trade balance in services for the United States. Studies by the United Nations Centre on Transnational Corporations show sales by U.S. service affiliates abroad (non-tradable services) to far exceed U.S. exports of services. More than half of U.S. service trade is accounted for in investment income, i.e., interest, dividends, and profits on loans and overseas investments.

Canada's services trade balance, by contrast, is in deficit, and the deficit has steadily grown over the past several decades. The non-tradable services have rapidly accrued debits, and the deficit is increasing; the tradable services, though also in deficit, have not increased their losses over the 1980s.

The services trade deficit amounted to $7 billion in 1987, more than half of which was composed of interest, business dividend and other business service payments. Overall, 62% of business service payments to non-residents was attributable to foreign-controlled firms operating in Canada. In research and development transactions, the deficit rose from $296 million to $429 million between 1986 and 1987. Most payments were by Canadian subsidiaries to U.S. parent companies, and most of the deficit was attributable to American business services located in Canada.

The balance is not modified by a corresponding return on Canadian investments elsewhere. The service industries in 1985 accounted for 29% of Canada's total direct investment abroad, just under half going to the United States, and about a third to South America and Central America. By comparison, these industries accounted for 44% of total U.S. foreign direct investment, 47% of West Germany's, and 52% of Japan's in 1985. Contrary to the trend in most other OECD countries, including Australia with its similar resource-based economy, Canada's share of services as a component of total foreign direct investment slightly declined over the 1980s.

433

Service industries located elsewhere do return profits to their Canadian parent firms, and in dollar terms, these returns have climbed upward, but they do not offset the outflow from foreign firms located in Canada, and in comparison to other industrial countries, Canada's returns are low.

While trying to find a route for profitable external services investment by Canadians, the 1982 task force concluded that Canada's non-tradable services sector had little chance of showing a reduction in the deficit. Canada's exports as a whole account for nearly a third of the GNP, consisting largely of raw materials and energy, except in Ontario where the transference between units of multinational manufacturing firms includes component parts assembled there. In the view of the task force, Canada's failure to develop independent manufacturing industries reduces its capacity to sustain international service industries. Canada lacks the vertical linkages to establish viable service systems or capture follow-up service sales on exports.

It may seem somewhat paradoxical in the age of a global economy, when information services are instantaneously transmitted everywhere, that physical proximity to customers is still crucial to business success. Such services as hotels must be physically located in host countries. Advertising, rental and leasing, engineering, tourism, utilities, and data processing services typically require local outlets for their provision. With overproduction in many manufacturing sectors—computer chips, for example—survival depends on the competitive advantages of locating service outlets close to ultimate customers. The same is true of automobiles and electrical goods: successful competition depends on the follow-up services. Canada's declining services account occurs because the original goods-producing companies are not in place; there is nothing to follow, there are no linkages to serve.

The task force then turned to the tradable services, which show a constant rather than increasing deficit over most of this time. It considered the potential for services embodied in goods (primarily cultural, such as recordings, books, computer tapes and films); services complementary to trade in goods (including transportation, financing, insurance, advertising); services substituting for trade in goods (franchising, chartering, leasing, and repairs and maintenance); and services traded without a relationship to goods (banking, professional services, telecommunications, data processing, information, travel). However, even in these, Canada's lack of linkages to the goods-producing firms elsewhere puts its service firms at a disadvantage.

Telecommunications and computer services are the high-technology areas now expanding on a global scale. They become tradable commodities primarily in the consulting, construction and implementation of systems. Here, as elsewhere, Canadian companies operating primarily or only in Canada are, for the most part, not vertically integrated and cannot fully capture such downstream trade benefits; as well, they compete with global companies which can do so either through internal or contracted systems.

Engineering firms and real estate developers have had greater success on the international market. In the early 1990s the bankruptcy of the Olympia and York real estate empire, though headquartered in Toronto, with its huge holdings in New York and London, England, has cast a pall here as well. Canada's experience in building massive hydroelectric dams and other physical infrastructure in rough terrain has created an expertise that has global recognition. The real estate developments might be understood as the obverse side of high foreign ownership in the manufacturing industries: Canadian capital has concentrated in real estate in place of goods-production.

The most prominent service industries are associated with international finance. Canadian banks were among the 30 major global banks during the 1960s and 1970s. During the 1980s, these banks declined relative to banks originating in Japan and Europe. The expanding banks were following the manufacturing companies and providing follow-up services to them. With deregulation of the financial sector throughout industrial countries and finally including Japan, banks have become transnational corporations and the world financial market has been substantially integrated.

The five transnational banks of Canadian origin that were prominent in international lending in the 1970s have suffered a double fate: like other banks, they have suffered from the debt crisis in the Lesser Developed Countries (LDCs), but unlike Japanese and European banks, they have not reaped the benefits of increased foreign direct investment in other industrial and service sectors. Since there are relatively few Canadian firms abroad to be serviced, Canadian banks have less power within the banking community now than they had in the early 1970s.

American leadership in the services sector has dominated Canada, but on a global scale it is declining. Investment in the United States by external service firms has risen, and by 1985 accounted for more than 50% of total inward foreign direct investment. American production within the United States has also declined, especially in high-technology services, but only partly because of Japanese and European competition. Global operations of American firms in these industries are having the same impact as off-shore sourcing in manufacturing industries did in the 1970s and early 1980s. Airlines, computer entry data services, credit-card applications and other services for U.S. companies are now being produced in the Newly Industrializing Countries (NICs) for export to the industrialized centers.

The impact of off-shore sourcing is experienced in Canada as well as the United States. The services themselves are becoming global, in the sense that single companies (often joint ventures, involving capital originating in various locations) operate on a world scale, but an international division of labor is already in evidence. Research and development is being centered in cities in the United States and Japan (Europe is not prominent), labor-intensive operations are being performed in the NICs, and countries such as Canada are recipients rather than providers of international services.

In the hope that these trends may be reversed, Canadian consulting and technical service companies, arguing that their business is inhibited by the telecommunications and other policies of foreign governments, urge governments to push for dismantling of non-tariff barriers elsewhere. These complaints are reflected in the 1982 task force report and a possible alternative route is promoted: channeling contracts through the World Bank or other international agencies.

For Canadian companies, these agencies are very often the preferred routes to obtain business in LDCs as most of the trade impediments imposed on normal government procurement disappear or are substantially reduced.

Thus we can understand the FTA and GATT discussions in the context of the interest of service firms in expansion to other countries. To break down their barriers, harmonization of entry and treatment rules is a prerequisite; failing that, reliance on international banks becomes a possible means of entry into indebted countries. The major push behind free trade in services comes from the United States. American service firms continue to show profits where merchandise accounts are declining, and they are poised to operate on a global scale. At the moment, Canadian service firms appear less able to benefit from the changing international environment, though Canadian banks and telecommunications companies pushed hard for the North American Free Trade Agreement (NAFTA) in the early 1990s in the belief that they could penetrate the Mexican market.

COST OF SERVICES

The cost of services overall has risen steadily relative to the cost of manufactured goods over the past four decades, and also has risen faster in industrial than in developing countries. There are several possible reasons for the relative rise in prices for services. Most obviously, many services are labor intensive. In an expanding economy, wages tend to rise across the board, so that if services employment is increasing faster than employment in production and primary sectors, and if their base level were lower to begin with, we could attribute the rise simply to quantities.

That is a problematic explanation where the services are more in the nature of transformations from in-house components to external contracts. What occurs then is simply that the accounting changes, and what was earlier attributed to the cost of production, is now attributed to services commercially obtained. The cost of external services, since it now includes profits for the commercial contractor, may actually be higher than the in-house cost. Immediate costs notwithstanding, the practice of contracting out became more frequent throughout the private sector in the 1970s and in the public sector in the 1980s.

Labor, especially organized labor, has lost ground in this move, since the small contractors are not unionized for the most part, nor could labor employed in small contract operations be easily serviced by unions. Successful unionization of the public sector in Canada and Europe, and the general security of employment in all Developed Market Economies (DMEs), have provided means for increases in civil service as well as private sector wages. Security of tenure has generally improved. These trends are stalled by the practices of contracting out. Since the contractor has limited-time agreements and no legal capacity to ensure longevity, both governments and large companies can obtain their services without taking on long-term commitments to labor. This is advantageous to the employer when production technologies are rapidly changing, and future labor requirements are either unpredictable or inconsistent with interim needs. The practice of off-shore sourcing for data entry services is a direct reflection of this process. The off-shore sources are in regions that have low labor costs.

Beyond that, there is the investment cost involved in knowledge: since it is knowledge-intensive service sectors that are growing most rapidly, we can assume it is here that the cost of services has grown most markedly. Where there is high capital investment there is a demand for skilled service workers. Thus we might anticipate that as capital intensity increases in the goods-producing sectors, so does the cost of labor in services as well as production.

Labor costs may not, in fact, be the major component of service costs in knowledge-intensive industries of the 1990s. Where engineering and ar-chitectural designing is computerized, where banking is likewise auto-mated to a high degree, and other information-based services are embedded in high-cost machinery, much of the cost is in the capital itself. What may be necessary to explain rising service costs is a combination of labor costs for some traditional activities and capital costs for technologically more advanced activities.

But even that combination will not explain the rising costs of business and financial services. There, the high cost of services lies in interest rates, dividends, management fees and the like; it has little to do with either capital intensity (though that is important) or skilled workers. In the highly lucrative business of financing leveraged takeovers and similar transactions that have characterized international investments since the mid-1970s, it is the high level of profit anticipated by the buyers and proportionately de-manded by the bankers that makes the service so expensive.

A trade agreement has recently come into effect between the United States and Canada which guarantees rights to establishment and national treat-ment for service firms. These rights are controversial because they have the potential result of decreasing public control of services presently under gov-ernment management. Current practices of privatization and contracting out of components of public sector services appear to lead in the same direction.

While developments in telematics facilitate transmission of information without physical presence, many services still require local presence by vir-tue of their nature rather than as a condition of national restrictions. For these, Canada's historical situation as a host country to foreign investment has resulted in continuing deficits attributable to interest, dividend, man-agement, and other service payments. Canada, along with the United States, has focused on the need to remove barriers elsewhere in hopes of expanding opportunities for investment income from services in place. Expansion would involve contracts with foreign governments and the facilitating aid of in-ternational agencies and banks.

Canada's lack of linkages between service and manufacturing sectors con-tinues to inhibit Canadian presence on the international circuits, and this affects even the dominant banking industry. In short, Canada is the recipient of service industry foreign investments, but has a very small and apparently declining role in the global marketplace for services.

Within North America, the bi-national bodies established under the Canada-U.S. agreement will, in all likelihood, become vital regulators of economic policies, displacing national, state and provincial governments. The regulations eventually emerging from these international governing bodies could take many forms (the European Community is already contemplating new labor legislation for a single market); what they will not provide is protection of national differences. Most likely to be affected by this change are Canada's greater reliance on public services, and the related cultural differences between Canada and the United States.

FURTHER READING

Cameron, Duncan, ed. *The Free Trade Papers.* Toronto: James Lorimer, 1986.

Canada. *The Canada-U.S. Free Trade Agreement.* copy 10-12-87. Ottawa, 1988.

————. *Task Force on Trade in Services, Background Report.* Ottawa, October 1982.

Clairmont, Frederick F., and John H. Cavanagh. *Transnational Corporations and Services: The Final Frontier.* United Nations: UNCTAD, 1984.

Cohen, Marjorie Griffin. *Free Trade and the Future of Women's Work: Manufacturing and Service Industries.* Part two. Ottawa: Garamond Press and the Canadian Centre for Policy Alternatives, 1987.

Ontario, Government of. Ministry of Treasury and Economics. *Ontario Study of the Service Sector.* 1986.

Statistics Canada. *Canada's International Transactions in Services 1986 and 1987.* Cat. 67-203 annual.

————. *Canada's International Trade in Services: 1969 to 1984.* June 1986.

United Nations Center on Transnational Corporations. *Foreign Direct Investment, The Service Sector and International Banking.* Series A:7 (May 1987). New York: United Nations.

ENERGY

G. BRUCE DOERN

Energy development in Canada is a function of four political-economic imperatives that in the 1990s are joined increasingly by a fifth. The four that have prevailed for all of Canada's modern energy history are: a rich and diverse energy endowment of oil and gas, hydroelectric, coal and nuclear fuels; a Canadian dependence on U.S. continental markets to make feasible most energy developments; divided political jurisdiction over energy policy between the federal and provincial governments but with powerful resource ownership powers residing in the hands of the latter; and the pan-Canadian spatial reality of energy resources in regions distant from consumer population centers, thus triggering huge transportation problems but also entrenched political-economic divisions among Canada's regions, especially between the producer regions of Western Canada and the heavily populated consumer regions of Ontario and Quebec. The fifth imperative, certainly present in the past but more evident in the 1990s, is the desire for a better marriage between energy and the environment.

Each of these imperatives is discussed briefly and then related to three broad periods of energy development since World War II: 1945 to 1973, 1973 to 1984, and 1984 to 1990. These periods correspond roughly to different levels of reliance on markets versus government intervention to influence the pace and nature of development. The first and last periods have been very market oriented, while the middle period, influenced greatly by the two world oil crises of 1973 and 1979–80, witnessed a surge of government intervention. Each period can also be seen as embracing the emergence of a new "ascending" or dominant fuel. But cumulatively a situation has evolved in which, in the 1990s, there are more and more economic opportunities for inter-fuel substitution in industrial production and consumer use.

THE FIVE IMPERATIVES

The Rich Fuel Endowment: The Problem of Too Many Choices?
Canada's huge landmass is a resource haven. Its abundant supplies of all fuels—oil and gas, coal, hydroelectricity and uranium for nuclear power—give it energy assets that are the envy of most countries. At the same time

the immense continental expanse and northern cold climate make it one of the world's most prodigious per capita energy users and wasters. Canada has used its energy base as an explicit development strategy leading many to conclude that successive efforts to "live off" its resources have resulted in a lack of national attention to the manufacturing components of its economy. Even as lately as 1981 the federal government defined its "industrial" policy as spinoffs from resource mega-projects. According to this policy, several planned giant energy projects would be the engine of a national strategy. Past energy developments, in concert with other resource development in the grains and minerals sector, have also led to "boom and bust" cycles of economic activity in response to price changes and world sales.

Countries with lesser energy endowments have little choice but to choose the obvious. Canada's multiple endowments have often led to the problem of too many choices or at least a tendency to think that the country's endowment allowed the luxury of shielding itself from energy realities. In both the 1973 and 1979–80 energy crises, it was argued by many that Canada tried to shield itself unrealistically from the effects of rising world prices by establishing a two-price policy for exports versus domestic users of oil and gas.

Dependence on United States Continental Markets
The unalterable fact that the United States has 10 times the population of Canada combined with the equally unalterable fact that Canada's resources are usually located in the more sparsely populated parts of Canada has meant that Canadian energy decisions are almost always simultaneously American decisions. The fact that the Canadian oil and gas industry has been extensively American-owned only adds to this energy market dependence. Foreign ownership has been as high as 70%; it was reduced in the 1970s and 1980s to about 40% but is edging upward in the 1990s.

Any major energy development beyond the exploration stage—in short, any decisions regarding the financing and building of production facilities, pipelines and related transportation facilities—involves not only American influence but decisions by American authorities and regulators. Over 40% of oil and gas transported from one part of Canada to another part of Canada traverses the United States. While hydroelectric development was for a long period somewhat isolated from these continental realities, it too has increasingly been tied to the desire of provincial governments, which own these utilities, to export increasing amounts of electrical power to the United States. The huge James Bay projects in Quebec typify this trend.

Canadian energy development has also been adversely affected by U.S. energy protectionism. This has come in the form of import taxes and fees, regulatory rules, and outright prohibitions. To a significant extent, when U.S. energy policy changes, Canadian energy policy changes too, albeit not always lock-step. For example, the partial deregulation of natural gas in the United States in the late 1970s and early 1980s certainly helped precipitate the Canadian effort to deregulate in 1985 and 1986.

Divided Political Jurisdiction
Compared with other Western federal countries, Canada probably has the most divided and decentralized jurisdictional arrangement for making energy policy. This arises primarily because of the great extent of direct provincial ownership of lands containing energy resources and of strong provincial managerial powers over resource extraction. The federal government has some strong powers too that can directly and indirectly influence energy development.

More specifically, provincial powers are derived from section 109 of the Canadian constitution, which confers all lands, mines, minerals, and royalties to the provinces. Provincial ownership is reinforced by the property and civil rights clause (92-13), the power to levy direct taxes (92-2) and authority over the management and sale of public lands (92-5). Federal power resides in the trade and commerce clause (91-2), which confers powers over interprovincial trade, and clause 91-3, which enables the federal government to tax by any mode or means, as well as emergency and declaratory powers and treaty powers. The federal government also has direct ownership of the vast Canada Lands (the north and offshore), in which it has all the powers that a province has and the powers of the owner as well. Some of these latter powers have been in dispute in two senses: in some cases offshore areas, such as those off Newfoundland, raise provincial-like disputes; and in other cases Native people's land claims are in dispute.

Divided jurisdiction means that energy policy-making is always a process of federal-provincial bargaining. This has been most intense over oil and gas issues. In the realm of hydroelectric power, which is also a classic area of a monopoly economic activity, provincial ownership has been the norm. Moreover, with only limited interprovincial trade in electricity, it has generally escaped significant federal-provincial dispute. With regard to uranium and aspects of nuclear power development, the federal government has the upper hand mainly due to powers granted at the dawn of the nuclear age during World War II. Even here, however, there are important elements of shared power. For example, Ontario is by far the largest producer and user of nuclear power and Saskatchewan has huge uranium reserves.

Regional/Spatial Realities and Producer-Consumer Tensions
Within Canada, the major population concentrations are in Ontario and Quebec and most of this is located in the Montreal-to-Windsor corridor hugging the American border. Energy sources, on the other hand, tend to be in the less populated west (especially for oil, gas and coal), in remote hinterland regions within each province (hydroelectric projects) or in the vast northern and offshore territories known as the Canada Lands.

One consequence of this, in concert with divided jurisdiction, is that Canada has replicated within its borders some of the basic producer-consumer conflicts seen on the world stage between the Western OECD consumer countries and OPEC producer countries. Canada's western producer provinces and its eastern consumer provinces frequently have fundamentally different interests. These different material interests emerged most starkly when world oil prices shot up in 1973 and then again in 1979–80. Western producer interests believed they should have been entitled to receive the world price, but they were denied it by national (in their view "eastern") policy. These resentments are not just a product of energy issues. They reflect a larger historic view, especially in western Canada, that national economic policy as a whole has favored eastern Canada, especially Ontario and Quebec. Thus battles over energy become extremely emotional and symbolic in interregional terms.

The second result of these spatial imperatives is that most energy developments involve large transportation links to bring the energy fuel to market. Individual projects, usually mega-projects, therefore become very visible because of their cost and risk. Both political and business careers are "on the line" with the full glare of national and regional media coverage. Governments at the federal and provincial levels have both risen to, and fallen from, power on the basis of the promises, successes and failures of such projects.

Energy and the Environment
There is a strong sense, as Canadians sit near the American border, that the north and its energy and other resources *are* Canada's environment. This is true even though most Canadians have never actually visited the far north. With the political emergence of an environmental movement in the late 1960s, the sense of linkage between energy and the environment has only intensified and become more specific. The increased political visibility of the moral case advanced by Native peoples for their land claims in energy-rich areas has also enhanced the links.

Environmental-energy issues first peaked on the national political-economic agenda in the mid-1970s when a major commission of inquiry, the Berger Commission, examined the desirability of building the huge proposed Mackenzie Valley gas pipeline. Because of the Berger hearings and the sensitivities they raised, the project was put on hold. In the early 1990s, the Cree Indians of northern Quebec and North American environmentalists combined to halt further development of James Bay hydroelectric power for export to the United States.

In the 1980s, there was a gradual increase in regulatory requirements at both the federal and provincial levels to protect environmental values. In the late 1980s, the federal government formally committed itself to adopting the "sustainable development" concept advocated by the prestigious Brundtland World Commission on the Environment.

These then are the five imperatives for understanding the economics and politics of Canadian energy development. Each of the following three historical periods must be viewed with these imperatives fully in mind.

WORLD WAR II TO 1973

As the post-World War II period began, the dominant fuel was coal, with significant use of electrical power within each province. All this changed with the discovery of major oil and gas reserves in Alberta. Almost immediately, these discoveries in 1947 resulted in a battle for jurisdiction. Alberta strengthened its powers with legislation to ensure that Albertans had primary access to their own resource. It also established the Alberta Gas Trunk Line (now NOVA) as a single-system gas gatherer within the province. The federal government also passed laws to ensure its role over interprovincial and international energy trade.

Federal policy differentiated clearly between oil and gas, especially as they concerned the early approval of the first pipelines. The main concern with oil was to move it and sell it efficiently so as to earn the highest rate of return. Thus the early pipelines were linked to U.S. markets. For natural gas, however, federal policy was different. Natural gas would not move across the border until the government was convinced that "there was no economic use present or future for that gas within Canada." This difference in policy was partly due to greater concerns about conservation regarding gas. But it was also a function of the different economic characteristics of gas production and sales. The heavy front-end capital and transportation facility costs necessitated long-term contracts of 15 to 20 years.

The first postwar decade ended with a major national political battle over the construction of the TransCanada pipeline. The government wanted an all-Canadian route but had to compromise somewhat on this promise. This plus the sponsoring minister's arrogance in pushing the legislation through Parliament eventually led to the defeat of the previously entrenched Liberal government of Prime Minister Louis St. Laurent. With the election of the Conservative Diefenbaker government in 1957, and the tabling of the report of a Royal Commission on Energy, national energy policy entered a period of relative serenity.

The focus of policy from 1960 until 1973 was almost exclusively oriented toward the expansion and development of the oil industry. Within the decade, oil became the dominant fuel, supplanting coal. The central piece of this development was the National Oil Policy (NOP). The NOP ensured that consumers east of the Ottawa Valley would be served by cheaper Venezuelan imports (as the U.S. major oil companies were urging) while consumers to the west were supplied by Alberta oil. Alberta oil was more expensive and hence Ontario consumers would pay a premium price for national development purposes. All the main industry and national and regional players were accommodated by this policy. In 1959 the National Energy Board (NEB) was also established to preside over this basically dynamic developmental phase of nation building, much as an earlier era had seen the building of the national pan-Canadian railways.

The other major feature of this period, developing largely out of sight of national political attention, was the consolidation and expansion of provincial hydroelectric utilities and their increasing use as tools of provincial economic development. While the timing varied among the provinces, most of the hydros had been brought under provincial ownership by the 1960s.

Electricity, unlike oil and gas, is a natural monopoly and is characterized by significant economies of scale. Pressures for public ownership came from the business community that feared monopoly exploitation. This was certainly the impetus in Ontario, where ownership by the province dates back to 1904. Later takeovers by other provinces also arose out of fears over foreign or nonprovincial ownership and also out of positive desires to use the hydros as tools of development. The nationalization of hydroelectric utilities in Quebec in the 1960s and the later development of the huge James Bay projects were a central feature of Quebec nationalist sentiment.

The main developmental tool concerning the hydros was pricing policy. Promotional rate structures were introduced in which major customers were charged lower rates for each succeeding block of power purchased. These policies lured major customers such as forestry and mineral companies. Pricing policy was also intended to keep electrical prices for general consumers as low and as equal as possible across the province in question. By the early 1970s, the hydros were among the largest of Canada's corporations; virtually all were state owned, and they were key players in the political economy of each province. For the most part, however, they were energy traders within their own provincial areas rather than interprovincially or internationally.

1973 TO 1984: THE ENERGY CRISES AND GOVERNMENT INTERVENTION

The benchmark events for Canadian energy development during this period were the two energy crises. The first occurred in 1973 when the OPEC oil embargo helped precipitate a sudden fourfold increase in the world price of oil. The second occurred in 1979–80 when, in the wake of the revolution in Iran, the world price doubled. Both of these price shocks led to bursts of policy intervention and international and federal-provincial political conflict.

Criticized for its lack of preparedness, the federal government responded in 1973 by announcing in quick succession a series of initiatives including oil export controls, a freeze on domestic oil prices, an oil import compensation program to protect consumers who were dependent on imported oil, and the establishment of a new state-owned oil company, Petro-Canada. Many of these initiatives were the result of the federal government's frustration over its own lack of good information about Canada's reserves, and over its dependence on a largely foreign-owned industry for strategic information.

The federal policy initiatives were viewed by the main producing provinces as a major invasion of their areas of jurisdiction. The old NOP consensus of the 1960s was decimated. The provinces strengthened their own legislation and added their own provincially owned energy companies to fend off Ottawa. In subsequent negotiations over prices later in the 1970s, Ottawa pulled back from its two-price position and gradually let oil prices approach quite closely to the then prevailing world level. Then suddenly came the second oil crisis when, following the Iranian revolution of 1979, world prices shot up again.

The intensity of this next interregional conflict in Canada was initially illustrated by the fact that not even the newly elected Conservative government under Prime Minister Joe Clark, himself an Albertan, could solve the growing dispute with fellow Conservative and Albertan, Premier Peter Lougheed. The Clark government, after barely nine months in office, was defeated in the House of Commons, in part over its budget proposals for new energy taxes. The core political issue, as in 1973, was that Alberta believed it was entitled to ask the world price for its depleting resource while the federal government pressed again for lower prices to assist central Canadian consumers and industries. There was also intense dispute over how the new resource revenues should be managed to promote economic development.

Both of the political protagonists had their own new institutional symbols that served to gall the other. The Liberal government of Pierre Trudeau had, in the latter part of the 1970s, facilitated the expansion of Petro-Canada through takeovers of private oil companies. This angered the oil patch as well as free enterprise Albertans, and the Clark government had promised to privatize Petro-Canada. For its part, Alberta had established a Heritage Trust Fund in which was put some of its burgeoning oil and gas revenues. The exponential growth of this fund meant that any Alberta claims that it was somehow an aggrieved and economically vulnerable region fell upon deaf ears in eastern Canada.

The sudden defeat of the Clark government in 1980 brought with it the equally sudden return to power of a refurbished Trudeau Liberal government, with virtually no representation in it from western Canada. In its first budget in the fall of 1980 the Liberals announced its National Energy Program (NEP). The NEP was a massive act of federal intervention premised on the Liberals' campaign promise of fair "made in Canada" prices; 50% Canadian ownership of the oil and gas industry; and a promise to promote energy security, including self-sufficiency in oil by 1990. The NEP was also premised on absolutely bullish expectations about rising future energy prices—which failed to materialize.

The NEP turned energy incentives on their head. The emphasis changed from a tax-based to a grant-based system, with grants favoring Canadian firms, and preference given for drilling in the frontier areas under federal jurisdiction. A new two-price regime was put into effect and a massive new array of energy taxes was imposed, including production taxes. The NEP also included new conservation and oil substitution incentives. Canadianization measures not only included the grants but also enhanced Canadian ownership through a special levy that would allow Petro-Canada to take over more private energy companies.

With the NEP, the federal Liberals had thrown down the gauntlet. It precipitated angry negotiations and acts of political brinkmanship which seriously threatened national unity. Nonetheless, a pricing agreement was eventually reached in September 1981, in part because both the federal government and Alberta believed their own forecasts of ever-increasing prices and hence thought they were sharing a very big revenue pie. The NEP also angered the newly elected free-enterprise-oriented Reagan administration in the United States as well as major parts of the energy industry and Canadian business community as a whole. It was, however, initially a popular policy in Ontario and Quebec.

The NEP was barely under way, however, when many of its underpinnings fell away. High interest rates and the 1982 worldwide recession dealt an initial blow. Oil prices softened due to reduced demand caused by the recession itself, by political splits in OPEC, and by the cumulative effects of past conservation programs and the discovery of new world supplies. When combined with the new energy taxes and the uncertainties of the new NEP regime, the energy industry in Canada nosedived. By mid-1982 the Liberal government was already offering to change some of its NEP provisions so as to aid the oil and gas industry, especially small producers.

The NEP did increase Canadian ownership and did produce a level of exploration in the frontier areas that increased knowledge of the reserves that exist there. The gas industry infrastructure was expanded further into Quebec, and Petro-Canada became a formidable and symbolic presence in the consciousness of Canadians. But the great majority of professional energy policy opinion was that the NEP was a mistaken and seriously flawed policy. The view increasingly was that energy issues were too volatile economically and that no policy could anticipate or encompass all the changes going on. Massive intervention only made things worse. The stage was being set for the return of pro-market energy policy.

Politically, however, the NEP left a bitter taste especially regarding relations between central and western Canada. It became the quintessential example, especially in western Canada, of how not to make policy. It was seen as a combative unilateral act by an unsympathetic eastern-dominated government. This lesson was a major contributing factor in later discussions in 1987–88 when energy free trade was secured through the Canada-United States free trade agreement. From the western Canadian perspective this ensured that there could never again be "another NEP."

Operating far in the background, but nonetheless still important to Canadian energy development in the 1970s and early 1980s, was Canada's nuclear industry. Following its earlier research and development phase under federal auspices at Atomic Energy of Canada Ltd. (AECL), the industry moved into its commercial stage. The Canadian-designed CANDU reactor became the basis for Ontario Hydro's extensive movement into nuclear power. Ontario became Canada's main nuclear province. The federal government also tried to persuade and induce other provinces to adopt the CANDU but only New Brunswick and Hydro-Quebec did, the latter to only a very limited extent.

Ottawa's ambitions for developing foreign markets for CANDU reactors did not enjoy much success. In part this was because of the novelty of the CANDU system compared to other dominant reactor systems and to the general drying up of the world reactor market following worldwide environmental concerns raised by the shutdown of the Three Mile Island plant in the United States. But to an even greater extent it was also caused by the ambivalence of Canada's views about reactor sales and nuclear proliferation. This came to a head in the mid-1970s when India, using nuclear materials from a Canadian-sponsored research reactor, exploded its first nuclear weapon. The issue of nuclear safeguards escalated even further into policy consciousness and divided the Cabinet over just how hard to push sales, especially to countries that had demonstrated dubious records on non-proliferation issues.

To these dilemmas were added some serious financial and accountability problems at AECL. Questionable sales practices and costly oversupply problems concerning heavy water brought AECL into political disrepute. By the mid-1980s the CANDU program and AECL were facing at best a steady-state situation and at worst a seriously deteriorating one.

HEADING INTO THE 1990S: PRO-MARKET ENERGY POLICIES

Each era of Canadian energy policy reacts to the previous period while at the same time guessing what the future might bring. At the same time it is propelled by realities that may bear only limited resemblance to the rhetoric used to describe that reality. The election of the Mulroney Conservative government to a massive majority victory in 1984 certainly brought a new energy agenda. Ideologically it favored a return to strong pro-market polices on energy and the economy. Politically, especially regarding western Canada, it sought national reconciliation and an end to the energy wars. And internationally, it sought closer relations with the United States.

In their last days of opposition and in the transition period to power, the Mulroney Conservatives probably spent more concerted time on developing their energy policy than on any other policy field. A task force had worked for over a year in close cooperation with the oil and gas industry. Accordingly, once in power, they moved swiftly and sure-handedly on the energy front, with the prime task being the dismantling of the NEP. The decisive pro-market conciliatory slant of federal policy was reflected in four initiatives, the net effects of which have been to create a free market in energy trade that exceeds even the pre-1973 era when the national oil policy was in operation.

The first initiative was the signing of the Western Accord between Ottawa and the western producer provinces. This accord deregulated oil and restored continental oil markets. The Atlantic Accord was an agreement primarily with Newfoundland which settled the long festering and divisive issue of jurisdictional control and management of offshore resources. This was not itself particularly pro-market in its content but certainly exhibited commitments to national reconciliation.

The Western Accord was followed by an agreement to phase in the deregulation of gas. This would allow more direct buy-sell relationships between gas producers and gas users with a consequent weakening of some of the previous monopoly powers of the pipelines and distribution companies. Because of long-term contracts, this new gas policy was difficult to implement, but it is nonetheless a significant change. The extent of gas deregulation eventually included an end to the past postwar policy which had required surplus reserve tests for exports of gas. These had required a 25- to 30-year domestic supply cushion before exports were allowed.

The final arrow in the Mulroney energy policy bow came in the provisions of the Canada-United States Free Trade Agreement (FTA) which came into effect January 1, 1989. It further opened the continental boundaries, mainly by preventing the future use of two price systems and by restraining the Americans from using many restrictive measures that they had resorted to in the postwar era regarding Canadian oil and gas (and uranium) exports. The quid pro quo for this long-sought-after, more secure access to the huge American market was the so-called proportionality clause. It provided that Canada could not arbitrarily cut off contracted American buyers of Canadian oil and gas. If declared shortages occurred, Canada could only reduce supply in proportion over an agreed three-year base period. The FTA does protect Canada's existing foreign ownership laws regarding energy investments, but for the most part the FTA provides the capstone to the Mulroney government's pro-market energy policies, in effect "constitutionalizing" them.

The degree to which this was achieved in the FTA is in part the result of the anger left from the political legacy of the NEP. The federal government may have given up more of its energy powers in the negotiations over the FTA than it would have had to had the Liberals practiced a more conciliatory approach in 1980. In any event, there is little doubt that by the 1990s, the pro-market approach was clearly in the ascendancy.

One of the policy events that further reflected the intellectual underpinning for the pro-market focus was the Energy Options report published in 1988 by the minister of energy's Energy Options Advisory Committee. After an elaborate public consultative exercise it concluded that energy policy participants had rejected the "hoarding" approach for a "development" approach. By a development approach it meant an appoach that relied on free markets. By a hoarding approach, it meant policies that slow the rate of development below what is economic under prevailing conditions to ensure that future generations are left with an adequate supply. The Energy Options committee concluded that these policies were fundamentally flawed for four reasons. First, they presumed that policymakers had the wisdom to forecast the future. Second, they frustrated the very mechanism, namely market pricing, most likely to bring on the growth of needed oil and gas reserves. Third, they divided the nation by frustrating the needs and aspirations of the producing regions. And finally, they assigned to governments the responsibility for prescribing choices as opposed to allowing Canadian producers and consumers to generate the needed solutions through their diverse market interactions.

While the implicit and explicit claims for the development model are somewhat overstated in the above critique, they nonetheless capture real changes in energy markets and in views about how past policy had worked or failed to work. For example, unknown to the general public, profound changes had occurred in energy markets in the 1980s. Several layers beneath the policy rhetoric, by both interventionist and pro-market forces, a situation of massive new opportunities had emerged in Canada for interfuel substitution. Policy no longer just fostered or followed the rise of a newly dominant fuel—first coal, then oil, then gas. There was a new maturity to markets in which one could now more readily say that interfuel "energy" markets truly existed. Industrial production could increasingly switch to different fuels depending on price and other factors. Conservation and softer energy alternatives were beginning to have an effect on the range of energy choices available.

While the overall direction of energy development is market oriented, there is one contrary trend that implies potentially greater, rather than reduced, governmental roles in Canadian energy development. These arise out of federal and provincial governmental adoption in principle of the concept of "sustainable" development in their environmental policy. As defined by the world Brundtland Report, sustainable development is development which ensures that the utilization of resources and the environment today does not damage prospects for their use by future generations. In theory, this is a radical concept, but its meaning in practice will depend upon a host of decisions and bargains by public and private decision makers.

The adoption of more strenuous environmental regulations and assessment processes throughout the public policy process seems highly likely in the 1990s. This is not just because leaders of Western nations uttered the appropriate words at summit meetings but rather because there was a growing body of public opinion in Canada and elsewhere that regarded a better energy-environmental mix as being politically and economically essential.

FURTHER READING

Bregha, François. *Bob Blair's Pipeline*. Toronto: Lorimer, 1980.

Canada. *Energy and Canadians Into the 21st Century*. Ottawa: Minister of Supply and Services Canada, 1988.

Doern, G. Bruce, and Glen Toner. *The Politics of Energy*. Toronto: Methuen, 1985.

Doern, G. Bruce, and Brian Tomlin. *Faith and Fear: The Free Trade Story*. Toronto: Stoddart, 1991.

Economic Council of Canada. *Connections: An Energy Strategy For the Future*. Ottawa: Minister of Supply and Services Canada, 1985.

Lermer, George. *Atomic Energy of Canada Limited: The Crown Corporation as Strategist in an Entrepreneurial, Global Scale Industry*. Ottawa: Supply and Services Canada, 1987.

National Energy Board. *The Regulation of Electricity Exports*. Ottawa: Supply and Services Canada, 1987.

Pearse, Peter H. "Property Rights and the Development of Natural Resource Policies in Canada." *Canadian Public Policy* 14 (September 1988): 307–20.

Richards, J., and L. Pratt. *Prairie Capitalism*. Toronto: McClelland and Stewart, 1979.

TRANSPORT AND COMMUNICATIONS

GARTH STEVENSON

Canada's history and its national identity, more than those of any other political community in the world, have been associated with the development of transport and communications. The country's vast size, its harsh physical environment, the geographical barriers between its regions, and its origins as a producer of bulky commodities for export all contributed to the early preoccupation with transport. The need to provide the infrastructure of transportation and communication, largely at public expense, has shaped the development of the Canadian state and provided much of its raison d'être. Transport and communications have been used to reinforce the rather tenuous bonds of national unity in a country the regions of which have fewer natural links with one another than with neighboring regions of the United States. As Professor Goldwin Smith, who favored union with the United States, commented a century ago: "Whether the four blocks of territory constituting the Dominion can forever be kept by political agencies united among themselves and separate from their Continent . . . is the Canadian question." Canadians tried to answer the question by building all-Canadian networks from the St. Lawrence to the Pacific by rail (1885), air (1939), pipeline (1958), television microwave (1958), paved highway (1962) and fiber-optic cable (1989). Subvention, regulation, and public ownership have been used, in varying proportions, to promote the development of all the different modes of transport and communication. Federal legislation requires that air carriers and broadcasting stations be Canadian-owned. Although British capital played a large role in building the railways, much of it was portfolio rather than direct investment. Canadian ownership has always predominated in the transport and communication industries generally.

Responsibility for transport and communication in Canada is shared by all three levels of government. The Constitution Act of 1867 asserts that "works or undertakings" connecting one province with another, or connecting Canada with a foreign country, can be regulated by the central government. Parliament can acquire jurisdiction over "works or undertakings" within a province simply by declaring them to be "for the general

450

advantage of Canada," a practice that in the railway age was used to bring practically all railways under federal control. Parliament also has responsibility for navigation and shipping. Subsequent judicial decisions have given the central government jurisdiction over aeronautics, broadcasting, cable television, and interprovincial trucks and buses, although the power to regulate trucks and buses was promptly delegated back to the provinces. The federal government owns the largest railway system and the largest broadcasting network, operates most of the airports and seaports, and regulates virtually every aspect of the communications industry. It has only recently sold the largest airline to private investors.

On the other hand, the provinces own and maintain the highways, which by a curious legal fiction are assumed to end and begin at each provincial boundary, even though the motorist may be scarcely aware of the transition from one to another. Ontario and British Columbia own important regional railways, and British Columbia owns a large fleet of ferries. Saskatchewan operates rural and intercity bus service. Ontario contracts with transportation companies to provide air transport in its northern regions and commuter trains around Toronto. Ontario, Quebec and Alberta operate "educational" television networks and Alberta, Saskatchewan and Manitoba own their telephone systems. One important and sometimes overlooked form of transport, the transmission of electricity over long distance, is entirely a provincial responsibility. Cities and metropolitan governments operate urban transit services, and a few of them own their telephone systems. There are also some municipal airports.

Canada has been a leader not only in communications, but in the study of communications. Harold A. Innis, who wrote his doctoral dissertation on the Canadian Pacific Railway and became Canada's most distinguished economic historian with his studies of the fur trade and the cod fisheries, turned in his last years to studying the role of communications in world history and their influence on patterns of thought. This aspect of Innis' work was carried on after his death by Marshall McLuhan, whose book *Understanding Media* attracted world renown in the 1960s. Today several Canadian universities have programs, schools or institutes of communications studies.

This chapter will discuss the development of the principal modes of transport and communication in Canada since 1945, a period of dramatic technological developments that have altered the relative importance of the different modes. Social changes, such as urbanization, and economic changes, such as the shift from a staple-producing to a more service-oriented economy, have also had an impact on transport and communications. Governments have tried to promote the development of newer modes while responding to the decline of older modes, with mixed success. The traditional policy instruments of subvention, regulation, and public ownership have become increasingly controversial, but none of the three is likely to be abandoned entirely. Advocates of more market-driven, and presumably less expensive, policies have won some victories. Their opponents have argued, with some success, that the fragile state of national integration, and the natural handicaps suffered by certain regions of Canada, make interventionist policies essential. A more recent complication in transport policy has been the growing concern that some modes (air transport, highways, pipelines, and electric power lines) may be detrimental to human health or to the physical environment.

It is appropriate to begin with the railways, because in 1945 they dominated Canadian transportation, and Canadian life generally, to an extent that is almost unimaginable today. The two major transcontinental systems, government-owned Canadian National and privately-owned Canadian Pacific, were Canada's largest enterprises and largest employers. Including their express companies, telegraph networks, hotels, and ships, they employed almost a quarter of a million Canadians, or 5% of the labor force. The overwhelming preponderance of freight and passenger traffic moved by rail, most of it behind steam locomotives, of which there were more than four thousand in active service. Canada had more rail trackage per capita than any other country in the world (a distinction that it has since lost to Australia) and few hamlets were too small to have regular freight and passenger service. Larger centers, with very few exceptions, enjoyed a choice between the competing freight and passenger services of the two systems. In most Canadian cities and towns the principal railway station was the focal point of the community and the center of its commercial and industrial economy. The railway hotel, in cities important enough to have one, was invariably the largest and best in town. The long express passenger trains, with their sleeping, dining and parlor cars, offered frequent glimpses of luxury, sophistication and elegance to the places where they paused for water or coal, to change crews or to pick up and let off passengers.

Railways also occupied a prominent place in the country's political debates. Spokesmen for the profitable Canadian Pacific asserted that the larger but less prosperous Canadian National was a burden on the taxpayers, and that Canadian National's deficits demonstrated the superiority of private enterprise. Canadian National's defenders replied that the deficits were caused by redundant trackage built prior to nationalization, and by the interest on inherited debts. They also pointed out that Canadian Pacific, in its early years, had received massive assistance from the state. Local or family tradition often dictated a preference for one or the other system, with Liberals, farmers, and westerners tending to prefer the Canadian National while Tories, urban residents and central Canadians were more partial to the Canadian Pacific.

Today most of this has changed or vanished. Thousands of miles of track have been abandoned, while thousands more are overgrown with weeds and used only occasionally. Most of the passenger service has disappeared, and most of what remains is operated by a government agency, the future of which is now in doubt, at heavy cost to the taxpayer. Hundreds of stations have been demolished or converted to other uses, and many of those that remain sit forlorn and dilapidated, far removed from the newer hotels and shopping centers and rarely visited by local residents. The railways no longer carry the mail, and their telegraph and express companies have been disbanded. Even much of the freight business has been lost to highway trucks, including most movement of manufactured end products, although the railways still carry vast quantities of grain, minerals and forest products, particularly west of Lake Superior. Railways are rarely mentioned in Parliament or the media except when a branch line or a passenger service is about to be abandoned.

Despite their diminishing importance, the imprint of the railways on Canada remains. Scores of towns and cities are named after railways, railway executives or railway financiers. Others, including Calgary and Vancouver, occupy locations that were chosen by railway surveyors. There is still a Railway Committee Room in the Parliament Building, and the Senate annually introduces a pro forma "bill relating to railways" to symbolize its independence from the Crown. As the popular historian Pierre Berton has observed, the country is even shaped like a train, with its provinces coupled end to end along a track.

The railways have tried to adapt to their changed circumstances, a process that the state has sometimes assisted and sometimes obstructed. Perhaps the easiest form of adaptation has been technological. Steam locomotives were completely eliminated by 1960, with diesel-electric units taking their place. New types of freight cars have been built for specialized traffics. Radio communication between trains, centralized traffic control, computers and intermodal freight containers have transformed many aspects of railway operation. Cabooses are now being eliminated from freight trains. Some main lines have been reconstructed with continuous welded rail and concrete ties, and the Canadian Pacific recently built the longest tunnel in North America to increase the capacity of its line between Calgary and Vancouver. Both major Canadian systems have consulting services that share their expertise with railways in Asia, Africa, Latin America and the South Pacific. Some new railways have even been built since 1945, mainly to reach mineral deposits in Labrador, the Northwest Territories, and the northern regions of Quebec, Manitoba, Alberta and British Columbia.

Until 1967 railways were very closely regulated by a federal agency, the Board of Transport Commissioners, on the assumption that they were powerful enough to dominate the transportation market to the detriment of consumers. Increases in freight rates invariably caused a political uproar, and governments found it expedient to provide subsidies rather than allowing increases that would permit profitable operation. The railways were also required to provide many services for which there was no longer much effective demand. In 1961 the Macpherson Royal Commission noted that the railways now faced serious competition from other modes, and recommended that they be given more freedom to set rates and abandon uneconomic services. The National Transportation Act, which took effect in 1967, partially implemented these recommendations. It also replaced the Board of Transport Commissioners with a new agency, the Canadian Transport Commission. The CTC was supposed to be responsible for all modes of transport (although the sections of the Act pertaining to highway transport were never implemented) and to conduct research and provide policy advice to the government, rather than merely making ad hoc decisions.

The most politically sensitive of the railways' tasks, the transport of prairie grain, was deliberately excluded from the terms of the National Transportation Act, and by the 1970s it had become highly unprofitable for the railways. A statute dating from 1925 required them to carry grain at rates set before the turn of the century. Like Dr. Johnson's dog walking on its hind legs, the railways did not do the job well, but it is surprising that they managed to do it at all. Apart from their effect on railway balance sheets, the low rates discouraged flour milling and livestock feeding on the prairies, where the grain was grown, and they discouraged any use of highway trucks to move grain, even for short distances. Pressure from other users of the railway system, and from the railways themselves, finally forced the government to adopt the Western Grain Transportation Act in 1983. This act allowed freight rates on grain to rise gradually to a somewhat more realistic level and paid massive subsidies to the railways, proportionate to the amount of grain carried. The railways are still burdened with excessive grain-related trackage, which they are forbidden to abandon until at least the year 2000, but the government has given them some financial assistance in rehabilitating this trackage. Prior to 1983 the federal government and the prairie provincial governments also purchased new hopper cars to move the grain, since the railways refused to do so until the rates were deregulated.

Initially the National Transportation Act of 1967 had a highly beneficial effect on railway finances, but by the early 1980s the effect had worn off. After the United States completely deregulated its railways in 1980, the two major Canadian railways urged the Canadian government to do likewise, particularly since they competed against the American systems for much of their traffic. A second National Transportation Act, adopted 20 years after the first, made it easier for the railways to abandon trackage (although no more than 20% of the total could be abandoned in the first five years) and allowed confidential contracts between railways and shippers. It also replaced the Canadian Transport Commission with a new, and smaller, National Transportation Agency.

The government-owned Canadian National has gradually become more profitable, and the contrast between it and Canadian Pacific is no longer significant. Mainly this is because in 1952, and again in 1978, the government relieved Canadian National of its accumulated debts. As a state enterprise, Canadian National must borrow rather than issuing share capital. By 1986 the burden of interest payments again exceeded operating revenues, but the Progressive Conservative government refused to assume more debt, and instead forced the railway to sell its hotels and telecommunications to Canadian Pacific as a means of paying off its debts. Canadian National has also been allowed to terminate all railway operations in Newfoundland and Prince Edward Island, where it had no hope of ever making a profit. Conceivably, Canadian National may be sold to private investors after some further pruning of its network.

Railway passenger traffic began to decline as soon as the Second World War ended. In the 1950s the railways hoped that diesel power and new rolling stock would stem the decline, but soon they, and particularly Canadian Pacific, became discouraged and began to abandon services, a process that required a public hearing in each case before the Board of Transport Commissioners. The Macpherson Royal Commission recommended that the railways be allowed to abandon all passenger service, except in remote areas without adequate highways. As this was considered too controversial by the government, the National Transportation Act of 1967 merely transferred responsibility for deciding on abandonments to the CTC and provided that the government could subsidize up to 80% of the losses of any passenger service that was retained.

The next decade saw gradual deterioration of passenger service and increasing subsidies. In 1978 the government adopted a different approach, borrowed from the United States. The railways sold their passenger rolling stock to a new crown corporation, Via Rail Canada, which assumed responsibility for providing the service. In effect this meant that the government would pay 100% of the operating losses, rather than 80%, but it was hoped that the service could be made more efficient and more popular. There was little evidence of this, and in 1981 the government suddenly discontinued about one-fifth of the passenger service by order-in-council. The new government that took office in 1984 restored most of the abandoned services, but by 1989 it too was considering massive cutbacks, or even the possibility of abandoning Via Rail entirely. Like the Macpherson Commission, it admitted that certain "remote" services would somehow have to be maintained, although these services are among the most spectacularly unprofitable. Early in 1990 the government terminated about one-half of Via Rail's services, including the daily transcontinental train between Montreal, Toronto, Calgary and Vancouver.

In addition to Via Rail, some regional railways still operate their own passenger services. Also, both Montreal and Toronto are served by commuter trains that use Canadian National and Canadian Pacific trackage. The railways provide operating crews while a government agency (provincial in Toronto and municipal in Montreal) owns the rolling stock. These commuter services carry several times as many passengers as Via Rail, albeit over shorter distances.

AIR TRANSPORT

Canadian air transport developed first in the northern regions of the country. There were hardly any roads or railways in those regions, but the many lakes left by the retreating glaciers facilitated the operation of light aircraft, equipped with floats in summer and with skis in winter. Such aircraft could carry passengers, mail, and even freight, particularly the products of Canada's oldest commercial industry, the fur trade. They were operated by a host of small, privately owned air carriers.

Several airports in southern Canada were built for military purposes, or as relief projects during the Depression. In 1937 the government organized

Trans-Canada Airlines, a subsidiary of the Canadian National Railways, to operate air service from coast to coast. Canadian Pacific, which had been invited to participate, decided to form its own airline instead, but until 1959 the government reserved the transcontinental route, and most international routes, for its own carrier. In fact the publicly owned carrier, renamed Air Canada in 1964 as part of the government's policy of bilingualism, retained special privileges until as late as 1979.

In the early postwar years air travel was still a somewhat esoteric novelty, used only by the most time-sensitive, and courageous, travelers. The largest aircraft carried only 40 passengers. Speeds were slow, stops frequent, noise levels high and pressurization erratic. Passengers were allowed only 20 kilograms (44 pounds) of luggage. Fatal accidents were fairly common, and flights were frequently delayed or canceled because of weather conditions.

Despite these difficulties, the Canadian industry grew rapidly. TCA added branches to its main transcontinental route and extended its operations into Western Europe, the Caribbean and the United States. Its main rival, Canadian Pacific Airlines, was allowed to fly to Japan, Australia, New Zealand, South America, and Europe, even before a change of government permitted its entry to the transcontinental market in 1959. Several other significant carriers operated local services, particularly in the north. Turboprop aircraft were introduced on domestic routes in 1955 (the Vickers Viscount) and jet aircraft in 1960 (the Douglas DC-8). By the latter year Canadian air carriers were carrying 10 times as much passenger traffic as in 1947, and their passenger traffic for the first time exceeded that of the railways.

By the 1960s air travel had come of age. Higher incomes, faster, more comfortable and safer aircraft, and a decline in its cost relative to the costs of railway and steamship travel made it accessible to a mass market. Increasingly the public demanded "competition," such as existed in the United States, rather than the quasi-monopoly enjoyed by the government airline. The Progressive Conservatives, traditionally sympathetic to Canadian Pacific, had allowed that company to enter the transcontinental airline market in 1959 but the Liberals, returning to office in 1963, did not reverse this policy. Instead they gradually removed the restrictions on Canadian Pacific so that by 1979 it could compete on equal terms with Air Canada. Shortly before this a new Air Canada Act had separated Air Canada from Canadian National Railways, given it more independence vis-à-vis the government, and required it to apply to the CTC for new routes in the same way as any other air carrier.

Meanwhile, several other significant air carriers had emerged. In the 1960s the government recognized five of these as "regional airlines" and allowed them to acquire jet aircraft and to compete with the transcontinental carriers on certain routes. The five were Eastern Provincial, based in Newfoundland; Nordair and Quebecair, both based in Montreal; Transair, based in Winnipeg; and Pacific Western, originally based in Vancouver but moved to Calgary after its acquisition by the government of Alberta in 1974. Pacific Western, which controlled the lucrative route between Edmonton and Calgary, was the most successful of these, and acquired Transair in 1978. By 1986 Canadian Pacific Airlines had gained control of the other three regional carriers, whereupon it was itself sold by its parent railway company to Pacific Western, which had been privatized by the Alberta government in 1984. Pacific Western organized its various holdings into a new carrier known as Canadian Airlines International, which rivaled Air Canada in size. Most of the small local carriers using propeller aircraft were acquired by one or other of the two giants, and Canadian Airlines International acquired Wardair, a jet carrier operating mainly international routes. The airline industry has ended up as a duopoly, similar to that of the railway freight industry. A significant difference between the two is that the federal government is no longer involved in the airline business. The privatization of Air Canada took place in two stages and was completed in 1989. In the early 1990s, Air Canada initiated merger talks with Canadian Airlines International.

The traveling public demanded not only a choice of airlines, but lower fares. In the 1960s travel agents and various organizations began to buy large blocks of seats on international flights from the air carriers at low rates and retail them to the public. This practice made it cheaper, in certain circumstances, to fly across the Atlantic than to fly across Canada, an anomaly that attracted much criticism. In response Canadian air carriers, beginning in 1977, offered some domestic round trip tickets at lower rates, provided the traveler reserved well in advance and stayed a certain length of time at the destination. Although the airlines themselves had mixed feelings about the practice, it was popular with the public and was tacitly encouraged by the CTC. Within a few years passengers paying regular fares were a distinct minority, consisting mainly of expense account travelers, persons required to travel on very short notice because of some family emergency, and migrants with no plans to return to their original starting point. Everyone else traveled at low excursion rates.

Despite this fact, and despite the deteriorating financial position of the air carriers, the public developed an irrational belief that even lower fares would result from deregulation, or, in other words, from allowing new or existing carriers to enter any market regardless of the effect on existing carriers. When the United States deregulated its airlines beginning in 1979, it became a foregone conclusion that Canada would do the same. Such a policy was promised by the Liberals just before their electoral defeat in 1984, and actually was implemented by the Progressive Conservatives not long afterward. Neither lower fares nor more "competition" really resulted. In fact, as noted above, there were only two significant air carriers after deregulation, and no new ones emerged to take advantage of the opportunity to compete with them. By 1990 the government was considering the possibility of opening domestic routes to United States carriers, in return for access for the Canadian carriers to more routes in and to the United States.

Nonetheless, Canada now enjoys what is arguably the best domestic airline service of any country in the world. Jet aircraft of the two main air carriers connect all of the major urban areas, and a few minor ones, with

457

one another. Turboprop aircraft operated by the local subsidiaries of the major carriers provide connections to virtually every other place of any consequence, except for places within an hour's driving time of a major metropolitan airport.

The size, location and environmental effects of airports have become perhaps the most controversial aspects of the aeronautics industry. Mirabel Airport outside of Montreal opened in 1976 but is unpopular because of its remoteness from the city. Consequently the original plan to close Montreal's old Dorval Airport had to be abandoned, and Mirabel operates far below its capacity, handling only overseas traffic. Toronto's main airport, Lester B. Pearson International, is approaching the limits of its capacity, but it is already surrounded by suburban development, so that its expansion would be highly controversial. The building of another airport east of the city was considered in the 1970s, but the idea was abandoned because of local resistance. A new high-speed rail network in southern Ontario, perhaps extending into Quebec and the United States, may eventually prove to be the best solution to this problem.

HIGHWAYS AND HIGHWAY TRANSPORT

Despite the historic importance of the railways and the technological sophistication of the airlines, Canada's most important mode of transport is highway transport. It is difficult to say precisely how important it is, because neither the number of journeys made by individuals driving their own cars nor the amount of freight carried by business enterprises in their own trucks can be accurately measured. However, it is generally assumed that about 90% of intercity travel is by road, and even the for-hire truckers (those who sell their services to unrelated enterprises) have a total freight revenue exceeding that of the railways. (The railways still carry more tonnage, but most of it is bulky low-value commodities such as coal and grain, carried at low rates.)

In 1945 Canada had only one short stretch of modern limited-access highway, the Queen Elizabeth Way between Toronto and Fort Erie. Even that was broken into two segments by the absence of a bridge across Hamilton Harbour, an omission not rectified until a decade later. Outside of southern Ontario, few roads were even paved. North of Lake Superior there was no road at all, and the road from Vancouver to the Continental Divide was little more than a trail along the Fraser and Columbia rivers. The few people who drove from eastern to western Canada, or from the prairies to the Pacific, went through the United States.

Motor vehicle ownership expanded rapidly after the war with the end of gasoline rationing and the reconversion of automobile factories to civilian production. This naturally created a demand for more and better highways, which was reinforced by the rapid growth of the population. The building of roads, except on military bases and in national parks, was traditionally a provincial responsibility, but in 1949 Parliament adopted the Trans-Canada Highway Act, authorizing the federal government to share with the

458

provinces the cost of building a two-lane paved highway from St. John's, Newfoundland to Victoria, British Columbia, as well as a short section of highway on Prince Edward Island. Quebec did not join this scheme for more than a decade, since Premier Maurice Duplessis opposed conditional grants in principle. The project was completed in 1962 with the opening of the section of highway through Rogers Pass in British Columbia. Since that time the federal government has contributed to the upgrading of certain sections of the highway. It has also helped to build some other roads under the Roads to Resources program of the Diefenbaker government and later under regional development agreements with the provinces.

Nonetheless, most of the cost of highway building has been borne by the provinces themselves, and the cost has been considerable. Practically all important roads in Canada are now paved, apart from the Alaska and Mackenzie highways in the far northwest. A continuous multilane limited-access highway extends from Rivière du Loup, Quebec to Windsor, Ontario, a distance of 800 miles. Other major limited-access roads connect Montreal with Ottawa and Quebec City, Toronto with Georgian Bay, and Calgary with Edmonton. In contrast to many American states, the Canadian provinces do not charge tolls on their limited-access highways. Quebec formerly did so but abolished its tolls in 1985.

The improvement of highways, the diversification of the economy, and the availability of larger and more efficient vehicles have caused a tremendous growth in the trucking industry. Unlike railroading and scheduled air transport, trucking is characterized by a large number of small to medium-sized enterprises, rather than a few dominant carriers. Traditionally trucking was regulated by the provinces, an arrangement that was appropriate when the limitations of trucks and roads made trucking operations purely local in scope. A judicial ruling in 1954 that provinces could not regulate interprovincial or international highway transport embarrassed both levels of government. The federal government was not ready to accept responsibility, and delegated its jurisdiction back to the provincial highway transport boards, which had been exercising it before the judicial decision. After the Macpherson Royal Commission drew attention to the fact that trucks now competed seriously with railways, the federal government decided that it should regulate long-distance trucking after all. The National Transportation Act of 1967 provided for the CTC to assume this task, but opposition from the provinces and from within the federal bureaucracy, and the lukewarm attitude of the trucking industry itself, prevented the relevant sections of the act from ever being proclaimed. The provinces continued to regulate entry into the for-hire trucking industry, apart from Alberta, which allowed freedom of entry to every truck meeting certain technical standards. Truckers wishing to operate interprovincially had to secure separate licenses from each province in which they intended to operate.

As in the case of railways and airlines, the deregulation of trucking in the United States led inexorably to adoption of the same policy in Canada. By the second National Transportation Act of 1987 the federal government in effect threatened to use its constitutional powers to impose deregulation on the provinces if they did not deregulate the trucking industry themselves. The threat had the desired effect and deregulation is now proceeding in all provinces, apart from Alberta, where it took place many years ago.

These developments have not affected the intercity bus industry, which is still tightly regulated by the provinces. Competition has been allowed on only two routes, Calgary to Edmonton and Toronto to Sudbury, so that a number of regional monopolies have been created. Interprovincial routes are operated by Greyhound Lines (west of Toronto and Sudbury) and by Voyageur Colonial (east of Toronto and Sudbury). Profits from the main bus routes cross-subsidize the services to small towns, a fact that is often used as an argument in favor of monopoly. Since the establishment of Via Rail the bus companies, especially Voyageur Colonial, have complained frequently that subsidized rail competition threatens their survival. Bus service in Newfoundland is provided by a subsidiary of Canadian National.

URBAN TRANSIT

In 1945 all Canadian cities had electric street railways, some of which were privately owned. All are now owned and heavily subsidized by local governments and all except that of Toronto were converted from streetcars to buses by 1959. Toronto has retained and modernized its street railway system, which is now one of the largest in the world. Both Toronto and Montreal have extensive underground rapid transit rail systems and Vancouver has an innovative monorail system. Calgary and Edmonton have light rail transit lines; Edmonton's runs partially underground. Major Canadian cities have tended recently to favor improvement of public transit rather than building additional highways into the urban core.

WATER TRANSPORT

The construction and operation of canals were among the earliest activities of the colonial state in British North America and are still important today. Canada's most important canal, and one of the world's busiest, is the Welland Ship Canal between Lake Erie and Lake Ontario. Completed in 1932, it was the fourth canal to be built on approximately the same site, and is now operated by the St. Lawrence Seaway Authority, a federal crown corporation. The St. Lawrence Seaway itself was built to give ocean-going vessels access to Lake Ontario and the other Great Lakes. For many years Canada tried to interest the United States in this project, without success. In 1951 Canada decided to build the entire Seaway itself, whereupon the United States changed its mind and agreed to cooperate. The Seaway opened in 1959. The chief cargoes on both the Seaway proper and the Welland Canal are iron ore moving upstream from Labrador and grain moving downstream from the head of the Lakes. The Seaway closes for approximately three months every winter.

Canada has not had a salt water merchant marine since 1949, although there are some Canadian-owned ships under foreign flags. However, shipping on the Great Lakes is important, and the vessels used rival ocean freighters in size. About two-thirds of the bulk carriers on the lakes are Canadian. The most important carrier is Canada Steamship Lines, based in Montreal.

Another important sector of water transport is coastal shipping on the Atlantic and Pacific coasts, including services to Vancouver Island, Prince Edward Island and Newfoundland. There are also services connecting Nova Scotia and Vancouver Island with the United States. Most of the vessels used are actually ferries that carry cars, trucks and buses. At one time most of these services were operated by Canadian National and Canadian Pacific, but both railways have now abandoned coastal shipping. The main operator on the Pacific coast is now the provincial government of British Columbia, while on the Atlantic coast it is a federal crown corporation, Marine Canada Limited. Both operations are heavily subsidized.

PIPELINES

Canada is second only to the United States in the extent of its pipeline networks for oil and natural gas. Interprovincial and international lines are regulated by the National Energy Board, a federal agency. The main pipelines for both oil and gas extend east, south and west from Alberta, which is the major producer of both commodities. The oil pipelines were built first, in the early 1950s. The Trans-Canada gas pipeline, from Alberta to Montreal by an all-Canadian route, was completed in 1958. Later Trans-Canada built a second line south of the Great Lakes. Natural gas was not transported east of Montreal until 1983. Within Alberta the gas gathering system is operated by NOVA Corporation (known as Alberta Gas Trunk Line until 1980) and regulated by the provincial government.

COMMUNICATIONS

Communications, even more than transport, have been dramatically altered by technological developments over the last few decades. While their physical infrastructure is much less conspicuous than highways, railway lines and airports, their effect on the life of individuals and communities may be even greater. They are now probably more relevant than highways, railways or airports to the traditional objectives of uniting Canada along an east-west axis and keeping it separate from the United States. Governments appear to have recognized this fact, but rapidly changing and complex technology, the lack of clear distinction between different modes, and the uncertain boundary between federal and provincial responsibilities have all tended to hinder effective policy.

The only form of electronic communication that existed in 1867, the telegraph, is now effectively obsolete. For over a century, however, it was used to exchange personal greetings, to control the movements of trains, and to carry messages, sometimes in code, between governments. In the first half of the 20th century, when telegraphs were still important, they were operated in Canada by the transcontinental railways, the two parallel networks of which reached almost every Canadian community. Messages

461

were delivered by wire to the nearest telegraph office or railway station, and then by a messenger on a bicycle to the recipient. As business declined the messengers disappeared, and the telegraph offices began merely to telephone the recipients. By 1967 the railways no longer thought it worth their while to compete for the little business that remained, and their telegraph operations were merged. The entity that resulted, CN-CP Telecommunications, soon turned its attention to more sophisticated technologies.

Next in seniority after the telegraph was the telephone. This now ubiquitous device was invented in Canada, although Alexander Graham Bell, a Scottish immigrant, soon moved to the United States. Canada's largest telephone company, now known as Bell Canada, is its largest Canadian-owned private enterprise, since its revenues, including assorted subsidiaries, are now larger than those of Canadian Pacific. It serves most of Ontario and Quebec, and its subscribers and their families comprise more than half of Canada's total population. Its subsidiary, Northern Telecom, is an internationally competitive producer of communications equipment, with factories in Canada and the United States. The governments of Manitoba, Saskatchewan and Alberta own their respective telephone systems although Edmonton, Alberta's capital city, has its own municipal system. Various private enterprises provide telephone service in other parts of Canada.

More than half of all telephone utility revenue now comes from long-distance service, which has effectively replaced the telegraph. The nine major telephone companies in Canada operate a consortium, known as Telecom Canada, which provides all long-distance service across the country. The telephone companies and the federal government jointly own Telesat Canada, which is also a partner in Telecom Canada. Telesat was incorporated in 1969 and launched its first communications satellite three years later. Satellites are used to provide long-distance service to northern and remote areas. Telecom also operates a microwave radio network across the country and has just completed a fiber-optic cable line from coast to coast. Overseas telephone communications, by cable and satellite, are the responsibility of Teleglobe Canada, which was founded in 1949 as a federal crown corporation. It was sold in 1987 as part of the Progressive Conservative government's privatization program. The government rejected a bid from Telecom Canada and accepted one from a little-known firm, Memotec Data. Subsequently a controlling interest in Memotec was acquired by Bell Canada.

Another important communications network is that of CN-CP Telecommunications. As mentioned above, this enterprise was formed by merging the telegraph subsidiaries of the two railways in 1967. With the telegraph business in decline, CN-CP concentrated much of its attention on Telex. As this too has begun to decline, attention has shifted to still newer technologies, such as facsimile transmission. Also, in 1983 CN-CP applied to the Canadian Radio-Television and Telecommunications Commission (CRTTC), the federal regulatory agency which regulates electronic communications and broadcasting) for permission to offer long-distance telephone service in competition with Telecom Canada. The application was rejected in 1986 but the company did not give up. It continued to lay its own fiber-optic cable network across the country and submitted another application in 1989. Meanwhile Canadian National, under pressure from the government, sold its share of CN-CP Telecommunications in 1988. Since Canadian Pacific, under the original agreement, had the first option to purchase, the privately owned railway company became the sole owner.

Radio broadcasting in Canada was originally, and is still predominantly, conducted by private enterprise. The Canadian Broadcasting Corporation (CBC) was established before the Second World War as an instrument of national integration and to provide an alternative to the mainly American content of commercial radio. Today the CBC owns a network of 68 radio stations, offering a mixture of network and local programs. Seventeen affiliated stations also carry its programs. One important consequence of the CBC is the existence of French-language radio broadcasting across the country, even in areas where there are too few francophones to support a commercial operation. CBC's share of the total radio audience is relatively small, and seems to consist mainly of middle-aged university graduates. Commercial radio stations, which outnumber CBC stations by a ratio of seven to one, no longer broadcast network programs since the advent of television. The staple diet of commercial radio is now popular music (to which much of the population seems addicted) interspersed with weather and traffic reports, news, and local advertising. Also popular, particularly in the populist western provinces, are "open line" programs in which listeners may participate by offering their opinions on various issues via telephone.

Television in Canada was pioneered by the CBC, which began French-language television broadcasting out of Montreal and English-language television broadcasting out of Toronto in 1952. Both the English and French television networks now extend across the country, although most program production is still concentrated in Toronto and Montreal, respectively. The French-language network, known as Radio-Canada, is run as a virtually separate operation. CBC television, unlike CBC radio, accepts commercial advertising, but is still heavily dependent on subsidies from the state. The CBC completed its transcontinental microwave network in 1958. The first coast-to-coast broadcast, ironically, featured a popular French-language commentator, René Lévesque, who was subsequently the leader of Quebec's independence movement. CBC broadcasts later reached the north via communications satellite.

Like the Canadian National Railways and Air Canada, the CBC has traditionally been viewed more sympathetically by Liberals than by Progressive Conservatives. The Progressive Conservative government of John Diefenbaker was the first to give television licenses to private enterprises. A second network, known as CTV, had emerged by 1961, operating in English only. Its news and public affairs programs continue to have a somewhat more conservative orientation than those of the CBC. There are also two regional commercial networks, Global TV in Ontario and Quatre Saisons in Quebec, and some independent stations not affiliated with any network. Quebec, Ontario, and Alberta have "educational" networks run by agencies of the provincial governments. TV Ontario has a somewhat broader range of programs than the other two and resembles the PBS network in the United States. It is the only network, apart from CBC, that broadcasts in both English and French.

From the beginnings of television, stations located in the United States have had an important share of the Canadian television audience. At first Canadians located along the southern border, and particularly in the three largest cities, picked up American signals by mounting large aerials on their roofs. Today it is more usual to receive American signals via cable, which has made them available also to Canadians living too far from the border to use the earlier method. Three out of every five Canadian households subscribe to cable television services. The cable operators, of which there are almost a thousand, are required to reserve a certain number of channels for Canadian stations, including rarely-watched "community" programming, but there is little doubt that access to the American networks is the real attraction. Even before the advent of cable, the Canadian networks had begun in self-defense to broadcast popular American programs themselves, although they are required to offer a certain percentage of Canadian content. There are periodic suggestions that the CBC should broadcast Canadian programs exclusively, but since this would drastically increase its costs and reduce its advertising revenue, the idea has never been implemented.

Apart from reliable access to ordinary television signals, cable operators now offer a variety of other services, sometimes at extra cost. For example, there are closed-circuit channels devoted exclusively to sports and others that carry the debates of the House of Commons and of certain provincial legislatures.

The Canadian preoccupation with transport and communication is not likely to end soon, if ever. Growing economic ties with the United States, the increasing ethnic diversity of the population, and the rambunctious behavior of certain provincial governments have made the challenges to national unity more rather than less acute in recent years. Current trends toward deregulation and privatization may continue or may be reversed. The only certainty is that technological progress will continue, creating both new problems and new opportunities.

FURTHER READING

Bryan, Nancy. *More Taxes and More Traffic.* Toronto: Canadian Tax Foundation, 1972.

Darling, Howard. *The Politics of Freight Rates.* Toronto: McClelland and Stewart, 1980.

Kaplan, Harold. *Policy and Rationality: The Regulation of Canadian Trucking.* Toronto: University of Toronto Press, 1989.

Langford, John, and Ken Huffman. "Air Canada." In *Privatization, Public Policy and Public Corporations in Canada.* edited by A. Tupper and G. B. Doern. Halifax: Institute for Research on Public Policy, 1988.

Lukasiewicz, Julius. *The Railway Game.* Toronto: McClelland and Stewart, 1975.

McGregor, Gordon R. *The Adolescence of an Airline.* Montreal: Air Canada, 1970.

McLuhan, Marshall. *Understanding Media: The Extensions of Man.* New York: McGraw Hill, 1964.

Schultz, Richard. "Teleglobe Canada." In *Privatization, Public Policy and Public Corporations in Canada,* edited by A. Tupper and G. B. Doern. Halifax: Institute for Research on Public Policy, 1988.

Stevenson, Garth. "Canadian National Railways and Via Rail." In *Privatization, Public Policy and Public Corporations in Canada,* edited by A. Tupper and G. B. Doern. Halifax: Institute for Research on Public Policy, 1988.

————. *The Politics of Canada's Airlines.* Toronto: University of Toronto Press, 1987.

Weaver, R. Kent. *The Politics of Industrial Change.* Washington, Brookings Institute, 1985.

BANKING AND FINANCE

ALEX N. McLEOD

Canadians have long been the possessors of a sound and internationally competitive financial system. In the closing decade of the 20th century, however, a number of important issues that have attracted considerable public attention are not yet fully resolved. These include:

- Deregulation. Should the rules that have governed Canadian financial institutions in the past be relaxed, and if so then to what extent and in what ways?
- Ownership. Should widely-dispersed ownership be insisted on? If not, should commercial and industrial enterprises be allowed to control financial institutions? How do these questions relate to the concentration of general economic power in Canada?
- Inspection and supervision. To the extent that regulations are retained, how should the inspection and supervision of financial institutions be organized? The fact that Canada is a federal country adds complications to this question, since some of the institutions are under federal jurisdiction and some are under provincial jurisdiction.

The discussion of these issues may properly begin with a brief reference to the Report of the Royal Commission on Banking and Finance in 1964 (popularly known as the Porter Report, after its chairman, the Honorable Dana Harris Porter, Chief Justice of Ontario), because it marked the start of substantial changes in the Canadian financial system.

An outstanding feature of banking legislation in Canada is that it is customarily scheduled to expire 10 years after its most recent enactment, and must then be renewed, which means that it is regularly brought up to date. The Bank Act, as it is called, was due to lapse in 1964, and the government of the day decided that an extensive review of the entire financial system was desirable before it was revised. No such general review had been made since that of 1933, which had led to the establishment of Canada's central bank (the Bank of Canada); in the meantime changing conditions and the worldwide revival of monetary policy in the 1950s had raised a number of practical problems. Accordingly the Porter Commission was

466

established in 1961. It reported in 1964. The new Bank Act was delayed until 1967 as a consequence; the old Act was extended several times, while the new one was being drafted and debated.

With a few specific exceptions governed by other acts, only those institutions authorized under the Bank Act may use the title "bank," which is defined simply as one of the institutions listed in a schedule to the Act or incorporated in accordance with its provisions. They are known as "chartered" banks, and in 1964 there were only eight of them; the Act was their charter. They had wide lending and deposit-taking powers.

At that time, and until quite recently, the financial system was commonly described as consisting of four "pillars," meaning four types of institutions that operated in more or less separate compartments: banks, trust companies, insurance companies and investment dealers. Only the banks had full freedom in commercial lending. Only the trust companies could undertake discretionary fiduciary activities. Only the life insurance companies could underwrite life insurance and issue life-contingent annuities. Only investment dealers could underwrite corporate securities with full freedom, and be members of stock exchanges.

However, merely listing the four pillars gives an incomplete description of the system. For one thing, there are other financial institutions that do not fit neatly into those four categories: credit unions (and their Quebec counterparts, the *caisses populaires*), property-and-casualty-insurance companies, mortgage-loan companies, sales-finance companies, investment companies, pension funds and others. For another, the trust companies and many of the others offer deposit and loan services that compete very closely with one another and with those offered by the banks; they are often called "near-banks" for this reason.

In practice these institutions had all shown considerable ingenuity in devising instruments and techniques that would compete with one another. Nevertheless the structure of the financial system was unnecessarily rigid and this tended to restrict consumer choice. Competition among the banks themselves was rather limited, with tacit or explicit agreements on opening hours and other matters.

The Porter commissioners noted that there was no satisfactory definition of "bank" in Canadian legislation, and that other institutions carried on activities that were very similar to those of the chartered banks. They recommended that a suitable definition be introduced, which it was clearly within the competence of the federal parliament to do. They also recommended that all institutions doing "essentially a banking business" should be brought under the Bank Act, whether they were federally or provincially chartered, and be made subject to its system of supervision and inspection. This was expressly interpreted to include all institutions that accept checkable, demand, or short-term deposits. In addition, their report emphasized that the office of the Inspector General of Banks, where responsibility for bank supervision lay, would have to be enlarged and strengthened because of the increase this would entail in its duties.

In this context the commissioners recommended that the near-banks be allowed more scope to compete with the chartered banks, and that some of the restrictions on the latter be removed. Among other things, they suggested that the banks be eventually permitted to go into the trust business. In addition they made proposals to increase interbank competition.

In the 28 years since the Porter Report, many of its recommendations have been put into effect and other impediments to competition have been removed. The securities business has been opened up to ownership by other financial institutions, including foreign firms. New banks have been allowed to incorporate under less stringent restrictions than used to apply; instead of eight banks, there are now 66. The number of near-banks has also greatly increased, and many of the statutory restraints on their lending have been relaxed. However, significantly, they have not been brought under the Bank Act; if they had, some of the worst of the abuses that have recently plagued the financial system would have been avoided. There is still no satisfactory definition of a bank, thereby creating jurisdictional uncertainties. And the chartered banks are still excluded from the trust business.

The expansion of the near-banks has also been greatly encouraged by the introduction of deposit insurance in 1967. The Canada Deposit Insurance Corporation (CDIC) insures Canadian-dollar deposits maturing within five years in all chartered banks and virtually all trust and loan companies, up to $60,000; the main exceptions are institutions incorporated in the Province of Quebec, which operates its own parallel deposit-insurance plan. Credit unions also come under separate provincial plans. Depositors with relatively small sums to invest need have no qualms about placing their funds with any insured depository, no matter how small and unknown.

Securities dealers have long had a self-administered plan that protects their customers in the event of the failure of a member. Both the casualty-insurance and the life-insurance companies now have their own industry-sponsored plans.

Meanwhile the economic environment has changed materially. Many years of inflationary pressures led to instability in financial markets, which affected some institutions more than others and led them to seek greater diversification. Computerization and other technological advances have increased the possibilities for competition, both domestically and internationally. Holding companies have brought institutions in different financial sectors under one control, and have led to pressures for permission to coordinate their services. Economic ups and downs have affected some regions of the country more seriously than others, with adverse effects on some regionally based institutions.

Other pressures for deregulation have also been building, particularly from the fact that a substantial amount of deregulation has already occurred in competing financial markets in other countries. Some Canadian financial institutions are important players in world markets—especially the banks and the life-insurance companies—and would be severely hampered if they were subject to more stringent regulation than their competitors abroad.

For 15 years or so these changes and innovations seemed to go smoothly enough. Then between 1980 and 1985 disasters overtook a number of financial institutions. Some of them failed, others were liquidated, a few were able to remain in business after a reorganization. Mismanagement and over-appraised real-estate assets were commonly the cause, but in some cases it was a matter of outright fraud. Also, control of some financial institutions had passed into the hands of one or a few persons, which led to some glaring cases of self-dealing. In one instance (the notorious Grey-mac Affair in 1983) five related institutions in Ontario were seized after a series of spectacular and questionable real-estate deals.

Until 1984 the casualties were mostly provincially-regulated near-banks, but in that year one of the newer chartered banks underwent a restructuring and a management shakeup. In 1985 more near-banks were liquidated, and two of the smaller chartered banks encountered serious difficulties that eventually led to their failure—the first bank failures in over 60 years. Furthermore, the collapse of the Principal Group in Alberta in 1989 and Standard Trust in 1991 suggests that these problems may not all be behind us even yet.

By 1984 the federal government was showing some concern. In November of that year it issued a document entitled *A New Direction for Canada: An Agenda for Economic Renewal,* in which it indicated that it intended to work with the provinces, the public, and the financial community to ensure that financial legislation kept pace with changing conditions, and preliminary consultations followed.

In April 1985 the Department of Finance issued a "Green Paper," *The Regulation of Canadian Financial Institutions: Proposals for Discussion,* which identified a number of problem areas, acknowledged most of the problems that had arisen, committed itself to a set of basic objectives, and offered suggestions designed to stimulate discussion. The objectives were basically unexceptionable in themselves, but some of them are not entirely compatible with one another:

- Improve consumer protection.
- Strictly control self-dealing.
- Guard against abuses of conflicts of interest.
- Promote competition, innovation, and efficiency.
- Enhance the convenience and options available to customers in the marketplace.
- Broaden the sources of credit available to individuals and business.
- Ensure the soundness of financial institutions and the stability of the financial system.
- Promote international competitiveness and domestic economic growth.
- Promote the harmonization of federal and provincial regulatory policies.

Two official committees were already at work in some of these matters when the Green Paper was issued. Serious questions had arisen with respect to deposit insurance because of how some of the recent insolvencies had been handled, and the federal government had set up the Working Committee on the Canada Deposit Insurance Corporation (the Wyman Committee) to make recommendations. Also, the Ontario government had set up its Task Force on Financial Institutions (the Dupré Committee) in 1984. Then the House of Commons Standing Committee on Finance, Trade, and Economic Affairs and the Senate Standing Committee on Banking, Trade, and Commerce also initiated studies of the financial system, in response to the Green Paper.

All four of these committees issued reports in 1985 or 1986, in which they made extensive recommendations. There were significant differences and even disagreements in their proposals, but all four offered cogent analyses of the problems and made constructive contributions to their solution.

The Green Paper pointed out that there are three principal ways in which savers can be protected from insolvency risks. One is by ensuring that full information is available about the institution in which they are asked to put their funds, and about the terms they are offered. A second is to provide some assurance that the institutions observe suitable standards of prudence in their operations, as by a system of inspection and supervision. A third is by some guarantee of the securities or other obligations they offer, as with deposit insurance. However, each has its limitations or disadvantages. Even all three in combination cannot entirely remove the possibility of default. Variations on these themes are to be found in all four of the official reports, and in the proposals the government has since put forward.

The pressures for financial deregulation have already been noted. However, this objective must clearly be pursued with caution. The Green Paper contains an excellent defense of the fact that the financial sector has been more heavily supervised and regulated than other sectors of the economy. First, it occupies a central place through its role in allocating credit and operating the payments mechanism. Second, financial institutions are in a unique position of trust in handling funds belonging to the general public. Canadian governments from their earliest days have been concerned to ensure the solvency of major financial institutions, and to maintain public confidence in the system. Loss of confidence could lead to a breakdown that would harm not only the creditors of particular institutions but also the entire economy.

Any discussion of deregulation inevitably merges with questions about ownership and control, and the spate of failures in the 1980s focused attention on some of the problems in that field, in addition to solvency. There has long been concern in many quarters over the concentration of economic power in relatively few hands in Canada, not by any means limited to the financial sector. The presumption is that it leads to inefficiency, higher costs, less choice for consumers, and less innovation. However, large size may confer advantages of scale on a firm, which may be particularly important if it is active in competitive international markets. Also, large firms may be better able to diversify, both regionally and in their choice of activities, and may therefore be better able to withstand adverse developments in particular markets. Even if there are few firms in a given line of business, they may be subject to competition from firms in somewhat different lines or from foreign firms that are able to penetrate the domestic market.

All these considerations apply in some degree to Canada's financial system. In all four pillars a relatively few firms dominate, even where there are many smaller firms as well. Canadian banks and life-insurance firms are major players in international financial markets. The four pillars do compete with one another for many types of business. Foreign competitors are also significant, especially since the deregulations that have already occurred. In addition, however, close control of a financial institution raises possibilities of self-dealing in favor of its owners, and intercorporate affiliations permit conflicts of interest to the disadvantage of their customers, as recent events had amply demonstrated.

The ownership of Canada's chartered banks has for many years been widely dispersed among the public, and a strong majority of the issued shares has been jealously kept in Canadian hands. Under the 1967 version of the Bank Act, for example, not more than 10% of the shares of a bank were to be held by any one person or group of associated persons. Also, not more than 25% in total were to be held by nonresidents.* These requirements are widely regarded as a major defense against any one person or group getting control of one of the larger banks and using that control for self-dealing.

There are no comparable limitations on the ownership or the activities of most other financial institutions in Canada. In the 1960s some moves had been made toward applying ownership limitations to the trust companies, but they petered out ineffectively. (However, in August 1989 the government initiated a policy of ministerial review of any change in the shareholdings of any investor, domestic or foreign, holding more than 10% of any class of shares.) By now there are no trust companies, and few security dealers or life insurance companies (except the mutuals), that are not controlled by one person or a small group of associated persons—usually a financial or a commercial conglomerate.

A major takeover occurred even while the four official committees were deliberating over these and other issues. In 1985 Genstar, a diversified conglomerate that had recently acquired a major mortgage-loan company, bought Canada Trust and merged the two. Canada Trust was the largest trust company in the country, and by then was the only one not closely controlled. This created a financial-services giant, ranking just after the sixth largest chartered bank.

The authorities showed some concern, but apparently found themselves unable or unwilling to do anything about it. A few months later Imasco, a tobacco and retail conglomerate, took over Genstar *and* its newly enlarged trust company. This raised an even more fundamental question: the ownership of a major financial institution by what is not merely a single controlling shareholder, but also one whose primary interests are industrial and

---

*This limitation has been eliminated for U.S. investors, as part of the Canada-United States Free Trade Agreement, but remains in effect for investors from other countries.

commercial. That is a combination that has traditionally been opposed in British, U.S., and Canadian financial circles.

Furthermore, these developments must be viewed in the light of the torrent of mergers and takeovers that has overwhelmed most countries in recent years. Many observers are alarmed at this trend. Unlike the concentration of ownership in a single industry, which may at least promise some rationalization of productive facilities and other economies of scale, today's conglomerates often simply stitch together a jumble of unrelated enterprises that seem to have no rational justification.

For reasons that are well argued in the Green Paper, some minimum structure of regulations and restraints will always be necessary in order to ensure the solvency and efficient operation of all financial institutions. Inspection and supervision will therefore also be necessary, to ensure that the established standards are fully honored. In Canada some financial institutions come exclusively under federal jurisdiction, some exclusively under provincial jurisdiction, and some may be either federally or provincially incorporated (insurance companies, trust companies and mortgage-loan companies).

Logically, the jurisdiction under which a given institution is established will normally be responsible for its supervision. All jurisdictions should endeavor to establish more or less uniform standards, if for no other reason than because that will discourage a would-be entrant from shopping around for the one with the least onerous requirements. It is also necessary to ensure that all financial institutions and functions are adequately regulated, and that some do not fall between the cracks of alternative regulatory bodies.

Much more important than these jurisdictional problems, the rash of financial misadventures in the 1980s disclosed some glaring inadequacies in the supervisory facilities at both the federal and the provincial levels. It became clear, for example, that the staff provided to the inspector general of banks had not been sufficiently strengthened to cope with the increase in the number of institutions under his responsibility and the different characteristics of some of the new entrants. It also became clear that he needed additional powers in order to deal effectively with their changed circumstances. The same was true of the federal superintendent of insurance, whose jurisdiction included the federally chartered trust companies. Provincially, supervision and inspection varied greatly from one jurisdiction to another, but the problems encountered show that even the best systems were unsatisfactory.

Special mention must be made of the supervisory role of the CDIC. From its inception until 1988 it was required to insure all Canadian-dollar deposits maturing within five years at federally incorporated financial institutions. It was also empowered to insure similar deposits at such provincially incorporated institutions as the provinces permitted. It did have the right to refuse coverage for provincially incorporated applicants, and to terminate their coverage for cause, but had inadequate power to monitor them and to intervene less drastically if signs of trouble were detected. Insured deposit limits had been arbitrarily and retroactively raised by the federal gov-

472

ernment of the day from $20,000 to $60,000 in the midst of the Greymac Affair in 1983. Furthermore, acting on a mandate from a government spokesman that it "assist in maintaining the confidence and stability of the financial system," the CDIC had arranged to repay *all* the depositors *in full*. That saddled it with a heavy load of debt, which must ultimately be repaid by the remaining healthy insured institutions.

There were earlier precedents of a sort for such bailouts. Before the introduction of deposit insurance, in instances going back into the 19th century, it was a common practice for Canadian governments to rescue failing banks (and sometimes other financial institutions) by arranging or inviting a merger with a stronger institution. The justification for this practice was that it preserved confidence in the banking system as a whole, which was considered to be of overriding importance to the entire economy.

Presumably influenced by these precedents, the CDIC (occasionally helped by a contribution from the federal government) has bailed out all the depositors of failing institutions whose deposits it insured, with only one exception. (In the case of the two chartered banks that were liquidated in 1986, the federal government, or the general taxpayer), assumed some of the burden.) After the Greymac bailout, many critics, including some government officials in public statements, strongly objected, but the weight of precedent has prevailed so far. That will make it difficult to end the practice gracefully.

The logic of the argument in favor of such actions had already been undermined by the establishment of deposit insurance: small deposits now had their own protection, and the implication was that the owners of larger deposits were competent to look after their own interests. The cumulative effect of the repeated bailouts was to erode those principles and to virtually eliminate all discipline from the market. Prudence was placed at a discount. Business corporations, municipalities and wealthy individuals had no more reason than small savers to concern themselves with evaluating the potential risk against the promised yield.

That was basically the context in which the Wyman Committee was set up to study deposit insurance. It heard submissions from various Canadian interests, and studied the deposit-insurance plans of a number of other countries. It recommended that the CDIC be given greater autonomy, that its board of directors be enlarged by the addition of members from the private sector, and that its staff be enlarged and upgraded. It also suggested that financial institutions should have to apply to the CDIC for coverage, which should be granted only at the corporation's discretion, renewable annually, and terminable for cause.

The other three reports agreed substantially with the Wyman proposals. The main exception was that the Senate report proposed that the federal government cover the portion of the CDIC's deficit that could be attributed to the retroactive increase in coverage from $20,000 to $60,000 during the Greymac Affair, since it was a government decision.

In December 1986 the federal government issued a new document entitled *New Directions for the Financial Sector,* setting out the policies it proposed to embody in new legislation promised for the then-current session of parliament, after further consultation with the financial-services interests. It reflected consideration of the four committee reports, as well as representations already made by the affected institutions. However, it did some selective picking and choosing among the various recommendations offered it; not everyone would agree with all of its choices.

The basic thrust of the proposals was expressly toward deregulation, including easing the restraints on links between commercial and financial institutions. In principle, there were to be no restrictions on common ownership of regulated financial institutions; they might be held as subsidiaries of firms in other pillars, or be affiliated through holding companies. They were to be allowed to make consumer loans and, with some exceptions, commercial loans. Full networking (allowing financial institutions to act on behalf of one another) was to be permitted, except the retailing of insurance.

Small domestic banks were to be allowed to remain closely held until they grew to a substantial size before being required to move toward widely held status. Steps were to be taken with respect to trust, loan and insurance companies, now mostly closely held, to arrest the trend to concentrated ownership and to encourage a significant minority holding. Approval for the incorporation of new companies in these fields was not to be granted to applicants with significant commercial interests, and commercially-linked institutions with more than $50 million in capital were to be required to have 25% of their voting shares publicly traded and widely held. Those with no commercial links and more than $750 million in capital were to meet the same conditions. Cumulative voting was to be mandatory for the election of directors in any financial institution in which one shareholder owns more than 10% of any class of voting shares (that is, a group of shareholders may vote all their combined shares for a single candidate, in order to increase the chances that minority interests may elect at least one director).

Self-dealing was to be controlled by a three-tiered approach: a ban on most non-arm's-length transactions, internal controls for permitted classes of transactions and pre-clearance with supervisors for unusual transactions. The first category was to include most loans and investments and most sales or purchases of assets between the institution and influential parties. Controlled transactions were to include the sale or purchase of business services, subject to approval by independent or "outside" directors and certain specific restraints.

Abuses of conflicts of interest were to be handled by a combination of greater disclosure to the consumer, "Chinese Walls" (that is, restrictions that prevent the transfer of information between one division of an institution and another, or between institutions), and enhanced internal scrutiny. A large majority of board members were to be from outside the institution. At least one-third of the directors were to meet stringent criteria of independence: for example, they were not to be officers, employers or significant shareholders; they were not to have significant business links with the corporation; and they were not to be major legal advisers.

A committee of independent board members was to monitor the institution's affairs, provide guidelines to the auditors and review the auditors' reports.

New Directions proposed the amalgamation of the offices of the inspector general of banks and the superintendent of insurance, to form the Office of the Superintendent of Financial Institutions, with responsibility for supervising all those that are federally incorporated. The staff was to be increased and upgraded, and given greater powers. In case of actual or imminent insolvency the governor in council would have the power to vest all the capital of the institution in the CDIC.

The proposals reaffirmed that the mandate of the CDIC includes protecting depositors, enhancing the standards of member institutions, and contributing to the stability and competitiveness of the financial system. The corporation was to be given responsibility for federal institutions similar to that for provincial institutions, that is discretion as to whether to provide deposit insurance and (subject to the approval of the minister of finance) the power to terminate coverage. It was to be permitted to set premium levels by regulation, in order to retire its deficit, and the ceiling on its borrowings from the government's Consolidated Revenue Fund was to be doubled.

A number of other legislative changes were promised. The laws governing financial institutions other than banks were to be amended to ensure periodic review on the same cycle as the chartered banks. Trust companies and loan companies were to be brought under a single act. The two separate acts governing Canadian, British, and foreign insurance companies were to be consolidated. To the extent that credit unions come under federal supervision, they were to be subjected to the same general principles as other financial institutions.

The federal government did pass two new acts in 1987. The duties of the inspector general of banks and the superintendent of insurance were combined in the new Office of the Superintendent of Financial Institutions. The staff was enlarged and upgraded, and the office was given substantially improved enforcement powers over federally incorporated institutions. The CDIC was strengthened, pretty much as promised in *New Directions*. Its powers of supervision and enforcement were increased, though its direct monitoring capabilities are still quite limited and largely dependent on other supervisory authorities. Federal financial institutions were permitted to own securities-firm subsidiaries; the six major chartered banks promptly bought or established firms on their own, which now control some 80% of the business.

In December 1987 a draft of the proposed new trust-and-loan company legislation was circulated for discussion. However, the parliamentary bill was not introduced until September 1990, after extensive discussions with the financial sector; it was then accompanied by a revised policy paper on financial institutions. New draft banking legislation was introduced in the spring of 1991, followed by new draft insurance legislation.

These steps included some important policy changes. One was an undertaking to promote the harmonization of federal and provincial legislation, including the sharing of information. If effectively implemented, this would greatly improve the regulatory process. Another, on the other hand, was to remove the limited constraints on commercial-financial linkages that had been included in earlier proposals, to bring federal legislation in line with most provincial policies. This would be a major departure from a policy considered important in the past, and a further weakening of control over the concentration of economic power in few hands.

The larger provinces have taken advantage of the federal delays in enacting promised legislation, by moving vigorously into fields in which the federal authorities had traditionally been the leaders. Ontario and Quebec introduced new legislation governing trust and loan companies in 1988. Subsequently Quebec passed comprehensive new legislation governing credit unions, and innovative measures that increase the powers and the regulation of insurance brokers and stockbrokers. British Columbia has passed a bill to regulate its financial institutions. Alberta has released draft consumer-protection legislation for public comment. In all these cases the provinces' financial institutions are permitted to be closely held, and their ownership may be linked to commercial firms. Their institutions have also been granted wider powers, though in general they must be exercised through subsidiaries if they involve new core functions.

The new provincial legislation deals with questions of solvency, self-dealing, and conflicts of interest primarily by requiring fuller and more reliable disclosure of financial information, and by imposing more and clearer responsibilities on the directors and officials of the institutions themselves. Auditors are also given increased responsibilities in certifying the financial statements of these institutions.

In order to put these developments in perspective some parallels and contrasts with the recommendations of the four official reports presented in 1985 and 1986 may be noted, and some comments by independent observers added.

All four official reports approved departures from the four-pillars approach, mainly by allowing institutions to own subsidiaries that could undertake activities outside their normal core functions. However, the House of Commons Report qualified its stand by noting that holding companies do not operate as passive investors but as integrated firms with centralized policies; that makes it difficult to isolate financial affiliates from the fortunes of the rest of the organization. Only the Senate Report gave unequivocal support to all four major means of diversification: expanded in-house powers, subsidiaries, a variety of holding companies, and networking. (The Senate is an appointed, not an elected, body, and its members are strongly representative of business interests.)

The official reports were nearly unanimous in agreeing that widely-held ownership of other financial institutions has proven pretty effective in preventing self-dealing, but no attempt has been made to apply it to any institutions besides the banks. Of course, this is no panacea either. However, its proven record contrasts sharply with the uncertain promise of the measures on which *New Directions* relies. Confidence in the financial system is so important that all available defenses should be fully employed.

Most of the committees opposed permitting non-financial and financial companies to own one another. Independent critics point out that allowing certain powerful commercial interests to retain 60% ownership of major financial institutions offends this principle. Having 35% of its stock publicly traded may indeed ensure that professional financial analysts will monitor its operations, as the Senate Report argued, but that seems a pretty weak defense against self-dealing. Financial analysts are more concerned with monitoring profits than with monitoring ethics.

With one partial exception, however, the committees quailed at the thought of forcing divestiture of affiliates that had already been acquired. Since virtually all of the susceptible institutions were already closely controlled, their opposition to cross-ownership rang rather hollow. (The partial exception was that, after Imasco's takeover of Genstar, the House of Commons Committee came out strongly in favor of requiring the new owner to divest itself of Canada Trust.) It has been argued that divestiture should be insisted on, even though the acquisitions were perfectly legal at the time, on the grounds that this is not a mere matter of good sportsmanship, in which the rules ought not to be changed in the course of play, but a deadly serious matter of the soundness of the Canadian financial system and the fair treatment of the general public.

Criticisms have also been directed at reliance on legal prohibitions, self-regulation, committees of directors, Chinese Walls, and such techniques to control conflicts of interest. Recent widely publicized disclosures of frauds in insider trading demonstrate how ineffective such admonitions can be. So does the regularity with which the stock market anticipates the release of most corporate news, whether good or bad. Many of the economies of scale that corporate affiliations and networking are supposed to offer involve the use of the same personnel for different functions on behalf of the various entities, which would make it virtually impossible to prevent either tied selling (linking the purchase of one service to the purchase of another) or the transfer of confidential client data.

Curiously, none of these documents mentions the potential for conflicts of interest within security dealerships, in that they are active both in underwriting and selling corporate and other securities and in advising clients on their investment decisions. There is an obvious risk that their investment advice may be influenced by their interest in placing the new issues they have underwritten. This possibility is increased rather than decreased now that the major chartered banks control most of the stockbroking business, for the banks also participate in distributing new issues. There would seem to be a case for confining the underwriting function to specialized institutions or firms that are not involved in either selling the issues or offering investment advice.

Turning now to the question of inspection and supervision, the four committee reports were in substantial agreement that the regulatory authorities needed additional powers. With some differences of emphasis, they typically included the right to gain access to records, to issue cease-and-desist orders, to set ratios of liabilities to capital, to replace the management, and to enforce other remedial measures when needed. They also recommended that better standards of assessing and reporting an institution's exposure to risk be devised, and that there be better internal monitoring by boards of directors.

Between them, the Wyman Report and the House of Commons Report made a strong case for giving the CDIC effective powers of inspection and supervision of the institutions whose deposits it insures. The former spoke favorably of powers of regulation, supervision, rehabilitation and liquidation comparable to those of the Federal Deposit Insurance Corporation in the United States, though it accepted the present dispersion of responsibilities as a reasonable temporary situation. The latter proposed a much broader and more powerful agency, a National Financial Administrative Agency, which among other things would administer all deposit-insurance and similar plans, but its arguments in favor of wide regulatory and supervisory powers for that agency would transfer readily to the CDIC.

Even the Senate Report gave some indirect support to the idea, despite its generally negative comments, in that it recognized that the CDIC should participate in establishing early-warning systems for impending trouble, and become involved in supervisory and remedial action if a pre-established threshold were crossed. Elsewhere, while it agreed that the regulatory authorities needed additional powers, it argued that most of the problems encountered in the past had arisen from failure to use their existing powers effectively. In general it tended to downgrade the objectives of solvency and stability in favor of competition and efficiency.

The Dupré Commission repeatedly emphasized the need for the coordination of legislative and regulatory provisions among the federal and the provincial governments, particularly those of Ontario and Quebec. However, it rejected any regulatory role for the CDIC (and inferentially for the House of Commons Committee's National Financial Administrative Agency), on the grounds that it overlooked the responsibility of provincial governments for regulating the institutions under their jurisdiction, and that it would involve unnecessary duplication of effort.

The Senate Report and other observers, too, have objected to duplication of supervision, though the Senate Committee did acknowledge that an institution might have to be subject to different authorities with respect to activities outside its core function. Surely, however, this criticism can be overdone; this may be a case in which only too much is enough.

Without meaning to suggest that institutions in the United States necessarily offer valid models for Canada in all cases, their long experience of having to deal with bank failures may give Canadians some guidance here. There are at least four bank-inspecting authorities in every state in the union: state authorities for state banks, the Controller of the Currency for national banks, the Federal Reserve Board for member banks, and the Federal Deposit Insurance Corporation for insured institutions. Also, there are other regulatory bodies for various near-banks. Some institutions are subject to at least three separate inspecting authorities, each with substantial powers of intervention.

Serious criticisms have also been made in another important area: the effective harmonization and coordination of inspection and supervision among the 11 separate legislative and administrative jurisdictions. Despite much lip-service to the idea, little has been accomplished. This raises the risk that some institutions will seek to incorporate in whatever area offers the least onerous restrictions on their activities. Already some federally incorporated trust companies are known to be considering transferring to provincial jurisdiction. Also, since trust companies now have or soon will have virtually all the powers of chartered banks, it raises the possibility that Canada may soon see the evolution of a dual banking system: widely held chartered banks at the federal level, and closely held banks at the provincial level, each under a different system of inspection and supervision. An unappealing alternative is that the least onerous regulations will become the standard in all jurisdictions.

By the early 1990s the reform of federal financial legislation appeared to be finally on the way to completion. Some of the desirable objectives spelled out more than six years earlier in the Green Paper will apparently be well achieved, others will have fallen by the wayside. It would be comforting to think that the long delay in formulating and implementing these reforms has been well worthwhile, but that remains to be seen. Several years may pass before a clear judgment can be made as to where the successes and the failures lie, but it would seem that business interests will prove to have been better served than those of the general public. Nevertheless, despite the compromises that have been made and the opportunities that have been lost, Canadians can be confident that their financial system remains one of the strongest in the community of nations.

FURTHER READING

Canada. Department of Finance. *A New Direction for Canada: An Agenda for Economic Renewal.* Ottawa: Minister of Supply and Services, November 1984.

————. Department of Finance. *The Regulation of Canadian Financial Institutions: Proposals for Discussion* (Green Paper). Ottawa: Minister of Supply and Services, April 1985. *Technical Supplement,* June 1985.

————. Department of Finance. *New Directions for the Financial Sector.* Ottawa: Minister of Supply and Services, December 1986.

————. Department of Finance. *Reform of Federal Financial Institutions Legislation: Overview of Legislative Proposals.* Ottawa: Minister of Supply and Services, 1990.

————. House of Commons. Standing Committee on Finance, Trade, and Economic Affairs. *Canadian Financial Institutions* (House Report). Ottawa: Queen's Printer, November 1985.

————. Royal Commission on Banking and Finance. *Report of the Royal Commission on Banking and Finance* (Porter Report). Ottawa: Queen's Printer, 1964.

————. Senate. Standing Committee on Banking, Trade, and Commerce. *Deposit Insurance* (Senate Interim Report). Ottawa: Queen's Printer, December 1985.

———. Senate. Standing Committee on Banking, Trade, and Commerce. *Towards a More Competitive Financial Environment* (Senate Final Report). Ottawa: Queen's Printer, May 1986.

———. The Working Committee on the Canada Deposit Insurance Corporation. *Final Report of the Working Committee on the Canada Deposit Insurance Corporation (CDIC)* (Wyman Report). Ottawa: Minister of Supply and Services, August 1985.

Kennett, William. "Reform of Financial Sector Follows Decade of Upheaval, Indecision." *The Globe and Mail,* September 11, 1989, p. C2.

McLeod, Alex N. "Better Late than Never," *Canadian Public Policy* 12 (September 1986): 484–498.

Ontario. Task Force on Financial Institutions. *Final Report* (Dupré Report). Toronto: Ontario Task Force on Financial Institutions, December 1985.

TOURISM

JAMES R. MacGREGOR

ECONOMIC IMPACT OF THE CANADIAN TRAVEL INDUSTRY

Tourism and travel is the world's largest civilian industry. In 1991 its value was U.S. $2.5 trillion, with the global sale of goods and services representing 6% of the world economy. The travel industry is also the largest employer in almost every country and accounts for one out of every 16 jobs worldwide.

The travel industry is also extremely important to the Canadian economy. In 1988 foreign visitors and traveling Canadians spent more than $24* billion, which represents more than 7% of all personal expenditures on goods and services in that year. The Canadian travel industry is characterized by several impressive statistics:

- between 1975 and 1987 growth rates in tourism employment surpassed those in all major segments of the Canadian economy, and the rate was more than three times greater than that for transportation, construction and manufacturing;
- it is the single largest earner of foreign exchange outside of the automobile industry and is greater than either lumber or newsprint;
- in 1987 it generated $11 billion in tax revenues for provincial and federal governments, thus contributing significantly by reducing the national debt;
- it employs more than 630,000 Canadians in 60,000 businesses, most of which are small enterprises;
- it is the fourth largest industry in terms of economic impact.

In the 12-year period between 1976 and 1988, tourism receipts grew from $9.2 billion to more than $24 billion, and projections indicate that receipts will significantly exceed $40 billion by 1995.

---

*Figures are in Canadian dollars unless otherwise noted.

Canada's performance in the international tourism arena has also been impressive. The World Tourism Organization recently estimated that the total international receipts had grown by 55% between 1980 and 1987. Canada's international receipts, however, grew by 73% during the same period. Canada now is the ninth major generator of international tourism receipts in the world. In 1988, foreign visitors represented more than 28% of Canada's total tourism industry, compared to only 22.7% in 1980. They are now worth $8 billion annually. The 73% growth in international tourism receipts is particularly impressive when compared to other major competitors for the international tourism dollar. For instance, international tourism receipts grew by only 52% in the United States, 47% in the United Kingdom and 38% in France.

While the industry seems to be doing well—though it was certainly hurt by the recession of the early 1990s—recent research conducted by Tourism Canada indicates that when measured against the number of potential travelers worldwide, the Canadian travel product could realistically attract in excess of 31 million international visitors. Most of these (25 million) would come from the United States and another 6 million could come from the various overseas markets. Based on existing trends and assuming a stable international economy, the Canadian tourism industry is expected to attract 18.7 million international visitors by 1995 or a 2.5% annual increase from the 15.5 million visitors in 1988. If Canada achieves this growth, it would more than double the current international tourism receipts from $6.9 billion to $14.2 billion, or an annual increase of 10.9%.

The prospects of achieving these significant growth rates seem realistic. In the past few years, Canada has greatly enhanced its image as an international tourism destination. Events such as Expo '86 in Vancouver, British Columbia and the Calgary Olympics have brought international attention. As well, more Americans, Europeans and Japanese are realizing that Canada has a unique product in terms of multiculturalism, wilderness and scenic values. Tourism Canada in its draft statement, "Towards a National Tourism Development Strategy," has outlined four of Canada's distinct strengths in encouraging greater international visitation. They are frequently referred to as "Canada's tourism products" and include:

1. Touring
    Touring has traditionally been Canada's strongest tourism activity segment and accounts for almost half of all international travel to Canada. Typical trips include automobile and recreation vehicle touring and fly-drive and motorcoach package tours. Both Canadians and nonresident visitors tour Canada to experience its spectacular scenery, rugged coastlines, historic sites and multicultural attractions. Three regions of Canada that offer the greatest potential for this activity include:

    • the Great Lakes and St. Lawrence River Valley corridor including Niagara Falls, Toronto, Montreal and Quebec City
    • the four Rocky Mountain national parks and in particular the Jasper/Banff Corridor

482

- the southern corner of British Columbia, including Vancouver and Victoria.

2. Adventure Tourism and Ecotourism

Over the past decade, Canada has become increasingly recognized for the high-quality adventure/wilderness tourism offered by its wildlife and scenic resources, national parks and wilderness areas. Double-digit growth in this sector has contributed to the emergence of hundreds of new operators offering such activities as wildlife safaris, nature photography, hiking, canoeing, kayaking, whalewatching, hunting and fishing and mountaineering. Western Canada, and in particular British Columbia, has become a focus for these activities, although the eastern provinces are developing new products. As Canada improves its reputation as a nation that is concerned about the quality of the environment, it is certain that the Europeans and Japanese, in particular, will want to buy into its pristine wilderness-based tourism. The potential world market for Canada's adventure product may be as high as 7 million visitors.

3. Urban Tourism

The 1985 U.S. Pleasure Survey discovered some interesting characteristics about Canada's southern neighbor and largest international visitor base. The Canadian travel industry had generally believed that Americans were only interested in Canada's "moose, mounties and mountains." The study showed, however, that they were also interested in its cities. They were not only important as "hubs and staging areas" for the touring experiences, but were also significant destinations in themselves.

Toronto and Vancouver have become major destinations for the Japanese market, while Montreal and Quebec City offer a unique European flavor for the American and English Canadian tourist. Edmonton also has become a significant Western Canadian destination city because of its famous West Edmonton Mall, and it will soon become an international gateway with direct flights arriving from Japan's new Kensai Airport.

However, as the cities become more attractive and air links with international markets improve, it may tend to have a negative effect on Canada's rural areas. For instance, following Expo '86 and the subsequent "discovery" of Vancouver by Americans, in particular, recent studies show that Vancouver and Victoria are now attracting almost half of all travelers to British Columbia compared to a quarter in the pre-Expo '86 years.

4. Resort Development

Tourism Canada defines Canadian resorts as "somewhat unique in that they do not conform with the international perception that a resort must be located in a hot, sunny climate near a large body of water." In fact, the Canadian resort sector is extremely broad with product offerings ranging from naturalist lodges on the Arctic Ocean, to guest ranches and hotsprings, to beachfront properties on the west coast of Vancouver Island, to the traditional inns of Atlantic Canada.

With the increase in short getaway vacations and a focus on a variety of product offerings, the future of the resort industry appears very positive, particularly with those properties appealing to the Japanese and European markets. This is most evident with the increase of Swiss, German and Japanese investment in these resort facilities. Not only are these offshore investors building the properties, they are also directly marketing back to their country of origin and therefore assuring high occupancy rates.

Canadian domestic travel is performing almost as impressively as international travel. This has been substantiated by the 1988 Canadian Travel Survey. It indicates that Canadians took more trips within Canada in 1988 than any other year in the 1980s. They traveled on more than 133 million trips, 14% more than the record high reached in 1986, the year of the World Exposition in Vancouver. Domestic travelers also spent at least one night away on 80 million of these trips, resulting in a 6% growth in the 1986–88 period.

The high growth in day outings was responsible for much of the overall domestic travel increase. For instance, same-day excursions jumped 30% to almost 54 million in 1988, and, of course, these increases are even more dramatic when compared to the beginning of the 1980s.

Domestic business travel flourished during 1988, and business travelers took 12 million overnight business trips, an increase of 10% over 1986 and 25% over 1980. Canadians also took more trips to see friends or family: 32.4 million, up 8% from 1986. Pleasure travel, however, increased only slightly between 1986 and 1988 and was actually below the record 33.3 million trips in 1980.

Air travel is becoming increasingly popular for domestic trips. Canadians purchased airline tickets for 6 million of their domestic trips, representing an 8% increase from 1986 and 19% growth since 1980. Travelers also used trains more frequently than in 1986; however, recent cuts in the Canadian rail service will undoubtedly affect this growth in the future.

Automobile travel, which accounts for the bulk of Canada's domestic trips, rose 6% to almost 49 million overnight trips. Only bus travel declined from 1986, and this is due to the large number of packaged motorcoach tours that were generated by Expo '86.

In the Summer 1989 issue of *Travel-log,* a publication of Statistics Canada, Laurie McDougall notes that, "Perhaps one of the most notable changes in the '80s has been the change in the age of the traveling population." This has been reflected by a corresponding decline in the youth segment and an increase in older Canadian travelers. In 1988, those 65 and older took 4.7 overnight trips, 12% above 1986 and 56% over 1980. However, in the same period, youth travelers were down 7% from 1986 and 23% from 1980.

IMPACT OF TOURISM ON THE PROVINCES AND
TERRITORIES

The national importance of tourism is also reflected in the provincial economies. For example, the Conference Board of Canada suggests that it ranges from as high as 9.6% of the Gross Provincial Product, GPP, of Prince Edward Island to 3.3% of GPP of Quebec. It is also one of the largest industries in every province. In Prince Edward Island, it is the primary industry; it is the third largest in British Columbia, after lumber and pulp and paper; and it is the fourth largest industry in Ontario. In Nova Scotia, Saskatchewan and Alberta, it is the fifth largest industry, and it is the sixth in the remaining provinces other than Newfoundland, where it is seventh.

Ontario
Ontario has a significant lead in terms of overall provincial tourism expenditures with 36.2% (65% of Canada's foreign visitor receipts), followed by Quebec with 18.1%, British Columbia with 16.1% and Alberta with 11.3%. These four provinces draw heavily from their proximity to the United States.

For instance, Ontario has Niagara Falls, which alone attracts in excess of 14 million visitors per year. As well, such attractions as Canada's Wonderland, the Toronto Zoo and the nation's capital in Ottawa-Hull, and the appeal of Toronto itself to Americans from Detroit, Cleveland and Chicago, accounted for an $8 billion expenditure in 1988.

Toronto has become one of Canada's major destinations. Visitor expenditures in 1987 were $2.65 billion and the tourism industry now generates more than a billion dollars in tax revenue. Visitors are attracted to Toronto's cleanliness, low crime rate and ethnic mix (half the city's residents come from other countries).

Ontario tourism is also driven by the addition of recent attractions in Ottawa, where travel is now the second largest industry after government. Tourism receipts in 1987 were $400 million. The new Natural Gallery and Museum of Civilization are having a significant impact, as will a National Capital Region Aquarium, which is being promoted by the Canadian Museum of Nature.

Quebec
Quebec has always enjoyed popularity with U.S. visitors coming to experience the unique character of Quebec City, the nightlife of Montreal, and the high-quality ski resorts of Mont Ste.-Anne and the ski hills of the Laurentians. Heavy promotion in the Boston-New York-Washington corridor continues to generate high American visitation. In 1988, the provincial government provided the largest-ever marketing budget of $18 million. Quebec also draws visitors from Ontario and derives a substantial portion of its visitors from those en route to Atlantic Canada.

Montreal, with its 9,000 first-class hotel rooms (including the famous Queen Elizabeth, with 1,050 rooms), lively nighttime entertainment, restaurants and cultural mix, is Quebec's major attraction.

British Columbia
In the period since Expo '86, British Columbia has experienced remarkable growth in visitation from the western American states, Alberta and Asia. While 1988 visits were lower than in 1986, the year of Expo '86, Vancouver has become a domestic destination of close to 3 million trips. Albertans account for 41% of all interprovincial travel to Vancouver, while Ontario contributes the next largest visitor supply with 35%.

In terms of international overnight traffic, American visitors have increased 2% over 1987 to 1.2 million in 1988. While growth continues, it will be several years before British Columbia achieves the record 2.5 million visitors that arrived for Expo '86. However, compared to the years leading up to Expo, the accelerated growth continues, with much of this traffic crossing at the Pacific Highway gateway linking Vancouver to Seattle, Washington.

Air arrivals at Vancouver International Airport showed the most significant growth. American and overseas visitor arrivals increased by 15% in 1988 to approximately 800,000, making this airport the second busiest after Toronto. Again, while these figures are below those recorded in 1986 (835,000 visitors), the growth rates since Expo '86 suggests a major long-term potential in that market. Overseas air travel to British Columbia has not slowed down since 1986. Overseas arrivals in 1988 showed an increase of 16% from 1986 and 22% from 1987. Leading the flow of overseas travel to British Columbia have been the Asian nations and most notably, Japan.

The 30% growth rates from Japan are bound to continue into the next decade. The new Japanese traveler is intent on breaking from the mass packaged tours of the 1980s. More personalized itineraries in locations *not* visited by other Japanese will become increasingly popular. Canada can respond to this demand more than most nations can.

The Asian market now represents 43% of all offshore arrivals to British Columbia, while another 40% comes from Europe. The Japanese account for approximately one out of every four trips to Vancouver, while British Columbia residents are the next most frequent visitors at 16%. Rounding out the top five overseas visitors to British Columbia are Hong Kong with 9%, Germany with 10% and Australia with 7%.

Alberta
Alberta has also benefited from the growth in international travel to western Canada. The four Rocky Mountain national parks with their attractions of Lake Louise, Banff and Jasper continue to be among the most popular destinations in Canada. As well, the international exposure and legacy of the Calgary Olympics has created a "western" identity or image for this province that will continue to generate high volumes, especially in such lucrative markets as Germany, Japan and Switzerland.

Saskatchewan and Manitoba
Saskatchewan and Manitoba account for 3.7% and 3.5%, respectively, of expenditures generated by the Canadian travel industry. Statistics indicate that as little as 5% of this volume comes from outside Canada and as much

as 85% of all tourism expenditure is generated by interprovincial travel. It is estimated that 87% of all visitors to Saskatoon, Saskatchewan came from within the province while another 10% came from other provinces, with only 3% being international arrivals. Most of those were American recreation vehicle operators en route to Alaska via the Yellowhead Highway. On the other hand, the study also revealed that traffic on this highway is increasing at twice the rate as on the TransCanada Highway, suggesting the traditional route between eastern Canada and the U.S. Eastern Seaboard/ Midwest and western Canada and Alaska is shifting to the northern part of the Prairie Provinces.

Atlantic Canada
The four Atlantic Provinces account for a mere 7.3% of all of the Canadian travel industry. Nova Scotia is the most popular with 3%, followed by New Brunswick with 2.2%, Newfoundland-Labrador with 1.4% and Prince Edward Island with 0.7%. In 1987, Newfoundland attracted 290,000 overnight visitors, up 20,000 from 1986; Nova Scotia reported 800,000; and the small island of Prince Edward Island attracted 700,000. New Brunswick receives most of these tourists as pass-through visitors on their way from Quebec and Ontario; however, with attractions such as Magnetic Hill and the Acadian Village, they are making a significant effort to increase their overall visitor nights and length of stay.

Relatively lower volumes and expenditures in this region can largely be attributed to the perceived distances from major American markets and the lack of a strong image in Europe and Asia. Nevertheless, total expenditures inject $1.5 billion into the Atlantic Canada economy and provide more than 55,000 direct and indirect jobs. This compares favorably to other economic sectors, including forestry and fishing. Tourism growth in this region is approximately 3–5%, and these rates can be maintained if there is a strong economy in Ontario and Quebec, which are the major generators of interprovince visitation, and continued government support for the development of the industry.

Yukon and Northwest Territories
While expenditures in northern Canada's Yukon and Northwest Territories are only approximately 1% of the overall Canadian tourism industry, these regions have shown remarkable growth rates over the past five years in the high-yield adventure travel market.

According to the Product Development Plan for the Northwest Territories (NWT), the adventure market has grown by approximately 20% per annum since 1982. The industry is largely made up of 90 outfitters offering services in hunting, fishing, nature observation, dog sledding, etc. The most popular areas are the Baffin and Fort Smith regions, with the Western Arctic and Arctic coast having the most potential. The NWT currently captures approximately 6,000 U.S. outdoor adventure travelers. The Atlantic and eastern states are the principal markets for the Baffin and Keewatin, while the western Arctic, which has been experiencing 40–50% annual growth rates over the past five years, attracts visitors from the west coast states. Per trip expenditures are some of the highest in Canada at $1,500 (1986), providing the NWT with a $25 million industry.

The Yukon Territory travel industry is based on American travel up the Alaska Highway to the state of Alaska. While this market segment has remained relatively stable at approximately 200,000 visitors per year, the adventure market is growing at an estimated 20–25% annually, and many operators have experienced 100% increases in business volumes in the past two years. Trip expenditures are similar to those in the NWT and generally exceed $1,000 per person.

THE CANADIAN BUSINESS TRAVELER

The business traveler has a significant impact on domestic tourism. In 1988 more than 22 million Canadians traveled for business, up 14% from 1986. More than half of these trips were overnight—a 10% increase over 1986. Most business travelers tend to use a car (67%), but there was an appreciable growth in the use of aircraft, with a 1-million-trip increase taking place between 1986 and 1988.

Hotels are the preferred accommodation (54%) and growth in this area has resulted in a decrease in motel visitor nights. The rise in budget hotels may have influenced the decrease in motel use. High-quality restaurants are also benefiting from the business traveler, with 25% reporting that they had fine dining on their recent business trip.

Men still dominate the business market (76%), and 25% of the travelers have household incomes in excess of $70,000.

In 1988, business travelers spent more than $4 billion, representing 38% of overnight domestic travel expenditure. The average trip was $366.00 and their per-night spending of $132.00 was higher than market segments.

NEED FOR INCREASED MARKETING

While the international tourism industry experiences rapid growth, so does competition for the traveler's attention from other travel destinations. If Canada is to maintain, or even increase its market share, it must focus its marketing budgets on those regions offering the most potential for the Canadian travel product. For instance, in the United States, state tourism budgets exceeded $295 million in 1988–89. On the other hand, the Canadian federal advertising budget directed toward the United States was only $25 million in that same period, with an additional $8 million directed toward the overseas markets. However, it has been clearly demonstrated that those areas of the world experiencing the strongest growth in tourist arrivals (i.e., Asia Pacific, Europe and the Far East) are also spending increasingly larger sums of marketing. For instance, in 1988–89, the United Kingdom spent $51.5 million, Italy 47.5 million, Australia $38.2 million, and even Malaysia spent a significant $31.5 million.

CANADA'S COMMITMENT TO ENVIRONMENTAL PROTECTION

Over the past two years both the Canadian people and the government have demonstrated an increasing commitment to the concept of sustainable development. This promises to have a significant long-term impact on the Canadian industry. Market research in Canada's prime markets indicates the high value these consumers place on the pristine, natural environment. The ability to maintain this environmental and cultural base as well as to assume a leadership role in environmental protection worldwide will create a positive image for Canada as a tourist destination founded on its ability to preserve its natural heritage. As tourism becomes increasingly respected and recognized as an activity that produces major economic benefits, it will increasingly be used as a catalyst for sustainable economic development.

FURTHER READING

Bar-on, R. *Travel and Tourism Data: A Comprehensive Research Handbook on World Travel*. Phoenix, Ariz.: Oryx Press, 1989.
Boulton, Roger. *Canada Coast to Coast*. New York: Oxford University Press, 1982.
Mieczkowski, Zbigniew. *World Trends in Tourism and Recreation*. New York: Lang, Peter Publishing, 1990.

INTERNATIONAL DEVELOPMENT ASSISTANCE

CRANFORD PRATT

Canada's development assistance to Third World countries is a substantial affair. In 1989 the government spent $2.3 billion (U.S.) net on overseas development assistance (ODA), a sum equal to .44% of Canada's GNP and approximately 2% of the expenditures of the government of Canada. Not surprisingly, the spending of sums that large is a complicated exercise. Tables 1, 2 and 3 provide some indication of this complexity, with refer-

TABLE 1

Net ODA Disbursements by Type (1989)

			$US Million
1		Bilateral grant and grant-like	
	1.1	Technical assistance	246
	1.2	Food aid	131
	1.3	Administrative costs	184
	1.4	Other grants	1,036
2		New bilateral development lending	− 16
3		Contributions to multilateral institutions	
	3.1	Grants to UN agencies	274
	3.2	Grants to other international agencies	49
	3.3	Capital subscription to World Bank (excluding International Development Association, IDA)	13
	3.4	Capital subscription to IDA	169
	3.5	Capital subscription to regional banks	208
	3.6	Other capital subscriptions	26
		TOTAL	2,320

Source: *Development Cooperation 1990* (Paris: OECD, 1990), p. 254.

TABLE 2

Distribution of Canadian Aid by Major
World Regions (1988–89)

	%
Sub-Saharan Africa	39.8
South Asia	21.6
Other Asia and Oceania	12.6
Middle East and North Africa	8.5
Latin America and Caribbean	17.5

Source: *Development Cooperation 1990* (Paris: OECD, 1990), p. 195.

ence to types of disbursements, geographic distribution of disbursements and the major uses of Canadian aid.

Canada's aid program has for years been remarkably widely supported by Canadians. This is revealed by the substantial majorities that recurrently register their support for Canada's aid program in public opinion polls and by the active, varied and numerous nongovernmental organizations (NGOs) which engage in development and relief work and, in many cases, express solidarity with Third World peoples. It is also suggested by the broad interparty support for the work of the Canadian International Development Agency (CIDA). There are but few parliamentarians who are markedly hostile to the agency. They are concentrated in the extreme right wing of the Conservative Party, and the prime minister, Brian Mulroney, has been very careful to concede to them no influence on aid policies.

The basis of the public support for CIDA is predominantly ethical. Canadians have come to accept a measure of obligation toward those who live in poverty in other countries. A poll in 1980, for example, reported not only that a substantial majority of Canadians support Canada's aid program (a result that has been consistently produced by polls over the last 15 years at least) but, more interesting still, almost all of those who supported it did so for altruistic reasons. Only 4% felt that commercial advantage to

TABLE 3

Distribution of Canadian Aid by Major Uses
(1987–88)

	%
Social and administrative infrastructure	9.0
Economic infrastructure	22.7
Agriculture	27.2
Industry and other production	6.1
Food aid	12.9
Program assistance	22.1

Source: *Development Cooperation 1990* (Paris: OECD, 1990), p. 196.

Canada should be an important factor and only 2% wished political advantages to rank high. Canadian parliamentarians have reflected these same humanitarian sentiments. In 1986 a Special Joint Committee of the Senate and the House of Commons affirmed, and in the following year the Standing Committee on External Affairs and International Trade agreed unanimously—and, in its words, "emphatically,"—that meeting the needs of the poorest countries and people should remain the primary and overriding objective of the Canadian aid program. This humanitarian, ethical emphasis is echoed in the CIDA strategy paper issued in 1988 which asserts that policy is to be based "on a commitment to putting the alleviation of poverty first."

Yet despite all this, political and commercial objectives have always tended to intrude significantly into Canadian development assistance policies. Indeed the Standing Committee on External Affairs and International Trade opened its 1987 report on Canadian aid policies with the declaration that "Canadian official development assistance . . . is beset with confusion of purpose" and commented that "it is imperative that its impact not be diminished by tendencies and trends that would see it become dissipated, unfocused or diverted from its primary objective of helping the world's poorest to achieve self-reliance." The tendencies and trends that have had these unfortunate consequences have entailed an effort to achieve immediate Canadian political and commercial objectives while at the same time still promoting development. An important distinction is to be noted here. Many argue, surely correctly, that a good development program will in fact be in Canada's long-term political and economic interest, for it will promote a peaceful world and a stable and more developed global economy. These long-term political and economic interests are served by an aid program that diligently pursues its humanitarian and development objectives. In contrast, the political and commercial objectives that have intruded into Canada's aid program are immediate and specific; they divert CIDA from a single-minded pursuit of its humanitarian and development objectives and change the pattern of its allocations.

Pressures on CIDA to promote Canadian exports, augment Canadian influence and prestige, and reinforce the position of friendly regimes have been very significant, both from within the government and from powerful interests in society. To these influences in recent years has been added an important preoccupation with supporting the efforts of the International Monetary Fund (IMF) and the World Bank to pressure Third World governments to initiate structural adjustment policies as were judged necessary by these institutions. This chapter will attempt, by an overview of the main features of Canada's development assistance and by a review of its evolution since the early 1950s, to assess the shifting balance that has been effected among these varying and conflicting purposes that have between them given shape and detailed content to the aid program.

CANADA'S AID PROFILE

Five aspects of CIDA's activities provide both an awareness of their main characteristics and insight into the interplay of motives and objectives that have determined these characteristics. These aspects will be examined in turn. They are the scale and terms of Canadian aid; the choice of country recipients; the tying of Canadian aid to the purchase of Canadian goods and services; the linking of aid financing to export promotion; and finally, a number of more specific Canadian aid activities.

Scale and Terms of Canadian Aid

Canada had been neither a leader nor a laggard in regard to development assistance. The western aid donors separate themselves rather neatly into three clusters. The Netherlands, Norway, Sweden and Denmark have in recent years devoted from .9% to 1.1% of their GNP to ODA. In contrast, the United States and the United Kingdom have each allowed their aid in recent years to settle at about .2% of their respective GNPs. The rest of the western donors, including Germany and France, cluster between these upper and lower limits. Canada's .44% of its GNP thus places Canada rather squarely in the middle, a position Canada has tended to occupy for at least the past decade. Canada is, however, rather wealthier than most of the other aid donors. As a result, in 1989 although Canada has the fourth highest GNP per capita of the members of the Organization of Economic Cooperation and Development (OECD), its aid as a percentage of GNP ranks eighth.

Nevertheless, government enthusiasm for an expanding aid program has declined. In 1984 the new Conservative government pledged immediately to raise the level of aid to .5% of GNP and to raise the level to .6% by 1990 and .7% by 1995. On three subsequent occasions these targets have been pared down. The 1989 budget cuts proportionately slashed CIDA's allocation far more substantially than any other vote. In addition, the .7% target has been abandoned and the accomplishment of a .6% target has been postponed until the year 2000.

The pattern, of course, could have been worse. Had the primary motivation for Canadian aid been the political desire to be fully accepted as a member of the OECD club, then one might have expected Canadian aid to have drifted downward to a percentage of Canada's GNP that would not be much higher than that of the United States and the United Kingdom. This, however, has not happened. Not only have humanitarian considerations favored higher levels of aid; so also did another important political consideration. Canadian political leaders have tended to see relations with the Third World, or at least with selected Third World countries, as an arena within which Canada can demonstrate its capacity to play an independent role in international politics. Canada has long attached importance to its role in the Commonwealth and more recently in La Francophonie, the association of French-language states. Canadian leaders recurrently have sought to play a mediating role in North-South relations, as Prime Minister Pierre Elliott Trudeau did in the lead-up to the Cancun Conference of 17 world leaders in 1980 and as Prime Minister Mulroney sought to do on the issue of Third World debt. It is therefore not surprising that the leadership would see political advantage in holding Canadian aid at levels somewhat higher than those of the United States and the United Kingdom.

It helped to establish the credibility of Canada playing this sort of role on North-South issues.

Canadian aid, as indeed is the case with aid from all the OECD countries except Germany and Japan, is now almost entirely in the form of grants rather than loans. Canada, in fact, moved to grant aid a few years ahead of most of the OECD members and acted to convert to grants a greater portion of earlier aid loans than have most. The motivation for this has been a blend of developmental and political considerations, the political aspect being revealed by the fact that the Canadian initiatives in this regard have been closely related to Canadian prominence either at the Conference on International Economic Cooperation in 1975–76 or at the 1987 meetings of the Commonwealth and La Francophonie.

Country Selection

Almost from the start Canada has divided its bilateral assistance among a substantial number of countries. For years some 30 countries or regional groupings have been identified as core recipients. Canada has accepted a major aid commitment to each of these. By policy decision, they receive 75% of Canada's bilateral aid. A further 20% has gone to an additional 25 to 30 countries "in order to respond to the diverse objectives of Canadian foreign policy," as an official paper recently explained. The final 5% is divided among more than 50 countries "of minimal Canadian presence."

The list of the core countries makes clear that the selection has not been influenced primarily by commercial considerations. So also does Table 4, which lists the 20 countries that were the recipients of the largest amounts of Canadian aid in 1980–81 and 1985–86. The economies of most of these major recipients are clearly very undeveloped and are growing only very slowly. They are of far less commercial interest to Canada than the richer, middle- and higher-income less developed countries (LDCs). In 1979, for example, a report of a government-appointed committee complained that "most of the nations we assist are too undeveloped for much meaningful trade to result." One of the most interesting recent studies of Canadian aid policies, that by Réal Lavergne, demonstrates that very poor and slowly growing LDCs have received more aid per capita than have the economically stronger and the commercially more attractive LDCs. This has persisted despite very strong pressures on CIDA to move its aid substantially toward more prosperous recipients. The primary influence determining the selection of aid recipients does therefore seem to have been humanitarian and political. It cannot be claimed that it has been commercial. That clearly acknowledged, it should also be recognized that commercial motivations have nevertheless intruded. The deliberate identification of 20% of bilateral aid, recently increased to 25%, for commercially interesting middle-income countries illustrates this. Lavergne, in his study already mentioned, suggests that at least six of the core countries are on the list because of Canadian commercial interests. It is also the case that in recent years Canadian aid has tended increasingly to go to the less poor and commercially more interesting of the core countries. That Indonesia in 1985–86 was the sec-

TABLE 4
The Major Recipients of Canadian Bilateral Aid in order
of magnitude of aid received
% of total Canadian bilateral aid

1980–81		1985–86	
Bangladesh	5.0	Bangladesh	4.0
India	4.2	Pakistan	2.5
Pakistan	3.7	Indonesia	1.7
Sri Lanka	2.7	Jamaica	1.7
Kenya	2.0	Tanzania	1.7
Tanzania	2.0	China	1.5
Egypt	1.8	Ghana	1.3
Indonesia	1.6	Kenya	1.3
Cameroon	1.5	Morocco	1.3
Mali	1.1	India	1.2
Ghana	1.0	Mozambique	1.2
Zambia	1.0	Egypt	1.1
Jamaica	0.9	Senegal	1.1
Senegal	0.9	Thailand	1.1
Turkey	0.9	Cameroon	1.0
Zaire	0.9	Philippines	1.0
Malawi	0.8	Sri Lanka	1.0
Tunisia	0.7	Zambia	1.0

Source: *Development Cooperation 1990* (Paris: OECD, 1990), p. 234.

ond largest aid recipient and that Thailand was on the list at all, illustrates this.

Political interests have also influenced the selection of aid recipients. Canada has never acted on the advice, often offered, that its aid would be more effective if concentrated in far fewer countries. The foreign policy interest in having an aid presence in a large number of countries has always overruled that advice. Political factors also explain the importance of Commonwealth countries as aid recipients, as they do the substantial Canadian program in the Caribbean and the decision more than 15 years ago to have programs of approximately equal total value in Commonwealth Africa and in francophone Africa.

All of this suggests that political factors have been influential but that, along with commercial factors, they have been contained within a policy framework that has kept the bulk of bilateral aid going to low-income countries.

Aid Tying
No feature of Canadian development assistance has been more entrenched nor the focus of more sustained criticism than the requirement from 1970 until 1988 that 80% of all bilateral aid (except for international shipping costs) be spent on Canadian goods and services. Even as CIDA has some-

what modified this practice, it has not diluted the vigor of its defense of the practice. *Sharing Our Future,* CIDA's 1988 strategy paper, for example, roundly declares, "Canadians want to help developing countries but they do not want to see Canadian assistance going to buy the products of wealthy countries that are Canada's rivals for overseas markets.'

The basic criticism of aid-tying was expressed precisely and sharply in an official report produced in 1986 which said that the tying regulations made it impossible for CIDA to apply vigorously the directive "that the better part of bilateral aid be channeled towards the most disadvantaged populations of the Third World." The force of this point has long been recognized. If Canadian aid must be spent on Canadian goods and services, then it cannot assist many high-priority development projects. This is especially the case for those projects that seek to reach the poorest, for typically such projects require only small quantities of imports. International opinion has gradually come to recognize this fact. The Development Assistance Committee (DAC) of the OECD has long sought a simultaneous reduction of tying by all members so that the corporations of each country would gain the right to tender for aid projects financed by other countries at the same time as they lose their exclusive hold on the aid projects of their own country. Most countries, but not Canada, did in fact gradually relax their tying provisions, so that in recent years Canada, along with Austria, has had the most restrictive tying regulations of any OECD country.

Canada also resisted the DAC decision in 1972 that, as a stimulus to intra-Third World trade, each donor country should at least permit its aid monies to be used for Third World procurement of imports when they are competitive with its national products as a stimulus to intra-Third World trade. Canada refused to implement this DAC recommendation.

Public interest groups and informed individuals concerned with Third World development have long lobbied against Canadian tied aid policies. In 1986 this lobbying was decisively reinforced when the Standing Committee on External Affairs and International Trade (SCEAIT) of the House of Commons recommended a sharp relaxation in the tying regulations. In March 1988 a partial relaxation was announced, not as much as SCEAIT had urged but significant nevertheless. Under the new policy, half the bilateral aid to Africa and to least-developed countries elsewhere can be untied, as can a third of the balance of Canadian bilateral aid. This is being done primarily to permit the meeting of local costs from aid funds. No emphasis at all is given to the possibility that untied funds should also be used for competitive Third World procurement. Aid-financed procurement from other developed countries is even less likely.

Before these recent changes there were two important shifts in official thinking that related to tying. First, it was recognized that tied aid might well not be very helpful in promoting ongoing trade relations that would outlast the aid. Too often the Canadian firms that benefited from aid tying were unlikely to be able to sell competitively in Third World markets. In their cases, therefore, the aid relationship did not in fact lead to greater long-term trade relations. The Canadian government had much more interest in promoting long-term trade relations than it did in helping out uncompetitive Canadian exporters. As a result, CIDA in recent years has emphasized that its projects must be in sectors in which Canadian firms are likely to be competitive by the end of the aid contract. It is thus likely that while Canadian tying has continued to exclude Canadian involvement in many poverty-oriented projects, an effort has at least been made to channel it to sectors in which Canadian products are competitive.

The second development has been a widespread move away from project aid toward commodity aid and balance of payments support. These involve the extension of credits for the purchase of specific Canadian products or, more generally, for the purchase of whatever Canadian products or services are judged to be appropriate within a specified range of economic activities. This aid is thus still tied to Canadian goods and services, but it is not linked to new projects. Given the fact that so many Third World economies are under such severe strain, this is enormously advantageous, for it is very likely that most new projects, once the aid stops, quickly falter as the governments simply do not have the foreign exchange for the imports essential to the projects. The greater use of commodity aid and balance of payments support means that aid is to an ever greater extent financing imports and technical assistance programs needed to help resuscitate industries and productive activities that are already in place, but that are operating at a very low level of efficiency because of the country's foreign exchange crisis.

Commodity aid and program aid not only meet real development needs in this way, they are also attractive to CIDA, for they are forms of tied aid which, by their very nature, will likely be used for the purchase of Canadian imports that really are needed and are most nearly competitive in price. These are objectives less easily ensured with project aid.

Associated Financing
Since the late 1970s the OECD countries have developed a range of practices which in one way or another use aid funds as inducements to ensure that corporations from the country concerned are successful in competing for large capital contracts in LDCs. The techniques are varied: aid funds can be added to export credit funds (credit mixte), the aid agency can jointly finance a project with a government export development corporation (co-financing), or the agency can offer additional related projects on condition that a national corporation be awarded the main contract (parallel financing). The techniques thus vary but the purpose is constant: to secure for Canadian corporations contracts that they would otherwise not get, either because they were not price-competitive or because another country had "spoiled the market" by an offer of an aid-financed sweetener which then swung the decision in favor of the competitor from that country. Activities of this sort have been significant. From 1978 to 1986 CIDA and the Export Development Corporation (EDC) co-financed 22 projects with a total value of $1.5 billion, CIDA's participation being over $500 million. One project alone, the Chimera hydroelectric project in India, involved a $250-million CIDA grant plus $403 million in credit from the EDC.

497

After a good deal of internal debate and consultation with interested Canadian corporations, the Canadian government decided in 1986 not to involve CIDA directly in credit mixte or associated financing arrangements but instead to provide the EDC with the funds and responsibility for these trade-promoting activities. CIDA, however, is still to endeavor to link aid projects to possible EDC projects where this would help to ensure Canadian commercial involvement.

Other CIDA Initiatives

A number of important additional Canadian ODA activities have been initiated which further reveal the heterodoxy of the influences that have shaped Canadian aid policy. Four of these can be briefly mentioned:

1. The International Development Research Centre (IDRC) was created in 1970. It has become internationally renowned as a sensitive and imaginative research agency identifying and funding projects in key areas of development concern, with the research primarily being conducted by institutions within the Third World. It is a crown corporation with an independent board on which there is substantial Third World representation. Its budget for 1986–87 exceeded $100 million.
2. Petro-Canada International Assistance Corporation, a wholly-owned subsidiary of Petro-Canada, was created in 1981 to promote the use of Canadian technology and expertise by Third World countries anxious to lessen their dependency on imported oil. In 1986–87 its total expenditures were budgeted at over $58 million.
3. The Business Cooperation Branch, first created in 1984, has been a rapidly expanding unit within CIDA charged in particular, to quote from an internal 1986 document, "to ensure improved linkages between Canadian development assistance and Canadian economic objectives, particularly export promotion." A reaffirmation of the importance of securing greater Canadian business involvement in the aid program, and a promise of significant additional funds for this branch, have been featured in the several major policy statements on development assistance which the government issued in December 1987 and in March 1988.
4. Another CIDA activity that has expanded rapidly in recent years has been its program of cooperation with Canadian NGOs working in the Third World. This began in 1969 and, by 1986–87, $75 million was provided for it in CIDA's estimates, with a further $17 million to support international NGOs. The assistance to the Canadian NGOs was initially "reactive," that is, CIDA responded to requests from NGOs for project and program assistance which emerged from their intimate knowledge of the needs of those they were serving in the Third World. There has recently been a further development, initially called country-focus programming, which entails the enlistment of the skills, contacts and experience of NGOs to implement projects that are selected and financed by CIDA and reflect its

sense of priority and needs. In 1988, some $100 million was allocated to be spent as grants to NGOs. In recent years 11% of total ODA, excluding food aid, has been delivered through NGOs, a higher percentage than by any other major donor.

THE DETERMINANTS OF CANADIAN POLICIES

This chapter began with evidence that Canadians support CIDA's activities very substantially for humanitarian reasons. It is clear, however, from the aid profile just presented, that political and—even more—commercial considerations have had a major impact on these activities. Political considerations, for example, influenced the decision to hold Canadian aid at a percentage of GNP higher than that achieved by the United States and the United Kingdom. Political considerations were as well the major influence determining the selection of recipient countries.

Commercial considerations have been even more important. They are the primary explanation for Canada's policies toward aid tying and associated financing and for the creation and expansion of the Business Cooperation Branch. Their influence is clearly at work in the shifting of aid within the bilateral program toward those countries, such as Indonesia and Thailand, that are judged to be of greater long-term commercial interest in Canada.

This pattern is hardly surprising. Government decision-makers are bound to give prominence to considerations that concern the profitability of the Canadian economy and the international prestige and influence of Canada. These are the main professional preoccupations of Canadian foreign policy decision-makers. In addition, governments in Canada have always been particularly responsive to the lobbying of corporate interests in pursuit of special advantage. Foreign policy issues, including development assistance, have not been free of this pervasive characteristic of Canadian decision making.

Nevertheless, despite these factors, humanitarian and development considerations have not been overwhelmed. The public reaffirmation that aiding the poorest is the primary purpose of the aid program is surely not unimportant. In addition, the substantial number of low-income countries that have remained core country recipients of Canadian aid, though they are of little commercial interest to Canada, illustrates the strength still of a responsiveness to development and humanitarian considerations, as does the importance given to the IDRC and to disbursements through the NGO community.

The balance between these various influences has not been constant over the decades. Instead, a pattern is easily discernible in which one can trace the shifting comparative importance over time of these various determining influences.

The Years 1950–64

In the first decade and more after 1945, Canadian foreign policy was in many ways remarkably internationalist. Canada played a prominent role in the formation of the United Nations, the International Monetary Fund (IMF), the World Bank and the General Agreement on Tariffs and Trade (GATT).

499

Canada contributed to the various UN peacekeeping missions and was of crucial importance in the UN initiatives to restore peace in 1956, after the Israeli, British and French invasion of Egypt. Moreover, Canada had demonstrated a real capacity for generosity in 1946 and 1947, contributing 6.4% and 4.3% of its GNP to European relief and reconstruction loans.

However, Canadian humane internationalism was at that time not global in its reach. Instead it was very much focused on the Canada-United States-Europe relationship and on the containment of what was perceived as the threat of international communism. Assistance to Europe after the war was one thing, but the idea of giving similar assistance to the less developed countries was quite another. As one official recalls, "Most ministers felt on familiar ground when dealing with Europeans but hundreds of millions of Asians raised questions of a different type." Pearson in his memoirs wrote that the government wished "to stay out of the vanguard" in regard to development aid.

Canada certainly did stay out of the vanguard in these years. Canadian aid allocations grew but slowly in the 1950s and then in the first four years of the next decade. The net disbursements for external assistance in the years 1961–63 were significantly lower than the 1960 disbursements. The 1964 disbursements rose again and totaled slightly more than the 1960 figure ($77.9 million in contrast to $75.2 million). However, within that 1964 figure was a sizable contribution to the World Bank's International Development Association, so that in fact bilateral assistance was nearly 20% less in 1964 than in 1960.

The motivation behind Canadian aid in this first period was primarily political. Canada was taking part in an American-led effort to minimize the risk that the newly independent countries would turn to the Soviet Union for help rather than to the West. The Canadian government was none too anxious to be much involved in this effort, but it recognized that the existence of a reasonable aid program was part of the price of full acceptance in the western alliance. Given this attitude, it is not surprising that Canada had an aid program but that it kept its total low, tied it to the purchase of Canadian goods and services and sought, successfully, to have its recipients accept surplus Canadian wheat as a significant portion of Canadian aid. Humanitarian and developmental goals were emphasized in the rhetoric about Canadian assistance, but the operating motives were primarily political, with commercial considerations greatly influencing the details.

The Years 1964–75

Several major influences transformed Canada's development assistance programs in the decade immediately after 1964. Independence had been won throughout tropical Africa and the Caribbean in the years immediately preceding, so that Canada was drawn into an extension of its aid activities in these areas. The Americans and the British increasingly pressed Canada to "pull its weight" by augmenting the levels of its aid program. At the same time, Canada was, through the United Nations and the Commonwealth, becoming more truly global in its interests, while the Canadian govern-

TABLE 5
Canadian ODA Disbursements 1964–75
in $US millions

	1964	1967	1970	1974	1975
Net ODA	77.9	197.9	346.3	713	880

Source: DAC Annual Review, *Development Cooperation 1972 and 1978* (Paris: OECD, 1973 and 1979).

ment, because of the Vietnam War, was anxious to demonstrate the independence of its foreign policy. A much expanded development assistance program therefore was, for many different reasons, particularly appropriate.

Between 1964 and 1975 Canada ODA expanded at a prodigious rate, as Table 5 indicates. By 1970 Canadian aid had surpassed that of the United States and the United Kingdom as a percentage of their respective GNPs. By 1975 these percentages were 0.55 for Canada and 0.26 and 0.37 for the United States and the United Kingdom respectively. Canada was thus no longer primarily responding to a desire to achieve a respectable level of aid in contrast to those of its major allies. Instead the aid program had become itself an important component of Canada's foreign policy, expressing both the global reach of Canadian foreign policy interests and the expanding international component of Canadian humanitarianism.

Not only were Canadian aid allocations sharply increased, so also were the professionalism and commitment to development of the Canadian aid agency. First Prime Minister Pearson and then Prime Minister Pierre Elliott Trudeau appointed independent and outspoken persons, Maurice Strong and then Paul Gerin Lajoie, from outside the civil service to head the aid agency. The agency in turn acquired greater status and influence in 1968 when it became the Canadian International Development Agency under the secretary of state for external affairs and headed by a president with deputy minister status. Reinforced soon thereafter by the parallel emergence, in the World Bank and in the International Labour Office and the Development Assistance Committee of the OECD, of a more single-minded commitment to development, CIDA battled hard to make development and humanitarian objectives primary.

It was no easy struggle, for such departments within government as Finance and Industry, Trade and Commerce, along with politically powerful corporate interests, had a major stake in the continued responsiveness of CIDA to commercial interests. Nevertheless, CIDA did succeed, in 1975, in winning Cabinet acceptance of a strategy paper which signaled, or appeared to signal, that Canadian development assistance for the next five years would very much be concentrated on helping the poorest sectors of the lower-income developing countries to achieve greater productivity and autonomy. The balance seemed decisively to have been swung in that direction, away from a preponderant responsiveness to political and commercial concerns.

The Years 1975–90
CIDA, had, however, overreached itself. Very quickly, political and even more prominently commercial considerations reacquired major prominence. A great many specific decisions illustrate this: the failure, until very recently, to implement the 1972 DAC decision to permit Third World procurement on aid-financed projects; the extensive use of CIDA funds in a variety of ways to assist Canadian firms to secure major Third World contracts; the continued emphasis on food aid; the shift of bilateral aid toward commercially more interesting countries. At the same time as the government's particular responsiveness to immediate economic interests has generated this diffusion of objectives, there was nevertheless in 1986 and 1987 a strong reaffirmation by two important parliamentary committees that Canadian development assistance ought primarily to be concerned with aiding the poorest countries and the poorest peoples.

These two parliamentary reports, however, did not significantly shift Canadian aid policies in a humanitarian direction. Instead, most recently, Canada has moved much closer to the International Monetary Fund and the World Bank in its diagnosis of Third World development needs. Primary policy emphasis, as a result, has been to use Canadian aid as additional leverage to support the structural adjustment policies which the IMF has been requiring of any country hoping for its assistance. This most recent shift involves a downplaying of both the narrowly commercial and the directly humanitarian. Instead, the emphasis very much is on inducing Third World countries to limit severely state activities in the economy and to follow an outward-oriented market-dominated development strategy. Most recently, nearly 40% of Canada's bilateral aid was used for this purpose. Thus, Canadian aid policies, as with public policy in other areas, have moved into a much closer ideological rapport with the policies of the major industrialized states, the World Bank and the IMF.

FURTHER READING

Canada. House of Commons. Standing Committee on External Affairs and International Trade. *For Whose Benefit? A Report on Canada's Official Development Assistance Policies and Programs.* Ottawa, Queen's Printer, 1987.
————. *To Benefit a Better World. Response of the Government of Canada to the report of the Standing Committee on External Affairs and International Trade.* Ottawa, Minister of Supplies and Services, 1987.
Canadian International Development Agency. *Sharing Our Future.* Ottawa, Minister of Supplies and Services, 1988.
CIDA Task Force on Canada's Official Development Assistance Program. *Study of the Policy and Organization of Canada's Official Development Aid.* Hull, Québec, 1986.
Carty, Robert, and Virginia Smith. *Perpetuating Poverty: The Political Economy of Canadian Foreign Aid.* Toronto: Between the Lines, 1981.
Lavergne, Réal. "Determinants of Canadian Aid Policies." *Western Middle Powers and Global Poverty,* edited by Olav Stokke. Uppsala, Sweden. Scandinavian Institute of African Studies, 1989.

Pratt, Cranford. "An Eroding and Limited Internationalism." In *Internationalism Under Strain: The North-South Policies of Canada, the Netherlands, Norway and Sweden,* edited by Cranford Pratt. Toronto: University of Toronto Press, 1989.

Spicer, Keith. *A Samaritan State: External Aid in Canadian Foreign Policy,* Toronto: University of Toronto Press, 1966.

PART FIVE

SOCIAL AFFAIRS

ENVIRONMENT

DIXON THOMPSON

The Speech from the Throne of the Second Session of the 34th Parliament, April 3, 1989, identified environmental protection as the second of four fundamental objectives of the government of Canada. Specific references were made to sustainable development, stronger environmental legislation, international agreements to reduce pollution, cleanup of the Great Lakes and St. Lawrence River, environmentally friendly products, and legislation to ensure an appropriate environmental assessment review process. However, the government's critics have pointed out that there has been no net increase in the budget and the strength of the federal Department of Environment, that there has been no effective environmental assessment of very significant government actions (the cutbacks in the Via Rail passenger system), and that programs providing incentives for energy conservation and development of renewable energy have been slashed.

The government made two fundamental changes at cabinet level which must be recognized as very significant. For the first time there is a cabinet committee dealing with environmental issues and the federal minister of environment now sits on all major cabinet committees. While such changes do not guarantee adequate consideration of environmental aspects of cabinet decisions, at least there is a good possibility that such factors will get more than the cursory, after-the-fact consideration they have received in the past.

PARKS AND PROTECTED AREAS

There were early efforts to protect the more scenic parts of Canada's environment as a result of attempts by the Canadian Pacific Railway in the mid-1890s to develop a tourist industry in the Canadian Rockies. In 1887, the 1885 Order in Council which had established the Rocky Mountain National Parks (later Banff and Jasper) was formally passed by Parliament and given Royal Assent.

Canada's national parks, which are protected by legislation, play a key role in protecting natural areas for future generations. Some areas have been removed from the parks so that they could be exploited by commercial interests. Federal ministers have sometimes suggested that park lands be opened to forestry and mining operations and to increased commercial recreation development. However, the parks system has been steadily expanded and has for the most part been able to resist large-scale efforts to compromise its mandate. Although for the most part this is due to sympathetic and understanding federal ministers and stalwart civil servants, it is also due to the fact that the larger-scale proposals for developments within the parks have been short-sighted, carelessly developed, and put forward with no realistic tradeoffs provided. The minister, his civil servants, public interest groups and the general public would have to give serious thought to a development within a national (or provincial) park which had been subjected to a thorough environmental impact assessment, which provided for good management and public scrutiny, and which provided for generous expansion of the area of the park in compensation for infringement on the park which was required by the development.

Parks have been added to Canada's system in the past decade, and in 1988 the National Parks Act was strengthened. For example, fines for poaching were increased from $500 to $150,000 to make them an effective deterrent. However, much remains to be done if Canada is to have all natural regions represented in the national parks system and reach the Brundtland Commission's recommendation that 12% of the landscape be legally protected. At present, only 21 of 39 different natural terrestrial systems have representative areas protected and so at least 18 more parks are required. There are 45 national wildlife areas but a further 99 have been identified as requiring protection. Only 2 of 29 marine parks have been established. Provincially, New Brunswick, Prince Edward Island, Newfoundland and the Northwest Territories have not yet started any parks systems. Although provinces such as British Columbia, Alberta, Ontario and Quebec have extensive provincial parks systems, they are too easily subject to compromise for commercial purposes.

So far, Canada has "protected" only 2.6% of its surface area. Some protection is afforded in another 3.7% (for a total of 6.3%), but logging, mining and hunting are permitted. Therefore Canada is a long way from the Brundtland Commission's recommended 12%, which would require expansion from at least partial protection of 25 million square miles to the goal of 46 million. It has been argued that protection of such large areas puts too large a constraint on needed economic development, whether it be mining, logging, expansion of urban and commercial areas or transportation systems. On the other hand, although expanding tourism itself threatens protected areas, the economic benefits from keeping Canadian travel dollars in Canada and improving the country's balance of payments by bringing in foreign tourists is significant now and will become increasingly important in the future.

The role of national and provincial parks and other protected areas in promoting the economic benefits of tourism will continue to provoke serious debate and controversy and demand careful solutions to the problems posed. At the one extreme, such parks are seen as wilderness areas to be accessible to only a few under "primitive" conditions. Others see the areas' development as constrained only by commerce's capacity to maximize short-term returns in the most crass and garish manner possible. To that spectrum of unreconcilable extremes must be added the current occupants and users of any areas that are selected for new parks, particularly the aboriginal people. This seems to have been successfully resolved in the Arctic as far as Inuit occupation and use is concerned (Inuit hunting is permitted). However, on the Prairies a grasslands park has been held up by controversy, and on the St. Lawrence and in the Maritimes conflict has arisen over compensation of those whose land (and heritage) has been expropriated.

In contrast to the wilderness areas are Canada's cities. While these densely populated areas do have some of the country's worst pollution problems, the quality of life is still relatively good. In comparison to the cities in the United States, pollution levels and crime rates are much lower. Although cause-and-effect relationships are not clearly understood, factors which likely contribute to a higher quality of life in Canadian cities include a greater willingness to constrain development through planning, and a social support system which helps reduce poverty and thereby the pressures to seek marginal improvements by moving to major metropolitan areas. Most major Canadian cities have very large natural parks: Vancouver's Stanley Park and the Endowment Lands, Edmonton's North Saskatchewan River valley, Calgary's Fish Creek and Nose Hill parks, Toronto's Islands/Ravines and Montreal's Mount Royal. Such large natural areas within metropolitan centers are important in providing recreational opportunities for the relief of stress without the necessity of travel. They also provide essential educational opportunities.

AGENCIES FOR THE ENVIRONMENT

It was the environment movement of the late 1960s that led to the formation of government agencies and departments responsible for environmental matters. Alberta's Environment Conservation Authority (ECA) was the first such body in Canada, formed through the Environment Conservation Act 1970. The Federal Department of Environment (now Environment Canada) was established in 1971 through the Government Organization Act 1970. In the next four years all provinces passed legislation establishing departments responsible for environmental matters and most of them formed agencies responsible for public consultation. In the 1970s and 1980s, there were revisions and amendments which, with a few exceptions (notably Alberta's ECA), strengthened the legislation and regulations protecting the environment.

Four umbrella organizations provide relatively easy access to the many environmental groups in Canada. The Canadian Environmental Advisory Council is an appointed federal body which can provide contacts for the parallel advisory bodies at the provincial level. Many of the provincial organizations are either representative of the province's environmental groups or can provide contact with them. There are also organizations at the municipal level dealing with environment and health issues.

The Canadian Environmental Network (P. O. Box 1289 Station B, Ottawa, Ontario K1P 5R3), The Canadian Nature Federation (453 Sussex

Dr., Ottawa, Ontario K1N 6Z4), the Canadian Wildlife Federation (1673 Carling Ave., Ottawa, Ontario K2A 3Z1), the Canadian Arctic Resources Committee (111 Sparks Street, Ottawa, Ontario K1P 5B5) and the Canadian Environmental Law Association (234 Queen St. W., Toronto, Ontario M5V 1Z4) are good sources of information in their respective areas.

Several industry organizations deal explicitly with environmental issues or have significant environmental components to their organizations. Some of the latter include the Canadian Petroleum Association, the Coal Association, the Canadian Pulp and Paper Association, and the Canadian Chemical Producer's Association. Some of these organizations (the CPA for example) have established environmental codes of conduct for their members.

ENDANGERED SPECIES

The extermination of species is deplorable on moral and ethical grounds and because of the loss of ecological and genetic pool diversity. However, a more ominous concern is the fact that loss of species indicates a lack of control over change. Coal miners used canaries to check on air quality: the death of a bird was a warning to the miners. So the loss of species should be taken as a warning of deteriorating environmental quality.

In Canada, more than 180 species of plants or animals are now extinct, extirpated or endangered generally through hunting and/or loss of habitat. Species which are extinct largely due to hunting include the Labrador duck, great auk, passenger pigeon, plains grizzly, Dawson caribou and sea mink. Recently the white pelican has been removed from the endangered list. Programs or plans to reestablish viable populations of extirpated or endangered species include those for plains and wood buffalo, whooping crane, peregrine falcon, swift fox, sea otter, Vancouver Island marmot, and burrowing owl, among others. Reestablishment of viable populations requires the provision of habitat and food; protection from predators, hunting and disease; and a large enough gene pool that the species can thrive. Such programs demand intensive management to the point that they are much like farming. However, the objective of the programs is the establishment of a population which can survive on its own.

Zoos in Canada are playing and will continue to play a role in the survival of threatened species through participation in breeding programs which may be able to maintain an adequate gene pool until reintroduction programs can be started.

Although hunting has been a factor in endangering species in Canada, the most significant factors are now protection of habitat which is adequate for species survival and protection from pollution. This is in contrast to the larger species in Africa and Asia (elephant, rhino, large cats) and whales, all of which are threatened mainly by hunting. Canada's contributions in these areas can be through economic aid to reduce poverty-driven poaching and through support for the Convention on International Trade in Endangered Species (CITES) and other international agreements.

Both the habitat problem and the pollution problem also have international aspects for species that migrate, because air and water-borne pollu-

510

ENVIRONMENT

tants move across borders. Domestically, the protection of habitat must be provided through the system of national and provincial parks and other wilderness areas and wildlife preserves protected by legislation. Those systems are not yet extensive enough to provide the protection needed. The federal government's Environmental Assessment and Review Process, which should identify and recommend protection for important habitat threatened by large development projects, will also play a key role.

The problems with protecting species threatened by pollution go back to early identification of pesticides as a threat to North America's birds by Rachel Carson in her book *Silent Spring,* which was a key factor in starting the environment movement of the 1960s. Canada's elimination of use of some pesticides such as DDT has made a significant difference. However, DDT is still found in Canadian birds and fish because it is still being used in Mexico, Central America and Latin America. Serious pollution problems in the Great Lakes and the St. Lawrence River systems threaten wildlife, particularly such species as the beluga whales of the St. Lawrence River.

Climate change may introduce some critical factors if habitats change and wildlife are unable to move to suitable habitat because it is just not available, because they will not or cannot migrate (especially in the case of plants) or because migration corridors are not available. This may be one of the more difficult and the more unfortunate aspects of human-induced climate change. Clearly, the long-term history of species extinction due to climate change is a series of catastrophes of staggering proportions. However, if humans were to precipitate an unintended change resulting in species extinctions, it would not be justifiable by citing precedents.

Efforts to reintroduce extirpated species, to protect threatened or endangered species, and to maintain viable populations of all species must be distinguished from the radical elements of the animal rights movements, which demand protection of all members of all species through elimination of all hunting and trapping of wild animals. The successful efforts to ban the killing of baby harp seals with ongoing protests against sealing and trapping have had a devastating effect on fishing and sealing communities on Canada's east coast and on Native people in the North. These communities have maintained their lifestyle and culture and made a living from their environment on a sustainable yield basis for centuries. Their incomes have been cut by as much as 90% and their cultures put at risk because of the demands of urban dwellers, some of whom may be simply uninformed or misinformed.

Native groups in Canada (Inuit and Indian) have started a major campaign to try to offset the lobbying of animal rights and antitrapping groups. There is a very high emotional component that seems to have been accepted by governments in Europe, which have acted in response to pressure by vociferous minority groups. Interestingly, those same governments have refused to respond to Canadian government requests to cooperate in programs to protect declining commercial fishing stocks on Canada's east coast.

Canada's federal and provincial governments have displayed a similar inconsistency in their response to Native land claims. Native Canadians are a very small proportion of Canada's population and with few exceptions

511

(e.g., Vancouver) Native land claims are not being made in the populated areas. Mixed successes have been achieved in the Northwest Territories in part as a result of the Berger Commission's 1977 recommendation that economic development (a natural gas pipeline) be suspended until Native land claims were settled. The Northern Flood Agreement in Manitoba, which arose from the dispute over land claims and compensation for environmental damage caused by the flooding of Southern Indian Lake for hydroelectric development, is still under negotiation. The James Bay Agreement in northern Quebec has had Phase I completed but the lack of consensus on the adequacy of the settlement suggests that Phases II and III for expansions of the hydroelectric generation systems will be even more difficult. This is particularly the case as the skills and knowledge of Native groups and those supporting them increase.

The hunting of migratory birds and wildlife and fishing are generally permitted under regulation and with licenses outside national parks and other protected habitats. However, controversy has developed over whether or not the "farming" (private ownership and semi-domestication for commercial exploitation) of species not thought to be domesticated should be permitted. Those against the "farming" of wildlife argue that any introduction will encourage and facilitate poaching to the point where wild populations will be exterminated. They also argue that pollution of the wild gene pool will occur and that diseases will be introduced. On the other hand, proponents of wildlife "farming" (e.g. deer, elk) argue that it promotes economic development and employment, that the demand for oriental medicinal products derived from wildlife is better served by controlled production, and that poaching can be controlled. It is also argued that wildlife species may be better suited to some areas because they do less damage to habitat, soils and water bodies than domestic species such as cattle. It must also be noted that if grazing of land by cattle and sheep is the only grazing alternative, there will be demands for protection of cattle, etc. from predators, disease and parasites. Those protection programs can have very serious repercussions for wild populations.

MANAGEMENT OF THE ENVIRONMENT

During much of Canadian history, the natural environment was considered to be hostile and the "myth of infinite resources" dominated attitudes about its management. It was assumed that the land, forest and fisheries resources were so abundant that there was no need for conservation or the use of resource management practices with long-term considerations. Even with sustained public concern about environmental issues and recent government commitments to "sustainable development," renewable resource industries (fisheries, forestry and agriculture) have yet to come effectively to grips with the fact that these resources are being mined through short-sighted management practices. Although it is agreed that current practices will destroy the resource base for these industries, management systems that will ensure the economic benefits from these resources in perpetuity have yet to be implemented.

It has gradually become recognized that the mandates and resources of the established agencies responsible for environmental matters have not been sufficient to prevent the continued deterioration of environmental quality and abuse of renewable resources. Substantial improvements were made in certain areas, as shown, for example, through Environment Canada's State of the Environment Report published in 1986. However, the persistent nature of some problems (soil erosion, water pollution, hazardous wastes, endangered species, acid rain) and the recognition of pressing new issues such as global warming and concern about the ozone layer have led to the understanding that more fundamental problems had to be attacked.

Numerous federal and provincial government reports and efforts by non-governmental organizations (NGOs) and academics identified the need for sound environment and resource management. The Macdonald Commission (Royal Commission on Economic Union and Development Prospects for Canada) stated unambiguously that resource and environment issues were crucial to the long-term economic and social well-being of Canada and that environment and economic development decisions must be integrated. Canada provided extensive support for the United Nations Report of the World Commission on Environment and Development (Brundtland Commission) and followed one recommendation through the formation of the National Task Force on Environment and Economy and the subsequent establishment of "round tables" for discussions of problems and solutions for sustainable development at the federal and provincial levels. There are 13 Round Tables at the federal, provincial (10) and territorial (2) levels and some local governments are using that mechanism for dispute avoidance and resolution and for policy development. At the provincial level, most governments have started the development of comprehensive "conservation strategies." However, once again these strategies are not official policy; they are largely theoretical rather than practical documents, and they do not have timetables for implementation. In June 1989, a group of 28 environment and Native NGOs prepared a "Greenprint for Canada" which addressed the environment and resource management issues in the country and provided realistic proposals for helping to solve the problems that they had identified. In 1991 the federal government adopted Canada's Green Plan after extensive public consultation. Implementation has been impeded by budget constraints and concerns that it will slow economic growth.

CANADA's PARTICIPATION IN INTERNATIONAL EFFORTS

Canada has been involved in numerous international efforts to deal with environmental problems. Canadians played significant roles at the United Nations' Stockholm '72 and hosted "Habitat" in Vancouver in 1976. Vancouver was the site for major international environmental conferences and trade shows in March 1990 and March 1992

Canada was involved in the Law of the Sea Conference, although the government has not yet ratified that agreement; Canada also participated in the International Union for Conservation of Nature (IUCN)'s Conservation Strategy and is a signatory nation to the Convention on International

Trade in Endangered Species (CITES). The Montreal Protocol (1987) deals with the phasing out of CFCs (chloroflurocarbons), which are causing the deterioration of the ozone layer that protects all forms of life from too much damaging ultraviolet radiation. Although the protocol requires cutbacks in production of some CFCs and freezes the production levels of others, the target reductions are now under international review. Canada has announced complete elimination of controlled CFCs within the decade. Some Canadian corporations that were very large CFC users are leaders in the phaseout, which they expect to complete at the corporate level by 1994 without providing opportunities or incentives to move CFC use to other countries. The Montreal Protocol was followed by the UN General Assembly's "Malta Resolution" (January 1989) and the 24-nation Hague Declaration which formed the International Panel on Climate Change (IPCC). IPCC was jointly conceived by the World Meteorological Organization and the United Nations Environmental Program (UNEP) in response to growing demand for an effective international organ. This effort may be an outstanding example of international cooperation to fight a global problem. However, the cooperation from industry may be a result of forecasts of very large profits in the changeover as much as corporate enthusiasm for anticipating and avoiding environmental problems.

Toronto was the site of a conference on global warming that led to a 1988 agreement to have the industrialized nations reduce carbon dioxide emissions to 20% of 1988 levels by the year 2005. As the host to that conference, it would seem that Canada would have had a commitment to the results. However, federal and provincial energy officials are still meeting to discuss the practicality of such a reduction. It may be that government and corporate willingness to implement effective strategies to meet the Toronto target on carbon dioxide will be much less than that for reduction and elimination of CFCs. However, most of the world's leading climatologists now agree that the greenhouse effect is a sound theory and that prudent preventive measures are warranted. As the impacts of climate change become better understood, it is very likely that the targets for reduction of greenhouse gases will be increased and the rate of implementation will be increased. The major effects of climate change will be on renewable resources (agriculture, forestry, fisheries, wildlife and water resources) and indirectly from "environmental refugees" who are forced to move by the impacts of climate change, particularly the increase in sea levels.

Canada is also party to international protocols and agreements on sulfur dioxide (acid rain, in the Helsinki Protocol). Canada's action in this area places emphasis on reductions of sulfur dioxide emissions in the seven eastern provinces, and places a permanent national cap on total sulfur dioxide emissions by the year 2000.

The Sofia Protocol (1987) is an international agreement to hold emissions of oxides of nitrogen to 1987 levels. The Canadian Council of Ministers of the Environment produced a management plan for nitrogen oxides and volatile organic compounds in November 1990.

Canada was one of 105 countries that supported the March 1989 Basel Convention to regulate movement of hazardous wastes. Although now one of 37 nations to that have signed the UN Global Convention on the Control of Transboundary Movement of Hazardous Wastes, Canada has not yet ratified the agreement, probably because of concerns about how it would affect established patterns of movement of hazardous wastes between Canada and the United States. These problems are being addressed at the federal and provincial levels separately and in a coordinated fashion through the Canadian Council of Ministers of the Environment (CCME). In the August 1989 First Ministers Meeting (attended by the prime minister and provincial premiers), there was considerable provincial pressure for Canada to increase air quality controls to match those of California, which are the most stringent. This would follow the American lead toward using the California standard as a national one and may be the beginning of the setting of uniform standards north of the Rio Grande. It would be in line with the agreement between Canada and the United States on air quality, signed in March 1991. The normal mechanism for handling transboundary air and water pollution problems is the 1909 Transboundary Agreement, which was used to settle American claims for sulfur dioxide damage from smelters in British Columbia but which was specifically excluded from handling the more recent acid rain dispute in eastern Canada.

PUBLIC OPINION

Recent political and public opinion polls in Canada have shown that although environmental issues have been relatively high on the list of concerns of Canadians for the last couple of decades, it is now the top priority of about one-third of Canadians and 90–100% have heard about the issue and think that it is serious. A survey conducted in mid-1989 indicated that 60% or more of those surveyed would use unbleached paper, would pay 50% more for garbage collection, and would pay 10% more for safe packaging, 5 cents per liter more for gasoline, $1,000 more for a fuel-efficient car, $250 per year more for sewage treatment, and a 10% tax on energy. Some 71% would seriously consider a "green" political party, but only 27% were activists or enthusiastic supporters while 39% were apathetic, fatalistic or hostile. The remaining 35% were optimists or anxious but unable to involve themselves.

These political opinions are reflected in more and more political support for solving environmental problems. However, costs are a factor that keeps political support from becoming political action. One expert estimated in 1989 that the cost of a major effort to solve environmental problems would be $1,400 per household (in 1989 dollars), of which $575 per household would be spent by provincial and municipal governments mostly for water and sewage systems and waste disposal. A review of Great Lakes pollution problems has suggested that the total cost of Great Lakes cleanup will be more than $10 billion. However, these cost calculations have not included the cost of not doing the necessary cleanups, nor have the benefits to be derived been calculated. Calculations in the former German Democratic Republic estimated that 6–8% of the gross domestic product was lost as the result of environmental damage. If this were the same in Canada, environmental damage would be costing $33–44 billion per year.

Strong public opinion is reflected in some consumer action, much tougher legislation and enforcement with heavy fines and jail sentences. There have been changes in the values of corporate executives and employees. Some of the largest changes have been made by companies that were formerly among those with the worst track records for pollution and poor resource management.

A limited review of 1987 corporate annual reports noted that 13% had a specific section on environmental matters and 24% mentioned the issue. There are still corporations and executives who view environmental constraints as totally unnecessary inhibition of the god-given rights of free enterprise. However, those who have recognized the need for changes have done some or all of the following: placed sound environment and resource management as one of the corporate goals and/or as part of the corporate philosophy; combined health, safety and environment into one corporate unit; raised the executive responsible for health, safety and environment to vice president level; introduced annual, internal audits of corporate performance on environmental issues; introduced "green," environmentally friendly products; and made sincere efforts to consult with the public and public interest groups that might be affected by corporate activity.

A relatively small oil spill at Chadebucto Bay on Canada's east coast was studied thoroughly in 1971 and detailed recommendations were made for prevention of and response to oil spills. Almost 20 years later such spills still occur. One spill off the State of Washington in December 1988 hit the west coast of Vancouver Island, and federal government estimates of Canada's cleanup costs were $4.5–5 million. Again, these calculations do not account for losses due to the spill. The cleanup costs of one small spill would cover a very significant prevention and response program.

The spectacular nature of some environmental problems (the Exxon Valdez oil spill, for example) and the seriousness of the consequences of some pollutants (such as irreversible health effects) have led to what is probably a cycle of increased media attention and increasing public knowledge and concern. High-profile personalities such as David Suzuki now have large audiences for programs on television ("A Planet for the Taking") and radio ("It's a Matter of Survival"). Canadian newspapers contain articles on environmental issues daily and feature major "specials" and series. The major business publications (*Canadian Business, The Globe and Mail Report on Business Magazine, Financial Post*) have all featured significant articles on the environment, something which was almost unheard of only a few years ago.

STANDARDS

The question of standards in North America has been raised with respect to the Free Trade Agreement between Canada and the United States and was a major issue in the negotiations for the North American Free Trade

Agreement between Canada, the United States and Mexico. Although the FTA protects the right of the two countries to pass legislation protecting health, safety and the environment, it is missing a vital component, which would be a stipulation that any pressure for change in health, safety and environmental legislation would be toward the highest common denominator. Unfortunately, indications are that there will be corporate pressures to push such legislation and regulation toward the lowest common denominator. A very modest amendment to the agreement during any further negotiations could ensure that the changes under free trade are clearly in line with the expressed desire of both governments for greatly improved environmental quality. The environment is now on the table in the three-country negotiations to bring Mexico into the free trade agreement.

At the federal level, the first new piece of federal environmental legislation in over a decade was passed in 1988. The new legislation consolidates earlier pieces of legislation, provides heavy fines and jail sentences for violations, and moves to provide for control of hazardous substances. A 1989 court case on the Rafferty Alameda Dam in Saskatchewan ruled that the federal government was obliged in all cases of such projects to apply the Environmental Assessment and Review Process to ensure that to the extent possible, environmental problems are identified and managed. This is a very significant change which removes ministerial discretion in deciding whether to carry out a formal assessment and review of projects within federal jurisdication, involving federal land or financing, or involving other provinces or countries. The Canadian International Development Agency has decided to apply such standards to all of Canada's international aid projects, but the details of the implementation remain to be worked out. Further significant changes to the legislation governing the Environmental Assessment and Review Process are expected, although opposition within cabinet and government departments may cause delays and weakening of the proposed changes.

HAZARDOUS WASTE

In March 1989, Canada was one of 37 nations to sign the UN Global Convention on the Control of Transboundary Movement of Hazardous Wastes. Although wastes have moved between Canada and the United States for some time, recent concerns about fuels deliberately contaminated with polychlorinated biphenyls (PCBs) being shipped into Canada and PCB wastes being returned from the United Kingdom to Canada will likely further reduce the international movement of hazardous wastes.

The problems of storing, transporting and disposing of hazardous wastes has become increasingly focused through a series of unfortunate incidents. A PCB spill on the Trans-Canada Highway in Ontario in April 1985, the PCB-contaminated fuel imports of 1988–89, the closure of fisheries on the west coast due to dioxin contamination from pulp mill wastes, and the St. Basile-le-Grand fire and the return trip of the PCB wastes to the United Kingdom in 1988–89 have raised public concern and political awareness. There are waste sites all over Canada, including military sites in the Arctic.

The more industrialized provinces (Ontario and Quebec) have large volumes of hazardous wastes stored throughout their territory. However, neither province has been successful in selecting a site and building a disposal facility. This is in spite of a decade of work on the problem in Ontario. Alberta has been operating a Special Waste Treatment Facility at Swan Hills which received its full operating license in November 1988. It is the only such facility in Canada.

A very important environmental concern about waste disposal centers around the storage of nuclear wastes. AECL (Atomic Energy Canada Limited) is involved in the promotion and regulation of the nuclear energy industry (and other applications) in Canada. There is an ongoing and acrimonious debate about how nuclear wastes should be handled in Canada, if indeed the generation of such wastes should continue at all. Of course, even if the answer to the last question were no, existing wastes would have to be dealt with.

Under the new Canada Environmental Protection Act, there are 44 classes of chemicals on the priority substances list for stringent control. (This is compared with more than 300 in the United States). Two significant problems emerge here: one is scientific and economic, the other is political and perceptual. The scientific and economic problem is the time and cost and difficulty of proving that a chemical is hazardous. One way around the public cost and the delays is to move to systems more like that for food and drug legislation and demand "reverse onus." That is, use and release of chemicals would only be permitted after they had been shown to meet established standards for health, safety and the environment. The political and perceptual problem arises from the crisis-management nature of current political systems, in which issues have to be perceived as extremely serious before any action will be or can be taken. Under these conditions, for example, public fears have arisen nearly to the point of hysteria in some cases over chemicals such as PCBs. PCBs are in fact a health and environment concern, but their threat has been exaggerated.

Environmental and health concerns have led to limitations on or the banning of the use and/or the manufacture of at least nine chemicals or substances in Canada: non-biodegradable detergents, phosphates in detergent formulations, mercury in fungicides and industrial applications, lead in gasoline, PCBs, asbestos, UFFI (ureaformaldehyde foam insulation), insecticides such as DDT, and CFCs (chlorofluorocarbons). It is expected that that list will grow and that chemical producers and manufacturers will have to be increasingly aware of such constraints in the future to avoid serious economic difficulties.

In the workplace, the Workplace Hazardous Materials Information System (WHMIS) has been introduced to provide employees with Material Safety Data Sheets (MSDS) on all the substances they work with. Protection for the environment could be provided by establishing Zero Discharge as a long-term goal for Persistent Toxic Substances (PTS). Persistent toxic substances are those chemicals which are toxic and do not decompose, or decompose very slowly, in the natural environment. Zero discharge means stopping total release of PTSs to the environment by eliminating PTSs in wastes and in products.

SOLID WASTE

Crude statistics suggest that Canadians generate about 4.5 pounds of solid waste per person per day. This is second only to the United States. Moreover, only 2 to 3% of post-consumer waste (not waste generated within industry) is recycled. In 1989, the minister of the environment promised a 50% reduction in garbage generated, presumably to be achieved by reducing the waste generated and by recycling. This very high level of waste has been established because of relative affluence and high wages which make low-value, labor-intensive processes prohibitively expensive; low population densities and long distances between centers where waste is generated; low waste disposal costs, very cheap raw materials and the myth of infinite resources, which suggested there was no need for conservation; and an economy that is supported by government policies and strategies that emphasized exploitation of natural resources over anything else.

The lack of well-established recycling industries and markets for recyled materials prevents much of the public from acting on their declared willingness to reduce waste through recycling. In fact, with recycling, not only would the solid waste problem be reduced, but the energy demands and environmental damage of producing the raw material in the first place would be saved.

In Canada, municipal solid waste is 30–40% paper, 6–7% each of metals, plastics and glass, 20–30% food wastes and wastes that could be composted, and 10–15% wood, textiles and other wastes. The composition varies with the season.

Paper recycling is limited in all provinces. This could be changed by adding the stipulation, in licensing Canada's very large pulp and paper industry, that each company assist with recycling as a condition for exploiting the forest resources and the air and water resources associated with their historically very dirty industry. Some provinces, such as Alberta, require deposits on all metal, plastic and glass beverage containers, while others require it for only some containers. Canadians generate an estimated 300 million liters of waste motor oil (eight times the Exxon Valdez spill), but only limited quantities are recycled. Changes in demand for metals through more use of plastics in cars, and fiber optics for communications, have changed the metal recycling industry. Steel production technologies have been improved, but the demand for scrap iron and steel has been reduced as a result. The recycling of plastics remains a difficulty because there are so many different polymers used in plastics; they are difficult to distinguish, and plastics can only be used as recycled mixtures in a very limited number of ways.

Numerous studies have identified the loss of organic matter in soils as an increasingly serious problem for agriculture in Canada. Unfortunately, this problem has yet to be linked to the large volume of compostable wastes creating economic and environmental problems for many municipalities. Clearly, because the Canadian winter is so harsh, composting cannot be a straightforward, year-round operation, but it is another area in which changes can be expected.

RESOURCES

The myth of infinite spaces and limitless resources has, until recently, so dominated Canadian thinking that protection of the environment and conservation of renewable and nonrenewable resources was difficult. Water is an excellent example of this type of persistent fallacy, in which various authors have suggested that Canada has one-fifth of the earth's fresh water without providing any basis for that statistic. In fact, to the extent that averages mean anything, Canada has only slightly more than the world average of fresh water flows per unit of surface area: both the United States and the Soviet Union, for example, are "wetter." The average does not mean much without consideration of distribution. Just as average income does not mean much to those below the poverty line, average flows do not mean much to those in dry areas. The value of irrigation is very well established in the four western provinces, where the renewable nature of the resource and the existence of very large supplies in other parts of the country have not been of much use in extending the supply of the limited resource. Many water resource management problems stem from the fact that water has always been treated as a free good. Complete cost recovery for delivery systems, and charge for effluent disposal within pollution control regulations (not a license to pollute) would go a good deal of the way to solving water management problems and can be expected in the short to medium term.

Pollution remains an issue in many watersheds because of the well-established principle and practice of using the "assimilative capacity" for waste of bodies of water as a resource to be exploited. Because such capacity is difficult to assess, varies with conditions, time of day and season, and volume of flow, and is generally very poorly managed, pollution problems persist.

Furthermore, water pollution cannot be completely controlled until air quality is managed effectively. This is particularly the case with acid rain; air pollution controls are essential to reverse the very serious effects of sulfur dioxide in areas where soils, water and vegetation are sensitive. Some water pollution problems have certainly been reduced over the past two decades. Heavy metals such as mercury and lead have steadily decreased in water supplies throughout the country. Although problems remain, rivers (the North and South Saskatchewan and the Ottawa, for example) and lakes (such as Lake Erie) have seen definite improvements.

Multiple use of resources such as air, water and forests is discussed a good deal in the literature and by governments. However, because these resources are largely undervalued, and because there are no effective and binding mechanisms for resolutions of disputes between users, established practices of misuse and single-purpose use persist. This has been the case in areas where water resources have been dedicated to hydroelectricity generation or irrigation. In these industries, construction of reservoirs, diversions and delivery systems have been increasingly subjected to formal Environmental Impact Assessments. But other uses, particularly instream uses such as recreation, fish, wildlife, waterfowl and esthetics, often cannot compete.

With notable and regrettable exceptions, Canada is fortunate in having water and sewer services in almost all urban areas. However, the low cost of the supply and waste disposal and the political popularity of postponing unpopular taxes and service charges has led to two major problems. Canadians are very heavy water users: gross statistics suggest 120 gallons per person per day. Modest efforts at conservation could easily cut this by 20–25%. Not only would there be a savings in capital expenditures for water and waste water treatment systems, but operating costs would be reduced. The second problem is that of capital replacements of aging systems, where it is estimated that Canadians face $7 billion for costs in repairs and upgrading.

The mining, mineral processing and smelting industry has been an important contributor to the Canadian economy but at heavy cost to the environment. Lead, zinc, copper and nickel have contributed to acid rain and other water and air pollution problems. Gold mining and refining has contributed to very severe water pollution problems and to the devastation of watersheds through placer mining. Uranium use is characterized by all the problems associated with exposure of workers and radioactive wastes. Aluminium is produced at the cost of air pollution and the destruction of natural environments because of the high demands for cheap hydroelectric power.

Renewable resource-based industries (agriculture, forestry, fishing, tourism and hunting and trapping) are very important to the Canadian economy but face severe problems. Agriculture, forestry and fishing are suffering because of long-standing practices and policies that are based upon emphasizing short-term returns at the cost of long-term stability based upon sustainable yield. Canadian agriculture faces soil degradation, loss of high-quality land to other uses, and demands for constraints on chemical pesticides and fertilizers because of real and imagined health problems. Canadian forestry has been managed like a nonrenewable mining operation; about 25% of the area cut has been reforested. Basically all of the Atlantic hardwood forests are gone, and 90% of the southwestern Ontario resource, which are or were extremely high-value products, has been cut. Two-thirds of the west coast temperate rain forest has been cut, and much of what remains is difficult to access or is under demands for preservation or dedication to other uses or users.

Although the forest industry now claims that reforestation has been increased to cover almost half the cut area, the industry and the unions it supports have not gained any credibility with critics, who have good evidence that short-term planning has always dominated forest management.

The forest industry's adverse impacts on tourism and recreation, wildlife and water quality are that much more deplorable because they are largely avoidable.

Forest management is a major concern at the international level. Canadian critics of current management of tropical rain forests will suffer the same kind of credibility problems that the Canadian forest industry suffers until Canada itself establishes sound practices. But the international environmental critics cannot expect to receive a hearing with simplistic demands to stop clearing the forests or to stop logging. Developing countries should expect a contribution from Canada in terms of sound forest management, which can make a contribution to the pressing problems of poverty, debt load and the demands for economic development.

Canada's freshwater and saltwater fisheries are in decline from coast to coast to coast. Pollution, destruction of spawning routes or habitat, and overfishing are the problems to be solved to set Canada's oldest export industry on a sustainable basis.

Renewable and nonrenewable energy resources are being placed under more and more pressure to reduce environmental impact whether it be the coal-fired electricity sector (acid rain), hydroelectric generation and conflicts with other users or the oil industry from exploration to consumer products. For all the above there should be complete environmental impact assessments for all new projects. The Canadian Petroleum Association, the Canadian Coal Association and many of the electricity utilities are working hard on environmental problems, although there is still ample ground for criticism. The federal government is still presenting very mixed messages. It has stated the goal of reducing carbon dioxide emissions by 20%, yet in 1989 almost all federal programs for development and promotion of renewable energy systems were eliminated. With no action on renewable energy and energy conservation, Canada can expect a 25%–50% increase in carbon dioxide emissions, whereas modest action would cause a 20% decrease and concerted efforts a 30%–50% decrease or more.

Recreation and tourism are important factors in management of the environment because they are often part of multiple-use conflicts, because some forms of recreation that do not rely on gasoline or gunpowder generally generate considerable health benefits, and because outdoor recreation often creates in the user/doer an understanding of the environment and a willingness to provide support for its protection.

Population size and growth rates are very significant environmental concerns in much of the world. With a population of approximately 27 million and a birthrate less than needed for replacement, Canada is relatively well off. However, Canada's 3.9 million square miles of surface area and large open spaces exacerbate the problem of the myth of limitless resources and lead to recommendations for a much larger population through increasing the birth rate (especially among minorities) and increasing immigration. Those policies must be understood in light of the fact that Canada's climate and land characteristics dictate that most of its vast land is not easily inhabitable. Only 13% is suitable for agriculture; only 7% is arable, and 6% is only good for grazing. Canada has 33% as much agricultural land as

India, or 16% as much as the United States. Therefore the land must be used wisely if it is to support its future human and wildlife populations well.

FURTHER READING

Bankes, N., and J. O. Saunders. *Public Disposition of Natural Resources.* Calgary: Canadian Institute of Resources Law, 1984.

Bird, Peter M., and David J. Rapport. *State of the Environment Report for Canada.* Ottawa: Supply and Services Canada, 1986.

Brown, Lester R., et al. *State of the World 1991.* Cambridge, Mass.: Norton, 1991.

Canada. Senate. *Soil at Risk: Canada's Eroding Future.* Ottawa, 1984.

Carson, Patrick, and Julia Moulden. *Green is Gold: Business Talking to Business about the Environmental Revolution.* Toronto: Harper, 1991.

Dorcey, Anthony H. J., ed. *Perspectives on Sustainable Development in Water Management.* Vancouver: Westwater Research Centre, 1991.

Environment Canada. *Canada's Green Plan.* Ottawa: Supply and Services Canada, 1990.

Goudie, Andrew. *The Human Impact on the Natural Environment.* Cambridge, Mass.: MIT Press, 1990.

Healey, M. C., and R. R. Wallace, eds. *Canadian Aquatic Resources.* Ottawa: Fisheries and Oceans Canada, 1987.

Hummel, Monte, ed. *Endangered Spaces.* Toronto: Key Porter Books, 1989.

Lilley, J., and Calvin Webb. *Climate Warming? Exploring the Answers.* Edmonton: Environment Council of Alberta, 1990.

MacNeill, Jim, John Cox, and David Runnalls. *CIDA and Sustainable Development.* Halifax: Institute for Research on Public Policy, 1989.

Mungall, Constance, and Digby McLaren. *Planet Under Stress.* Don Mitls, Ontario: Oxford University Press, 1990.

Sanderson, K. *Acid-Forming Emissions: Transportation and Effects.* Edmonton: Environment Council of Alberta, 1984.

The World Commission on Environment and Development. *Our Common Future.* Oxford: Oxford University Press, 1987.

IMMIGRATION AND MULTICULTURALISM

HAROLD TROPER

An immigration debate is going on in Canada today. It is an important debate, but it is also muted and potentially divisive. Many argue that Canada, with its falling birthrate and aging population, will need to increase immigration to ensure a work force and tax base necessary to support projected expenditures. But, where will these new immigrants come from? If the recent past is any guide, the majority will be from the Third World. Accordingly, any discussion of increases in immigration is bound to ignite discussion of Canada's "absorptive capacity." But race and ethnicity are not the only issues shaping Canadian immigration. Since World War II, Canadian immigration policy, legislation and regulation have also reflected Canada's changing profile in the international community, pressures from organized business and ethnic lobbies, and humanitarian considerations.

This is little different from the experience of other western immigration-receiving nations, including the United States. But Canada is not the United States. Canada's international position and commitments are different. Canada, for example, neither has a common border with a Third World country nor has been direct party to American adventures in Cuba, Chile, Vietnam, El Salvador or Panama. Accordingly, Canada's reference points, when it came to admission of immigrants or refugees from these countries, have been very different from those of the United States.

Furthermore, there are unique facts of Canadian life which distinguish Canadian immigration experience. Not least of these differences is the fact of the United States itself. Canadian immigration policy always had to take the imposing American reality into account. Whether Canadians like it or not, Canadian immigration is forever riding the roller coaster of American economic fluctuations. The same can hardly be said in reverse.

The United States has also been a magnet to the world, passively drawing immigrants to its shores. Not so Canada. For many, Canada has been less a land of second chance than a land of second choice. Since World War II, indeed since the turn of the century, Canada has repeatedly intervened to direct the immigration flow, sometimes beating the bushes for immigrants it wanted. Canada's main competition was the lure of the United

524

States. Oddly, the drawing power of the United States sometimes worked in Canada's favor. When the American front door was locked, many saw Canada as a back door. Once in Canada, many of those who previously thought of Canada as the American doormat, instead took a look around and decided to stay.

Canadian postwar immigration experience was also shaped by distinctively domestic factors. Unlike American states, for example, Canadian provinces share jurisdiction for immigration with the federal government. The degree to which any one province choses to exercise that jurisdiction has varied from province to province and period to period. But, provincial concerns do influence immigration policy, sometimes directly and always indirectly.

Moreover, Canadian immigration law has traditionally left greater discretionary power in the hands of the minister responsible for immigration and his public servants than is true of the United States. The reach of this power is dramatic. In a majority government, the minister and his officials have been able to turn policy on its head without enacting new immigration legislation.

POSTWAR IMMIGRATION

Canada's postwar immigration policy did not arise, phoenixlike, out of the ashes of battle. It was rooted in an immigration policy reaching back before the war. Canada emerged from World War II a modern industrial power. But when it declared war on Nazi Germany in September 1939, Canada was in the depths of depression. With the collapse of the Canadian labor market, immigration into Canada had been closed to all but British and American nationals. This immigration restrictionism was not new. In the mid-1920s, after several decades of courting immigrants from Central Europe and Eastern Europe to farm the vast expanse of the Canadian prairies and work in Canada's extractive industries, the demand for labor had gradually eased and anti-foreign sentiment had grown rife. Immigration officials had responded with new draconian regulations which, without changing immigration legislation, had effectively closed Canada's doors to all but a very select group of would-be immigrants. The Chinese and other Asians had long been prohibited entry to Canada. To this list was now added most Eastern Europeans and Southern Europeans and all Jews, except those from the United States and Britain. During the depression, regulations were tightened still further. Indeed, restrictions were so tight that Canada remained virtually impervious to the victims of Nazism. In the end, Canada had arguably the worst record of all western nations in accepting prewar and wartime refugees.

In the immediate postwar period, immigration legislation and restrictive immigration regulations remained intact from the prewar period. What is more, immigration personnel who had cut their teeth in the era of immigration restriction remained in charge of the immigration department. Government policy planners of the day would not have it any other way. Inasmuch as postwar policy planning had taken immigration into account, which was not much, it was regarded as something to be avoided. Immigration meant imported laborers, and laborers were not wanted. Many feared that the end of massive government expenditures on the war effort would mean a sharp downturn in the Canadian economy. This, officials recalled, was exactly what had happened after World War I. In this atmosphere of apprehension, the idea of renewed immigration was unthinkable.

But the two postwar eras were not parallel. After a lumbering start, the post-World War II Canadian economy did not slide back into depression. In fact, the opposite happened. With exports leading the way, the Canadian economy surged ahead. Demand for Canadian raw materials and manufactured goods was strong in Britain and war-ravaged Europe. Demand became almost insatiable as the Marshall Plan spent millions of dollars to prop up the economic infrastructure of a non-communist Europe. Nor was the export market the only area of Canadian economic strength. Many Canadians had done well during the war, although forced savings plans and shortages of consumer products had kept a lid on spending. Now, in the postwar period, delayed gratification was cast aside. An orgy of consumer spending stoked the fire of economic growth. The problem was a shortage of goods, not of money.

By late 1946, labor-intensive industries, especially in the core economic sectors of agriculture, mining and lumbering, began to press government for a relaxation of restrictive barriers against imported immigrant labor. Canadians remained cautious. Would the economic recovery stand the test of time? Many had their doubts. For their part, immigration officials dug in their heels against any wholesale importation of immigrants. This was especially true when it came to those in camps for displaced persons from Germany and Austria. The camps were filled with many of the very Central European and Eastern European groups against which immigration barriers had been imposed in the first place. If the Canadian public might be sold on the economic benefits of renewed immigration, they were certainly hesitant about allowing in those who stood first in line to get out of postwar Europe: Slavs and Jews.

But unrelenting pressure from the business lobby demanding to bring labor to capital could not be denied. In the spring of 1947, the Canadian prime minister, Mackenzie King, informed the parliament of his government's decision to reopen Canada's door to immigration. But his was far from unqualified support. The purpose of Canada's immigration policy, he declared, must be to "enlarge the population of the country. It would be dangerous for a small population to attempt to hold so great a heritage as ours." But there must also be limits as to how wide to cast the immigration net. He cautioned that "it is of the utmost importance to relate immigration to absorptive capacity." And, in his mind, Canada's capacity to absorb immigrants was tied not so much to the number of immigrants as to their ethnic or racial origins. The prime minister was only reflecting the national mood when he observed that "the people of Canada do not wish to make a fundamental alteration in the character of their population through mass immigration." Discrimination and ethnic selectivity in immigration would remain. "It is not a 'fundamental human right' of any alien to enter

Canada. It is a privilege. It is a matter of domestic policy." There would be no lifting of restrictions against Asian immigration. Furthermore, care would be taken to ensure that immigration preference be given to applicants from groups which, in the past, had proven best able to assimilate into the existing Canadian society. In so many ways, the government's reopening of the door to immigration in late 1947 was less a giant leap forward than it was a throwback to the policy, regulations and racial priorities of an earlier era.

Yet, this inauspicious beginning precipitated almost revolutionary change in the Canadian community. In the 40 years since the genie of renewed immigration was let out of the government's bottle, the character of Canada's population has been transformed. Canada's population doubled from under 13 million at the war's end to 27 million by the early 1990s. Immigrants and their children account for much of that growth. Just as crucial, the ethnocultural composition of Canada's population has been recast. The proportion of Canadians not of British or French origin—that is, not descended from the two Canadian founding or charter groups—has increased dramatically, although the impact has been felt most in large Canadian urban centers.

Had the larger postwar civic culture known this would be the long-term result of short-term immigration initiatives, it is doubtful they would have so readily consented to re-open Canada to immigration in 1947, even on a limited and ethnically selective scale. But none could foresee the future and, more important, there were immediate problems of labor shortage that demanded solution. Thus, with less enthusiasm than determination to make the most of what all hoped would be a new era of economic prosperity, Canada re-opened its door to immigrant labor.

First priority was given those immigrants believed to be most adaptable to the Canadian "way of life." To this end, British, Americans and Northern Europeans were actively courted. Ontario was so concerned to get the type of immigrant it wanted that it flexed its jurisdictional muscle in immigration matters and inaugurated a highly publicized airlift of British settlers into the province. When British currency regulations threatened to choke off the flow of cash-starved prospective immigrants, the Canadian government negotiated special low air and ship passenger rates to stimulate the outflow. Similar currency regulations also hindered the ability of other "desirable" Western European groups to emigrate, particularly the Dutch. Again the Canadian government intervened. In 1948 a three-year bilateral agreement was signed with the Netherlands to ensure the orderly transplant of approximately 15,000 Dutch farmers and farm workers to Canada.

Labor-intensive industry was less concerned with the ethnicity of workers than with their numbers. Business interests demanded that government syphon off the best available labor from the displaced persons camps of Europe. Responding to this pressure, immigration officials reluctantly began to process the applications of displaced persons, while carefully monitoring the public mood for any negative reaction.

The arrival of displaced persons did not signal any liberalization in ethnic selectivity. There can be little doubt but that if there had been no labor shortages, few displaced persons would have been welcome to enter Canada. Enlightened self-interest had its ethnic limits. To ensure that those entering Canada did not tilt the ethnic balance in a way the government and public did not want, priority was given to Northern European refugees, in this case those from the Baltic republics, rather than to Jewish and Slavic refugees.

Unfortunately for government planners, the demand for labor was greater than could be met by those British or Northern European settlers ready to relocate to Canada. Nor was Canada the only game in town. As opportunities to migrate to the United States, Australia or elsewhere in the west opened up, Canadian immigration and labor officials suddenly found themselves fighting for their share of a shrinking labor pool. As a result, those previously seen as less desirable notched up the ladder of preference. In the face of continuing labor shortages, the door slowly swung open to Jews and Slavic immigrants, especially those with skills demanded by labor-starved industries or those willing to work in jobs that native-born Canadians rejected. By the time the displaced person admission program ended in 1948, tens of thousands had entered Canada and the routine processing of immigration from Europe was running smoothly. Reflecting the priority now accorded immigration, in 1950 the Immigration Branch of the Department of Mines and Resources, which had previously administered immigration policy, was integrated into a new Department of Citizenship and Immigration. The old guard was eased out and a new staff was introduced.

Before long, senior officials in the new department brought forward the draft of a new immigration act. The resulting Immigration Act of 1952 was designed to attract a continuing selective stream of immigrants under the general terms outlined by the prime minister in his 1947 policy statement. In keeping with a long-standing practice, the act allowed the minister of immigration and his officials wide discretionary powers which could open and close the door against virtually any group or individual. Although this "tap on, tap off" legislation was couched in the rhetoric of liberalism demanded of a signatory to the United Nations Charter, it was far less yielding of matters of race and ethnicity than advocates of a more progressive immigration policy might have hoped. At the discretion of the minister, individuals or groups might be rejected on account of nationality, geographic origin, peculiarity of custom, unsuitability of climate and the omnibus provision that any individual or group demonstrated an inability "to become assimilated."

Furthermore, in keeping with the cold war climate of the day, strict security checks were required of would-be immigrants. Security personnel acted much like a separate estate, accountable only to themselves and virtually immune to criticism. No credible mechanism for appeal was allowed those barred on security grounds. Rumor held that the security service was almost as concerned with race and ethnic selectivity as it was with security. But it was the threat from would-be immigrants tainted by any hint of left-wing political connections that preoccupied security personnel. In their zeal to guard against the left, however, they too often ignored if not abetted the admission of some whose World War II records should have set off alarms in Ottawa, but did not. Whatever these Nazis or Nazi collaborators might have done in the past, in the eyes of Canadian security authorities they were free of communism and many had proven records as anti-communists.

IMMIGRATION IN THE 1950S AND 1960S

Through the 1950s, the racial fears that underscored Canadian immigration policy gradually gave way. In a symbolic break with the past, and with an eye to the potential importance of newly independent Third World countries, both as possible trading partners and at the United Nations, where Canada was playing a high-profile role, in 1951 Canada introduced small but nonetheless important immigrant quotas for its non-white Asian Commonwealth partners, India, Pakistan and Ceylon (Sri Lanka). If the actual numbers of South Asian immigrants who entered Canada was small, the fact that the government approved a program for the admission of "visible minority" immigrants cannot be minimized. In the main, however, the government's attitude on race and ethnicity remained cautious.

Through the 1950s, officials predicated their planning on gradually reduced Canadian labor needs and on the continued inflow of settlers from Northern Europe. Both of these assumptions proved wrong. As prosperity returned to Northern and Western Europe in the 1950s, the number of persons seeking to emigrate declined. All the while, Canadian demand for labor remained strong. Labor-intensive industries clamored ever louder for more manpower and warned that continued prosperity hinged on immigration. But where would immigrants come from? The displaced person camps were emptied of desirable labor, Eastern Europe closed its borders to emigration and Western Europeans were arriving in smaller numbers. As a result, business interests began to eye the available pool of labor in Southern Europe and Italy in particular. After some initial resistance, the government responded. At first hoping to restrict intake to the more "Germanic" northern Italian, the government opened immigration offices. While security personnel warned against the strength of the Italian Communist Party and the potential for infiltration by subversives—a warning security personnel attached to virtually any new government immigration initiative—the flow of Italian immigrant labor to urban Canada began. In short order, the number of southern Italians arriving in Canada climbed into the hundreds of thousands. By the mid-1960s, in the industrial heartland of southern Ontario and urban Canada more generally, Italian labor became to the construction industry what an earlier generation of Jews had been to the needle trades and Ukrainians to the breaking of the prairie sod.

In 1956 the government immigration program faced a new challenge, this time as a result of the Hungarian uprising. The Soviet suppression of the Hungarian revolt set off a rush of refugees westward into Austria. This first major refugee crisis of the cold war era came at a fortuitous moment for Canada. Its economy was buoyant and the country was generally aroused in sympathy for the Hungarian "freedom fighters." But Canadian authorities remained uneasy. Again security personnel advised caution. They warned that the Soviets might use this refugee movement to smuggle subversives into unsuspecting western countries. The government, however, proved less concerned with spies than with the price of generosity.

As the government dickered over costs, the media and the general public were swept up in sympathy for the Hungarian refugees. Voluntary agencies pledged to pick up much of the cost of refugee resettlement, and both liberal and conservative media castigated officials for their fumbling of the Hungarian refugee issue. The government finally moved; and, like a freight train building up a head of steam, once the government got going, it swept every barrier out of its path. Setting aside the warnings of security personnel, the minister of immigration rushed off to Vienna, where the Hungarians were regrouping. He was followed by immigration teams mandated to skim the cream off the top of the refugee pool as quickly as possible.

The Hungarian refugee resettlement program was a success. However, it must be seen not as a product of routine Canadian immigration procedures but as an exception to them. Normal procedures, including medical and security clearances, were set aside or deferred until after arrival in Canada. In short order almost 37,000 Hungarians were relocated to Canada, most to urban Canada—which was, by the mid-1950s, home to most new immigrants. Canada did well by doing good.

In the early 1960s, the Canadian labor market began to shrink. Active immigrant recruitment was curtailed and many in Europe, without the resources necessary to finance a new beginning abroad, put aside plans of leaving for Canada. But even as active immigration work was scaled down and new arrivals fell by 50%, one major change was made in Canadian immigration policy. In 1962, largely as a spillover from federal and provincial human rights initiatives and the continually expanding Canadian presence on the international stage, racial and ethnic discrimination in the processing of independent immigrants was officially ended. Ethnic discrimination remained in effect in the case of family reunification, largely out of fear that any liberalization would open the door to a rapid growth in the small Chinese and South Asian communities in Canada. But, henceforth, all independent applicants were to be judged on the basis of individual skills or, more correctly, Canadian market needs.

The Issue of Discrimination
This, of course, did not eliminate administrative priorities that could result in de facto discrimination. For example, the resources of the immigration bureaucracy were concentrated in areas of traditional immigrant preference: the United Kingdom, the United States and Western Europe. By contrast, few on-site immigration services were available to the Third World. In 1960, Canada maintained 27 immigration offices outside of North America. Twenty-four were in Europe, two were in Asia and one was in Israel. There were no offices in Africa or South America. Thus, removal of discrimination from immigration required more than expunging of racism from the legislation and admission criteria. But the importance of officially striking overt racial discrimination from Canadian immigration regulations cannot be denied. And if these changes did not come soon enough or go far

enough to satisfy many of the government's critics, change did follow. A Canadian office was opened in Egypt in 1963; in 1967 in Japan; and in 1968 in Lebanon, the Philippines, the West Indies and Pakistan. The racial composition of Canadian immigration was about to change.

In 1964, with the economy still in a slump and immigration numbers leveled off, administrative responsibility for immigration was again transferred, this time to a newly established Department of Manpower and Immigration. The government's underlying intent was clear. Whatever the social impact of immigration on Canadian society, a first priority of policy planning and administration remained to dovetail immigration to short-term national employment priorities.

With the economy in the doldrums, one of the problems confronting immigration officials was illegal entrants, including those who overstayed their tourist visas, Asians smuggled into Canada, and extended family of persons in Canada who had misrepresented the closeness of their relationship in order to gain entry. Dealing with these illegal immigrants strained the resources of immigration authorities and clogged the administrative process. Furthermore, the government proved both unwilling to spend the money necessary to hire enough new staff to deal with the blizzard of paperwork created by the illegal immigrants, and reluctant to unleash the police in a wholesale crackdown on the illegal immigrants, many of whom were working as low-paid domestics or in other menial jobs. In hope of clearing the immediate mess, while allowing the bureaucracy a breathing space in which to reevaluate regulations and procedures, officials authorized the first of several amnesties for illegals. Although this amnesty succeeded in regularizing the status of many illegal immigrants, the problem of illegal entry defied easy solution. During the ensuing years several more amnesties were tried, but the problem persists.

The White Paper of 1966 and Anglo-conformity

Partly to deal with questions of illegal entry, the government commissioned a general review of all aspects of immigration. A White Paper on Immigration was released in 1966. The policy document, infused with the liberal spirit of the day, called for a complete and final overhaul of Canadian immigration regulations so as to exorcise any hint of discrimination on account of race or ethnicity. But it went further. Discrimination might be out but, again reflecting the 1960s, concern with overpopulation was definitely in. Although far from the Malthusian warnings of an earlier day and not meeting the demands of zero population growth advocates, the White Paper questioned Canada's long-term ability to absorb large numbers of job-hungry immigrants at the prime of their fertility cycle. As much in the name of population control as national economic self-interest, the White Paper called for still closer links between Canada's immediate labor needs and immigration. In this regard, it called for a tightening up of the family reunification regulations, considered by many immigration officials to be a loose cannon on the immigration deck. The White Paper recommended restricting the right of landed immigrants to sponsor any but immediate dependents and allowing Canadian citizens to sponsor only those relatives who met the educational and occupational standards demanded of independent immigrants.

The White Paper was referred to a parliamentary committee for discussion. The ensuing debate was explosive. In an unprecedented show of lobbying muscle, ethnic communities organized to let their elected officials know their displeasure at any suggestion of narrowing family and sponsorship categories. Warning that ethnic voters could not be taken for granted, church, labor and ethnic leaders united to demand not a narrowing but a broadening of these same categories. Members of Parliament, especially those from heavily immigrant or ethnic constituencies, withered in the political heat. They soon joined the chorus of those protesting against implementation of those White Paper recommendations that would limit sponsorship. The changes were set aside, at least in the form suggested in the White Paper.

Equally important, the retreat from alienating the immigrant and ethnic constituency signaled a new twist in Canadian political life. Postwar immigrants, joined by the increasingly urban, middle-class and well-educated children and grandchildren of yesterday's immigrants, suddenly represented a potent alliance of those too long denied access to the corridors of power. This so called "Third Force" of non-English and non-French heritage groups had long felt that they were in Canada but not part of Canada. Now, increasingly confident of their economic status, proud of wartime sacrifices made in common cause with other Canadians and infected by the spirit of tolerance which permeated civic discourse, ethnic spokespersons demanded a new deal. They rejected the long-standing Canadian policy of Anglo-conformity, the effort to recast the "foreigner" into a model Anglo Canadian as quickly, cheaply and painlessly as possible. Anglo-conformity was not only wrong-minded, they protested, it also did not work. Their ethnicity had proved more enduring than the assimilationist efforts of Canadian gatekeepers. In place of Anglo-conformity, ethnic leaders posited a new pluralist vision of Canada as a multicultural society, a mosaic of communities welded together to produce, in a cliché of the day, unity through diversity.

The Rise of Multiculturalism
The crusade for multiculturalism and political talk of a nascent "Third Force" reached its height during the heady days of the Royal Commission on Bilingualism and Biculturalism. The commission was set up in 1965 to examine the rocky state of relations between Canada's two charter groups, the English and French. It was soon besieged by organized ethnic communities demanding that their ethno-cultural heritages be accorded public recognition as equal partners in the nation building process. This campaign, led largely by the dispossessed minorities from Eastern Europe, pretended to a unity of ethnic political interest and potential for coordinated lobbying that was to prove fleeting at best. At the time, however, it looked very real indeed.

Confronted by the fact that fully one-third of all Canadians were of neither British nor French origin, politicians suddenly took notice. The Commission recommended that the "contribution of Canada's other ethnic communities" be acknowledged in government policy. In 1971 the federal government responded by declaring Canada to be a multicultural nation within a bilingual framework. Biculturalism was officially dead.

Detractors have dismissed the multiculturalism policy, together with its accompanying nickel-and-dime program of grants in support of ethnic cultural retention and sharing, as little more than a government game of smoke and mirrors. Some attacked multiculturalism as an unsuccessful federal effort to downplay the importance of French Canadian nationalism by equating it with other forms of ethnic self-assertion that were then demanding to be heard. Others have argued that multiculturalism was a crude and equally unsuccessful attempt to buy ethnic voters with their own money. Still others regarded multiculturalism as nothing less than cynical manipulation of the powerless by a Canadian power elite. According to this interpretation, multiculturalism was designed to keep "the ethnics" dancing in church basements instead of pressing for their legitimate place in the social, economic and political goverance of the nation.

Even if one or all of these charges is true, it does not negate the fact that these once-immigrant laborers and their children and children's children suddenly represented something of a political sleeping lion. The lion generally appeared friendly, but rare was the politician so reckless as to put his or her head into the lion's mouth to find out for sure. And at times, as during the White Paper debate on family reunification, politicians heard an ethnic roar and warned one another that "it's a jungle out there."

Family Reunification and Other Admission Policies
Although the specific recommendations on family reunification in the White Paper were dropped, other White Paper recommendations were incorporated into immigration regulations. In 1967 any and all vestiges of racial and ethnic discrimination were officially erased from the immigration regulations and procedures. Most particularly, racial discrimination was eliminated for sponsored immigration. Although the definition of first-degree relatives was reined in somewhat, all citizens and landed immigrants in Canada, including those from the Third World, were legally entitled to sponsor family members.

On the issue of family reunification, the government proceeded with caution. In the end, it took with one hand and gave with the other. The list of those entitled to entry into Canada as first-degree relatives was narrowed. But, a new class of immigrant, a nominated class, was announced. Nominated immigrants were primarily non-dependent family of those in Canada who could show a demonstrated ability to integrate with a minimum of difficulty. In effect, they were expected to have the strengths of independent immigrants but were granted priority admission. Their Canadian sponsor also had less legal liability for a nominated immigrant than was the case with dependent family.

The government also overhauled procedures by which independent applicants were admitted into Canada. Again, without enacting new legislation, immigration admissions were still linked closer to domestic economic fluctuations. A point system was introduced. The desirability of each independent applicant would henceforth be calculated on a sliding scale measuring short-term and long-term prospects for successful integration. In addition to education and employment experience, points were assigned for an individual's personal character, market demand for his or her particular skills, English and French language proficiency, age, proposed Canadian destination and prearranged employment. The point system could be adjusted on very short notice to reflect fluctuations in the Canadian economy. Although the immigration officer assessing each applicant retained some discretionary power in awarding points, the point system reduced the power of immigration officials to arbitrarily reject applicants without cause. Henceforth, all admissions were formally based on a universal system with objective selection criteria.

In late 1967, the key immigration issue was not routine processing of immigrants, but refugees. The end of the Prague Spring in 1968 sent a flood of Czechoslovakian refugees streaming westward in what seemed a repeat of the Hungarian refugee crisis of a decade earlier. Driven by a mixture of humanitarianism, cold war posturing and economic self-interest, the government geared up for action. This time there was no waiting for voluntary associations to underwrite costs. With the Canadian economy on the mend and a block of highly skilled labor ripe for the picking, immigration teams were fast off the mark. After the success of the Hungarian program, there was not even an objection from the security service. Again, waiving many of its immigration regulations, Canada resettled approximately 12,000 Czech refugees.

ADMISSION OF REFUGEES AND CHANGES TO POLICY IN THE 1970S

While many Canadians pat themselves on the back for the magnanimity of refugee resettlement programs, there remains a less flattering side to Canada's refugee activities. Liberal groups repeatedly charged the government with favoring the victims of communist or other high-profile and unpopular regimes over refugees from right-wing tyranny. Evidence to support this charge is not difficult to find. The uneven treatment of refugees escaping different political regimes was clearly apparent in the case of Ugandan Asian refugees expelled by Idi Amin in 1972 and Chilean refugees from the 1973 right-wing coup d'état against Salvador Allende's democratically elected left-wing government. In the case of the approximately 50,000 Asians with British passports expelled from Uganda, the British, fearing a backlash at the increase of Asian numbers in Britain, appealed to Canada for assistance. Building on the Czech experience, Canada moved quickly to identify candidates for easy integration and eventually processed about 5,600 Ugandan Asians. For the first time, the issue of race played almost no part in the government's decision. If its response was something less than a totally humanitarian gesture, the Canadian effort on behalf of Ugandan refugees was far from the kind of ethnically front-loaded displaced persons movement that previously had proved the model for most Canadian postwar refugee initiatives.

The Chilean experience a year later was different. The Canadian government may have become color-blind to race, but not to ideology. And when it came to Chileans, immigration and security personnel saw red. The overthrow of Allende's socialist government was engineered by the United States, Canada's closest ally, and Canada, with corporate interests at stake, was among the first to recognize the new Pinochet regime. It was not long before the problem of political refugees was front and center. Across Canada, a pro-refugee lobby coalesced under the wing of the Canadian Council of Churches and the academic community.

Contrast with Ugandan Asian refugees or with the earlier Czech and Hungarian programs is unavoidable. Perhaps uneasy about taking in any large group of left-leaning refugees, or concerned about a negative American reaction, the government proceeded with caution. Immigration authorities did not rush into Chile to process applications. Regulations were not waived. In spite of a storm of protest from liberal groups, immigration officials were slow to set up shop in Santiago and proved reluctant to forego stringent immigration procedures, including security checks. Two years after the ousting of Allende, and in the face of an international outcry at continuing wholesale abuse of civil liberties by the Pinochet government, fewer than 2,000 Chilean refugees were granted safe haven in Canada. Once again, many of those who finally did get into Canada were white-collar professionals with the kind of educational or work experience that might have won them entry into Canada as independent immigrants.

When the Chilean refugee crisis erupted, immigration policy was already under stress. The 1952 Immigration Act had been amended a number of times and the immigration regulations which directed the day-to-day operations of immigration work were under constant review. But, among public servants there was growing sentiment in favor of a major reformulation of Canadian policy and law. Indeed, the Canada which the 1952 act was designed to serve was no more; the social and economic assumptions which the legislation had been designed to complement no longer applied. In the 20 years since passage of the 1952 legislation, Canada had grown in population and international stature. The racial and ethnic priorities of those who had written the legislation seemed embarrassingly out of step in a liberal democracy. Nor were Canadian immigration priorities still dominated by the need for unskilled agricultural labor. Canada was now among the most urban of western states and immigrants streamed into Canada's major cities. To compete in an ever more technological and service-oriented world marketplace, Canada required skilled and capital-productive immigration. New thinking on immigration was required.

In September 1973, the minister of manpower and immigration announced a comprehensive public review of Canadian immigration policy. But the effort hardly seemed justified by the final product. After almost a year and a half of public hearings, reviewing expert briefs and wide discussion of immigration procedures and statistics, the review commission issued its four-volume *Report of the Canadian Immigration and Population Study.* Offered more as a discussion paper than as a blueprint for the future, the Green Paper on Immigration, as the report was commonly known, did not recommend nearly so radical a departure from existing immigration philosophy or procedures as many had hoped. It reaffirmed the need for a hand-in-glove relationship between immigration and labor supply. But, unlike the earlier White Paper, the 1973 document was bullish on the need for population increase through immigration. Pointing to the declining national fertility rate and an already low mortality rate, the Green Paper foreshadowed a time in which the resources of those generating wealth would be far outstripped by those requiring support. The Green Paper advised that "the number of immigrants Canada admits may progressively become, not only the main determinant of eventual population size, but also the chief factor responsible for the pace at which growth occurs."

The timing of the public debate on the Green Paper was unfortunate. It took place in the shadow of yet another economic recession. With unemployment rising, any increase in immigration numbers was a hard sell. The discussion of long-term Canadian demographic needs was drowned out in heated debate over immediate employment problems and charges that immigrants took away jobs from "real" Canadians. The debate also encouraged racists, hovering at the margins of respectable social discourse, to vent their hostility against the growing number of Third World immigrants entering Canada. Indeed, following the removal of racial criteria in immigration selection and the opening of immigration offices in areas of nontraditional Canadian immigration, the admission of visible minorities from the Third World increased quickly. In 1967, shortly after Canadian immigration operations were upgraded in Asia and the Caribbean, fewer than 15% of immigrants into Canada were black or Asian. By 1975, as the Green Paper debate raged, the percentage of visible minorities among Canadian immigrants had more than doubled. By 1985, the arrival of non-Europeans topped 60%. To its credit, the larger Canadian polity rejected appeals to racism. Of course, there is no denying that anxiety about the changing ethnographic face of Canada, especially urban Canada, exists. Canada also has a long way to go before systemic racism is eliminated. But there is virtually no credible support for turning back the immigration clock to an earlier era of racial and ethnic selectivity.

FROM THE IMMIGRATION ACT OF 1976 TO THE PRESENT

In 1976, even as echoes of the Green Paper discussion could still be heard, the government proceeded with its own immigration agenda. This included introducing a new immigration law. The Immigration Act of 1976 represents an important step in the history of Canadian immigration. Never before had an immigration act specifically delineated national responsibility for the immigrant as well as for the receiving society. The preamble to the new act pledged the government's commitment to family reunification and, for the first time, affirmed Canada's international obligations to ease the distress of refugees, the displaced and the persecuted.

Also for the first time, the act introduced a modified form of quota system. Each year the federal government, in consultation with the provinces, sets a target for the number of immigrants Canada will accept in the coming year. The number is more a guide than any exact promise of what is to be. Depending on prevailing conditions at home and abroad, the actual number might be above or below the target. However, it is hoped that a target figure will allow federal and provincial authorities to allocate their respective resources in a rational way.

Importantly, the act also recognized refugees as a class distinct from other immigrants and legally entitled to Canadian sanctuary. Each year a percentage of the total immigration quota is set aside for refugees, and the cost of their integration covered by the government. Provision is made for private nongovernmental agencies or individuals to sponsor additional refugees. While it was originally envisioned that most refugees who would come to Canada would be processed abroad, in refugee camps or by making a claim through a Canadian immigration office, the door was left open for those who made their way to Canada without prior screening to apply for immigrant status once in Canada.

In spite of the progressive tone of the preamble and the important breakthrough in the area of refugees, the act promised more of the same when it came to family reunification and economic issues. Certainly, much of the underlying policy was familiar. Those family members eligible for reunification with kin in Canada, aside from a spouse or dependent child under age 10, still must assure government personnel that their education, employment record or skills are an immediate asset to Canada. A new class of immigrant was created: the entrepreneurial class. Individuals proved to have sufficient capital to invest in an enterprise that would generate new employment and wealth were welcome to apply for Canadian immigration. In the first 10 years after the new legislation came into effect, the most prominent group of entrepreneurial-class immigrants to arrive in Canada came from Hong Kong. With the impending Chinese takeover of Hong Kong in 1997, many Hong Kong businessmen began hedging their bets on the future by placing capital into more secure investments abroad. Canada became a favorite destination for capital in flight. For some the chance to transfer both capital and citizenship also proved appealing. As a result, the past few years have witnessed an influx of well-off Hong Kong Chinese into Canada, particularly into Vancouver and Toronto.

For independent immigrants, not blessed with a minimum $250,000 to invest in Canada, the going got rough. Under immigration regulations, those of more modest means and no family or sponsor are increasingly out of luck unless they have a job waiting for them. This is not easy. Before offering employment to a would-be immigrant, a prospective employer must prove, to the satisfaction of immigration officials, that there is no satisfactory candidate in Canada able to take the job.

The refugee provisions of the 1976 Immigration Act, which came into effect in 1978, were soon put to the test. In 1979 the Vietnamese "boat people" crisis erupted. The outpouring of concern among Canadians took government by surprise. As the demand for action grow stronger, private individuals banded together and, under new immigration provisions allowing for private sponsorship of refugees, mobilized to receive thousands of individuals and families in need. Faced with this unprecedented outpouring of public sympathy, the government announced it would match voluntary sponsorships. Immigration officials were dispatched to the refugee camps that had been set up for the "boat people" in Hong Kong and Southeast Asia. By the end of 1980, more than 60,000 Vietnamese, Cambodians, Laotians and ethnic Chinese from Southeast Asia were admitted to Canada, the highest per capita "boat people" resettlement program of any nation— a truly humanitarian gesture on the part of the Canadian public.

But not all those claiming refugee status were equally welcome. Public enthusiasm for refugees began to wane as persons who might otherwise not be admissible to Canada entered illegally or as tourists only to claim refugee status once they had entered. As the number or refugee claimants grew, the refugee determination review system become clogged. Validation of legitimate refugee claims, often without access to documentation, took time. Dealing with fraudulent entrants only muddied the refugee waters still more.

Immigration authorities were particularly upset. They wanted to close the "loophole" in the immigration procedures which allowed individuals claiming refugee status to select Canada rather than requiring that immigration officials select them. Officials pressed for changes in the rules which would prevent individuals from applying for immigrant status from within Canada.

The pro-refugee lobby objected. Any change which would undermine the right of persons once in Canada to claim refugee status would also choke off the flow of legitimate refugees who needed immediate sanctuary. But, for immigration authorities, allowing persons to enter Canada on their own and then demanding to stay as refugees was just too messy. After two ships illegally landed their respective cargoes of Sikh and Tamil refugees on Canada's east coast, the federal government acted. Over the objections of pro-refugee advocates, new legislation was passed curtailing the right of refugees to seek asylum once in Canada and restricting other aspects of the refugee program. Many pro-refugee lobbyists believed Canada had taken a giant step backward from its recent commitment to refugee sanctuary.

Today, public attention remains fixed on the high-profile issues of refugees, the concentration of visible minority immigrants in Canadian cities and the social and economic impact of entrepreneurial immigrants, accused by some of buying their way into Canada. Obviously, each of these issues has racial overtones. Although some members of visible minority groups might disagree, public discussion has not yet turned into a moral referendum on white Canada's tolerance of non-whites. While many Canadians may have concerns for the future of their country, to date the civility of the Canadian polity remains intact. One cannot deny, however, that race and race-dominated issues have risen on the public agenda. Whether the public's commitment to multiculturalism will remain hearty enough to embrace a multiracial society remains to be seen.

As government monitors the public mood, policy planners are focusing on the future. Mindful of the race-related issues which hold the public eye, some explore the demographic and economic issues raised by a falling national birthrate and the need for immigrants to meet Canada's expected population shortfall. How these issues will be resolved, if they can be resolved, we cannot know. However, it is safe to assume that immigration and its social and economic fallout are not about to recede from government priority or public consciousness.

FURTHER READING

Abella, Irving, and Harold Troper. *None Is Too Many: Canada and the Jews of Europe, 1933–1948.* New York: Random House, 1983.

Dirks, Gerald E. *Canada's Refugee Policy: Indifference or Opportunism?* Toronto: University of Toronto Press, 1978.

Hawkins, Freda. *Canada and Immigration: Public Policy and Public Concern.* Toronto: University of Toronto Press, 1972.

Palmer, Howard, ed. *Immigration and the Rise of Multiculturalism.* Toronto: McClelland & Stewart, 1975.

Richmond, Anthony H. *Post-War Immigrants in Canada.* Toronto: University of Toronto Press, 1967.

Whitaker, Reg. *Double Standard: The Secret History of Canadian Immigration.* Toronto: Lester and Orpen Dennys, 1987.

EDUCATION

LIONEL ORLIKOW

THE ENVIRONMENT OF CANADIAN EDUCATION

There is no such thing as the Canadian educational system. Each of the ten provinces and the two territories has distinctive educational policies and programs.

No other federal state in the world is in such a position. There is no national office of education, no national strategy; there are no national goals. Canadian education is diverse, decentralized, yet dynamic. There is no national debate in Canada to reassess, to reorganize, to reinforce education, essential though that would seem. The whole should be more than the sum of its parts.

In its comprehensive *Review of Educational Policy of Canada* published in 1976, the Organization for Economic Cooperation and Development (OECD) analyzed the situation:

> The lack of educational policies for the future is striking. There is a need to define goals for education that fit a vision of national interest.
>
> Decisions now have to be taken concerning the destination of the Canadian school system within an ordered view of the Canadian nation.
>
> Politicians, parties and governments will not be able to avoid much longer taking some political stands, and that means also nationwide, and not simply province-oriented positions. They need to give Canadian answers to Canadian problems. Without political leadership and responsibility a severe backlash against future educational development in Canada may be unavoidable.

How has a nation of 12 education systems in which policy is made by 12 sets of legislatures and officials, plus hundreds of local community school boards, evolved?

Canadians today have, on the whole, accepted that theirs is a nation of differences. This willingness to accept diversity may well be one of the distinguishing marks of the Canadian national identity—a contrast to the pressures toward conformity that characterize many other national cultures. This emphasis upon pluralism is rooted in historic, geographic, cultural and political factors.

First, Canada is spatially the second largest country in the world, with a land areas as large as Europe's. Immense variations in resources, human and natural, facilitate parochialism and decentralization in politics and administration over five time zones. Internal variations abound. To cite one: one quarter of the 27 million Canadians reside in the cities of Montreal and Toronto, whereas the province of Prince Edward Island has 130,000 inhabitants. This province employs fewer bureaucrats to service its schools than do individual large school districts in Ontario.

Strong regionalism persists in Canada. Uneven economic activity has meant that different regions have separate economic causes to advance. Physical remoteness often exacerbates tensions among the provinces and between the provinces and federal government. Fiscal capacities differ, as do shares allocated to education budgets.

Second, ethnic and linguistic cleavages are a continuing reality. Canada is essentially a society of two cultures, francophone and anglophone. Francophones, in particular, jealously guard their linguistic and cultural differences. Although the two founding ethnic groups represent the main cultural divisions, other groups make up a quarter of the total population. To varying degrees, they, too, cherish their own traditions and utilize the education systems to do so. Successive federal governments, since 1971, have promoted multiculturalism in a bilingual country.

Third, the fact that most Canadians live within 100 miles of the United States facilitates transborder flows of products, pollution, capital investment, ideas and ideals. The penetration of U.S. mass media, the existence of a shared language, and simply the relative size of the two populations produce for Canada a porous Canada-U.S. border. There are frequent interactions as Canadian educators go south to attend conferences, read U.S. journals, and even appropriate research produced in that different milieu.

Fourth, Canada is a federative system that constitutionally shapes the intrusions by the federal government in education. The Constitution Act of 1867 provides that "in and for each Province, the legislature may exclusively make laws in relation to Education," a power that has not been modified by the Constitution Act of 1982. Provincial authenticity in education only is limited to certain qualifications respecting the rights and privileges of denominational schools and respecting official minority language (English or French) educational rights where numbers warrant.

Constitutional flexibility has permitted many federal moves into provincial systems of education. The federal parliament has responsibility for the national interest, which is not necessarily, and often is not, the same as that of any one or more of the provinces. The federal government has spending power not only in the very few areas in which, according to the constitution, it has specific jurisdiction but also in others in which only the provinces have legislative power. In addition, under the clause giving the federal parliament authority "to make Laws for the Peace, Order, and good Government of Canada" it has power to legislate regarding matters which are in the interest of more than one of the provinces.

Given such complexity in an absence of national direction, it is a wonder that education works at all. But it does. In 1941, only 48% of the population aged 15 and older had some high school education, compared with 81% in 1985. The percentage of people with some postsecondary education more than tripled in the same period.

At least one in every three Canadians is currently a student in the country's education network. In addition to six million full-time students enrolled in more than 16,000 schools, colleges, and universities, there are more than three million adults furthering their education on a part-time basis.

Still, generalizations about Canadian education are hazardous. Much that is written fails to capture the diversity in practice not just among provinces, but also within local school systems. A mandated course often is taught with different content and standards in classrooms even in different schools in the same school district.

THE PROVINCES IN EDUCATION

The absence of a strong federal government direction, buttressed by diverse historic developments and by differing geographic, social and economic conditions has produced 12 unique educational systems.

The policies and powers of the provinces are embodied in university and college legislative acts, school or education acts, or cabinet orders-in-council. The governmental regulations that flow therefrom are extremely critical in setting details.

Great diversity is perpetuated by structured fragmentation. Administration, standards and curriculum context differ markedly among the twelve. Courses required for graduation, the scope of provincially-set external tests, regulations on compulsory attendance, and the proportion of school revenue to be raised by the local taxpayer, are just a few of these essential elements.

Nevertheless, the 12 systems do have common features, although there are exceptions to every statement that can be made.

Universal free schooling is available across Canada from kindergarten (age 5) to grade 12 (grade 11 in Quebec, grade 13 in Ontario). A few local school districts offer classes for 4-year-olds, and a number encourage more mature adults to return and complete high school.

Schooling is compulsory from age 6 or 7 to 14 or 16. A school year extends from 185 to 200 days, September 1 to June 30.

Schools are organized in many ways. Generally elementary school includes Kindergarten through grades 6 or 8. Secondary, or high, school contains grades 9 or 10 to 12. Junior high, grades 7 to 9, or middle schools, grades 6 to 8, are found in some school districts. Kindergarten through grade 12 schools are located in less populated rural communities. Larger high schools, about 800 plus in enrollment, schedule a range of academic and vocational programs, whereas smaller ones only give courses directed toward university studies.

The overwhelming majority of elementary pupils attend self-contained classes, where they receive most instruction from one teacher. Starting at grade 7, students go to approximately six classes a day, 40 to 50 minutes each, with specialist teachers. Their courses generally include English, math, social studies (history and geography), general science, French, physical education, and electives drawn from art, music, workshop and computers.

High school courses resemble those at the junior level, although there now are streams such as technical, business, and advanced academic. Most students are tracked into several levels, although critics maintain that streaming had implicitly begun much earlier. Those planning to go on to university pursue more science (physics, chemistry), higher mathematics, French, and literature. Taking vocational options could lead to community college. A third track with a diluted academic curriculum attracts students who do not do well in school, or whose academic plans are not well formulated. About 30% of school graduates go on directly into full-time post-secondary education.

Most schools are trying to plan for the exceptional children, especially the learning disabled and handicapped, but including the gifted as well. Generally elementary classrooms integrate the disabled into regular classrooms more successfully than do high schools.

While English remains the chief medium of instruction outside Quebec and in the English schools of that province, French is increasingly found as a language of instruction everywhere in Canada for francophones, and in immersion schools and classes attended by English-speaking children.

Languages other than English and French are almost extinct in Canadian schools. So-called heritage languages help ethno-cultural groups retain their languages, but are not designed to encourage other Canadians to share the contributions of these groups in Canada. Close to 50 heritage languages are taught in Ontario's public schools.

There is much rhetoric about the situation in which ethnic groups can retain their distinctiveness and yet be Canadian, in contrast to the United States' melting pot. Mulculturalism in its many forms has been encouraged in many ways. A few groups, such as the Hutterites in western Canada, manage to balance provincial requirements and their distinct cultural demands. Yet Canadian schools remain a major force in assimilation.

More schools are frequently called upon to deal with social ills—sexual abuse, drug education, nutrition—that place added burdens on schools and staffs already in difficulty in meeting academic standards. Extras have been added without benefit of either extra time or integration with existing courses.

Some homogenization is happening today under the banners of "standards" and "back to the basics." The results are a reduction of curricular diversity, a direct control of teachers and a narrowing of the objectives of schooling. "Discipline" and "moral education" are popular slogans increasingly used by elected officials. Music, art and physical education are threatened, often viewed as expendable "frills."

Several provinces allow tax support of schools on a denominational basis. The first tax-supported school in a district is designated the public school; the second, the separate school. Denominational is interpreted to mean Roman Catholic and Protestant. Newfoundland has a more diversified system, where tax support is available for specific religious denominations as well as for groups of denominations. Non-sectarian public education is provided in five provinces.

Although they must meet provincial standards, private schools are independent, fee-charging institutions. Some provinces give partial financial aid to such schools. Private schools include religious schools (e.g., a recent surge by small fundamentalist Christian churches), rigidly academic schools, schools emphasizing the arts, and schools based on specific pedagogical philosophies and practices (e.g., Montessori). A recent increase in the number of private schools in Canada is significant, reaching 5% of children of elementary and secondary school age. Ninety percent of these students reside in British Columbia, Ontario and Quebec.

Provincial governments have constitutional responsibility for administering school systems. A department or ministry of education (some provinces divide responsibilities into two departments, postsecondary and elementary secondary) are headed by a minister of education, an elected member of the provincial legislature appointed to the cabinet. While the minister has general authority, administration is carried out by civil servants under one or more deputy ministers. Functions of the department usually include supervision and inspection of schools, general policies on curriculum and school organization, preparation and approval of new courses, finance, correspondence courses, and teacher certification.

The province provides most of the funds to schools. Their contribution nearly doubled since 1960 to about 70% of total outlays borne by local governments. Wide variations exist. New Brunswick and Prince Edward Island assume full financing of school board revenue, in contrast to 51% in Ontario.

The growing provincial cash responsibility for schooling has largely been a consequence of two factors. The one has been a desire for some equality both in expenditures per student (student equity) and in the tax burden on people (taxpayer equity). The other has been a recognition that the financial capability of local communities to spend on schooling varies immensely. Municipal areas in which residential property values are comparatively high may be able to afford higher expenditures per pupil than can poorer districts.

Provincial authority over education has the power to delegate power to local school boards composed, for the most part, of elected trustees from 3 to 15 in number. Usually boards manage the delivery of educational services; appoint a professional as superintendent, or director, and other staff; initiate proposals for construction of facilities; purchase supplies; implement and adapt the provincial curriculum; set local tax rates; bargain collectively with staff (salaries are set provincially in some provinces); and so forth.

Most school boards in Canada are functionally specialized governing bodies autonomous from general municipal governments. This separation is justified in the view that education is too important a public function to be left to city/town governments and that schools are more likely to prosper under the administration of school boards separately established under the provisions of provincial education laws.

In the abstract, local boards are responsible for setting school district policy. In fact, school trustees seldom are well enough informed or have sufficient time to engage in much policy setting. The members are citizens serving with modest financial compensation, meeting once a week.

New Brunswick and Ontario have parallel systems of administration in ethnically divided communities. French and English children can receive instruction in their native language; as well, their school administration functions in those languages.

Within the provinces, provincial authority was strengthened in the 1980s after two decades of decentralization. A few moves to centralization include: reimposition of central examinations; more compulsory courses and mandatory topics to be covered; and reviews and monitoring on effectiveness of board expenditures and programs.

Local boards face other challenges. Several provinces have raised their financial contributions to private schools, thereby attracting pupils away from public schools. At another level, a few boards themselves have decentralized through the transference of designated administrative responsibilities to individual school-parent-teacher councils.

Provinces also are assuming stronger control over postsecondary education. All institutions of higher education are dependent upon provincial governments for the main portion of their budgets. Since the late 1940s there has been rapid growth of these institutions; there are now more than 250, including universities, community colleges, and technical institutes (now largely absorbed by the colleges). More than 20% of Canadians of university age attend these postsecondary institutions full-time.

Community colleges are public institutions that offer two to three years of employment preparation for a diploma in trades and technologies as well as a variety of vocational courses, such as art or domestic crafts. Transfer for university credit is possible in some cases. As their name implies, community colleges attempt to be responsive to the needs of the region or local community, facilitated by local representatives on the board of governors.

The backbone of the postsecondary system is the university. Most were founded as private religious institutions but have since become heavily dependent on public funding, and almost all have been obliged to sever their denominational ties.

Universities range in size and complexity from a few with less than 1,000 students, providing first-degree courses in the liberal arts, to half a dozen multiversities enrolling more than 20,000 students and providing programs in arts, science and the professions, leading to the baccalaureate, the master's degree, and the doctorate. They set their own admission requirements, a situation that usually means an applicant's high school academic record at the end of grades 12 or 13. Final admission is based on specific courses completed and a grade point average achieved. The quality of university education is quite uniform across Canada.

In addition to colleges and universities there is an uncoordinated tertiary system. Continuing education opportunities are furnished by a wide range of institutions and organizations, such as school boards, departments of government, nonprofit organizations, private trade schools, employers, unions, museums and church groups. Participation in this sector surpasses those in colleges and universities, as adults participate on a credit or noncredit basis, full-time or part-time, either in order to secure useful qualifications or simply out of personal interest.

A unique public institution in Quebec for students choosing to study beyond the secondary level is the CEGEP (collège d'enseignement général et professionnel). This institution provides two-year courses toward entry into a university and a three-year vocational program for entry into the labor force.

A fundamental restructuring in education that government officials cannot hope to manage or massage is occurring among aboriginal communities. These people are recasting their values, traditions and future hopes in terms of indigenous constitutions. The federal government, on the basis of its special relationship under the constitution, is transferring control of some schools and postsecondary education to the aboriginal communities. An example is the establishment of the Saskatchewan Indian Federated College at the University of Regina, which offers a range of degrees including social work, business and education. The place of education under principles of self-government over large areas also is being worked out in northern Quebec and the Territories.

The federal government has attempted to raise the level of interest in, and knowledge about, lifelong learning, particularly through paid educational leave. Various encouraging reports were circulated in the early 1980s, but not much advance has been made in actual programs.

Provincial governments generally have established intermediary bodies between themselves and the universities. They differ in function. In Quebec and Ontario, they are advisory with respect to the allocation of funds to the universities, while those in six other provinces enjoy delegated authority with respect to such allocation. In no case, however, is the intermediary empowered to determine the total amount to be allocated to the universities. This is the government's prerogative. Community colleges, despite delegation of powers by government, have always been regarded as a part of broader provincial economic plans.

Postsecondary education has been especially pinched by the fiscal squeeze. Government grants to colleges and universities each increased by only 2.5% in real collars in the 10 years to 1987, while enrollments grew by 36% and 27% respectively. No relief is in sight.

The private sector could represent an alternate source of funding in Canada. Canadian governments by the late 1980s, both federal and provincial, were more private-sector oriented than their predecessors. Federal employment and training policy now calls for greater private-sector participation in educational activities that have been traditionally the preserve of public institutions.

THE FEDERAL GOVERNMENT IN EDUCATION

Education is a function consciously omitted from the role of the central government in the constitution. Federal entry into this highly sensitive arena was gradual and unpretentious, usually justified under many guises. Education was slipped under fiscal transfers, federal responsibilities for defense, regional development, the national economy, or cultural identity. These special national interests, often funded entirely by Ottawa, are accepted by the provinces as they do not appear to threaten the legal control of provincial government.

The few controls set by Ottawa were very loosely defined in application, thereby contributing to inconsistent standards and services across Canada. Provincial programming also was maintained because it was provincial departments of education that channeled federal dollars to local schools and postsecondary institutions. The federal government only provided less than 10% of the direct contribution for education in 1988, and this expenditure was selective in nature.

Yet federal contributions managed to change key sectors of Canadian education after World War II. The acceleration in growth of vocational schools and community colleges came with grants to improve manpower training. Promoting Canadian unity offered the umbrella for the federal government to subsidize official language (English and French) teaching, a virtual revolution now reaching 15% of Canadian anglophone schoolchildren alone. Extensive adult student financial loans came on the grounds of greater accessibility to qualified Canadians in need.

Moreover, the federal effort has been critical in many modest ventures. The Department of Health and Welfare assisted with reports and information to various organizations regarding needed provisions for exceptional children. School broadcasts through the Canadian Broadcasting Corporation were an early form of long-distance education. The Department of Secretary of State funded several reviews on Canadian content.

The success of these federal programs contained the seeds of retrenchment. Growing demands for more help from poorer provinces, awareness of little political credit to the federal funder, a feeling that some provinces diverted moneys to other sectors, a rising deficit, all contributed to new federal-provincial arrangements in the 1980s. In the federal government's support of postsecondary education, its funding proposals sought a linkage between federal funding increases and more provincial expenditures. These demands were not taken up by the provinces and funding cuts to the provinces followed. Federal manpower training dollars also were diverted from community colleges to private sector employers.

The Charter of Rights and Freedoms of 1982 provides a fresh activist route for the federal government in provincial education. The possible placement of "national" education standards and policy on provincial and local school districts through federal court rulings may induce profound social and cultural changes at all levels of Canadian society.

In the first years of the charter, official language minorities, the French outside of Quebec and the English inside Quebec, made most use of its provisions. These groups initiated successful challenges against language policies of their respective provincial governments.

The equality provisions in Section 15 of the charter may have more impact on education than all the other provisions of the charter combined. A host of challenges is possible in the protection of the constitutional rights of students, teachers and other employees of the school district, and parents for equal access and treatment; and on matters relating to discrimination on race, sex, and physical characteristics.

Consequently a broad definition of conditions for learning will allow the Federal Court to become involved in areas which have been traditionally the prerogative of school authorities, such as school financing, school curriculum, school personnel policies, and streaming or tracking of students.

In order to counter federal initiatives in funding training and postsecondary education, the provinces in 1967 organized the Council of Ministers of Education. This interprovincial agency provides a meeting ground for ministers and their staffs for consultation on subjects of mutual concern. No recommendations are binding on provincial departments.

Other national organizations, such as the Association of Canadian Community Colleges, the Canadian Teachers' Federation, and the Canadian Association of University Teachers, also act as forums for the exchange of ideas. Again, responsibility for action remains with member bodies at the provincial level.

In summary, Canada does not have a federal department of education, which might have responsibility for coordinating and directing federal initiatives in education, collecting educational data and disseminating information, promoting trans-Canadian research in education, maintaining continuous liaison with provincial departments of education and, in general, providing overall leadership and a national perspective on education. Provincial departments of education only fill a very small part in this void.

NATURE OF POLICY FORMATION

Education is the most accessible of Canada's public institutions, yet parents feel remote from their children's education. Education usually is nonpartisan and pragmatic; the major interest groups, teachers and trustees, work with whoever is in power. Yet education is heavily politicized.

Many provinces in the 1970s and 1980s witnessed a consultative process whereby officials of the provincial ministries of education met on a wide variety of committees with the leadership of teachers', trustees' and school administrators' organizations. The subjects covered included curriculum development, financial distribution formulas, certification of teachers—in short, all the nuts and bolts of a provincial school system.

Education was usually removed from politics of the legislature. Rare legislative debates on education typically centered upon "more"—a lower teacher-pupil ratio, higher salaries, etc. Consensus politics let the minister of education assure his cabinet colleagues that education was a non-issue. Public policy statements generally had been vetted by major interest groups.

Conflict does erupt occasionally. Some subjects, such as government aid to private schools, are so divisive that nonpartisanship is reinforced. Politicians have found that education usually costs votes, and does not win them.

An apolitical mood is reinforced at the local level. Most trustees are elected without benefit of political party affiliation. They campaign for office without platforms for which they can be held accountable.

Notwithstanding teachers' rights to bargain granted by legislation in the provinces, wage bargaining was severely curtailed in the 1980s. All provinces imposed wage restraints.

Some teachers' organizations have since broken with tradition by assuming a more active role in provincial elections, by financial contributions to, or the endorsing of, a party.

Meanwhile, relationships between provincial governments and the school boards are becoming more ambivalent. Local boards of education generally are directly elected, but formal, legal control over education rests in the hands of the province, which delegates whatever power it thinks fit to the boards of education. Provincial governments seem to want control without responsibility, and local school districts get responsibility without control.

ASSESSMENT OF EDUCATION

It is impossible to know what is happening in Canadian schools. Input data suggest that materially most of the system does well in terms of staff-student ratios (18:1 in schools, 13:1 in universities), staff salaries, classroom supplies, and physical plant. But, little information is available about educational outcomes, primarily student performance.

Educational research and evaluation remain a relatively underdeveloped discipline. Consequently, supporting documentation for a new program frequently relies upon imported studies based on the U.S. education system's legal frameworks, public finance structures, social relations, and other models which are inappropriate to the Canadian situation.

Most educational research is carried out by university faculties of education, but some is undertaken also by provincial departments of education, larger school boards, and organizations of teachers and school trustees. Federal support for research in education has been quite limited.

A few interprovincial educational research bodies, non-provincial and non-federal, had brief lives. It is small wonder that various reports have concluded that the relative ineffectiveness of Canadian educational research is a result of underfunding, underdevelopment, and too much attention to parochial issues.

Generally provinces and local boards have avoided implementation of a comprehensive set of externally imposed exams for graduation and tests as checkpoints through the grades. Student evaluation relies upon a variety of methods, including student assignments, tests, and final examinations, set at the school level.

Public concern over students' mastery of basic skills in the 1980s encouraged a return to provincial examinations that had been abolished in the late 1960s. Some departments of education are sampling designated grades and subjects on a rotational basis for their own information about curriculum mastery. Other provinces are setting final exams for all major subjects in specified grades.

A number of school districts have developed their own system-wide tests, in fact replacing a provincial standard with a local standard. Usually these large school units also have taken the initiative in curriculum development.

Small and rural districts usually followed faithfully the provincial curriculum.

Consequently, there is no comprehensive Canadian survey of secondary education, as evaluation of students is done by teachers individually or in very small groups. There is little agreement among teachers on criteria for excellence, and furthermore, few teachers have had training in test construction.

But, there are noteworthy national achievements. Specifically, unique Canadian experience with French immersion programs has been extensively evaluated and their success has been documented. The goals of the different forms of immersion programs largely have been met, namely to develop high levels of French proficiency at no cost to students' English proficiency or academic achievement in other academic subjects.

One of the largest curriculum studies ever undertaken in Canada, and one of the few such studies to take a national rather than a provincial perspective, was completed in the late 1980s as the Canadian component of the Second International Science Study of the International Association for Education Achievement. This isolated moderate effort was unique. Currently the Council of Ministers of Education, in cooperation with the provinces, is designing a set of standardized tests that will be applied nationally. Data comparing student performance at the national, provincial and local levels will be facilitated.

Education shares in the adverse effect of general underfunding of research and development in Canada. It is not too difficult to guesstimate the situation where the level of investment in research and development is smaller than the OECD average. The dependency of many education researchers upon the government public trough discourages thorough examination of such a startling fact as why Canadians suffer from distinctively low rates of school attendance from age 17 onward in comparison with 23 other industrialized nations.

Until now Canada has managed to create an extensive educational system within a political system that discourages extensive planning and debate. Change and improvement flowed out of economic growth and an abundance of resources.

This climate encouraged most educators, as well as the public, to view Canadian education through rose-colored glasses. Serious debates, nationally, provincially, and locally, rarely occurred. An absence of good data analyses, together with a narrow range of participants, restricted significant critique and disagreement about alternative ends and means.

SUMMARY

The period after World War II through the late 1970s in Canadian education was one of unprecedented contrasts. It began as a period of considerable activity in education, accompanied by massive increases of expenditures.

Major features of the period are paradoxical:

- A dramatic increased involvement of the federal government in education, which led to a strengthening of provincial bureaucracies to manage many new programs.
- A significant commitment of finance to programs at all levels of education, but relatively modest improvement in programs for the less fortunate, notably Canada's aboriginal people.
- A reduction in external controls over schools partly through a reduced use of external examinations, but a reluctance by many local boards to take advantage of flexibility in these arrangements.
- Alternative approaches—a sensitivity to multiculturalism, or open education—which then triggered the critics' call for standardization and the "basics."
- Admission of nontraditional students into high schools and postsecondary institutions actually became antidemocratic in the creation of dual tracks both in high schools and postsecondary institutions.

Canadians in the 1980s did not heed the warning made by OECD examiners in 1976.

> The general tone of policy making appears to be adaptations to short-term pressures, doing a little more of what already has been done, and above all, pressing for economies and reductions of expenditures.
> The further development of Canadian educational policy is therefore clearly approaching a danger zone, in which more is at risk than simply the quantity of finance available.

It is unlikely that impressive growth can continue. The federal government is withdrawing from a number of major financial supports to education. Fresh demands in education also will confront public support for slower growth in provincial spending; slow growth in the national and certain regional economies; and demographic change, with an aging population (new entrants to the labor force will decline by 25% by 2000 A.D.).

Canadian education is unprepared to resolve dramatic change in its national and international environment. Traditional methods and increased spending cannot develop new and better ways necessary for educating society in the 1990s.

FURTHER READING

Canadian Education Association. *An Overview of Canadian Education*. Toronto: CEA, 1984.

Council of Ministers of Education. *The Financing of Elementary and Secondary Education in Canada*. Toronto: The Council, 1985.

Devereaux, M. S., *One in Every Five: A Survey of Adult Education in Canada*. Ottawa: Minister of Supply and Services, Canada, 1985.

Federal Cultural Policy Review Committee. Report (1982). Ottawa: Ministry of Supply and Services, 1982. The report is popularly known as the Applebaum-Hebert Report.

Lam, Jack Y. L., ed. *The Canadian Public Education System: Issues and Prospects.* Calqary: Detselig Enterprises, 1990.

Organization for Economic Cooperation and Development. *Review of National Policies for Education: Canada.* Paris: OECD, 1976.

Pineo, Peter, and John Goyder. "The Growth of the Canadian Education System: An Analysis of Transition Probabilities." *The Canadian Journal of Higher Education* 28 (1988).

Stewin, Leonard L., and Stewart J. McCann, eds. *Contemporary Educational Issues: The Canadian Mosaic.* Toronto: Copp C. Pitman, 1987.

Williams, Tom R., and Holly Millincoff, *Canadian Schools: Report Card for the 1990s: A CEA Opinion Poll.* Toronto: Canadian Education Association, 1990.

UNIONS AND INDUSTRIAL RELATIONS

JOHN R. CALVERT

INTRODUCTION: THE UNIQUE CHARACTERISTICS OF CANADIAN LABOR RELATIONS

In recent years, industrial relations in Canada has become the subject of growing international attention, primarily because it has evolved in a manner significantly different from industrial relations in the United States and, perhaps, from what might have been anticipated in Canada several decades ago. Explaining the divergent tendencies of Canadian labor relations, compared to developments in other jurisdictions, has become a major focus of recent industrial relations literature, both internationally and within Canada.

Of course, it is true that Canadian industrial relations has been shaped by broad social and economic developments shared by all industrial nations. The impact of industrialization, urbanization, technological innovation, growing internationalization of economic activity, and other, more industry specific influences common to Western Europe, the United States and Japan has been equally evident in Canada. Yet despite numerous parallels with other jurisdictions, what is most interesting about the postwar Canadian experience is how much it reflects political, economic, social and historical developments unique to the Canadian setting.

THE POLITICAL, ECONOMIC AND LEGISLATIVE FRAMEWORK OF CANADIAN INDUSTRIAL RELATIONS: A BRIEF OVERVIEW

The fact that Canada has a federal, rather than unitary, system of government has had a profound impact in shaping Canadian industrial relations. The federal political system has permitted a variety of legislative arrangements at federal and provincial levels, allowing far more experimentation and innovation in labor law and public policy than would be the case within a unitary state. Indirectly, the federal structure has also deeply affected the pattern of unionization and the membership of specific unions.

Under the Canadian constitution, the federal government's jurisdiction over industrial relations is restricted to its own employees and to employees in federal crown corporations and federally regulated industries, such as transportation, banking, broadcasting and telecommunications. Fully 90% of workers in Canada are employed in industries that fall under provincial jurisdiction. The provinces have thus had considerable scope to shape industrial relations policies according to their specific political and economic circumstances. This has given rise to significant diversity in legislation and in the application of labor law and industrial relations practices.

Canada's political federalism has been paralleled by the existence of significant regional differences within the country. These differences have also profoundly shaped the evolution of labor relations. The unique historical, economic and social experiences of the various regions has been reflected in notable variations in the level and pattern of unionization, in the extent of industrial conflict and in the role of unions and employers in the broader political arena.

The historical, linguistic and cultural characteristics of the province of Quebec have added a further dimension to the Canadian mosaic of labor relations, particularly with respect to the emergence of a separate, Quebec-based labor movement. Although many Quebec workers are members of unions affiliated to national labor bodies, Quebec is unique among the provinces in having its own autonomous labor federations which represent almost half of the unionized labor force.

Like many other areas of Canadian society, Canadian labor relations has been deeply influenced by the United States. This influence has many dimensions. There has been considerable "spillover" of U.S. labor relations practices in the management of firms, partly as a result of the high level of U.S. ownership and partly as a result of the influence of U.S. management and labor relations models on the thinking of Canadian managers, politicians and industrial relations specialists.

Taylorism, Human Relations, Job Enrichment, Quality of Working Life Experiments and, more recently, the "union-free" approaches of a growing number of U.S. firms have influenced Canadian managers. Many Canadian firms have also followed the U.S. lead in trying to improve their international competitiveness by cutting wage and benefit costs, demanding concessions and rollbacks and by pressing for the adoption of more flexible working practices.

The influence of the U.S. is seen in other ways. Canada's postwar labor legislation was modeled on the U.S. Wagner Act. The legalistic approach to collective bargaining and dispute resolution reflects the U.S. practice, rather than that of Great Britain, even though Canada's legal system was principally based on the British model.

Until quite recently, the majority of unionized workers and the largest unions in Canada were affiliated to U.S.-based international unions associated with the AFL-CIO. Canada's labor movement, particularly outside Quebec, was deeply influenced by the "bread and butter" business unionism approach of American unions, which focused on making pragmatic gains through collective bargaining and eschewed political action based on theories of class.

However, there are other factors which have worked to limit the influence of the United States in shaping the development of Canadian industrial relations. In contrast to the United States, but in common with much of Western Europe, Canada has had a strong social democratic party. The 1944 election victory of the Co-operative Commonwealth Federation (CCF) in Saskatchewan (where the government proceeded to enact some of Canada's most pro-union labor legislation) and the popularity of the CCF toward the end of World War II at the federal level have been widely interpreted as major factors pushing Prime Minister Mackenzie King's Liberal federal government into granting unions legal recognition and establishing a new framework for collective bargaining.

The CCF's successor, the New Democratic Party (NDP), was cofounded by the Canadian Labour Congress (CLC), Canada's largest union central, in 1961. The NDP has acted, in part, as the political expression of the labor movement, which, in turn, provides it with much of its financial and organizational support. During the past two decades, provincial NDP governments in Saskatchewan, Manitoba, British Columbia and, most recently, Ontario have all made labor relations reform a key element in their programs. Their innovations have had a broader, national influence. The British Columbia Labour Code, enacted in the mid-1970s, for example, profoundly affected labor law reforms enacted federally and in most other provinces whose governments did not share the NDP's social democratic politics.

While recent NDP labor legislation has not always pleased the labor movement—and particularly unions in the public sector—the election of social democratic provincial governments has continued to create an opening for legislative reforms generally supportive of unions.

In Quebec, postwar labor relations has been somewhat different. Social democratic politics did not emerge until the 1960s, with the growth of the separatist Parti Québécois (PQ). Quebec's trade union movement evolved according to a European model of plural unionism with three major union federations, rather than a single dominant union central as in English-speaking Canada.

Quebec labor legislation, which had been extremely restrictive of union activity until the early 1960s, was dramatically transformed by the Liberal provincial government of Jean Lesage, as part of the Quiet Revolution that swept Quebec politics during that period. The Quebec labor movement was extremely militant during this period, with many of its key leaders ending up in jail for disobeying back-to-work legislation and court injunctions.

The 1976 election of the PQ, to which the unions were strongly aligned, resulted in further changes in labor legislation, including a ban on employers hiring new, nonunion employees during a strike, the so-called "Anti-Scab" provisions.

The structure of the Canadian economy has also been a major factor influencing the development of labor relations. Canada's economy is still characterized by reliance on capital-intensive resource extraction industries such as mining, oil and gas, forestry and fishing. Resource industries are vulnerable to erratic fluctuations in international demand and price, a fact that has been partly responsible for the very high incidence of industrial conflict in this sector in Canada.

The pattern of unionization has, to a significant degree, reflected the structure of the Canadian economy. With the significant exception of oil and gas production, the major resource extraction industries are highly unionized. In provinces such as British Columbia, where forestry, mining and fishing have been the foundation of the economy, provincial industrial relations have been critically shaped by the fortunes of these industries and by the militant union traditions that have characterized their workforces—traditions that have many parallels in countries with similar resource-based industries.

In other provinces, key resource disputes, such as Quebec's 1949 asbestos strike, or the 1981 Inco Nickel strike at Sudbury, Ontario, have become symbols, and rallying points, for the labor movement.

However, as a source of employment—and union influence—the resource sector is diminishing, largely due to the increasingly capital-intensive nature of the industries concerned, the impact of technological change, and the reluctance of the major firms to invest in more labor-intensive downstream processing and manufacture of the raw materials.

Although Canada has a substantial, if increasingly besieged, manufacturing sector, most of this sector is concentrated in the belt of land in central Canada stretching from Windsor in southwestern Ontario through Hamilton and Toronto to Montreal. Many regions of the country have little or no manufacturing, and are heavily dependent on resources, agriculture and other primary industries.

Canada's manufacturing sector, which was the center of many of the famous union recognition disputes during and immediately after World War II, is highly unionized. Until recently, the high level of U.S. ownership of manufacturing was accompanied by a corresponding dominance of U.S.-based international unions.

The private, service sector of the economy has grown dramatically in recent years. In this regard, Canada is part of a well documented international trend toward a more service-based economy. Relatively high levels of unemployment, the highly competitive labor market and strong opposition to unionization by many of the larger employers have combined to result in a relatively low level of unionization. Fewer than 10% of workers in commercial services are union members, for example.

The virtual absence of unions in banking, insurance, financial services and services to business contrasts sharply with the much higher levels in manufacturing, resources and the public sector. While some private-sector services, such as hotels, restaurants and retail outlets, are partially organized, there is little evidence to suggest that private services will see any substantial growth in unionization in the near future.

In contrast, the public sector of the economy is very highly unionized. Approximately 70% of public-sector workers are members of unions. Canadian legislation permits unionization of all levels of government, with the exception of the armed forces, security services and some, but not all, police officers. The relatively high level of public-sector unionization should also be viewed in light of the fact that Canada's public sector is, proportionately, a good deal larger than its U.S. counterpart (although smaller than its counterpart in many European countries).

Notable among the more recent economic developments affecting Canadian industrial relations is the continuing trend toward the integration of the U.S. and Canadian economies, particularly as a result of the 1989 Canada-U.S. Free Trade Agreement and the possible extension of this agreement to include Mexico and other Latin American countries. Continental integration is bringing to Canada many of the competitive pressures which have shaped the bargaining climate in the United States. Whether the new economic pressures will lead to a corresponding decline in union density in Canada's manufacturing sector remains in question.

THE LEGISLATIVE FRAMEWORK OF CANADIAN INDUSTRIAL RELATIONS

The Establishment of Collective Bargaining Rights in the Private Sector

Although a number of important pieces of labor legislation were passed in Canada before World War II, the contemporary labor relations system can be traced to Privy Council Order 1003 of 1944, known as the Wartime Labour Relations Regulations. This legislation marked a major turning point in government policy toward trade unions. Previously, unions had been treated with suspicion and public policy toward them had been one of restricting union growth and curtailing their economic influence, while protecting the interests of employers.

Privy Council Order (P.C.) 1003 drew heavily from the U.S. Wagner Act of 1935. It included: legal recognition and certification for trade unions representing workers in the private sector; an obligation on employers to bargain in good faith with trade unions; a two-stage compulsory conciliation process to assist the parties in reaching a legally binding collective agreement; the concept of unfair labor practices; and a grievance procedure for resolving disputes during the term of a collective agreement without recourse to a strike or lockout.

The emergency federal wartime legislation (which applied in provincial jurisdictions as well) provided the model for subsequent labor legislation at both levels of government. The experience and precedents of P.C. 1003 encouraged the provinces to grant legal recognition to unions and establish a broadly similar collective bargaining framework when the federal government's emergency powers expired in early 1948.

P.C. 1003 was a response to union pressure under the wartime conditions of skill shortages, full employment and substantial price inflation. But the way in which it accommodated labor's demands critically shaped the development of the emerging collective bargaining process and, to a degree perhaps not realized at the time, decisively influenced the future development of the labor movement.

Although Canadian labor legislation drew very extensively from the U.S. model, it differed—and continues to differ—in certain important respects. Whereas in the United States, workers were permitted the right to strike over grievances during the term of a collective agreement, a right which U.S. unions customarily sign away as a condition of achieving a settlement, Canadian labor law, with the exception of Saskatchewan, is more restrictive. It bans strikes during the term of an agreement. Canada also continued its own practice, established early in the century, of compulsory conciliation, or in some provinces, mediation, requiring this process to be completed before the parties engaged in a strike or lockout.

Yet if some aspects of the Canadian system placed additional limitations on unions, other parts of the Canadian system came to be more supportive of union activities, particularly in contrast to a U.S. framework, which became increasingly restrictive after World War II. Certain rights granted to U.S. workers under the Wagner Act were subsequently circumscribed by the passage of the Taft-Hartley Act after the war. Enacted in response to vigorous employer lobbying and influenced by the cold war fear that unions were becoming dominated by subversive elements, Taft-Hartley was designed, in part, to redress what U.S. employers saw as the too favorable treatment given to unions by President Franklin Roosevelt's earlier legislation.

Moreover, U.S. labor and constitutional jurisprudence has tended, in recent years, to erode earlier union gains. For example, during union organizing drives, employers have the right to lobby employees, a practice which is viewed as the legitimate exercise of the employers' constitutional "freedom of speech." Similar activities can be ruled as unfair labor practices under Canadian labor law.

Union certification is easier under Canadian legislation, because most labor boards have been empowered to grant recognition without a vote, if they have clear evidence—normally through signed cards—that a majority of workers supports unionization. In some provinces they are even empowered to grant certification if employer interference has been so blatant that the employees have been denied a fair vote. Similarly, the definition of unfair labor practices by employers is broader in Canada and easier to enforce.

The comparatively easier legal requirements for certification in Canada provide one explanation for the growing difference in union density between the two countries. In the early postwar period the United States had a level of unionization of about 35%, slightly higher than Canada's. However, a divergent trend began to emerge during the late 1960s. Recent estimates suggest that U.S. union density has fallen to about 16% or less than half the 1990 Canadian figure of 36.2% of the nonagricultural paid workforce.

The Second Phase of Labor Legislation: Bargaining Rights for Public-Sector Workers

While private-sector workers achieved collective bargaining rights by 1945, it was not until the 1960s that workers in the public sector began to achieve similar rights. (The exception was Saskatchewan's CCF, which granted such rights in 1944.) In 1965, the Quebec government extended collective bargaining to the provincial public sector.

This decision was influenced by the fact that increasingly militant public-sector workers were simply ignoring the existing "consultative mechanisms" and striking illegally. The labor relations framework had become unenforceable largely because union opposition had become so widespread. The change was also influenced by the argument that there was no justification for denying public-sector workers the same rights enjoyed by workers in the private sector.

Change came at the federal level soon after the Quebec legislation. The recommendations of the federally appointed Heeney Commission, the example of Quebec, and the reality of escalating illegal strikes by postal workers and other federal employees persuaded the Liberal government to grant collective bargaining rights for federal government employees in 1967.

However, the legal framework establishing public-sector bargaining was considerably more restrictive than in the private sector, with a number of key areas such as job classifications, pensions, staffing levels, the use of part-time and casual employees, and seniority being retained as the unilateral prerogative of the government. In addition, the government set up a process whereby certain workers could be "designated" as essential and required to work during a strike of their bargaining unit.

By the middle of the 1970s, the other provinces had followed the precedent of Quebec and the federal government and granted collective bargaining rights to public employees. However, as at the federal level, the rights granted were generally much more limited than in the private sector, with many provinces substituting compulsory arbitration for the right to strike. Some provinces also followed the federal model by establishing a system for designating essential workers.

Recent Developments: The Retreat From Collective Bargaining

If the period until the mid-1970s was one of legislative reform encouraging—or at least acquiescing to—unionization and the spread of collective bargaining, the ensuing years have been characterized by a notably less supportive approach by governments and employers toward unionization. Concerns over the presumed inflationary impact of high wage settlements, over Canada's international competitive situation, over government budget deficits and over the disruptive use of the strike weapon, particularly in the essential services within the public sector, have come to overshadow earlier commitments to the promotion of collective bargaining.

Since the late 1970s, federal and provincial governments have felt it increasingly necessary to end strikes through "back-to-work" legislation, often imposing contracts unilaterally on striking workers. Sanctions against unions have become more frequent and the labor relations climate, especially in the public sector, has been characterized by polarization and frequent conflicts, particularly around wage controls.

Recently, a number of provincial governments, most notably British Columbia and Saskatchewan, have enacted far-reaching amendments to their labor codes, imposing new restrictions on the exercise of the strike weapon and further limiting the bargaining rights of public-sector workers. From having what were arguably the most pro-union labor codes, these provinces have adopted much more restrictive labor legislation. The public policy objective is now to reduce the level of unionization and curtail the bargaining power of the trade union movement in order to minimize labor disputes and attract foreign investment. In 1991, however, both British Columbia and Saskatchewan elected NDP governments that are more supportive of unions.

Others provinces which had been less enthusiastic in promoting collective bargaining, such as Alberta, New Brunswick and Newfoundland, have also retreated significantly from the bargaining framework enacted in the 1970s, particularly with respect to workers in the public sector. In Quebec, the province has expanded the scope of its essential services restrictions to cover additional groups of public-sector workers. While the federal government has not dramatically changed the Canada Labour Code and the Public Service Staff Relations Act, it has imposed strict wage guidelines on its own employees.

The retreat from public policy supporting collective bargaining has not been universal, however. Pressure from women's organizations and unions has led Manitoba and Ontario to introduce new and far-reaching pay equity legislation. Although initially implemented in the public sector, the intent is to apply it to private industry as well.

Under the previous government in Ontario, unions were given the right to request first contract arbitration in cases where employers refused to negotiate in good faith with a newly certified bargaining unit. This was to deal with situations where the employer was intent on reversing a unionization vote by simply refusing to negotiate a first contract or by forcing a strike or lockout with the intention of eventually decertifying the new union.

The newly elected New Democratic Party (NDP) government of Ontario, which has close ties with the trade unions, has indicated its intention to introduce a number of measures designed to expand the collective bargaining rights of workers. Legislation for a wage protection fund to protect workers who lose their jobs through the bankruptcy of their firms has been introduced.

Still, the trend from the late 1970s has been toward establishing a legislative environment more sympathetic to the concerns of employers.

THE ADMINISTRATION OF LABOR LEGISLATION

While the preceding has discussed some of the key policy matters associated with labor legislation in Canada, it has not explained how labor law is administered. The Canadian system, while highly legalistic in many respects, has generally chosen to minimize the direct role of the courts in labor relations matters. Instead, various quasi-judicial bodies have been established to regulate the certification of unions and the administration of labor disputes.

In this regard, labor relations boards play a central role in the operation of the Canadian industrial relations system. Boards have the legal authority to administer the labor acts. The rationale behind establishing labor relations boards is that they offer a more flexible and pragmatic approach to resolving complex industrial disputes than do the courts. Because unions and employers have an ongoing relationship, a major policy objective of labor policy has been to find ways to settle differences that promote cooperation and minimize sources of future friction between the parties.

While usually appointed by the relevant minister of labor, boards normally draw their members from both employers and unions, to provide a balance of views and experience. Regardless of their past affiliation, board members are expected to behave impartially.

The labor relations boards administer the law in matters such as the certification and decertification of unions, determining the scope of bargaining units, ruling on the legality of a strike or lockout, adjudicating unfair labor practices and a wide range of other industrial relations matters. They also oversee the work of conciliation and mediation officers employed to assist the parties in reaching a collective agreement. Board officers frequently provide assistance to unions and employers during disputes.

As in other countries, a great deal of the public policy and legislative activity of governments in Canada has focused on broad employment issues not directly associated with collective bargaining. For example, the provincial and federal ministries of labor play a significant role in administering the wide range of labor standards governing hours of work, vacations, statutory holidays, maternity leave, minimum wages, overtime payments, health and safety, and a variety of other employment matters.

Separate quasi-judicial boards and commissions have also been established to administer Canada's system of workers' compensation insurance. This supplants the civil liability of employers for injuries incurred by their employees by a system designed to provide payments to injured or disabled workers based on income loss and the extent of disability.

There is also a federally administered system of compulsory unemployment insurance. It is funded by levies imposed on workers and employers and administered by a national Unemployment Insurance Commission. Finally, the provincial and federal human rights commissions are also increasingly engaged in providing advice and hearing cases over issues involving workplace discrimination.

THE IMPACT OF THE NEW CHARTER OF RIGHTS AND FREEDOMS

One very specific change to Canada's constitutional framework merits special mention. The enactment in 1982 of a U.S.-style Charter of Rights and Freedoms has introduced a new and clearly very important influence into Canadian industrial relations. The full impact of the charter is by no means yet clear and it will take decades for the courts to address the many areas in which it conceivably may apply to labor relations.

Formally, the charter applies only to relations between government and individuals. However, because the public sector is such a large component of the Canadian labor relations system and because the system itself is based on extensive government legislation and regulation, the impact of the charter will be quite significant.

561

Potentially, a very wide range of labor legislation, government administrative activity, employer labor relations policies and union activity are encompassed by its various provisions. Many long-standing industrial relations practices are now being reviewed in the courts to determine if they violate provisions of the charter.

Several issues have quickly come to the fore. The charter provides for freedom of association, but does not specify that the right to collective bargaining and the right to strike are encompassed within this provision. In response to legislation suspending collective bargaining or barring the right to strike in the public sector, unions have pressed for rulings from the courts clarifying that the right of freedom of association includes the right to bargain collectively and to go on strike. Thus far, Supreme Court decisions have not supported this view.

Another area of contention has been the right and obligations of individual workers to the unions which bargain on their behalf. Many agreements include union security provisions requiring that all employees must either be union members or contribute dues to support the union that acts as their bargaining agent. Several individuals, in different provinces, have challenged the right of unions to use any part of this dues money for activities outside collective bargaining, defined in a very narrow way, on the grounds that they should not be forced, through compulsory union dues contributions, to support political and social causes they may oppose. Other provisions of the internal constitutions and practices of unions have also been subject to charter appeals.

The statutory powers of labor boards, and particularly their authority to enforce certain decisions on employers or unions, has also been the subject of court challenges. For example, the right of the Manitoba board to impose a first contract on a reluctant employer was the subject of a constitutional challenge. The case was appealed to the Supreme Court, which affirmed the board's jurisdiction.

The charter has also led a reexamination of legislation and collective agreement provisions which might be construed as discriminating against individuals by virtue of age, race, sexual orientation, disability, ethnic origin and other factors. In sum, the new charter is beginning to have a major impact on a wide range of labor relations issues. The jurisprudence can be expected to expand substantially in the coming years, with results which are not entirely predictable at this juncture.

WORKER ORGANIZATIONS: RECENT DEVELOPMENTS IN THE CANADIAN LABOR MOVEMENT

A Profile of the Membership and Organization of Trade Unions
Approximately four million workers belong to trade unions in Canada, representing about 36.2% of the employed labor force. The number of organized workers has increased at a rate paralleling the growth of the labor force since the mid-1970s. As a consequence, the percentage of organized workers has remained relatively stable over the past decade, with perhaps a slight decline beginning to appear at the beginning of the 1990s. The

relatively stable union membership in Canada contrasts with the precipitous decline in union density during the 1980s in the United States, United Kingdom, Japan and other jurisdictions.

The figures on union density do conceal some major changes within the composition of the organized workforce, however. In some industries, such as forestry, mining and construction, the number of union members has fallen. In contrast, union membership has continued to rise in certain service industries, especially in the public sector.

Approximately 37% of union members are now women, almost double the percentage organized scarcely 20 years earlier. Women constitute four-fifths of new union recruits. Perhaps not surprisingly, this increase has been accompanied by new affirmative action policies within unions and a notable increase in bargaining demands addressing issues of concern to women, such as pay equity, sexual harassment, child care and new hiring and promotion provisions in agreements.

The Canadian labor movement is divided between unions affiliated to U.S.-based internationals or autonomous Canadian unions. For most of the period following World War II, international unions based in manufacturing, resources and transportation dominated the Canadian labor scene. In 1961, more than 70% of all unionized workers in Canada were in international unions.

However, due to the growth of the public sector and the granting of bargaining rights to government employees, the membership of autonomous Canadian public-sector unions has increased dramatically over the past three decades. Disaffiliation of a number of Canadian sections of international unions coupled with the decline in employment in economic sectors where the remaining internationals are concentrated have had the combined effect of reducing the percentage of workers in international unions to 32% of total union membership in Canada.

The major labor central is the Canadian Labor Congress (CLC), which currently represents just over 2.4 million workers, or about three-fifths of the total unionized labor force. It is composed of international unions, national unions and a few small independent Canadian locals. Because of its size and the key sectors of the economy represented by its affiliated unions, the CLC has been the principal representative of organized labor at the national level in Canada.

In addition to the national organization, CLC affiliates in each province are organized into provincial federations of labor. This is in part necessitated by the fact that so much labor legislation and public policy on industrial relations issues is in the hands of the provinces. The provincial federations of labor are responsible for coordinating the activities of member unions, providing support during disputes, representing the interests of labor to the respective provincial government and implementing policies established by the national body.

There are also several much smaller labor centrals, including the 211,000-member Canadian Federation of Labour (CFL), which represents a number of construction trades unions affiliated to the AFL-CIO. This central is composed of unions that broke away from the Canadian Labor Congress in the early 1980s over disagreements about the political direction of the CLC and its system of representation.

In Quebec, there is another independent labor central, the Confederation of National Trade Unions (CNTU), which represents about 212,000 workers, largely in the public sector. And the Quebec teachers also have their own provincial labor organization separate from other teachers' unions in the rest of Canada, with a membership of 103,000 in 1990. Since its emergence during the period of the Quiet Revolution in the 1960s, the Quebec labor movement has been strongly separatist, with many of its unions favoring an independent Quebec state.

During the 1960s and 1970s the Quebec union centrals frequently espoused a Marxist economic and political analysis quite different from the more "bread and butter" approach of unions in the rest of Canada. In recent years, however, they have tended to downplay these views as the Quebec political spectrum has moved sharply to the right. Their current priority is independence, which they see as a precondition to progressive labor reform in the future.

Aside from the major national and Quebec-based labor centrals, there are also a number of independent unions, some of which are loosely associated at the national level. Nurses, teachers, university faculty and various smaller professional and semiprofessional employees form the bulk of these organizations.

Reasons for the Continuing High Level of Union Membership

One of the most interesting features of the labor movement in Canada during the 1980s has been its success in recruiting new members. This success contrasts sharply with the United States, where membership has declined sharply. A number of reasons have been suggested for this situation. First, the Canadian legal and public policy environment has been more favorable, at least until the late 1970s. Canadian labor law has made it easier for unions to obtain certifications and more difficult to lose them.

Second, a much larger part of the public sector in Canada is unionized. Moreover, as Canada's public sector is about one-third greater, proportionately, than that of the United States, this has had a significant impact on overall union density.

Third, the existence of a social democratic party has created the political opening for more progressive labor legislation to be enacted. Indeed, the broader political culture of Canada, which has permitted discussion of socialist and social democratic ideas more freely than in the United States, may have also been significant in maintaining public support for trade unions.

A final factor that has been suggested is that the unions themselves within Canada have been more effective in defending their gains, partly through a more militant orientation and their willingness to build bridges with other popular-sector organizations. While in the United States a right-wing backlash, beginning in the late 1940s, replaced many of the more militant organizers of U.S. unions, the impact in Canada of McCarthyism was much less pronounced. This, too, may have been a contributing factor.

Whatever the complex reasons, unions in Canada still seem to be able to persuade current and prospective members that being organized can make a difference to their terms and conditions of employment. As a consequence, they have remained attractive to workers.

The "Canadianization" of the Canadian Labor Movement

One of the key developments during the 1980s has been the gradual weakening of formal ties with the U.S. trade union movement through the disaffiliation of key unions such as the Canadian Auto Workers. Many reasons have been advanced for this occurrence. But according to the unions themselves, a major reason has been that they reject the more conservative political, social and collective bargaining orientation of their U.S. counterparts.

As noted earlier, a key feature of the Canadian trade union movement is that it has followed a more explicitly social democratic political agenda than its American counterpart. This has also meant attempting to influence the broader public policy direction of governments in a wide range of areas outside labor relations.

Canadian unions have also been notably more critical of employer proposals for concessions at the bargaining table, preferring a more adversarial approach, compared to what they view as collaboration with employers. For the same reason, new industrial relations approaches such as "quality of working life" and "team concepts" have met considerable skepticism in many unions.

Union militancy in Canada during the past decade has been particularly notable in the public sector, with regular and major confrontations between governments and their employees at all levels. Illegal strikes and back-to-work orders have been frequent. This has occurred despite an increasingly hostile economic and public-policy environment.

In sum, the Canadian labor movement appears intent on following a very different approach from its U.S. counterparts.

RECENT TRENDS IN COLLECTIVE BARGAINING IN CANADA

Wage Developments

Although Canadian trade unions have done comparatively well in maintaining membership, they have had notably less success in preventing inflation from eroding real wages. While the pattern varies significantly from region to region and from one sector of the economy to another, on average, unionized workers have lost approximately 10% of their real purchasing power since the mid-1970s.

This fall is less precipitous than that experienced by unionized workers in the United States (and particularly the highly unionized "Rust Belt"), but it compares unfavorably with the experience of workers in much of Western Europe and Japan. Unorganized workers have seen a comparable decline in real wages.

The decline can be attributed both to deliberate government policies designed to restrain wage increases and to the more difficult circumstances facing the Canadian economy in recent years.

The first major wage restraint legislation was enacted by the federal government in October 1975. Claiming that inflation was a national emergency, it passed the Anti-Inflation Act, which, like the War Measures Act, enabled it to override provincial jurisdictions and impose limits on all negotiated wage increases in the public and private sectors of the economy for a three-year period.

At the expiry of the program, federal and provincial governments imposed a new series of wage-restraint measures on the public sector, either directly through legislated wage controls in some jurisdictions or, indirectly, through limiting the wage and salary component of departmental and program budgets. At the same time they urged the private sector to follow their "lead" by adhering to similar guidelines.

While wage settlements were restricted by policy in the public sector, negotiated increases in the private sector were also affected by the much less favorable bargaining climate initiated by the very severe 1981–82 recession. Faced with massive layoffs in manufacturing and resource industries and a sharp increase in unemployment, many unions were forced to accept settlements significantly below the rate of inflation, changing their focus to job security, severance pay and fighting back employer demands for contract concessions.

On average, negotiated wage settlements failed to keep up with inflation throughout the prolonged period of economic recovery, which continued until the end of the decade of the 1980s. Unemployment remained high despite rapid economic growth. And, even when it finally began to fall toward the end of the decade, the bargaining climate had changed so dramatically, as a result of other factors, that unions found it difficult to recoup their losses.

The beginning of the 1990s has witnessed what may become the most severe recession since World War II. Unlike the 1981–82 downturn, this recession has been accompanied by massive structural adjustments associated with the Canada-U.S. Free Trade deal. The federal government has imposed de facto wage controls that could cut real wages of public employees by between 5 and 10% over the next three years. Seven provinces have chosen to establish similar—in some cases more stringent—controls policies. Only NDP-led Ontario has explicitly rejected a policy of public-sector controls.

Private-sector settlements in manufacturing began to plummet by the middle of 1991 as a result of the unprecedented loss in manufacturing jobs, particularly in Ontario. Rising unemployment and the deepening recession are likely to have a continuing effect in dampening down wage increases during the early 1990s in the private sector, while conservative fiscal policies and budget deficits will likely result in continuing controls in the public sector.

For unorganized workers, the pattern has been broadly similar. While wages rates in the unorganized workplace reflect market forces, at the bottom end of the scale they are also significantly influenced by government labor standards which set minimum wages. Since the late 1970s, provincial and federal governments have allowed minimum wage levels to fall significantly behind inflation, with the result that real wages for nonunion workers, particularly in the low-wage service sector, have declined significantly, a fact exacerbated by the growing use of part-time and temporary workers.

Bargaining Trends On Other Issues
During the 1980s employers became much more aggressive at the bargaining table, demanding contract concessions such as two-tier wages, cuts in employee benefits, more flexibility in the deployment of labor, the erosion of seniority rights, exclusion of temporary and part-time workers from benefit plans, and significant amendments to union security and employee grievance procedures.

Privatization, cuts in staffing, the wholesale closure of certain public services and government fiscal restraint policies have the public-sector equivalent of increased competitive pressures. Bargaining, as noted earlier, has been highly confrontational throughout the 1980s, with many lengthy and bitter strikes, frequently accompanied by back-to-work legislation.

This is not to suggest that unions have abandoned their efforts to make real gains. In areas such as maternity and parental leave, pay equity, benefits for part-time workers, pensions, and health and safety, unions have negotiated significant improvements. There have also been reductions in the length of the work week for hourly paid employees in parts of the public and private sectors. However, these have tended to be much more incremental in nature than the major wage and benefit gains of the 1960s and early 1970s. Moreover, they have often been offset by bargaining setbacks in other areas.

Collective bargaining trends have also become more regionalist and decentralized, partly in response to the very uneven economic recovery that characterized the latter part of the 1980s. Wages (and the level of union organization) in the construction industry in the western provinces, for example, have plummeted, while the booming Ontario economy experienced settlements rising slightly above the rate of inflation during the final years of the 1980s and the beginning of the 1990s. These developments suggest that many of the traditional national bargaining relationships are becoming severely strained or actually are dissolving.

CONCLUSION: CANADA'S ADVERSARIAL SYSTEM WILL CONTINUE TO PRODUCE CONFLICT DURING THE 1990S

The future of labor relations in Canada will be critically influenced by the response of employers, unions and governments to the restructuring of the Canadian economy, particularly as a result of the Canada-U.S. Free Trade Agreement and its possible extension to Mexico. The FTA is already integrating the two economies at an accelerating pace. In the process, it is unleashing new competitive pressures on labor.

There is already considerable evidence that businesses operating in Canada are becoming much more aggressive in their efforts to cut labor costs. The harmonization of the two economies, when viewed in light of the transfer of production and jobs within the U.S. to the Sun Belt and Mexico, will lead to the abandonment of certain kinds of labor-intensive manufacturing within Canada, and to greater pressure on Canadian workers to accept concessions.

However, attempts to reduce real wages as part of a strategy of making labor costs in Canada more competitive with other jurisdictions will be strongly resisted by the trade union movement, both at the bargaining table and in the political arena. While trade union growth has been arrested during the 1980s, there has been no loss in union members parallel to that which has occurred in the United States and the United Kingdom. The recent history of labor conflict in Canada suggests that unions will not readily abandon their longstanding gains.

In the private sector, disputes over job security, work rules and employer demands for concessions will, therefore, be a central factor of labor relations. Significant confrontations between public employees and governments over wages, working conditions and the funding of services will, if anything, escalate, as disputes by postal workers, nurses, hospital workers, railway employees and other provincial and federal government employees have recently demonstrated. How the increasingly divergent demands of economic harmonization and union aspirations will be resolved remains unclear. What is clear is that labor relations in the 1990s in Canada will be anything but boring.

FURTHER READING

Adams, G. W. *Canadian Labour Law: A Comprehensive Text.* Aurora, Ontario: Canada Law Book, 1985.

Anderson, John C., Morley Gunderson, and Allen Ponak. *Union-Management Relations in Canada.* Don Mills, Ontario: Addison-Wesley, 1989.

Boivin, J., and Jacques Guilbault. *Les Relations patronales-syndicales au Québec.* Chicoutimi, Quebec: Gaetan Morin, 1982.

Carrothers, A. W. R., E. E. Palmer, and W. B. Rayner. *Collective Bargaining Law in Canada.* Toronto: Butterworths, 1986.

Commission Consultative sur le Travail. *Rapport.* Québec: Editeur officiel, Gouvernement du Québec, 1985.

Craig, Alton. *The System of Industrial Relations in Canada.* Scarborough, Ontario: Prentice-Hall, 1983.

Giles, Anthony, and Gregor Murray. "Towards an Historical Understanding of Industrial Relations Theory in Canada." Quebec: Laval University Department of Industrial Relations, 1987.

Ison, T. G. *Workers' Compensation in Canada.* Toronto: Butterworths, 1983.

Jamieson, Stuart. *Industrial Relations in Canada.* 2nd ed. Toronto: Macmillan, 1973.

Kumar, P., M. L. Coates, and D. Arrowsmith, eds. *The Current Industrial Relations Scene in Canada.* Kingston, Ontario: Industrial Relations Centre, Queen's University, 1988.

Panitch, Leo, and Donald Swartz. *The Assault on Trade Union Freedoms.* Toronto: Garamond Press, 1988.

Swimmer, Gene, and Mark Thompson, eds. *Conflict or Compromise: The Future of Public Sector Industrial Relations.* Montreal: The Institute for Research in Public Policy, 1984.

Weiler, Paul. *Reconcilable Differences: New Directions in Canadian Law Reform.* Agincourt, Ontario: Carswell, 1980.

Woods, H. D. *Report of the Task Force on Labour Relations.* Ottawa: The Queen's Printer, 1968.

WOMEN

LORNA R. MARSDEN

STATUS OF WOMEN ISSUES

The status of women in Canada compares favorably with that in most OECD countries. Canadian women, while well situated in comparison to most of the world's women, nonetheless hold a secondary status compared to men regardless of their social class, ethnicity or age. While the early history of women in Canada tells of struggles for equality, the years since the end of the Second World War have seen major changes in the status of women.

Women constitute more than half of the Canadian population. At birth the proportion of females is slightly less than males, but with each succeeding decade women predominate more and more, until about two-thirds of Canadians over the age of 75 are women. In the most recent generation, the life expectancy of women has increased to nearly 80 years. Girls born in 1985 can expect to live almost seven years longer than boys born at the same time. Changes in fertility have been especially important to women and their families since 1945. The postwar baby boom was a significant departure from a long-term downward trend in average family size. After the war this rose to a high of 3.9 in 1959, but the average has dropped to 1.7 since the early 1980s. Childbirth and its complications used to be a leading cause of death among adult women. In 1940, 400 women died per 100,000 live births in Canada. By 1970 that figure had been reduced to 20.2 and by 1988 to 5.0. Women are much more likely now to die of cancer of the lung or breast and heart disease. The health status of women is one good indicator of the improved status of women in Canada overall.

From our knowledge of Native women before European settlement in Canada, to the pioneering years of European settlement, and throughout our history, Canadian women have played a crucial economic role not only in the household but in the larger economy of Canadian society. This role has increased dramatically since 1945. The economic role of women, both in the household and outside, is a crucial factor in explaining the status of women in the community and in the family.

Over the past 40 years, there has been a dramatic increase in female labor force participation rates, so that women now constitute just less than half of all of Canada's labor force participants, and almost 60% of adult women in Canada work for pay. But the pattern of labor force participation has changed even more dramatically. The cohort of women born in the 1930s entered the labor force after leaving school, dropped out of the labor force to have children, and then some of them returned to paid work when their children were grown. All subsequent cohorts show increasingly permanent attachment to the labor force. By 1988, the participation rate for married women with children under school age was 62% and for single-parent mothers with children in school about 72%. Women's permanent attachment to the paid labor force shows in the participation rate but also in the increasing concern among women for their opportunities, wages, pensions and benefits from paid work.

The wages of Canadian women are, on average, about 65% of the wages of men. Even among equally qualified professional workers, women on average earn about 65% of men's salaries. Some of this difference is accounted for by segregation within occupations (for example, women lawyers tend to be specialized in less well paying family law, while men are more highly concentrated in corporate law), but, among all workers, much of the difference in women's wages is accounted for by occupational segregation. Almost three-quarters of women in Canada work in clerical, sales and other low-wage service occupations. Some of the wage difference is accounted for by the lower proportion of women with postsecondary degrees and specialized education. But when all such variables are held constant there is still a wage gap attributed to discrimination in Canadian society. This has been a focus of attention of those interested in women's equality.

Because the wages of women are lower than those of men, pensions are also lower. Canadian women in the paid labor force contribute to the Canada Pension Plan, and universal old-age security is available for all men and women over age 65. But for women not in the paid labor force, or women who drop out for the purpose of raising families, retirement income is low. In the past decade a number of adjustments to pensions have been made and older women are no longer the poorest group of Canadians, although they are among the poorest. Now it is single mothers who are the poorest group of Canadians.

Another indicator of the status of women concerns education. The amount of education women have is closely linked to the type of occupations they hold and therefore their incomes. But the correlation between education and occupation and income is not as high for Canadian women as it is for men, or to put it in terms of human capital, the returns to education for women are not as great as they are for men comparing lifetime earnings. In general, women are more likely than men to complete high school. In most provinces, the legal minimum school leaving age is 16 but the full primary and secondary education program requires between 11 and 13 years, so normal school leaving age is between 17 and 19.

School dropouts, or those who leave before the end of high school, constitute one of the groups with high rates of unemployment or underemployment in Canada. However, while women are considerably more likely than men to finish high school, many fewer have skills in subjects considered crucial for many contemporary occupations, such as math and physics.

It is at the level of postsecondary education that gender differences become most significant. In the Canadian postsecondary education system, which varies from province to province, there are apprenticeships, community colleges (or collèges d'enseignement général et professional—CEGEP—in the province of Quebec), and universities.

Among Canadian women as a whole, the great majority has a high school education only; about one in five has less than nine years of education (considered the minimum level of literacy in Canada); and in 1988, only 10% of women 15 years or older were university graduates (compared to almost 14% of men). However, among the younger age cohorts the picture is rather different. By the mid 1980s, among women aged 25–34, only 7% had less than 9 years of education; 52% had high school graduation and nearly 40% had some kind of postsecondary qualification.

In apprenticeship programs, women constitute less than 5% of those enrolled and, even there, are concentrated in such traditional female trades as cook and hair stylist. Several provincial governments are making concerted efforts to attract women into skills training, and into nontraditional jobs. In the face of increased competitive pressure on Canadian workers for productivity and increased technical skills, retraining for female workers in low-skill jobs is a major concern of governments and such voluntary organizations as the Canadian Congress for Learning Opportunities for Women.

The community college system is a phenomenon of the 1960s and was originally male dominant, but by 1984–85, women made up more than half of the full-time students. In 1988–89, however, this dropped to 46%. As in the high schools and universities, women in the community colleges are enrolled in traditional areas of study in health sciences and the arts and humanities.

At major universities women have been admitted as degree students since the 1880s. But the proportion of university women remained quite small in all fields except those particularly designed for women. The latter include teaching, household science, librarianship, nursing, physical and occupational therapy and such of the arts as were considered appropriate for women. At the end of the Second World War, returning veterans were granted special support and priority to help them acquire university degrees. Although about 50,000 Canadian women had joined the services during the war, only a tiny proportion took advantage of the university education. The rapid expansion and popularization of university education in the postwar period changed the nature and meaning of a university degree. Women increased in numbers but declined as a proportion of university students. Between 1950 and 1980, the attendance of women increased gradually, and women became a majority in undergraduate faculties by the mid-1980s. During the 1980s, women's enrollment in professional programs, such as law, engineering and pharmacy, increased rapidly. The proportion of older women returning to university on a part-time basis rose dramatically in the 1980s, and women now dominate in part-time postsecondary education.

In Quebec, education was under the control of the church until 1964 and women were encouraged to fulfill traditional roles and to remain in the domestic arts programs. The Quiet Revolution of the 1960s in Quebec rapidly changed women's roles, and the professions and universities opened to include a large proportion of women students. Quebec is now considered the most progressive province in many areas of women's rights and female representation in the professions.

It is in the master's and doctoral degrees that women fall behind, especially in scientific fields. The relatively small proportion of women receiving doctorates in Canada is echoed in the very small proportion of women full-time faculty in the universities. Less than 20% of university faculty are women and a very small percentage attain the highest ranks. While at least one woman has held full professorship in virtually every field in Canada, university teaching is dominated by men except in "female" disciplines.

The postwar period in Canadian education is characterized by major reforms in most provinces, pushed by the baby boom that followed the end of the war. The very large cohort of children swelled demand for schools and teachers and a major recruiting program was undertaken. With time, there was a demand for upgrading the qualifications of teachers, and both men and women returned to universities to complete their bachelor's and master's degrees of arts or education. Teaching has become increasingly specialized, with demand in the areas of science, languages and specialized areas in the arts. The demand for an upgrading of science teachers is the long-term effect in all of North America of the science race associated with the Cold War and the upgrading of requirements in industrial jobs. In the 1950s and 1960s this led to great demand for more technical and advanced education among young men, but as the science-based technologies of the contemporary period spill into the service, financial, health and social science areas, an increasing proportion of young women are being trained in fields linked to science and technology.

The civil status of women is largely a product of the Roman Catholic tradition in Quebec, the British traditions imposed on Canadian political life and, from the 1850s forward, the demands made by women for increased equality. The right to vote and the right to own and control property were issues settled everywhere, except in Quebec, by 1927. Canadian women won the vote first in the province of Manitoba in 1916 and in all provinces, except Quebec, in the next few years. The federal vote was won in 1918. Quebec women, who had periodically held voting rights, lost the vote at the end of the 19th century and regained it in the province of Quebec only in 1940. The much more complex question of the rights of single and married women to own and control their own property, bank accounts and economic life has been the subject of almost continuous reforms throughout the provinces. In the area of marriage laws, change continues. Even quite recently, the right to divorce was more easily available to husbands than wives. Until 1969 divorce required an act of parliament, and that process varied by province. The question of support after divorce is a provincial matter and puts women in an invidious position because of their restricted access to the labor market and constrained ability to gain support from their former husbands. The contemporary solution to this issue has been to require women to be economically independent and make divorce available on a no-fault basis with the support of children divided between the parents.

By these traditional measures of the status of women (income, education, occupation, civil status and life expectancy), Canadian women emerge not as equal with men but with a status greatly improved in the years since 1945.

SOURCES OF CHANGE IN THE STATUS OF WOMEN

To understand the changes in the status of women, three features of Canadian society must be understood. These underlie the pressures for change in Canada and, to a large extent, determine the form and timing of change. The first is the nature of the Canadian economy, which can be described as semi-peripheral, closely linked to the core economy of the United States. The influence on the work of Canadian women is both direct and indirect: directly, through employment in foreign-owned firms and through imported management systems, and indirectly through U.S. media views of desirable consumption and work practices.

The second factor is the importance of regional allegiances in Canada. The issues of language, multiculturalism and social class differences find their most immediate expression through provincial or regional cultures and their governments. In comparison to other modern societies, government in Canada is highly decentralized. Most of the issues that affect daily life, such as health, education, employment, civil justice, welfare and housing, are under the constitutional jurisdiction of provincial legislatures. Provincial legislatures devolve some issues to municipal governments. So Canadians identify more closely with provincial organizations, governments and cultures than with national institutions.

This is reflected in most voluntary associations with their powerful provincial branches and endemic regional, language and ethnic rivalries. Keeping a national focus on the concerns of Canadian women is an expensive undertaking of great complexity within established organizations such as political parties, unions, churches, women's organizations and even major corporations. Since the Report of the Royal Commission on the Status of Women in 1970, governments have established coordinating agencies and councils to focus on the status of women issues, but in voluntary associations only a small number of women have the time or money to participate in national organizations. This creates a structure of national elites who dominate nearly all national institutions. It makes it particularly difficult for women who are members of minorities to have their voices heard at the national level.

The third factor is the Canadian social movement, which influences public policy, and private life. National women's organizations of a secular and nonpartisan nature have been present in Canada for well over a century. Up until the end of the Second World War the cause of women was couched in the language of social reform and social betterment. In the 1960s, however, the form and substance of the argument for the improvement in the status of women changed.

THE MODERN WOMEN'S MOVEMENT

What is often called "second-wave feminism" in Canada emerged in the 1960s from the activism of women of the postwar generation. To a great extent, the contemporary women's movement uses the language of equality of rights and opportunity borrowing language from the civil rights movement of the United States and from the struggle of francophones for recognition and equality in Canada. While the objectives of the struggle and the major rationale for action shifted, the traditional women's organizations, which had existed in Canada from the days of suffrage, have stayed strong and involved.

The modern women's movement emerged in a variety of ways. In the early 1960s the peace movement organized by the Voice of Women, the rise of secular women's organizations in Quebec and the dissatisfaction of women with the domestic life which had been created by the postwar consumerism reactivated feminist concerns. The desire to give men returning from the war every opportunity in the economy had pushed women from the labor force, and the baby boom had kept them in the household. Their concerns were focused in the magazine *Chatelaine,* which, under the editorship of Doris Anderson, debated the public role of women at home. Finally, the many active Canadian women banded together to form the Committee on Equality for Women, led by Laura Sabia from St. Catharines, Ontario. This committee drew together leaders from the major women's organizations across the country and made representations to government on a number of matters. The catalyzing event was their success in having formed a Royal Commission on the Status of Women in Canada (RCSW).

The Royal Commission was begun under Prime Minister Lester Pearson in 1967. The commission was headed by Florence Bird, a well-known broadcaster (and subsequently senator), and the commissioners were from across the country, including Jeanne Lapointe, a Quebec academic and veteran of Quebec's Parent Commission on Education; Elsie Gregory MacGill, the first woman aeronautical engineer, former president of the Canadian Federation of Business and Professional Women's Clubs, and third-generation feminist; Judge Doris Ogilvie of Nova Scotia; and Lola Lange, a farm leader from the Prairies, among others.

The RCSW is significant not only for its 167 recommendations, which continue to influence the public agenda to this day, but for its public hearings, which roused the women of Canada to a common cause. Many hearings were broadcast on the Canadian Broadcasting Corporation, and, for the first time, women at home and at work realized how much their troubles were held in common. The rise of radical feminists with a new agenda and method of consciousness raising mobilized young women. By the late 1960s student activists had realized that the men of the new left movements were as patriarchal as their fathers had been, and the women left to organize for themselves.

A major concern of women was birth control and abortion, which became legal for women in Canada only in 1969 under highly regulated conditions. In 1970, an Abortion Caravan arrived in Ottawa and in a vigorous demonstration closed down Parliament, while in Quebec a similar demonstration took place. So even as the RCSW report was building common cause among women, the political division between the indépendantiste, or separatist, movement in Quebec and the federalist movement in Canada was evident. This division is a persistent theme in Canadian life.

When the RCSW reported, Laura Sabia and her committee developed an effective organizational strategy consisting of two parts. First, since many of the recommendations were directed to the provincial jurisdiction, they helped women organize provincially (e.g., the Ontario Committee on the Status of Women was formed early in 1971 to lobby the provincial government). Second, they got federal funding for a national conference on follow-up to the RCSW recommendations. The Strategy for Change Conference was held in Toronto in April 1972. From that conference emerged a common purpose among most women's groups in Canada, a network of relationships between generations and across regions, and the founding of the National Action Committee on the Status of Women (NACSW). NACSW is an umbrella organization of women's groups which has grown to represent indirectly more than five million Canadian women. It lobbies government on women's issues, provides information and materials for action, and analyses legislation at the federal level. Fraught with divisions among regions, among the main language groups, and among economic and ethnic groups, it nonetheless has grown to be one of the most powerful voices on Parliament Hill and an influential element in the public agenda.

To a large extent, the agenda of the women's movement until the early 1980s followed the recommendations of the Royal Commission, and with considerable success. In October 1979, the Advisory Council on the Status of Women published a report, *Ten Years Later*, which indicated the extent to which the recommendations had been implemented. Monitoring continues.

Among the key subsequent events has been movement on the constitutional front, a move not anticipated by the RCSW.

CONSTITUTIONAL RIGHTS FOR WOMEN

Over most of Canada's history, the relationship of Canadian women to the constitution has not been a matter of great importance to either women or governments. Constitution-making has been for and about relations between the federal and provincial governments. The rights of citizens and individuals were not, until 1982, embodied in the constitution. Women had sought equality rights by appealing to the courts on the basis of the Canadian Bill of Rights. The Bill of Rights, passed into law in 1960 in the Diefenbaker government, stated strong principles of equality, but in the courts the bill was treated as "just another statute." The bill therefore does not override other laws, such as the Indian Act, which entrenched sexual inequality. Furthermore, it does not apply to provincial laws, which cover most employment and other crucial issues. Women were not in a position to claim constitutional rights.

The movement for constitutional reform in Canada for many years had been an unsuccessful search by governments for patriation of the British North America Act from Great Britain and for an amending formula that would satisfy all governments involved. In 1980, however, the ongoing struggle over separation of the province of Quebec from the rest of Canada was taken to a referendum by the Quebec government. On one side, the Parti Québécois led by Premier René Lévesque sought a mandate to negotiate a form of sovereignty-association with Canada; on the other, the federalists led by the Trudeau government in Ottawa sought to renegotiate the nature of Canada to include Quebec and French language and culture in the national institutions of the country.

Women's rights emerged as an issue in the referendum debate when the minister responsible for women's issues in Quebec, fighting for the indépendantiste side, referred to women on the federalist side as "Yvettes." The character "Yvette" appeared in the standard primary school reader of the province of Quebec as a good little girl, firmly sex-stereotyped in the traditional mold. Women on the federalist side, enraged by this comparison, vowed to demonstrate the full participation of federalist women in the struggle. In a rally held in the Montreal Forum on April 7, 1980, 14,000 women cheered speakers and waved huge banners in a revolutionary expression of feeling about women, their role in nation-building, and the solidarity of Canadians. Meanwhile, many of Quebec's intellectual women who had brought about some of the great reforms for the women of the province worked on the separatist side.

When the separatist side lost that referendum, the response at the federal level was to move for constitutional reform to include not only patriation and an amending formula but also a Charter of Human Rights and Freedoms entrenched in the constitution.

For women, the entrenchment of equality rights became the focus of debate. The Trudeau government's original draft of the charter included rights for women, but the struggle was over two major questions: was the wording sufficiently strong to guarantee equality between the sexes in law and practice, and what was the process for securing those rights? Because of the elite nature of Canadian politics, the process was the most troublesome question. The premiers bargained among themselves and with Prime Minister Pierre Elliott Trudeau over the question of charter rights and trade-offs. Compromises unacceptable to women took place at several points.

As legal and constitutional issues, as opposed to economic issues, became more central, the leadership of the women's movement changed. The National Association of Women and the Law had been formed in 1974 and its members, in various organizations, provided expert knowledge on the charter. They had addressed cases taken under the Bill of Rights, and marital property laws, as key issues.

There was division among women on the constitutional questions. Many women espoused the cause of their provincial political leaders, and the women of Quebec, in particular, were skeptical of the federal initiatives. On the other hand, women across Canada were aware of the dangers for women in this constitutional process. Only a year earlier, at the February 1979 constitutional meeting, the prime minister had suddenly proposed moving the jurisdiction for divorce to the provincial level, and only fierce lobbying by feminists had prevented what would have been a major setback for women. So in preparation for a common front among women on the constitution, the government-appointed Canadian Advisory Council on the Status of Women commissioned research papers, and many groups joined in a campaign to arouse consciousness. When a joint committee of the Senate and House of Commons began public hearings, women proposed a series of changes to the government's constitutional resolution to strengthen the rights of women. The government responded in part to these requests in January 1981, but when an important conference on the question was canceled, a public furor arose. An ad hoc committee came forward with a plan for a constitutional conference on February 14, 1981. In the best tradition of the women's movement, with almost no resources or time, 1,300 women from across the country traveled to the Ottawa conference. With this conference and the backing of the major women's groups, the government accepted advice to draft an additional section of the constitution (Section 28) to ensure women's rights.

But the battle was not won. After various court decisions on aspects of constitutional change, the premiers and Prime Minister Trudeau reconvened for another bargaining session, which produced an accord on November 5, 1981. This accord contained an override section which put into jeopardy the hard-won women's rights, and once again women had to mobilize to fight, this time with the premiers. By focusing on each provincial premier in turn, women were able to split the solidarity of the premiers and free Section 28 from the override clause.

This battle was of fundamental importance to the new powers of the courts. The Canada Act, or the patriated constitution embodying the Charter of Human Rights and Freedoms, was signed and proclaimed by Queen Elizabeth II in Ottawa on April 17, 1982. But Quebec had refused to sign the constitution.

A new group, the Women's Legal Education and Action Fund (LEAF), was formed to take charter cases useful to women to the courts. Before a major case defining women's rights could reach the Supreme Court, however, another round of constitutional negotiations again threatened women's equality rights.

In the September 1984 election the Liberals were defeated. With their large majority, the Conservative government began negotiations to get Quebec to sign the new constitution, and an accord was signed in early 1987 proposing a series of changes. It appeared at once that the Meech Lake Accord, as it came to be called, was most unsatisfactory for numbers of women. Women's rights were threatened since the Meech Lake amendments included as an interpretive clause a description of Quebec as a "distinct society," an undefined term. The problem was that a hierarchy of rights would be created by the court system and, as feared by feminists in the 1980–82 negotiations, women's equality might be overridden by cultural concerns, in this case by Quebec, which would affect Supreme Court decisions covering all Canadian women.

The accord was deeply unpopular, and after tense last-minute compromises by the premiers, it was defeated in June 1990 by the actions of Elijah Harper, a Manitoba legislator and aboriginal spokesperson, who stalled action until time ran out. His actions were strongly supported by English Canadian feminists, who were, by now, part of a coalition of "equality seekers." This included women, aboriginal peoples, people with disabilities and ethnic minorities who felt excluded by the processes of executive federalism. Renewed attempts to amend the constitution continue.

WOMEN AND PUBLIC LIFE

As property owners had the municipal vote in Canada, some women had the vote early in Canadian history, Since 1940 all women have had the vote, but by the time of the Royal Commission Report only a handful had been elected to office. The RCSW had some sharp comments to make about this situation, since it was well established that women were the backbone of the political parties and were highly effective organizers. Between 1970 and 1988, 71 women were elected at the federal levels. Since 1979, women have formed about 14% of candidates in the federal elections, and in the 1988 election women gained more than 13% of the seats in the House of Commons. Women have held a number of important cabinet posts, including External Affairs, Justice, Health and Welfare, and Employment and Immigration. Prime Minister Trudeau appointed Jeanne Sauvé the first woman speaker of the House of Commons in 1980.

The RCSW was critical of government's inaction in the area of appointments. Between 1970 and 1991, 23 women were made senators. At present 16 out of 104 seats are held by women. Appointments of judges have increased substantially, and since 1982 three women have joined the Supreme Court of Canada. In 1990 of the 859 judges appointed by the federal government, 81 were women.

The federal and provincial governments have a very large number of appointments to boards and commissions, to the senior public service, and to a variety of special task forces. The advisory committees at the federal and provincial level keep a watch on these appointments, and governments have become more sensitive to the issue. Nonetheless, women remain a tiny proportion of senior appointments in Canada.

In political parties, women have been active since before the franchise and have consistently worked in elections and between elections. Women have held office, including elected office in political parties, but usually at the constituency level. In 1980, the Liberal Party of Canada elected Iona Campagnolo, a former cabinet minister, as its first female national president. The New Democratic Party elected its first woman president shortly thereafter. All three parties have had separate women's organizations both at the provincial and federal levels. In the second wave of feminism, the parties absorbed the women's groups into their national executives through a variety of means, and women sit on the national executives of all parties. Since 1980, women have held the position of executive assistant to cabinet ministers—a position that is an apprenticeship post for senior political and public office jobs—and women work on the policy side of party and public life. While all jobs are open to women, the appointment of women to top jobs in political life is still a matter of comment rather than a matter of course.

CONTEMPORARY ECONOMIC ISSUES

The rapid entry of women into the paid labor force in Canada has changed public policy in two directions. On one hand, women are demanding better access to training and good jobs, and more equitable pay and benefits in the labor market, and on the other hand, parents are demanding better and more child care spaces for their children.

Pay equity has been an issue for Canadian women since at least the First World War. In the post-World War II era, the Canadian Federation of Business and Professional Women's Clubs mounted a concerted campaign on provincial governments to provide equal pay laws, since about 90% of Canadian workers are under provincial jurisdiction. The majority of governments responded, and by the 1960s there were laws requiring equal pay for equal work across Canada. The problem, of course, is that the work is not equal for women. Occupational segregation, which has increased over the years, makes it impossible to compare the work of men and women in most cases. In 1972, Canada signed International Labor Organization (ILO) Convention 100, which requires a new form of pay equity from its signatories: equal pay for work of equal value. The women's movement in Canada pressed hard to have that written into the law, and quite recently this has occurred. The job of educating public servants and politicians about the meaning of this concept continues, but the province of Manitoba brought in mandatory equal pay for work of equal value in the public sector in 1985 and Ontario had made it mandatory in both the public and private sector by 1990.

The federal government has a voluntary form of pay equity which, like most voluntary exercises, has little impact. But the Abella Commission on Employment Equity has been turned into a mandatory program at the federal level. Judge Rosalie Silberman Abella was commissioned to study the employment inequalities among women, visible minorities, Native people and people with disabilities and to determine the course of action appropriate to the Canadian context. The comparison was with the U.S. affirmative action program but in a totally different legislative and economic context. The Abella Report came out in 1984 recommending the establishment of remedial action, goals and timetables, and reporting to the federal government. In 1986, an Act Respecting Employment Equity was passed which requires all employers of 100 or more in the federal jurisdiction to report annually on the four target groups. These data are then compared with external availability data for the region in which the employer hires, and, if progress is not being made toward more employment and advancement of the target groups, a case may be heard before the Canadian Human Rights Commission. The only penalty in the legislation is for failure to file an annual report, however, and only when the mandatory legislative review is complete will one know whether or not the law is effective in changing the long-term situation of women and other groups.

Furthermore, since 90% of workers are in the provincial domain and mandatory employment equity is not yet in provincial legislation except for the public service, the gap between men and women in the Canadian labor market, which has existed since records were first kept, is closing only very slowly and reflects the continued secondary treatment of women in the Canadian economy.

Issues that continue to affect the lives of Canadian women lie in pressures of economic life, the lessening gap between the public and private spheres expressed in such ways as the demand for child care, and the growing consciousness of visible minority women, women with disabilities, older women and lesbian women, of the special problems they face. The rich tradition of writing about the situation of women in Canada in the postwar period has expressed the evolution of women's cultures and values. Novels such as *The Tin Flute* by Gabrielle Roy, *The Stone Angel* by Margaret Laurence, *La Sagouine* by Antoine Maillet, *The Handmaid's Tale* by Margaret Atwood and *Lives of Girls and Women* by Alice Munro are only some of the literature—to which are added plays, painting, poetry, songs and dance— that capture the dilemma of women in their times. Women have more recently become filmmakers and directors and are active in all the visual arts. Analysis of the situation of women is expressed in scholarly research by academics and women's studies programs at many Canadian universities. These programs, born in the 1970s, have grown into degree-granting programs in some universities but have become centers of scholarship elsewhere in many fields of science and humanities. More popular analysis is found in columns for newspapers and magazines, no longer sex segregated as much as before, and in a lively underground press.

REACTIONS TO CHANGE

There have always been those who resisted change in women's status, including anti-suffrage groups and groups opposed to easing the laws on divorce, birth control and entry of women into the labor market. At the time of the RCSW, the leader, Laura Sabia, was able to gain at least temporary commitment of the majority of Canadian women. Sabia, who is a Roman Catholic, card-holding member of the Conservative Party and a committed capitalist, symbolized the characteristics quite opposite to the popular image of the feminist. Shortly after the founding of the National Action Committee, however, those totally opposed to abortion left the coalition. This divisive issue has risen to prominence once again. The 1969 law that made abortion legal under a set of restrictive conditions was struck down by the Supreme Court in the 1988 Morgentaler decision. In the absence of federal law, some provincial courts allowed injunctions against women seeking abortions, which were overturned by the Supreme Court. The federal government reintroduced an abortion law, which passed the House of Commons but was defeated in the Senate by a tied vote in 1990. Abortion has remained the issue which most deeply divides women in Canada and, in reaction to the obvious success of the second wave of feminism on the public agenda, new groups opposed to feminism have sprung up.

There are two main opposition coalitions. Those who oppose abortion, child care, working mothers and the claims of women to be able to compete with men are found in groups such as REAL Women (Realistic Equal Active for Life), while a number of young right-wing women are to be found in the post-feminist groups. The latter argue that the battles have been won and women need no special legislative consideration to work and live equally. Since 1984, these groups have received a great deal of attention in the media, but there is no indication that the majority of Canadian women will move from the moderate, reformist position which they have occupied for many generations.

FURTHER READING

Abella, Rosalie Silberman. *Equality in Employment: A Royal Commission Report*. Ottawa: Minister of Supply and Services, 1984.

Armstrong, Pat, and Hugh Armstrong. *The Double Ghetto: Canadian Women and their Segregated Work*. Toronto: McClelland and Stewart, 1978.

Canadian Advisory Council on the Status of Women. *Ten Years Later*. Ottawa, October 1979.

Cleverdon, Catherine L. *The Woman Suffrage Movement in Canada, The Start of Liberation 1900–20*. Toronto: University of Toronto Press, 1950.

Cooke, Katie, et al., *Report of the Task Force on Childcare*. Ottawa: Minister of Supply and Services, 1986.

Fudge, Judy, and Patricia McDermott, eds. *Just Wages, A Feminist Assessment of Pay Equity*. Toronto: University of Toronto Press, 1991.

Hosek, Chaviva. "Women and the Constitutional Process." In *And No One Cheered*, edited by Keith Banting and Richard Simeon. Toronto: Methuen, 1983.

Jones, Charles, Lorna Marsden, and Lorne Tepperman. *Lives of their Own*. Toronto: Oxford University Press, 1990.

ABORIGINAL PEOPLES

MEL WATKINS

In the nature of things, aboriginal peoples have been in the place now called Canada longer than anyone else. At times, notably in the bygone days when the fur trade was dominant, they played a crucial role in the economic development of the country. But in due course they were pushed aside by settlers and ignored. Outside the mainstream of society, they became almost invisible.

Yet today, in spite of their comparatively small numbers, Canada's aboriginal peoples are highly visible. That is because they have become increasingly militant and well organized politically, and insist on being seen and heard.

In the space of a few months in the summer of 1990, two events took place that gave Canada's aboriginal peoples a profile unprecedented in contemporary times. An ambitious attempt to amend the Canadian constitution called the Meech Lake Constitutional Accord was tearing English-speaking Canada and Quebec apart while doing nothing for aboriginal people. It required the unanimous consent of all the provinces. The death blow was dealt by the refusal of Elijah Harper, an aboriginal member of the Manitoba legislature, to consent to the matter being voted on by that legislature. His refusal made it impossible for Manitoba to vote consent, and the accord was stopped in its tracks. To opponents of the accord, who included not only aboriginal peoples but also the majority of English-speaking Canadians, Harper was a modern hero.

Then, at the village of Oka near Montreal, Mohawks from the Kanesatake reserve that straddles the Canada-United States border took up arms to stop further loss of their lands to the construction of a golf course. In an armed confrontation with the Quebec police, a policeman was killed, and the Canadian army was sent in to restore the peace. There was surprising support among Canadians for the masked Mohawk warriors whom Canadians saw each night on their television sets, though, again, support was greater in English-speaking Canada than in Quebec.

Now, as Canada attempts in the '90s to rewrite its constitution with the possibility of radically restructuring its polity, the one group that sits at the table with elected premiers and parliamentarians is the leadership of the aboriginal peoples. Happily, polls show that most Canadians have accepted aboriginal participation; they know, finally, that aboriginal peoples have been badly treated and are entitled to redress.

Why the plural of the title? Because aboriginal people have always been many peoples and still are. Above the treeline in the Arctic and Subarctic live those who were called Eskimos but now, at their insistence, are known as the Inuit (meaning "the people" in the language of Inuktitut). Below the treeline are the peoples who were falsely called Indians because of Columbus' great historic blunder. They were, in any event, not a single people but many "tribes," as numerous and various as the nations of Europe. In fact, they were likewise "nations," and were so recognized initially by imperial authorities. (The famous Royal Proclamation of 1763 by which Britain attempted to contain its American colonists refers to "the several tribes and nations of Indians with whom we are connected.")

Today, significantly, they call themselves First Nations, and their main, pan-Canadian political organization is called the Assembly of First Nations. They use their own words to name themselves—such as Dene, Innu, Wet-'suwet'en, Teme-Augama Anishnabai—and they talk of self-determination, sovereignty and self-government. Just as their historical loss of the right to name themselves deprived them of a most basic human right, their successful reassertion of that right can be seen as an important victory symbolically and substantially.

There are, as well, the people called the Métis, who are the offspring of the encounter between aboriginal and European peoples going back to fur-trade times. They have always defined themselves as aboriginal people—Louis Riel, the great leader of two Native rebellions in the latter part of the 19th century, was a Métis—but they can also be regarded as the first made-in-Canada Canadians.

These peoples define themselves as aboriginal; so too does Canada's written constitution. Section 35 of the Canadian Charter of Rights and Freedoms, which has been part of the Canadian Constitution since 1982, defines the aboriginal peoples of Canada whose rights are "recognized and affirmed" as "the Indian, Inuit and Métis peoples of Canada."

How many are there of these peoples and what is the present condition of their lives? The federal Department of Indian and Northern Affairs estimated their total population in 1991 as 802,852, or some 3% of the Canadian population. Their numbers are growing rapidly, having more than doubled in the last 25 years; their birthrates are running double the Canadian average.

The 1991 estimate shows 490,178 status Indians, 32,619 Inuit, 59,745 Métis and 220,310 non-status Indians. "Status Indians" (or "treaty Indians") is a classification going back to the Indian Act of 1876. Basically, it means that their ancestors signed treaties recognizing them as distinct people, though many of those treaties, by assigning the people to reserves, recognized them in ways that treated them as inferiors and made them worse off. Indeed, they could neither vote nor legally consume alcohol prior to 1961, even if they had fought for Canada in one of the world wars.

Today only about three-fifths of these status people actually live on the more than 2,000 reserves scattered across Canada. This is down from two-thirds only five years earlier and is indicative of the limited economic opportunities on the reserves in the face of rapid population growth. That, in turn, is not unrelated to the fact that the reserves constitute less than 0.2% of the landmass of Canada—in contrast to aboriginal people in total comprising 3% of the population and status people about 1.5%

The number of Métis and non-status Indians who live off the reserves exceeds the number of off-reserve status Indians. The Native Council of Canada, which represents these people politically, believes that, if all those with a substantial Indian heritage were counted, the number might be as high as one million. Some Métis and non-status people live in remote rural communities with a life-style comparable to that of reserve Indians. Like the status people, a significant and growing minority live in urban or semi-urban areas.

The Inuit mostly still live in their far northern communities in the Northwest Territories, northern Quebec and Labrador.

Compared to other Canadians, aboriginal peoples on the average live poorly, often abjectly so. Of course, some prosper. To take a striking example, the Samson Cree Nation in Alberta runs a trust company with assets approaching $200 million, which services Native businesses. In view of the hardship and barriers they face, those who do well economically deserve much credit for their achievement. For the harsh reality is that aboriginal people in Canada rank in material terms below any other ethnic group, including the most recent immigrants.

There is, manifestly, overwhelming evidence of conditions that suggest—some would say prove—systematic discrimination and racism from the beginning. (Much of this has been powerfully portrayed in a book by Toronto *Globe and Mail* reporter Geoffrey York. The book is entitled, properly and pointedly, *The Dispossessed,* and is subtitled, hauntingly, *Life and Death in Native Canada.*)

The life expectancy of an aboriginal person is 10 years less than that of an average Canadian; he or she is 50% more likely to die before age 65. The infant mortality rate is twice that of non-Native Canadians; the death rate for Indian children to age 14 is four times that for non-Natives. Demographically, the situation of aboriginal people is more like that of the Third World than of the affluent First World, which Canada clearly inhabits. Indeed, Canada's aboriginal people sometimes describe themselves as being in a Fourth World of indigenous people impoverished within a First World country.

In fact, diseases such as tuberculosis, gastroenteritis and pneumonia, which are now widespread only in the Third World, abound among aboriginal people in Canada. A Native Canadian is ten times more likely than a non-Native to contract turberculosis; the rate on Indian reserves is said to be higher than in Tanzania.

Inuit women in Canada's North have an incidence of lung cancer six times higher than the general population in Canada. The rate is the second highest in the world, only behind that for the Native population of New Zealand. Cigarette packages in Canada carry strong health warnings in English and French, but not in Native languages.

The latest disease that some fear may devastate aboriginal peoples is AIDS. In Vancouver, where Indians gather from around British Columbia, the HIV infection rate for aboriginals living on the street is believed to be the highest for any ethnic group in Canada. AIDS is now manifesting itself in many of the small aboriginal communities in British Columbia.

The average income of an aboriginal person is about one-half that of a non-Native's. More than half of Indian families are on welfare. They live disproportionately in poverty and unemployment, on reserves and in the skid rows of cities. One-third of all houses on reserves have no running water, and outdoor latrines are common. Half of such houses have no central heating, and there are frequent fires and deaths from unsafe stoves.

Impoverishment and oppression breed hopelessness. The suicide rate among Canada's Indians is the highest of any racial group in the world. It is a veritable epidemic among youth, with suicide rates for Native people between the ages of 15 and 24 five to six times greater than for non-Natives in the same age group. Accidental and violent deaths among Native people account for more than one-third of their deaths, compared to one in 20 for non-Natives—a higher rate than is found anywhere in the Third World. There is serious alcohol abuse, and gas-sniffing is pervasive among children. It has been estimated that an aboriginal Canadian is three times more likely to land in a jail cell than in a high-school graduating class. Aboriginal people are, in the words of a recognized authority, Professor Tony Hall of the University of Lethbridge, "grotesquely overrepresented in jails, child-welfare agencies and morgues."

Canada's own Human Rights Commission calls Canada's treatment of its aboriginal peoples a national tragedy. International human rights groups, including the United Nations, have criticized Canada for its inadequate and discriminatory Native policies. Amnesty International brands Canada's treatment of its Native people "barbaric" and has put Canada on a list of countries it will watch. A 1991 report by two United Nations agencies—the UN Center on Transnational Corporations and the UN Center for Human Rights—lumps Quebec with Brazil and India in its disregard for indigenous peoples whose lives are disrupted by mammoth hydroelectric projects. Considerable sums are spent by governments, notably the federal government, on "Indian Affairs," and there is a large federal bureaucracy that goes by that name, but it is evidently of slight avail.

Georges Erasmus, shortly before he stepped down in 1991 as National Chief of the Assembly of First Nations, wrote, "I would not want to leave the impression that Native people are making no progress at all. It remains true, however, that every step forward must be made in face of enormous discouragement." Still, since Erasmus made that observation, the federal government has, under strong pressure from aboriginal peoples and in the face of much militancy, appointed a Royal Commission on Aboriginal Peoples with a sweeping mandate. It is cochaired by Erasmus, and four of its seven members are aboriginal people.

Announcing the formation of the commission, Prime Minister Brian Mulroney himself spoke of what he called "Third World conditions" on Indian reserves "that we would deplore anywhere else." Constitutional Affairs minister Joe Clark concedes the unhappy plight of aboriginal people but says, "That is not just a portrait of a people in pain. It is a portrait of people who have been denied the instruments to control their own destiny." He advocates recognition of an aboriginal right to self-government.

Notwithstanding their dismal lot, it has usually been understood that aboriginal people had aboriginal rights, and that the rationale for their having them was that they would thereby be helped rather than hurt.

True, as recently as 1969, the just-elected Trudeau government announced its intention to abolish all special status for Indians in order to assimilate them into mainstream society. Aboriginal peoples were so repelled by this policy that they organized in an unprecedented way to defeat it, and, ironically, they have remained ever since more vigilant and insistent. Shortly thereafter, a split ruling by the Supreme Court of Canada in the 1973 Calder case created the possibility that Nishga land rights in British Columbia had not been extinguished. This caused even Prime Minister Trudeau to concede that there were extant aboriginal rights.

But what are these aboriginal rights? Do they make aboriginal people Citizens Minus—in the ways outlined above—or Citizens Plus, to use the language of the claim put forward by one group of aboriginal people? Are they traditional rights, to hunt and fish and gather and trap, and even then only to the extent that the right can be exercised in the face of encroachments? Or are they modern rights to the use of land, perhaps even including the political right of sovereignty? Should they—can they—be extinguished? Or should they—must they—be recognized? Such questions are not rhetorical flourishes. They are precisely the issues that aboriginal Canadians and all Canadians are grappling with in the '90s.

Now the "rights of the aboriginal peoples" that are constitutionally recognized are actually "aboriginal and treaty rights." What is meant by treaty rights? When the European powers and settlers arrived, the lands were not empty but were being occupied and used by aboriginal peoples. This is known to be so from historical evidence. It can further be presumed to be so because even today, when developers want to open mines or build pipelines or dam rivers in remote areas that are thought to be wilderness, it invariably turns out that these projects cannot be undertaken without interfering with aboriginal land use. From the viewpoint of the new claimants, however, the treaties had been signed to permit access to aboriginal lands.

Much Indian land, particularly in Ontario and the Prairie Provinces, was covered by such treaties. A good deal was not, and no treaties were signed with the Inuit. Aboriginal rights where there are no treaties hinge on court interpretations of what rights remain in the face of de facto occupation by non-Natives, and on contemporary land-claims negotiations.

As for the treaties, in a curious way they first affirmed that Indians had title, and then extinguished that title. Most of the land was taken away; a small amount was returned as reserves. Likewise, small amounts of cash and guarantees as to schools and health care were included in the treaties.

In the opinion of the dominant society, these treaties cleared the way for "progress," and if they seemed to confine Native people to reserves, that depended on what Native people chose to do. Some viewed the treaties as ways that Native people were being helped (some would use the stronger word "coerced") to join, and be assimilated by, mainstream society. Perhaps not surprisingly, the treaties were regarded by Native people in a very different way—as assurances of friendship and as affirmations of their rights.

Given the thrust of the settlers and the inexorable march of the dominant society, there was a logic, maybe even some virtue, to these treaties. Regardless, Native societies stood to be swamped. Certainly Native people today want to make the best of them. But the more that is known about the history of treaty-making, the more it is evident that Native people often did not realize that there were clauses in the treaties extinguishing their title. In many cases these clauses were never read out to them, and, even worse, their signatures (their marks, to be precise, since they were illiterate) were sometimes forged. Worst of all, food was sometimes withheld from starving peoples pending ratification of the treaty. Finally, after the treaty had been ratified, in numerous cases the lands allocated for Indians, though typically niggardly, were not fully allocated, or were subsequently taken away without the Indians' proper consent.

It follows from this historical litany that if the 1982 constitution means that treaty rights should be restored and redressed, that is far from nothing. It could be a means both to return lands lost and to recognize that the aboriginal peoples who signed the treaties were, and still are, distinct and sovereign peoples.

Canada's dominant society and aboriginal peoples no longer make treaties; today they negotiate land claims. In ways that are mostly problematic for aboriginal rights, land claims settlements resemble the treaties inasmuch as they extinguish aboriginal title. This is simply unacceptable to some aboriginal people, such as the Dene in the southern part of the Mackenzie Valley in the Northwest Territories, who want their title, and rights, affirmed. Land claims settlements categorize the land, taking much of it away. They give some back with full title. They give some more with hunting, fishing and trapping rights—so long as they can be exercised while development progresses. They are signed when the dominant society wants access to lands, typically for some mega-project, and they guarantee that the mega-project can proceed. In the case of the great James Bay hydroelectric development on Cree lands in northern Quebec in the 1970s, the project was started before negotiations even began. Still, in 1991, when Hydro-Québec and the Quebec government wanted to proceed with the vast Great Whale extension of the James Bay development without a full environmental assessment, the Federal Court of Canada held that to do so would violate the terms of the 1975 land claims settlement with the Cree.

As with the treaties, with claims settlements there is the risk that the parties involved will perceive the claim differently. In fact, the very meaning of "land" is so perceived. For the mainstream white society—particularly dominant corporate and state interests—"land" means real estate that can be bought and sold and can be expropriated by the state with fair compensation. For aboriginal peoples, land is integral to their being, inseparable from themselves; it is not a commodity but a way of life. The point is made poignantly by Robert Calihoo when he describes his childhood feelings about the reserve, on the one hand, and the bush life and the connection with nature on the other hand:

> The shacks were awful and conditions inside were like a nightmare. But out on the land, it was different. It was clean. Being out there, alone, with the wind in your hair, listening for the small sounds in the bush and watching for movements that might portray a groundhog in the waving grass, easing up quietly toward the top of the hill to peer down the other side and see if anything was moving, swimming in the lake—even if it was so cold it took your breath away—lying on your back in the still-damp, still-cold earth, looking up at the clouds gliding over the tops of last year's dry grass, a whisky-jack bucking the west wind . . . or at night with all the universe up there hanging like broken chandeliers or falling with infinite slowness toward you, that was something special.

Still, the claims settlements that have been made, or those for which ratification is presently pending—a half dozen in total—are typically much more generous both in land and in cash than were the treaties. Funds are available, particularly through royalties, for economic development. Local political control and even some real powers over environmental protection are part of the new deals. The Inuvialuit (the Inuit people in the Mackenzie Delta of the Western Arctic), under a comprehensive agreement signed in 1984, have been able to stop oil drilling in the Beaufort Sea which they think is unsafe. The pending Yukon settlement has innovative features that promise to greatly facilitate community development under Native control. Traditional activities are supported—as through an innovative minimum-income plan for hunters and trappers in the James Bay Agreement—while development corporations invest money in Native-run businesses to assist in providing wage employment for the rapidly growing aboriginal population involved.

There is no escaping the fundamental ambiguity of these settlements and everything that comes in their wake. Indian bands that have made a settlement are materially better off than similarly placed bands that have not. The Cree in Quebec, the signers of the first and most comprehensive of the modern settlements, would seem, objectively, to be better off, perhaps considerably more so than before, though there is still widespread poverty, and educational, medical and social services are inadequate. But to a degree no one anticipated, flooding from dams has released mercury, which has contaminated the fish and threatens the health and the very way of life of the Cree. The Cree have made it abundantly clear that they want no further hydroelectric development, no further imposed progress. At the time, and perhaps still, many Cree would apparently do without the 1975 land claims settlement if they were allowed to do without the dams.

A comprehensive settlement is very complicated and can take a decade or two to negotiate and ratify. Some 50 settlements remain to be made. At the present rate of negotiation—the federal government has had a policy of not dealing with more than six at a time—it has been estimated that it will take at least a century and a half. This more than tries the patience of aboriginal peoples.

In the attempt to prove and define their aboriginal rights, aboriginal peoples have recourse to the courts; in their attempt to strengthen their rights, they insist on being actively involved in any rewriting of the Canadian constitution.

Historically, the court route has not been very helpful. The rights have had to be proven on the basis of use and occupancy, and they must not have been ceded, knowingly or unknowingly, by ancestors. Even when proven, the courts may decide that the rights have been lost because the dominant society has acted, by settlement and legislation, as if that were so. Even when they are admitted to exist, the courts may decide their content is severely constrained; specifically, aboriginal claimants equate their rights with full ownership, but the courts limit them to historic uses of land and resources.

Since 1982, as we have seen, aboriginal rights have been entrenched in the constitution. But they are mostly there because aboriginal peoples put them there. Prime Minister Pierre Trudeau, who was engaged in the broader exercise of giving Canada a made-in-Canada constitution, wanted a Charter of Rights and Freedoms. He needed the consent of the provinces, and some of the premiers, notably from western Canada, where aboriginal peoples tend to be a higher percentage of the population, balked at including aboriginal rights, fearing that to do so would interfere with provincial control over resources. The result was a proposed charter that failed to enshrine the human rights of those people with demonstrably the least respected human rights of any Canadians. Public pressure, spearheaded by aboriginal peoples themselves, got their rights back in the charter.

But what, in fact, were these entrenched rights? Everyone agreed that this had to be clarified, and a series of special constitutional conferences of first ministers (the prime minister of Canada and the premiers of the provinces) and aboriginal leaders was mandated. Four conferences were held, but to no avail. Aboriginal leaders wanted their rights to be defined as meaning fundamentally the right of self-government. Prime Minister Brian Mulroney agreed, but too many provinces did not. Alberta, British Columbia and Newfoundland objected (with the premier of Alberta actually threatening to secede), and Quebec, which would have been supportive, was absent for unrelated reasons.

The frustration and bitterness this engendered among aboriginal peoples explains why they played a key role in defeating the Meech Lake Constitutional Accord in 1990. The first ministers, unable to give aboriginal people anything more in the constitution, were prepared to rewrite it to recognize Quebec as a "distinct society." Having both French-speaking and English-speaking Canadians was said to be "a fundamental characteristic of

Canada" but the fact that aboriginal people had been in Canada before either of these groups did not merit similar recognition.

In the flurry of another round of constitution-making in the '90s to try to hold the country together after the failure of the Meech Lake Accord, aboriginal people have won the right to be at the table. When they speak of their right to aboriginal self-government and list what that would mean in terms of real powers, some powerful politicians concur. Canada's Constitutional Affairs minister Joe Clark is on the record as to what he thinks aboriginal self-government would mean: "We are not talking about separation here, nor about a state within a state. But make no mistake about it. Neither are we talking about feathers and folk dances. We are talking about the negotiated exercise of real power by aboriginal communities over matters that affect them directly. That might include education, economic development, health and social services, land and justice systems." Such an impressive list of newly won powers would create a level of aboriginal government analogous perhaps to that of the provinces themselves.

Meanwhile, both federal and provincial governments can negotitate self-government agreements with Indian bands, and in some cases have done so. The social democratic government elected in Ontario in 1990 has gone the farthest in this regard by signing an overall agreement with Ontario chiefs that recognizes "the inherent right to self-government of the First Nations [that] flows from the Creator and from the First Nations' original occupation of the land."

Amid the plethora of proposals to give aboriginal peoples more political clout is one that would grant them a guaranteed number of seats in the Canadian Parliament, both in the House of Commons and a reformed Senate.

Also pending is the issue of creating further provinces out of the Yukon Territory and the Northwest Territories, with fuller rights of self-government in the North. This matters to aboriginal peoples because the Northwest Territories has a majority aboriginal population. In fact, the Northwest Territories is a vast area, with Dene people in the Mackenzie Valley and Inuit in the Arctic. Sentiment among these aboriginal peoples favors a split, creating a new territory called Denendeh in the western part of the Northeast Territories and one called Nunavut in the central and eastern part. Both could then evolve into provinces. Nunavut would have a clear majority of Inuit. Unlike Manitoba and British Columbia, which began as provinces with an aboriginal majority, Nunavut is sufficiently inhospitable to non-aboriginal settlement that it could then remain as the only aboriginal province. Granting such sovereign rights to the Inuit might be seen as fitting recompense for the unwitting role they have played in maintaining Canada's sovereign claims to the North. That includes an unsavory chapter in the early 1950s when the federal government uprooted 87 Inuit from their communities in northern Quebec and relocated them in the Far North. The Inuit, some experts assert, were being used as flags to strengthen Canada's claims to sovereignty in the face of a burgeoning U.S. military presence and of nomadic Greenlanders wintering on Ellesmere Island.

Meanwhile, the Charter of Rights and Freedoms and the changing times—judges can be presumed to follow the news and have some sense of how the political winds are blowing—seem finally to be making the courts somewhat more receptive to aboriginal rights. In the landmark 1989 Sparrow decision dealing with aboriginal fishing rights, the Supreme Court of Canada held that the aboriginal right to fish has precedence over others' right to fish, and can only be constrained in the interest of conservation. It further observed that the aboriginal right cannot be extinguished incidentally by regulation; that the right should be interpreted not in a literal historical sense but in a contemporary fashion; that the government's relationship with aboriginal peoples should be not adversarial (as in land claims negotiations) but trust-like; and that aboriginal rights could be affirmed, not just extinguished (as land claims settlements presently do).

Aboriginal people are increasingly asking for their own justice system, and there is a growing willingness among other Canadians to consider that. The failures of the present system can no longer be glossed over. The prisons are full of aboriginal people, though that has long been the case. But what has shocked Canadians in recent years is repeated evidence of racist treatment of Native people by the police and the justice system in general.

Donald Marshall, a Nova Scotia Micmac, was imprisoned for 11 years for a 1971 murder he did not commit. It has now been established that local police and the Royal Canadian Mounted Police were more interested in convicting Marshall and in keeping him in prison than they were in telling the truth or investigating evidence of injustice, and that this had to do with the fact that Marshall was an aboriginal person. Marshall was freed and granted compensation for life.

In 1991 Manitoba's official Aboriginal Justice Inquiry reported on the 1971 sex slaying of Cree teenager Helen Betty Osborne, and on the 1988 shooting of Native leader J. J. Harper by a Winnipeg constable. It took 16 years for Osborne's assailants to be brought to justice. The inquiry report says bluntly: "It is clear that Betty Osborne would not have been killed if she were not aboriginal," nor would it have taken so intolerably long to deal with the perpetrators of the crime. J. J. Harper, who had done no wrong, was stopped by the police and ended up dead. Again, bluntly, the report reads, "What started as an unnecessary, racially motivated approach to an aboriginal citizen on a city street has had profoundly disturbing results." Overall, the report roundly condemns the Manitoba justice system: "We have investigated the administration of justice in Manitoba and have come to the conclusion that it does not deliver justice to Manitoba's aboriginal people."

The report concludes that no reform of the existing system would be sufficient and calls instead for a separate Native justice system; aboriginal people would be given complete control over all aspects of justice in their own communities, including the criminal courts and police. Aboriginal peoples are 12% of the Manitoba population, but they make up at least 50% of the prison population. A Native justice system that reduced the number of aboriginal people in provincial courts and jails could justify itself on cost-saving grounds alone.

Also in 1991, two official reviews of how Native people fared within the Alberta justice system found that racism was pervasive, and that there was a damaging "lack of cultural empathy" on the part of police in their daily dealings with aboriginal peoples.

Not even the churches have emerged unscathed from recent revelations of the maltreatment of aboriginal peoples. Until a short time ago, most Native children went to residential schools run by the religious orders. They were removed from their parents without consent, were punished for speaking their native languages and, it is now revealed, in some cases were subjected to sexual abuse. To their credit, today's churches are atoning for these sins by being in the vanguard of organizations supporting aboriginal rights.

The colonists who came to Canada did so to exploit its rich natural resources. Contemporary Canada is an industrialized, urbanized country, but its economy still depends to a remarkable degree on the export of these resource staples, and giant resource-exploitation projects are still touted as the means to create growth. This is the backdrop against which the relations of aboriginal peoples with the larger society are played out.

The Indians and the Métis were needed to carry out the fur trade, and they benefited from the goods they acquired in trade for the furs. But the great fortunes accrued to the Hudson's Bay Company and the Montreal business class; and, in due course, as the fur trade gave way to other activities, aboriginal peoples were left in the hinterlands, poor and abandoned. Relentless pursuit of the beaver mapped out the boundaries of Canada; while the country's name was Indian, its people were mostly not. And today some of those people, in the name of animal rights, campaign against the trapping of wild fur, putting at risk an important source of cash income to Canada's aboriginal people.

Subsequent staples—timber, wheat, hydroelectricity, oil and gas, minerals—have not even served the aboriginal interest in passing. In Canada, as elsewhere, the Indians suffer, in the words of the Latin American writer Eduardo Galeano, "the curse of the wealth of the lands they inhabit." In the late 1980s, the Toronto *Globe and Mail* reported that the 470-member Ouje-Bougoumo band in Northern Quebec "has been forced to relocate seven times in the past 40 years because of gold-mining in the area, and the Indians now live in tents and tarpaper shacks, without running water, electricity or toilets, alongside a highway."

It might be thought that the problem, unfortunate though it may be, is largely the consequence of aboriginal peoples' inability or unwillingness to adapt to the exigencies of an industrial economy. But historians show that it was not that simple. Prairie Indians who could find no buffalo to hunt and wanted to become farmers were denied good land and proper machinery. Indians in British Columbia were actively excluded from the fisheries and faced severe wage discrimination in the canneries. The Indian

Act itself was—and is—riddled with constraints imposed on aboriginal peoples that simply disadvantaged them more than they already were in competing with settlers. Even when aboriginal peoples were willing to adapt, they faced systematic discrimination and racism.

It is obviously not easy to alter long-standing patterns of behavior, but these are changing in the '90s, with widespread ramifications. The most dramatic case is the James Bay affair. Premier Robert Bourassa and a coalition of Quebec business groups insist that it is intolerable that a small minority of aboriginal people could block further development of the great James Bay hydroelectric project, with its alleged economic benefits for Quebecers. But many environmentalists, in both Canada and the United States (the generated power is to be exported there), insist that aboriginal people, in resisting the project, are making the best decision not only for themselves but for the larger public interest. The transborder coalition of aboriginal people and environmentalists, with an assist from the Canadian courts, has already managed to delay the project. The stakes are high and the future is problematic, even fraught with danger: should Quebec move to independence, the northern Quebec Cree may say they want to stay in Canada.

In another example of behavior and attitudes facing change, non-aboriginal commercial fisherman feel threatened by court rulings that give preference to Native fishing. Sports hunters resent the preference given Native hunters and resist the possibility that at some point in the future they may have to apply to aboriginal people for a hunting license. Tourists who want to escape from it all into wilderness parks discover that aboriginal people have an unextinguished right to pursue their traditional activities there.

The 1990s mark half a millennium since John Cabot "discovered" the great fishing banks off Newfoundland. Off-shore fishing led to on-shore fishing and to settlement. The aboriginal inhabitants of Newfoundland were the Beothuk. (They painted their bodies with red ochre and may be responsible for North American Native people being called Red Indians.) Denied access to their fish, harassed, perhaps slaughtered by the settlers, the last of them died in 1829. This is a sad story. But today, at last, there is a strong and growing sentiment in Canada to grant to its aboriginal citizens the space, physically and politically, that will permit them to flourish both as aboriginal peoples and as Canadians.

FURTHER READING

Brody, Hugh. *Living Arctic: Hunters of the Canadian North.* Seattle: University of Washington Press, 1987.

Comeau, Pauline, and Aldo Santin. *The First Canadians: A Profile of Canada's Native People Today.* Toronto: Lorimer, 1990.

Dickason, Olive Patricia. *Canada's First Nations: A History of Founding Peoples from Earliest Times.* Toronto: McClelland and Stewart, 1992.

Hunter, Robert, and Robert Calihoo. *Occupied Canada: A Young White Man Discovers His Unsuspected Past.* Toronto: McClelland and Stewart, 1991.

Little Bear, Leroy, Menno Boldt, and J. Anthony Long, eds. *Pathways to Self-Determination: Canadian Indians and the Canadian State.* Toronto/Buffalo: University of Toronto Press, 1984.

McMahon, Kevin, *Arctic Twilight: Reflections on the Destiny of Canada's Northern Land and People.* Toronto: Lorimer, 1988.

Miller, J. R. *Skyscrapers Hide the Heavens: A History of Indian-White Relations in Canada.* Toronto/Buffalo: University of Toronto Press, 1989.

Miller, J. R., ed. *Sweet Promises: A Reader on Indian-White Relations in Canada.* Toronto/Buffalo: University of Toronto Press, 1991.

Purich, Donald. *The Metis.* Toronto: Lorimer, 1988.

Richardson, Boyce. *Strangers Devour the Land: A Chronicle of the Assault Upon the Last Coherent Hunting Culture in Northern America, the Cree Indians of Quebec, and Their Vast Primeval Homelands.* New York: Knopf, 1975. Reissued with foreword by Winona LaDuke Kapashesit and epilogue by Boyce Richardson. Vancouver/Toronto: Douglas & McIntyre, 1991.

Richardson, Boyce. ed. *Drum Beat: Anger and Renewal in Indian Country.* With introduction by Georges Erasmus. Toronto: Summerhill Press and the Assembly of First Nations, 1989.

Task Force to Review Comprehensive Claims Policy. *Living Treaties: Lasting Agreements.* Ottawa: Department of Indian Affairs and Northern Development, 1985.

York, Geoffrey. *The Dispossessed: Life and Death in Native Canada.* Toronto: Lester and Orpen Denys, 1989.

RELIGION AND PUBLIC LIFE

ROGER HUTCHINSON

If anyone had attempted to write an article on religion and Canadian public life before 1850, a central theme would have been the attempts of the "founding races" to plant their French and British versions of Christendom in the "New World." A complementary theme would have been the way forces such as the Methodist and Baptist evangelical revivals and various reform movements challenged the monopolistic aspirations of the Anglo-Saxon Protestant and French Catholic established orders. By the time of Confederation in 1867 the Church of England had lost its battle to be the church as by law established, while the Roman Catholic church had secured its hold upon French Canada.

During Canada's first century public life was characterized by clearly defined Anglo-Saxon Protestant and French Catholic spheres of influence, and by the continuing assumption that there was a close relationship between Christianizing and Canadianizing Native peoples and new immigrants. As the upwardly mobile Methodists and Baptists became increasingly integrated into the Canadian mainstream, the Salvation Army, Jehovah's Witnesses and Pentecostal groups emerged on the margins of society to challenge conventional approaches to poverty, salvation and religious conversion.

By the time Canada celebrated its 100th birthday in 1967, two world wars, the depression of the 1930s, changing patterns of immigration and successive waves of technological change had produced a radically changed society. One of the signs that the old Anglo-Saxon Protestant–French Catholic dualism was giving way to a multicultural Canada was the increasing proportion of the population who were Roman Catholic but not French. Between 1951 and 1971 the number of non-French Roman Catholics increased from 1.89 million to 4.16 million (an increase from 13.5% to 19.3% of the Canadian population), while the five largest Protestant denominations (Anglican, Baptist, Lutheran, Presbyterian and United Church) increased from 6.67 million to 8.57 million (a decrease from 47.6% to 30.1% of the Canadian population). During the same period French Catholics in-

596

creased in numbers from 4.17 million to 5.78 million, but decreased as a percentage of the Canadian population from 29.8 to 26.9.

A major contribution to the non-French Roman Catholic population came from the sharp increase in Italian immigration following changes in immigration regulations during the 1960s. Between 1951 and 1971 the Italian population increased from 152,245 to 730,820, and 679,910 of these were Roman Catholics. Thus, by 1971 Italians had replaced Ukrainians as the fourth largest ethnic group. Persons with German ancestry continued to be the third largest group. These figures demonstrate the loss of hegemony of the earlier Anglo-Saxon Protestant and French Catholic spheres of influence; and the increased ethnic diversity of the Canadian population. They also serve as a reminder that the Roman Catholic religion, which once had to fight for minority rights, now makes up almost 50% of the Canadian population.

By the third decade of Canada's second century, it had become less common to assume that North America was discovered by Europeans or that human society there began with their arrival. Native Canadians are now part of a worldwide struggle for aboriginal rights, which include the right to retrieve their own religious traditions. Changing immigration patterns have altered the basic character of the Canadian population. In relation to earlier periods of Anglo-Saxon Protestant and French Catholic hegemony, or Protestant and Catholic multiculturalism, Canadian society is now both multicultural and religiously diverse. Whereas census data for 1951 showed that 95.6% of the Canadian population identified with a Christian group, in 1981 the figure had dropped to 86.3%. New religious groups such as Sun Myung Moon's Unification Church, the Church of Scientology and the International Society for Krishna Consciousness (Hare Krishna) have failed to attract more than 1% of the Canadian population, but they have added color to city streets and they have increased the diversity of Canadian religious life.

The fact that fewer than one-third of the Canadians identified as Christians by Census Canada show up on church membership roles provides a further challenge for anyone wishing to understand the nature and role of religion in Canadian society. On the one hand, there is general agreement that Canada has become a secular, pluralistic society. Formerly mainstream Christian traditions have moved from the center to the margins of Canadian life. Anglo-Saxon Protestant and French Catholic spheres of influence have given way to an ethnically and religiously diverse society in which—in metropolitan areas at least—Christians, Jews, Hindus, Muslims, Sikhs, and others, plus the 1.8 million Canadians who reported no religious preference in 1981, live side by side as neighbors.

On the other hand, how one thinks about religion and Canadian public life will be affected by what one means by secularization and pluralism, and by which aspect of these interrelated processes one chooses to emphasize. A widely shared understanding of secularization is that public life is no longer under church control or guided by a dominant set of beliefs in a transcendent power. Some observers go on to conclude that religion, therefore, must be a purely private affair. Once religion has been banished to the private realm, religious diversity poses no particular problem for public life. Sikhs, who want to continue to wear their turbans and ceremonial daggers as members of the Royal Canadian Mounted Police, must simply be reminded that Canada is a secular society and that religious beliefs and rituals should not affect the ability to conform to the demands of our public roles.

Other observers accept this definition of secularization, but do not conclude that religion is merely a private matter. For this group, the absence of a single dominant set of religious beliefs means, not that religion is private, but that public meanings and practices must be negotiated. Pluralism becomes a key factor insofar as participation in public debate, and in the determination of public practices such as dress codes for the police, ought to include members of different religious traditions. The interesting question, then, for anyone interested in religion in Canada is how particular religious groups relate to the public realm of this modern or postmodern, secular, pluralistic society.

MEMBERSHIP AND AFFILIATION TRENDS

Statistics provided by Census Canada, by church membership figures and by pollsters and survey researchers provide the bases both for claiming that Canadian society has become increasingly secular and pluralistic, and for being somewhat cautious about that claim. The most dramatic support for the secularization argument is the extent to which active membership and participation levels have steadily declined. Results of nationwide polls indicate that the number of Canadians claiming to have attended church or synagogue in the preceding seven days declined from 67% in 1946 to 61% in 1956, 55% in 1965, 41% in 1975 and 32% in 1985. The figures for Roman Catholic respondents were (in percentages): 83, 87, 83, 61 and 43; and for Protestants (in percentages): 60, 43, 32, 25 and 29. Part of this percentage decline can be accounted for by the changing nature of the Canadian population, and by the fact that after 1971 it was easier to register a preference for no religion. However, the greatest drop-off in membership occurred among those persons who continued to report their traditional religious affiliation to the census taker.

The transition of large numbers of Canadians from active church membership to inactive identification with the religion of their youth does not in itself prove that church teachings no longer influence the beliefs and attitudes of these "secular" Christians. University of Lethbridge sociologist Reginald Bibby has reported that active and nonactive members hold similar views on selected public issues, and that their views are very similar to the views of other Canadians. This similarity in the views of active and inactive members, and of nonmembers, prompted Bibby to conclude that religion has "ceased to be life-informing at the level of the average Canadian," and that "religion in Canada is saying very little to culture that

598

culture is not already saying to itself."[1] He could have drawn the opposite conclusion. He could have used the fact that church members and non-members hold similar views on public issues to support the claim that religion was continuing to have an important impact on Canadian culture.

It is not necessary to resolve the debate over the nature and meaning of secularization to agree that the role of Christianity in Canada has changed, and that the changes are related to a number of factors. A very significant factor is the increased diversity of the Canadian population. It is conventional wisdom in Canada that the Atlantic provinces and rural Ontario have retained their Anglo-Saxon Protestant character, Quebec its Roman Catholic flavor in spite of the anticlericalism and decline in active membership associated with the Quiet Revolution of the 1960s; and that large urban areas and British Columbia are the most religiously diverse. Census data confirms this general picture. The Quebec population in 1981 was 88% Roman Catholic, 6% Protestant and 4% other. The Protestant, Catholic and "other" percentages for the Atlantic provinces were, respectively. Newfoundland, 63, 36, 0; Prince Edward Island, 50, 47, 3; Nova Scotia, 58, 37, 5; and New Brunswick, 43, 54, 3. British Columbia, on the other hand, reported 55% Protestants, 20% Catholics and 25% other. Ontario, Manitoba, Saskatchewan and Alberta had respectively, 12%, 12%, 10% and 16% in the "other" category.

The distribution of Sikhs and of other religious or spiritual groups (such as Native religions, New Thought-Unity-Metaphysical, pagan, Fourth Way and theosophy) illustrates the different degrees of religious diversity in Quebec and the Atlantic provinces on the one hand, and in Ontario and British Columbia on the other. In 1981, 60.5% of Canada's Sikh's were in British Columbia; 24.6% were in Ontario; and 2.6% and 0.6% were in Quebec and the Atlantic provinces, respectively. Whereas Sikhs made up 1.51% of the British Columbia population and 0.195% of Ontario's, they represented only 0.028% of Quebec's population and 0.018% of the population of the Atlantic provinces. As will be readily seen, these percentages remain quite small even in provinces with the largest number of non-Christians. The extent to which Canadian society as a whole has become pluralistic must be further qualified by the predictable fact that most of the diversity occurs in the large urban areas.

In Nova Scotia three out of five Jews, 315 of the 450 Buddhists, and 645 of the 1,025 Hindus live in Halifax. The figures for British Columbia reveal a similar concentration of non-Christian residents in Vancouver ($\frac{2}{3}$ of the Buddhists, $\frac{7}{9}$ of the Hindus, $\frac{11}{13}$ of the Muslims and over one-half of the Sikhs). However, visibility is not related only to numbers. Most Canadians are very aware of the presence of the Salvation Army, even though that group makes up only half of one percent of the Canadian population. Visible minorities, and groups with distinctive dress codes and rigorously

---

[1] Reginald W. Bibby, *Fragmented Gods: The Poverty and Potential of Religion in Canada* (Toronto: Irwin Publishing, 1987) pp. 5 and 203.

observed rituals, are present to Canadians whether or not their numbers remain small. Groups such as the Sikhs combine growing numbers and visibility. In Vancouver there are about five times as many Sikhs as there are members of the Salvation Army (22,390 as opposed to 4,475). In Ontario the 16,650 Sikhs living in Toronto and the 5,030 outside of Toronto provide a visible reminder of the changing Canadian population.

On the whole, however, there continue to be sections of the Canadian population that do not yet experience the diversity increasingly taken for granted in urban areas. This difference in daily experience is reflected in tensions within most of the larger denominations over church policies regarding issues such as immigration, refugees, prayer in the public schools, interfaith dialogue, and the acceptance of homosexuals as full members of church and society.

ECUMENICAL DEVELOPMENTS IN THE 1960s AND 1970s

Ecumenical and interfaith developments during the 1960s and 1970s were characterized by new levels of cooperation between Protestants and Roman Catholics; between formerly mainstream churches and minority groups such as the Mennonites and Quakers; and among Christians, Jews, Muslims and members of other religions. On the other hand, issues such as abortion and public funding for secondary schools rekindled old suspicions and produced new alignments pitting Roman Catholics and conservative Protestants against liberal churches.

Just as the first three decades of the 20th century had been the formative period for the Protestant social gospel, the 1970s were the golden years for ecumenical cooperation. Anglican, Lutheran, Presbyterian, Roman Catholic and United churches did an end run around slow-moving plans for closer integration of the Roman Catholic church into the Canadian Council of Churches, by creating a number of jointly sponsored, issue-oriented social action coalitions. These distinctively Canadian organizations each have a small, highly trained staff, and an administrative committee consisting of representatives from each sponsoring denomination. The best way to appreciate the present range of ecumenical activities sponsored by Canadian churches is to recall some of the developments during the heady days of the late 1960s and early 1970s when it seemed possible to change the world.

Protestant-Catholic cooperation emerged after World War II against a background of suspicion and isolation. When seven Protestant churches created a Committee on Protestant-Roman Catholic Relations in 1945, its initial purpose was to "discern the trend of Protestant-Roman Catholic tensions" and to "assist churches in combating any threatened encroachment on Protestant rights." By 1964, "in conformity with the new religious climate," the committee had shifted its emphasis to discovering "ways and means of improving Protestant-Roman Catholic relations." The fact that Roman Catholics were occasionally "invited to present their viewpoints" illustrates both a more tolerant attitude and the isolation normally experienced by Protestants and Catholics.[2]

A number of developments in the post-Vatican II period brought Protestants and Catholics into closer contact with one another. Canadian Protestant observers at Vatican II, and Roman Catholic observers at World Council of Churches events (e.g., Faith and Order, Montreal, 1963; Church and Society, Geneva, 1966), contributed to the growing enthusiasm for ecumenical cooperation. By the late 1960s a Joint Working Group of the Canadian Council of Churches and the Canadian Catholic Conference had been created as a formal channel for discussing Protestant-Catholic relationships. In the mid-1980s, after 15 years of active cooperation through jointly sponsored social action coalitions, the Canadian Conference of Catholic Bishops became an associate member of the Canadian Council of Churches.

The ecumenical social witness of the 1960s was characterized both by Protestant-Roman Catholic cooperation and by concentration on key issues. The 1965 Working Conference on the Implications of a Health Charter for Canadians was timed to coincide with the release of the report of the Royal Commission on Health Services. This conference, cosponsored by 10 churches and 10 other voluntary organizations, provided timely support for the commission's major recommendation: "That as a nation we now take the necessary legislative, organizational and financial decisions to make all the fruits of the health sciences available to all our residents without hindrance of any kind."

By the late 1960s poverty had been rediscovered not only in the Third World but at home. In May 1968, 12 churches plus the federal government and several provincial governments cosponsored a Canadian Conference on Church and Society on the theme "Christian Conscience and Poverty." Reports from working groups on food, education, health, housing, and aid and trade, plus plenary addresses by international figures such as Barbara Ward and Archbishop Helder Camara, identified most of the issues the churches would attempt to address in the following decades.

The most significant follow-up to the Montreal poverty conference was the creation of a Canadian Coalition for Development. In a brief presented to the Special Senate Committee on Poverty, in April 1970, the churches outlined their hopes for the new coalition. They explained that in the summer of 1969 "the idea of a working partnership of churches and other intermediate organizations in the voluntary sector was explored with national leaders of business, cooperatives, labor, welfare and related fields." Responses were positive, "provided that this cooperation did not involve yet another super-agency and assuming an open-ended *ad hoc* approach was taken." At meetings in the fall and winter of 1969, four priority issues were identified: "tax reform that gives a fair deal to low-income Canadians, effective cooperation with new citizens' groups at local levels, . . . a greater

---

[2] Quotations in this and the following paragraphs are documented in Roger Hutchinson, "Ecumenical Witness in Canada: Social Action Coalitions," *International Review of Mission* 71 (1982): 344–53.

Canadian role in world development, and united support of native peoples."

The Coalition for Development, launched with such high hopes in 1970, failed to survive as a national organization. However, the coalition model became an important part of the churches' strategy for addressing public issues. Canadian church observers at the third meeting of the U.N. Committee on Trade and Development discovered a glaring gap between the Canadian government's professed concern about the poor nations and its tendency to support the self-serving policies of other rich industrial nations. The churches decided that it would be timely to focus on trying to influence Canadian trade and aid policies in preparation for the next round of talks of the General Agreement on Tariffs and Trade (GATT). The name GATT-Fly was chosen for the new interchurch coalition, to symbolize both the gadfly role of the churches and the desire to urge the government of Canada to support more progressive policies at the GATT meetings; by the 1990s, the declining role of GATT in the global economy led to GATT-Fly's rechristening as the Ecumenical Coalition for Economic Justice. The Inter-Church Committee on World Development Education—also called Ten Days for World Development because of its focus on a 10-day period during the Lenten season—was given a similar mandate to raise the consciousness of Canadians regarding world development issues.

An important Roman Catholic initiative during the early 1970s added a new dimension to the emerging ecumenical consensus. The United Nations' plans for a World Population Conference in Bucharest in 1974 focused world attention on the population explosion. Roman Catholic leaders reacted against what they saw as a one-sided emphasis on controlling population growth in poor countries. In addition to their traditional negative stance regarding birth control, Catholic leaders pointed out that it was the wasteful consumption patterns of affluent members of rich countries, rather than the large numbers of poor people, that posed the greatest threat to global survival. The preoccupation of Western industrial nations with the population problem of poor nations diverted attention from the need for a new economic order. The 1972 consultation on population sponsored by the Catholic bishops was a first step toward articulating an alternative policy that would shift the emphasis from controlling population growth to changing global economic structures. Rather than focusing primarily on the influence of population on employment, price levels, housing, health care, environment, etc., an alternative policy would look at the impact of economic and social policies on people, especially on the poor.

This social-justice perspective on the relationship between population growth and development was given wide circulation through the church leaders' brief, "Development Demands Justice," submitted to the Canadian government in 1973. The ability of Protestants and Roman Catholics to go beyond their traditionally polarized pro-family planning and anti-birth control positions cleared the way for the creation of the Inter-Church Project on Population (ICPOP) in the summer of 1973. Following a second population policy consultation in the fall of 1973, cosponsored by ICPOP and the Washington-based Center of Concern, ICPOP was asked by the

Canadian government to help conduct public hearings designed to involve more Canadians in the process of developing a Canadian population policy for the 1974 World Population Conference in Bucharest. Meanwhile, GATT-Fly was working on alternatives to the food policies of the rich industrial nations, for which it lobbied with some success at the 1974 World Food Conference in Rome.

Growing concerns about the racism of the South African apartheid system, human rights abuses in Latin America, and threats to northern Native communities posed by proposals for massive resource extraction projects, led to the creation of three additional jointly sponsored social-action coalitions in the mid-1970s. The Taskforce on the Churches and Corporate Responsibility was formed to enable the churches to promote jointly the efforts of groups such as the United Church and the YWCA to discourage bank loans to South Africa. Within the context of a disciplined focus on corporate responsibility, and on government policies regulating corporate behavior, the Taskforce provided the kind of research and continuity that enabled the churches to exert steady pressure on corporations and governments.

The Inter-Church Committee on Chile was created in response to the 1973 coup in that country. In 1976 it became the Inter-Church Committee on Human Rights in Latin America, with a mandate to deal with human rights violations anywhere in Latin America. Increased demand for hydroelectric power from northern Manitoba and Quebec rivers, the discovery of oil and natural gas in Alaska and the Mackenzie delta, and renewed demands for a just settlement of their land claims on the part of Native peoples prompted the churches to rethink their relationship to Native Canadians. Within a few decades the mainstream Christian churches went from being the religious arm of the state—running residential schools and legitimizing attempts to assimilate Natives into an alien culture—to being allies of the Natives in their attempts to block development schemes until land claims had been settled.

In 1975 an interchurch project on Native rights and northern development, called Project North, was created by the Anglican, Roman Catholic and United churches, and was later supported by the Lutherans, Mennonites, Presbyterians (who subsequently withdrew their support), Jesuits, the Oblate Conference in Canada, the Council of Reformed Churches in Canada, and the Quakers. Between 1975 and the fall of 1987, when its mandate was ended by the sponsoring churches, Project North played an active role as a link between northern Natives and their southern supporters. In 1989, the Aboriginal Rights Coalition, a new interchurch coalition to deal with aboriginal rights was launched by the churches and located in Ottawa.

During the affluent, expansive 1960s and 1970s new church-sponsored activities could be launched without a high degree of centralized coordination and without too much worrying about priorities. In the late 1980s the churches entered a period of restraint and neoconservatism in which it no longer seemed obvious that the world could be changed. The coordination of coalition activity and attempts to determine ecumenical priorities received more attention. However, there continued to be a solid base of support in the churches for traditional concerns about economic justice and world peace, and there was a new level of alarm about the environmental crisis. As the churches entered the 1990s they attempted to consolidate the work of the 1980s in these areas.

JUSTICE, PEACE AND THE INTEGRITY OF CREATION

The concerns of the Canadian churches are concisely expressed in the World Council of Churches' call for its member churches to renew their efforts to promote justice, peace and the "integrity of creation." Integrity of creation refers both to the churches' response to the environmental crisis, and to renewed interest in ecological ethics and ways of thinking about and relating to the cosmos as a whole. At its Sixth Assembly, which met in Vancouver in 1983, the World Council invited Christians and all concerned persons around the world to realize that there could be no peace without justice; that security could not be based upon the ability of the superpowers to incinerate the world; and that the natural environment must be protected from unsustainable rates and types of exploitation.

The churches' campaigns for justice cover topics ranging from traditional concerns about crimes committed by individuals to the organized activities of governments and corporations. Crimes of violence against innocent victims must be denounced, and the people who commit them must be brought to justice. However, a society is also judged by how it treats those who break its rules and violate its core values. The churches continue to participate actively in public discussions about the nature and purpose of the criminal justice system. Ecumenical work in this area illustrates the ability of churches with different traditions and theologies to cooperate with one another for specific purposes. The Presbyterians, for example, believe that the state has the right to impose the death penalty for certain crimes. Since the early 1960s, however, they have argued that Canada can afford to respond in a more civilized way to people who commit murder. The Quakers, on the other hand, withhold from the state the right to execute murderers, and argue that prisons themselves should be abolished. Presbyterians and Quakers worked together to abolish capital punishment, and they continue to cooperate with nine other churches in the Church Council on Justice and Corrections. This national, bilingual organization coordinates the churches' efforts to create a more just and humane criminal justice system.

Another way in which the churches' concern for justice finds expression is in the treatment of refugees and refugee claimants. The Inter-Church Committee for Refugees was created in 1980 by the Anglican, Christian Reformed, Presbyterian and United churches, the Canadian Baptist Federation, the Canadian Conference of Catholic Bishops, the Canadian Friends Service Committee, the Mennonite Central Committee, and the Salvation Army. Their close cooperation with Canada's Jewish and Muslim communities on immigration and refugee issues illustrates a nonsectarian, humanitarian conviction that all persons seeking refuge and a better life deserve to be treated justly.

Even during earlier periods, when missionaries built hospitals in distant lands as a means to convert Africans or Asians to Christianity, there was an underlying humanitarian conviction that God willed the fullness of life for all people regardless of race or creed. In recent decades the emphasis on the part of most Canadian churches has shifted from good works as a missionary strategy to good works and human rights advocacy as ends in themselves: People should have food, shelter, adequate health care and civil rights because otherwise they would be hungry, homeless, unhealthy and oppressed.

This focus on meeting human needs for the sake of the people in need has prompted theologically conservative Christians to complain their mission has been reduced to liberal do-gooding and that social justice advocates are simply reviving an earlier social gospel belief in progress through human effort. Church reformers insist that they do not rely on a simple belief that progress is inevitable or easily achieved. They insist that what is required is the gift of courage to persevere in the face of entrenched indifference and evil. The churches' efforts to have human rights criteria applied to decisions about loans made by international financial institutions (IFIs) such as the World Bank and the International Monetary Fund illustrates the patience required to work for justice in the context of global economic structures.

From the time of their creation at the Bretton Woods Conference in 1944 until recently, IFIs have insisted that human rights considerations would unnecessarily politicize their work and infringe upon the sovereignty of donor and recipient nations. During the 1970s the United States in particular began to press for the relevance of human rights considerations. In 1972 Robert McNamara, then president of the World Bank, insisted that the plight of the poorest of the poor was of concern to the bank. During the presidency of Jimmy Carter, the U.S. executive director of the World Bank and of the regional development banks opposed 118 loans because of human rights reasons (34% would have been to "leftist" and 31% to "rightist" governments).

The Canadian government has frequently insisted that human rights concerns are an important part of Canadian foreign policy. However, Canada has been reluctant to put this into practice by instructing its representatives to consider human rights criteria when voting on IFI loan applications. Since the early 1980s the churches, through the Taskforce on the Churches and Corporate Responsibility, have been pressing the Canadian government to articulate and to justify its policies regarding IFIs. The churches have drawn public attention to certain inconsistencies in government policy. For instance, Canadian representatives provided key votes for the approval of a controversial line of credit to South Africa. Yet at the same time Canada was insisting that it did not want to support the apartheid regime. The churches' role in a religiously diverse society is not to impose an authoritative interpretation of Christian values to resolve disputes about public policy. They feel called to witness to the truth and to fight for justice on behalf of those who lack power and prestige. They do this by challenging all participants in the public realm to seek justice, and by exposing the ways in which governments, corporations and the churches themselves fail to live up to their professed intentions to be on the side of justice.

Such painstaking attempts to expose gaps between profession and practice, on the part of governments and corporations, complement the more crusading style of other church-sponsored campaigns for justice. For example, Project North's campaign to block the Mackenzie Valley pipeline, crusades against testing cruise missiles and against the Canada-U.S. Free Trade Agreement, and the efforts of pro-choice or anti-choice/anti-abortion activists to open or close abortion clinics presuppose clearly identified allies and enemies. Sometimes tensions within the churches and between church and society are related to differences in style; and sometimes deep underlying differences are involved. In both cases, by pressing debates to the level of basic convictions and world views the churches are not introducing extraneous religious divisions into the public realm. They are contributing to the struggle for justice and peace by helping to clarify the values and views of reality that actually shape public lives.

For the churches, justice and peace are intertwined. The close relationship between economic justice, economic development, national security and global peace was illustrated in major church briefs submitted to the Special Joint Committee on Canada's International Relations. In its 1985 Green Paper, *Competitiveness and Security: Directions for Canada's International Relations,* the federal government initiated the first major review of Canada's international relations since the 1970 White Paper, *Foreign Policy for Canadians.* It provided the occasion for the churches to reflect upon the broad scope of their concerns during the intervening 15 years, and to articulate insights gained from the specialized work of the various denominational agencies and interchurch coalitions. The Canadian Council of Churches called its brief: "Canada's International Relations: An Alternative View, an Enhanced Role for Canada." In calling for an alternative to the government's narrow focus on Canada's economic self-interest, the brief reiterated the churches' concerns about trade and aid policies. To underline the importance of a comprehensive approach to peacemaking it stressed the relevance of human rights criteria for multilateral institutions and for Canadian policies on aid and military exports; and it drew on the work of denominational and ecumenical personnel with direct involvement in mediating disputes and providing humanitarian aid in Asia, the Middle East, Africa and Latin America.

In response to the Green Paper's emphasis on Canada's "collective security" as a member of the Western alliance facing a Soviet threat, the churches drew on the work of an interchurch coalition, Project Ploughshares, to suggest a shift in imagery to common security. No one can be secure unless an international order exists that can ensure the security of all. In a world made insecure by poverty and by the militarization of the pursuit of national interest, emphasis should shift from nuclear deterrence to measures to control the arms trade and to counteract the militarization of the earth's commons.

606

A similar brief, called "Reflections on Canada's Role in Developing a New International Order based on Justice and Peace," was presented by the Canadian Conference of Catholic Bishops in cooperation with other national Catholic organizations (the Canadian Catholic Organization for Development and Peace; the Canadian Religious Conference; and L'Entraide Missionnaire, Inc.). Both briefs combined general statements about the need to stress economic justice and human rights with the results of detailed research and lobbying in relation to particular policies.

As political scientists Robert Matthews and Cranford Pratt have pointed out, while the churches no longer whisper in the ear of the king from positions of great power or influence, neither do they simply utter the private preferences of a religious remnant. They are raising basic questions about the direction of Canada's international relations and the nature of Canada's public life.

Just as Canada and the United States rediscovered poverty in the 1960s, environmental problems moved to the front burner in the 1980s. In the tradition of Rachel Carson's *Silent Spring* (1962) and the Club of Rome's *Limits to Growth* (1972), voices ranging from the Brundtland Report's sober calls for reform to David Suzuki's apocalyptic radio and television specials once again drew attention to the ecological crisis. Whereas the desacralizing impact of Christian teachings was blamed for producing a culture in which humans exploit rather than care for the rest of nature, Christians themselves found resources in the biblical tradition for more balanced relationships among God, humans and the rest of God's creation. The 1977 United Church Task Force on the Environment pointed out that, just as Western Christians have abandoned their imperialistic attitude toward their "partners in mission" in other parts of the world, humans should think of themselves as partners with rather than as lords over the rest of nature.

There is a sense in which recent calls for a partnership model of inter-denominational and interfaith relations, and of the relationship between humans and the rest of nature, bring the story of religion and Canadian public life full circle. The conviction that people with different religious beliefs and practices can live together as friends without feeling that one religion must triumph over the others represents a return to the spirituality of the Native peoples who initially welcomed their European visitors. Similarly, the notion that humans should live in harmony with nature is a central theme of Native religions. It would be satisfying to think that the era of a male-dominated industrial society, with its religiously sanctioned belief in the divine right of technologically advanced peoples, is coming to an end. Progress has been made toward the inclusion of Native peoples, women and ethnocultural minorities into Canadian society; however, even the commitment to inclusiveness illustrates continuing tensions and ambiguities in the religious life of the nation.

Anti-abortion crusaders appeal to the commitment to inclusiveness in their insistence that full state protection should be granted to each human life from the time of conception. Pro-choice critics of the move to recriminalize abortion stress the importance of including women as responsible moral agents in a community that recognizes that abortion can be a morally responsible option. From their point of view, since fetuses are not full members of the community they should not be granted full legal protection by the state. Although there are dissenting minorities within each church, the abortion issue is a burr under the ecumenical saddle. Mainline Protestant denominations, such as the Anglican, Presbyterian and United churches, believe that women should have access to legal, safe abortions, particularly in the early stages of pregnancy. The official stance of the Roman Catholic church is that abortion ought to be a criminal offense at any stage in the pregnancy except in increasingly unusual cases when the life of the mother is threatened.

Attempts to extend the boundaries of the community in another direction have been equally disruptive. The debate over the nature of homosexuality and the rights of gay men and lesbians reached a crescendo in 1988 when the General Council of the United Church adopted a resolution saying that homosexual orientation was not in itself grounds for excluding gays and lesbians from full membership in the United Church—including eligibility to be ordained or commissioned as ministers. By dealing openly with the status of self-proclaimed, sexually active homosexuals, the United Church precipitated a vigorous debate within its own ranks. However, the issue is also a source of tension between liberal and conservative churches.

Issues such as abortion and homosexuality illustrate the fact that a general commitment to becoming a more inclusive community will not resolve all conflicts. Debates over such issues within and between religious groups also show how no particular religious organization has the power or the authority to determine the outcome of public policy debates.

Although the mainstream churches have moved from the center to the margins of Canadian society, religion has not disappeared from the public realm. Canadian society has become secularized in the sense that no single religious tradition enjoys the status of a legal establishment, and no single set of beliefs in a transcendent power exerts monopoly control over the hearts, minds and public institutions of Canadians. This does not, however, mean that religion has become private or irrelevant.

In a pluralistic society no single religious tradition provides the dominant language for expressing the society's basic convictions and dreams. Members of different religious traditions participate in public debates on the basis of shared commitments to justice, peace and care for the earth, and in relation to their own reasons for supporting some policies and opposing others. In the late 20th century the important question for inhabitants of the shared public space is not who is religious but how one understands one's own relationship to the task of nurturing and shaping a just, peaceful and sustainable society.

FURTHER READING

Bibby, Reginald W. *Fragmented Gods: The Poverty and Potential of Religion in Canada.* Toronto: Irwin Publishing, 1987.

Canadian Council of Churches/Council Canadian des Eglises. *Directory 1988–Annuaire 1988.* (A directory of national interchurch social-action coalitions and other ecumenical groups.) 1988.

Grant, John Webster. *The Church in the Canadian Era.* Burlington, Ontario: Welch Publishing Company, Inc., 1988.

Hutchinson, Roger. "Ecumenical Witness in Canada: Social Action Coalitions. *International Review of Mission* 71 (1982): 344–53.

Matthews, Robert. *"The Christian Churches and Human Rights in Canadian Foreign Policy." Journal of Canadian Studies* 24,1 (Spring 1989): 5–31.

Matthews, Robert, and Cranford Pratt, eds. *Church and State: The Christian Churches and Canadian Foreign Policy.* Toronto: Canadian Institute of International Affairs, 1982.

Mol, Hans. *Faith and Fragility: Religion and Identity in Canada.* Burlington, Ontario: Trinity Press, 1985.

Pratt, Cranford, and Roger Hutchinson, eds. *Christian Faith and Economic Justice: Toward a Canadian Perspective.* Burlington, Ontario: Trinity Press, 1988.

Pratt, Renate. *"International Financial Institutions."* In *Human Rights in Canadian Foreign Policy,* edited by Robert O. Matthews and Cranford Pratt. Kingston and Montreal: McGill-Queen's University Press, 1988.

Westfall, William, et al., eds. *Religion/Culture: Comparative Canadian Studies/Etudes canadiennes comparées. Canadian Issues/Themes canadiennes,* vol. 7. Ottawa: The Association of Canadian Studies, 1985.

WELFARE STATE
POLICIES AND TAXATION

LEONARD SHIFRIN

In terms of geography, Canada is only slightly closer to Europe than is the United States. In its social philosophy, though, it is very much closer, and that is reflected in the scope and design of its social programs. Canadian measures have more often been modeled on those across the Atlantic than on those across the American border..

The United States has, nonetheless, been a significant factor in the development of the Canadian welfare state. Sometimes, as in recent years, it has cast a conservative pall. For the most part, though, its influence has been positive, with progressive currents unleashed south of the border sometimes having more impact when their ripples reached Canada than they achieved in their own country. The critical factor shaping the welfare state in Canada, however, has been federal-provincial relations, providing the essential impetus at some junctures and an immovable impediment at others.

The impact of Canada's tax and transfer-payment programs can be readily seen in the income shares of the five quintiles of the income ladder. Figures for 1989 show that the income share of the poorest 20% of households increases fourfold as a result of government transfer payments, and increases further after the progressive income tax is taken into account. The top quintile has its share significantly reduced.

The programs that produce this result are almost entirely the product of the postwar period. In 1939, when Canada entered World War II, its welfare system was rudimentary. Today, the federal government operates comprehensive pension, unemployment insurance and child benefit programs, and contributes to the universal health insurance programs that are run by the provinces under national guidelines. It also pays half the cost of provincial social assistance and social services programs.

Part of what led to a federal government dominance in social policy, despite a 19th-century constitution that saw health and welfare as local matters and put them under provincial jurisdiction, was a dominant federal fiscal capacity resulting from the permanence of the "temporary" income tax established during World War I. That fiscal dominance has eroded in

610

PERCENTAGE SHARES OF INCOME BY QUINTILES, ALL HOUSEHOLD UNITS, 1989

	Income Before Transfers	Income After Transfers	Income After Tax
Lowest quintile	1.2	4.8	5.6
Second quintile	8.7	10.5	11.6
Middle quintile	16.9	16.9	17.6
Fourth quintile	26.0	24.6	24.5
Highest quintile	47.2	43.2	40.7

recent decades, as the central government ceded increasing shares of its income tax room to the provinces, and the consumption and property taxes on which provincial and local government relied grew in importance. The ten provincial governments now raise roughly the same amount of revenue as does the federal government, while the municipalities—which are creatures of the provinces—raise about a quarter as much as do their mentors.

Income taxes account for two-thirds of federal government revenues, and sales and commodity taxes account for one-third. The personal income tax is a source of two-thirds of these income tax revenues, while the corporate income tax and employer-employee premiums for unemployment insurance each generate half of the balance. The Progressive Conservative government of Brian Mulroney, which took office in 1984, both reduced the progressivity of the personal income tax and increased the role of consumption taxes. In 1988, the ten brackets of the personal income tax system were cut to three, with the spread between top and bottom brackets being dramatically reduced. The manufacturers' sales tax was substantially increased in the early years of the Mulroney government and then was replaced, in 1991, by a far more comprehensive value-added tax that extends to the retail level and covers services as well as goods.

Although the building of Canada's welfare state was essentially a postwar phenomenon, the process began during the war. There was no unemployment insurance program in Canada during the Depression because jurisdiction for such a program lay with the provinces, and none of them was willing to risk putting its industries at a competitive disadvantage by introducing the employer levies the measure would entail. After an attempt by the federal government to establish a national program was rejected by the courts in 1937, some provinces were ready to endorse a constitutional amendment giving the federal government the power to create such a program, but others were not. Only a crucial change of government in Quebec, in an election dominated by war-related issues, enabled the amendment to pass and the program to be established in 1940.

The 1942 Beveridge Report in Britain is credited with inspiring that country's postwar welfare state with its vision of a fairer, more compassionate country at the end of the wartime suffering. It also inspired the Canadian government to commission a similar study. The Marsh Report of 1943 was as visionary as its British counterpart, but it faced one huge disadvantage. Beveridge's report went to a government that needed only the will to implement it. Marsh's report was presented to a government that had no constitutional authority to act on its proposals for social insurance programs covering everything from health care to retirement income. Only the proposed children's allowance was clearly within federal jurisdiction.

The wage mechanism is incapable of taking into account the difference in needs between a single person and the breadwinner for a large family; and too many mouths to feed can relegate a household to poverty. The practice of government providing a flat-rate monthly payment for each child, while novel in a North American context, was well established in Europe and had already spread to Australia when Canada's family allowance program began, in 1945.

While it may seem strange that so much of the Marsh report called for the central government to do what it was constitutionally barred from doing, it was not so strange at the time. The events of the depression years demonstrated the failings of the 1867 division of constitutional powers. The provinces, particularly those in the Atlantic region and the prairies, lacked the financial resources to carry out their responsibilities, while the federal government lacked the constitutional authority to perform the role for which it was financially equipped. In the wake of the court's rejection of the initial attempt to create a nationwide unemployment insurance plan, the federal government established a Royal Commission on Dominion-Provincial Relations, which presented its report in 1940. Among other things, it called for a transfer to the central government of authority for measures dealing with unemployment and old age.

Although the effect of the war in ending depression conditions substantially undercut the prospect, such a constitutional reshuffling remained a possibility at the time Marsh designed his proposals. It was only in 1944, with the return to office of the pre-1939 provincial rights government of Maurice Duplessis in Quebec, that the death knell for such a transfer was sounded. At that point, the Marsh report ceased to be a prospective blueprint for Canada's postwar welfare state and became instead an agenda. With a system of universal family allowances already in place at war's end, a comprehensive old-age pension emerged as the top item on that agenda.

It took six years before the Old Age Security (OAS) pension was established. In striking down the first attempt to create an unemployment insurance plan, the courts had held that provincial jurisdiction extends to all forms of insurance, which meant the federal government could not create a pension plan based on the social insurance approach of employer and employee contributions. Universal payments out of federal general revenues—the family allowance approach—would be constitutionally acceptable, but those who regarded fiscal conservatism as a form of morality argued for some kind of earmarked contribution to finance the measure. The compromise result was that a specified portion of personal and corporate income taxes and federal sales tax was earmarked as a fund for the universal pension payments. Although some would contribute more to the fund than others, all would receive equal benefits.

Constitutional authorities were confident the courts would not regard this form of contribution as making the scheme insurance, but they were not absolutely sure. As a precaution, the federal government therefore asked for a constitutional amendment permitting it to legislate old-age pensions. For a province to refuse, and be responsible for keeping its seniors from receiving payments, was beyond the pale politically—even for Maurice Duplessis. Before agreeing, though, he insisted that the amendment specify that if federal pension legislation were ever to conflict with provincial legislation, the provincial law would prevail. The proviso seemed purely symbolic at the time, but it was destined to play a key role in later events.

The next item on the welfare state agenda was health insurance, and it came in two stages, a decade apart, starting with the less controversial part: hospital care. There was never any question that these programs would be operated by the provinces. The years of haggling were over how much the federal government would contribute and what conditions it would require provinces to meet in order to qualify for those contributions. In the end, it paid half of the costs, and required that provincial plans be comprehensive in what they covered, universal in who they covered, and run by nonprofit public agencies. To counter the charge that it was imposing its agenda on the provinces, the federal hospital insurance legislation provided for federal contributions to begin only when a majority of the provinces containing a majority of the population established such plans.

In the 1957 federal election, with qualifying programs in place in five of the ten provinces covering a majority of the population, the Liberal government came under attack for legislation that was still withholding payments. When the Conservatives won, they promptly amended the law to remove the condition. This had no real significance at the time, as the necessary sixth province was by then proceeding with a hospital insurance plan, but it proved a precedent with important repercussions a decade later, when a restored Liberal government followed suit by omitting the condition in the medical care legislation covering doctors' services.

The loudest screams about that medical care bill came from the Conservative premier of Ontario, who wanted federal contributions for a noncomprehensive, nonuniversal plan that would be largely run by private insurance companies. Because it had almost 40% of Canada's population, Ontario would have needed the backing of only one or two other provinces to immobilize a federal cost-sharing scheme that was subject to the condition of a decade earlier. With no such provision in the medical care legislation, however, Ontario had to adopt a conforming plan or see the federal taxes paid by its citizenry supporting health plans in other provinces, but not its own.

The Liberals might not have adopted such an explicit set of conditions for provincial medical care plans to qualify for cost sharing if the New Democratic government of Saskatchewan had not pioneered a comprehensive, universal, publicly administered plan in 1962, and if the province's doctors had not responded with a strike. By the time the beaten doctors returned to their practices, a month later, the Saskatchewan plan was established in the public's mind as the national model.

The 1960s were a watershed in the building of Canada's welfare state. The momentum that was born of depression conditions and nurtured on postwar prosperity reached full flowering in the five remarkable years of Lester Pearson's minority Liberal government, from 1963 to 1968. After their half-dozen years in opposition, the Liberals returned to power with a raft of social policy commitments and a dependence on the parliamentary support of either the social democratic third party in the House of Commons, the New Democrats, or a Quebec-based populist group, the Créditistes.

Along with medical care insurance, another campaign pledge Pearson brought to office was creating an earnings-related, contributory Canada Pension Plan to supplement the modest universal OAS payments. The new measure was to be based on a pay-as-you-go approach, with annual contributions roughly matching annual payments. In Quebec, Maurice Duplessis was dead, his Union Nationale party was in disarray, and the province's Quiet Revolution had begun. A rejuvenated Liberal party was in office under Jean Lesage, who wanted to establish a fully-funded Quebec Pension Plan and use the accumulating cash to finance the infrastructure of the province's modernization. Because the 1951 constitutional amendment had given paramountcy to provincial pension legislation, and because it did not give the federal government authority to legislate related aspects of a pension plan, such as dependents' and survivors' benefits and disability pensions, Lesage held a strong hand.

The prospect of a Canada Pension Plan that operated only in nine provinces, while a drastically different pension scheme operated in Quebec, was seen in Ottawa as a national disaster, a Great Wall inhibiting the free flow of labor between Quebec and the rest of Canada. The result was a compromise on all counts. There would be separate but matching Canada and Quebec pension plans. They would be partially funded, and the nine provinces participating in the Canada plan would be able to borrow their shares of the excess contributions as Quebec was drawing on its surplus. In order that the Canada plan could contain the same survivor, dependent and disability provisions as Quebec's, the provinces would agree to a further constitutional amendment broadening the 1951 old-age pension provision.

The Canada and Quebec pension plan promised a rosier retirement to future generations of retirees, but they offered nothing to those who were already retired, and little to those on the verge of retirement. Even when the plans were fully mature, benefits for widowed spouses of low-income workers, for example, could be less than adequate. To fill such gaps, the federal government introduced the Guaranteed Income Supplement for the Aged (GIS). Patterned on the guaranteed income plans then being tested in several localities in the United States as part of its War on Poverty, the amount of GIS benefit declined by 50 cents for each dollar of other income (apart from the universal OAS payment). In combination with the OAS, it was a guaranteed annual income for those over 65.

In addition to the Canada Pension Plan, GIS and medical care insurance, the Pearson government's war on poverty included creation of the Canada Assistance Plan. Over the years, the federal government had extended 50%

cost sharing to provincial social assistance programs for various categories of the poor. The Canada Assistance Plan abolished the categories and provided federal sharing for provincial aid given to anyone in need, whatever the cause. It also provided for the federal government to contribute half the cost of social services for persons who were in need or were likely to be in need if the service was not provided. In the case of child care services, Ottawa defined need so broadly that provinces could get federal sharing of subsidized day care for half the population. Unfortunately, no provincial subsidization measures ever came close to the federal income limits.

The five years of Pearson government were a golden age of expansion for Canada's social program system. But in 1968, when Pearson was succeeded by Pierre Elliott Trudeau, it seemed they were only the prelude to an even more remarkable era to come. Charismatic and intellectual, Trudeau had ceased calling himself a socialist only three years earlier, when he had left academia, joined the Liberal party and been elected to Parliament. Campaigning on the promise to create a "Just Society," he swept into the party leadership and carried it to a landslide victory in the ensuing election.

Among the Trudeau administration's major inheritances was the report of the federal government's Royal Commission on Taxation. Known as the Carter report, after its chairman, erstwhile conservative accountant Kenneth Carter, it was a remarkably far-reaching document, and particularly so for its time. Its central thesis was "a buck is a buck," and it contended that all increments to wealth should be treated equally—earnings, dividends, even capital gains, which in those days were not taxed at all.

Another report, in the public domain and waiting to be acted upon, dealt with unemployment insurance, calling for a major expansion of the program. The third study was carried out within government and never released, although its contents came to be widely known. After the passage of the GIS for senior citizens, Prime Minister Pearson had asked the top civil servant in the social sector to prepare a road map for the rest of a guaranteed income. His report suggested that the children's portion come next, either by adding a counterpart of the GIS on top of the universal family allowance, or by abolishing the universal benefit and replacing it with a much larger one that declined as family income rose.

If Pierre Trudeau had wanted a social policy agenda for his Just Society, it was there waiting for him. The surprise was that he did not want it. The former law professor's passions turned out to be entirely lawyerly. His notion of a Just Society revolved around such things as French-English bilingualism and constitutional reforms that would include a charter of rights, and he had little interest in the tax or social program systems. Those who were threatened by Kenneth Carter's tax proposals did, though, and they mounted a ferocious attack.

When the government issued a White Paper on tax reform, backing down a long way from Carter's proposals, the business community renewed its attack and won a further watering down of the reforms. The one-sided debate and shambling government retreat continued through the legislative process, cobbling a result that was a far cry from what Carter had called for. A buck was not to be a buck after all. Some loopholes were closed, but capital gains and dividends would continue to receive preferential treatment; and marginal tax rates for those in highest-income brackets would be substantially reduced to compensate for the changes that did survive.

A decade later, when the Trudeau government was in the last of its four terms in office and had acquired a more reformist bent, that process would be repeated, with a virtual carbon copy result. The 1981 move against tax expenditure provisions that enabled thousands of Canada's wealthiest citizens to pay no tax at all was again accompanied by a proposed reduction in top marginal tax rates to cushion the blow. And again, the counterattack was so powerful that the government retreated in disarray, abandoning huge chunks of its loophole-closing package while letting the rate reductions stand.

As for unemployment insurance reform and the guaranteed income proposals, the first-term Trudeau government decided it was willing to commit itself to only one major income security measure, and it chose unemployment insurance—mainly because it expected that to be far less costly. Unemployment insurance eligibility rules were substantially relaxed, benefit levels and durations were significantly extended, and provisions for sickness and maternity benefits were added to the program. But the authors of the legislation believed none of that need entail extra cost for the government, because its contribution would be tied to unemployment rates. If these proved lower than they had been in the past, employer and employee premiums would meet almost all the costs, and the federal treasury might actually contribute less than it had under the previous system.

As it turned out, the 4% average unemployment rate of the 1960s would never be seen again, and the government found itself paying far more for unemployment insurance than it had anticipated. Within a year of the new act coming into force, the Trudeau government was ruing the choice it had made, and trying to change it.

In his first term in office, Pierre Trudeau almost achieved his goal of constitutional reform; but the federal-provincial agreement collapsed at the last moment when Quebec raised objections on the social policy front. The provincial government had developed its own plan for a guaranteed income and wanted a major financial transfer from Ottawa to help pay for it, including being given the funds the federal government spent on family allowances in the province, so that it could distribute them differently. When Trudeau came within a hair's breadth of losing the 1972 election to the Conservatives, and found himself dependent on New Democratic Party support to survive in Parliament, both problems argued for the same solution: a major social policy initiative.

The federal government was well aware that nothing endeared it to many Quebecers so much as the checks it sent to the province's households, and it had no intention of giving up that role in the case of family allowances. Negotiations with the Quebec government produced an accommodation. Federal family allowances would be increased, and provinces would be permitted to dictate variances of their amount on the basis of children's ages or family size. By reducing benefits for first children, Quebec was able to introduce a steep escalation of payments for each additional child in a family.

The federal government also called for an income supplementation program for the working poor and indicated that it was prepared to operate and fund the program. When the provinces refused to cede it the jurisdiction, the federal government offered to provide the bulk of the funds for such programs to be run by the provinces, subject to ground rules developed jointly by federal and provincial governments. Three years of intergovernmental task forces and working groups later, Ottawa offered to pay two-thirds of the cost of programs meeting the agreed-upon criteria. But only three provinces proved willing to come up with the balance of the money for a program—and one was Quebec, which objected to the national criteria. At that point, the Trudeau government abandoned the income supplementation initiative and withdrew its cost-sharing offer.

By then, it had reestablished its parliamentary majority in a new election and was no longer dependent on support from the left. It had also pushed legislation through Parliament, cutting back some elements of the unemployment insurance program—including an end to the provision of higher benefits to those with dependents, which had existed since the original 1940 act. Further cutbacks followed, reducing benefit levels, raising eligibility requirements and reducing durations of entitlement, though not enough to entirely undo the 1971 reforms.

When the federal-provincial negotiations collapsed, Ottawa promised to pursue a federal avenue to supplementing the incomes of working poor families. Two years later, it introduced the refundable child tax credit for low- and middle-income families. Compared to the major income supplementation program it had proposed a few years earlier, the credit was a modest initiative—and all the more so for its being funded by a reduction in the universal family allowance and a cutback in the existing income tax provisions for dependent children. Nonetheless, its effect was to shift some benefits from high- to low-income households, and as the first refundable credit in the federal tax system, it demonstrated how the tax mechanism can be used to deliver benefits as well as collect money.

The failure of the income supplementation negotiations was unprecedented. It was the first time a social program proposal had suffered such a fate, and it reflected the breakdown of an intergovernmental consensus that dated back almost half a century. The generation of federal and provincial officials who had shared the experience of the Depression and hailed the Marsh report as their postwar agenda had been replaced by a new generation with no such unity of purpose. For the management generalists of the new welfare bureaucracy, there was nothing unthinkable about letting an antipoverty measure slip away. Before the decade was out, such impasses would become the norm.

By the mid-1970s, provincial governments had begun to complain that the two federal cost-sharing programs for health care, one covering all services performed in hospitals and the other all services performed by doctors, led to inefficiencies. Services by non-doctors in non-hospital settings—having nurses provide home care, for example—was being discouraged because the cost was not shareable. Ottawa agreed to negotiate an extension of the cost-sharing arrangements to cover such gaps, but the talks quickly bogged down as some provinces balked at the federal government drawing any lines at all. In the end, Ottawa threw up its hands and offered to replace item-by-item cost sharing with block grants, the size of which would be tied to the growth of the national economy rather than to actual provincial health expenditures.

At the same time these negotiations were taking place, other talks were going on, aimed at removing the social service provisions from the Canada Assistance Plan, broadening some, and putting them all in a new Social Services Act. Again, the process collapsed when the provinces refused to accept the principle that had animated shared-cost programs over the years: that the federal banker has a right to say what is to be bankrolled. And again, Ottawa threw up its hands and offered a block funding arrangement.

Social service advocates were appalled. The extended cost sharing of a national social services act would have led to an expansion of services, they said; giving the money to the provinces with no strings attached would lead to reductions. Block grants might be all right for health programs that are already well established, but it was no way to encourage investment in new services. As it turned out, the social services block funding proposal fell through for financial reasons. This was fortunate, because experience would soon show that even in the health field the consequences of block grants were disastrous.

The federal government's health care cost-sharing rules had never prohibited extra charges. If the provinces, which financed hospitals and negotiated fee schedules with doctors, chose to impose small user fees at hospitals or permit doctors to charge patients a few dollars more than what the insurance plan provided, that did not offend the federal law. However, every dollar a province saved that way reduced the federal contribution by 50 cents, so the province was giving its voters a dollar's worth of dissatisfaction for a 50-cent saving, and that was sufficiently poor politics that there was very little extra charging—until block grants replaced cost sharing.

Suddenly, federal funds were no longer contingent on provincial outlays. Every dollar the provincial government saved was its to keep; and hospital user fees and extra billing by doctors began to escalate. Provinces were holding the line on the fees they agreed to pay doctors, and telling them to get the rest of what they wanted from their patients. For years, polls had reported that health insurance was by far the most popular of all government services, so it was not surprising that its erosion led to a massive outcry.

It is both logically inexplicable and totally characteristic that the outcry was aimed at Ottawa. Just as, a half-century earlier, Canadians had ignored the fact that jurisdiction for unemployment insurance lay with the provinces and demanded that the federal government "do something," in the 1980s they saw provinces letting their health plans shrink and demanded that Ottawa "do something."

At first, the Trudeau government tried gentle persuasion, offering to negotiate "reasonable limits" to extra charging. Then the Conservative health minister in Alberta made a gaffe of classic proportions. Declaring that the province's hospitals had to live within their means, he said they would be permitted to charge patients substantial sums if necessary to balance their books. When cries of outrage greeted his announcement, he responded that as long as rates were less than at the Holiday Inn, they were a bargain. In the wake of the nationwide eruption triggered by that remark, the Trudeau government decided to move against extra charging. The Canada Health Act, which it introduced, imposes no prohibitions on the practice, as this would be unconstitutional. What the act does is reduce the federal block grant by the full amount of any extra charges levied in a province.

All ten provincial governments fiercely opposed the legislation. The public overwhelmingly supported it; and so did every member of Parliament when it came to a vote. Many Liberals had hoped the Conservatives, usually quick to champion provincial rights, would oppose the bill and alienate the electorate, but they declined to cut their own throats. Within three years of the act becoming law, every province had banned extra charges. The chief battleground this time was Ontario, and again the doctors carried out a spectacularly unsuccessful, month-long strike before accepting the new rules.

When Pierre Trudeau retired, in the summer of 1984, the Liberals had been in power for 42 of the 49 years since a Depression-era Conservative government was put out of office in 1935. A large part of the reason for that, the Conservative party pollster freely acknowledged, was the Tory reputation of hostility to social programs. Escaping that image was essential for victory, he insisted, and the new Conservative leader, Brian Mulroney, agreed. While the Liberals were hoping he would fall into the trap of opposing the Canada Health Act, Mulroney welcomed the high-profile opportunity to endorse it. That, plus one significant election plank and a surprising declaration during the televised leaders' debate, was all it took to establish the new image. The declaration was that he supported a minimum tax on the rich. The promise was to extend the guaranteed income system for seniors that the Liberals had been building.

The OAS-GIS guaranteed income level for seniors had been raised a number of times during the Trudeau years, as well as being indexed to increases in the cost of living. In addition, a Spouse's Allowance had been added for couples in which the pre-pensioner partner was aged 60 to 65. If the couple's income was low enough, the younger spouse received a benefit that gave the same guaranteed income as a couple who were both over 65. If a spouse began receiving the benefit and then was widowed, the benefit continued. If a person was widowed before age 60, however, he or she was ineligible. Mulroney promised to extend eligibility to all widows and widowers aged 60 to 65. It was a modest promise, because most poor 60-to-65-year-olds are married to other people below the age of 65, have never been married or are divorced; but it was enough to register the message. The new-look Conservatives won a huge victory.

Six months later, though, the government was showing very different colors, and pensioners were demonstrating by the thousands on Parliament Hill, protesting the Mulroney government's plan to de-index the universal

OAS benefit and thereby cut inflation protection for even the poorest seniors. The outcry against that move was so overwhelming that the government was forced to back down, but it did manage to de-index children's benefits. It also cut them back for all but the poor, largely through the tax reform exercise, the chief objective of which was to reduce top marginal tax rates. A capital gains exemption was also created, and the so-called minimum tax, promised so dramatically during the election, turned out to be a seven-year income-averaging device.

As well, the ceiling for tax-exempt contributions to Retirement Savings Plans will more than double between 1990 and 1996, raising the earnings level necessary for maximum contributions from $38,000 to $87,000—from twice the 1990 national median earnings level to more than four times. Meanwhile, a new round of social expenditure restraint legislation, introduced in 1989, further restricted unemployment insurance and clawed back, through a repayment provision, up to 100% of family allowances and OAS benefits from middle-income as well as upper-income households; the clawback threshold was only partially indexed, so it caught more recipients each year. In its 1992 budget, the federal government announced it was abandoning universality in favor of monthly payments to low-income families.

Then there are the Mulroney government's two big initiatives: a 1989 free trade pact with the United States, and an aborted constitutional amendment package known as the Meech Lake Accord, whose threat to national social program standards continues despite the accord's demise.

Social program supporters fear that the free trade pact threatens Canada's social policy independence. Canadian businesses will insist they cannot meet American competition when fettered by such things as Canada's higher minimum wage, maternity leave and workplace health and safety standards. At the same time, U.S. companies could initiate countervail actions, claiming to be injured by the "unfair advantage" conferred on their Canadian competitors by government contributions to unemployment insurance, by publicly funded health care saving them from the costliest of fringe benefits and so on.

The Mulroney government, of course, denies any of this will happen, and points out that the one challenge to a Canadian social program in an American countervail action—a challenge to fishermen's benefits under Canada's unemployment insurance program—was rejected by the U.S. trade tribunal. Opponents of the treaty, however, note how often the tribunal has reversed itself in recent years, and wonder about the "coincidence" that only a few months after the trade deal's ten-year implementation process began, Ottawa cut back unemployment insurance and eliminated the government funding provision.

As for the Meech Lake Accord, it would have given the provinces a role in a number of areas of federal jurisdiction, from immigration to the appointment of Supreme Court justices. Most of the opposition to the pact revolved around the extent to which its recognition of Quebec as a "distinct society" within Canada would erode the effect in that province of the Charter of Rights that Pierre Trudeau had finally managed to get into the constitution. For those in the social program field, however, it was two other provisions in the Accord that were anathema.

One provided that in the event of federal-provincial agreement to the transfer of an area of legislative jurisdiction from the provinces to Ottawa, any province that disapproved could opt out and receive the money the federal government would have spent in the province. Only three such transfers of provincial powers have ever taken place, and all of them dealt with social programs: the 1940 amendment for unemployment insurance, and the 1951 and 1964 amendments for pensions. If Meech Lake's proposed provision had existed a half-century ago, none of these programs might now exist. Certainly it is inconceivable that the provincial-rights government of Maurice Duplessis would have agreed to the 1951 amendment if it had had the option of the Quebec treasury pocketing the federal pension money.

The other Meech Lake provision that threatened the social sector would have entitled any province to opt out of a federal-provincial cost-sharing program in an area of its jurisdiction and receive full compensation if it had a "compatible initiative." According to the illustration given by the Quebec government, if Ottawa were offering funds for building sidewalks and Quebec wanted to build bridges instead, that would be a sufficiently compatible initiative to qualify. Even with a far more restrictive interpretation than that, clearly Canada's national medical care insurance program would never have come about if such a provision had been in force in the 1960s. The Ontario Conservatives' noncomprehensive, nonuniversal, insurance-company-run scheme would have constituted a compatible initiative and entitled it to the federal funds.

Although the Meech Lake Accord narrowly failed to win ratification, that failure created a constitutional crisis, with a real prospect of Quebec seceding from Canada. A new set of constitutional proposals is currently being developed, and it is expected to include provisions as restrictive for national social programs as the Meech Lake measures. Whatever comes of that process, there is little imminent prospect of a return to the days of strong federal leadership in areas of provincial social-sector jurisdiction. With the exception of the Canada Health Act—a unique measure, aimed at shoring up an existing program that was unraveling, rather than extending the safety net—there has not been a successful federal initiative in more than 20 years.

Quebec has generally led the resistance to federal action, but it has not been alone in its opposition. Unlike the other provinces, though, Quebec's unwillingness to accept substantive federal intervention has reflected a social policy agenda of its own. When a federal initiative might be used to advance Quebec's agenda—as with income supplementation for the working poor—it has been willing to tolerate the effrontery.

The central thrust of the Quebec policy is pro-natalist. It sees the dramatic drop in the province's birthrate—from the highest in Canada to the lowest—as threatening the preservation of the French fact in North America, and aims to boost births by removing financial disincentives to parenthood and, particularly, to large families. Borrowing an idea from France, it has introduced a system of birth bonuses, and these rise steeply for third and subsequent children.

Income programs in the other provinces are more basic. In addition to all provinces having social assistance measures and employer-funded Workers' Compensation programs for injuries suffered on the job, six provinces provide pension top-ups, raising the federal OAS-GIS guarantee level, and two have family allowance supplements for lowest-income households. Subsidized prescription drug programs and free dental care for school children are also provided in several provinces.

The building of Canada's welfare state is incomplete, and the process is stalled, but the achievements are nonetheless evident. Since the introduction of the universal health care system, indexes of the nation's health, from child mortality to the life expectancy of seniors, have registered major gains. Evidence of the system's efficiency is that in 1989, only 9.0% of the gross national product was required to provide comprehensive health care to all Canadians, whereas the United States spent 11.6% of its gross national product on a system of private health care that left 15% of its population uncovered, and many others with only partial coverage. The measure of the success of Canada's guaranteed income program for the aged is the spectacular drop in poverty among seniors, who used to have the country's highest poverty rates.

The quality of life enjoyed today by those who would once have been doomed to deprivation, insecurity and ill health makes the Canadian welfare state a success story, albeit an unfinished one, the final chapters of which remain to be written.

FURTHER READING

Armitage, Andrew. *Social Welfare in Canada.* 2d ed. Toronto: McClelland and Stewart Publishers, 1988.

Banting, Keith G. *The Welfare State and Canadian Federalism.* 2d ed. Montreal and Kingston: McGill-Queen's University Press, 1987.

Boadway, Robin W., and Harry M. Kitchen. *Canadian Tax Policy.* 2d ed. Toronto: Canadian Tax Foundation, 1984.

Brooks, W. Neil, ed. *The Quest for Tax Reform.* Toronto: Carswell Publishers, 1988.

Bryden, Kenneth. *Old Age Pensions and Policy-Making in Canada.* Montreal and Kingston: McGill-Queen's University Press, 1974.

Guest, Dennis. *The Emergence of Social Security in Canada.* 2d ed. Vancouver: University of British Columbia Press, 1985.

McQuaig, Linda. *Behind Closed Doors: How the Rich Won Control of Canada's Tax System.* Markham, Ontario: Viking, Penguin Books Canada, 1987.

Ross, David P., *The Working Poor: Wage Earners and the Failure of Income Security Policy.* Toronto: James Lorimer & Co., 1981.

Taylor, Malcolm. *Health Insurance and Canadian Public Policy.* 2d ed. Montreal and Kingston: McGill-Queen's University Press, 1987.

LANGUAGE POLICY

RONALD WARDHAUGH

Although it is officially and constitutionally a bilingual English-French state, Canada is nevertheless predominantly English-speaking. There is a very strong French presence in Quebec, but within the country as a whole, and especially within the wider context of the entire North American continent, that presence is a minority one. Quebec is a "French island in an ocean of English," and almost every effort the French Canadians have made to spread their language beyond the confines of that island has met with resistance. Furthermore, the English Canadians and their language have constantly assaulted the French within their own territory to the extent that in recent years the French there have sought to adopt measures designed to resist further assault. Today, a majority of Quebecers feel that they must be constantly on guard if Quebec is to remain French-speaking. Currently, what we observe in Canada is a kind of organized rearguard action to preserve French language and culture in North America, an action which has had both successes and failures but one from which the French themselves can seek no respite.

The linguistic situation in Canada is further complicated by the presence of languages other than English and French, comprising scores of languages brought by immigrants and more than 50 indigenous languages. Although Canada is officially "bilingual," it is not officially "bicultural"; rather, it is officially "multicultural," that is, there is an explicit recognition that cultures other than those associated with the populations of English and French descent have a role to play in the life of the country. However, in practice, all cultural traditions other than the English and French—and all other languages too—inevitably must seek to locate themselves within the overriding English-French framework.

THE HISTORICAL SETTING

Within Canada two official languages, English and French, exist in a fundamentally unequal relationship, historically and demographically, and in that inequality lies the explanation of much of the discontent that has characterized the relationship between the government of Quebec and the federal government in Ottawa since the 1960s. The two languages are official languages at the federal level of government and are enshrined as such in the 1982 constitution. However, English is the language of the majority of Canadians. It is also the official language of nine of the ten provinces. French is also an official language in two of the provinces: in Quebec it is the sole official language (although English also has very strong constitutional guarantees there), and in New Brunswick both English and French have been official languages since that province passed its own Official Languages Act in 1969. French has also some long-standing legal rights in Manitoba, Saskatchewan, and Alberta, rights which the Supreme Court of Canada has recently ordered to be recognized once more.

Geographically, however, the English and French languages in Canada are divided territorially. Most francophones live within Quebec itself or in an adjacent "bilingual belt," comprising for the most part areas in western New Brunswick and northeastern Ontario, and most anglophones live in the rest of the country. Moreover, the territorial separation of the two languages appears to be increasing rather than decreasing, and this at a time when the constitution commits the federal government to protect official-language minorities, which in practice means promoting policies that safeguard the use of French in anglophone Canada. Such policies are designed to allow francophones there to deal with the federal government and its numerous agencies in French. They also require that where numbers warrant, certain educational opportunities be provided to francophone students. Anglophone minorities in francophone areas receive similar protection, as indeed they have always done, but whether the two minorities are, or should be, treated equally has proven to be a divisive issue within the country as a whole.

If we go back to the origins of Canada, we find that the English and French competed in colonizing the northern part of North America. That competition ended in 1759 when the English finally conquered the French in a decisive battle on the Plains of Abraham and captured the city of Quebec. Canada came into existence at that time; it was a British possession to the north of those colonies that were soon to break away from the Crown and unite to form a new country, the United States of America. Canada stayed loyal and gradually expanded to include other British possessions in North America and to fill the prairies to the north of the United States.

Canada actually dates its origin as a virtually independent state to 1867, the year of the British North America Act. This act of the British Parliament was the last of a series of constitutional arrangements made in London to provide some kind of governing structure for this British colonial possession in North America. The 1867 constitution established a framework for self-government, but it was actually not until 1982 that the government of Canada and the government of the United Kingdom finally "patriated" the Canadian constitution, that is, gave Canada complete charge of its own constitutional affairs, with the passing of the Constitution Act and the Canadian Charter of Rights and Freedoms.

Under the arrangement made in 1867, the French in Canada seemed assured of opportunities to spread their language and culture as the country itself developed westward. They were guaranteed the right to use their language in their own province of Quebec, although strong rights to use English there were also entrenched, and they were encouraged to believe that as French settlers moved west they would find adequate guarantees of their linguistic rights elsewhere in Canada. Since the French tended to have large families, natural population growth would also favor them. The French viewed the 1867 agreement as one between two "founding peoples" and they looked forward to an era in which English and French would be in a position of perfect equality in the developing country.

Such hopes were soon dashed. For example, in the last few years of the 19th century the newly created province (1870) of Manitoba abrogated what rights the French had to their language in that province, rights that were not restored until 1985. Increasingly the French in Canada found themselves confined to Quebec, itself dominated by the English of Montreal. Only the high birthrate in that province, the "revenge of the cradles," kept the French relatively secure there, compensating for both the considerable emigration of francophones to the United States, Quebec's "fatal hemorrhage," and the increase in the anglophone population in the province. As the French found themselves more and more confined to Quebec and saw the progressive loss of French speakers outside that province to English, they became acutely conscious of the danger they faced, that of the extinction of their language in North America.

Although certain accommodations were made to ensure a French presence in the government, courts, the military, and other official bodies, the overall Canadian system, was one in which the English clearly had the ascendancy in an evolving federalism of nine anglophone provinces and a solitary francophone one. It was also a system of majority rule in which the French were clearly outnumbered. The result was "two solitudes" in Canada, two peoples largely cut off from each other, each with its own view of Canadian history and identity. For a long time there appeared to be little chance of reconciliation, and occasionally there was even open antagonism, e.g., over the issue of conscription in both world wars when French Canadians were much less willing than English Canadians to fight what many of them perceived to be Britain's wars.

THE OFFICIAL LANGUAGES ACT

By the 1960s it was evident that serious attention had to be given to the relationship between the English and the French in Canada. The French language was in rapid decline outside Quebec and in less rapid but still serious decline within. There were two further threatening factors within the province of Quebec. The first was that the birthrate there had fallen to become the lowest in Canada and one of the lowest anywhere in the world; the French in Canada were beginning to fall significantly below their historic 30% proportion of the overall Canadian population. The second was that immigrants to Quebec from outside Canada were settling in Montreal and learning English, the language of the anglophone elite of that city, rather than French. In this way the already strong English minority in the province was gaining converts from those who were of neither English nor French origin. Immigrants to Quebec saw the English language rather than the French language as offering a better future for themselves and their children. This choice was the obvious one everywhere else in Canada; it was particularly threatening to the French that it would also seem so obvious in Montreal.

In 1963 the government of Canada appointed a Royal Commission on Bilingualism and Biculturalism to examine the relationship between the English and French in Canada and make recommendations for changes that seemed called for. In its report to Parliament the commission completely rejected any "territorial" solution to the problems the country faced with regard to languages. Its recommendations led to the Official Languages Act of 1969 (updated in a new act with the same name in 1988), which named English and French as equal official languages and guaranteed official-language minorities everywhere in the country certain basic rights in dealing with the federal government and its various agencies. But, of course, it was the francophone minority outside Quebec that really needed such guarantees. The act proposed a number of measures to guarantee support of the French language outside Quebec, measures that would in some way provide this minority with some of the support that the English minority in Quebec itself had enjoyed since 1867. Parliament's intention was to provide a measure of security for the French language outside Quebec by placing it on an equal footing with English so far as the federal government was concerned and, in doing so, appease those in Quebec itself who were beginning to seek a new deal for the province within the federal structure.

Parliament also appointed a commissioner of official languages, a kind of national linguistic ombudsman, to report annually to it on the progress, or lack of progress, that is being made in carrying out the numerous provisions of the act. Over the years since its passage the implementation of the act has brought about much controversy and much strife, most notably a crisis over the language, or languages, of air traffic control in June 1976 and accusations by some anglophones that the act is being used to "force French down our throats." The act has also been criticized by many who are of neither English nor French origin for giving the French language a status it no longer appears to merit in certain parts of Canada, particularly those parts in which speakers of languages other than English or French outnumber francophones or in which the francophone population has become virtually extinct as a result of previous policies and attitudes.

Whatever the controversies and disagreements, when Canada finally patriated its constitution in 1982 certain rights of the French to their language in Canada were enshrined in that document. In future, the language rights of official-language minorities in Canada can be changed only after a complicated process of constitutional amendment; they can no longer be changed merely by a simple majority vote in any parliamentary session. The government that was then in power in Quebec, headed by René Lévesque of the Parti Québécois refused to sign the new constitutional agreement because it did not appear to go far enough to protect what the Quebecers felt was Quebec's unique place within Canada. The failed Meech Lake Accord of 1987, which, among other provisions, proposed that Quebec be recognized as a "distinct society," was an attempt to patch up some of these differences and make Quebec a signatory to the 1982 constitution.

QUEBEC AND THE OTHER PROVINCES

At the same time as the government of Canada was guaranteeing French rights throughout the country as a whole, the government of Quebec was taking measures to reduce the use of English within that province. Quebec had modernized during the Quiet Revolution of the early 1960s and created a new sense of purpose, a national sentiment, an intelligentsia, and its own cultural outlets. It was also time to put its linguistic house in order. While the federal government saw its mission as one of extending bilingualism across Canada, the provincial government of Quebec saw its task to be that of protecting the French language within the province where it was also under attack. Successive Quebec governments therefore passed a variety of bills designed to do such things as make French the language of work in Quebec and require residents of Quebec to be educated in French except when they had a constitutional right to be educated in English. The last of these laws, Bill 101, the Charter of the French Language, was passed in 1977 by a Parti Québécois government that had swept into power in 1976 on an indépendantiste, or separatist, platform. Bill 101 established an Office de la Langue Française to promote the use of French in the workplace. It also banned English from signs in the province. However, it was the provisions in the bill that dealt with education that became the first major issue between the governments of Quebec and Canada because Quebec opted for a very narrow interpretation of the constitutional right to education in English within the province. In 1984 the Supreme Court of Canada ruled that Quebec's new legislation was too narrow and it voided those parts of Bill 101 that had restricted anglophone rights to an education in English in Quebec to those who could demonstrate that they had such rights because their parents had been educated in English within the province. The "separatist" ambitions of the Parti Québécois were also thwarted in a 1980 referendum when 59.5% of the provincial electorate voted against seeking such a solution to Quebec's problems through "sovereignty association," i.e., a politically independent Quebec still in a close economic relationship with the rest of Canada. The Parti Québécois finally lost power in 1985.

In 1988 the Supreme Court of Canada struck down those provisions of Bill 101 that required the use of "French only" in public and commercial signs and advertising within the province. The new Liberal government of Quebec proceeded in Bill 178 to use the "notwithstanding" or "override" clause of Section 33 of the Canadian Charter of Rights and Freedoms in order to continue to give French visual predominance within the province. The use of this clause, though permitted by the constitution, provoked a strong reaction outside Quebec, being viewed as a deliberate attempt to infringe minority-language rights, in this case the right to use English within Quebec; this contributed to the defeat of the Meech Lake Accord.

Elsewhere in Canada, in Manitoba, the French had been denied certain rights that had been guaranteed to them under Section 23 of the Manitoba Act when that province was created in 1870. In 1985 the Supreme Court ruled that these rights, which had been taken away in 1890, had to be restored even though the demographic composition of the province today is quite different from what it was when the rights were abrogated. There are very few francophones left in Manitoba—about 5% of the province's population—so it is not surprising that this decision of the Supreme Court appeared to some observers to be a classic case of "closing the stable door after the horse has gone." Restoring the rights would also be a costly process, one that many Manitobans felt to be no longer appropriate given the number of francophones in the province and the likelihood that this number would continue to decline regardless of the court's decision. In 1988 both Alberta and Saskatchewan proceeded to restrict minority-language French rights after the Supreme Court decision in the Mercure case, concerning Section 110 of the old North-West Territories Act, declared existing government practices regarding the use (or rather the non-use) of French in the provincial legislatures and courts to be an unconstitutional infringement of historical obligations.

Canada's most populous province, Ontario, continues to refuse to declare itself officially bilingual. Governments of all political persuasions have feared the possible political repercussions that might follow such a move. The use of French though has been extended into virtually all areas of government activity so that, while there is not de jure bilingualism in Ontario, there is considerable de facto bilingualism.

THE CONTINUED LANGUAGE IMBALANCE

Figures from the decennial 1981 census show clearly that the historic decline of French in Canada is still continuing in spite of efforts by both the government of Canada and the government of Quebec to prevent further erosion. (Census figures regarding language distributions and uses are very important in Canada: it would be unthinkable that a Canadian census could ignore language issues or for the particular questions that are asked and the findings not to be subject to prolonged scrutiny.) The percentage of residents of Canada who gave French as their mother tongue was 28.1% in 1961; it fell to 26.9% in 1971, to 25.7% in 1981, and to 25.1% in 1986 (in the interim census of that year). However, during the same period there was an increase in Quebec in those who gave French as their mother tongue, from 81.2% in 1961 to 82.8% in 1986, with the decline to 80.7% in 1971 apparently having been reversed. But, whereas Quebec had become just a little more French-speaking over this period of time, Canada outside Quebec had become less French-speaking. The 6.6% of the total Canadian population outside Quebec who gave French as their mother tongue in 1961 had declined to 6.0% in 1971, to 5.3% in 1981, and to 5.0% in 1986. Between 1971 and 1981 the French-speaking population of Canada actually grew by 8% with 85.4% of all such francophones concentrated in Quebec; however, the English-speaking population grew by 15% in the same period, mainly as a result of language shifts and transfers toward English.

English is the language that draws speakers of other languages to it everywhere outside Quebec, both francophones and allophones (that is, those whose first language is neither English nor French). In Canada as a whole the most used language in the home is English, 68.9% reporting such use in 1986 in contrast to 67.0% in 1971. French was so used by 24.0% in 1986 in contrast to an earlier 25.7% in 1971. Outside Quebec, English use in the home increased between 1971 and 1986 from 87.2% to 88.6%, and French use declined from 4.3% to 3.6%. In Ontario, Canada's most populous province, there were in 1981 only 475,000 out of 7.2 million who claimed French as their mother tongue; this 5.5% compares with 6.3% in 1971. Inside Quebec, however, there was an increase in the use of French as the language of the home between 1971 and 1986, from 80.8% to 82.8%, and a decrease in the use of English, from 14.7% to 12.3%. This increase in the use of French in Quebec has continued into the 1980s partly as a result of the province losing about 10% of its anglophone population in the first five years of the decade as many anglophones chose to relocate themselves elsewhere in Canada because of Quebec's language policy. Within Quebec three-quarters of the anglophones are concentrated in Montreal. Also of interest is the fact that in 1986, 7.1% of the population of Canada gave a language other than English or French as the language of the home. It is very likely that most of these will eventually convert to English. Even in Quebec itself English has considerable attraction for many of those who responded this way.

One of the conclusions that Canada's commissioner of official languages drew from the 1981 census in his 1985 report to the Parliament of Canada was that official bilingualism in Canada was poised between an honest, linguistic partnership and the distinct danger of linguistic territorialism on the Belgian model, a model that the Royal Commission on Bilingualism and Biculturalism deliberately rejected. Such a conclusion seems to be entirely warranted. The tendency of the two languages in Canada to divide on a territorial basis has been apparent throughout the 20th century. It was certainly very obvious when the Royal Commission on Bilingualism and Biculturalism was working and deliberating in the middle and late 1960s. The commission deliberately set out to recommend measures designed to reverse the historic trend toward separation of the two languages. So far there has been no reversal and there is considerable evidence to suggest that English will continue to gain at the expense of French outside Quebec. Moreover, the French within Quebec will likely have a difficult task in maintaining their language there in sufficient numbers to keep the French people and their language close to their historic proportion within the Canadian population. English is no less a threat today to French in Canada than it has ever been.

A further disturbing fact for the French in Canada has been the growth in power of the federal government since the end of World War II. Even though in the federal government itself, and particularly at senior levels, there has been a significant increase in the use of French, this growth still

629

threatens French Canadians as a whole since it puts them increasingly into a minority position within the country. It makes them less and less equal with the English and drives them further away from achieving any kind of parity as one of the two "founding nations" of Canada. Quebec has become just one of ten equal provinces with which the federal government must deal, and when Quebec disagrees with either the federal government or with the other provinces, it usually finds itself in very much a minority situation. Insofar as the wording of the Meech Lake Accord recognized Quebec as a "distinct society," this minority situation appeared to find some remedy. However, many Canadians were reluctant to accept such a distinctiveness, not knowing what it could mean in the absence of any explanation by those who proposed the term.

NON-OFFICIAL LANGUAGES

Just like the United States and Australia, Canada is a nation of immigrants, but in this case those immigrants entered a country split linguistically between the English and the French languages. In the French view, Canada is a country built by two equal founding nations; in the English view, it is a country built through conquest, of the French by the English, and then developed to fill the empty spaces to the north of the United States. In neither view is it a country intended to be multicultural, and recent moves to declare that it is such a country have met, it can be argued, with little enthusiasm from the majority of Canadians.

The traditional pattern of immigration has been one that brought immigrants to the English-speaking part of Canada. Except for the city of Montreal itself, the province of Quebec has never been attractive to immigrants and early acquired and then kept a reputation for xenophobia. Immigrants settled mainly in Ontario and the provinces to the west. They built farms, did much of the dirty work, and populated the country. They brought a variety of European languages with them, mainly those of Northern Europe at first, because immigration policy was deliberately selective. People were later allowed into Canada from Central Europe and Eastern Europe, and still later from the Mediterranean area, but Orientals and Asiatics were almost entirely excluded on strictly racial grounds.

It is part of the Canadian myth that these new immigrants were invited to form part of a "cultural mosaic" that has come into existence in the country, that is, that they were encouraged to maintain many of their cultural characteristics in the new land. According to this myth, it is this fostering of a diversity of cultures and a concomitant lack of pressure to conform to a single narrow ideal that above all characterize the Canadian approach to immigration. Many Canadians claim that such an approach is quite different from the one practiced by Canada's southern neighbor, the United States, with its "melting pot" approach to immigrants out of which emerges a single nation *(E pluribus unum)*. In practice, however, it seems that from the beginning a policy of Anglo-conformity prevailed in English Canada: English was taught in the schools, the Union Jack was saluted, "English" virtues and values were lauded, and the English monarchy was glorified. Such a policy was particularly in evidence in the early 20th century, when there was considerable immigration.

One consequence was that immigrants found it very difficult to maintain the languages they brought with them. Isolated attempts to found schools in which these languages would be used as languages of instruction were quickly abandoned. The developing school systems insisted on English as the only language of instruction and disfavored much of the cultural baggage that many immigrants brought with them. Even the French outside Quebec fell victim to this same insistence on English and English ways, suffering a particularly severe defeat to their aspirations in Manitoba, where all languages except English were virtually wiped out of the schools.

Until the period of immigration after World War II, little consideration was given to immigrants and their special needs. They were a ready source of labor and were particularly useful in filling in many of the vast empty spaces the country had. They could be praised for their quaint ways of dressing and foods, but any special ambitions they had, cultural and linguistic ambitions in particular, were not to be taken seriously. If anything, immigrants were often regarded as posing "problems" of one kind or another: some harbored "radical" ideas, others were suspect in their loyalties in times of war, and still others were sometimes regarded as breeders of disease in the terrible urban conditions in which they were compelled to live through no fault of their own.

Following World War II, Canada gradually liberalized its immigration policy. Overt racial discrimination was ended and in the prosperous 1950s and 1960s immigrants began to arrive from many different parts of the world. Not only did people come from traditional sources such as the British Isles and Northern Europe, but large numbers also arrived from Italy, Greece, Portugal, Yugoslavia, and elsewhere. Later, West Indians, various Asiatic peoples, and South and Central Americans were also well represented among the immigrants and refugees who came. Before 1960, 90% of all immigrants had come from Europe. By the late 1980s, 43% came from Asia and only 29% from Europe; however, those from the British Isles still made up the largest single group. By the end of the 1980s immigration had also increased to about 155,000 a year, double what it had been earlier in the decade, but still far less than the record 282,000 of 1957.

About half of the new arrivals settle in Ontario and about half of these in Toronto, so that by 1981 38% of Toronto's population was foreign born. Altogether three-quarters of those who arrive settle almost immediately into cities of over 100,000 in population no matter what their origin, urban or rural, or whether from Europe, Asia, or the Caribbean. Toronto, Montreal, Vancouver, Edmonton, and Winnipeg are the most preferred cities. In 1986 15.6% of Canada's population were foreign born, a percentage that has remained fairly constant over a quarter-century but one still well below the 22% of the period between 1911 and 1931.

A considerable effort has gone into teaching English to new immigrants. Outside Quebec—and even within, in the Protestant schools—the language of school instruction is usually English. Until the Quebec government with Bill 101 put an end to the practice, even those immigrants who settled in Montreal tended to opt for their children to be schooled in English rather than in French. They might be Roman Catholic, they might work with French speakers, but they recognized the value of English in the overall Canadian society.

Immigrants soon became familiar with the pattern of language loss in Canada. In general, in the absence of continued immigration by the group and sometimes even in spite of such continued immigration, an immigrant language has a lifespan of less than three generations. The children of immigrants quickly become bilingual and their children often become unilingual in English. With minor variations all immigrant languages in Canada have experienced this pattern of loss. Languages survive only when those who speak them manage to isolate themselves on the vast plains, as did the German-speaking Hutterites, or receive regular replacements from new immigrants.

In the 1960s there was a widespread feeling that a valuable cultural and linguistic resource was going to waste in Canada and that something should be done about it. The Royal Commission on Bilingualism and Biculturalism did address some of the concerns, but it was not until 1971, when the government of Canada announced a policy of "multiculturalism within a bilingual framework," that an attempt was made to deal with the new realities. Canada was to have two official languages but no official culture; it was to be "multicultural," whatever that meant. By that time those of neither English nor French origin in Canada—some 27% of the total population—had come to number almost as many as those of French origin— some 28%—and those of English origin had actually become a minority (in numbers at least) in Canada as a whole.

The new policy, later to be incorporated into the Multiculturalism Act of 1988, was designed to enhance "Canadian identity" by preserving and enhancing what immigrants bring to the country. This enhancement has required government support, but that support has always been token in nature and the multiculturalism portfolio in the federal government has always been a junior portfolio. Critics often complain that what little money is spent goes largely to window-dressing of various kinds, to buying off or coopting ethnic entrepreneurs, and to promoting the government's image in the ethnic press. Provincially sponsored programs also exist but these too have met with many of the same criticisms.

It might appear that immigrants would be natural allies of the French in their fight to preserve their cultural and linguistic heritage. However, such has not been the case. Many of those who speak on behalf of immigrants consider that the French in Canada, particularly the French outside Quebec, should have no privileges, so far as language is concerned, that they themselves do not enjoy. This feeling is particularly strong in parts of western Canada. Outside Quebec those of other origins vastly outnumber those of French origin and the language that predominates is English. The 1981 census figures show that in the four western provinces of British Columbia, Alberta, Saskatchewan, and Manitoba, 79.8% are of English mother tongue but only 2.7% are of French mother tongue, with the remaining 17.5%, of course, neither.

Federal efforts to promote multiculturalism are undoubtedly superficial. That they should be so is not at all surprising. The government has failed to grapple with what it would mean to have a genuinely multicultural society. It is also a multicultural policy without a solid language base, and is therefore essentially an ambiguous policy. But possibly more important is the fact that the major linguistic effort of the federal government must necessarily be directed toward working out the ongoing relationship between the English and French people and languages in Canada. The French are particularly resistant to the idea that other languages should get much attention at all until their language needs have been satisfied. They also object strongly to the fact that the French language outside Quebec is often placed in the same category as Ukrainian, Italian, and other languages of immigration—that is, being sometimes subsumed under a policy of "multiculturalism" rather than one of "bilingualism." For their part speakers of languages other than English or French outside Quebec often resent what they feel to be the entirely undeserved position that French has. It is less spoken in some parts of Canada than certain other languages such as Italian, German, Ukrainian, Chinese (Cantonese), and Portuguese, but those who speak it have access to resources denied to other languages. Perhaps the federal government's lack of enthusiasm and leadership in multicultural matters is entirely understandable. It would be in a no-win situation if it tried to do more.

Trying to do more also would not necessarily guarantee that the particular federal government that did more would increase its electoral support through its efforts. In general, Canadians have shown little enthusiasm for multiculturalism and show little willingness to support the spending of public money on teaching through the medium of languages other than English or French. Education is, of course, a provincial matter in Canada and provisions for language education vary from province to province. Several provinces do make some provision for the teaching of "heritage languages," i.e., the languages spoken by various immigrant groups, but the introduction of such teaching within the regular school day can be a very controversial matter. In Toronto, for example, years of debate have still not brought about a consensus on this issue. Whether or not heritage languages should be taught as part of the regular school curriculum also tends to be overshadowed by the issue of teaching French to anglophones or English to francophones, particularly in "immersion" programs in which English-speaking children are taught entirely in French in their first few years of schooling or, much less frequently, French-speaking children are taught in English. Apparently, many Canadians see much more merit in programs designed to foster some kind of bilingualism in the two official languages than in preserving immigrant languages and fostering multiculturalism. It is one thing to spend small sums to encourage folk dancing and ethnic foods; using large sums and part of the regular school day to maintain "exotic" languages is quite another matter!

INDIGENOUS LANGUAGES

The 1981 census revealed that about 2% of Canada's population declared themselves to be of aboriginal descent, some half-million people with 59.6% of these status Indians—a person of aboriginal descent registered under the Indian Act as an Indian and consequently entitled to certain benefits— 20.0% Métis, 15.3% non-status Indians—a person of aboriginal descent not qualified for registration as an Indian under the Indian Act—and 5.2% Inuit. These people, often referred to as the "Native peoples," are widely scattered throughout Canada. The greatest concentrations are in the Northwest Territories, where they comprise 58% of the population in 1981, the Yukon (17.5%), Manitoba (6.5%), Saskatchewan (6.2%), and Alberta and British Columbia (about 3%). East of Manitoba they comprise less than 1% of the population. In 1981 there were approximately 154,000 speakers of 53 indigenous languages within 11 language families. However, only two Algonquian languages, Cree with 55,000 speakers and Ojibway with 30,000 speakers within Canada and about half as many again outside the country, and Inuktitut, an Eskimo-Aleut language, with 16,000 speakers within Canada and 47,000 speakers outside, are not currently endangered. Some of the indigenous languages actually have far fewer than a hundred speakers, such as Delaware, Tagish, Sarcee, Tuscarora and Squamish.

As a result of their historic treatment by the federal government, teachers, missionaries and other authorities, the majority of Native peoples— some six out of every ten—learn English as their first language. In 1981 only three out of every ten claimed an indigenous language as their mother tongue and a quarter of these used English in the home. Except for the three languages mentioned above, indigenous languages in Canada seem headed for extinction. Although some attempt has been made in recent years to slow this process, the Native peoples of Canada have been more preoccupied recently with land claims than with the erosion of their languages. In the absence of a settlement of such claims within the near future, giving Native peoples much more control over their lives, their languages will continue their rapid disappearance.

The fundamental language issue in Canada continues to be that of the relationship of the English and French peoples and languages. Within Canada, English is by far the more vital of the two languages; it gains speakers from all other language groups and remains an attractive language even within Quebec. Only in Quebec does French maintain its vitality, but still it does not gain there at the expense of all the other languages combined; everywhere else in Canada, French continues to lose speakers to English, but, because of the Official Languages Act, not so drastically as do the nonofficial languages there. Measures taken since the passage of that act in 1969 may have slowed the decline of French in Canada somewhat—although one cannot be absolutely sure even of that because of countervailing forces at work in Canadian society—but they certainly have neither arrested that decline nor come anywhere near to reversing it. Paradoxically, the consolidation of French in Quebec may even harm the language outside the province in that it discourages French emigration from Quebec or English immigration into the province and further "hardens" the English-French territorial distribution in Canada. Outside Quebec all languages other than English decline and only substantial ongoing immigration offers any protection against this process. English is the great gainer from the decline of other languages.

As far as personal bilingualism in the two official languages is concerned, it is still French Canadians who most exhibit this characteristic. In the 1981 census, of the close to four million self-declared bilinguals in the two official languages, 85% of francophones outside Quebec reported that they also spoke English, as did 28.7% of francophones within Quebec. Within Quebec, 53.4% of anglophones claimed to be bilingual, but outside the province the percentage of anglophones claiming to be bilingual ranged from 1.8% in Newfoundland to 8.9% in New Brunswick. Within Canada as a whole one in every three francophones also claimed facility in English; in contrast fewer than one in every twelve anglophones claimed to be able to speak French. In Canada there is actually considerable bilingualism outside Quebec but the languages involved are not English and French but rather English and some other language.

FURTHER READING

Berry, J. W., R. Kalin and D. M. Taylor. *Multiculturalism and Ethnic Attitudes in Canada*. Ottawa: Minister of Supply and Services, 1977.

Bourhis, R. Y., ed. *Conflict and Language Planning in Quebec*. Clevedon: Multilingual Matters, 1984.

Breton, R., J. G. Reitz, and V. F. Valentine. *Cultural Boundaries and the Cohesion of Canada*. Montreal: Institute for Research on Public Policy, 1980.

Commissioner of Official Languages. *Annual Report 1971–* . Ottawa: Minister of Supply and Services, 1972– .

Joy, R. J. *Languages in Conflict*. Toronto: McClelland and Stewart, 1972.

Lachapelle, R., and J. Henripin. *The Demolinguistic Situation in Canada*. Montreal: Institute for Research on Public Policy, 1982.

Wardhaugh, R. *Language and Nationhood*. Vancouver: New Star Books, 1983.

REGIONAL DEVELOPMENT POLICY

DONALD J. SAVOIE

The Canadian experience of regional economic development is markedly different from that of other countries. It is, for example, very different from that of the United States, despite 4,000 miles (6,400 kilometers) of common border. Canada has not shared with the United States the continuous movement of population into frontier areas. This is not to suggest that Canada has been any more successful than other countries in alleviating regional disparities. It has not. Canada's population and manufacturing center is still today concentrated between Toronto and Montreal. While the Toronto region, for example, has been able to develop a highly sophisticated urban structure and a strong industrial base, the Gaspé Peninsula and northern New Brunswick, some 1,200 miles (1,920 kilometers) to the east, suffer from chronic unemployment, a weak or nonexistent urban structure and a heavy reliance on natural resources. The economic conditions there are more akin to those found in the Third World or developing countries than to the modern sophisticated economy of southern Ontario. Canada's inability to attenuate such disparities has not, however, been for want of trying.

Government efforts to promote regional development in Canada have been varied, costly and never-ending since they were first introduced in the late 1950s. The efforts have continued even in the face of government restraint measures and many studies that point to their lack of success. Today, depending on how one defines regional development, the federal government spends anywhere between $2 billion and $12 billion annually on regional development. Even the election of a right-of-center government in 1984 led only to temporary cutbacks in the area. In fact by the end of its first four-year mandate, the government had unveiled new and ambitious regional development efforts.

One would be hard pressed to argue that Canada's regional development programs have been guided by clearly stated policy objectives, designed to raise productivity, employment, and incomes in regions with unsolved problems or unexploited potential. Rather, the forces fueling federal government regional development efforts in Canada have been political and institutional.

636

Provincial governments reject out of hand any notion that their respective economic circumstances are shaped by the market forces and by the geographically neutral policies of the federal government. In fact, provincial governments of the four Atlantic provinces, the four western provinces, and now Quebec, firmly believe that federal economic policies actually retard regional development and favor growth in southern Ontario.

Canada's federal system has also ensured that the country's economic debates are not simply concerned with the functional efficiency of national economic policies; federal-provincial relations have contributed to the notion that there should be an equitable regional distribution of the economic benefits of federalism. It is hardly possible to overstate the importance of federal-provincial relations in economic policy-making. The premiers of the 10 provincial governments now meet at least once a year with the prime minister to discuss the economy. These meetings are national media events and they provide the premiers an ideal forum to point to all the shortcomings of federal economic policies when viewed from the perspective of 10 provinces. Provincial premiers can usually count on the support of their electors whenever they take dead aim at federal policies to explain the underdevelopment of their respective regions. As a result, long-standing real or perceived historical grievances regarding the impact of federal policies on their economy are brought up by the Atlantic premiers and remedial action is demanded. Quebec premiers have blamed national economic policies for the weakness of their industrial sector and premiers from the west have argued that national defense spending in their provinces is inadequate when compared with the national average or that their provinces are not getting their fair share of federal government purchases. Ontario premiers argue that national economic policies are not putting proper emphasis on national economic strengths. In short, provincial governments nearly always evaluate federal policies and initiatives in terms of their impact on their own provinces and regions. As Professor Allan Tupper points out: "the provinces' singular obsession with their own wellbeing often leads them to discount the possibility that federal decisions, while not necessarily conferring equivalent short-term benefits on all the provinces might, over the long term, strengthen the national economy." Indeed, when a provincial government considers that its economic interests have been slighted by the federal government, it will make a case for compensation to Ottawa under the welcome glare of the national television cameras. Experience has shown that Ottawa often tries to compensate the province under the banner of regional development programming.

The public pressure stemming from federal-provincial conferences often spills over, not only into the media, but into the federal cabinet as well. The most powerful cabinet ministers in Canada are the 10 "regional ministers," so named because they hold political responsibility for the provinces they represent. Regional ministers often sit on the most powerful cabinet committees. They are expected to defend their province's interests before their cabinet colleagues and they make full use of their political clout to get more federal projects and funding for their regions. Prime Minister Brian Mulroney did away with the designation of "regional ministers" when he came to power in 1984. Political pressure, however, forced him to reinstate it a few years later. Political scientist Herman Bakvis defines regional representation in the cabinet as "obtaining as many visible projects as possible for their particular region. Personal ambition and the wish to do things for one's region, to help redress the economic imbalances within confederation, merge into one. In this respect, it demonstrates that federal leaders can be just as regionally centered, perhaps even parochial, if not more so, as their provincial counterparts."

It is against this backdrop that one must review Canadian regional policy.

THE BEGINNING

Only after World War II did the federal government begin to show a real concern for regional balance in economic activity, perhaps because regional differences became much more apparent in these years.

This recognition of serious imbalance was brought home by the fiscal weakness of the poorer provinces following the harsh Depression years. The Rowell-Sirois Royal Commission on Dominion-Provincial Relations had been established in 1937 to reexamine "the economic and financial basis of Confederation and . . . the distribution of legislative powers in the light of the economic and social developments of the last seventy years." Essentially pessimistic about the capacity of governments to work together efficiently in joint activities, the commission had favored a clear delimitation of power. It had concluded that the Canadian fiscal system should enable every province to provide an acceptable standard of services, without having to impose a heavier-than-average tax burden. It had recommended a strengthening of the federal government's economic powers and a series of national grants to the poorer provinces so that they could offer public services broadly equivalent to those in the richer provinces.

Another royal commission was to come forward with suggestions about establishing special development plans. The Royal Commission on Canada's Economic Prospects (the Gordon Commission) reported in 1957 that "a bold and comprehensive and coordinated approach" was needed to resolve the underlying problems of the Atlantic region, which required special measures to improve its economic framework. Those measures included a federally sponsored capital project commission to provide needed infrastructure facilities to encourage economic growth. The commission also called for measures to increase the rate of capital investment in the region. In many ways, the commission was breaking new ground in advocating special measures to involve the private sector in promoting development in slow-growth regions. Perhaps for this reason the commission remained cautious in its recommendations: "Special assistance put into effect to assist these areas might well adversely affect the welfare of industries already functioning in most established areas of Canada."

A few years later, the federal government decided to accept some of the recommendations of the Gordon Commission. The country was facing a recession. All regions felt the effect of the recession, but nowhere was it as severe as in the four Atlantic provinces.

The 1960 budget speech unveiled the first of many measures Ottawa has developed to combat regional disparities. The budget permitted firms to obtain double the normal rate of capital cost allowances on most of the assets they acquired to produce new products—if they located in designated regions (those with high unemployment and slow economic growth).

Shortly after this measure was introduced, Parliament passed the Agriculture Rehabilitation and Development Act (ARDA). It was an attempt to rebuild the depressed rural economy and represented Ottawa's first "regional" development program. ARDA began as a federal-provincial effort to stimulate agricultural development in order to increase income in rural areas. It aimed to increase small farmers' output and productivity by providing assistance for alternative use of marginal land, by creating work opportunities in rural areas, by developing water and soil resources and by setting up projects designed to benefit people engaged in natural resource industries other than agriculture, such as fisheries. Later, in 1966, the program was renamed the Agricultural and Rural Development Act, and its objectives were adjusted to include nonagricultural programs in rural areas, designed to absorb surplus labor from farming. Thus, to reduce rural poverty became ARDA's overriding objective. Notwithstanding these adjustments, however, some Ottawa decision-makers believed that ARDA had one serious drawback: it lacked an appropriate geographical focus. It was, in the words of one federal official, "all over the Canadian map."

The Fund for Rural Economic Development (FRED), introduced in 1966, would deal with this concern. The program could be applied only in designated regions, those with widespread low incomes and major problems of economic adjustment. In the end, five regions were identified under FRED: the Interlake region of Manitoba, the Gaspé Peninsula in Quebec, the Mactaquac and northeastern regions of New Brunswick, and all of Prince Edward Island. Separate "comprehensive development plans" were then formulated for those five regions, to develop infrastructure and industry.

The federal government introduced in 1962 yet another development initiative: the Atlantic Development Board (ADB). Unlike other regional development programs, this board would be active only in the four Atlantic provinces, as its name implied. Largely inspired by the Gordon Commission, the ADB was initially asked to define measures and initiatives for promoting economic growth and development in the Atlantic region. A planning staff was put together, mainly from within the federal public service. Considerable research was undertaken on the various sectors of the regional economy, and some consultations were held with planners at the provincial level.

Shortly after its creation, the board was given an Atlantic Development Fund to administer. By and large, the fund was employed to assist in the provision or improvement of the region's basic economic infrastructure. More than half of the fund, which totaled $186 million, was spent on highway construction and water and sewerage systems. Some money was spent on electrical generating and transmission facilities and in servicing new industrial parks at various locations throughout the region.

The federal government introduced still other measures to promote regional development under the Area Development Incentives Act (ADIA), and under the Area Development Agency (ADA) within the Department of Industry. Legislation establishing ADIA was passed in 1963. The central purpose behind these initiatives was to turn to the private sector to stimulate growth in economically depressed regions. This was to be done by enriching existing tax incentives and by introducing capital grants in designated areas.

Regions of high unemployment and slow growth were targeted: only those reporting unemployment rates above a specified threshold level would become eligible. Manufacturing and processing firms were then invited to locate or expand operations in these regions. Three kinds of incentives were applied sequentially: accelerated capital cost allowances, a three-year income-tax exemption, and higher capital cost allowances. In 1965, a program of cash grants was introduced over and above the capital cost allowances.

Assistance was provided automatically on a formula basis. It was applied in a nondiscretionary manner to areas chosen solely on the basis of unemployment levels, and Ottawa quickly discovered that it had limited potential as a development tool. Virtually no opportunity existed to relate assistance to development planning. In addition, because of the program's regional formula, the areas eligible for assistance did not include main population or industrial centers within slow-growth regions, where new manufacturing initiatives could be expected to have a better chance of success.

THE TRUDEAU LEGACY

Throughout the 1968 election campaign, which saw the election of the first Trudeau government, Pierre Elliott Trudeau stressed time and again the importance of regional development to national unity. He went so far as to suggest that the problem of regional development was as threatening to national unity as were the language issue and English-French relations. In fact, he saw the issues as somewhat interwoven, in that regions which were predominantly francophone were also economically underdeveloped.

Once elected, Trudeau moved quickly to establish a new department with specific responsibilities for regional development: the Department of Regional Economic Expansion (DREE). It was clear early on that the Trudeau government had ambitious intentions for regional development. It would attempt to accomplish more than had been done to date. Politically, the government had made regional development and language policy central to its goal of giving Canadians a "Just Society." Economically, it was possible to stress regional development because, in the late 1960s, the national economy was buoyant, the federal treasury was, relatively speaking, burgeoning, and the trend in policy development was in the direction of explicit redistributive priorities. The first DREE minister, Jean Marchand, summed up the situation by pointing out that "because things are boiling over in central Canada, monetary conditions have to be tightened in order to head off inflation. The restraint may be felt here [Atlantic Canada] even though, far from the economy boiling over, there is persistent and severe unemployment."

Because of these economic circumstances and because of its high-priority status, funding for regional development initiatives was never a problem in DREE's early years. DREE integrated the various regional development programs administered by several departments and agencies and introduced two new major ones.

Underpinning the very purpose of these two new programs was the "growth pole" concept. Inspired by the works of French economist François Perroux, the growth pole concept was one that would see growth concentrated around certain focal points. Perroux suggested that if efforts were made to strengthen these focal points, a process of self-sustaining economic growth would be set in motion.

Marchand and senior DREE officials embraced this concept and came forward with a "special areas" program and one for "regional industrial incentives." The two programs shared the same objective: to encourage manufacturing and processing industries in selected communities in slow-growth regions with growth potential.

With the required infrastructure in place, the regional industrial incentives program, through cash grants, would then be able to attract new manufacturing industry to the selected centers. The cash grants would lower the cost of setting up production. The intent was to compensate the investor for locating in economically weak regions through a grant sufficiently large that the new production facility would generate the same return on investment that it would have had, had the firm located in southern Ontario without the grant.

The special areas program was delivered through federal-provincial agreements. A great variety of projects were sponsored, including highways, water systems, industrial parks, tourist attractions, servicing of industrial land, sewer systems and schools. Funding arrangements were also varied.

The second Marchand program, one that remained important throughout the life of DREE, was a regional incentives program (RDIA). This provided grants to companies calculated on the basis of new jobs created in a designated region and on capital cost of the new or expanded plant. Later, a loan guarantee program was added to the regional incentives scheme.

Only a few years after the two programs were introduced, however, DREE came under persistent attack on at least one program: the special areas program. Provincial governments in particular argued that the program was highly discriminatory in that it favored certain communities over others. The provinces were also highly critical of DREE's approach to federal-provincial relations. Ottawa, provincial governments insisted, had adopted a "take it or leave it" approach to federal-provincial relations in the area of regional development that made close federal-provincial cooperation impossible. The provinces wanted to extend federal-regional development programs to more communities while the federal government, pressed by permanent officials, sought to restrict them to a limited number.

There was also no convincing evidence, after three or four years of operation, that the two programs had contributed in any significant fashion to the reduction of regional disparities. Though the time lapse was short, Atlantic Canadians in particular were growing impatient with the results and began to call for more effective measures to "ensure" that the region's economy would catch up to the rest of the country. They pointed out that standard indicators of economic well-being, such as unemployment and per capita income, had widened, rather than lessened, among the different regions.

A major policy review of regional development programming was launched inside DREE in 1972. In a federal election of that year, the Trudeau government barely clung to power, was returned in a weak minority position in the House, and suffered particularly heavy losses in western Canada.

Trudeau immediately set out to recapture public support. In the area of regional development, he moved Marchand out of DREE and replaced him with another powerful minister, Don Jamieson of Newfoundland. Jamieson pressed on with DREE's major policy review. Its conclusions were twofold: first, that the special areas program had too narrow a focus and did not lend itself to new and imaginative ways of pursuing development opportunities; and second, that federal regional development programming had to be pursued in close harmony with provincial governments.

It was this policy review that gave rise to the General Development Agreements (GDAS) and to the decentralization of DREE. GDAs were broad enabling documents that permitted the federal government and individual provincial governments to sponsor a variety of projects under individually negotiated subsidiary agreements. These subsidiary agreements could be province-wide in scope or could concentrate solely on a specific sub-provincial area, an economic sector, or even a single industry.

Provincial governments applauded the GDAs and the kind of federal-provincial cooperation that they entailed. From a provincial perspective, the GDAs had numerous attractive features. They meant new discretionary spending in a high profile field: economic development. They had the provincial governments actually delivering the project, so that the governments were viewed as the benefactors. By and large, the provinces came forward with proposals and the federal government responded, with the cash.

The GDA approach was not without its problems and critics, however. In Ottawa, the GDAs were criticized for being little other than enabling documents. Senior officials in economic departments, including the Finance and Treasury Board, were puzzled by the hodgepodge approach of the GDAs. They had hoped that the GDAs would "harden" over time and evolve into strategic documents or at the very least into guides to preferences or priorities for sponsoring initiatives. Thus viewed from Ottawa, the GDAs represented little more than a new source of funding for provincial governments to tap for whatever development initiative they desired, whether or not it corresponded to a coherent strategy.

The scope and type of activities sponsored by the GDAs is mind-boggling. They covered virtually every economic sector. In Newfoundland, the

GDA sponsored initiatives in tourism, forestry, recreation, fisheries, highways, special projects for Labrador, ocean research, special projects for St. John's, mineral development, industrial development, rural development, agriculture, and federal-provincial planning. Nova Scotia's GDA supported mineral development, special projects for the Halifax-Dartmouth area, the Strait of Canso and Cape Breton, agriculture, industrial development, forestry, tourism, energy, dry dock development, and special measures for Sydney Steel Corporation and for Michelin Tires.

Even wealthy Ontario signed several regional development subsidiary agreements. One was designed to strengthen the urban system of northern Ontario by providing for new industrial parks and new water and sewer systems in Parry Sound, Timmins, Sudbury and North Bay. A forestry subsidiary agreement promoted projects to improve forest management, accelerate reforestation, and construct new forest access roads. Community and rural resource development became the subject of another subsidiary agreement: the Upper Ottawa Valley and the Kirkland Lake areas benefited from industrial land development studies, geo-scientific surveys, and hardwood forest renewal schemes. A $180-million subsidiary agreement for strengthening the competitive position of the province's pulp and paper industry was also signed.

The list of GDA projects goes on and on. More than 130 subsidiary agreements were signed between 1974 and 1982, with a total financial commitment of close to $6 billion.

There is little doubt that the strength of the GDA system was in its flexibility. One senior DREE official remarked that the problem of regional economic disparity is economic and not constitutional. "Jurisdictional lines," he insisted, "ought to be blurred so that appropriate, viable and coordinated measures to stimulate economic development [could] be brought forward." The GDAs certainly did this.

The one recurring criticism, however, that was leveled at GDAs by less-developed provinces was that DREE had spread its efforts too thinly and had moved away from its firm commitment to the Atlantic provinces. If one compared DREE spending with the pattern established by Marchand, then this criticism had some validity. By 1977–78, DREE was spending 39% of its resources in the Atlantic provinces, 31% in Quebec, 5% in Ontario and 21% in the western provinces. In 1970–71, the breakdown had greatly favored the Atlantic provinces, which received more than 50% of DREE funds, with Quebec following at 23%; Ontario received less than 5%, and the western provinces about 16%.

Criticism of the GDAs was also heard frequently in Ottawa. Many thought that provincial DREE officials had become too imbued with local attitudes. They were simply echoing provincial governments' priorities and were unable to bring a national, or even interprovincial, perspective to their work. How else could one explain the "hodgepodge" of projects DREE was supporting? From an Ottawa view, not one of the GDAs pointed to an overall development strategy. They supported rural development if a provincial government favored it, or tourism projects, or highways construction. Simply put, no one could discern a central and coherent purpose in any of the

GDA strategies. Viewed from Ottawa, provincial DREE and provincial government officials employed the concept of development opportunities to justify whatever project they wanted approved. In short, the GDAs hardly constituted a guide for action in regional development. They certainly did not represent clearly stated objectives for both orders of government to pursue and against which to test proposed initiatives.

It is important to bear in mind that by the late 1970s, economic circumstances had changed considerably from when DREE was first established. In fact, by then, there were a number of factors at work that were having a profound impact on the future direction of Canadian regional policy. "Stagflation" had crept into the economic vocabulary, describing the difficult position of having at the same time both inflationary pressure and slow, or no, growth. An international recession had struck. Canada's industrial structure was found wanting, with some of its major components no longer capable of competing internationally. There was increasing talk about the need for government intervention to assist in the restructuring of Canada's industrial heartland of southern Ontario and southern Quebec. The country's textile industry was in some difficulty, as were the automotive industry and heavy appliance sector. Thus, in some ways the regional problem had spread from eastern Quebec and the four Atlantic provinces into regions that had traditionally led the nation in economic performance.

At the political level in Ottawa, it was fast becoming obvious that cabinet ministers and government members of Parliament were less than enthusiastic about the GDA approach. Essentially, they regarded it as an instrument substantially financed with federal funds but clearly favoring the political profile of provincial governments. Even Pierre de Bané, the new minister of DREE appointed in 1980, suggested publicly that: "[he] would be surprised if 10 percent of Canadians [were] aware that DREE grants to business account for only 20 percent of the department's budget, the rest going to the provinces."

The above forces led the federal government to launch a second major review of its regional development policy. This review revealed that the regional balance in the national economy was changing and that now both problems and opportunities existed in all regions. The opportunities were thought to lie in the anticipated economic benefits stemming from "megaprojects," which were primarily energy-related. The Atlantic provinces, for instance, were expected to benefit from a number of such projects, associated with offshore resources. To deal with this development, the review recommended that regional economic development concerns should be central to public policy planning at the federal level. A key element of the review was federal-provincial relations. On this point, the review stressed the importance of close federal cooperation but stated that "joint implementation of economic development programming may not always be desirable."

Shortly after the policy review was completed in early 1982, Trudeau, who was then prime minister, unveiled a major reorganization of the federal government. DREE would be disbanded, the GDAs would be replaced by a new and simpler set of federal-provincial agreements, a new central agency charged with the responsibility of ensuring that regional development concerns would be central to decision making in Ottawa was to be established, and a regional fund would be set up. DREE, the prime minister explained, had not been able to launch a sustained effort at promoting regional development. As a simple line department, it had been incapable of directing the departments to contribute to Ottawa's overall regional development policy. The new central agency, the Ministry of State for Regional and Economic Development (MSRED), would now be able to ensure a "government-wide" focus on regional development, thus strengthening Ottawa's commitment to regional development, and a new line department, the Department of Regional Industrial Expansion (DRIE), would deliver regional and industrial development programs.

The cabinet established MSERD by adding regional policy and coordination to the functions of the existing Ministry of State for Economic Development. That ministry had been set up in late 1978 to coordinate and direct economic development policy and to manage the economic policy "expenditure envelope." The envelope system integrated into a single process the separate functions of setting priorities, establishing spending limits, and making specific expenditure decisions. Within the envelope system, thus, MSERD was to advise deputy ministers and ministers on Ottawa's economic development budget and recommend allocation of funds between programs.

New "Economic and Regional Development Agreements" (ERDAs) would replace GDAs so as to clear the way for the federal government to deliver specific initiatives directly. In practically every other aspect, however, they would resemble the GDAs. In fact, the legal format of the ERDAs and the federal-provincial coordinating mechanism at the officials level are virtually identical to the GDAs.

A regional development fund was also established. The purpose of the fund was to support special regional and economic development efforts and would be funded by "money freed up as the existing GDAs expire." In other words, it involved no new funding but was simply a continuation of the funding level established for the various GDAs.

The new Department of Regional Industrial Expansion was formed through the amalgamation of the regional programs of DREE with the industry, small business, and tourism components of the Department of Industry, Trade and Commerce (IT&C). The first DRIE minister was Ed Lumley, who rose in the House of Commons on June 27, 1983 to explain Ottawa's new industrial and regional development program. Lumley cautioned that "combatting regional disparities is difficult even in good economic times. . . . It is much more difficult in a period when, because of a worldwide downturn [Canada's] traditional industries are suffering from soft markets, stiff international competition, rapid technological change and rising protectionism from the countries that make up our market." A new program to meet these circumstances would have to be one that he could "clearly recommend to the business community, to the Canadian public and to Members of Parliament." DRIE, Lumley reported, had come up with such a program. It was a "regionally sensitized, multifaceted program of industrial assistance in all parts of Canada. . . . This is not a program available only in certain *designated* regions. Whatever riding any Member of this House represents, his or her constituents will be eligible for assistance." The program could accommodate a variety of needs, including investment in infrastructure, industrial diversification, the establishment of new plants, and the launching of new product lines.

THE MULRONEY SOLUTIONS

During the 1984 election campaign, Brian Mulroney outlined a number of specific regional development measures which a Progressive Conservative government would implement. DRIE, he revealed, would be given a "specific legislative mandate to promote the least developed regions" and "every department [would] be required to submit to the Standing Committee of Parliament on Economic and Regional Development annual assessments of the effect of departmental policies on specific regions." DRIE would also be given a wide range of new policy instruments. For instance, in addition to incentive grants, DRIE would be able to offer tax incentives. In the case of the four Atlantic provinces, efforts would be made to improve the economic infrastructure of the region. Such efforts would include facilities for transportation and communications, as well as training programs, improved market research, and other similar measures. Commitments were also made to assist communities suffering from chronic unemployment and very little economic activity.

By the time the Mulroney government assumed office, several ERDA agreements had already been signed. The new government did not attempt to change or to urge the provinces to change the substance of these agreements. In fact, it moved quickly to sign ERDAs with the three remaining provinces, namely, Ontario, British Columbia and Quebec. The three new ERDAs follow the administrative format and program approach of the seven signed earlier. The Mulroney government also inherited a fully implemented Industrial and Regional Development Program (IRDP).

In line with its election pledge to promote the least developed regions, the Mulroney government unveiled some adjustments to IRDP in November 1984. The new DRIE minister, Sinclair Stevens, pointed out that the adjustments were designed in part to ensure that support is provided in areas of the country where it is most needed. Important restrictions were applied to "tier one" regions, or the most developed areas of the country. For instance, "modernization" and "expansion" projects are no longer eligible for assistance in these regions.

By 1986, the government concluded that mere adjustments to DRIE programs would not suffice. For one thing, regions such as Atlantic Canada were becoming increasingly critical of DRIE, which they insisted was an industry department primarily concerned with sectoral, rather than regional, issues. For another, it was also evident that such economic recovery as was taking hold was largely concentrated in central Canada. It was becoming obvious that the premise underpinning the policy shift that had seen the doing away of DREE and the establishment of DRIE was false.

Resource-based mega-projects did not transform the economy of Atlantic Canada. That of southern Ontario and southern Quebec was demonstrating remarkable resilience and not the "unprecedented softness" that had been predicted earlier.

In response to these developments, the prime minister embarked on a multi-stop tour of Atlantic Canada, where he met with provincial premiers and community leaders. The premier of New Brunswick urged Mulroney to establish a new economic development agency that would be specifically concerned with Atlantic Canada. Shortly after his visit, the prime minister unveiled his government's plans to establish the Atlantic Canada Opportunities Agency (ACOA).

Several months later, in June 1987, the prime minister announced the details of the agency. There would be a federal commitment of $1.05 billion over five years in new money for regional development for Atlantic Canada. Effective decision making would be decentralized to the region with the head of the agency holding the highest rank available in the Canadian Public Service. The agency's head office was to be located in the region—in Moncton, New Brunswick—rather than in Ottawa. The head of the agency in turn would report directly to a cabinet minister and not through another permanent official. The work of the agency, it was explained, would be guided by an advisory board made up of Atlantic Canadians.

The agency would play a dual role—one of advocacy to ensure that national economic policies are adjusted to correspond to the economic circumstances of Atlantic Canada and the other to put in place programs designed to assist entrepreneurs or would-be entrepreneurs to launch new businesses in the region. The agency also assumed full responsibility for the ERDAs. In addition, most of the DRIE programs, including IRDP, were transferred to the new agency. It was made clear, however, that the agency had the mandate to define new programs for Atlantic Canada. It was also made clear that the programs would have few built-in restrictions, so as to allow maximum flexibility to the decision makers in the region. The agency's efforts were to be on developing an entrepreneurial spirit among Atlantic Canadians and to rely less and less on attempts to lure outside investors to the region.

The Atlantic agency paved the way for similar agencies in other regions of the country. Two months after ACOA was unveiled, the prime minister announced a new economic development agency to assist in the industrial diversification of western Canada. The goal of the Western Diversification Office (WDO) is to help move the western economy away from the volatile resource and agriculture sectors. The prime minister released a background paper on opportunities for diversification in the west at the same time he announced the establishment of the agency. Funding for the WDO was set at $1.2 billion.

At about the same time the WDO was established, the prime minister also announced more new measures for promoting development, this time in Canada's north, and unveiled special "regional development" measures for northern Ontario, including the establishment of a new "office" for northern Ontario and a special development fund. The northern Ontario scheme cost $100 million over five years. Key features of the program include $40 million in direct loans and grants and $60 million in loan guarantees for small and medium-sized business from the region. A Northern Ontario Advisory Board was also set up to guide program implementation. Specific initiatives directly involving the private sector, it was announced, would be put in place "as soon as possible."

In 1988, a major regional development effort, totaling $515 million, was announced for Quebec. Federal funds were spent on a host of projects in virtually every economic sector in the province. Within a few months, the federal government announced that it would spend billions to kick-start major energy projects in Atlantic Canada and the west. Since they were not considered economically viable, these energy projects were quickly labeled "regional development measures." They required, the media reported, government "handouts" to proceed. Canada's leading English-language newspaper, the *Globe and Mail,* ran an editorial the day after the announcement with regard to such an energy project in Newfoundland, arguing that "Brian Mulroney did not even try to pretend . . . that Hibernia was an energy project. It is a regional development project at heart . . . in the full context of Canadian policy, the question is not whether Hibernia is good, but how good at this price."

Shortly after announcing the establishment of the WDO, the prime minister declared that DRIE would be "replaced" by a new department, the Department of Industry, Science and Technology (IST), which would be concerned with growth prospects in the "high tech" sector. The department will have offices in "all" regions (i.e., provinces) and will try to promote growth in traditional slow-growth regions. It is generally assumed, however, that the department will concentrate its efforts in southern Ontario. The result is that all regions, and even some sub-regions (such as northern Ontario and the Gaspé Peninsula), have their own federal government agencies for regional development.

The Mulroney government was returned to office with another majority mandate in the fall of 1988. The government made no attempt to alter, in any significant fashion, the various regional development measures it had introduced since first coming to office in 1984. The minister of finance, however, unveiled a series of spending cuts to the regional development agencies (i.e., $80 million in the case of ACOA). The agencies were simply asked to absorb the cuts without cutting programs.

SOME CONCLUDING OBSERVATIONS

This review of the evolution of Canada's regional policy confirms that it has been guided not by economics, but by politics. Clear policy goals have not been evident. The measure of the federal government's commitment to regional economic development is, instead, displayed on pocket calculators, with each region keeping a close watch on federal spending to ensure that it gets its fair share. The result is that regional development is viewed, not in terms of strengthening the national economy, but of redividing the national pie, with most regions in full competition to get a bigger piece. In short, Canadian regional policy does not look at less developed regions for the purpose of developing a comprehensive study of both regional problems and potential in order to develop realistic ways of using their resources.

When the federal government pours funds into a region in the name of "regional equity," another region is certain to come calling for federal funds with the same justification. The process is never-ending, and every region in the country has over the past 15 years been able to lay claim to federal funds for regional development. In addition, federal funds are now made available for virtually every conceivable economic development project in every region. The regional development banner is employed to support all kinds of projects, from the redevelopment of the port of Montreal to the cleanup of Halifax harbor, to economically unviable energy projects in the west and off the Atlantic coast. Regional development has become in Canada the convenient "catch-all" for governments to support any number of high-profit projects.

The federal government introduced regional development measures in 1960, in a somewhat hesitant fashion. It was then concerned that the active promotion of regional development would be harmful to the national economy and would unduly interfere in the operation of the marketplace. It was widely believed then that the efforts would need to be modest and restricted to a handful of communities or economically depressed areas. Gradually this concern gave way, and as we saw, the efforts have now been stretched to cover virtually every economic sector in every region. There are political forces made strong by Canada's political institutions and conventions pushing and pulling the federal government into every region with funds for economic development projects. These forces are not likely to diminish in the years ahead. Canada's Constitution Act of 1982 commits both levels of government to "promoting equal opportunities . . . and further economic development to reduce disparity in opportunities." Provincial governments can now turn to the constitution to support their claims for more federal funding for development in their respective regions. They are likely to continue to push for more federal funds in various forums, including on the annually televised first ministers' conferences on the economy.

The fact that shifting national and international economic forces make it impossible for development opportunities to be equal in all regions, or that there may not be sufficient opportunities for development in a region to warrant more federal funds, will likely matter little. What does matter in Canadian regional policy is not so much what can realistically be done to develop the economic potential of an economically depressed regions. Rather, it is what the pocket calculator reveals about federal government spending in one region over another.

FURTHER READING

Bakvis, Herman. "Regional Minister, National Policy and the Administrative State." Paper presented to the Annual Meeting of the Canadian Political Science Association, University of Manitoba, June 1986.

Brewis, Thomas N. "Regional Development in Canada in Historical Perspective." In *Regional Economic Policy: The Canadian Experience,* edited by N. H. Lithwick. Toronto: McGraw-Hill Ryerson, 1978.

———. *Regional Economic Policies in Canada.* Toronto: Macmillan, 1969.

Canada. Department of Finance. *Economic Development for Canada in the 1980s.* Ottawa: Department of Finance, 1981.

Canada. *Report of the Royal Commission on Canada's Economic Prospects,* 1957.

Canada. *Report of the Royal Commission on Dominion-Provincial Relations,* 1940.

Careless, Anthony. *Initiative and Response: The Adaptation of Canadian Federalism to Regional Economic Development.* (Montreal: McGill-Queen's University Press, 1977.

Matthews, Ralph. *The Creation of Regional Dependency.* Toronto: University of Toronto Press, 1983.

Savoie, Donald J. *Establishing the Atlantic Canada Opportunities Agency (ACOA).* Report submitted to the Prime Minister of Canada, May 1987.

———. *Federal-Provincial Collaboration: The Canada-New Brunswick General Development Agreement.* Montreal: McGill-Queen's University Press, 1981.

———. *Regional Economic Development: Canada's Search for Solutions.* Toronto: University of Toronto Press, 1986.

Tupper, Allan. *Public Money in the Private Sector.* Kingston: Institute of Intergovernmental Relations, Queen's University, 1982.

Walton, Frank. "Canada's Atlantic Region: Recent Policy for Economic Development. *The Canadian Journal of Regional Science* 1, 2 (Autumn 1978).

CANADA AND THE
UNITED STATES
COMPARED

SEYMOUR MARTIN LIPSET

There is much to be gained, empirically and analytically, from a systematic comparative study of Canada and the United States. They share many ecological and demographic conditions, have similar levels of economic development and social mobility, and have much in common culturally as well. However, there are consistent patterns of difference between the two.

The central argument of this essay is that Canada has been a more class-aware, elitist, law-abiding, statist, collectivity-oriented, and particularistic (group-oriented) society than the United States, and that these fundamental distinctions stem in large part from the event that divided British North America: the American Revolution. The social effects of this division have subsequently been reflected in, and reinforced by, variations in literature, religious traditions, political and legal institutions, and socioeconomic structures between the two countries.

THE BACKGROUND

Given the contrasts between American and Canadian history, it is not surprising that the peoples of the two countries formed different self-conceptions. The American emphasis on individualism and achievement, crystallized in the Declaration of Independence, provided a basis for a populist format throughout subsequent American history. Canadians, having rejected the revolution, continued to define themselves by reference to what they are not—that is, American—rather than in terms of their own national history and tradition. French-speaking Canada, largely under the leadership of Catholic clerics, isolated itself from the anticlerical democratic values of the French Revolution.

The United States remained, through the 19th and early 20th centuries, the extreme example of a classically liberal or Lockean society which rejected the alliance of throne and altar, ascriptive elitism, mercantilism,

651

noblesse oblige and communitarianism. These values are precisely what Canadians sought to preserve by reacting against the liberal revolutions.

If early American history can be seen as a triumph of the more leftist Jeffersonian-Jacksonian tendencies, many Canadian historians and sociologists have emphasized the dominance of conservative forces north of the border until deep into the 20th century. Canada was no more homogeneous politically than the United States, but its 19th-century populist reform movements, such as the Mackenzie and Papineau rebellions of the 1830s, failed while equivalent groups or movements in the United States triumphed. The founding fathers who established the Dominion of Canada and drew up a constitution were pro-empire Conservatives. As Frank Underhill summed up this Canadian history:

> Our forefathers made the great refusal in 1776 when they declined to join the revolting American colonies. They made it again in 1812 when they repelled the American Invasion. They made it once again in 1837 when they . . . opted for a staid moderate respectable British Whiggism which they called "Responsible Government." They made it once more in 1867 when the separated British colonies joined to set up a new nationality in order to preempt expansionism. . . .

Patterns of emigration and immigration reinforced right-wing trends north of the border. Bourgeois, rationalist and Huguenot elements left Quebec after the British conquest, and conservative priests arrived from France in reaction to adverse events there. In anglophone Canada, most pro-Revolution Congregational clergy moved to New England, and an estimated 50,000 Loyalists—including many Anglican priests—crossed the new border in the opposite direction.

Canada evolved gradually as an independent nation. The link with Britain inhibited the emergence of a distinctive Canadian identity. Until 1982 the constitution of the Canadian confederation was the British North America Act, written by Canadian leaders but enacted by the Parliament in London and proclaimed in 1867 by Queen Victoria. Until the adoption of the Constitution Act of 1982, Canadians had to petition the British House of Commons for any amendment to their constitution. Before 1949, the ultimate court of appeals for Canada was the Privy Council of Great Britain. The 1978 Immigration Act gave Canadians a distinct citizenship for the first time, and not until 1980 did "O Canada" replace "God Save The Queen" as the national anthem. Toryism remained an enduring influence. As political scientist Reg Whitaker points out:

> Toryism was not . . . an economic doctrine masquerading as a philosophy. . . . The emphasis on *control* of the processes of national development, the element of the collective will of the dominant class expressed through the public institutions of the state, . . . was crucially relevant to . . . a frontier colony struggling on the fringes of a growing economic and political power to the south.

Some of the scholars who see Canada as a more British- or European-type conservative society stress that the values inherent in Tory conservatism give rise to support for social democratic redistributive and welfare policies. Gad Horowitz, in his penetrating analysis of Canadian politics, notes that "socialism has more in common with Toryism than with [classical] liberalism, for liberalism is possessive individualism, while socialism and Toryism are variants of collectivism." A dominant laissez-faire Lockean tradition is antithetical to such programs.

Other analysts correctly point to the need to consider also the impact of variations in the ecology, demography and geography of the two nations. Canada controls an area that, though larger than the United States, is much less hospitable in terms of climate and resources. Its greater size, smaller population base, and fear of an American takeover have reinforced a Tory statist tradition of direct government involvement in the economy. South of the border, the anti-statist, classically liberal revolutionary ideology was not challenged by the need for state intervention to protect the nation's independence against a powerful neighbor.

A comparison of the frontier experiences of the two countries encapsulates the ways in which values and structural factors have interacted to produce different outcomes. Since Canada was on constant guard against American expansionism, it could not leave its frontier communities unprotected or autonomous. Law and order in the form of the centrally-controlled North West Mounted Police accompanied settlers into the Canadian frontier, and their presence contributed to a deeper respect for the institutions of law and order. South of the border, frontier lawlessness epitomized American individualism and disrespect for authority.

The diffusion of values through rapid transportation and almost instantaneous communications are promoting a common Western culture. National differences, however, continue. As journalist Richard Gwyn writes, Canadians have become "a quite distinct kind of North American . . . utterly unlike [those in the United States] in their political cultures so that they are as distinct from each other as are the Germans from the French, say, even though both are European just as Canadians and Americans are both North Americans."

The debate as to the sources and nature of the differences continues. The cultural (values) and structuralists approaches are not mutually exclusive frameworks. Harold Innis, Canada's leading economic historian, although emphasizing structural factors in his discussion of cross-national variations, also noted the importance of "the essentially counter-revolutionary traditions, represented by the United Empire Loyalists and by the Church in French Canada, which escaped the influences of the French Revolution."

LITERATURE AND MYTHS

Northrop Frye has argued that "a culture founded on a revolutionary tradition, like that of the United States, is bound to show very different assumptions and imaginative patterns from those of a culture that rejects or distrusts revolution." Many literary critics have pursued the revolution-counterrevolution theme in their comparative analyses of North American literatures. The novelist Margaret Atwood has stressed the difference in the way the two societies look at authority. She points out that unlike Americans, Canadians do not see authority or government as an enemy. Rebels or revolutionists are not heroes in Canadian literature.

Literary critic Russell Brown agrees that the variations in national literatures stem from "crucial differences between American and Canadian societies. . . ." Thus, south of the border, novels emphasize rejection of the father by the sons, much as the Americans overthrew the British King; i.e., the themes are Oedipal. Canadian writing, on the other hand, reflects the story of Telemachus. Telemachus' problem is that "the King, his father, has departed, has left him to grow up fatherless in his mother's home for reasons he cannot fully grasp. . . ." Hence he sets out in the *Odyssey* to find his father. Brown cites various Canadian novels as reflecting the Telemachus syndrome, including Hugh MacLennan's *Each Man's Son,* Robert Kroetsch's *Badlands* and Margaret Laurence's *Diviners.*

Mary Jean Green, an American student of Quebec literature, while pointing to the same differences in content, suggests that the family tension myth north of the border reflects the stress of the mother-daughter relationship rather than the father-son relationship. The theme of many recent novels in both anglophone and francophone Canada has been the feminine theme "of rejection and reconciliation," resembling Canada's relationship to Britain, rather than the more masculine sharp break, found in American fiction, which corresponds to the American revolutionary overthrow of British rule. Green suggests that one reason that women are much more prevalent among Canadian authors than among American authors is that Canadian fiction is more likely to involve feminine themes.

Canadian novelist Hugh MacLennan contends that Canadian literary culture reflects the fact that its three founding nationalities, the English, the French and the Scots, are defeated peoples: the English by the Americans, and the French and Jacobite Scots by the English. Atwood notes that the heroes of Canadian novels "survive, but just barely. They are born losers failing to do anything but keep alive."

A similar point has been made about English Canadian motion pictures. Film critic Robert Fothergill argues that film content points to a "sense of limitation and inadequacy experienced half-consciously by Canadians in their real lives," to a "defeatist fantasy." Critic Geoff Pevere finds that Fothergill's thesis helps "to account for the losers roaming around Canadian films." He also notes the "persistent proliferation of outsiders as heroes in Canadian movies. . . . And unlike the romantic American version of the outlaw . . . the Canadian outcast is defined by his being less and not greater than those communities that have rejected him."

Literary critics A. J. M. Smith and Ronald Sutherland call attention to the recent effects of a new nationalism north of the border that is producing more radical writing. But, ironically, as Sutherland points out, these changes are making Canada and its fiction more American, involving a greater emphasis on values such as pride in country, self-reliance, individualism, independence, and self-confidence. This new nationalism, often linked among intellectuals to socialism and Toryism, seeks to resist American takeover of

Canada's economy and increased cultural and media influence by the traditional Canadian remedy of state intervention.

Harold Innis wrote that a "counter-revolutionary tradition implies an emphasis on ecclesiasticism." Historically, the majority of Canadians have adhered to the Roman Catholic or Anglican churches, both of which are hierarchically organized and, until recently, had a strong relationship to the state. As student of religion John Webster Grant notes, Canada has

> never succeeded in drawing with any precision a line between areas in which the state has a legitimate interest and those that ought to be left to the voluntary activities of the churches . . . Few Canadians find "the separation of Church and State" an acceptable description of their situation or of their ideal for it.

Both the Roman Catholic church and the Church of England, traditional state churches, endorsed the established political and social orders up to the post-World War II era. Hence one found mutually reinforcing conservative forces at the summits of the class, church and political structures. The Anglican Church has declined greatly in modern times, with the ecumenical United Church, formed from a union of Methodists, Congregationalists and Presbyterians, emerging as the largest Protestant denomination.

On the other hand, American tradition and law emphasize separation of church and state. A large majority of Americans belong to "non-conformist" Protestant sects that opposed the established state church in England. These groups have a congregational structure and promote the concept of a personal relationship with God. Tocqueville pointed out that all American denominations are minorities, and hence have an interest in liberty and a weak state.

Just as religious practices and institutions can reinforce general value orientations prevalent in a national community, so too can the latter influence the former, as is demonstrated in a comparative study of the Roman Catholic church in North America. Sociologist Kenneth Westhues suggests that there has been an "acceptance by the American Church of the role of voluntary association. . . ," not state related as the Church has been in Europe. Thus, the Roman Catholic church in the United States has taken over many of the characteristics of Protestantism, including a strong emphasis on individual moralism. As a result, the Vatican has frowned somewhat on the American Church and has, in fact, not treated it as well as the Canadian affiliate in terms of honors (e.g., number of cardinals and saints).

Religion in both countries has become more secularized in tandem with increased urbanism and education. Canadian Catholicism in Quebec had modified the nature of its commitment to communitarianism from a link to agrarian and elitist anti-industrial values to a tie to leftist socialist beliefs. Public opinion research suggests that francophone Catholics have given up much of their commitment to Jansenist puritanical values, especially as they affect sexual behavior and family size. Similar trends are observable within the other two major Canadian denominations, the Anglican and the United Church. Secularizing trends, although generally observable in both countries, have been less noticeable in the United States, particularly among evangelical Protestants, who are very much stronger south of the border than in the north. Americans, according to data from sample surveys, are more likely to attend church regularly than are Canadians, and to adhere to fundamentalist beliefs. There is a consistent pattern in these data: Americans far outnumber Canadians generally in giving expression to such sentiments, with anglophones more likely than francophones to hold such views. Congruent with the variation in religious practice and belief, Americans appear to be more puritanical than Canadians; and among Canadians, francophones appear to be the most tolerant with respect to sexual behavior.

LAW AND DEVIANCE

The concern of Canada's founding fathers with "peace, order, and good government" in their preamble to the Constitution of 1867 implies control of and protection for the society. The parallel stress by America's founding fathers on "life, liberty, and the pursuit of happiness" suggests upholding the rights of the individual. The American commitment to personal rights, including those of political dissidents and people accused of crime, is inherent in the "due process" model, involving various constitutional inhibitions on the power of the police and prosecutors. The "crime control" model, more dominant in Canada and Europe, emphasizes the maintenance of law and order and is less protective of the rights of the accused and of individuals generally.

The lesser respect and deference accorded to the law in the United States are inherent in a system that values egalitarianism and lacks diffuse elitism. The greater lawlessness and corruption in America may also be attributed in part to a greater emphasis on achievement. The American sociologist Robert Merton has noted that achievement orientation means that the "moral mandate to achieve success thus exerts pressure to succeed, by fair means if possible and by foul means if necessary."

Americans are more prone than Canadians to commit violent offenses such as murder, robbery and rape and to be arrested for the use of illegal drugs such as opiates and cocaine. For example, in 1987 the murder rate for Canada was 2.5 per 100,000 population; in the United States it was 8.3. The United States not only has a much higher rate of homicide than Canada; it also has a considerably higher level of political violence.

The lower rates of crime and violence in Canada are accompanied by a greater respect for police and a higher level of support for gun control legislation. In the United States, gun ownership has been regarded as a "right" linked to a constitutional guarantee established to protect citizens against the state. Canadian policy is based on the belief that "ownership of offensive weapons or guns is a privilege, not a right," and the latter possess far fewer arms than the former.

Canada has been involved during the 1980s in a process of changing its fundamental rules. The adoption of a comprehensive Charter of Rights and Freedoms in the new Constitution of 1982 was designed to create a basis, absent from the British North America Act, for judicial intervention to protect individual rights and civil liberties, one which Canadian courts have actively begun to practice. The charter, however, is not the American Bill of Rights. While placing many comparable restrictions on government action, it still is not as protective of individuals accused of crime. For example, as sociologist Edgar Friedenberg has noted:

> The American Bill of Rights provides no person shall "for the same offense be twice put in jeopardy of his life or limb." A similar provision under Section 10(h) of the Canadian Charter of Rights and Freedoms is made ineffective in preventing . . . "double jeopardy" by the [provision that] the process is not considered final till the Crown has exhausted its right to appeal [an acquittal]. . . .

Canadian law under the charter still retains some of the traditional Canadian emphasis in favor of collective (group) rights. The Constitution of 1867 had provisions protecting specific linguistic and religious minorities. The charter protects many individual rights, but "the collective rights of minorities . . ." continue to enjoy preeminence. These include aboriginal rights and rights to sexual equality. The charter also explicitly authorizes affirmative action programs. Although the constitution permits individual rights to be overridden by Parliament or provincial legislatures, group rights may not.

Not surprisingly, analyses of variations between the Canadian and American economies can be distinguished based on whether they stress structural or cultural factors. The structural explanation of North American affluence emphasizes the advantages possessed by settlers occupying a continent open to development, with enormous agricultural, animal, and mineral resources. Within this shared context, the greater size of the American market has given business in the United States a considerable advantage compared to that in Canada.

The cultural interpretation, by contrast, points to the congruence noted by Max Weber between the Protestant sectarian and the capitalist ethos, reflected in the presence of a more hardworking capital-maximizing population south of the border. Canada, as noted earlier, has been less Protestant sectarian than has America and, consistent with Weber's thesis, has developed more slowly. The Weberian logic also suggests that Quebec and the American South were economically less advanced because of Catholicism in Quebec and slavery in the American South, and their residues in values and structures. Friedrich Engels, recording his impressions of a brief visit to North America in 1888, emphasized the sharp variation between the "spirit of the Americans" and that of the Canadians. He noted that north of the border, one imagines that one is in Europe again, and then one thinks that one is in a positively retrogressing and decaying country. Here one sees how necessary the *feverish speculative spirit* of the Americans is for the rapid development of a new country.

He pointed to the "economic necessity for an infusion of Yankee blood" for Canada to grow.

The nature of Canadian society has affected the way its citizens have done business. Historical and recent survey evidence indicates that Canadian entrepreneurs have been less aggressive, less innovating, and less willing to take risks than Americans have been. The Science Council of Canada, assessing impediments to innovation, emphasized the "prudence" of Canadians as a major obstacle. Data drawn from opinion polls reinforce observations about Canadian economic prudence. They suggest that Americans are more likely than Canadians to express attitudes reflecting greater absorption of the values of the business industrial system. Canadians are somewhat more hostile than Americans to private enterprise.

Canadians have been much more disposed than Americans to call on the state to handle economic and other matters. The Tory orientation and the smaller population relative to landmass north of the border have meant a larger role for the state in the Canadian economy since Confederation. As of 1987, the proportion of Canadian gross domestic product in government hands was 47%, compared to 37% in the United States. Moreover, while there is some government ownership of industry in both countries, it has been much more common in Canada. According to urbanologists Michael Goldberg and John Mercer, in Canada, "of 400 top industrial firms, 25 were controlled by the federal or provincial governments. . . . For financial institutions 9 out of the top 25 were federally or provincially owned or controlled. . . ." While below the norm for OECD countries, Canadian subsidies to business and employment in public enterprise were five times the level of those in the United States during the 1970s.

Similar variations occur with respect to welfare policies. Welfare experts Robert Kudrle and Theodore Marmor conclude that specific welfare policies were adopted earlier in Canada than in America, and tend to be "more advanced in terms of program development, coverage and benefits." Seeking to account for these variations, they stress ideological differences: "In every policy area it appears that general public as well as elite opinion . . . [has been] more supportive of state action in Canada than in the United States."

Differences related to party affiliation in both countries also emphasize the cross-national variations. Canada has an electorally viable social democratic party, the New Democratic Party (NDP), reflecting in part the strength of the Tory-statist tradition and the stronger collectivity orientation north of the border. Summarizing surveys of high-level civil servants and federal, state and provincial legislators, Canadian political scientist Robert Presthus shows that, during the 1970s, Canadian Liberal legislators scored much higher than American Democrats on economic liberalism, and Canadian Conservatives were much higher than Republicans. Conservatives and Republicans in each country were lower in economic liberalism than were Liberals and Democrats, but Canadian Conservatives were higher than American Democrats.

STRATIFICATION

Much of the comparative discussion of North America refers implicitly, if not explicitly, to variations in stratification, patterns of class sentiments, hierarchy, and inequality. Goldberg and Mercer conclude that "Canadians are much more tolerant of ruling elites and oligarchs than Americans." In a study of two communities situated on different sides of the border, sociologists Craig Crawford and James Curtis report that Americans are lower than Canadians on an elite orientation scale, and higher on achievement orientation. Neil Guppy, another Canadian sociologist, has studied the degree of consensus across the social hierarchy with respect to the prestige rankings given to different occupations by cross-national samples. He concludes that the evidence supports the argument that "in the United States less emphasis is placed on hierarchical patterns of deference."

Cross-national polls conducted over the past 15 years point to strong and continuing differences between Americans and Canadians on support for meritocracy in contrast to equality of result. Therefore, it is not surprising that Americans, being more achievement oriented, have placed more emphasis than Canadians on education as the primary mechanism for social mobility, whereas the northern country has been more engaged in redistributive policies. The differences between the Tory/social democratic elitist tradition and the classically liberal, laissez-faire populist one are reflected in the greater emphasis on state-supported welfare and group equality in the north. Canada has been much less divided than the United States on a parliamentary level over efforts to foster government health care or affirmative action policies for minorities and women.

Canada resembles Britain in recruiting its business and political administrative elites disproportionately from among those without a professional or technical education. Studies of business leaders reveal that the Canadians not only have less specialized education than the Americans, but also that the former are much more likely to have an elitist social background. As of the mid-1970s, 61% of the Canadian top executives were of upper-class origin compared to 36% of the Americans. Similar results were reported for top civil servants in studies done during the late 1960s and the '70s.

These findings on stratification and elite behavior are relevant to the cross-national variation in trade union strength and the presence or absence of electorally viable socialist or social democratic parties. While Canada falls behind Europe on both items, its trade union movement has encompassed a significantly larger proportion of the nonagricultural labor force than has the American movement for most of the years from 1918 to the present (35% to 17% as of the start of the '90s). Canadian labor officials, moreover, repeatedly endorsed the principle of independent labor political action from the turn of the century on, and were much more favorable to state intervention than were the American union leaders. Although the great majority of Canadian and American trade unionists once belonged to the same international unions, and 32% of the northerners still do, the affiliates in the two countries have varied ideologically in ways that reflect the diverse national traditions.

The American social structure and values foster a free market and competitive individualism, an orientation that is not congruent with class consciousness, support for socialist or social democratic parties, or a strong trade union movement. The country changed during the Great Depression, which introduced a "social democratic tinge" into American party politics in the form of New Deal welfare and planning policies. But evidence from election results (seven Republican victories in the ten presidential elections held from 1952 on) and the findings of opinion polls suggest that the postwar economic prosperity has given Americans renewed faith in their country as an open meritocratic society. Support for statism, nationalization of various industries, and socialism have declined. Trade union membership has also fallen from 1955 to the present, down from one-third of the employed nonagricultural labor force to one-sixth as of 1990.

In contrast to the American experience, the postwar economic boom did not precipitate a return to the values of classical liberalism in Canada because they have never constituted the national tradition north of the border. All Canadian political parties, including the now-governing Tories, remain committed to an activist welfare state. Prime Minister Brian Mulroney has referred to it as "our sacred trust." In spite of improved economic conditions, Canadian socialism has held its own nationally, generally obtaining between one-fifth and one-quarter of the vote in English Canada, and securing 43 seats in the House of Commons in the 1988 elections, the highest yet. The NDP won control of the government of Ontario, the most populous and wealthiest province, in 1990. Social democracy gained a new bastion in French Canada with the rise of the Parti Québécois, which has been the government or main opposition party since the 1970s.

MOSAIC AND MELTING POT: CENTER AND PERIPHERY

Canada's particularism, emphasizing group affiliations and loyalties, as opposed to American universalism, is reflected in (a) the Canadian concept of the "mosaic" applied to the right to cultural survival of ethnic groups, as compared to the American notion of the "melting pot"; (b) the more frequent recurrence and survival of strong regionally-based third parties in Canada than in the United States; and (c) the greater strength of provinces within the Canadian union, compared to the relative weakness of the states and the nationalization of parties, i.e., the decline of regionalism, in America.

The greater support for the perpetuation of minority cultures in Canada, derivative from the founding commitment to guarantee the rights of the francophones and Catholics, has affected groups as diverse as the Native populations, Jews, and Mennonites. The 1982 Charter of Rights and Freedoms explicitly singles out "the Indian, Inuit and Métis peoples of Canada" for special protection and guarantees aboriginal treaty rights. The Canadian aboriginal communities, larger in size and supported by the values implicit in multiculturalism, have done better than their American counterparts.

The Canadian Jews are much better organized than their American co-religionists. A single national organization, the Canadian Jewish Congress, represents all Jews in Canada; there is no comparable group in the United States. The small size of the Jewish community in Canada should have led to greater assimilation, but the emphasis on particularistic group organization subsumed in the mosaic seemingly helps to perpetuate a more solidaristic Canadian Jewish community.

The two North American countries are more disparate than before with respect to the importance of the federal and state and provincial governments; the power of the latter has steadily declined in the United States, but has increased in Canada. An American political scientist, Samuel Beer, has asserted that political and economic modernization inherently lead to a growth in authority at the center and a reduction in state and provincial power, and he cites the United States as an example of this process. But in Canada, as Donald Smiley points out, "modernization had not led to centralization in the . . . federal system but rather to the power, assertiveness, and the competence of the provinces. Furthermore, the provinces where modernization has proceeded most rapidly are the most insistent about preserving and extending their autonomy."

The differences between the two countries in this respect show up strikingly in government revenue. While American federal authorities control most of the funds raised and spent by state and local governments, in fiscal terms Canada is a highly decentralized federation: the provinces and municipalities exceed the federal government in total spending and tax revenue. As of 1985, the federal share of total Canadian tax revenue, not including social security funds, was 47.6%; the equivalent figure for the United States was 56.3%.

Canadian provinces have also been more disposed than American states to challenge the power of the federal government. Movements advocating secession have recurred in this century not only in Quebec, but in part of the Maritimes, the Prairies, and British Columbia as well. Public sentiment in Canada remains much more territorial than in the United States.

The discrepancy between the experience of the two countries has led social scientists to ask what has accounted for these contradictory developments. Two variables appear to be most important. One is the role of the French Canadians. Smaller anglophone provinces, seeking to protect their autonomy, have been able to do so because Quebec has always been in the forefront of the struggle for greater provincial power. The other is the difference between the American presidential-congressional system and the British parliamentary model. The greater propensity of Canadian provinces to engage in recurrent struggles with the federal government and to generate third parties may be explained by the fact that regional interests are much less protected in Parliament than in Congress. Given the different consequences of the national party discipline imposed by a parliamentary system as compared with the American divided powers presidential system (which permits members of Congress to vote against their party leaders,

661

including the president), Canadians are forced to find a way of expressing their special regional or other group needs outside of the House of Commons. The Canadian solution has frequently been to support different parties on a provincial level from those which they back nationally, so that provincial governments may carry out the regional representation tasks that in the United States are fulfilled by cross-party Congressional interest blocs.

There can be little doubt that, regardless of how much emphasis is placed on structural or cultural factors in accounting for variations, Canada and the United States continue to differ considerably. Since World War II, substantial changes in economic productivity, in urbanization, in education and in rates of upward social mobility have indeed reduced the structural gap. But there has been no consistent decline in the pattern of differences in behavior and values. Significant dissimilarities remain across the border with respect to a broad range of societal conditions. These variations in values and behavior can be linked to different reactions to the American Revolution.

The United States and Canada remain two nations formed around different organizing principles. Although some will disagree, there can be no argument. As Margaret Atwood concludes: "Americans and Canadians are not the same, they are products of two very different histories, two very different situations."

FURTHER READING

Banting, Keith G., ed. *State and Society: Canada in Comparative Perspective.* Toronto: University of Toronto Press, 1986.

Doran, Charles F., and John H. Sigler, eds. *Canada and the United States: Enduring Friendship, Persistent Stress.* Englewood Cliffs, N. J.: Prentice-Hall, 1985.

Fogel, Stanley. *A Tale of Two Countries: Contemporary Fiction in English Canada and the United States.* Toronto: ECW Press, 1984.

Friedenberg, Edgar. *Deference to Authority.* White Plains, N. Y.: M. E. Sharpe, 1980.

Gibbins, Roger. *Regionalism: Territorial Politics in Canada and the United States.* Toronto: Butterworths, 1982.

Goldberg, Michael A., and John Mercer. *The Myth of the North American City: Continentalism Challenged.* Vancouver: University of British Columbia Press, 1986.

Handy, Robert T. *A History of the Churches in the United States and Canada.* New York: Oxford University Press, 1972.

Hartz, Louis. *The Founding of New Societies.* New York: Harcourt, Brace and World, 1964.

Horowitz, Gad. *Canadian Labour in Politics.* Toronto: University of Toronto Press, 1968.

Lipset, Seymour Martin. *Continental Divide: The Values and Institutions of the United States and Canada.* New York and Toronto: Routledge, 1990.

————. *The First New Nation: The United States in Historical and Comparative Perspective.* New York: Basic Books, 1963; expanded paper ed., New York: W. W. Norton, 1979.

Michalos, Alex C. *North American Social Report: A Comparative Study of the Quality of Life in Canada and the USA from 1964 to 1974.* 5 vols. Dordrecht, Netherlands: D. Reidel, 1980–82.

Presthus, Robert, ed. *Cross-National Perspectives: United States and Canada.* Leiden, Netherlands: E. J. Brill, 1977.

Preston, Richard A., ed. *Perspectives on Revolution and Evolution.* Durham, N. C.: Duke University Press, 1979.

Schwartz, Mildred. *The Environment for Policy-Making in Canada and the United States.* Montreal: C. D. Howe Research Institute; Washington, D. C.: National Planning Association, 1981.

THE CONTEXT OF CULTURAL POLICY: ENGLISH-SPEAKING CANADA

JOHN HUTCHESON

Let us, for the sake of this essay, consider culture in the form of entertainment provided by professionals. What does Canada have to offer in the closing years of the 20th century? A useful assessment might be made by considering the entertainment menu offered to a citizen of, or a visitor to, Toronto, Canada's largest city.

Depending on the season, the consumer might opt for a visit to a major league baseball game—non-Canadian players competing in the American League, but in a Canadian domed stadium complete with a state-of-the-art retractable roof. Or perhaps a hockey game—a mostly Canadian team playing in what is called the National Hockey League, though the majority of teams are located in the United States. Or a football game—a Canadian variant of the game with a Canadian league in which the stars are mostly American also-rans.

But, despite the continuing allure of professional sports and their place in the imaginations of many Canadians and in the pages of newspapers, the representative cultural consumer would now more likely purchase a ticket to a theater, or a concert hall, or visit a museum or art gallery, or visit a bookstore to take home some entertainment in the form of a book or magazine.

For the opera fan or ballet enthusiast there are major Canadian companies—not yet, it is true, housed in a suitable building—playing an international repertoire, with some luminous Canadian stars interspersed with distinguished visitors and a large local supporting cast. The "serious music" devotee can visit a new concert hall named after the late Roy Thomson, also known as Lord Thomson of Fleet. (Thomson began his career in Canada, where he proved that it is possible to make a lot of money out of a lot of small newspapers. Then, after moving into the ownership of British papers, he demonstrated that a British television license was a license to print one's own money.) In the hall an excellent resident orchestra, supplemented by Canadian and foreign soloists, presents an internationally familiar repertoire, combined with the occasional work by a Canadian composer, the latter appearing in the same category as "difficult," "modern" music, needing to be sandwiched with more digestible fare. The less prominent citizens who attend popular music concerts can from time to time catch well-known, mostly foreign, visiting groups playing in a variety of large buildings around the city.

The stages of the city offer a dozen or so possibilities: a few Canadian productions, with mostly Canadian casts and sometimes Canadian directors, of mega-hits from the London stage; the now occasional visit of a bound-for-Broadway show or the usually tired revival of a past-Broadway hit; and a variety of resident theater groups, playing in theaters that run from the plush to the barely comfortable, offering excellent professional theater with a high proportion of first-run Canadian plays.

A much larger audience, however, finds its way into theaters with screens. Here the bill of fare is almost entirely the product of Hollywood, even if some viewers will recognize the occasional name of a Canadian actor or director or cameraman who has "made it" in the "big time." Canadian movies are located in the category of "foreign" movies, shown mostly in the kind of theater where audiences are accustomed to subtitles, though Canadian movies do not have subtitles, unless they come from Quebec.

If none of the above suit the cultural consumer, there are many alternatives, usually operating on a smaller scale: dance groups, poetry and fiction read by the author, small dinner theaters, club performances. There are also galleries and museums, from the larger institutions, which might be hosting or presenting a major exhibition, to the small galleries showing work of local artists.

Opting to stay home, or in the hotel room, with a book or magazine, the reader will discover that the many bookstores carry titles by such reputable authors as Robertson Davies, Alice Munro and Margaret Atwood, as well as an impressively long list of Canadian authors who are less likely to be known outside the country. There is also, although found in a smaller number of the stores, a wide selection of Canadian magazines to suit a variety of tastes and interests. But it will also be obvious that the share of the shelf space for Canadian authors and Canadian magazines is very small in proportion to that allocated to the internationally recognizable titles.

Finally, for the stay-at-home consumer, there is the most pervasive of all cultural activities: television, now backed up by video recordings. Pushing the buttons in the hope of finding some reflection of Canadian life, the viewer may chance upon a few of Canada's theater stars—Eric Peterson or Bruno Gerussi, for example—who have made the transition to a better-paid medium; or he may find one of the current affairs programs that interpret Canada and the world from a Canadian perspective. But it is much more likely that he will see the screen filled with the familiar fare of the American networks that finds its way into households around the world. The video market merely repeats the situation in the film theaters.

The choice of the entertainment market in Toronto is not made with the intention of antagonizing those many Canadians who do not live in the city and who are frequently, it appears, united, as by little else, by a dislike

665

(some might say envy) of Toronto and all its works. Of course, the cultural market varies from one place to another, although it would be fair to say that, as is usually the case, smaller towns offer less choice, however much that choice is valued by their residents (and, in the Canadian case, less choice means less choice of Canadian products).

CORPORATE INDUSTRIES AND GOVERNMENT FUNDING

A reflection on the choices available to the consumer of entertainment emphasizes the point that, in our age, most culture is the product of cultural industries. Those industries are shaped by technology and, importantly, by the corporate organizations that come into being to produce and distribute the products using the available technology. There are many forms for such corporations, ranging from state monopoly to small-scale private enterprise. Distribution can vary from exclusive lists to free broadcasting. But typically, though with significant exceptions, the Industrial Revolution put more and more aspects of culture in the hands of corporations formed to produce and distribute their products for profit, seeking the widest available market.

A distinctive feature of the Canadian cultural marketplace is that, as media analyst Paul Audley has shown in his study of broadcasting, publishing, recording and film, the structure of the domestic production and distribution industries is geared to the supply of imported material. Fewer than 30% of books and magazines sold are Canadian, less than 3% of film screen time is filled with Canadian films, fewer than 10% of sound recordings are Canadian and less than 30% of all programming available in the English language on television screens is Canadian.

A second distinctive feature of the country is that what Canadian production there is, is to a remarkable extent dependent on subsidies from the various levels of government in Canada.

In searching for an adequate set of policies for culture and communications, the Canadian government was naturally forced to take into account the prevailing international and domestic circumstances. For most of this century the dominant external concern of the Canadian government was the decline of the British Empire and the accompanying establishment of a "Pax Americana." The complicated footwork that was demanded of the Canadian government as it changed partners in that obligatory historical dance was made even more demanding by the need to pay simultaneous attention to the atonal music of domestic politics, where there were two dominant themes. The first of these, unique to Canada, although with echoes of "national" conflicts elsewhere, concerned the relations between English-speaking Canadians and French-speaking Canadians. The second domestic issue was the common coin of politics almost everywhere, namely a wide-ranging struggle over the meaning of a democratic society. All of these large issues, external and internal, had to be resolved within the constitutional framework of a federal state that gave very considerable powers to the provincial governments.

Notwithstanding these constraints, the Canadian government has played a fundamental role in the evolution of Canada's cultural industries. A 1986 Task Force on Funding of the Arts—with the latter defined as the performing arts, museums, art galleries, visual arts and creative writing—estimated that these activities constituted a $1.1 billion industry, even before indirect economic effects are taken into account. Thirty thousand Canadians were found to be at work as painters, sculptors, actors, musicians, dancers or writers. Necessary to the understanding of this large industry is the fact that only half of its revenues are derived from purely commercial activities, that is, from theaters, galleries or festivals that receive no government subsidies. Of equal importance, and of greater significance artistically, are nonprofit arts organizations receiving government funding. Although their audiences continue to grow, nonprofit arts activities receive only 35% of their total revenue directly from consumers. Fifty-six percent of their revenue comes from government sources. A large hidden subsidy for many of the activities comes from the artists themselves, who work for low pay under often unfavorable conditions. But federal and provincial government policies have been crucial to these cultural industries.

A major factor in this cultural subsidization is the activity of the Canada Council. The establishment of an arts council in the form of an independent, government-financed organization to aid the performing and creative arts was originally proposed by the artists themselves. The concept was furthered by the influential Royal Commission on the Arts, Letters and Sciences (the Massey Commission, discussed below), and in 1957 the Canada Council came into being with a mandate to "foster and promote the study and enjoyment of, and the production of works in, the arts." At the end of its first 30 years, the disbursements of the Canada Council had reached more than $90 million annually, and since its founding it has dramatically changed the financial circumstances of a wide range of artistic activities including dance, music, theater, visual arts, writing and publishing. In some provinces the work of the Canada Council is supplemented by provincial arts councils, and a Social Sciences and Humanities Research Council that was separated from the Canada Council in 1978 and reunited with it in 1992.

There are further means by which cultural activities are sheltered from the full blast of the marketplace. The music-recording industry, for example, depends not only on direct sales but on the related issue of regulation of radio broadcasting. Most recordings played by radio stations are produced by multinational corporations which would, in the absence of regulation, have little incentive to produce Canadian music or international music played by Canadians. The conditions of licensing require that for AM radio, 30% of the musical content must be Canadian. For FM radio there are adjustable quotas for various categories of music.

The Canadian magazine industry, which is a low-profit activity, is heavily dependent on an amendment to the Income Tax Act, commonly known as Bill C-58, which affects advertising revenues. Advertising revenues are "protected" by the fact that Canadian advertisers can claim income tax deductions for advertising costs only for those advertisements that are placed in Canadian publications. While still subject to the loss of revenue attributable to "spillover" advertising—the capacity for U.S. advertisers to reach Canadian audiences directly through the many U.S. publications that circulate in Canada—Bill C-58 penalizes U.S. publishers who attempt to reach Canadian audiences through Canadian editions of U.S. magazines. Magazines have also benefited from federal sales tax exemptions and postal subsidies—though both policies were revised in the late 1980s.

Bill C-58 also has implications for broadcasting from U.S. border stations, preventing the "escape" of advertising dollars from Canadian advertisers to border stations that reach Canadian audiences, and a similar tax provision exists for newspapers. The newspaper industry, which is both highly concentrated in the hands of some large Canadian-owned corporations and highly profitable, is also the recipient of further benefits in the form of postal rates and federal sales tax exemption.

FILMS, THEATER, PUBLISHING

Canada's film industry—however fleeting its manifestations on the screen—does have a long history of involvement with the government. A National Film Board (NFB) was created in 1939 in circumstances that determined that its work would be essentially confined to documentaries related to World War II. It was clear from the outset that the Canadian government did not imagine that the existence of the NFB constituted a policy with respect to Canadian film in general, far less that it had any implications for the Canadian market for Hollywood productions. The NFB did, however, notwithstanding considerable political turmoil, gradually evolve into a production unit that combines internationally acclaimed documentaries and short films with feature-length dramatic films. About 80% of its budget is a grant from the federal government.

Commercial film production in Canada goes back to the 1890s, but production remains sporadic and Canada has not developed an industry using centralized studio production. No Canadian government has ever introduced effective legislation for the production, distribution or exhibition of Canadian films. In the face of such vertical integration of the film industry in Hollywood, and given the expansion of the distribution and exhibition arms of that industry into Canada, the Canadian film market became a region of the United States. As with other aspects of communications, and indeed following the pattern clearly evident in many industries, a combination of U.S. corporate expansion and Canadian government compliance colluded to integrate the two economies.

The federal government does now play a role in the commercial film industry through a funding agency—Telefilm Canada—and has attempted to link film and television broadcast policy. In addition, federal and provincial governments have juggled tax regulations in order to encourage commercial investment in the industry. But if some form of subsidization has been constant, so too has the fear of regulations that, through an impact on distribution and exhibition, would touch on trade and investment policy.

The support of the Canada Council and other sources of government funding has had a profound impact on the evolution of the Canadian theater's community of writers, directors, designers, actors and stage crew. It is self-evident that access to theaters and audiences will determine the prospects for the growth of the community. Until the 1950s, theaters and audiences in Canada had long been devoted to the visits of sometimes distinguished, but always well-promoted, visiting artists. Canadians who looked for a career in the theater had little choice but to leave the country. Amateur theater groups existed and a few actors attained a semiprofessional status, but there were few opportunities on the stage and, it is important to note, few of the supplementary activities that existed in some other countries. The Canadian film industry barely existed. It was the radio network of the Canadian Broadcasting Corporation (CBC) that began, in the 1940s, a significant process of change by creating regular work for some actors and writers as well as technical staff and promoting the development of an audience for Canadian productions. The Canada Council was able to build on this momentum.

The result of the subsidization by the Canada Council, and other government sources, has been the emergence of a tripartite professional theater community: the major festival theaters, such as the Stratford Festival Theatre and the Shaw Festival, both in Ontario within reach of the metropolitan Toronto audience and substantial tourism from the United States; a series of civic showcase theaters in many of the larger cities across the country; and a large number of small theater companies, most of them in the larger cities. Debates continue about the adequacy of subsidies and the role of corporate sponsorship, about the allocation of subsidies among the three sectors, about commitment to Canadian theater as opposed to theater in Canada; but the size of the community and its audience has continued to grow.

Policies of support from the Canada Council and other sources of funding from both federal and provincial governments, acting in combination with the expansion of universities and other levels of education, have also greatly widened the opportunities for Canadian writers and for Canadian book publishers. It is now possible for Canadian writers to write for a Canadian audience, rather than, as in the past, having to assume that the majority of readers would have to be sought outside the country. Some writers perhaps found this of little consequence because their work traveled well: L. M. Montgomery, the creator of *Anne of Green Gables,* is a prominent example. Others knew—Hugh MacLennan has made this point—that they would have to explain some of their themes and assumptions to readers who would not be familiar with the Canadian terrain. The consequence of the shift has been a proliferation of diverse voices from within Canada speaking to many different aspects of the national imagination.

In 1985, the *Annual Report of the National Advisory Committee on Cultural Statistics* estimated that the overall annual expenditures for "arts and culture" by the three levels of government—federal, provincial and municipal—were in the region of $2.9 billion. Even allowing for the difficulty of determining what is or is not "'arts and culture," this is an impressive figure.

There can be little doubt that the emergence of the Canada Council in the 1950s marks a major turning point in cultural policy and that the consequences have been immense for Canadian writers, performers, and artists of many kinds. Still, in some cultural industries there are limits to the effectiveness of subsidization. In book publishing, for example, the limits of government policy are dictated by the fact that the Canadian market is considered by American publishers to be an extension of their own. Subsidiary publishers occupy a prominent place in the Canadian industry, there is a cost advantage for the publisher who imports foreign books, and Canada alone imports half of all U.S. book exports. In fact it seems clear from an examination of the cultural industries that subsidies and regulations are not synonymous with trade and investment policies.

TELEVISION

If the role of cultural subsidies has been to encourage Canadian production while leaving a large part of the cultural market open to imported material, there can be little doubt that television is both a typical and an extreme example of Canada's cultural industries. It is typical because what Canadian share of the market exists does so because of subsidy and regulation; it is extreme because of the overwhelming part played by television in the shaping of the imagination.

Television has dominated the cultural marketplace since the 1950s. Television viewing time for Canadians from infancy on averages 22 hours a week. Yet, as the 1986 report of a Task Force on Broadcasting Policy indicates, only 28% of all the programming available on English-language television is Canadian and less than one-third of the total time spent watching television is devoted to Canadian programming.

The issues raised by these simple statistics can best be approached by means of a quick look at the origins of broadcasting in the days of radio, which began when the first radio station in Canada—CFCF in Montreal—was licensed in 1919. From the outset radio broadcasting posed a policy dilemma: Private broadcasters could not raise sufficient revenue to pay for Canadian programs. Although the Canadian National Railway, a crown corporation, established a public broadcasting network for train passengers and hotel guests, private stations found it profitable to affiliate with the emerging U.S. networks. In the course of a campaign for Canadian radio which was fought in the 1930s, one of the main proponents of the campaign, Graham Spry, coined the slogan "The State or the United States." The Canadian government opted for the State at least to some extent by determining that the airwaves were a publicly owned natural resource, that broadcasting should be under national control, and that a publicly owned system was necessary. The Canadian Broadcasting Corporation came into existence in 1936 with a mandate to produce a national radio service and regulate the private sector. What did not change, however, was the financial advantage that resided in selling American programs to the Canadian public. Private broadcasters still had an interest in distributing the product of the United States and so, to some extent, did the CBC.

The national radio networks of the CBC now stand in sharp contrast to the many local private stations by being funded through a government grant and thus free of the need to seek advertising. Through a variety of magazine-format shows, as well as through their news services, the CBC radio networks open up opportunities for Canadian voices to reflect the sensibility of the country.

The experience of radio was to be repeated in television but in an exacerbated form as a result of the high cost of television production and without the emergence of the CBC as a noncommercial alternative.

From the beginning of television broadcasting in the United States, U.S. border stations were accessible to many Canadians, and a market for American programs had been created before the CBC went on the air. By an extension of its powers over radio broadcasting, the CBC controlled the television airwaves, but policy was shaped by many factors. Some of the early technical decisions had momentous consequences. The CBC opted for the 525-line transmission signal used by U.S. broadcasters and, like the United States, chose the Very High Frequency (VHF) band, reserving Ultra High Frequency (UHF) for later use. The consequence was technological integration and the direct import of programs from the United States. In addition, from the outset the CBC coexisted with private broadcasters. The mixture of public and private broadcasters ultimately undermined the centrality of the CBC. To begin with, the private stations were affiliates of the CBC, but by the 1960s the CBC had lost its regulatory authority over the private sector and in 1961 a private network was permitted. Finally, the CBC had made it a policy to contain its own costs of production and to sustain its own audience by providing American programs in prime time. The advent of cable television further fragmented the Canadian market, by the wholesale provision of U.S. television networks to Canadian audiences.

The Canadian government did not abandon its stated object of regulating television broadcasting in the public interest. The 1968 Broadcast Act attempted to reformulate government policy in the light of the changes in the preceding years; the act brought cable systems under control as "broadcast-receiving undertakings" and it established a new regulatory agency. The Canadian Radio-Television Commission, restyled the Canadian Radio-Television and Telecommunications Commission in 1976, was mandated to "safeguard, enrich, and strengthen the cultural, political, social, and economic fabric of Canada." But if the CBC had had trouble juggling the unstable mixture of public broadcasting, American technology, and American programming, the CRTC quickly showed itself incapable of stopping, or unwilling to stop, the flood of American programming.

One key issue for cultural policy is that of the cost and availability of programs. The 1986 Report of the Task Force on Broadcasting Policy suggests that "a general rule of thumb is that it costs ten times as much to produce a Canadian show as it costs to buy an American show." The available American shows are in fact being sold for a fraction of their production costs, by companies that are able to cover the costs in the U.S. market. Changing the balance in programming available to Canadians viewers would require an enhancement of one or both of the two strands of policy now in place: either to considerably increase the grants to the public broadcasters (primarily the CBC but also provincial networks such as TVOntario), or to film producers (either private or the NFB), who now produce the bulk of Canadian programs; or to regulate the access to Canadian distribution networks of some portion of imported programs.

NEW TECHNOLOGY, SAME ISSUES

Much is in flux at the moment. In the 1980s, the combination of the microchip, the computer satellite and optical fiber circuits began a digital revolution that is transforming communications networks in Canada as elsewhere. The boundaries between the media are being blurred. The creation of a binary digital language for computers and the ability to process that language through transistors and microchips have in effect computerized a vast number of products, some of which have been around for a hundred years and some of which are very recent. These computerized technologies can be linked together in long-distance networks because communications satellites and fiber-optic cables have dramatically reduced the cost of transmitting multiple signals. In the United States, "software"—the information or entertainment that can be processed through the digital systems—is regarded as a commercial product.

The Canadian government's response to the digital revolution will ultimately include a new broadcasting act, a copyright act and new legislation on telecommunications. In addition a new goods and services tax already impinges on the culture and communications sector. But what will not be resolved is the question of which information and which programs flow through the networks. The answer is of fundamental importance for the future of Canadian culture.

Although it was the advent of television that was to provide the major challenge for cultural policy after 1950, the contours of a communications and cultural policy had of necessity been laid out in the century before as new communications technologies, and their corporate organization, interacted with political forces. The telegraph, the telephone, mass circulation newspapers and magazines, the movies and radio broadcasting had all in their time posed questions for Canadian governments. Each new technology created a new network of communications and it was inevitable that governments would pay attention to questions of ownership, the geographical routes along which the networks were established, and the social, economic and political implications of the "traffic" that was carried around the networks.

It is widely believed that by creating the transcontinental Canadian Pacific Railway in the 1880s, using an all-Canadian route—financed by a combination of private capital and government largesse in cash and land grants, and sustained by pervasive regulation—the government of Sir John Macdonald had established an east-west axis for Canadian unity offsetting the influence of north-south commercial ties. In his novel *Barometer Rising,* written during the years of World War II though set in World War I, Hugh MacLennan offers a stark statement of this theme, describing the railway line as a "tenuous thread, which bound Canada to both the great oceans and made her a nation." The passage goes on to describe Canada as a "beadlike string of crude towns and cities tied by nothing but railway tracks, [a] nation undiscovered by the rest of the world and unknown to itself, [a] people neither American nor English . . ." It is also often said, though perhaps less widely believed, that the Canadian Broadcasting Corporation holds a position analogous to that of the Canadian Pacific Railway in forging an east-west articulation of Canadian identity. There is much to be said for this point of view, both with respect to the CPR and the CBC, though both institutions have managed in their time to provoke considerable regional grievances and the reality is, inevitably, more complexly shaded than the mythology.

The mere existence of Canadian transport or communications networks, even those with all-Canadian routes, has not been sufficient to offset those continentalist forces that link Canada to the networks of the United States. The telegraph lines that followed the railways became conduits for the news services and linked Canadian newspapers to the major wire services outside of Canada, in the process shaping Canada's view of the world. The telephone systems of the U.S.-owned Bell Company extended into the central provinces of Canada. (Bell Canada became a Canadian-owned company in the 1970s.)

One of the remarkable features of the Canadian historical experience in communications policy is the lesson that it offers regarding the limits of regulatory power. Government regulation has been pervasive: the telegraph and telephone networks, for example, were seen as "public utilities" and were required to provide services at "just and reasonable rates"; even government ownership has coexisted with private corporate control as in the case of provincially owned telephone companies, provincially and federally owned documentary film units, and the CBC. But the flow of information has essentially been determined by commercial considerations which have been fueled by the industrial development of the United States and the corresponding accumulation of political power.

That political power has been a significant factor in the international arena in the years since 1945. As U.S. media analyst Herbert Schiller notes in his *Mass Communications and American Empire,* in staking a claim for freedom, U.S. policy sought to extend "the American way." That included the acceptance of broadcasting time as a source of income, information as a commodity and audiences as a market. Hollywood had pioneered a global market. Broadcasting, radio and television would be the American newspaper writ large, with a global audience and an American editorial policy. The barriers to the expansion would be those governments, both "friendly" and hostile, that sought, for diverse reasons, to retain some elements of sovereignty in the realm of communications.

MASSEY AND INNIS

Perhaps the most prominent Canadian to see the need for cultural policies to maintain essential aspects of sovereignty was Vincent Massey. Massey, the scion of the wealthy agricultural implements manufacturing family, was schooled in the appreciation of the power shifts along all three sides of the North Atlantic triangle by holding diplomatic appointments in both Washington and London. While others in Ottawa worried about U.S. demands for bases and military integration, in 1949 Massey persuaded the government to appoint a royal commission of inquiry on the arts, letters and sciences. The commission was to have a major impact on cultural policy after 1950 by creating an interventionist "defense" to offset the wholesale importation of the cultural products of the United States.

The Massey Commission called for the establishment of an arts council; the national gallery and national museums were to be developed; public records and historical sites were to be expanded; aid to universities and for scientific research was to come from the federal government; the CBC was to continue to control national and private radio broadcasting; and the introduction of television was to be under the direction of the CBC in order to "avoid excessive commercialism and to encourage Canadian content and the use of Canadian talent."

Clearly a major issue was control of broadcasting, both radio and the newly arrived television. Given that the imported goods were overwhelmingly populist in character and could profitably be sold to large numbers of Canadians, Massey's reputation as "plus royalist que le roi"—he was later, most fittingly, the first Canadian to be appointed governor general—gave strength to those who argued that interventionist cultural policies were elitist and merely promoted the interests of an unrepresentative minority. But that was to miss the point. What the Massey Commission had done was to raise, in a very sharp political manner, one of the most troubling aspects of the exercise of sovereignty by any community: namely, how can a community draw a boundary between the desire to maintain its "cultural integrity" on the one side, and a threat of creating an oppressive "closed" society on the other. There was little danger that Canada would became a closed society—its trade and investment patterns required open boundaries. The dilemma was that trade routes are, as economic historian Harold Innis knew, also communications routes, and that imperial trade routes between the centers of empire and its margins bring, as an inevitable consequence, imperial communications policies.

Harold Innis was in many respects the complete opposite of Vincent Massey. Shaped by growing up on a small farm and making his way through the regional school system and into university, his life was profoundly altered by his experience in the trenches of World War I. Innis emerged from those horrifying events and his perception of Canada's role in them with a determination to create an approach to economic history that would explain Canada's unique place in the world. In a series of studies of transportation and resource industries, Innis set out what came to be known as the "staple theory" of Canada's development: Canada had developed at the "margin" of the world economy, exporting raw materials at prices set in an economic system dominated by a series of "center" countries. Each staple product—be it cod, fur, wheat, newsprint or minerals—had its own rhythm of development and brought with it its own pattern of immigration, capital movements, financial and political institutions and communications.

In the years before his death in 1952, Innis devoted much of his time to the study of communications and also to implications for Canada of the dramatic shift in world power. In *Changing Concepts of Time,* published in 1952, Innis arrived at a conclusion that was strikingly similar to one of the main themes of the report of the Massey Commission: "We are indeed fighting for our lives. The pernicious influence of American advertising . . . and the powerful persistent impact of commercialism have been evident in all the ramifications of Canadian life . . . We can only survive by taking persistent action at strategic points against American imperialism in all its attractive guises."

Canadian society has found neither the means nor the political desire to resist that "attractive" commercialism. The cultural border has been kept open by historical circumstance as well as by Canada's political culture and the open border is now formalized in the 1989 Free Trade Agreement between Canada and the United States The demands for retention of significant elements of Canadian sovereignty, however—including a degree of cultural sovereignty—remain part of the political agenda in Canada. The issue, as both Harold Innis and Vincent Massey recognized, is a question of adapting political organization to the circumstances created by technology and commercial organization.

FURTHER READING

Audley, Paul. *Canada's Cultural Industries: Broadcasting, Publishing, Records and Film.* Toronto: Canadian Institute for Economic Policy, 1983.

Canada. Department of Communications. *Report of the Federal Cultural Policy Review Committee.* Ottawa, 1982.

Canada. Ministry of Supply and Services. *Report of the Task Force on Broadcasting Policy.* Ottawa, 1986.

Peers, F.W. *The Public Eye: Television and the Politics of Canadian Broadcasting, 1952–1968.* Toronto: University of Toronto Press, 1979.

Siegel, Arthur. *Politics and the Media in Canada.* Toronto: McGraw-Hill Ryerson, 1983.

INDEX

Entries are filed letter-by-letter. **Boldface** locators indicate extensive treatment of a topic. Locators followed by a **b** indicate biographical sketches. Locators followed by t indicate table.

A

Abella, Rosalie Silberman 580
Abella Commission on Employment Equity 580
Abella Report (1984) 580
Aberhart, William 12, 14
ABM defense *See* antiballistic missile defense
Aboriginal Justice Inquiry (Manitoba) 592
aboriginal peoples *See* native peoples; *province, region, and group names*
Aboriginal Rights Coalition 603
abortion 175t, 576, 581, 582, 606–608
Abortion Caravan 576
Acadians: New Brunswick 25, 27, 28, 35; Nova Scotia 120, 232; Prince Edward Island 52
Acadian Village (New Brunswick) 487
accidents 178t
acidification 280
acid rain 286, 292, 296, 297, 419, 513–515, 520–522
ACOA *See* Atlantic Canada Opportunities Agency
Act Respecting Employment Equity (1986) 580
Acts of Parliament 346, 347 *See also specific acts*
Acuma (New Brunswick) 30
ADA *See* Area Development Agency
ADB *See* Atlantic Development Board
ADIA *See* Area Development Incentives Act
advanced industrial materials 409, 410t
Advocate (Deer River, Alberta) 21
AECL *See* Atomic Energy of Canada Ltd.
Afghanistan 291
AFL-CIO *See* American Federation of Labor-Congress of Industrial Organizations
Africa: Commonwealth of Nations 214, 301, 495; development assistance 491t, 495, 496, 500, 606; endangered species 510; immigration policy 530; La Francophonie 304, 305, 495; missionaries 605; railways 453
agencies (environmental) 509–510 *See also specific agencies*
Agricultural and Rural Development Act (1966) 639
agriculture **379–396** *See also individual provinces, regions and crops*; agribusiness 215, 388–391; Commonwealth of Nations 302; crisis in 1980s 391–393; employment 427; environment 512, 514, 519, 521, 522; farms and farm families 382–387; foreign trade 381, 395, 397, 403, 430; future of 393–396; history 205, 222, 248, 398, 406, 411; immigration 525, 526, 535; industrial structure 399, 402; international development assistance 500; labor relations 556; physical resources 379–380; privatization 432; production 380–382; provincial government and 3, 4; regional development policy 639; statistics 192t, 393t, 394t, 400t, 404t, 405t, 415t; transportation 460; U.S. trade 372
Agriculture Rehabilitation and Development Act (1961) 639
Agriculture Rehabilitation and Development Agency (ARDA) 639
AIDS (acquired immune deficiency syndrome) 586
Air Canada 45, 86, 101, 125, 139, 206, 456, 457, 463
Air Canada Act (1977) 456
Air Command 316
Air-Sea Transportable Combat Group (CAST) 314
Aishihik (Yukon Territory) 166
Alaska Highway 113, 164, 166, 242, 274, 488
Alberta **9–22**: agriculture 15–16; banking and finance 469; biographical sketches 22; climate 9, 11; comparative statistics 173–196; constitution and 339, 347, 417; economy 14–15; education 20–21; employment 19; energy 16–18, 222, 237, 271, 417, 442–445; environment 508, 509, 519; ethnic composition 11; federal government and 4, 13, 247, 250,

256; foreign trade 19, 414, 417; forestry 18–19; geography 9; health care 20, 619; history 13–14, 215, 238, 272; housing 20; judicial system 5, 13, 357, 593; labor relations 560; language 11, 624, 628, 632; local government 12–13; manufacturing 18; map 10; mass media 21, 451, 462, 463; mining 16–18, 271; national leaders 223; native peoples 11, 585, 590, 593, 634; political parties 12, 205, 216n, 334, 335; population 11; prices 19; provincial government 12; religion 11, 599; service sector 19; taxation 5–6; tourism 485, 486; transportation 216, 453, 456, 457, 459, 460, 461; welfare services 19–20
Alberta Gas Trunk Line *See* NOVA
Alberta Heritage Savings Trust Fund 15
Alberta Report (magazine) 21
Alberta University (Edmonton) 21
Alcan Aluminum Ltd. 70, 85
Alder Lodge 88
alfalfa 16
Algeria 221
Algonquian Indians: language 634; New Brunswick 25; Prince Edward Island 52; Quebec 234
Allende, Salvador 534, 535
Alliance Française 304
Allooloo, Titus **117b**
aluminum: British Columbia 77, 86, 422; environment 521; industrial structure 403, 418; Prince Edward Island 57; Quebec 70, 72, 422; statistics 418t, 422t; world production share 421
Amauligak oil field (Northwest Territories) 113
American Federation of Labor (AFL) 217, 217n
American Federation of Labor-Congress of Industrial Organizations (AFL-CIO) 554, 563
"Americanization" 213, 218
American League (baseball) 664
American Revolution 25, 234, 236, 327, 651, 652, 662
Amherst (Nova Scotia) 125, 128
Amin, Idi 534
ammonium phosphate 154
Amnesty International 307, 586
Anderson, Doris 575
Anglicans *See also individual provinces*: abortion 608; American Revolution and 652; decline of 655; early North America and 242; ecumenical cooperation 600, 603, 604; education 201; statistics 596; U.S. comparison 656
Anglo-conformity 531, 532, 630
anglophones *See* language policy; *individual provinces*
animal feed 154
animal oil 242
Annapolis Royal tidal power project (Nova Scotia) 122, 124
Anne of Green Gables (L.M. Montgomery) 211, 669
antiballistic missile (ABM) defense 319
Antigonish (Nova Scotia) 128
Anti-Inflation Act (1975) 566
antimony 30, 112, 166
"Anti-Scab" provisions 555
anti-Semitism 216n–217n
apples 82
aquaculture: New Brunswick 33; Yukon 166
Arctic College (Northwest Territories) 116
Arctic Cooperation Treaty 285
Arctic Environmental Strategy 280
Arctic Winter Games 114
Area Development Agency (ADA) 640
Area Development Incentives Act (ADIA) 640
area (provincial and national) 176t, 177t
Argentia (Newfoundland) 101

677

J

DATE DUE